# "A Few Acres of Snow"

# "A FEW ACRES OF SNOW"
## *Documents in Pre-Confederation Canadian History*

Second Edition

*Edited by*

## Thomas Thorner
with assistance from Thor Frohn-Nielsen

broadview press

**National Library of Canada Cataloguing in Publication**
"A few acres of snow": documents in pre-confederation Canadian history / edited by Thomas Thorner; with assistance from Thor Frohn-Nielsen. — 2nd ed.
First ed. published 1997 under title: "A few acres of snow": documents in Canadian history, 1577-1867.
Includes bibliographical references.
ISBN 1-55111-549-2
1. Canada—History—Sources. I. Thorner, Thomas II. Frohn-Nielsen, Thor, 1955-
FC18.F49 2003     971  C2003-902025-8 . F1003.F49 2003

Broadview Press Ltd. is an independent, international publishing house, incorporated in 1985. Broadview believes in shared ownership, both with its employees and with the general public; since the year 2000 Broadview shares have traded publicly on the Toronto Venture Exchange under the symbol BDP.

We welcome comments and suggestions regarding any aspect of our publications—please feel free to contact us at the addresses below or at broadview@broadviewpress.com.

**North America**
*Canada*: PO Box 1243, Peterborough, Ontario, Canada K9J 7H5
*United States*: 3576 California Road, Orchard Park, NY, USA 14127
Tel: (705) 743-8990; Fax: (705) 743-8353
e-mail: customerservice@broadviewpress.com

**UK, Ireland, and Continental Europe**
Plymbridge Distributors
Estover Road
Plymouth, UK  PL6 7PZ
Tel: 44(0) 1752 202301; Fax: 44(0) 1752 202333
e-mail: orders@plymbridge.com

**Australia and New Zealand**
UNIREPS, University of New South Wales
Sydney, NSW, Australia  2052
Tel: 61 2 9664 0999; Fax: 61 2 9664 5420
e-mail: info.press@unsw.edu.au

**www.broadviewpress.com**

Broadview Press Ltd. gratefully acknowledges the financial support of the Government of Canada through the Book Publishing Industry Development Program for our publishing activities.

This book is printed on acid-free paper containing 30% post-consumer fibre.

Eco-Logo Certified
30% Post

Printed in Canada

# Contents

# Not Another Edition

Many publishers annually incorporate relatively minor changes to produce yet another edition of their textbooks. This usually prevents students from selling their old editions and from purchasing cheaper, used books for courses. In this case well over half of the material is entirely new. The idea of a revised edition originated with a number of specific problems. First, one of the most compelling documents in the original collection turned out to have been fabricated. Without any hint of its fictional nature, Gerald Keegan's diary can still be found in one of the best anthologies concerning the Irish in Canada. Yet its authenticity sparked a major controversy in Ireland during the early 1990s. The "diary" turns out to have been written as a short story by a Scottish immigrant 50 years after the events it describes, and was not the account of a genuine Irish famine victim. The Keegan material also leaves the impression that the main motives for migration centred upon dispossession, nationalism, and Anglo-phobia, a version sharply contradicted by the De Vere account which now forms part of this new edition. Second, students wanted to hear more from the perspective of native peoples. Therefore a new opening chapter comparing cultural perspectives as well as an entire chapter devoted to native dissent was added. Third, some critics thought that a single chapter on the early Maritime colonies was grossly inadequate. In its place are four new chapters. With the volume covering the period after 1867, many readers sought more material on classic Canadian issues and coverage beyond 1982 (which still remains the termination date for our post-Confederation history at Kwantlen University College). Another common suggestion was to include study questions, which previously had been available only in the study guides provided to instructors.

The first edition also failed to provide sufficient acknowledgement to the library staff at Kwantlen—in particular Margaret Giacomello and Jean McKendry—as well as Karen Archer, Jacinta Sterling, Kathie Holloway, Ann McBurnie, Judy Issac, and Nancy Smith—who always managed to keep the interlibrary loan material, upon which so much of this book was based, flowing.

# INTRODUCTION

> "You realize that these two countries have been fighting over a few acres of snow near Canada, and they are spending on this splendid struggle more than Canada itself is worth."
>
> Voltaire, *Candide*, 1759

Voltaire's remark, although unflattering, remains one of the best-known descriptions of early Canada. The modern reader must find it ironic that one of the leading thinkers of the Enlightenment could utterly dismiss an area, which he never visited, that would come to be one of the world's wealthiest and most highly developed societies. Published in 1759, when French dreams of a religious utopia or commercial success in North America lay in shambles, the remark could be attributed to bitterness or Eurocentrism. Yet many high-ranking French government officials shared his assessment of Canada. With this short incisive remark, Voltaire also satirized his fellow philosophers such as Montaigne and Rousseau who romanticized about the garden paradise and natural goodness found in the New World. But four years after *Candide* Voltaire published another novel, *L'Ingénu*, that contradicted his earlier views. Its protagonist, a French Canadian raised by Huron native people, employs his morality and ingenuity to rise above the corrupt Parisian environment he is forced to confront.[1]

Nonetheless, Voltaire's image has served as and still remains a powerful characterization of this country. Whether they wrote exploration diaries, natural histories, guide books, immigration tracts, or essays, early Canadian writers often concentrated upon the physical environment. As the ink froze in her pen, Anna Brownell Jameson recorded that human character and behaviour "depend more on the influence of climate than the pride of civilized humanity would be willing to allow" and went on to pity the poor immigrants who were as "yet unprepared against the rigour of the season."[2] While some such as Catharine Parr Traill experienced "infinite delight … contemplating these pretty frolics of Father Frost,"[3] many other Canadians perceived their relationship with winter in hostile terms. One is reminded of Thomas Keefer's lament that "from Canada there is no escape: blockaded and imprisoned by Ice and Apathy."[4] A partial explanation for these varying opinions may be that Canadian winter meant different things to different people. According to Judith Fingard, "To the successful merchant and his family winter represented a time of entertainment, sport, cultural activity or, at worst, boredom," while to the labourer winter was "synonymous with hardship, cold, hunger, and gloomy unemployment or underemployment."[5] What meaning indigenous people placed upon winter is not as well documented, but they too experienced vast differences. The winter village ceremonies of the West Coast would, for example, contrast sharply with those of the Cree hunting bands of the prairies.

The bleakness inherent in the image of "a few acres of snow" is also in harmony with the disappointment and subsequent transiency of the colonial population. Some like Susannah Moodie described Upper Canada as a "prison house." Whether it was groups such as Black Loyalists who chose Sierra Leone over Nova Scotia or individuals such as Samuel Cunard or Thomas Chandler Haliburton, many sought to escape the limitations of Canada and moved elsewhere. For the Irish arriving at Grosse-Île or the gold mines of British Columbia, as the following accounts reveal, the promise of a better life was often illusionary.

What follows is a volume that attempts to bring together compelling excerpts of divergent eyewitness perspectives on specific topics in Canadian history. The fascination of primary sources like the Voltaire quote lies in their personal perspective and the immediacy of experience they convey. However lacking in objective insight they may be, they were written by people at or close to the source of the events they describe.

Many collections of Canadian readings on the market today reprint articles from academic journals as models of scholarship. Although such articles may certainly be of great value, they naturally tend to be written with a scholarly audience in mind. Coupled with standard survey texts, the near-total reliance upon secondary sources has had wide-ranging consequences. A student registering for a course on the Victorian novel would, no doubt, expect to read Victorian novels, not simply digest what secondary sources had to say about them. Even if the raw materials were as dense, drab, and dull as the popular perception of Canadian history makes them out to be, bypassing them would be disturbing. But the primary sources are far from dull. What historians usually find most enjoyable about the craft is research—the labyrinthine quest in primary sources for answers about the past. In the same way, readers of this book are encouraged to analyze the arguments and information in the sources for themselves.

This is still very much a book aimed at those largely unfamiliar with the subject. In order to make available the greatest possible amount of original material that is interesting and important, some less pertinent passages have been deleted. Exercising even a minimal shaping hand will sacrifice some dimensions of the past, but even if the occasional reader feels uncomfortable that the integrity of some documents has been violated, one hopes that in the interests of engaging a wider readership and lifting the veil of boredom from Canadian history, the end will have justified the means.

Some may also wish to hear less in a volume such as this one from the voices of white men. Despite efforts to the contrary, the unfortunate fact is that for many topics one has to rely upon the opinions of the white, male elite. Even those women who did provide detailed records of their experiences in early Canada often reflected their origin and class more closely than their gender. On the rare occasions when one comes upon a substantial native commentary, it has invariably been transcribed by Europeans, rendering its contents highly suspect.

Editors of document collections such as this must also be sensitive to Emma Larocque's criticism that reproducing historical documents such as these perpetuates negative images, particularly about native people, and as such constitutes hate literature.[6] Without a doubt many documents written by ethnocentric Europeans, with their emphasis on native violence, are elements of a literature of hate written to justify white domination. But it hardly follows that reprinting these inaccuracies constitutes disseminating hate literature. Instead these documents may provide a means of exposing these lies, of demonstrating the basis of intolerance, and of understanding that prejudice is commonplace. In some respects these documents may be used to confront the current complacency or smugness of Canadians who assume that, especially compared to the United States, ours has been a kinder, gentler history and therefore lacks the foundation for bigotry and racism.

## Notes

1. Greg Gatenby, *The Wild is Always There* (Toronto: Alfred A. Knopf, 1993) 177, 458–459. For some the qualifier "near Canada" in the famous *Candide* quote has also been taken to invalidate its wider application. On this debate, Gatenby cites "L'Opinion de Voltaire sur le Canada," *Séances et Travaux de L'Académie des Sciences Morales et Politiques: Compte Rendu* (Paris, 1900). Even if the *Candide* remark did not refer exclusively to Canada, the association between Canada and snow is unequivocal in Voltaire's remark of October 13, 1759: "We French had the bright idea of establishing ourselves in Canada, on top of the snow between the bears and the beavers."

2. Anna Brownell Jameson, *Winter Studies and Summer Rambles in Canada,* Volume 2 (London: Saunders and Otley, 1838) 27–28.

3. Catharine Parr Traill, *The Backwoods of Canada* (London: Charles Knight, 1836) 245.

4. Thomas Keefer, *Philosophy of Railroads* (Montreal: Armour and Ramsay, 1850), 1.

5. J. Fingard, "The Winter's Tale: The Seasonal Contours of Pre-Industrial Poverty in British North America, 1815–1860," *Canadian Historical Association Papers* (1974) 65.

6. Emma Larocque, "On the Ethics of Publishing Historical Documents," in J. Brown and R. Brightman, eds., *"The Orders of the Dreamed": George Nelson on Cree and Northern Ojibwa Religion and Myth 1823* (Winnipeg: University of Manitoba Press, 1988).

*Chapter One*

# "So Blind and So Ignorant": Looking into Other Eyes

1. Paul Le Jeune, *Jesuit Relations*, August 6, 1634.
2. Agwachiwagan, *Jesuit Relations*, September 21, 1643.
3. Christien Le Clerq, *New Relations of Gaspesia*, 1691.
4. Micmac Chief, *New Relations of Gaspesia*, 1691.
5. Baron Lahontan, *Some New Voyages to North America*, 1703.
6. Adario, *Some New Voyages to North America*, 1703.

## Introduction

When did Canadian history start? Certainly not with the arrival of Europeans. White contact may have been a pivotal event, but for many previous centuries indigenous cultures existed across the width and breadth of this continent. Surely a volume of primary research materials on Canada's history should begin with an examination of the cumulative knowledge that Native people passed orally from generation to generation. However, historians dealing with this early period face a difficult problem: some accept oral history as the Native equivalent to European documents and as the only means to reconstruct Native perspectives; others still rely on traditional European "hard evidence" and counter that the indigenous version of events is essentially unknowable. Recently in a landmark case, the Supreme Court of Canada ruled in favour of the significance of Native oral history which had previously been rejected as simple hearsay. Yet many historians remain uncomfortable with this legal precedent. Primary sources are typically eyewitness accounts created by specific individuals at specific times. They retain their original form for all subsequent generations to assess. Oral history, meanwhile, evolves over time through its retelling, and for some historians fits much better into the category of secondary rather than primary evidence. Whether non-Natives are even capable of assessing the cultural context of Native oral histories also raises serious evidentiary questions. Often classified as sacred and personal, some Native groups are now increasingly reluctant to share their histories with historians or anthropologists. Therefore, for better or worse, this documentary analysis begins with European accounts.

Unlike early explorers who had limited contact with North America and its inhabitants, French missionaries, soldiers, and administrators spent long periods not only observing and commenting upon the culture of local Native groups, but also recording the words spoken by individual Natives.

Can two wildly different cultures accurately perceive or interpret one another; and if they can, what are the limitations to using the evidence they presented at the time? What did Natives and Frenchmen see when they gazed upon each other for the first time? Early French records portrayed Native North Americans as "Noble Savages" from whom Europeans could learn much, but who could learn even more from Europeans—particularly about Catholicism and "civilization." Some adherents of this interpretation even stressed the "noble" prefix and elevated Native culture above French. Early eighteenth-century writers like Baron Lahontan, for example, transformed the Huron from a people who, in reality, tortured their captives to "children of nature" and "noble savages" who lived in a blissful state of natural grace and harmony, unencumbered by the stultifying trappings of French culture. Historical descriptions changed with time. The "noble savages" slowly gave way to pejorative depictions of a people that were "ruthless heathens," not noble at all.

The extremely few Native observations from this period remain highly suspect since they had to be translated and may have reflected more of what the recorder wished to hear rather than truly representing any Native perspective. While "Adario" may have been a partial anagram for the famed Huron orator, Kondiaronk (aka "The Rat"), whose speeches Lahontan did attend, most historians contend that these Native speeches were most likely invented as a subtle means for their French authors to critique their own societies and evade censorship. Nor is this issue merely about the dangers of motivation. Native spoken words may lose nuances when translated into written French and semantics evolve over time. The French word "sauvage," or "savage," for example, carried fewer negative connotations, and indeed some positive implications, in the seventeenth century. However, when we read the word with our modern sensibilities, we automatically wince at what we may perceive as European bigotry—which may be entirely untrue. As well, *Jesuit Relations,* the voluminous annual missionary reports sent to Rome, were heavily edited by priests who had never seen the New World but wished to encourage further missionary endeavours.

Post-modernist historians claim that there is no objective "truth" because truth exists in the eye of the beholder and is therefore relative to everyone else's truth. They argue that it is impossible to distinguish between truth and falsehood since reality is up to the individual perceiving it, and ethnocentrism, among other things, hopelessly biased the Jesuit and other early accounts of Native people. To this group, the Jesuits' effort to understand Indian culture is entirely unacceptable and amounts to "cognitive imperialism" and "academic colonization." This post-modernist approach, not surprisingly, wholeheartedly supports using Native oral history, even by itself, because the oral tradition gives equal voice to players who traditionally found themselves silenced. Furthermore, they say, because missionaries and their historians were, and are, cultural imperialists, oral history is an essential tool to correct the distorting biases promulgated by centuries of one-sided and agenda-laden interpretations.

It is, however, possible to make a few tentative observations on the Native view. Historians can ascertain, for example, that some Natives converted, abandoning their traditional religious values for new and foreign life patterns. Others accepted aspects of Christianity, though often not the central tenets, either for ideological reasons, or because lip service to Catholicism might improve trade. Most indigenous people, however, generally clung to their religion as tenaciously as the missionaries tried to convert them. They repeatedly reaffirmed their own pantheon, and strenuously resisted Christianity, either by avoiding the missionaries or by refusing to accept their teachings. They remained deeply suspicious of the message of the "Black Robes," and clearly recognized the cruel irony that promised them heaven and also brought them hell as both an abstract concept and a reality, as disease often arrived in unison with the European clergy.

## Discussion Points

1. Which aspects of Native society did Le Jeune, Le Clerq, and Lahontan admire? Which did they dislike? Did their descriptions serve to justify French domination and the conversion of Native people to Christianity?
2. Some argue that early Europeans never understood anything about Natives. Do these three documents tell us more about French society and its values, rather than Native culture?
3. From the perspective of Agwachiwagan, the Micmac chief, and Adario, what impact did French colonization have upon the North American Native population?
4. What indicates that these Native speeches may have been fabricated?
5. Consider the audience for whom these accounts were published. At that time who had the ability to read? What would these

readers have expected to find in literature from the New World? Would the characteristics of the reading public and their expectations have affected these accounts?

## Documents

### 1. Paul Le Jeune, *Jesuit Relations*, August 6, 1634.

... we begin with physical advantages, I will say that they possess these in abundance. They are tall, erect, strong, well proportioned, agile; and there is nothing effeminate in their appearance....

As to the mind of the Savage, it is of good quality. I believe that souls are all made from the same stock, and that they do not materially differ; hence, these barbarians having well formed bodies, and organs well regulated and well arranged, their minds ought to work with ease. Education and instruction alone are lacking. Their soul is a soil which is naturally good, but loaded down with all the evils that a land abandoned since the birth of the world can produce. I naturally compare our Savages with certain villagers, because both are usually without education, though our Peasants are superior in this regard; and yet I have not seen anyone thus far, of those who have come to this country, who does not confess and frankly admit that the Savages are more intelligent than our ordinary peasants.

Moreover, if it is a great blessing to be free from a great evil, our Savages are happy; for the two tyrants who provide hell and torture for many of our Europeans, do not reign in their great forests,—I mean ambition and avarice. As they have neither political organization, nor offices, nor dignities, nor any authority, for they only obey their Chief through good will toward him, therefore they never kill each other to acquire these honors. Also, as they are contented with a mere living, not one of them gives himself to the Devil to acquire wealth.

They make a pretence of never getting angry, not because of the beauty of this virtue, for which they have not even a name, but for their own contentment and happiness, I mean, to avoid the bitterness caused by anger....

Whoever professes not to get angry, ought also to make a profession of patience; the Savages surpass us to such an extent, in this respect, that we ought to be ashamed. I saw them, in their hardships and in their labors, suffer with cheerfulness. My host, wondering at the great number of people who I told him were in France, asked me if the men were good, if they did not become angry, if they were patient. I have never seen such patience as is shown by a sick Savage.

You may yell, storm, jump, dance, and he will scarcely ever complain. I found myself, with them, threatened with great suffering; they said to me, "We shall be sometimes two days, sometimes three, without eating, for lack of food; take courage, Chihiné, let thy soul be strong to endure suffering and hardship; keep thyself from being sad, otherwise thou wilt be sick; see how we do not cease to laugh, although we have little to eat." One thing alone casts them down,—it is when they see death, for they fear this beyond measure; take away this apprehension from the Savages, and they will endure all kinds of degradation and discomfort, and all kinds of trials and suffering very patiently....

They are very much attached to each other, and agree admirably. You do not see any disputes, quarrels, enmities, or reproaches among them. Men leave the arrangement of the household to the women, without interfering with them; they cut, and decide, and give away as they please, without making the husband angry. I have never seen my host ask a giddy young woman that he had with him what became of the provisions, although they were disappearing very fast. I have never heard the women complain because they were not invited to the feasts, because the men ate the good pieces, or because they had to work continually,— going in search of the fire wood for the fire, making the Houses, dressing the skins, and busying themselves in other very laborious work. Each one does her own little tasks, gently and peacefully, without any disputes. It is true, however, that they have neither gentleness nor courtesy in their utterance; and a Frenchman could not assume the accent, the tone, and the sharpness of their voices without becoming angry, yet they do not.

Tell a Savage that another savage has slandered him, and he will bow the head and not say a word; if they meet each other afterward, they will pretend not to know anything about it, acting as if nothing had been said. They treat each other as brothers; they harbor no spite against those of their own nation.

They are very generous among themselves and even make a show of not loving anything, of not being attached to the riches of the earth, so that they may not grieve if they lose them....

They do not open the hand half-way when they give,—I mean among themselves, for they are as ungrateful as possible toward strangers. You will see them take care of their kindered, the children of their friends, widows, orphans, and old men, never reproaching them in the least, giving them abundantly, sometimes whole Moose. This is truly the sign of a good heart and of a generous soul.

As there are many orphans among these people,—for they die in great numbers since they are addicted to drinking wine and brandy,—these poor children are scattered among the Cabins [dwellings] of their uncles, aunts, or other relatives. Do not suppose that they are snubbed and reproached because they eat the food of the household. Nothing of the kind, they are treated the same as the children of the father of the family, or at least almost the same, and are dressed as well as possible.

They are not fastidious in their food, beds, and clothes, but are very slovenly. They never complain of what is given them; if it be cold, if it be warm, it does not matter. When the food is cooked, it is divided without waiting for any one, not even the master of the house; a share is reserved for him, which is given to him cold. I have never heard my host complain because they did not wait for him, if he were only a few steps from the Cabin. They often sleep upon the ground, at the sign of the stars. They will pass one, two, and three days without eating, not ceasing to row, hunt, and fatigue themselves as much as they can. It will be seen in the course of this relation, that all I have said in this chapter is very true; and yet I would not dare to assert that I have seen one act of real moral virtue in a Savage. They have nothing but their own pleasure and satisfaction in view. Add to this the fear of being blamed, and the glory of seeming to be good hunters, and you have all that actuates them in their transactions.

The Savages, being filled with errors, are also haughty and proud. Humility is born of truth, vanity of error and falsehood. They are void of the knowledge of truth, and are in consequence, mainly occupied with thought of themselves. They imagine that they ought by right of birth, to enjoy the liberty of Wild ass colts, rendering no homage to anyone whomsoever, except when they like. They have reproached me a hundred times because we fear our Captains, while they laugh at and make sport of theirs. All the authority of their chief is in his tongue's end; for he is powerful in so far as he is eloquent; and, even if he kills himself talking and haranguing, he will not be obeyed unless he pleases the Savages.

I do not believe that there is a nation under heaven more given to sneering and bantering than that of the Montagnais. Their life is passed in eating, laughing, and making sport of each other, and of all the people they know. There is nothing serious about them, except occasionally, when they make a pretense among us of being grave and dignified; but among themselves they are real buffoons and genuine children, who ask only to laugh. Sometimes I annoyed them a little, specially the Sorcerer, by calling them children, and showing them that I never could place any reliance upon all their answers; because, if I questioned them about one thing, they told me about something else, only to get something to laugh and jest about; and consequently I could not know when they were speaking seriously, or when they were jesting. The usual conclusion of their discourses and conversations is: "Really, we did make a great deal of sport of such and such a one."

I have shown in my former letters how vindictive the Savages are toward their enemies, with what fury and cruelty they treat them, eating them after they have made them suffer all that an incarnate fiend could invent. This fury is common to the women as well as to the men, and they even surpass the latter in this respect. I have said that they eat the lice they find upon themselves, not that they like the taste of them, but because they want to bite those that bite them.

These people are very little moved by compassion. When anyone is sick in their Cabins, they ordinarily do not cease to cry and storm, and make as much noise as if everybody were in good health. They do not know what it is to take care of a poor invalid, and to give him the food which is good for him; if he asks for something to drink, it is given to him, if he asks for something to eat, it is given to him, but otherwise he is neglected; to coax him with love and gentleness, is a language which they do not understand. As long as a patient can eat, they will carry or drag him with them; if he stops eating, they believe that it is all over with him and kill him, as much to free him from the sufferings that he is enduring, as to relieve themselves of the trouble of taking him with them when they go to some other place. I have both admired and pitied the patience of the invalids whom I have seen among them.

The Savages are slanderous beyond all belief; I say, also among themselves, for they do not even spare their nearest relations, and with it all they are deceitful. For, if one speaks ill of another, they all jeer with loud laughter; if the other appears upon the scene, the first one will show him as much affection and treat him with as much love, as if he had elevated him to the third heaven by his praise. The reason of this is, it seems to me, that their slanders and derision do not come from malicious hearts or from infected mouths, but from a mind which says what it thinks in order to give itself free scope, and which seeks gratification from everything, even from slander and mockery. Hence they are not troubled even if they are told that others are making sport of them, or have injured their reputation....

Lying is as natural to Savages as talking, not among themselves, but to strangers. Hence it can be said that fear and hope, in one word, interest, is the measure of their fidelity. I would not be willing to trust them, except as they would fear to be punished if they failed in their duty, or hoped to be rewarded if they were faithful to it. They do not know what it is to keep a secret, to keep their word, and to love with constancy,—especially those who are not of their nation, for they are harmonious among themselves, and their slanders and raillery do not disturb their peace and friendly intercourse.

I will say in passing that the Montagnais Savages are not thieves. The doors of the French are open to them, because their hands can be trusted; but, as to the Hurons, if a person had as many eyes as they have fingers on their hands, he could not prevent them from stealing, for they steal with their feet. They make a profession of this art, and expect to be beaten if they are discovered. For, as I have already remarked, they will endure the blows which you give them, patiently, not as an acknowledgment of their fault, but as a punishment for their stupidity in allowing themselves to be detected in their theft.

Eating among the Savages is like drinking among the drunkards of Europe. Those dry and ever-thirsty souls would willingly end their lives in a tub of malmsey, and the Savages in a pot full of meat; those over there, talk only of drinking, and these here only of eating. It is giving a sort of insult to a Savage to refuse the pieces which he offers you ... the greatest satisfaction that they can have in their Paradise is in the stomach. I do not hesitate to exclaim: Oh, how just is the judgment of God, that these people, who place their ultimate happiness in eating, are always hungry, and are only fed like dogs; for their most splendid feastings are, so to speak, only the bones and the leavings of the tables of Europe! Their first act, upon awakening in the morning, is to stretch out their arms toward their bark dish full of meat, and then to eat. When I first began to stay with them, I tried to introduce the custom of praying to God before eating, and in fact I pronounced a blessing when they wanted it done. But the Apostate said to me, "If you want to pray as many times as they will eat in your Cabin, prepare to say your benedicite more than twenty times before night." They end the day as they begin it, always with a morsel in their mouths, or with their pipes to smoke when they lay their heads on the pillow to rest.

The Savages have always been gluttons, but since the coming of the Europeans they have become such drunkards, that,—although they see clearly that these new drinks, the wine and brandy which are brought to them, are depopulating their country, of which they themselves complain,—they cannot abstain from drinking, taking pride in getting drunk and in making others drunk. It is true that they die in great numbers; but I am astonished that they can resist it as long as they do. For, give two Savages two or three bottles of brandy, they will sit down and, without eating, will drink, one after the other, until they have emptied them ... those whom I have met are very lewd, both men and women. God! What blindness! How great is the happiness of Christian people! How great the chastisement of these....

Their lips are constantly foul with these obscenities; and it is the same with the little children. So I said to them, at one time, that if hogs and dogs knew how to talk, they would adopt their language. Indeed, if the shameless Sorcerer had not come into the Cabin where I was, I should have gained thus much from my people, that not one of them would dare to speak of impure things in my presence; but this impertinent fellow ruled the others. The older women go almost naked, the girls and young women are very modestly clad; but, among themselves, their language has the foul odor of the sewers. It must be admitted, however, that if liberty to gorge oneself in such filth existed among some Christians, as it does among these people, one would see very different exhibitions of excess from what are seen here; for, even despite the laws, both Divine and human, dissoluteness strides more openly there than here. For here the eyes are not offended.

Now, as these people are well aware of this corruption, they prefer to take the children of their sisters as heirs, rather than their own, or than those of their brothers, calling in question the fidelity of their wives, and being unable to doubt that these nephews come from their own blood. Also among the Hurons,—who are more licentious than our Montagnais, because they are better fed,—it is not the child of a Captain but his sister's son, who succeeds the father.

The Sorcerer told me one day that the women were fond of him, for, as the Savages say, it is his demon that makes the sex love him. I told him that it was not honorable for a woman to love anyone else except her husband; and that, this evil being among them, he himself was not sure that his son, who was there present, was his son. He replied, "Thou hast no sense. You French people love only your own children; but we all love all the children of our tribe." I began to laugh, seeing that he philosophized in horse and mule fashion.

They are dirty in their habits, in their postures, in their homes, and in their eating; yet there is no lack of propriety among them, for everything that gives satisfaction to the senses, passes as propriety.

I have said that they are dirty in their homes; the entrance to their Cabins is like a pig-pen. They never sweep their houses, they carpet them at first with branches of pine, but on the third day these branches are full of fur, feathers, hair, shavings, or whittlings of wood. Yet they have no other seats, nor beds upon which to sleep. From this it may be seen how full of dirt their clothes must be; it is true that this dirt and filth does not show as much upon their clothes as upon ours.

As to their postures, they follow their own sweet wills, and not the rules of good breeding. The Savages never prefer what is decent to what is agreeable. I have often seen the pretended magician lie down entirely naked—except a miserable strip of cloth dirtier than a dish-cloth, and blacker than an oven-mop—draw up one of his legs against his thigh, place the other upon his raised knee, and harangue his people in this position, his audience being scarcely more graceful.

As to their food, it is very little, if any, cleaner than the swill given to animals, and not always even as clean. I say nothing in exaggeration, as I have tasted it and lived upon it for almost six months. We had three persons in our Cabin affiicted with scrofula,—the son of the Sorcerer, whose ear was very disgusting and horrid from this disease; his nephew, who had it in his neck; and a daughter, who had it under one arm. I do not know whether this is the real scrofula; whatever it is, this sore is full of pus, and covered with a horrible-looking crust. They are nearly all attacked by this disease, when young, both on account of their filthy habits, and because they eat and drink indiscriminately with the sick. I have seen them a hundred times paddle about in the kettle containing our common drink; wash their hands in it; drink from it, thrusting in their heads, like the animals; and throw into it their leavings; for this is the custom of the Savages, to thrust sticks into it that are half-burned and covered with ashes; to dip therein their bark plates covered with grease, the fur of the Moose, and hair; and to dip water therefrom with kettles as black as the chimney; and after that, we all drank from this black broth, as if it were ambrosia. This is not all; they throw therein the bones that they have gnawed, then put water or snow in the kettle, let it boil, and behold their hippocras. One day some shoes, which had just been taken off, fell into our drink; they soaked there as long as they pleased, and were withdrawn without exciting any special attention, and then the water was drunk as if nothing whatever had happened. I am not very fastidious, but I was not very thirsty as long as this malmsey lasted.

They never wash their hands expressly before eating, still less their kettles, and the meat they cook, not at all,—although it is usually (I say this because I have seen it hundreds of times) all covered with the animal's hairs, and with those from their own heads. I have never drunk any broth among them, from which I did not have to throw out many of these hairs, and a variety of other rubbish, such as cinders, little pieces of wood, and even sticks with which they have stirred the fire and frequently stirred up the contents of the kettle. I have occasionally seen them take a blazing brand and put it in the ashes to extinguish it, then, almost without shaking it, dip it into the kettle where our dinner was simmering.

When they are engaged in drying meat, they will throw down upon the ground a whole side of the Moose, beat it with stones, walk over it, trample upon it with their dirty feet; the hairs of men and of animals, the feathers of birds, if they have killed any, dirt and ashes,—all these are ground into the meat, which they make almost as hard as wood with the smoke. Then when they come to eat this dried meat, all goes together into the stomach, for they have not washed it. In fact, they think that we are very foolish to wash our meat, for some of the grease goes away with the water.

When the kettle begins to boil, they gather the scum very carefully and eat it as a delicacy. They gave some to me as a favor, and during our famine I found it good; but since then, when I sometimes happened to decline this present, they called me fastidious and proud. They take delight in hunting rats and mice, the same as rabbits, and find them just as good.

## 2. Agwachiwagan, *Jesuit Relations*, September 21, 1643.

... I learn that your village is moved by the discourses of the black gowns; that several have already received Baptism; that a larger number desire it; and that you yourselves lend ear to discourses that, in sooth, charm them at first. But you are doubtless ignorant, my brothers, to what these promises of eternal life tend. I have been among the French at Quebec and at the Three Rivers. They have taught me the very substance of their doctrine. I know everything about matters of the Faith. But, the more I fathomed their mysteries, the less clearly did I see. They are fables, invented to inspire us with real fear of an imaginary fire; and, in the false hope of good that can never come to us, we involve ourselves in inevitable dangers. I do not speak without having had experience of it. Some years ago, you saw the Algonquins in such numbers that we were the terror of our enemies. Now we are reduced to nothing; disease has exterminated us; war has decimated us; famine pursues us, wherever we go. It is the Faith that brings these misfortunes upon us. That you may not doubt that what I say is true, when I went down to Quebec two Years ago, to see what had been the result of the Faith of the Montagnais and Algonquins who had received Baptism, I was shown a house full of one-eyed, lame, crippled, and blind persons; of fleshless skeletons; and of people who all carried death on their countenances. Such are the appanages of the Faith. That is the House that they esteem (he spoke of the hospital built near Quebec for the sick); "those are the people upon whom they fawn, because to resolve to be a Christian is to resign oneself to all those miseries. Besides that, one must expect to be no longer lucky either in fishing or in hunting. Finally, my brothers," he added, "if today I saw the whole of your village become Christian I would be satisfied to be considered the greatest impostor in the world if one of you remained alive before the end of the third year. For my part, I foresaw those misfortunes caused by the Faith. In vain did I predict them to those who, after refusing to believe me, acknowledged but too late, after their misfortune, that they were deceived. Has any Christian escaped, as I have, from the clutches of a thousand deaths prepared for him? If their God be in reality the Almighty, why does he leave them in opprobrium, why does he not break their chains? why is he not their liberator? why does he not show in a country where he wishes to be acknowledged that it is truly good to have him for one's Sovereign? But since those who refuse to worship him are happier than those who are his subjects, if you, my brothers, like me, have any feeling and love for yourselves, for your children, and for your country, choose with me to consider him rather as an enemy than as a friend."

## 3. Christien Le Clerq, *New Relations of Gaspesia*, 1691.

No matter what can be said of this reasoning, I assert, for my part, that I should consider these Indians incomparably more fortunate than ourselves, and that the life of these barbarians would even be capable of inspiring envy, if they had the instructions, the understanding, and the same means for their salvation which God has given us that we may save ourselves by preference over so many poor pagans, and as a result of His pity; for, after all, their lives are not vexed by a thousand annoyances as are ours. They have not among them those situations or offices, whether in the judiciary or in war, which are sought among us with so much ambition. Possessing nothing of their own, they are consequently free from trickery and legal proceedings in connection with inheritances from their relatives. The names of sergeant, of attorney, of clerk, of judge, or president are unknown to them. All their ambition centres in surprising and killing quantities of beavers, moose, seals, and other wild beasts in order to obtain their flesh for food and their skins for clothing. They live in very great harmony, never quarrelling and never beating one another except in drunkenness. On the contrary, they mutually aid one another in their needs with much charity and without self-seeking. There is continual joy in their wigwams. The multitude of their children does not embarrass them, for, far from being annoyed by these, they consider themselves just that much the more fortunate and richer as their family is more numerous.... [T]hey are also free from all those anxieties which we give ourselves in connection with the accumulation of property for the purpose of elevating children in society and in importance.... This duty, which in Europe is considered too onerous, is viewed by our Indians as very honourable, very advantageous, and very useful, and he who has the largest number of children is the most highly esteemed of the entire nation. This is because he finds more support for his old age, and because, in their condition in life, the boys and girls contribute equally to the happiness and joy of those who have given them birth....

It is certainly true that our Gaspesians had so little knowledge of bread and wine when the French arrived for the first time in their country, that these barbarians mistook the bread which was given them for a piece of birch tinder, and became convinced that the French were equally cruel and inhuman, since in their amusements, said the Indians, they drank blood without repugnance. It was thus they designated wine. Therefore they remained some time not only without tasting it, but even without wishing to become in any manner intimate, or to hold intercourse, with a nation which they believed to be accustomed to blood and carnage. Nevertheless, in the end, they became accustomed gradually to this drink, and it were to be wished that they had still to-day the same horror of wine and brandy, for they drink it even to drunkenness, to the prejudice of their salvation and of Christianity; and it makes them commit cruelties much greater than those which they had imagined in the conduct of the French....

The months of January and February are for these barbarians, as a rule, a time of involuntary penitence and very rigorous fasting, which is also often very sad as well, in view of the cruel and horrible results which it causes among them. Nevertheless they could very easily prevent its unfortunate consequences if they would but follow the example of the ants, and of the little squirrels, which, by an instinct as admirable as it is natural, accumulate with care in summer the wherewithal to subsist in plenty during the winter. But, after all, our Gaspesians are of those people who take no thought for the morrow, though this is much more because of laziness in collecting good provisions than through zeal in obeying the counsel which God has given thereon in His Holy Gospel. They are convinced that fifteen to twenty lumps of meat, or of fish dried and cured in the smoke, are more than enough to support them for the space of five to six months. Since, however, they are a people of good appetite, they consume their provisions very much sooner than they expect. This exposes them often to the danger of dying from hunger, through lack of provision which they could easily possess in abundance if they would only take the trouble to gather it. But these barbarians, being wanderers and vagabonds, do not plough the ground, nor do they harvest Indian corn, or peas, or pumpkins, as do the Iroquois, the Hurons, the Algonquins, and several other nations of Canada. In consequence they are sometimes reduced to so great need that they have neither the strength nor the spirit to leave their wigwams in order to go seek in the woods the wherewithal for living. It is then impossible to behold without compassion the innocent children, who, being nothing more than skin and bone, exhibit clearly enough in their wholly emaciated faces and in their living skeletons, the cruel hunger which they are suffering through the negligence of their fathers and mothers, who find themselves obliged, along with their unhappy children, to eat curdled blood, scrapings of skin, old moccasins, and a thousand other things incompatible with the life of man. All this would be little if they did not come sometimes to other extremes far more affecting and horrible.

... those who imagine a Gaspesian Indian as a monster of nature will understand only with difficulty the charity with which they mutually comfort one another. The strong take pleasure in supporting the feeble; and those who by their hunting procure many furs, give some in charity to those who have none, either in order to pay the debts of these, or to clothe them, or to obtain for them the necessaries of life. Widows and orphans receive presents, and if there is any widow who is unable to support her children, the old men take charge of them, and distribute and give them to the best hunters, with whom they live, neither more nor less than as if they were the actual children of the wigwam. It would be a shame, and a kind of fault worthy of eternal reproach, if it was known that an Indian, when he had provisions in abundance, did not make gift thereof to those whom he knew to be in want and in need....

For it is true that these people are distinguished in their manner of living by an uncleanness which turns the stomach. I cannot believe that there is any nation in the world so disgusting in its manners of drinking and eating as the Gaspesian, excepting, perhaps, some other peoples of this new world. Hence it is true that of all the troubles which the missionaries suffer at first in order to accustom themselves to the manner of life of the Indians for the sake of instructing them in the maxims of Christianity, this is without a doubt one of the most difficult to endure, because it very often causes a rising of the stomach. Our Gaspesians never clean their kettles except the first time they use them, because, they say, they are afraid of the verdigris, which is in no danger of attaching itself to them, when they are well greased and burnt. Nor do they ever skim it off, because it seems to them that this is removing grease from the pot, and just so much good material is lost. This causes the meat to be all stuffed with a black and thick scum, like little meat balls which have nearly the appearance of curdled milk. They content themselves with removing simply the largest moose hairs, although the meat may have been dragged around the campfire for five or six days, and the dogs also may have tasted it beforehand. They have no other tables than the flat ground, nor other napkins for wiping their hands than their moccasins, or their hair, on which they sedulously rub their hands. In a word there is nothing that is not rough, gross and repellent in the extraordinary manner of life of these barbarians, who observe neither in drinking nor in eating any rules of politeness or of civility....

The Gaspesians do not know how to read nor how to write. They have, nevertheless, enough understanding and memory to learn how to do both if only they were willing to give the necessary application. But aside from the fickleness and instability of their minds, which they are willing to apply only in so far as it pleases them, they all have the false and ridiculous belief that they would not live long if they were as learned as the French. From this it comes that they are pleased to live and to die in their natural ignorance.... [A]nd it can be said with truth that there are seen in Gaspesia as fine children, and persons as well built, as in France; whilst among them there are as a rule neither humpbacks nor crippled, one-eyed, blind, or maimed persons.

They enjoy a perfect health, not being subject to an infinity of diseases as we are. They are neither too stout nor too thin, and one does not see among the Gaspesians any of those fat bellies full of humours and of grease. Consequently the very names of gout, stone, gravel, gall, colic, rheumatism, are entirely unknown to them.

They all have naturally a sound mind, and common sense beyond that which is supposed in France. They conduct their affairs cleverly ... our Gaspesians can call themselves happy, because they have neither avarice nor ambition—those two cruel executioners which give pain and torture to a multitude of persons. As they have neither police, nor taxes, nor office, nor commandment which is absolute (for they obey, as we have said, only their head men and their chiefs in so far as it pleases them), they scarcely give themselves the trouble to amass riches, or to make a fortune more considerable than that which they possess in their woods. They are content enough provided that they have the wherewithal for living, and that they have the reputation of being good warriors and good hunters, in which they reckon all their glory and their ambition. They are naturally fond of their repose, putting away from them, as far as they can, all the subjects for annoyance which would trouble them. Hence it comes about that they never contradict anyone, and that they let everyone do as he pleases, even to the extent that the fathers and the mothers do not dare correct their children, but permit their misbehaviour for fear of vexing them by chastising them.

They never quarrel and never are angry with one another, not because of any inclination they have to practise virtue, but for their own satisfaction, and in the fear, as we have just said, of troubling their repose, of which they are wholly idolaters.

Indeed, if any natural antipathy exists between husband and wife, or if they cannot live together in perfect understanding, they separate from one another, in order to seek elsewhere the peace and union which they cannot find together. Consequently they cannot understand how one can submit to the indissolubility of marriage.... In a word, they hold it as a maxim that each one is free: that one can do whatever he wishes: and that it is not sensible to put constraint upon men. It is necessary, say they, to live without annoyance and disquiet, to be content with that which one has, and to endure with constancy the misfortunes.... In a word, they rely upon liking nothing, and upon not becoming attached to the goods of the earth, in order not to be grieved or sad when they lose them. They are, as a rule, always joyous, without being uneasy as to who will pay their debts....

It is not the same, however, when they are ill-treated without cause, for then everything is to be feared from them. As they are very vindictive against strangers, they preserve resentment for the ill-treatment in their hearts until they are entirely avenged for the injury or for the affront which will have been wrongly done them. They will even make themselves drunk on purpose, or they will pretend to be full with brandy, in order to carry out their wicked plan, imagining that they will always be amply justified in the crime which they have committed if they but say to the elders and heads of the nation, that they were tipsy, and that they had no reason or judgment during their drunkenness ...

They are so generous and liberal towards one another that they seem not to have any attachment to the little they possess, for they deprive themselves thereof very willingly and in very good spirit the very moment when they know that their friends have need of it. It is true that this generous disposition is undergoing some alteration since the French, through the commerce which they have with them, have gradually accustomed them to traffic and not to give anything for nothing; for, prior to the time when trade came into use among these people, it was as in the Golden Age, and everything was common property among them.

They are naturally fickle, mockers, slanderers, and dissimulators. They are not true to their promises except in so far as they are restrained either by fear or by hope; and they believe any person would have no sense who would keep his word against his own interest.

... [I]n fact they do not know what civility is, nor decorum. Since they consider themselves all equal, and one as great, as powerful, and as rich as another, they mock openly at our bowings, at our compliments, and at our embracings. They never remove their hats when they enter our dwellings....

They are filthy and vile in their wigwams, of which the approaches are filled with excrements, feathers, chips, shreds of skins, and very often with entrails of the animals or the fishes which they take in hunting or fishing. In their eating they wash their meat only very superficially before putting it upon the fire, and they never clean the kettle except the first time that they use it. Their clothes are all filthy, both outside and inside, and soaked with oil and grease, of which the stink often produces sickness of the stomach. They hunt for vermin before everybody, without turning aside even a little. They make it walk for fun upon their hands, and they eat it as if it were something good. They find the use of our handkerchiefs ridiculous; they mock at us and say that it is placing excrements in our pockets. Finally, however calm it may be outside of the wigwam, there always prevails inside a very inconvenient wind, since these Indians let it go very freely, especially when they have eaten much moose....

There is no one, however, more to be pitied than the sick persons, who endure without complaint the hubbub, the noise, and the fuss of the juggler [somewhat analogous to a shaman] and of those in the wigwam. It seems indeed that our Gaspesians, who in other respects seem sufficiently humane and kindly, are lacking in regard to charity and consideration for their sick. It can in fact be said that they do not know how to take care of them, they give them indifferently everything which they desire, both to drink and to eat, and whenever they ask it. They take the sick persons along, and carry or embark them with themselves on their voyages when there is any appearance of recovery. But if the recovery of the sick man is wholly despaired of, so that he can no more eat, drink, nor smoke, they sometimes break his head, as much to relieve the suffering he endures as to save themselves the trouble which they have in taking him everywhere with them.

Nor have they any better idea what it means to comfort a poor invalid, and from the moment when he no longer eats or smokes any more tobacco, or when he loses speech, they abandon him entirely, and never speak to him a single word of tenderness or comfort....

### 4. Micmac Chief, *New Relations of Gaspesia*, 1691.

I am greatly astonished that the French have so little cleverness, as they seem to exhibit in the matter of which thou hast just told me on their behalf, in the effort to persuade us to convert our poles, our barks, and our wigwams into those houses of stone and of wood which are tall and lofty, according to their account, as these trees. Very well! But why now, do men of five to six feet in height need houses which are sixty to eighty? For, in fact, as thou knowest very well thyself, Patriarch—do we not find in our own all the conveniences and the advantages that you have with yours, such as reposing, drinking, sleeping, eating, and amusing ourselves with our friends when we wish? This is not all, my brother, hast thou as much ingenuity and cleverness as the Indians, who carry their houses and their wigwams with them so that they may lodge wheresoever they please, independently of any seignior whatsoever? Thou art not as bold nor as stout as we, because when thou goest on a voyage thou canst not carry upon thy shoulders thy buildings and thy edifices. Therefore it is necessary that thou prepares as many lodgings as thou makest changes of residence, or else thou lodgest in a hired house which does not belong to thee. As for us, we find ourselves secure from all these inconveniences, and we can always say, more truly than thou, that we are at home everywhere, because we set up our wigwams with ease wheresoever we go, and without asking permission of anybody. Thou reproachest us, very inappropriately, that our country is a little hell in contrast with France, which thou comparest to a terrestrial paradise, inasmuch as it yields thee, so thou sayest, every kind of provision in abundance. Thou sayest of us also that we are the most miserable and most unhappy of all men, living without religion, without manners, without honour, without social order, and, in a word, without any rules, like the beasts in our woods and our forests, lacking bread, wine, and a thousand other comforts which thou hast in superfluity in Europe. Well, my brother, if thou dost not yet know the real feelings which our Indians have towards thy country and towards all thy nation, it is proper that I inform thee at once. I beg thee now to believe that, all miserable as we seem in thine eyes, we consider ourselves nevertheless much happier than thou in this, that we are very content with the little that we have; and believe also once for all, I pray, that thou deceivest thyself greatly if thou thinkest to persuade us that thy country is better than ours. For if France, as thou sayest, is a little terrestrial paradise, art thou sensible to leave it? And why abandon wives, children, relatives, and friends? Why risk thy life and thy property every year, and why venture thyself with such risk, in any season whatsoever, to the storms and tempests of the sea in order to come to a strange and barbarous country which thou considerest the poorest and least fortunate of the world? Besides, since we are wholly convinced of the contrary, we scarcely take the trouble to go to France, because we fear, with good reason, lest we find little satisfaction there, seeing, in our own experience, that those who are natives thereof leave it every year in order to enrich themselves on our shores. We believe, further, that you are also incomparably poorer than we, and that you are only simple journeymen, valets, servants, and slaves, all masters and grand captains though you may appear, seeing that you glory in our old rags and in our miserable suits of beaver which can no longer be of use to us, and that you find among us, in the fishery for cod which you make in these parts, the wherewithal to comfort your misery and the poverty which oppresses you. As to us, we find all our riches and all our conveniences among ourselves, without trouble and without exposing our lives to the dangers in which you find yourselves constantly through your long voyages. And, whilst feeling compassion for you in the sweetness of our repose, we wonder at the anxieties and cares which you give yourselves night and day in order to load your ship. We see also that all your people live, as a rule, only upon cod which you catch among us. It is everlastingly nothing but cod—cod in the morning, cod at midday, cod at evening, and always cod, until things come to such a pass that if you wish some good morsels, it is at our expense; and you are obliged to have recourse to the Indians, whom you despise so much, and to beg them to go a-hunting that you may be regaled. Now tell me this one little thing, if thou hast any sense: Which of these two is the wisest and happiest—he who labours without ceasing and only obtains, and that with great trouble, enough to live on, or he who rests in comfort and finds all that he needs in the pleasure of hunting and fishing? It is true, that we have not always had the use of bread and of wine which your France produces; but, in fact, before the arrival of the French in these parts, did not the Gaspesians live much longer than now? And if we have not any longer among us any of those old men of a hundred and thirty to forty years, it is only because we are gradually adopting your manner of living, for experience is making it very plain that those of us live longest who, despising your bread, your wine, and your brandy, are content with their natural food of beaver, of moose, of waterfowl, and fish, in accord with the custom of our ancestors and of all the Gaspesian nation. Learn now, my brother, once for all, because I must open to thee my heart: there is no Indian who does not consider himself infinitely more happy and more powerful than the French.

## 5. Baron Lahontan, *Some New Voyages to North America*, 1703.

All the savages are of a Sanguine Constitution, inclining to an Olive Colour, and generally speaking they have good Faces and proper Persons. 'Tis a great rarity to find any among them that are Lame, Hunch-back'd, One-ey'd, Blind, or Dumb. Their Eyes are large and black as well as their Hair; their Teeth are White like Ivory, and the Breath that springs from their Mouth in expiration is as pure as the Air that they suck in in Inspiration.... They are neither so strong nor so vigorous as most of the French are in raising of Weights with their Arms, or carrying of Burdens on their Backs; but to make amends for that, they are indefatigable and inur'd to Hardships, insomuch that the Inconveniences of Cold or Heat have no impression upon them; their whole time being spent in the way of Exercise, whether in running up and down at Hunting and Fishing, or in Dancing and playing at Foot-ball, or such Games as require the Motion of the Legs.

The Women are of an indifferent Stature, and as handsom in the Face as you can well imagine; but then they are so fat, unwieldy and ill-built, that they'l scarce tempt any but Savages. Their hair is rolled up behind with a sort of Rib-band, and that Roller hangs down to their Girdle; they never offer to cut their Hair during the whole Course of their Lives, whereas the Men cut theirs every Month.

The Savages are very Healthy, and unacquainted with an infinity of Dis-eases, that plague the *Europeans*, such as the *Palsey*, the *Dropsey*, the *Gout*, the *Phthisick*, the *Asthma*, the *Gravel*, and the *Stone*: But at the same time they are liable to the *Small-Pox, and to Pleurisies.* If a Man dies at the Age of Sixty Years, they think he dies young, for they commonly live to Eighty or an Hundred; nay, I met with two that were turned of an Hundred several Years. But there are some among them that do not live so long, because they voluntarily shorten their Lives by poysoning themselves....

The Savages are utter Strangers to distinctions of Property, for what be-longs to one is equally anothers. If anyone of them be in danger at the Beaver Hunting the rest fly to his Assistance without being so much as ask'd. If his Fusee bursts they are ready to offer him their own. If any of his Children be kill'd or taken by the Enemy, he is presently furnish'd with as many Slaves as he hath occasion for. Money is in use with none of them but those that are Christians, who live in the Suburbs of our Towns. The others will not touch or so much as look upon Silver, but give it the odious Name of the *French Serpent.* They'l tell you that amongst us the People Murther, Plunder, Defame, and betray one another, for Money, that the Husbands make Merchandize of their Wives, and the Mothers of their Daughters, for the Lucre of that Metal. They think it unac-countable that one Man should have more than another, and that the Rich should have more Respect than the Poor. In short, they say, the name of Savages which we bestow upon them would fit ourselves better, since there is nothing in our Actions that bears an appearance of Wisdom. Such as have been in France were continually teazing us with the Faults and Disorders they observ'd in our Towns, as being occasion'd by Money. 'Tis in vain to remonstrate to them how useful the Distinction of Property is for the support of a Society: They make a Jest of what's to be said on that Head. In fine, they neither Quarrel nor Fight, nor Slander one another. They scoff at Arts and Sciences, and laugh at the differ-ence of Degrees which is observ'd with us. They brand us for Slaves, and call us miserable Souls, whose Life is not worth having, alledging, That we degrade our selves in subjugating our selves to one Man who possesses the whole Power, and is bound by no Law but his Own Will; That we have continual Jars among our selves; that our Children rebel against their Parents; that we Imprison one another, and publickly promote our Own Destruction. Besides, they value themselves above any thing that you can imagine, and this is the reason they always give for't, *That one's as much Master as another, and since Men are all made of the same Clay there should be no Distinction or Superiority among them.* They pretend that their contented way of living far surpasses Our Riches; That all Our Siences are not so valuable as the Art of leading a peaceful calm Life. That a Man is not a Man with us any farther than Riches will make him; but among them the true Qualifications of a Man are, to run well, to hunt, to bend the Bow and manage the Fusee, to work a Cannoo, to understand War, to know Forrests, to subsist upon a little, to build Cottages, to fell Trees, and to be able to travel an hundred Leagues in a Wood without any Guide, or other Provision than his Bow and Arrows. They say, we are great Cheats in selling them bad Wares four times dearer than they are worth, by way of Exchange for their Beaver-skins: That our Fusees are continually bursting and laming them, after they have paid sufficient Prices for them.

The greatest Passion of the Savages consists in the Implacable Hatred they bear to their Enemies; that is, all Nations with whom they are at Open War: They value themselves mightily upon their Valour; insomuch that they have scarce any regard to any thing else. One may say That they are wholly govern'd by Temperament, and their Society is perfect Mechanism. They have neither Laws, Judges, nor Priests; they are naturally inclin'd to Gravity, which makes them very circumspect in their Words and Actions. They observe a certain Medium between Gayety and Melancholy. The *French* Air they could not away with; and there was none but the younger sort of them that approv'd of our Fashions.

They are as ignorant of *Geography* as of other *Sciences,* and yet they draw the most exact Maps imaginable of the Countries they're acquainted with, for there's nothing wanting in them but the Longitude and Latitude of Places: They set down the True *North* according to the *Pole Star*; The Ports, Harbours, Rivers, Creeks and Coasts, of the Lakes; the Roads, Mountains, Woods, Marshes, Meadows, and counting the distances by Journeys and Half-journeys of the Warriers, and allowing to every Journey Five Leagues. These *Chorographical Maps* are drawn upon the Rind of your Birch Tree; and when the Old Men hold a Council about War or Hunting, they're always sure to consult them.

This People cannot conceive that the *Europeans*, who value themselves upon their Sense and Knowledge, should be so blind and so ignorant as not to know that Marriage in their way is a source of Trouble and Uneasiness. To be ingag'd for one's Life time, to them is matter of Wonder and Surprise. They look upon it as a monstrous thing to be tied one to another without any hopes of being able to untie or break the Knot.

## 6. Adario, *Some New Voyages to North America*, 1703.

I am ready to hear thee, my dear Brother, in order to be inform'd of a great many things that the Jesuits have been Preaching up for a long time; and I would have us to discourse together with all the freedom that may be. If your Belief is the same with that of the Jesuits, 'tis in vain to enter into a Conference; for they have entertain'd me with so many Fabulous and Romantick Stories, that all the credit I can give 'em, is to believe, that they have more Sense than to believe themselves.

How do you mean, without the Knowledge of the True God? What! are you mad? Do thou believe we are void of Religion, after thou hast dwelt so long amongst us? Do'st not thee know in the first place, that we acknowledge a Creator of the Universe, under the Title of the Great Spirit or Master of Life; whom we believe to be in every thing, and to be unconfin'd to Limits? That we own the Immortality of the Soul. That the Great Spirit has furnished us with a Rational Faculty, capable of distinguishing Good from Evil, as much as Heaven from Earth; to the end that we might Religiously observe the true Measures of Justice and Wisdom. That the Tranquility and Serenity of the Soul pleases the Great Master of Life: And on the other hand, that he abhors trouble and anxiety of Mind, because it renders Men Wicked. That Life is a Dream, and Death the Season of Awaking, in which the Soul sees and knows the Nature and Quality of all things, whether visible or invisible. That the utmost reach of our Minds can't go one Inch above the Surface of the Earth: So that we ought not to corrupt and spoil it by endeavouring to pry into Invisible and Improbable things. This my dear Friend is Our Belief, and act up to it with the greatest Exactness. We believe that we shall go to the Country of Souls after death; but we have no such apprehension as you have, of a good and bad Mansion after this Life, provided for the good and bad Souls; for we cannot tell whether every thing that appears faulty to Men, is so in the Eyes of God. If your Religion differs from ours, it do's not follow that we have none at all. Thou knowest that I have been in *France*, *New York* and *Quebec*; where I Study'd the Customs and Doctrines of the *English* and

*French*. The *Jesuits* allege, that out of five or six hundred sorts of Religions, there's only one that is the good and the true Religion, and that's their own; out of which no Man shall escape the Flames of a Fire that will burn his Soul to all Eternity. This is their allegation: But when they have said all, they cannot offer any Proof for it.

How do you mean, *without contradicting one another*! Why! That Book of Holy Things, is not it full of Contradictions? These Gospels that the Jesuits speak of, do not they occasion discord between the *French* and the *English*? And yet if we take your word for it, every Period of that Book Sprung from the Mouth of the Great Spirit. But if the Great Spirit mean'd that his Words should be understood, why did he talk so confusedly, and cloath his Words with an ambiguous Sense? One or two things must follow from this advance. If he was born and died upon the Earth, and made speeches here, why, then his discourses must be lost; for he would certainly have spoke so distinctly and plainly, that the very Children might conceive his meaning. Or, if you will have the Gospels to be his genuine Words, and contain nothing but what flow'd from him; why, then he must have come to raise Wars in the World instead of Peace; which cannot be. The *English* have told me that tho' their Gospels contain the same Words with the French, yet there's as great a difference between their Religion and yours, as between Night and Day. They say positively that their's is the best; and on the other hand, the Jesuits allege, that the Religion of the *English*, and of a thousand Nations besides, is good for nothing. If there be but one true Religion upon Earth, who must I believe in this case? Who is it that do's not take their own Religion to be the most perfect? How can the Capacity of Man be able to single out that Divine Religion from among so many more, that lay claim to the same Title? Believe me, my dear Brother, the Great Spirit is Wise, all his Works are perfect; 'tis he that made us, and he knows perfectly well what will become of us. 'Tis our part to act freely, without perplexing our thoughts about future things. He order'd thee to be Born in *France*, with intent that thou shouldest believe what thou neither seest nor conceivest; and me he has caus'd to be Born a *Huron*, to the end that I should give credit to nothing but what I understand, and what my reason teaches me.

I perceive then, the words of the Son of the Great Spirit are chargeable with self-contradiction or obscurity; for as much as you and the *English* dispute about his meaning with so much heat and animosity: And this seems to be the principal Spring of the hatred that these two Nations bear to one another. But that is not what I insist upon.

As for my own part, I have always maintain'd that if 'twere possible that the

Great Spirit had been so mean, as to descend to the Earth, he had shewn himself to all the Inhabitants of the Earth; he had descended in Triumph, and in publick view, with Splendour and Majesty; he had rais'd the dead, restor'd sight to the blind, made the lame to walk upright, cur'd all the diseases upon the Earth: In fine, he had spoke and commanded all that he had a mind to have done, he had gone from Nation to Nation to work these great Miracles, and to give the same Laws to the whole World. Had he done so, we had been all of the same Religion, and that great Uniformity, spread over the face of the Earth, would be a lasting Proof to our Posterity for ten thousand years to come, of the truth of a Religion that was known and receiv'd with equal approbation in the four Corners of the Earth. But instead of that Uniformity, we find five or six hundred Religions, among which that Profess'd by the *French*, is according to your Argument the only true one, the only one that is good and holy.

For when they allege that God, who can't be represented under any Figure; could produce a Son under the Figure of a Man: I am ready to reply, that a Woman can't bring forth a Beaver; by reason that in the course of Nature, every Species produces its like. Besides, if before the coming of the Son of God all men were devoted to the Devil, what reason have we to think that he would assume the Form of such Creatures....

In the next place, as for Working on the days set apart for Worship, I do not find that you make any difference between Holy-Days and Work-Days; for I have frequently seen the *French* bargain for Skins on your Holy-Days, as well as make Nets, Game, Quarrel, beat one another, get Drunk, and commit a hundred extravagant Actions.

And as to the business of Lying, I affirm it for a truth, that there is not one Merchant in this Country that will not tell you twenty Lies in felling the worth of a Beaver's Skin in Goods....

You feel we have no Judges; and what's the reason of that? Why? We neither quarrel nor sue one another. And what's the reason that we have no Law Suits? Why? Because we are resolved neither to receive nor to know Silver.

Ha! Long live the Hurons; who without Laws, without Prisons, and without Torture, pass their Life in a State of Sweetness of and Tranquility, and enjoy a pitch of Felicity to which the French are utter Strangers. We live quietly under the Laws of Instinct and innocent Conduct, which wise Nature has imprinted upon our Minds from our Cradles. We are all of one Mind; our Wills, Opinions and Sentiments observe an exact Conformity; and thus we spend our Lives with such a perfect good understanding, that no Disputes or Suits can take place amongst us....

[T]he *French*, who like Beasts, love only to eat and to drink, and have been brought up to Softness and Effeminacy. Prithee, tell me what difference there is between lying in a good Hutt, and lying in a Palace; between Sleeping under a Cover of Beaver-Skins, and Sleeping under a Quilt between two Sheets; between Eating Boil'd and Roast Meat, and feeding upon dirty Pies, Ragou's, and dress'd by your great Scullions? Are we liable to more Disorders and Sickness than the French, who are accommodated with these Palaces, Beds and Cooks? But after all, how many are there in *France* that lye upon Straw in Garrets where the Rain comes in on all hands, and that are hard put to't to find Victuals and Drink? I have been in France, and speak from what I have seen with my Eyes. You rally without reason, upon our Cloaths made of Skins, for they are warmer, and keep out the Rain better than your Cloth; besides, they are not so ridiculously made as your Garments....

You conclude, in pretending that the *French* prevent our Misery by taking pity of us. But pray consider how our Ancestors liv'd an hundred years ago: They liv'd as well without your Commodities as we do with 'em; for instead of your Fire-Locks, Powder and Shot, they made use of Bows and Arrows, as we do to this day: They made Nets of the Thread of the Barks of Trees, Axes of Stone; Knives, Needles and Awls of Stag or Elk-Bones; and supply'd the room of Kettles with Earthen Pots. Now, since our Ancestors liv'd without these Commodities for so many Ages; I am of the Opinion, we could dispense with 'em easier than the *French* could with our Beaver Skins; for which, by a mighty piece of Friendship, they give us in exchange Fusees, that burst and Lame many of our Warriors, Axes that break in the cutting of a Shrub, Knives that turn Blunt, and lose their Edge in the cutting of a Citron; Thread which is half Rotten, and so very bad that our Nets are worn out as soon as they are made; and Kettles so thin and slight, that the very weight of Water makes the Bottoms fall out....

What signifies your Pepper, your Salt, and a thousand other Spices, unless it be to murder your Health? Try our way of living but one fort-night, and then you'll long for no such doings. What harm can you fear from the Painting of your Face with Colours? You dawb your Hair with Powder and Essence....

Ay, most certainly, you are of a different Mould from us; for your Wines, your Brandy, and your Spices, make us Sick unto death; whereas you can't live forsooth without such Drugs: Besides, your Blood is Salt and ours is not; you have got Beards, and we have none. Nay farther; I have observ'd that before you pass the Age of thirty five or forty, you are Stronger and more Robust than we; for we can't carry such heavy Loads as you do till that Age; but after that your Strength dwindles and visibly declines, whereas ours keeps to its wonted pitch

till we Count fifty five or sixty years of Age. This is a truth that Our young
Women can vouch for. They tell you that when a young *French-man* obliges 'em
six times a night, a young *Huron* do's not rise to above half the number; and
with the same Breath they declare, that the *French* are older in that Trade at
thirty five, than the *Hurons* are at fifty years of Age.

## Readings

Anderson, K. *Chain Her by One Foot: The Subjugation of Women in Seventeenth-Century New France.* London: Routledge, 1991.

Axtell, J. *After Columbus: Essays in the Ethnohistory of Colonial North America.* New York: Oxford University Press, 1988.

Axtell, J. *Beyond 1492: Encounters in Colonial North America.* New York: Oxford University Press, 1992.

Axtell, J. *The Invasion Within: The Contest of Cultures in Colonial North America.* New York: Oxford University Press, 1985.

Bailey, A. *The Conflict of European and Eastern Algonkian Cultures, 1504–1700: A Study in Canadian Civilization.* Second edition. Toronto: University of Toronto Press, 1969.

Beaulieu, A. *Convertir les fils de Cain: Jesuites et Amerindiens en la Nouvelle France, 1632–1642.* Quebec: Nuit Blanche, 1994.

Blackburn, C. *Harvest of Souls: The Jesuit Missions and Colonization in North America, 1632–1650.* Montreal: McGill-Queen's University Press, 2000.

Bonvillain, N. "The Iroquois and the Jesuits: Strategies of Influence and Resistance," *American Indian Culture and Research Journal* 10, 1 (1986).

Campeau, L. *La Mission des Jesuites chez les Hurons* Montreal: Bellarmin, 1987.

Conklin, R. "Legitimacy and Conversion in Social Change: The Case of French Missionaries and the Northeastern Algonkian," *Ethnohistory* (1974).

Delage, D. *Bitter Feast: Amerindians and Europeans in Northeastern North America, 1600–1664.* Vancouver: University of British Columbia Press, 1993.

Dickason, O. *The Myth of the Savage and the Beginnings of French Colonialism in the Americas.* Edmonton: University of Alberta Press, 1984.

Dorsey, P. "Going to School with Savages: Authorship and Authority among the Jesuits of New France," *William and Mary Quarterly* 3 (July 1998).

Doxtator, D. "Inclusive and Exclusive Perceptions of Difference: Native and Euro-Based Concepts of Time, History and Change," in G. Warkentin and C. Podruchny, *Decentering the Renaissance: Canada and Europe in Multidisciplinary Perspective, 1500–1700.* Toronto: University of Toronto Press, 2001.

Gagnon, F-M. *La Conversion par L'Image. Un Aspect de la Mission des Jesuites aupres des Indiens du Canada au XVII siecle.* Montreal: Bellarmin, 1975.

Goddard, P. "Canada in Seventeenth-Century Jesuit Thought: Backwater or Opportunity," in G. Warkentin and C. Podruchny, *Decentering the Renaissance:*

*Canada and Europe in Multidisciplinary Perspective, 1500–1700.* Toronto: University of Toronto Press, 2001.

Goddard, P. "Converting the Sauvage: Jesuit and Montagnais in Seventeenth-Century New France," *Catholic Historical Review* 84, 2 (April 1998).

Grant, J. *Moon of Wintertime: Missionaries and the Indians of Canada in Encounter since 1534.* Toronto: University of Toronto Press, 1984.

Heidenreich, C. "The Beginning of French Exploration out the St. Lawrence Valley: Motives, Methods, and Changing Attitudes Towards Native People," in G. Warkentin and C. Podruchny, *Decentering the Renaissance: Canada and Europe in Multidisciplinary Perspective, 1500–1700.* Toronto: University of Toronto Press, 2001.

Jaenen, C. "Amerindian View of French Culture in the Seventeenth Century," *Canadian Historical Review* 55, 3 (September 1974).

Jaenen, C. "Education for Francization: The Case of New France in the Seventeenth Century" in J. Barman et al. eds., *Indian Education in Canada: The Legacy.* Vancouver: University of British Columbia Press, 1986.

Jaenen, C. *Friend and Foe: Aspects of French-Amerindian Cultural Contact in the Sixteenth and Seventeenth Century.* Toronto: McClelland and Stewart, 1976.

Jaenen, C. "Problems of Assimilation in New France, 1603–1645," *French Historical Studies* (1966).

Jaenen, C. *The Role of the Church in New France.* Toronto: McGraw-Hill Ryerson, 1976.

Jaenen, C. "Thoughts on Early Canadian Contact," in C. Martin, ed., *The American Indian and the Problem of History.* New York, Oxford University Press, 1987.

Mali, A. "Strange Encounters: Missionary Activity and Mystical Thought in Seventeenth Century New France," *History of European Ideas* 22, 2 (1996).

Martin, C. "Ethnohistory: A Better Way to Write Indian History," in A. Hurtado and P. Ivenson, eds., *Major Problems in American Indian History.* New York: Houghton and Mifflin, 1994.

Martin, C. "The Metaphysics of Writing Indian-White History," in C. Martin, ed., *The American Indian and the Problem of History.* New York, Oxford University Press, 1987.

Mealing, S., ed. *Jesuit Relations and Allied Documents.* Toronto: McClelland and Stewart, 1963.

Morantz, T. "Plunder or Harmony: On Merging European and Native Views of Early Contact," in G. Warkentin and C. Podruchny, *Decentering the Renaissance: Canada and Europe in Multidisciplinary Perspective, 1500–1700.* Toronto: University of Toronto Press, 2001.

Morrison, K. "Montagnais Missionization in Early New France," in A. Hurtado and P. Ivenson, eds., *Major Problems in American Indian History.* New York: Houghton and Mifflin, 1994.

Ouellet, R., and M. Tremblay. "From the Good Savage to the Degenerate Indian: The Amerindian in Accounts of Travel to America," in G. Warkentin and C. Podruchny,

*Decentering the Renaissance: Canada and Europe in Multidisciplinary Perspective, 1500–1700.* Toronto: University of Toronto Press, 2001.

Rhonda, J. "We Are As We Are: An Indian Critique of Seventeenth-Century Christian Missions," *William and Mary Quarterly* 3, 34 (1977).

Sayre, G. *Les Sauvages Americaines: Representations of Native Americans in French and English Colonial Literature.* Chapel Hill: University of North Carolina Press, 1997.

Steckley, J. "The Warrior and the Lineage: Jesuit Use of Iroquoian Images to Communicate Christianity," *Ethnohistory* 39 (Fall 1992).

Therien, G. "Memoria as the Place of Fabrication of the New World," in G. Warkentin and C. Podruchny, *Decentering the Renaissance: Canada and Europe in Multidisciplinary Perspective, 1500–1700.* Toronto: University of Toronto Press, 2001.

Trigger, B. *The Children of Aataentsic: A History of the Huron People to 1660.* Montreal: McGill-Queen's University Press, 1976.

Trigger, B. "Early Native North American Responses to European Contact: Romantic versus Rationalistic Interpretations," *Journal of American History* 77, 4 (March 1991).

Trigger, B. *Natives and Newcomers: Canada's Heroic Age Reconsidered.* Montreal: McGill-Queen's University Press, 1985.

*Chapter Two*

# "Advantages and Inconveniences": The Colonization of Canada

1. Samuel de Champlain, "To the King and the Lords of His Council," 1618.
2. Pierre Boucher, *True and Genuine Description of New France Commonly Called Canada*, 1664.
3. Jean Talon, "Memoir on Canada," 1673.
4. Jacques Duchesneau, "To the Minister," November 10, 1679.
5. Jacques-Rene de Brisay de Denonville, "Memoir Respecting Canada Prepared for the Marquis de Seignelay," January, 1690.
6. Ruette d'Auteuil, "Memoir to His Royal Highness the Duc d'Orleans, Regent of France," December 12, 1715.
7. P.F.X. de Charlevoix, "Letter X," Montreal, April 22, 1721.
8. "Memoir of the King to Serve as Instructions for Sr. Hocquart, Commissary General of the Marine and Ordonnateur in New France," March 22, 1729.
9. Gilles Hocquart, "Memoir to the Minister Containing a Characterization of the French Canadian Population," November 8, 1737.

## Introduction

What role did France see its North American possessions playing within the context of the wider French empire and the geo-political realities of the seventeenth and eighteenth centuries? The answer depended upon a variety of factors and changed over time. Thus Champlain's aims and objectives in 1608, when he founded New France on the banks of the St. Lawrence, varied considerably from Hocquart's more than a century later. New rulers, circumstances, and philosophies shifted world views and led to different emphasis and opportunities. However, common threads throughout the following documents that cumulatively weave a tapestry of French aspirations, successes, fears, and failures with their colony of New France.

After an abortive attempt to settle in present day Nova Scotia, Samuel de Champlain returned to Canada in 1608. This time he and his crew settled at what is now Quebec City where they founded New France. It appeared to be a logical location: defensible, hopefully at the entrance to the transcontinental passage, close to Native allies, and with good agricultural potential. Problems immediately emerged, however. As with the first settlement efforts at Port Royale, the newcomers suffered terribly from scurvy, cold, hunger, isolation, and internal conflict. Then Champlain supported his new Huron friends by launching a series of raids against their Iroquois enemies, thereby embroiling New France in a desperate conflict that raged for the next half century. It was indeed an inauspicious beginning, and while his promotionally-minded dispatches outlined his hopes and dreams for New France, their realization is a matter of some debate. Certainly, settlement began, but to what extent? His little post clung to life, and even disappeared entirely for several years after an attack by English privateers led by the Kirke brothers. Agriculture essentially did not exist by the end of his life, despite his best efforts, but the fur trade did expand and became New France's economic lifeblood.

The crux of the problem lay in the fundamentally ambiguous and contradictory nature of the colony's purpose: it was to be settled and Frenchified under the king's auspices while simultaneously generating profit for private companies that received a monopoly over the area with the proviso that they absorb the expenses. The king followed this policy in order to save state funds, but the system virtually guaranteed that the colony would develop along lines that put profit before investment despite what the trade monopoly stipulated. Simply put, colonizing was expensive, requiring a significant investment in finding, transporting, and settling immigrants, who then needed an extensive and costly support infrastructure at the other end. A handful of traders in a fort, on the other hand, could generate huge profits from the fur trade with minimal financial outlay.

Nor were traders the only ones to balk at settling their new lands. Emigration remained a hard-sell. North America, after all, generated horror stories of "savages," monsters, desperate winters, and it was far removed from the perceived security and community of France. To be uprooted from their known world, remained frightening to an overwhelmingly illiterate and superstitious French populace. And those who did cross the Atlantic? They faced the prospect of years of lonely, backbreaking work creating a farm versus the siren temptations of the fur trade with its bonhomie, excitement, and supposed easy profit. The cumulative result was desperately slow settlement and a transient, male-dominated French population out to make a quick buck unlike the situation in the New England colonies to the south where settlement proceeded apace and along different lines.

Prevailing seventeenth-century economic models also discouraged a vibrant New France. Mercantilism held that colonies supplied raw materials and never competed against home-country businesses. Thus economic diversification along the St. Lawrence remained very difficult as French businessmen zealously guarded their interests and had colonial administrators shut down perceived competitors. New France thereby had to rely upon French imports for virtually everything but the homegrown bare essentials, which led to a debilitating negative cash flow from the colony to the motherland just as French commercial leaders demanded. Mercantilism indeed tolled the death knell to any chance of colonial self-sufficiency. If that was not bad enough, transportation costs drove prices upward, and the St. Lawrence froze for many months, bringing most trade to a halt for part of every year. Last, but certainly not least, interminable raids by the Iroquois, culminating in the brutal destruction of Huronia in the 1640s, all but killed New France by strangling the fur trade.

Things improved when Louis XIV, the dynamic and aggressive young "Sun King," made New France a royal province in 1663 after repeated pleas of support from settlers. Regal sanction constituted a major psychological, financial, and sociological boost to the fledgling settlement and guaranteed a measure of stability heretofore unknown. The royal province of New France received access to state funds, security forces, and gained the same administration as existed in French provinces. This affected the little colony's administrative tone as religious grounds for maintaining New France became secondary to commerce. The new structure did foster growth and the boundaries of the colony ballooned. This occurred for commercial and military reasons. Intendant Talon established an exploration program that annexed the heart of modern Canada, the Ohio country of the present United States, and the river network flowing southward to the Gulf of Mexico and France's possession of Louisiana. The expansion offered New France a back door to the St. Lawrence, prevented England from exploiting the land, and opened up new trade areas with indigenous people. It also meant, in theory at least, that New England found itself hemmed in by hostile French territory.

Mercantilism remained the economic order of the day throughout this phase, but in a slightly different guise: private enterprise, not the state, took more responsibility to fund and fuel trade and progress. Government still encouraged expansion, but not at the expense of the royal purse. This was, in other words, an era of cutbacks, restraint, cost-cutting, and His Majesty's bureaucrats doing more-with-less. The emphasis became political stability and peaceful commercial rivalry and coexistence with the old foe, England despite suspecting the illusory nature of that peace. Commercial success should now spring from a closely integrated empire with vibrant trade between all French Atlantic possessions, plus less emphasis on the fur trade in favour of agriculture and industry. This policy did, in fact, see some success.

## Discussion Points

1. List the potential benefits colonization of Canada had for France. What impediments had to be overcome?
2. Did the French image of Canada remain the same or change between 1618 and 1737? What, if any, trends emerged in these views?
3. According to these documents, in what respects was life in New France different from that in France? Would an average French citizen have been better off in Canada or not?
4. Which of these accounts seem most reliable? Least?

## Documents

### 1. Samuel de Champlain, "To the King and the Lords of His Council," 1618.

Sire: The Sieur de Champlain represents to you most humbly that for sixteen years he has toiled with laborious zeal as well in the discoveries of New France as of divers peoples and nations whom he has brought to our knowledge, who had never been discovered save by him; which peoples have given him such and so faithful report of the north and south seas that one cannot doubt but that this would be the means of reaching easily to the Kingdom of China and the East Indies, whence great riches could be drawn; besides planting there the divine worship ... in addition to the abundance of merchandise from the said country of New France.... Should this said country be given up and the settlement abandoned, for want of bestowing upon it the needed attention, the English or Flemings, envious of our prosperity, would seize upon it, thereby enjoying the fruits of our labours, and preventing by this means more than a thousand vessels from going to the dry and green fisheries, and for whale-oil....

Firstly.—His said Majesty will establish the Christian faith among an infinite number of souls, who neither hold nor possess any form of religion whatsoever, and nevertheless wish only for the knowledge of divine and human worship, according to the reports of all those who have made the voyage to the said New France.

Secondly.—The King will make himself master and lord of a country nearly eighteen hundred leagues in length, watered by the fairest rivers in the world and by the greatest and most numerous lakes, the richest and most abundant in all varieties of fish that are to be found, and full also of the greatest meadows, fields, and forests, for the most part of walnut-trees, and very pleasant hills upon which there is found a great abundance of wild vines, which yield grapes as large as or larger than ours, cultivated as these are.

Thirdly.—The Sieur de Champlain undertakes to discover the South Sea passage to China and to the East Indies by way of the river St. Lawrence, which traverses the lands of the said New France, and which river issues from a lake about three hundred leagues in length, from which lake flows a river that empties into the said South Sea, according to the account given to the said Sieur de Champlain by a number of people, his friends in the said country; whom he has visited and become acquainted with, having ascended the said river St. Lawrence for more than four hundred leagues into the said lake of three hundred leagues in length, on which voyage he found numerous fortified towns, encircled and enclosed with wooden palisades ... which towns can furnish two thousand men armed after their fashion; others less.

That His said Majesty would derive a great and notable profit from the taxes and duties he could levy on the merchandise coming from the said country, according to the memorial submitted, as likewise from the customs' duties on the merchandise that would come from China and from the Indies, which would surpass in value at least ten times all those levied in France, inasmuch as all the merchants of Christendom would pass through the passage sought by the Sieur de Champlain, if it please the King to grant them leave to do so, in order to shorten the said journey by more than a year and a half, without any risk from pirates and from the perils of the sea and of the voyage, on account of the great circuit it is necessary now to make, which brings a thousand inconveniences to merchants and travellers....

The Sieur de Champlain humbly begs to be heard concerning certain facts which he wishes to present to you for the honour and glory of God, for the increase of this realm and for the establishment of a great and permanent trade in New France, as is specified in the following articles:

The advantage that would accrue in the first place from the cod-fishery, which would be carried on annually thanks to the permanent settlement of the people inhabiting the said country of New France, where salt could be made in considerable quantity, and two kinds of fishing could be carried on, namely dry and green, ... and through the industry of the fishermen more than a million livres would be earned annually.

Likewise the salmon fishery, which fish are in such abundance in the harbours and rivers that one could produce annually 100,000 livres.

Likewise the sea-sturgeon fishery, as also that of the sea-trout, which are so abundant in most places that they might be sold ... in regions where this fish is much in demand, annually for 100,000 livres.

Likewise eels, sardines, herrings and other fish are so plentiful that there could be obtained annually for 100,000 livres.

Likewise the whale-oils, in which the country abounds of which one can make in the said country annually to the value of 200,000 livres.

Likewise whale-bone from the said whales, and walrus-tusks, which are better than elephant's teeth ... and an abundance of seals; and of these commodities there might be taken annually to the value of 500,000 livres.

Likewise from the forests, which are of marvellous height, a number of good vessels might be built, which could be laden with the above-mentioned merchandise and other commodities, as will be stated below. From the said forests could be made ships' masts of several sizes, beams, joists, planks of many varieties, such as oak, elm, beech, walnut, plane, maple, birch, cedar, cypress, chestnut, hemlock, pine, fir and other woods; there could be made stave-wood, sawed oak for window frames and wainscoting and for other interior decoration, for which the most part of the said woods are suitable; and there would be obtained from them annually to the value of 400,000 livres.

Likewise there could be obtained a quantity of gum, the smell of which resembles incense.

Likewise of the useless woods one could make ashes, from which there could be obtained annually to the value of 400,000 livres.

From the pines and firs could be obtained pitch, tar and resin to the value annually of 100,000 livres.

As for the nature of the soil, it is certain that it yields to the native tillers corn, maize, beans, peas, roots the dye of which makes a colour similar to cochineal; and if the said root were cultivated one could obtain from it annually to the value of 400,000 livres.

Likewise a notable profit could be gained from the hemp, which the same soil yields without cultivation and which in quality and texture is in wise inferior to ours; and there could be obtained from it annually to the value of 300,000 livres.

In addition is to be considered the profits to be derived from several kinds of mines, such as those of silver, steel, iron which yields 45 per cent., lead which yields 30 per cent., copper 18 per cent., and whatever other minerals, or things not yet come to our knowledge which a permanent settlement in the country may discover; and there could be derived from the said mines annually more than 1,000,000 livres.

Likewise cloths, such as sail-cloths, could be made from the hemp of the said country; as well as cables, ropes, and rigging for all sorts of vessels, to the value of more than 400,000 livres.

Likewise the traffic and trade in furs is not to be scorned, not only marten, beaver, fox, lynx and other skins, but also deer, moose and buffalo robes, which are commodities from which one can derive at present more than 400,000 livres.

Likewise from the said country can be obtained marble, jasper, alabaster, porphyry and other kinds of valuable stones; and a notable profit may be made therefrom.

Vines are in abundance in the said country, which the soil yields of itself; and if they were cultivated they would yield great profits; as likewise corn and other things, which the permanent settlements will be able to supply through the industry of the inhabitants of the said country.

Besides all these things one may expect in the future the same abundance of cattle that is seen in Peru since the Spaniards introduced them there ... and from the Spaniards' account more than a million in gold is obtained annually from the hides. For New France is so well watered everywhere that the fertility of the meadows ensures the feeding and multiplying of the said cattle, whenever they are introduced here....

## 2. Pierre Boucher, *True and Genuine Description of New France Commonly Called Canada*, 1664.

... But how can we make money there? What can we get out of it all? This is a question that has often been put to me, and that gave me an inclination to laugh every time it was put to me; I seemed to see people who wanted to reap a harvest before they had sowed any thing. After having said that the country is a good one, capable of producing all sorts of things, like France, that it is healthy, that population only is wanting, that the country is very extensive, and that without doubt there are great riches in it which we have not been able to bring to light, because we have an enemy who keeps us pent up in a little corner and prevents us from going about and making discoveries; and so he will have to be destroyed, and many people will have to come into this country, and then we shall know the riches of it; but some one will have to defray the cost of all this; and who shall do it if not our good King? He has shown an inclination to do it, and may God be pleased to keep him still of the same mind.

Our neighbours, the English, laid out a great deal of money at the outset on the settlements they made; they threw great numbers of people into them; so that now there are computed to be in them fifty thousand men capable of bearing arms; it is a wonder to see their country now; one finds all sorts of things there, the same as in Europe, and for half the price. They build numbers of ships, of all sorts and sizes; they work iron mines; they have beautiful cities; they have stage-coaches and mails from one to the other; they have carriages like those in France; those who laid out money there, are now getting good returns from it; that country is not different from this; what has been done there could be done here....

It seems to me that I hear some one say: "you have told us much about the advantages of New France but you have not shown us its disadvantages, nor its inconveniences, yet we know well that there is not a country in the world however good it may be, in which something that is disagreeable is not met with." I answer that you are right. It has been my study all along to make these things known to you; but in order to enable you to understand them more clearly, I shall here specify in detail what I consider the most troublesome and disagreeable things....

The first is that our enemies, the Iroquois keep us so closely pent up that they hinder us from enjoying the advantages of the country. We cannot go to hunt or fish without danger of being killed or taken prisoners by those rascals; and we cannot even plough out fields, much less make hay, without continual risk: They lie in ambush on all sides, and any little thicket suffices for six or seven of those barbarians to put themselves under cover in, or more correctly speaking in an ambush, from which they throw themselves upon you suddenly when you are at your work, or going to it or coming from it. They never attack but when they are the strongest; if they are the weakest they do not say a word; if by accident they are discovered they fly, leaving every thing behind them; and as they are fleet of foot it is difficult to catch them; so you see we are always in dread, and a poor fellow does not work in safety if he has to go ever so little a way off to his work. Wives are always uneasy lest their husbands, who have gone away to their work in the morning, should be killed or taken prisoners and they should never see them again; and these Indians are the cause of the greater number of our settlers being poor, not only through our not being able to enjoy the advantages of the country as I have just said, but because they often kill cattle, sometimes hinder the gathering in of the harvest, and at other times burn and plunder houses when they can take people by surprise. This is a great evil, but it is not beyond remedy, and we expect one from the benevolence of our good King, who has told me that he wishes to deliver us from it. It would not be very difficult to do so, for there are not among them more than eight hundred or nine hundred men capable of bearing arms. It is true they are warlike men, and very dexterous at fighting in the woods; they have given proof of this to our Commanders from France who despised them; some of these were killed and others were forced to admit that one must not neglect to take precautions when one goes to war with them, that they understand the business, and that on this score they are not barbarians; but after all a thousand or twelve hundred men well led would give occasion for its being said, "they were but they are not"; and to have exterminated a tribe that has caused so many others to perish and is the terror of all these countries, would raise the reputation of the French very high throughout New France....

Here is another set of questions that have been put to me, namely: how we live in this country whether justice is administered, if there is not great debauchery, seeing that numbers of worthless fellows and bad girls come here, it is said.

I will answer all these questions one after the other, beginning with the last. It is not true that those sort of girls come hither, and those who say so have made a great mistake, and have taken the Islands of Saint Christophe and Martinique for New France; if any of them come here, they are not known for such; for before any can be taken on board ship to come here some of their relations or friends must certify that they have always been well-behaved; if by chance there are found among those who have, some who are in disrepute, or who are said to have misconducted themselves on the voyage out, they are sent back to France.

As for the scapegraces, if any come over it is only because they are not known for what they are, and when they are in the country they have to live like decent people, otherwise they would have a bad time of it; we know how to hang people in this country as well as they do elsewhere, and we have proved it to some who have not been well behaved.

Justice is administered here, and there are Judges; and those who are not satisfied with their decisions can appeal to the Governor and the Sovereign Council, appointed by the King, and sitting at Quebec.

Hitherto we have lived pleasantly enough, for it has pleased God to give us Governors who have all been good men, and besides we have had the Jesuit

Fathers who take great pains to teach the people what is right so that all goes on peaceably; we live much in the fear of God, and nothing scandalous takes place without its being put to rights immediately; there is great religious devotion throughout the country.

Several persons after having heard me speak of New France, whether they felt inclined to come to it or not, have put these questions to me: "Do you think I would be fit for that country? What would have to be done in order to get there? If I took four or five thousand francs with me, could I with such a sum make myself tolerably comfortable?" And after these several other questions which I shall mention after having answered these.

You ask me in the first place whether you are fit for this country. The answer I make you is that this country is not yet fit for people of rank who are extremely rich, because such people would not find in it all the luxuries they enjoy in France; such persons must wait until this country has more inhabitants, unless they are persons who wish to retire from the world in order to lead a pleasant and quiet life free from fuss, or who are inclined to immortalize themselves by building cities or by other great works in this new world.

The people best fitted for this country are those who can work with their own hands in making clearings, putting up buildings and otherwise; for as men's wages are very high here, a man who does not take care and practice economy will be ruined; but the best way is always to begin by clearing land and making a good farm, and to attend to other things only after that has been done, and not to do like some whom I have seen, who paid out all their money for the erection of fine buildings which they had to sell afterwards for less than the cost.

I am supposing myself to be speaking to persons who would come to settle in this country with a view to making a living out of it, and not to trade.

It would be well for a man coming to settle, to bring provisions with him for at least a year or two years if possible, especially flour which he could get for much less in France and could not even be sure of being always able to get for any money here; for if many people should come from France in any year without bringing any flour with them and the grain crops should be bad here that year, which God forbid, they would find themselves much straitened.

It would be well also to bring a supply of clothes, for they cost twice as much here as they do in France.

Money is also much dearer; its value increases one third, so that a coin of fifteen sous is worth twenty, and so on in proportion.

I would advise a man having money enough to bring two labouring men with him, or even more if he has the means, to clear his land; this is in answer to the question whether a person having three thousand or four thousand francs to employ here could do so with advantage, such a person could get himself into very easy circumstances in three or four years if he choose to practice economy, as I have already said.

Most of our settlers are persons who came over in the capacity of servants, and who, after serving their masters for three years, set up for themselves. They had not worked for more than a year before they had cleared land on which they got in more than enough grain for their food. They have but little, generally when they set up for themselves, and marry wives who are no better off than they are; yet if they are fairly hard working people you see them in four or five years in easy circumstances and well fitted out for persons of their condition in life.

Poor people would be much better off here than they are in France, provided they are not lazy; they could not fail to get employment and could not say, as they do in France, that they are obliged to beg for their living because they cannot find any one to give them work; in one word, no people are wanted, either men or women, who cannot turn their hands to some work, unless they are very rich.

Women's work consists of household work and of feeding and caring for the cattle; for there are few female servants; so that wives are obliged to do their own house work; nevertheless those who have the means employ valets who do the work of maidservants....

The land is very high in relation to the river, but quite level. The little of it that is under cultivation produces very good grain and vegetables but is not fit for fruit trees that do not grow in clayey soil. There is eel fishing, but it is not plentiful. There are all types of wood, which are sold at Quebec....

In relation to the great size of the settlement, there is not one-quarter of the workmen required to clear and cultivate the land.

Farmers do not cultivate the land with enough care. It is certain that one *minot* as sown in France would produce more than two as sown in Canada.

Since the seasons are too short and there is much bad weather, it would be desirable that the Church allow the performance of essential works on feast days. There are not ninety working days left from May, when sowing begins, to the end of September, after allowance is made for holy days and bad weather. Yet, the strength of the colony hinges on that period.

It would be necessary to compel neglectful habitants to labor on the land by depriving them of the right to go on voyages, which exempt them from work. They earn thirty or forty écus on a voyage of two or three months but waste the farming season, and land remains fallow as a result....

Oblige the seigneurs, in order to facilitate the establishment of their seigneuries, to give sufficient common land at low prices and to build mills and other public conveniences. Many persons lose up to a third of their time traveling fifteen or twenty lieues to mill their flour....

Order the grand voyer to apply himself to building the roads and bridges necessary for the public, which is something very essential....

The subordination of the vassal to his seigneur is not observed. This error is the result of seigneuries being granted to commoners, who have not known how to maintain their rights over their tenants. Even the officers of militia, who are their dependents, have for the most part no consideration for their superiority and wish on occasions to be regarded as independent.

### 3. Jean Talon, "Memoir on Canada," 1673.

... It has appeared to me that one of the principal intentions of His Majesty was to form over the years a large and populous colony, full of men suited for all types of professions in the army, the navy, and the fisheries, and strong enough to engage in all types of work.

The girls sent from France by the king and the marriages they contracted with the soldiers who have voluntarily chosen to settle in the colony have so greatly increased the number of settlers that when taking the census in 1671 I found by the birth certificates that seven hundred children had been born in that year. At present I have reason to believe that one hundred marriages between young men and girls born in the colony are possible annually....

His Majesty further intended that the settlers of his colony of New France should enjoy the felicity of his reign to the same degree as his subjects of the old; that ... the southern part of America should be supported by the northern part, which can produce clothing and the necessities of life of which the southern part finds itself deprived by its exposure to the sun and a tropical climate; that stationary fisheries be established, so that the kingdom may not only do without the fish it buys from foreign countries for considerable sums, but also send to the Levant the dried fish that is consumed there in great quantities....

He also had in view the support of his navy with the wood that grows in Canada, the iron that could be discovered there, the tar that could be manufactured, and the hemp that could be grown for the making of ships' riggings. With these four products, he would no longer have to obtain from the princes of the Baltic, with an appearance of dependence, what is necessary to sustain his navy, which is such an important element of his glory and of his state's support.

In all this Canada seems to have responded well enough to the hopes of His Majesty. Hemp is being cultivated with success, cloth is being woven, cable and rope are being produced. The tar which has been manufactured has been tested both here and in France and found to be as good as that drawn from the north. Iron has been discovered, which master forgers consider to be suitable for all purposes. Vessels, which have now been sailing for six years, have been built for individuals who opened up the trade of Canada with the islands. At present there is one of 450 tons and forty-two guns being built for the king, which will put to sea next summer, and there is almost enough material in the yards for another. Before leaving, I established two workshops. During the present winter the first, of twenty-eight men, should produce 1,000 to 1,200 pieces of lumber suitable for the construction of a vessel of 600 to 700 tons, of which his Majesty has seen the model; from the labors of the second, we may hope for 25,000 to 30,000 feet of sheathing....

Stationary fisheries, which are so useful since dried cod is consumed almost everywhere in Europe, have been started before my departure....

Opening a trade between Canada and the Antilles is no longer considered a difficult thing. It was done by me in 1668 with a vessel built in Canada which successfully carried a cargo of this country's products. From there it sailed to Old France with a load of sugar and then returned to the New with the products of the kingdom of which this country stands in need. Every year since, as a result of this example, this commerce has been carried out by two or more vessels ...

This commerce is made up of the excess quantities of peas, salmon, salted eels, green and dried cod, planks and cask wood, and will be increased by excess wheat which will be converted into flour. It is estimated that Canada could export 30,000 *minots* each year if the crops are not ruined by bad weather. Peas could amount to 10,000 *minots*, and salted beef and pork will not in the future make up the smaller portion of this trade. Sales in the islands being favorable, I expect that Canada could soon supply pork, since it now does without that of France from which it formerly drew up to 1,200 barrels annually. The inhabitants of Port Royal in Acadia could supply salted beef. I obtained sixty quintals at twenty-two deniers a pound from there two years ago, which was as good as that of Ireland.

Beer could also profitably enter into this trade. I can guarantee 2,000 barrels a year for the islands and more if the consumption is greater, without altering the supply to the colonists of New France. It is by these methods that His Majesty will succeed in his aim of destroying the trade of the Dutch with our islands, without depriving his subjects residing there of the support they derived from it.

With all the provisions, which Canada will be able to supply in proportionately greater quantities as she develops, the islands will be provided with the necessities of life and will only lack a few accessories like spices, olive oil, wine, and salt. There is even the possibility of establishing salt works in Acadia if the king judges that it would not be prejudicial to Old France to make this new colony self-sufficient in this respect and to enable it to provide by itself for all its needs. I say all its needs not even excluding clothing which, we may hope, will be manufactured not only for the Canadians but in a few years for the islanders as well. For crafts have already been established for the fabrication of cloth, linen, and shoes; we already have enough leather to manufacture on the average 8,000 pairs of shoes annually; we will have as much hemp as we will care to grow; and the sheep which His Majesty sent have bred very well and will provide the material for the sheets and other cloths which we have begun to weave.

And all these things taken together will form the essence of a trade that will be useful to all His Majesty's subjects and will make for the happiness of those of New France. Thanks to the king's care and support, they live in peace and no longer suffer from those pressing needs which they felt for almost everything when his troops first landed in the colony.

Potash, which has successfully undergone a series of tests, can be used to wash linen or can be converted into a soft soap for bleaching or for cleaning silks and sheets. It can be produced in Canada in sufficient quantities to enable Paris to do without Spanish sodium, on which it spends a considerable sum. It could also enable Douay, Lille, Tournay, Courtrai, and other cities in Flanders and even in France where cloth is bleached to dispense with the potash of Muscovy and Poland, which increases the trade of the Dutch who accept this product in partial exchange for the beaver and spices they trade in those countries.

Potash should be received all the more favorably in Paris since all laundry-women know very well that Spanish sodium is very acrid and wears out the cloth, something which potash does not do....

Such, approximately, are the results of His Majesty's first attempt to make of a country that is crude, savage, and pagan the commencements of a province, and perhaps of a kingdom, that is refined, happy, and Christian.

## 4. Jacques Duchesneau, "To the Minister," November 10, 1679.

... The greater part of the officers of the Sovereign Council and the inferior justices, although they ought to apply themselves principally to their vocation and to instructing themselves in it, are prevented by their poverty, the wages they are paid being very small, which makes them occupy themselves as much as possible with commerce and with improving their living.

Several of the *gentilhommes*, officers retired on half pay and owners of seigneuries, since they accustom themselves to what is called in France the life of a country gentleman which they have practised and wish to continue to practise, make their chief occupation that of hunting and fishing. Because their manner of life and clothing, and that of their wives and children, does not enable them to live on so little as the simple habitants, and since they do not apply themselves entirely to household work and to improving their lands, they mix themselves up in trade, running into debt on all sides, exciting young habitants to become *coureurs de bois*, and lastly sending their own children to trade in furs, in the Indian villages and in the depths of the forest, in spite of prohibitions of His Majesty, and yet nevertheless they are in great poverty.

The merchants living in the country, with the exception of five or six at the most, are poor. The artisans, if one excludes a small number who are inn-keepers, because of the social pretensions of the women among whom there is no class distinction here, and their own debauchery, spend everything they make. Consequently, their families are in great misery and are not settled down.

Whenever the labourers apply themselves assiduously to the land, they subsist not only more honestly but are without comparison happier than those who are called good peasants in France. But, in the spirit of this country of taking life easily, and having much of the savage temperament which is unsteady, fickle and opposed to hard work, seeing the liberty that is taken so boldly to run the woods, they debauch themselves with the others and go to look for furs as a means of living without working. This causes the land to be left uncleared and beasts not to multiply as they should and no industries can be established here.

To turn to those who come into the country for profits only with no intention of establishing themselves, and who are called foreign merchants, there is no doubt that their only interest is to fix up their affairs and afterwards return to live more comfortable in France with their families.

On all this you may observe, Monseigneur, if it pleases you, that among so many different interests, the chief and common interest of those who have chosen this country to live in, when they think seriously, must be to establish good order in the colony, to cultivate the soil, to raise and increase the number of livestock, to establish manufacturing and to attract the savages to trade in the French villages....

In truth, Monseigneur, it is deplorable to see this country in its present state, when this colony which could become so important because of its advantages, of which I have so often informed you, is so little established.

## 5. Jacques-Rene de Brisay de Denonville, "Memoir Respecting Canada Prepared for the Marquis de Seignelay," January, 1690.

... Exclusive of the inability of the Governor-General to protect the country when obliged to act on the defensive, the great difficulty in controlling the people arises from the Colony being allowed to spread itself too much; and from every settler maintaining himself, isolated and without neighbours, in a savage independence. I see no remedy for this but to concentrate the Colony, and to collect the settlers, forming good inclosed villages. Whatever obstacle may be encountered herein, must be overcome if we would not hazard the destruction of the entire population....

The weakness of that country arises from isolated settlements adjoining interminable forests. If under such circumstances it be desired to continue the occupation of remote forts, such as that of Cataracouy or Fort Frontenac, it will add to the weakness of the country and increase expenses which cannot be of any use to us, whatever may be alleged to the contrary; for those posts cannot do injury to hostile Indians but to ourselves, in consequence of the difficulty of reaching, and the cost of maintaining, them.

Nothing is more certain than that it was a great mistake to have permitted, in time past, the occupation of posts so remote that those who occupy them are beyond the reach of the Colony and of assistance. The garrisons have thus been necessitated to enter into the interests of those Tribes nearest to them, and in that way to participate in their quarrels in order to please and conciliate them. We have, thus, drawn down on ourselves the enmity of their enemies and the contempt of our friends, who not receiving the assistance they were made to expect or might desire, have on divers occasions embarrassed us more than even our enemies. This has been experienced more than once.

It had been much better not to have meddled with their quarrels, and to have left all the Indians to come to the Colony in quest of the merchandise they required, than to have prevented their doing so by carrying goods to them in such large quantities as to have been frequently obliged to sell them at so low a rate as to discredit us among the Indians and to ruin trade; for many of our Coureur de bois have often lost, instead of gained, by their speculations. Moreover, the great number of Coureurs de bois has inflicted serious injury on the Colony, by physically and morally corrupting the settlers, who are prevented marrying by the cultivation of a vagabond, independent and idle spirit. For the aristocratic manners they assume, on their return, both in their dress and their drunken revelries, wherein they exhaust all their gains in a very short time, lead them to despise the peasantry and to consider it beneath them to espouse their daughters, though they are themselves, peasants like them. In addition to this, they will condescend no more to cultivate the soil, nor listen, any longer, to anything except returning to the woods for the purpose of continuing the same avocations. This gives rise to the innumerable excesses that many among them are guilty of with the Squaws, which cause a great deal of mischief in consequence of the displeasures of the Indians at the seduction of their wives and daughters, and of the injury thereby inflicted on Religion, when the Indians behold the French practicing nothing of what the Missionaries represent as the law of the Gospel.

The remedy for this is, not to permit, as far as practicable, the return of any person to the Indian country except those who cannot follow any other business, nor to allow ill conducted persons to go thither; to oblige all to bring to the Governor and Intendant a certificate of good behaviour and good morals from the Missionaries; to find employment for the youth of the country; which is a very easy matter, for the cod and whale fisheries afford a sure commerce, if closely attended to and made a business of. There is reason to believe that the wisest and oldest merchants of the country are tired of sending into the bush, but there will be always too many new and ambitious petty traders, who will attempt to send ventures thither, both with and without license. It is very proper that an ordinance be enacted holding the merchants responsible for the fault of unlicensed Coureurs de bois, for did the merchants not furnish goods, there would not be any Coureurs de bois....

As regards Acadia, that country is in great danger inasmuch as it has no fort of any value, and the settlers there are scattered and dispersed, as in Canada. It would be desirable that the King had a good fort at La Heve for the security of ships. That post would be much more advantageous than Port Royal, which it is not easy to get out of to defend the Coast from pirates, and to be more convenient to the Islands of Cape Breton and Newfoundland as well as the Great Bank.

Fish is so abundant on all the coasts of the King's territory, that it is desirable that the King's subjects only should go there to catch them, and that his Majesty were sufficiently powerful in that Country to prevent Foreigners fishing on the Great Bank. They ought to be deprived, at least, of fishing on the King's coasts. The Spaniards go every year to those of Labrador adjoining the Straits of Belle Isle. The English trade there more than we.

Hitherto, all the people of Acadia as well as those of Canada have paid more attention to the Beaver trade and to the sale of Brandy than to the establishment of Fisheries, which, nevertheless, afford the most certain and most durable profit, and are best suited to the inhabitants of the country, and to the augmentation of the Colony. For what each settler might realize annually would supply him most abundantly with clothes; and as the fishing season being only after the sowing and terminates before the harvest, every individual of any industry would find means to drive a profitable business, without abandoning agriculture, as the Coureurs de bois do. The Canadians are adroit and would become in a short time as expert as the Basques in whaling, were they to apply themselves to it. If the establishment of this fishery be persevered in, there is reason to hope that they will turn their attention to it, being encouraged by the stimulus of gain. But he who is desirous of commencing it, is not wealthy, and will find it difficult to defray its expense....

### 6. Ruette d'Auteuil, "Memoir to His Royal Highness the Duc D'Orleans, Regent of France," December 12, 1715.

Patriotism is such a common sentiment that all we can hope for is that those who read this memoir will appreciate the zeal of the Canadian ... who wrote it hoping to correct the erroneous, and publicly stated view, that Canada was worth nothing.

This vast stretch of country is immensely wealthy ... but restricting ourselves only to those areas actually inhabited by Frenchmen, and of the Gulf and Saint Lawrence River linked to the trade with the indigenous inhabitants, we can easily conclude that if the affairs of the country are in a poor condition it is not due to the nature of the land, but rather to the poor management of those who have directed the colony....

Commercial endeavours in Canada ... may be divided into two sections: those involving the indigenous inhabitants and those carried on independently of them.

Since the first discovery of Canada the trade of European merchandise for beaver skins has been the most striking commercial endeavour because of the large profits that may be realized ... a commerce, that in some years, has had a value of 5 or 600,000 livres....

As to the commercial endeavours which are carried on independently of the indigenous inhabitants they are divided as follows.

First there is agriculture, which produces maize, wheat, rye, barley, peas and other grains, meat, and wood, all of which are loaded on ships to be sent to the fishing grounds of the Gulf, and presently to Île Royale and to the French West Indies.

The second is that which is procured, and can be procured, from the River and Gulf of the Saint Lawrence ... cod, salmon, herring, mackerel, and other fish which can be salted ... and which can be said, without exaggeration, to be inexhaustible....

To this must be added the construction of ships ... and forest products which can be sent to France for shipbuilding, masts, and planks ... for the forests of Canada can furnish all kinds of wood ... and the rivers emptying into the Saint Lawrence facilitate their transportation....

To this may be added ... the exploitation of varied mineral reserves, for there are excellent iron ore deposits, and in a bay called Michigan and at Lake Huron almost pure copper mines have been found....

No doubt it will be objected: 1—that the country is very cold; 2—that population growth has been slow; 3—that commerce languishes.... The objections may be answered by saying that the first is not a drawback and that the inconvenience of the others cannot be blamed on the country or on the inhabitants, and that their remedy lies at hand....

## 7. P.F.X. de Charlevoix, "Letter X," Montreal, April 22, 1721.

... Thus it appears, Madam, that every one here is possessed of the necessaries of life; but there is little paid to the King; the inhabitant is not acquainted with taxes; bread is cheap; fish and flesh are not dear; but wine, stuffs, and all French commodities are very expensive. Gentlemen, and those officers who have nothing but their pay, and are besides encumbered with families, have the greatest reason to complain. The women have a great deal of spirit and good nature, are extremely agreeable, and excellent breeders; and these good qualities are for the most part all the fortune they bring their husbands; but God has blessed the marriages in this country.... There are a greater number of noblesse in New France than in all the other colonies put together.

The King maintains here eight and twenty companies of marines, and three *états-majors*. Many families have been ennobled here, and there still remain several officers of the regiment of Carignan-Salières, who have peopled this country with gentlemen who are not in extraordinary good circumstances, and would be still less so, were not commerce allowed them, and the right of hunting and fishing, which is common to everyone.

After all, it is a little their own fault if they are ever exposed to want; the land is good almost everywhere, and agriculture does not in the least derogate from their quality. How many gentlemen throughout all our provinces would envy the lot of the simple inhabitants of Canada, did they but know it? And can those who languish here in a shameful indigence, be excused for refusing to embrace a profession, which the corruption of manners and the most salutary maxims has alone degraded from its ancient dignity? There is not in the world a more wholesome climate than this; no particular distemper is epidemical here, the fields and woods are full of simples of a wonderful efficacy, and the trees distill balms of an excellent quality. These advantages ought at least to remain in it; but inconstancy, aversion to a regular and assiduous labour, and a spirit of independence, have ever carried a great many young people out of it, and prevented the colony from being peopled.

These, Madam, are the defects with which the French Canadians are, with the greatest justice, reproached. The same may likewise be said of the Indians. One would imagine that the air they breathe in this immense continent contributes to it; but the example and frequent intercourse with its natural inhabitants are more than sufficient to constitute this character. Our Creoles are likewise accused of great avidity in amassing, and indeed they do things with this view, which could hardly be believed if they were not seen. The journeys they undertake; the fatigues they undergo; the dangers to which they expose themselves, and the efforts they make, surpass all imagination … Thus there is some room to imagine that they commonly undertake such painful and dangerous journeys out of a taste they have contracted for them. They love to breathe a free air, they are early accustomed to a wandering life; it has charms for them, which make them forget past dangers and fatigues, and they place their glory in encountering them often. They have a great deal of wit, especially the fair sex, in whom it is brilliant and easy; they are, besides, constant and resolute, fertile in resources, courageous, and capable of managing the greatest affairs. You, Madam, are acquainted with more than one of this character, and have often declared your surprise at it to me. I can assure you such are frequent in this country, and are to be found in all ranks and conditions of life.

I know not whether I ought to reckon amongst the defects of our Canadians the good opinion they entertain of themselves. It is at least certain that it inspires them with a confidence, which leads them to undertake and execute what would appear impossible to many others. It must however be confessed they have excellent qualities. There is not a province in the kingdom where the people have a finer complexion, a more advantageous stature, or a body better proportioned. The strength of their constitution is not always answerable, and if the Canadians live to any age, they soon look old and decrepit. This is not entirely their own fault, it is likewise that of their parents, who are not sufficiently watchful over their children to prevent their ruining their health at a time of life, when if it suffers it is seldom or never recovered. Their agility and address are unequalled; the most expert Indians themselves are not better marksmen, or manage their canoes in the most dangerous rapids with greater skill.

Many are of opinion that they are unfit for the sciences, which require any great degree of application, and a continued study. I am not able to say whether this prejudice is well founded, for as yet we have seen no Canadian who has endeavoured to remove it, which is perhaps owing to the dissipation in which they are brought up. But nobody can deny them an excellent genius for mechanics; they have hardly any occasion for the assistance of a master in order to excel in this science; and some are every day to be met with who have succeeded in all trades, without ever having served an apprenticeship.

Some people tax them with ingratitude, nevertheless they seem to me to have a pretty good disposition; but their natural inconstancy often prevents their attending to the duties required by gratitude. It is alleged they make bad servants, which is owing to their great haughtiness of spirit, and to their loving liberty too much to subject themselves willingly to servitude. They are however good masters, which is the reverse of what is said of those from whom the greatest part of them are descended. They would have been perfect in character, if to their own virtues they had added those of their ancestors. Their inconstancy in friendship has sometimes been complained of; but this complaint can hardly be general, and in those who have given occasion for it, it proceeds from their not being accustomed to constraint, even in their own affairs. If they are not easily disciplin'd, this likewise proceeds from the same principle, or from their having a discipline peculiar to themselves, which they believe is better adapted by carrying on war against the Indians, in which they are not entirely to blame. Moreover, they appear to me to be unable to govern a certain impetuosity, which renders them fitter for sudden surprises to hasty expeditions, than the regular and continued operations of a campaign. It has likewise been observed, that amongst a great number of brave men who distinguished themselves in the last wars, there were very few found capable of bearing a superior. This is perhaps owing to their not having sufficiently learned to obey. It is however true, that when they are well conducted, there is nothing which they will not accomplish, whether by sea or land, but in order to do this they must entertain a great opinion of their commander....

There is one thing with respect to which they are not easily to be excused, and that is the little natural affection most of them shew to their parents, who for their part display a tenderness for them, which is not extremely well managed. The Indians fall into the same defect, and it produces amongst them the same consequences. But what above all things ought to make the Canadians be held in much esteem, is the great fund they have of piety and religion, and that nothing is wanting to their education upon this article. It is likewise true, that when they are out of their own country they hardly retain any of their defects. As with all this they are extremely brave and active, they might be of great service in war, in the marine and in the arts; and I am [of the] opinion that it would redound greatly to the advantage of the state, were they to be much more numerous than they are at present. Men constitute the principal riches of the Sovereign, and Canada, should it be of no other use to France, would still be, were it well peopled, one of the most important of all our colonies.

## 8. "Memoir of the King to Serve as Instructions for Sr. Hocquart, Commissary General of the Marine and Ordonnateur in New France," March 22, 1729.

… One of the greatest benefits that the Canadians can procure for France can come from the establishment of fisheries. Those of porpoises and seals that have been started in different places can provide the kingdom with an abundant quantity of fish oils, which are always in great demand but which for the most part are supplied by the Dutch. This commerce is likely to become very extensive and can never be too greatly encouraged. Besides oils it also provides sealskins, which can be used in a number of ways. In every respect, then, the commerce can only be most advantageous.

There are also masts and lumber to be drawn from Canada, not only for the royal shipyards, but also for private enterprise. In 1724 His Majesty sent the sr. de Tilly, a naval lieutenant, and a carpenter to Canada to inspect the forests and prepare wood for masts. This enterprise was beset by great difficulties and their efforts met with little success. The wood that was cut was of poor quality or wasted before being placed aboard the ships. As a result, there appeared reason to believe that obtaining masts from Canada would have to be deferred until the colony was more densely populated.…

Various crops can also be grown in Canada that will be of great utility to France, such as flax and hemp, which must be purchased in the north for considerable sums. In the past, His Majesty sent both types of seed to Quebec. The habitants, who were already in the habit of growing hemp, began to cultivate flax seven or eight years ago. In order to encourage them to increase this cultivation, His Majesty had set its price at sixty livres per quintal up to September 14 of last year and at forty livres after that date. He had ruled that this price would be maintained during the present year and lowered to twenty-five livres beginning on January 1, 1730, which is still higher than its cost in France. However, since this is a sizeable reduction, which might induce the habitants to discontinue this crop, His Majesty will approve if the sr. Hocquart sets the price at thirty-five livres or even at forty livres in 1730.... His Majesty is prepared to incur this expense because of the future utility of this crop, but it would be in vain if the habitants continued to prepare their hemp as badly as they have done until now. Every year complaints have been received.... The sr. Hocquart will do what he can to remedy this situation and will inform the habitants that His Majesty will not buy their hemp at any price if they are not more careful....

Tar is also made in Canada from the pine trees that grow there in quantity. His Majesty recommends that he maintain the habitants in this habit so that in the future this produce may be available for the shipyards....

His Majesty has been informed that sheep in Canada grow a good type of wool. Since there is a great consumption of this product in the kingdom, His Majesty wishes him to encourage as much as he can those who own suitable pastures to raise sheep. Eventually, this can procure considerable wealth for the colony and a more comfortable life for the habitants.

His Majesty recommends that he increase as much as possible the vegetable crops that have already been started in the colony. These not only procure abundance for the habitants but also give rise to a profitable trade with Île Royale and the West Indies, consisting of shipments of wheat, biscuit, and peas....

Before concluding this article on cultivations, His Majesty will observe to him that the Canadians have not until now realized the progress that could have been expected. Long wars, verily, have hindered the growth of the colony. The habitants became accustomed to wielding weapons and to going on expeditions and felt no inclination to remain on the land after the return of peace, although this is what is most enduring and can best contribute to the concentration of strength which the colony requires as protection against the hostile enterprises of its neighbors. With this in mind, the sr. Hocquart must encourage and favor cultivation and the increase of the population as matters most important for the safety of the colony.

It is very important to prevent all manner of trade between the inhabitants of Canada and the English, since the latter would necessarily supply merchandise that can be drawn from the kingdom....

### 9. Gilles Hocquart, "Memoir to the Minister Containing a Characterization of the French Canadian Population," November 8, 1737.

The population of the colony of New France is about 40,000 people of all ages and sex among which there are 10,000 men capable of bearing arms. The Canadians are husky, well built, and of a vigorous temperament. As trades are not dominated by specialization, and since, at the establishment of the colony, tradesmen were rare, necessity has made them ingenious from generation to generation. The rural inhabitants handle the axe very adroitly. They make themselves most of the tools and utensils needed for farming, and build their own houses and barns. Many are weavers and make linen, and a large cloth which is called *droguet* which they use to clothe themselves and their families.

They love honours and praise, and pride themselves on their courage, and are extremely sensitive to criticism and the least punishment. They are self-seeking, vindictive, subject to drunkenness, make much use of liquor, and are not the most truthful people.

This characterization suits the majority, especially the rural inhabitants. Those in the cities have few faults. All are attached to religion. One sees few perfidious people. They are fickle, and have too high an opinion of themselves, which lessens their abilities to succeed in trade, agriculture, and commerce. Add to this the idleness occasioned by the long and rigorous winters. They love hunting, sailing, and travelling and are not as gross and rustic as our peasants of France. They are amenable enough when we flatter them and govern them with justice, but are by nature indocile.

It is more and more necessary to establish the respect due to authority especially amongst the people of the countryside. This aspect of administration has always been most important and the most difficult to implement. One means of achieving this is to choose the officers of the administration for the countryside from amongst the inhabitants who are wise and capable of commanding, and to give all the attention possible to supporting their authority. It can be said that a lack of firmness by the governments in the past has contributed to insubordination. For several years now crimes have been punished, disorders have been checked by suitable chastisements. Policing of public roads, cabarets, etc., has been better, and in general, the inhabitants have been controlled better than in the past. There are few noble families in Canada, but they are so large that there are many gentlemen.

## *Readings*

Altman, I., and J. Horn, eds. *To Make America: European Emigration in the Early Modern Period*. Berkeley: University of California Press, 1991.

Benes, P., ed. *New England/New France, 1600–1850*. Boston: Boston University, 1992.

Bishop, M. *Champlain: A Life of Fortitude*. Toronto: McClelland and Stewart, 1962.

Bosher, J. *Business and Religion in the Age of New France*. Toronto: Canadian Scholar's Press, 1994.

Bosher, J. *The Canadian Merchants, 1713–1763*. Oxford: Clarendon Press, 1987.

Charbonneau, H., et al. *The First French Canadians: Pioneers in the St. Lawrence Valley*. Newark: University of Delaware Press, 1993.

Dechene, L. *Habitants and Merchants in Seventeenth Century Montreal*. Kingston and Montreal: McGill-Queen's University Press, 1992.

Eccles, W. *Canada Under Louis XIV*. Toronto: McClelland and Stewart, 1964.

Eccles, W. *Canadian Frontier 1534–1760*. Revised edition. Albuquerque: University of New Mexico Press, 1984.

Eccles, W. *Canadian Society during the French Regime*. Montreal: Harvest House, 1968.

Eccles, W. *Essays on New France*. Toronto: Oxford University Press, 1987.

Eccles, W. *France in America*. New York: Harper and Row, 1972.

Hamilton, R. *Feudal Society and Colonization: The Historiography of New France*. Gananogue: Language Press, 1988

Harris, R. "The Extension of France into Rural Canada," in J. Gibson, ed., *European Settlement and Development in North America*. Toronto: University of Toronto Press, 1978.

Harris, R. *The Seigneurial System in Early Canada: A Geographical Study*. Second edition. Kingston and Montreal: McGill-Queen's University Press, 1982.

Mattieu, J. *La Nouvelle-France*. Quebec: Presses de l'Universite Laval, 1991.

Miquelon, D. *New France 1701–1744: "A Supplement to Europe."* Toronto: McClelland and Stewart, 1987.

Moogk, P. *La Nouvelle France: The Making of French Canada*. East Lansing: Michigan State University Press, 2000.

Moogk, P. "Reluctant Exiles: Emigrants from France in Canada before 1760," *William and Mary Quarterly* 3 series 46, 3 (July 1989).

Trudel, M. *The Beginnings of New France*. Toronto: McClelland and Stewart, 1973.

Trudel, M. *Histoire de la Nouvelle-France*. Montreal: Fides, 1997.

Trudel, M. *Introduction to New France*. Toronto: Holt, Rinehart and Winston, 1969.

## Chapter Three

# "An Afflicted People": The Acadians

1. Paul Mascarene, *Description of Nova Scotia*, 1720.
2. Minutes of His Majesty's Council at Annapolis Royal, September 25, 1726.
3. Le Marquis de la Jonquiere, "Ordonnance," Quebec, April 12, 1751.
4. Acadians, "Memorial to Nova Scotia Governor Charles Lawrence," June 10, 1755.
5. Governor Charles Lawrence, "To the Governors on the Continent," August 11, 1755.
6. Governor Charles Lawrence, "To the Board of Trade," Halifax, October 18, 1755.
7. John Baptiste Galerm, "A Relation of the Misfortunes of the French Neutrals, as laid before the Assembly of the Province of Pennsylvania," 1758.

## Introduction

The forcible expulsion of the Acadian people during the Seven Years' War still generates controversy and debate among historians and the public; most portrayals cast the British as nefarious and imperialistic bullies attacking hapless and innocent victims. Loaded words like "genocide" and "ethnic cleansing" appear in books, periodicals, and at conferences now interpreting the event. Such inflammatory language is not mere hyperbole: courts in the Hague presently prosecute and incarcerate soldiers and politicians for such crimes, whether they take place in Bosnia or Rwanda, and an indictment, apart from assaulting national prestige, logically invites the issue of restitution for the victims, even long after the incident transpired. Canada set a precedent of sorts too, by compensating Japanese-Canadians for their inappropriate relocation during the Second World War. Why not offer similar restitution to Acadian descendants if the expulsion can be proven to have been unwarranted: to have been genocide rather than a tragic but strategically legitimate act of war.

France claimed and settled Acadia with a smattering of immigrants during the seventeenth century. The colony encompassed what is now peninsular Nova Scotia and the north shore of the Bay of Fundy, the inland borders of present day New Brunswick remaining ill-defined. Île Royale and Île Saint-Jean, now Cape Breton, and Prince Edward Islands, anchored this tenuous outpost of France's North American empire. French administrators considered the colony less important than New France on the St. Lawrence River and consequently tended to ignore it prior to 1713. Thus communication between the two areas, such as it was, remained slow and infrequent, and though nominally administrated from Quebec, Acadia evolved rather autonomously, generating a culture of self-sufficiency among its officially French population. The people, who originated from a small corner of southwest France and who spoke a dialect distinct from New France's, established a working relationship with the British New England colonies to the south, as well as with their motherland's North American headquarters at Quebec.

While religion, language, and history bound the Acadians far more to France than to England, their geographical location compromised that political allegiance because Acadia formed a natural buffer separating New England from New France. Such zones tend to hold strategic value and often end up as military hot spots, particularly when the protagonists are mortal enemies and competitive imperialists such as were England and France. The politically expedient solution to avoid becoming a battlefield, the Acadians believed, was to nurture their independentist spirit based upon a centrepiece of political neutrality. This potentially offered significant dividends: neutrality, for example, should double their economic activity by facilitating trade with both English and French possessions. As well, France and England had a history of squabbling over the land and nonalignment should keep the Acadians uninvolved, or at least from ending up on the wrong side after an ownership change, which seemed to occur with monotonous regularity.

A good part of Acadia changed hands in 1713 as a result of French losses and the armistice Treaty of Utrecht. The Union Jack once again fluttered over the peninsula, which Britain dubbed New Scotland or Nova Scotia, though Îles Saint Jean and Royale remained French, as did the north shore of the Bay of Fundy and land stretching into what is today the American state of Maine. An uneasy no-man's border zone soon emerged at the northern end of the isthmus of Chignecto, both nations eventually building fortifications that allowed soldiers in Fort Beauséjour to stare down their British counterpoints at Fort Lawrence, a short distance away.

Now Britain had to contend with the Acadians living in its newly conquered territory. On the one hand, a stable population, particularly of farmers such as they were, could furnish agricultural products to the English garrison, and would encourage later growth through the community's very existence. Expelling them would disrupt the established trade between Acadia and New England. And if the Acadians left, their number would simply strengthen French possessions elsewhere in North America which is hardly what an English military strategist should encourage. Finally, the Acadians seemed sufficiently docile and friendly not to constitute a threat to English security. On the other hand, however, France was the enemy. The Acadians were French and Catholic, they had weapons, and the French busily built forts in the vicinity which the Acadians willingly supplied with goods. How loyal was that? Catholic priests sent from Quebec repeatedly incited the Acadians and the Micmac Indians against their new masters. Meanwhile, the British garrison was initially so small that a tiny but determined band of rebellious subjects could possibly push it into the Atlantic. Did the benefits of the Acadian presence really outweigh the dangers?

The Acadians, many of whom were multi-generational settlers, did not wish to leave an area they considered home, regardless of the official ownership. They simply wished to get on with life. The only ones, in fact, who definitely wanted the Acadians out, now that the area was British, were the French who did not want to provide the English with easy provisions and a servile local population. No, the French argued, the Acadians should do the correct thing and remove themselves to Île Royale where they could support the massive new fortifications of Louisburg.

Local British administrators ultimately concluded that the advantages of keeping the Acadians on site did, in fact, outweigh the dangers if they hedged their bets. Britain would treat the Acadians magnanimously while insisting that their new subjects swear an oath of fidelity to the British crown. The most contentious aspect of the oath was the implication that "fidelity" could force Acadians to take up arms for England and against the French, which the former Frenchmen patently refused to countenance. The two sides overcame the ensuing diplomatic impasse through a tacit agreement, locally drafted, whereby the Acadians swore the oath but with a proviso exempting them from military service. This did not sit well with a British government that declared its citizens as either loyal or disloyal, period, though London chose not to force the issue. The modified oath was good enough for the "neutral" Acadians, however, who naively settled down to their new reality, seemingly oblivious to their status as expendable pawns in a much bigger geo-political chess game.

Time caught them out and their neutrality became a terrible liability. France and Britain stood poised for battle by the 1740s, and both manoeuvred ever more ferociously for the Acadians' loyalty. England increasingly believed that "neutral" definitely meant "enemy" in times of war, particularly after a number of suspicious incidents in which Acadians appeared to support French military efforts. British governors repeatedly pushed for the oath of complete fidelity which the Acadians refused without their traditional exemption. Tensions ratcheted upward. Rather than evict the Acadians, thereby strengthening the enemy, Governor Lawrence instead had them rounded up, packed onto waiting ships, and dispersed in small groups throughout the thirteen English colonies where, in theory, they were to be integrated with the local population and eventually disappear. The expulsions began in 1755 and carried on for several years until virtually the entire Acadian population disappeared. Some Acadians did successfully flee to Île Royale or Île Saint Jean during the initial evacuation, but their luck ran out when British forces overran both islands and expelled them from there too. It was not until well after the end of the war before Acadians were permitted to return, and when they did, they as often as not found others holding legal title to their old homesteads.

## Discussion Points

1. Who or what bears primary responsibility for the Acadian dilemma? How much was Britain to blame? The Acadians? The French?
2. Was Britain justified in its final actions or did the Acadians deserve different treatment? Were there other solutions? Was deportation inevitable?
3. Galerm raises the issue of compensation for Acadian losses. Is the Acadian deportation another example of an historical injustice for which we (or the British government) should provide compensation or an apology?
4. Historians often use the term "history from below" when discussing the perspectives of ordinary people like Galerm. In what respects would documents left by such people be better and/or worse historical sources than accounts from prominent government officials such as Lawrence?

*Documents*

## 1. Paul Mascarene, *Description of Nova Scotia*, 1720.

There are four considerable settlements on the south side of the Bay of Fundy, Annapolis Royal, Manis, Chignecto, and Cobequid which shall be treated on separately. Several families are scattered along the Eastern Coast which shall be also mentioned in their turn.

The Inhabitants of these Settlements are still all French and Indians; the former have been tolerated in the possession of the lands they possessed, under the French Government, and have had still from time to time longer time allowed them either to take the Oaths to the Crown of Great Britain, or to withdraw, which they have always found some pretence or other to delay, and to ask for longer time for consideration. They being in general of the Romish persuasion, can not be easily drawn from the French Interest, to which they seem to be entirely wedded tho' they find a great deal more sweetness under the English Government. They use all the means they can to keep the Indians from dealing with the British subjects, and by their mediation spreading among the Savages several false Notions tending to make them diffident, and frighten them from a free intercourse with them and prompting them now and then to some mischief which may increase that diffidence, and oblige them to keep more at a distance.

There are but two reasons which may plead for the keeping those French Inhabitants in this Country. 1st. The depriving the French of the addition of such a strength, which might render them too powerful neighbours, especially if these people on their withdrawing hence are received and settled at Cape Breton; and secondly, the use that may be made of them in providing necessaries for erecting fortifications, and for English Settlements and keeping on the stock of cattle, and the lands tilled, till the English are powerful enough of themselves to go on, which two last will sensibly decay if they withdraw before any considerable number of British subjects be settled in their stead, and it is also certain that they having the conveniency of saw mills (which it will not be in our power to hinder being destroyed by them, at their going away) may furnish sooner and cheaper the plank boards &c. requisite for building.

The reasons for not admitting these Inhabitants are many and strong, and naturally deriving from the little dependence on their allegiance. The free exercise of their religion as promised to them, implies their having missionaries of the Romish persuasion amongst them, who have that ascendance over that ignorant people, as to render themselves masters of all their actions, and to guide and direct them as they please in temporal as well as in spiritual affairs. These missionaries have their superiors at Canada or Cape Breton, from whom it is natural to think, they will receive such commands as will never square with the English interest being such as these, viz., Their forever inciting the Savages to some mischief or other, to hinder their corresponding with the English; their laying all manner of difficulties in the way when any English Settlement is proposed or going on by in citing underhand the Savages to disturb them, and making these last such a bugbear, as if they (the French) themselves durst not give any help to the English for fear of being massacred by them, when it is well known the Indians are but a handful in this country. And were the French Inhabitants (who are able to appear a thousand men under arms) hearty for the British Government, they could drive away, or utterly destroy the Savages in a very little time. The French Inhabitants besides are for the generality very little industrious, their lands not improved as might be expected, they living in a manner from hand to mouth, and provided they have a good field of Cabbages and Bread enough for their families with what fodder is sufficient for their cattle they seldom look for much further improvement.

It is certain that British Colonists would be far more advantageous to the settling this Province, and would besides the better improvement of it, for which their Industry is far superior to the French who inhabit it at present, lessen considerably the expense in defending of it, not only in regard to fortifications, but also in regard to Garrisons, because the English Inhabitants would be a strength of themselves, whereas the French require a strict watch over them. This would also reconcile the native Indians to the English, which the other as mentioned before, endeavour to keep at a distance.

The neighbouring Government of the French at Cape Breton is not very desirous of drawing the Inhabitants out of this Country so long as they remain in it under a kind of Allegiance to France, especially if they are not allowed to carry their cattle, effects, grain, &c., which last would be more welcome in the barren country than bare Inhabitants, but is opposing with all its might and by the influence of the Priests residing here, their taking the oaths of Allegiance to Great Britain, and if even that oath was taken by them, the same influence would make it of little or no effect. That Government is also improving by the same means the diffidence of the Indians, and will make them instruments to disturb the British Settlements on the Eastern Coast of this Government, or any other place, which might check the supplies they have from hence for their support on their barren territories besides the jealousy in trade and fear of this Government being too powerful in case of a War.

It would be therefore necessary for the interest of Great Britain, and in order to reap the benefit, which will accrue from the acquisition of this country, not to delay any longer the settling of it, but to go about it in good earnest to which it is humbly proposed, viz.:

That the French Inhabitants may not be tolerated any longer in their non-allegiance, but may have the test put to them without granting them any further delay, for which it is requisite a sufficient force be allowed to make them comply with the terms prescribed them, which force ought to be at least six hundred men to be divided to the several parts already inhabited by the French and Indians, and might be at the same time a cover to the British Inhabitants who would come to settle in the room of the French. For an encouragement to those new Inhabitants, should be given free transportation, free grants of land, and some stock of Cattle out of what such of the French who would rather choose to withdraw, than take the oaths, might be hindered to destroy or carry away.

The expense this project would cost the Government, would be made up by the benefit, which would accrue to trade, when the country should be settled with Inhabitants, who would promote it, and would be a security to it and in a little time a small force of regular troops would be able to defend it, with the help of loyal Inhabitants.

The great expense the Government has been at already on account of this country, and the little benefit that has accrued from it is owing for the most part, to its being peopled with Inhabitants that have been always enemies to the English Government, for it's evident from what has been said of the temper of the Inhabitants and the underhand dealings of the Government of Cape Breton, that what orders are or may be given out by the Governor of this Province, without they are backed by a sufficient force, will be always slighted and rendered of non effect....

## 2. Minutes of His Majesty's Council at Annapolis Royal, September 25, 1726.

At a Council held as aforesaid in His Majesty's Town of Annapolis Royal on Sunday the 25th of September 1726 ... The Honourable Lt. Governor of the Province acquainted [them] that he this day expected the deputies and the inhabitants with their answer conform to the appointment on Wednesday last and therefore desired the advice of the board what he should [do] in case they refused signing and taking the oaths of His Majesty.

The board thought that the only method to be used, was to demonstrate to them first the necessity of their so doing, and invite them thereunto by laying before them the many advantages and privileges of English subjects to which they by taking the oath of fidelity to His Majesty King George were as fully and freely entitled to as if they were the natural born subjects of Great Britain, as also the free exercise of their religion, estates and fortunes, otherwise they must of necessity retire immediately out of the province conform to His Majesty's directions for if arguments and promises of kind usage did not prevail, it would be to no purpose to pretend compelling them by force further than telling them what they might expect; and if thereby those who have plenty and good estates should be once engaged, the others would be either the more easily wrought upon or forced to be gone....

His Honour the Lieutenant Governor of the Province with the Honourable Lt. Governor of His Majesty's Town and Garrison of Annapolis Royal with the other members of the Council met at the Flag Bastion according to adjournment where the deputies [of the Acadians] with a number of the inhabitants being also present.

The Honourable Lt. Governor of the Province told them that he was glad to see them and that he hoped they had so far considered their own and children's future advantages, that they were come with a full resolution to take the oath of fidelity like good subjects....

Whereupon at the request of some of the inhabitants a French translation of the oath required to be taken was read unto them. Upon which some of them desiring that a clause whereby they might not be obliged to carry arms might be inserted.

The Governor told them that they had no reason to fear any such thing as that it being contrary to the laws of Great Britain that a Roman Catholic should serve in the army, His Majesty having so many faithful Protestant subjects first to provide for, and that all that His Majesty required of them was to be faithful subjects, not to join with any enemy, but for their own interest to discover all traiterous and evil designs, plots and conspiracies any ways formed against His Majesty's subjects and government and so peaceably and quietly to enjoy and improve their estates.

But they upon that motion made as aforesaid still refusing and desiring the said clause.

The Governor with the advice of the Council granted the same to be written upon the margin of the French translation in order to get them over by degrees. Whereupon they took and subscribed the same both in French and English.

### 3. Le Marquis de la Jonquiere, "Ordonnance," Quebec, April 12, 1751.

The representations which the French Acadians have made to us concerning the ill treatment that they have received from the English principally on account of the Apostolic and Roman Catholic religion that they profess having been frequently reiterated, we have determined to put them under the protection of the King our Master so that they will be sheltered from all insults from the English. This joined to the considerable expenses which His Majesty has undertaken in order to maintain them on their lands and to provide them with sustenance and everything which is necessary to them, does not permit us to entertain doubts as to the zeal and faithfulness of the said Acadians. But we have learnt with great sorrow that certain amongst them and notably Jacob Maurice, wishing to make themselves independant have refused to take the oath of fidelity to the King our Master, which makes them, in every view, guilty of the worst ingratitude and unworthy of participating in the graces of His Majesty.

And since we must punish such subjects WE DECLARE by the present ordinance that all Acadians who (within eight days of the publication of this) have not taken the oath of fidelity and are not incorporated within the Militia companies which we have created, will be declared rebels to the orders of the King and as such expelled from the lands which they hold. To which end we Order S. Deschaillons de St. Ours, Commandant at Beauséjour and all our other posts to fulfil this fully and that our intentions shall be known by all, the reading of this present ordinance shall be made everywhere where it has need to be. In faith of which we have signed, and placed the seal of our arms and our secretary has countersigned.

### 4. Acadians, "Memorial to Nova Scotia Governor Charles Lawrence," June 10, 1755.

"To His Excellency Charles Lawrence, Governor of the Province of Nova Scotia or Acadie, &c. &c.
"Sir,—
"We, the inhabitants of Mines, Pisiquid, and the river carard, take the liberty of approaching your Excellency for the purpose of testifying our sense of the care which the government exercises towards us.

"It appears, Sir, that your Excellency doubts the sincerity with which we have promised to be faithful to his Britannic Majesty.

"We most humbly beg your Excellency to consider our past conduct. You will see, that, very far from violating the oath we have taken, we have maintained it in its entirety, in spite of the solicitations and the dreadful threats of another power. We still entertain, Sir, the same pure and sincere disposition to prove under any circumstances, our unshaken fidelty to his Majesty, provided that His Majesty shall allow us the same liberty that he has granted us. We earnestly beg your Excellency to have the goodness to inform us of His Majesty's intentions on this subject, and to give us assurances on his part.

"Permit us, if you please, Sir, to make known the annoying circumstances in which we are placed, to the prejudice of the tranquillity we ought to enjoy. Under pretext that we are transporting our corn or other provisions to Beauséjour, and the river of St. John, we are no longer permitted to carry the least quantity of corn by water from one place to another. We beg your Excellency to be assured that we have never transported provisions to Beauséjour, or to the river St. John. If some refugee inhabitants at the point have been seized, with cattle, we are not on that account, by any means guilty, in as much as the cattle belonged to them as private individuals, and they were driving them to their respective habitations. As to ourselves, Sir, we have never offended in that respect; consequently we ought not, in our opinion, to be punished; on the contrary, we hope that your Excellency will be pleased to restore us the same liberty that we enjoyed formerly, in giving us the use of our canoes, either to transport our provisions from one river to the other, or for the purpose of fishing; thereby providing for our livelihood. This permission has never been taken from us except at the present time. We hope, Sir, that you will be pleased to restore it, especially in consideration of the number of poor inhabitants who would be very glad to support their families with the fish that they would be able to catch. Moreover, our guns, which we regard as our personal property, have been taken from us, notwithstanding the fact that they are absolutely necessary to us, either to defend our cattle which are attacked by the wild beasts, or for the protection of our children, and of ourselves.

"Any inhabitant who may have his oxen in the woods, and who may need them for purposes of labour, would not dare to expose himself in going for them without being prepared to defend himself.

"It is certain, Sir, that since the savages have ceased frequenting our parts, the wild beasts have greatly increased, and our cattle are devoured by them almost every day. Besides, the arms which have been taken from us are but a feeble guarantee of our fidelity. It is not the gun which an inhabitant possesses, that will induce him to revolt, nor the privation of the same gun that will make him more faithful; but his conscience alone must induce him to maintain his oath.

An order has appeared in your Excellency's name, given at Fort Edward June 4th, 1755, and in the 28th year of his Majesty's region, by which we are commanded to carry guns, pistols etc. to Fort Edward. It appears to us, Sir, that it would be dangerous for us to execute that order, before representing to you the danger to which this order exposes us. The savages may come and threaten and plunder us, reproaching us for having furnished arms to kill them. We hope, Sir, that you will be pleased, on the contrary, to order that those taken from us be restored to us. By so doing, you will afford us the means of preserving both ourselves and our cattle. In the last place, we are grieved, Sir, at seeing ourselves declared guilty without being aware of having disobeyed. One of our inhabitants of the river Canard, named Piere Melançon, was seized and arrested in charge of his boat, before having heard any order forbidding that kind of transport. We beg your Excellency, on this subject, to have the goodness to make know to us your good pleasure before confiscating our property and considering us in fault. This is the favour we expect from your Excellency's kindness, and we hope that you will do us the justice to believe that very far from violating our promises, we will maintain them, assuring you that we are very respectfully,

Sir,

Your very humble and obt. servants,"

Signed by twenty-five of the said inhabitants.

## 5. Governor Charles Lawrence, "To the Governors on the Continent," August 11, 1755.

Sir: The success that has attended his Majesty's arms in driving the French from the Encroachments they had made in this province furnished me with a favorable Opportunity of reducing the French inhabitants of this Colony to a proper obedience to his Majesty's Government, or forcing them to quit the country. These Inhabitants were permitted to remain in quiet possession of their lands upon condition they should take the Oath of allegiance to the King within one year after the Treaty of Utrecht by which this province was ceded to Great Britain; with this condition they have ever refused to comply, without having at the same time from the Governor an assurance in writing that they should not be called upon to bear arms in the defence of the province; and with this General Philipps did comply, of which step his Majesty disapproved and the inhabitants pretending therefrom to be in a state of Neutrality between his Majesty and his enemies have continually furnished the French & Indians with Intelligence, quarters, provisions and assistance in annoying the Government; and while one part have abetted the French Encroachments by their treachery, the other have countenanced them by open Rebellion, and three hundred of them were actually found in arms in the French Fort at Beauséjour when it surrendered.

Notwithstanding all their former bad behaviour, as his Majesty was pleased to allow me to extend still further his Royal grace to such as would return to their Duty, I offered such of them as had not been openly in arms against us, a continuance of the Possession of their lands, if they would take the Oath of Allegiance, unqualified with any Reservation whatsoever; but this they have most audaciously as well as unanimously refused, and if they would presume to do this when there is a large fleet of Ships of War in the harbor, and a considerable land force in the province, what might not we expect from them when the approaching winter deprives us of the former, and when the Troops which are only hired from New England occasionally and for a smalltime, have returned home.

As by this behaviour the inhabitants have forfeited all title to their lands and any further favor from the Government, I called together his Majesty's Council, at which the Honble. Vice Adml. Boscawen and Rear Adml. Mostyn assisted, to consider by what means we could with the greatest security and effect rid ourselves of a set of people who would forever have been an obstruction to the intention of settling this Colony and that It was now from their refusal to the Oath absolutely incumbent upon us to remove.

As their numbers amount to near 7000 persons the driving them off with leave to go whither they pleased would have doubtless strengthened Canada with so considerable a number of inhabitants; and as they have no cleared land to give them at present, such as are able to bear arms must have been immediately employed in annoying this and neighbouring Colonies. To prevent such inconvenience it was judged a necessary and the only practicable measure to divide them among the Colonies where they may be of some use, as most of them are healthy strong people; and as they cannot easily collect themselves together again it will be out of their power to do any mischief and they may become profitable and it is possible, in time, faithful subjects.

As this step was indispensably necessary to the security of this Colony, upon whose preservation from French encroachments the prosperity of North America is esteemed in a great measures dependent, I have not the least reason to doubt of your Excellency's concurrence and that you will receive the inhabitants I now send and dispose of them in such manner as may best answer our design in preventing their reunion.

## 6. Governor Charles Lawrence, "To the Board of Trade," Halifax, October 18, 1755.

My Lords,

Since the last letter I had the honor to write your Lordships of the 18th of July, the French deputys of the different districts have appeared before the Council to give a final answer to the proposal made them, of taking the Oath of Allegiance to his Majesty which they persisted in positively refusing; and tho' every means was used to point out to them their true interest, and sufficient time given them to deliberate maturely upon the step they were about to take, nothing would induce them to acquiesce in any measures that were consistent with his Majesty's honor or the security of his Province. Upon this behaviour the Council came to a resolution to oblige them to quit the Colony, and immediately took into consideration what might be the speediest, cheapest and easiest method of giving this necessary resolution its intended effect. We easily foresaw that driving them out by force of Arms to Canada or Louisbourg, would be attended with great difficulty, and if it had succeeded would have reinforced those settlements with a very considerable body of men, who were ever universally the most inveterate enemies to our religion and Government, and now highly enraged at the loss of their possessions.

The only safe means that appeared to us of preventing their return or their collecting themselves again into a large body, was distributing them among the Colonies from Georgia to New England. Accordingly the Vessels were hired at the cheapest rates: the embarkation is now in great forwardness, and I am in hopes some of them are already sailed, and that there will not be one remaining by the end of the next month. Herewith I transmit your Lordships a Copy of the Records of Council which contain a very particular account of this whole transaction.

I have taken all the care in my power to lessen the expense of the Transportation of the inhabitants, the vessels that have been taken up for that purpose, were most of them bound to the places where the inhabitants were destined, and by that means are hired greatly cheaper than the ordinary price. They have hitherto been victualled with their own provisions and will be supplied for the passage with the provisions that were taken in the French Forts at Chignecto as far as they will go.

In order to save as many of the French cattle as possible, I have given some of them among such of the Settlers as have the means of feeding them in the winter. As soon as the French are gone I shall use my best endeavours to encourage People to come from the continent to settle their lands, and if I succeed in this point we shall soon be in a condition of supplying ourselves with provisions, and I hope in time to be able to strike off the great expense of the Victualling the Troops. This was one of the happy effects I proposed to myself from driving the French off the Isthmus and the additional circumstance of the Inhabitants evacuating the Country will I flatter myself greatly hasten this event as it furnishes us with a large quantity of good land ready for immediate cultivation, renders it difficult for the Indians who cannot as formerly be supplied with provisions and intelligence, to make incursions upon our settlers, and I believe the French will not now be so sanguine in their hopes of possessing a province that they have hitherto looked upon as ready peopled for them the moment they would get the better of the English. I think it my duty to acquaint your Lordships that it will be highly necessary for the security of the province to fortify the Isthmus of Chignecto as early in the Spring as possible. The French Forts at Beauséjour and upon the Bay Verte are put into the best repair that the time would permit, but they are neither strong enough nor will they contain a sufficient number of men to resist any considerable force. It is also of the highest importance that there should be a Fort of some strength at St. John's River to prevent the French resettling there, as well as to awe the Indians of that district. I am very sensible that making these Fortifications will create a very considerable expense and therefore cannot be undertaken without orders, but if your Lordships should think it necessary to be done you may depend upon its being set about with the greatest economy....

As the Three French Priests, Messrs. Chauvreulx, Daudin & Le Maire were of no further use in this Province after the removal of the French Inhabitants, Admiral Boscawen has been so good as to take them on board his fleet & is to give them a passage to England. I omitted in the paragraph about the French Inhabitants to mention to your Lordships my having wrote a circular letter to the Governors of the provinces to which they were destined, & directed one to be given to the master of each transport. In this Letter I have set forth the reasons which obliged us to take the measures we have done, and I enclose a copy of it for your Lordship's perusal. I am in hopes the provinces will make no difficulties about receiving them as they may in a short time become useful & beneficial subjects.

## 7. John Baptiste Galerm, "A Relation of the Misfortunes of the French Neutrals, as laid before the Assembly of the Province of Pennsylvania," 1758.

About the Year 1713, when Annapolis Royal was taken from the French our Fathers being then settled on the Bay of Fundi, upon the Surrender of that Country to the English, had, by Virtue of the Treaty of Utrecht, a Year granted to them to remove with their Effects; but not being willing to lose the Fruit of many Years Labour, they chose rather to remain there, and become Subjects of Great Britain, on Condition that they might be exempted from bearing Arms against France (most of them having near Relations and friends amongst the French, which they might have destroyed with their own Hands, had they consented to bear Arms against them). This Request they always understood to be granted, on their taking the Oath of Fidelity to her late Majesty Queen Anne; which Oath of Fidelity was by us, about 27 Years ago, renewed to his Majesty King George by General Philipse, who then allowed us an Exemption of bearing Arms against France; which Exemption, till lately (that we were told to the contrary) we always thought was approved of by the King. Our Oath of Fidelity, we that are now brought into this Province, as well at those of our Community that are carried late into the neighbouring Provinces, have always inviolably observed, and have, on all Occasions, been willing to afford all the Assistance in our Power to his Majesty's Governors in erecting Forts, making Roads, Bridges, &c., and providing Provisions for his Majesty's Service, as can be testified by the several Governors and Officers that have commanded in his Majesty's Province of Nova Scotia; and this notwithstanding the repeated Solicitations, Threats and Abuses which we have continually, more or less, suffered from the French and French Indians of Canada on that Account; particularly, about ten Years ago, when 500 French and Indians came to our Settlements, intending to attack Annapolis Royal, which, had their intention succeeded, would have made them Masters of all Nova Scotia, it being the only Place of Strength then in that Province, they earnestly solicited with us to join with, and aid them therein; but we persisting in our Resolution to abide true to our Oath of Fidelity, and absolutely refusing to give them any Assistance, they gave over their Intention and returned to Canada. And about seven Years past, at the Settling of Halifax, a body of 150 Indians came amongst us, forced some of us from our Habitations, and by Threats and blows would have compelled us to assist them in Way laying and destroying the English, then employed in erecting Forts in different parts of the Country; but we positively refusing, they left us, after having abused us, and made great Havock of our Cattle, &c. I myself was six weeks before I wholly recovered of the blows I received from them at that time. Almost numberless are the Instances which might be given of the Abuses and Losses we have undergone from the French Indians on Account of our steady Adhearance to our Oath of Fidelity; and yet notwithstanding our strict Observance thereof, we have not been able to prevent the grievous Calamity which is now come upon us, which we apprehend to be in a great Measure owing to the unhappy Situation and Conduct of some of our People settled at Chignecto, at the bottom of the Bay of Fundi, where the French, about four Years ago, erected a Fort; those of our People who were settled near it, after having had many of their Settlements burnt by the French; being too far from Halifax and Annapolis Royal to expect sufficient Assistance from the English, were obliged, as we believe, more through Compulsion and Fear than Inclination, to join with and assist the French; which also appears from the Articles of Capitulation agreed on between Colonel Monckton and the French Commander, at the Delivery of the said Fort to the English, which is expressly in the following Words.

"With regard to the Acadians, as they have been forced to take up Arms on Pain of Death, they shall be pardoned for the Part they have been taking." Notwithstanding this, as these People's Conduct had given just Umbrage to the Government and erected Suspicions, to the Prejudice of our whole Community, we were summoned to appear before the Governor and Council at Halifax, where we were required to take the Oath of Allegiance without any Exception, which we could not comply with because, as that Government is at present situate, we apprehend that we should have been obliged to take up Arms; but we are still willing to take the Oath of Fidelity, and to give the strongest Assurance of continuing peaceable and faithful to his Britannick Majesty, with that Exception. But this, in the present Situation of Affairs, not being satisfactory, we were made Prisoners, and our Estates, both real and personal, forfeited for the King's Use; and Vessels being provided, we were some time after sent off, with most of our Families, and dispersed amongst the English Colonies. The Hurry and Confusion in which we were embarked was an aggravating Circumstance attending our Misfortunes; for thereby many, who had lived in Affluence, found themselves deprived of every Necessary, and many Families were separated, Parents from Children, and Children from Parents. Yet blessed be God that it was our Lot to be sent to Pennsylvania, where our Wants have been relieved, and we have in every Respect been received with Christian Benevolence and Charity. And let me add, that not withstanding the Suspicions and Fears which many here are possessed of on our Account, as tho' we were a dangerous People, who make little Scruple of breaking our Oaths. Time will manifest that we are not such a People: No, the unhappy situation which we are now in, is a plain Evidence that this is a false Claim, tending to aggravate the Misfortunes of an already too unhappy People; for had we entertained such pernicious Sentiments, we might easily have prevented our falling into the melancholy Circumstances we are now in, viz: Deprived of our Subsistance, banished from our native Country, and reduced to live by Charity in a strange Land; and this for refusing to take an Oath, which we are firmly persuaded Christianity absolutely forbids us to violate, had we once taken it, and yet an Oath which we could not comply with without being exposed to plunge our Swords in the Breasts of our Friends and Relations. We shall, however, as we have hitherto done, submit to what in the present Situation of Affairs may seem necessary, and with Patience and Resignation bear whatever God, in the course of his Providence, shall suffer to come upon us. We shall also think it our Duty to seek and promote the Peace of the Country into which we are transported, and inviolably keep the Oath of Fidelity that we have taken to his gracious Majesty King George, whom we firmly believe, when fully acquainted with our Faithfulness and Sufferings, will commiserate our unhappy Condition, and order that some Compensation be made us for our Losses. And may the Almighty abundantly bless his Honour the Governor, the Honourable Assembly of the Province, and the good People of Philadelphia, whose Sympathy, Benevolence and Christian Charity have been, and still are, greatly manifested and extended towards us, a poor distressed and afflicted People, is the sincere and earnest Prayer of John Baptiste Galerm.

## Readings

Arsenault, B. *History of the Acadians*. Quebec: Lemeac, 1966.

Arsenault, G. *The Island Acadians, 1720–1980*. Charlottetown: Ragweed, 1989.

Barnes, T. "'The Dayley Cry for Justice': The Juridical Failure of the Annapolis Royal Regime," in P. Girard and J. Phillips, eds., *Essays in the History of Canadian Law*. Volume 3. Toronto: Osgoode Society, 1990.

Barnes, T. "Historiography of the Acadians' Grand Derangement, 1755," *Quebec Studies* 7 (1988).

Blanchard, J. *The Acadians of Prince Edward Island*. Ottawa: LeDroit and LeClerc, 1976.

Brown, D. "Foundations of British Policy in the Acadian Expulsion: A Discussion of Land Tenure and the Oath of Allegiance," *Dalhousie Review* (1977).

Daigle, J., ed. *The Acadians of the Maritimes: Thematic Studies*. Moncton: Centre for Acadian Studies, 1982.

Ferguson, C. "The Expulsion of the Acadians," *Dalhousie Review* 25, 2 (1955).

Grant, H. "The Deportation of the Acadians," *Nova Scotia Historical Quarterly* (1975).

Griffiths, N. *The Acadian Deportation: Deliberate Perfidy or Cruel Necessity?* Toronto: Copp Clark, 1969.

Griffiths, N. *The Acadians: Creation of a People*. Toronto: McClelland and Stewart, 1973.

Griffiths, N. *The Contexts of Acadian History 1686–1784*. Kingston and Montreal: McGill-Queen's University Press, 1992.

Griffiths, N. "The Golden Age: Acadian Life 1713–1748," *Social History* 17, 33 (May 1984).

Keefer, J. "The Ideology of Innocence: Anglophone Literature and the Expulsion of the Acadians," *Revue de l'Universite Sainte-Anne* (1984–85).

Plant, G. *An Unsettled Conquest: The British Campaign Against the Peoples of Acadia*. Philadelphia: University of Pennsylvannia Press, 2001.

Reid, J. *Acadia, Maine and New Scotland: Marginal Colonies in the Seventeenth Century*. Toronto: University of Toronto Press, 1981.

*Chapter Four*

# "THE RUIN OF CANADA":
# LAST DECADES OF NEW FRANCE

1. François Daine, "To Marshal de Belle Isle," Quebec, May 19, 1758.
2. M. de Capellis, "Memoir," 1758.
3. Louis-Joseph de Montcalm, "To Marshal de Belle Isle," Montreal, April 12, 1759.
4. Michel-Jean-Hughes Péan, "Memoir on the Condition of Canada."
5. M. de Beaucat, "Mémoire sur le Canada," 1759.
6. Unknown, "Memoir on Canada."
7. Marie de la Visitation, *Narrative of the Doings During the Seige of Quebec, and the Conquest of Canada.*

## Introduction

The battle for North America between France and England, despite flaring up two years before the war officially began, was a sideshow to a greater European struggle. Thus the two home governments tended to let local commanders take charge of their American theatres, often without supplying the necessary logistical support. This served New England far better than New France. The English colonies had a population vastly greater than the French, concentrated in one major area, and with a diversified economy that promoted a high degree of self-sufficiency. New France, on the other hand, stretched for miles along the Saint Lawrence, a river frozen solid for months at a time during which outside communication stopped. Though agricultural, the colony's economic mainstay remained the fur trade and mercantilism discouraged both diversification and self-sufficiency. Thus New France, unlike New England, depended upon its umbilical cord to Europe, a cord the English Royal Navy effectively severed in mid-Atlantic.

As if this were not bad enough, all manner of internal strife and confusion racked New France during the final years—as the following documents suggest. The locally born governor, Vaudreuil, and the French aristocratic senior military commander, Montcalm, hated one another, found it impossible to agree on common strategy, and periodically sabotaged each other's efforts. The militia and professional forces disliked and distrusted each other, and native allies proved unpredictable. The economy lay in shambles, partly because Intendant Bigot and his cronies of the Grand Society pilfered the colony blind. Locally produced supplies disappeared as a result of hoarding, and from too many habitants serving in the militia when they were needed on their farms. Critical imports dried up due to the British blockade, inflation ran rampant, and last, but certainly not least, a pall of defeatism and terror hung over the entire New France population like a dark cloud.

The English eventually chose a three pronged pincer movement along the traditional invasion routes into the heart of New France Lawrence: via the Great Lakes; up the Richelieu River; and by sea through the Gulf of St. Lawrence. Year by year inching their way northward, eventually General Wolfe stood at the opposite shore from Quebec in the summer of 1759. Then began a summer-long cat-and-mouse game as Wolfe attempted to force the French into open battle by trying to land on the north shore and draw them out from the protective cover of the massive fort—which he pounded with artillery. French General Montcalm deftly parried every thrust until Wolfe, desperate for an advantage as winter freeze-up approached, took a catastrophically dangerous gamble and successfully scaled the cliffs below the Plains of Abraham. Montcalm was surprised to find the British on his doorstep and responded by hurling his garrison troops against them. The disciplined British regulars with the cliffs of the St. Lawrence at their backs, held their fire until the enemy came within range, then opened with a series of withering volleys that decimated the charging French troops. Although Quebec City fell shortly thereafter, that was not quite the end of New France.

What remained of the French forces fled to Montreal to regroup, hoping for reinforcements the following spring—reinforcements that never came. Several fierce but unsuccessful battles fought in the spring of 1760 failed to dislodge the British and New France formally surrendered. But that was still not quite the end. This war was, after all, a European conflict still raging on the other side of the Atlantic. New France, despite now being under British control, might revert to France through victory or diplomacy. In the meantime, the English garrison and the local Canadians at Quebec eyed each other suspiciously but generally resigned themselves to waiting. The habitants, however, should have remembered Voltaire's dictum that New France was a mere "few acres of snow." Had they done so, their futures might have been clearer—though no more comforting. France not only lost the war in 1763, but then bargained away New France at the peace table in favour of more desirable properties else-where. By the Peace of Paris, habitants found themselves officially ruled by their traditional enemy: the nation that had aided the Iroquois in the seventeenth century had expelled their brethren in Acadia; scorched the agricultural lands south of Quebec; and bombarded the city into rubble.

## Discussion Points

1. In the 1750s France again had to assess the value of its colonies in North America. Summarize the pros and cons of retaining New France.
2. Some historians hold Montcalm directly responsible for the col-lapse of New France. To what extent were other factors more significant?
3. How did Sister Marie's account differ from those of the various government officials? Could these differences be attributed to gender, occupation, personal experience, or other factors?

## Documents

### 1. François Daine, "To Marshal de Belle Isle," Quebec, May 19, 1758.

Nothing is more melancholy or more afflicting than the actual condition of this Colony, after having passed a part of last autumn and winter on a quarter of a pound of bread per person a day, we are reduced, these six weeks past, to two ounces. This country has subsisted, up to the present time, only by the wise and prudent economy of our Intendant, but all resources are exhausted and we are on the eve of the most cruel famine, unless the succors which we are expecting from our monarch's bounty and liberality arrive within fifteen days at farthest.

I am at a loss for terms to describe our misfortunes. The supply of animals is beginning to fail; the butchers cannot furnish a quarter of the beef necessary for the subsistence of the inhabitants of this town, though they pay an exorbi-tant price for it; without fowls, vegetables, mutton or veal, we are on the eve of dying of hunger.

To make up for the want of bread, beef and other necessaries of life, our Intendant has ordered 12 or 1500 horses to be purchased; these he has had distributed among the poor of this town at a rate much below what they cost the King. He is now having distributed among the same poor, a quarter of a pound of pork, and half a pound of cod fish a day, but that cannot last long. The mechanics, artisans and day-laborers exhausted by hunger, absolutely cannot work any longer; they are so feeble that 'tis with difficulty they can sustain themselves.

We have not yet any news from Europe, and are ignorant of the projects of the English on this continent. We have learned only by 2 Indians belonging to the Five Nations, who have been to trade with the English near Fort Bull, that Mr. Jeanson, who was there, had told them that we were without provisions and would not receive any succors from France this year, in consequence of the measures adopted by the Court of London to intercept them; that a formidable fleet would blockade the river, and that none of our ships would be able to pass; they had last fall captured three of them from us richly laden; that as regarded themselves, they enjoyed abundance of everything and were preparing to visit their village for the purpose of conveying rich presents thither, and that the Indians should not want for anything if they would abandon the French....

Our situation becomes more and more unfortunate and we are actually, my Lord, on the eve of perishing of hunger. Bread will cease to be furnished to the public on the first of June....

## 2. M. de Capellis, "Memoir," 1758.

France is not able to populate a country as vast as Canada.

Until today, this colony has produced little for the state in time of peace, for reasons which I cannot go into in this memoir, and has cost enormous sums for more than ten years. The money spent on that colony which the King is about to lose represents the greater part of the funds allotted to the navy. If the money had been used to build vessels and to establish solidly our maritime forces, we would have been respected and even feared by our enemies, who seem inclined to flout us. We can, then, cede this land to England, but here is what we should ask for in return, and I dare say that the King will not lose in the exchange....

The colony of St. Domingue has produced for the state in peacetime over twenty million livres annually. This amount can be doubled and some day may even exceed fifty million livres. Can we ever hope that Canada will sell that much to France? ... The island of Newfoundland will provide us with abundant fisheries.... France would derive an immense profit from the sale of salted fish for which she could find markets in Spain, Italy, and in part of Germany. The fisheries are also a nursery of seamen, and that is perhaps their greatest value.

The more extensive our fisheries become, the more sailors we will have. This class of men can never become too numerous.... It has also been said that there are beavers in the interior of the island and I have no reason to doubt this.... It can also be assumed that the lands in the interior are covered by immense forests, which would provide wood for masts and planks.... We could also extract pitch, tar, and resin.... We might eventually draw from Newfoundland what we presently import from northern Europe....

The advantages that the King's subjects would derive from the establishment of Newfoundland and from the cession of the Spanish part of St. Domingue would be far greater than those which the English would obtain from the cession of a part of Canada. I even dare advance that the island of Newfoundland and half of St. Domingue are worth much more than all of Canada; and I do not believe that we should hesitate to give it up entirely to obtain the other two establishments.

### 3. Louis-Joseph de Montcalm, "To Marshal de Belle Isle," Montreal, April 12, 1759.

Canada will be taken this campaign, and assuredly during the next, if there be not some unforeseen good luck, a powerful diversion by sea against the English Colonies, or some gross blunders on the part of the enemy.

The English have 60,000 men, we at most from 10 to 11,000. Our government is good for nothing; money and provisions will fail. Through want of provisions, the English will begin first; the farms scarcely tilled, cattle lack; the Canadians are dispirited; no confidence in M. de Vaudreuil or in M. Bigot. M. de Vaudreuil is incapable of preparing a plan of operations. He has no activity; he lends his confidence to empirics rather than to the General sent by the King. M. Bigot appears occupied only in making a large fortune for himself, his adherents and sycophants. Cupidity has seized officers, store-keepers; the commissaries also who are about the River St. John, or the Ohio, or with the Indians in the Upper country, are amassing astonishing fortunes. It is nothing but forged certificates legally admitted. If the Indians had a fourth of what is supposed to be expended for them, the King would have all those in America; the English none.

This interest has an influence on the war. M. de Vaudreuil, with whom men are equal, led by a knavish secretary and interested associates, would confide a vast operation to his brother, or any other Colonial officer, the same as to Chevalier de Levis. The choice concerns those who divide the cake; therefore has there never been any desire to send M. de Bourlamaque, or M. de Senezergues, commandant of the battalion of La Sarre, to Fort Duquesne, I did propose it; the King had gained by it; but what superintendents in a country, whose humblest cadet, a sergeant, a gunner, return with twenty, thirty thousand livres in certificates, for goods issued for the Indians on account of his Majesty.

This expenditure, which has been paid at Quebec by the Treasurer of the Colony, amounts to twenty-four millions. The year before, the expenses amounted only to twelve or thirteen millions. This year they will run up to thirty-six. Everybody appears to be in a hurry to make his fortune before the Colony is lost, which event many, perhaps, desire, as an impenetrable veil over their conduct. The craving after wealth has an influence on the war, and M. de Vaudreuil does not doubt it. Instead of reducing the expenses of Canada, people wish to retain all; how abandon positions which serve as a pretext to make private fortunes? Transportation is distributed to favorites. The agreement with the contractor is unknown to me as it is to the public. 'Tis reported that those who have invaded commerce participate in it. Has the King need of purchasing goods for the Indians? Instead of buying them directly, a favorite is notified, who purchases at any price whatever; then M. Bigot has them removed to the King's stores, allowing a profit of one hundred and even one hundred and fifty percent, to those who it is desired to favor. Is artillery to be transported, gun-carriages, carts, implements to be made? M. Mercier, commandant of the artillery, is the contractor under other people's names. Everything is done badly and at a high price. This officer, who came out twenty years ago a simple soldier, will be soon worth about six or seven hundred thousand livres, perhaps a million, if these things continue. I have often respectfully spoken to M. de Vaudreuil and M. Bigot of these expenses; each throws the blame on his colleague. The people alarmed at these expenses, fear a depreciation in the paper money of the country; the evil effect is, the Canadians who do not participate in those illicit profits, hate the Government. They repose confidence in the General of the French; accordingly, what consternation on a ridiculous rumor which circulated this winter that he had been poisoned....

If the war continue, Canada will belong to the English, perhaps this very campaign, or the next. If there be peace, the Colony is lost, if the entire government be not changed....

The general census of Canada has been at last completed. Though it has not been communicated to me, I think I'm correct, that there are not more than 82,000 souls in the Colony; of these, twelve thousand, at most, are men capable of bearing arms; deducting from this number those employed in works, transports, bateaux, in the Upper countries, no more than seven thousand Canadians will ever be collected together, and then it must not be either seed time or harvest, otherwise, by calling all out, the ground would remain uncultivated; famine would follow. Our eight battalions will make three thousand two hundred men; the Colonials, at most, fifteen hundred men in the field. What is that against at least fifty thousand men which the English have!

### 4. Michel-Jean-Hughes Péan, "Memoir on the Condition of Canada."

... in the month of August last, the Colony remained in the most critical situation; the farmers, after having furnished the last bushel of their wheat for the subsistence of the troops which were marching against the enemy, were supporting themselves only by the aid of some vegetables and wild herbs; eighteen months ago the people, without excepting a single officer, had to be reduced to four ounces of bread a day; they have been reduced of late to two ounces only. During the winter it had become necessary to deprive the troops of bread, and to subsist them on beef, horseflesh and codfish.

The provisions brought by several ships during the year have been immediately forwarded to the armies, but Quebec has always remained in its melancholy situation.

Yet, people have to defend themselves at Carillon against thirty thousand men; against ten thousand at Fort Duquesne and against six thousand towards Chouaguen. The capture of Louisbourg, the settlements pretended to have been made by the English at Gaspé and on the Island of Anticosty, at the entrance of the Gulf of St. Lawrence, have rendered the situation of Canada much more afflicting, but the late misfortune experienced at Fort Frontenac by the Colony, is the most prejudicial of those it has been threatened with, and 'twill run the greatest risks if that fort be not retaken, as it served as an entrepôt for all the King's forts and Indian posts, and as the English will close all the passages. Then, the Indians, who constitute our principal force, finding themselves deprived of all they want, by failure of the succors the French would furnish them, will not fail to go over to the English, and will come and scalp at the very gates of the towns in which the people will be obliged to shut themselves up.

'Twill probably cost a great many men and much money to retake that fort, but it is of such great necessity for the preservation of Canada, that 'tis impossible to dispense with making every effort to retake it.

The harvest is reported very bad, and we must not be surprised at that, if we observe that all the farmers have been obliged to march to oppose the efforts of the enemy.

'Tis therefore to be presumed that this Colony is about to be exposed to much more serious suffering than it has experienced in preceding years, during which people have been under the necessity of consuming all the cattle.

Many persons have died of hunger, and the number would have been much greater had the King not subsisted a greater part of the people.

The land in Canada is in general, very good, and has often supplied in time of peace, provisions to other colonies, and almost always to Isle Royale; but not having had the good fortune to participate in the last peace, and being forced since fifteen years into continual war, which has employed almost all the farmers, the land could not be cultivated, and the failure of the crops which has ensued, has augmented so considerably the price of provisions and rendered them so excessively dear, that the officer can no longer subsist there without running considerably in debt; this is not the case with the soldier to whom too considerable an allowance, and one too expensive to the King has been made.

'Tis certain that Canada will, next year, have to fight more than sixty thousand men, as the English have just sent thither additional troops; no more than fifteen to eighteen thousand men can be employed in its defence, because many will be required for conveyance of provisions and ammunition, in consequence of the difficulty of the roads and the distance of the different posts.

Supposing the English are not yet at Gaspé, we may rest assured that they will seize it in the spring, and then they will be able to impede the navigation so much, that 'tis to be feared they will capture the greater portion of the succors which will be on the way to Quebec.

## 5. M. de Beaucat, "Mémoire sur le Canada," 1759.

There are about 60,000 inhabitants in Canada, 180,000 acres of farmland, and 20,000 of pasture. The annual crop, on the average, consists of 400,000 bushels of wheat, 5,000 of corn, 130,000 of oats, 3,000 of barley, 6,000 of peas, 100,000 quintals of tobacco, 120,000 of flax, and 5,000 of hemp.

The value of beaver and other types of pelts does not exceed 1,500,000 livres. The seal fisheries are of very little account.

Canada has very little timber that is suited for construction, and it is very greasy. A few frigates and vessels are built there at costs that are as great as those that prevail in France. Furthermore, those ships do not last half as long as those built in Europe.

In years of drought the crops fail and we are obliged to send flour to Canada. The trade of this colony is so slight that in 1755, when colonial commerce was in a most flourishing state, sixty vessels were dispatched from France and over half of these had to return by way of St. Domingue to find cargo for their return voyage. In passing, we might note that this island has only 18,000 settlers, but its trade is so great that it occupies 400 vessels of 500 tons.

The cost of maintaining troops in the Canadian forts is also very great.

… All of Canada is covered by a thick blanket of snow during half the year, and the Gulf of St. Lawrence is impassable during that time. The settlers are confined to their houses and only venture outdoors to hunt or to exchange a few pelts with the Indians. On this colony have we spent men and money in such great quantities! The Canadians are brave, vigorous, and active, but they lack the means of enriching themselves by commerce or agriculture. They live from day to day, so to speak, and in time of war are exposed either to dying of hunger or at least to doing without the most basic necessities of life.

### 6. Unknown, "Memoir on Canada."

*First Question*: Is it of importance to preserve Canada?

There have been, from all time, people who have thought, and perhaps there are some still who are of opinion, that the preservation of Canada is of little importance to France. Some allege that it costs the King a great deal, and that it will eventually cost more; that it yields nothing, or next to nothing; that, in 1755, 1756, 1757 and 1758, probably more than fifteen millions have been expended yearly, which might have been better employed in the centre of the Kingdom. Others say that the Kingdom, which is itself stripped of people, is being depopulated to settle a country which is extremely rough, full of lakes and forests, frequently subject to the greatest scarcities; that there are within the Kingdom good lands which remain uncultivated; that the Indian trade is little worth; that, so far from increasing, it will always diminish, as the trade in peltries cannot last a century; they add, that the Canadian voyages are long, fatiguing and dangerous.

Finally, the third pretend that, in all the wars we shall have with the English, Canada will be taken, at least in part; that t'will always be the cause of preventing France, at the peace, preserving European conquests. Besides, that when Canada will be well settled, it will be exposed to many revolutions; is it not natural that Kingdoms and Republics will be formed there, which will separate from France? …

1st. It is certain that if France abandon Canada, heresy will establish itself there; Nations known and unknown, will remain in Paganism or adopt the religion of England. How many souls eternally lost! This reflection may strike a Christian Prince.

2nd. France possesses, in North America, more territory than is contained in the European continent. Its riches are not yet known; the best spots are not yet settled; the King's glory seems to require that so extensive a country be preserved notwithstanding the immense expenditure incurred there; it is always painful to behold the enemy aggrandizing themselves at our expense; besides, these expenses might considerably diminish; and, after all, this object is not so remarkable in times of peace; it would even be easy for those who are acquainted with finance to demonstrate that the trade and consumption of goods which is going on in Canada, produces for the King in time of peace, much more than is expended. This is the place where general reasons might be adduced to prove that it is of importance to a state to possess Colonies. 'Tis wrong to object, that it is depopulating the kingdom. One year of European war causes the loss of more men than would be required to people New France. It might be complained that no care has ever been taken to increase its population; that might be easily done now in a perceptible manner, because the Colony begins to grow in numbers. How many thousands of useless men within the heart of the Kingdom and in other states! Every year the English are transporting into foreign parts a great number of families whom they encourage to settle in New England. Were New France peopled, there is no country so easy of preservation; naval forces essentially necessary to Old France, would guard Acadia, Louisbourg; and it may be asserted that if Canada be lost to France the latter will require a larger naval force than ever, because the English will become absolute masters of the sea....

3rd. Supposing, in fact, that Canada will never be of much use to France; that it will cost even a trifle, must it be reckoned as nothing, the preventing a rival nation aggrandizing itself, establishing, on the seas, a despotic empire and monopolizing all the trade?

The English, once masters of Canada, will necessarily take Louisiana and the Islands, because, being no longer disturbed by the Canadians, they will direct all their weight against the Islands, which are an object of importance for France. For the same reason it may be relied on, that the English will soon wrest New Mexico from Spain, and Portugal may truly be affected by it.

Our immense forests, our vast prairies, once in the hands of the English, will carry abundance everywhere, and facilitate forever the construction of all the ships they will desire.

Were it only the codfishery, this would be an object of infinite importance and which we should lose. Of all commerce, this is the richest, the easiest, the least expensive and the most extensive. As early as 1696, the trade of the Island of Newfoundland alone amounted yearly to 15 millions. Canada once taken, all the fishing ground must be renounced.

Without knowing all the branches of trade which is and can be carried on throughout New France, it may be said that if the King lose that country, the commerce of England will soon be augmented more than 150 millions.

A thousand other reflections present themselves to the mind, but it is unnecessary to abuse the patience of those who will read this Memoir.

*Second Question*: Should the war continue in 1759, will Canada be able to defend herself?

The number of men in that Colony bearing arms has perhaps been exaggerated. I dare assert that there are not fifteen thousand of them, but at least eleven thousand must be deducted from that number for the reasons following:

1. We must strike off 4,000, to wit: the old men, those necessary in the country, the sick, the husbands of sick women, the servants of the parish priests, the sextons, those who hide themselves to avoid being called out, those who find means to be exempted, the pilots for navigating the river, sailors for a great many sloops and bateaux, those at outposts, who watch the signal fires day and night.

It is, in general, doing much to levy more than two-thirds of the men.

2. Of the eleven thousand men to be levied, nearly 1,000 must necessarily be deducted for the Upper and Lower posts, and usually these are the best; it would be easy to enumerate them.

3. 1,500 mechanics of different sorts, carpenters for bateaux, artillery work, blacksmiths, gate-keepers, cartmen in the towns, must also be deducted; again add to these, 1,500 domestics for the officers, the town's people, necessary couriers, clerks, writers.

4. Again, 3,000 men must be employed for the transportation of provisions, utensils and all the necessaries for the camps.

We have 4,000 leagues of country to preserve; we have scarcely 78 settled; the current must be surmounted, the wind is oftenest contrary; sloops are frequently a month going up to Montreal....

Add to this, that we have in Canada scarcely 5 months of the year suitable for transportation.

It follows that, supposing eleven thousand men could be raised in Canada, 4,000 only of them will be fit to fight, the others being occupied elsewhere, and, in fact, they are perhaps never met in the camps.

The 8 battalions of French Regulars, the forty companies of the Marine, hardly form a corps of 6,000 men; 'tis a great deal, still, to add two thousand fighting Indians.

I ask now, if it be possible for twelve thousand men to resist the enemy's army, which certainly amount to sixty thousand men....

I refer to the last question what regards our scarcity of provisions and liquors and presents for the Indians. I will not say that there is every prospect that no ploughing will be done this year, that the enemy will prevent this and the putting in seed the early part of spring.

*Third Question*: Is it easy for France to relieve Canada in 1759?

Troops and provisions are required; all must arrive in May; the examination of this article will point out the difficulty.

It is not too much to demand an augmentation of eight thousand troops. On arriving at Quebec, they will probably be reduced, by death or disease, to 6,000; consequently, we shall have only 18,000 to oppose against 60 thousand. Is this too much? Is it sufficient? The situation of the country must be relied on, and calculations made on the mistakes of the enemy.

Men-of-war or merchantmen are necessary for conveying 8,000 men; if the former be employed, 300 on board each, exclusive of the crew, is a liberal allowance; 27 ships will be required; if merchantmen, they will carry only 200, and 40 of them will be necessary; but will it be possible to dispense with having them convoyed by ships of the Line, Isle Royale and Gaspé being actually in the hands of the English?

The Contractor-General of Canada demands 40 ships for his share alone, but how many of these will be intercepted? 20 at least will be required by the merchants; here are at once 100 ships of 300 tons required, exclusive of those which are to carry the munitions of war; still more are necessary for the conveyance of provisions, for though the harvest be good, it is not sufficient for the Colony and for extra mouths. This has been proved in 1756.

The difficulty of transportation in Canada occasions a great consumption of provisions by pure loss, and it is impossible to remedy it; the necessity of employing Indians is another occasion of wasteful consumption. A party of Indians [is sent] to make prisoners, with 15 days' provisions; it returns at the end of 8 days victorious, or without striking a blow; it has consumed everything and demands provisions. How are they to be refused? Another inevitable abuse: Our domiciliated Indians are unwilling to go to fight unless we feed their women and children, so that if you have 2,000 Indians, it will require provisions at least for

6,000. It is not flour alone that is wanting, the Colony is very bare of oxen and sheep, and at the close of 1759, hardly any will be found for refreshments for the troops or the ships, and 'tis certain, if the war continue, the Colony will be obliged to live on salt meat, which will have to be imported from France, and in that case what a number of ships will be required. Finally, supposing France could furnish all those vessels, will they arrive in sufficient season? ... It is to be feared that they will meet the enemy on quitting France; some they will find about the roadsteads of Halifax; others will be about Louisbourg and Gaspé. Should those succors be sent altogether, a strong convoy will be required, and it will happen that many vessels will be separated by fogs and storms; it will happen that those ships will not be ready soon enough to sail together, and though they should be, their voyage will be a great deal longer. All these succors are necessary; can France furnish them? If an attempt be made to recover Louisbourg or Gaspé, or if any considerable diversion be made on the coasts of New England by a considerable fleet, then the whole of the succors I have enumerated may not be wanting; but has France ships and seamen? Enough for the seas of America and Europe.

*Detached Thoughts*

... It is almost impossible to retake Louisbourg; we possess no port in those seas; the enemy has, or will have, 8,000 men there, and doubtless after our example, will keep some ships of the line in that port.

Acadia is entirely ruined, stripped of all domestic animals; most of the inhabitants dead; 'twill cost immense sums to reestablish the few of them that remain.... Indeed, New England must be very weary of the wars our Indians are waging against it. It sees in its midst nearly 4,000 of its frontier families bewailing their kindred who have been massacred and whose properties have been laid waste. It knows that in taking Canada it will be rid of the cruelty of the Indians and enjoy forever the sweets of peace.

Quebec is not a strong place; all our hope depends on preventing the landing and having outside a flying camp of 4,000 men, to annoy the enemy in their march and during the siege; it is very improbable that the enemy is ignorant of the strength of the fleets which will be sent; 'tis natural that they will oppose stronger ones, especially as they can station them in the most advantageous ports.

To send succors in divisions is to run the risk of losing all in detail; to send them together, is to expose ourselves to a general action and to lose all at once; it is to expose oneself to a very long voyage....

Canada has but one very narrow outlet, that is the gulf. If the English preserve Louisbourg and Acadia, 'twould be difficult to receive any relief by that way.

'Tis to be feared that the English will leave in New England 15 or 18 thousand Regulars, which they will, on declaring war, push suddenly into Canada; what means of resistance are there, if we do not keep up 8 or 10 thousand troops; but unfortunately the Colony will be unable to feed them except in the most abundant years, and supplies of provisions, all the implements and munitions of war necessary for 10,000 men, will be required from time to time from France. It will be necessary to think seriously of establishing granaries or magazines of reserve, on account of the scarcities which frequently overtake us.

The people of Canada must naturally be quite tired of the war, many have perished in it; they are burdened with the most harassing works, have not time to increase their property nor even to repair their houses; a portion of their subsistence has been wrested from them, many have been without bread for 3 months, the troops that incommode them are quartered on them, they have not throughout the year as much food as they think they need; they are told that the English will allow them freedom of religion, furnish them goods at a cheaper rate and pay liberally for the smallest service. These ideas are spreading. Some persons above the populace do not blush to speak in the same style; it is natural for the people to murmur and allow themselves to be seduced; the inhabitants of the cities will be the most easily debauched.

### 7. Marie de la Visitation, *Narrative of the Doings During the Siege of Quebec, and the Conquest of Canada.*

My very reverend Mothers,
… The General Hospital is situated in the outer limits of Quebec, about half a mile from the walls.

The fire, from which our Sisters in Quebec have lately suffered, having rendered it impossible for them to continue their charge of the sick, Mr. Bigot, the Intendant of the country, proposed that we should receive them in our hospital. We readily agreed so to do; being desirous of rendering service and zealously fulfilling the duties of our calling, the Sisters lost no time in entering upon the sacred work. His Majesty, attentive to the wants of his subjects, and being informed of the preparations making by the English, did not fail to forward succour to the country, consisting in numerous vessels, laden with munitions of war and provisions, of which we were entirely destitute; and several regiments, who landed in a deplorable state, unfit for service, a great many men having died soon after. They were suffering from malignant fever. All the sick, officers and privates, were conveyed to our hospital, which was insufficient to contain them; we were therefore compelled to fill most parts of the building, even to the church, having obtained the permission of the late bishop Pontbriand, our illustrious prelate....

Thereupon, the enemy, despairing of vanquishing us, ashamed to retreat, determined to fit out a formidable fleet, armed with all the artillery that the infernal regions could supply for the destruction of human kind. They displayed the British flag in the harbour of Quebec on the 24th May, 1759. On the receipt of intelligence of their arrival, our troops and militia came down from above. Our Generals left garrisons in the advanced posts, of which there is a great number above Montreal, in order to prevent the junction of their land forces, which it was understood were on the march, from Orange. Our Generals did not fail to occupy most points where the enemy might land; but they could not guard them all. The sickness suffered by our troops, lately from France, and the losses they sustained in two or three recent actions with the enemy, though victorious, weakened us considerably; and it became necessary to abandon Point Levi, directly opposite to and commanding Quebec. The enemy soon occupied it and constructed their batteries; which commenced firing on the 24th July, in a manner to excite the greatest alarm in our unfortunate Communities of religious ladies ...

The only rest we partook of, was during prayers, and still it was not without interruption from the noise of shells and shot, dreading every moment that they would be directed towards us. The red-hot shot and carcasses terrified those who attended the sick during the night. They had the affliction of witnessing the destruction of the houses of the citizens, many of our connexions being immediately interested therein. During one night, upwards of fifty of the best houses in the Lower Town were destroyed. The vaults containing merchandise and many precious articles, did not escape the effects of the artillery. During this dreadful conflagration, we could offer nothing but our tears and prayers at the foot of the altar at such moments as could be snatched from the necessary attention to the wounded.

In addition to these misfortunes, we had to contend with more than one enemy; famine, at all times inseparable from war, threatened to reduce us to the last extremity; upwards of six hundred persons in our building and vicinity, partaking of our small means of subsistence, supplied from the government stores, which were likely soon to be short of what was required for the troops. In the midst of this desolation, the Almighty, disposed to humble us, and to deprive us of our substance, which we had probably amassed contrary to his will, and with too great avidity, still mercifully preserved our lives, which were daily periled, from the present state of the country....

The enemy, more cautious in their proceedings, on observing our army, hesitated in landing all their forces. We drove them from our redoubts, of which they had obtained possession. They became overwhelmed, and left the field strewed with killed and wounded. This action alone, had it been properly managed, would have finally relieved us from their invasion. We must not, however, attribute the mismanagement solely to our Generals; the Indian tribes, often essential to our support, became prejudicial to us on this occasion. Their hideous yells of defiance tended to intimidate our foes, who instead of meeting the onset, to which they had exposed themselves, precipitately retreated to their boats, and left us masters of the field. We charitably conveyed their wounded to our hospital, notwithstanding the fury and rage of the Indians, who, according [to] their cruel custom, sought to scalp them. Our army continued constantly ready to oppose the enemy. They dared not attempt a second landing; but ashamed of inaction, they took to burning the country places. Under shelter of darkness, they moved their vessels about seven or eight leagues above Quebec....

After remaining in vain nearly three months at anchor in the Port, they appeared disposed to retire, despairing of success; but the Almighty, whose intentions are beyond our penetration, and always just, having resolved to subdue us, inspired the English Commander with the idea of making another attempt before his departure, which was done by surprise during the night. It was the intention, that night, to send supplies to a body of our troops forming an outpost of the heights near Quebec. A miserable deserter gave the information to the enemy, and persuaded them that it would be easy to surprise us, and pass their boats by using our countersign. They profited by the information, and the treasonable scheme succeeded. They landed on giving the password; our officer detected the deceit, but too late. He defended his post bravely with his small band, and was wounded. By this plan the enemy found themselves on the heights near the city. General de Montcalm, without loss of time, marched at the head of his army; but having to proceed about half a league, the enemy had time to bring up their artillery, and to form for the reception of the French. Our leading battalions did not wait the arrival and formation of the other forces to support them, they rushed with their usual impetuosity on their enemies and killed a great number; but they were soon overcome by the artillery. They lost their General and a great number of officers. Our loss was not equal to that of the enemy; but it was not the less serious. General De Montcalm and his principal officers fell on the occasion.

Several officers of the Canadian Militia, fathers of families, shared the same fate. We witnessed the carnage from our windows. It was in such a scene that charity triumphed, and caused us to forget self-preservation and the danger we were exposed to, in the immediate presence of the enemy. We were in the midst of the dead and the dying, who were brought in to us by hundreds, many of them our close connexions; it was necessary to smother our griefs and exert ourselves to relieve them. Loaded with the inmates of three convents, and all the inhabitants of the neighbouring suburbs, which the approach of the enemy caused to fly in this direction, you may judge of our terror and confusion. The enemy masters of the field, and within a few paces of our house; exposed to the fury of the soldiers, we had reason to dread the worst. It was then that we experienced the truth of the words of holy writ: "he who places his trust in the Lord has nothing to fear." ...

The loss we had just sustained, and the departure of that force, determined the Marquis De Vaudreuil, Governor General of the Colony, to abandon Quebec, being no longer able to retain it. The enemy having formed their entrenchments and their Camp, near the principal gate; their fleet commanding the Port, it was impossible to convey succour to the garrison....

The principal inhabitants represented to him that they had readily sacrificed their property; but with regard to their wives and children, they could not make up their minds to witness their massacre, in the event of the place being stormed; it was therefore necessary to determine on capitulation.

The English readily accorded the articles demanded, religious toleration and civil advantages for the inhabitants. Happy in having acquired possession of a country, in which they had on several previous occasions failed, they were the most moderate of conquerors. We could not, without injustice, complain of the manner in which they treated us. However, their good treatment has not yet dried our tears....

The reduction of Quebec, on the 18th September, 1759, produced no tranquillity for us, but rather increased our labours. The English Generals came to our Hospital and assured us of their protection, and at the same time, required us to take charge of their wounded and sick.

Although we were near the seat of war, our establishment had nothing to fear, as the well understood rights of nations protected Hospitals so situated, still they obliged us to lodge a guard of thirty men, and it was necessary to prepare food and bedding for them. On being relieved they carried off many of the blankets, &c. the officer taking no measures to prevent them. Our greatest misfortune was to hear their talking during divine service....

Let us now return to the French. Our Generals not finding their force

sufficient to undertake the recovery of their losses, proceeded to the construction
of a Fort, about five leagues above Quebec, and left a garrison therein, capable of
checking the enemy from penetrating into the country. They did not remain
inactive, but were constantly on the alert, harassing the enemy. The English
were not safe beyond the gates of Quebec. General Murray the commander of
the place, on several occasions was near being made a prisoner; and would not
have escaped if our people had been faithful. Prisoners were frequently made,
which so irritated the Commander, that he sent out detachments to pillage and
burn the habitations of the country people.

The desire to recover the country and to acquire glory, was attended with
great loss to our citizens. We heard of nothing but combats throughout the
winter; the severity of the season had not the effect of making them lay down
their arms. Wherever the enemy was observed, they were pursued without relaxation; which caused them to remark, "they had never known a people more
attached and faithful to their sovereign than the Canadians."

The English did not fail to require the oath of allegiance to their King;
but, notwithstanding this forced obligation, which our people did not consider
themselves bound to observe, they joined the flying camps of the French, whenever an opportunity offered.

The French forces did not spare the inhabitants of the country; they lived
freely at the expense of those unfortunate people. We suffered considerable loss
in a Seigneurie which we possessed below Quebec. The officer commanding
seized on all our cattle, which were numerous, and wheat to subsist his troops.
The purveyor rendered us no account of such seizures. Notwithstanding this
loss, we were compelled to maintain upwards of three hundred wounded sent to
us after the battle of the 13th September....

Reverend Mothers, as I give you this account, merely from memory, of
what passed under our eyes, and with a view to afford you the satisfaction of
knowing that we sustained with fortitude and in an edifying manner the painful
duties, imposed upon us by our vocation; I will not undertake to relate to you all
the particulars of the surrender of the country. I could do it but imperfectly, and
from hearsay. I will merely say that the majority of the Canadians were disposed
to perish rather than surrender; and that the small number of troops remaining
were deficient of ammunition and provisions, and only surrendered in order to
save the lives of the women and children, who are likely to be exposed to the
greatest peril where towns are carried by assault.

Alas! Dear Mothers, it was a great misfortune for us that France could not
send, in the spring, some vessels with provisions and munitions; we should still

be under her dominion. She has lost a vast country and a faithful people, sincerely attached to their sovereign; a loss we must greatly deplore, on account of our religion, and the difference of the laws to which we must submit. We vainly flatter ourselves that peace may restore us to our rights; and that the Almighty will treat us in a fatherly manner, and soon cease to humble us; we still continue to experience his wrath. Our sins, doubtless, are very great, which leads us to apprehend that we are doomed to suffer long; the spirit of repentance is not general with the people, and God is still offended. We, however, yet entertain the hope of again coming under the dominion of our former masters....

## Readings

Eccles, W. "The French Forces in North America during the Seven Years' War," in F. Halpenny, ed., *Dictionary of Canadian Biography*. Volume III. Toronto: University of Toronto Press, 1974.

Fregault, G. *Canada: The War of Conquest*. Toronto: Oxford University Press, 1969.

Gwyn, J. "French and British Naval Power at the Two Seiges of Louisbourg, 1745 and 1758," *Nova Scotia Historical Review* 10, 2 (1990).

Macleod, P. *The Canadian Iroquois and the Seven Years' War*. Toronto: Dundurn Press, 1996.

Nicolai, M. "A Different Kind of Courage: The French Military and the Canadian Irregular Soldier during the Seven Years' War," *Canadian Historical Review* 70, 1 (March 1989).

Pritchard, J. *Anatomy of a Naval Disaster: The 1746 French Expedition to North America*. Kingston-Montreal: McGill-Queen's University Press, 1995.

Stacey, C. *Quebec, 1759: The Seige and the Battle*. Toronto: Macmillan, 1959.

Stanley, G. *New France: The Last Phase, 1744–1760*. Toronto: McClelland and Stewart, 1968.

Steele, I. *Guerillas and Grenadiers: The Struggle for Canada, 1689–1760*. Toronto: Ryerson, 1969.

Steele, I. *Warpaths: Invasions of North America*. New York: Oxford University Press, 1994.

*Chapter Five*

# "THE ABUNDANT BLESSINGS OF BRITISH RULE": QUEBEC'S NEW ADMINISTRATION

1. General James Murray, "Report of the State of the Government of Quebec in Canada," June 5, 1762.
2. Joseph-Octave Plessis, Bishop of Quebec, "Sermon on Nelson's Victory at Aboukir," 1799.
3. Selkirk, "Diary," February 10, 1804.
4. Anglo-Canadiensis, "To the Editor of the *Quebec Mercury*," *Le Canadien*, November 29, 1806.
5. John Lambert, *Travels Through Lower Canada and the United States of North America in the Years 1806, 1807, and 1808.*
6. Hugh Gray, *Letters from Canada Written During a Residence There in the Years 1806, 1807 and 1808,* 1809.
7. P-S. Bédard, "Memorandum In Support of the Petition of the Inhabitants of Lower Canada," 1814.

## Introduction

In 1945 Canadian writer Hugh MacLennan published the quintessentially Canadian "Two Solitudes," a novel exploring Quebec's cultural schism of Anglophones and Francophones living side by side in Montreal without mixing, comprehending, or even seeing one another. The parallel societies existed as two solitudes. MacLennan's observation, of course, was hardly new and Canadians still struggle with the great national conundrum: how to get two cultures with a long history of mutual animosity, and where one is conquered the other the conqueror, to live together peaceably and in harmony.

After the Conquest, many British civilian and military administrators charged with running the new colony expressed exasperation over the French-Canadians whom they perceived as ignorant, lazy, priest-ridden, backward, and harbouring questionable loyalties. Their response to the Quebeçois was, as often as not, defensive irritation at what they saw as the habitants' stultifying inertia and ingratitude for the "abundant blessings of British rule." Thus, if given the benefit of the doubt, the essence of British social legislation hinged on a genuine wish to save French-Canadians from themselves through assimilation.

Many French-Canadians, meanwhile, did not wish to be saved at all. They interpreted the Conquest as a humiliating defeat threatening their very cultural existence through an invasion of foreign rules, money, people, language, and mores. That they were a subservient people whose leaders abandoned them after the Conquest exacerbated this situation, they argued, by leaving them foundering rudderless in an incoming tide of Anglos. Later French-Canadian nationalist historians likened it to a body with its head decapitated, a situation, they say, that left the Quebeçois vulnerable to easy exploitation and subjugation. With attitudes like that, it is hardly surprising that many French-Canadians erected physical and psychological bulwarks against what they feared as cultural genocide—and always remembered who they were. It is not by chance that Quebec's provincial motto, stamped on every license plate, is: *je me souviens*. The two peoples, British and French-Canadian, could not, or would not, empathize with each other and invariably dug in their heels, retreated behind their cultural barricades, and periodically lobbed inflammatory rhetoric at one another.

In fairness to both, empathizing with a foreign culture is very difficult because it involves an inherent contradiction, and it is particularly troublesome, if not impossible, when the strangers find themselves involuntarily tossed together as a result of war. Could Governor Murray possibly understand an habitant's world view and vice versa? Perhaps it is asking too much for them to perceive each other objectively and to develop a *modus vivendi* based upon that.

Three profoundly important pieces of legislation dominate the period between the Conquest and the early nineteenth century and help anchor an understanding of the social dilemmas of the day: the Royal proclamation of 1763; the Quebec Act of 1774; and the Constitution Act of 1791. They, plus the American Revolution, greatly influenced the face of Quebec as it emerged in its new Britannic guise.

The Royal Proclamation of 1763 took no one by surprise, though it confirmed the Quebeçois' worst fears. Now conquered, they were to be Anglicized as rapidly as possible through the elimination of the elements that codified their society: the Catholic church; their legal code; system of land tenure; and administrative structure. The Proclamation essentially swept the French regime asunder, replacing it with British institutions consistent with those in the rest of the

Empire. A small coterie of British administrators and military men were to see the changes implemented—which they did not, fearing it would foment revolt among the habitant majority. Their fears were well founded as increasing numbers of New Englanders to the south called for independence from Britain and logically urged the Quebeçois to join in.

Quebec's governor in the 1770s, Guy Carleton, wooed the remaining French-Canadian leadership as a way of guaranteeing habitant loyalty. Getting the seigneurs and the clergy on side, however, required abrogating the hated Royal Proclamation, which Carleton achieved with the Quebec Act of 1774. This new document defined the nature of the colony and still serves, to many French-Canadians, as proof of their distinct society. The Quebec Act stipulates that Quebec would, in fact, be different from the rest of the Empire, not the same: French civil law ruled in a British colony; the Catholic church received recognition; the seigneurial system was retained; and without an elected Assembly, democracy lay off in the future. Despite concerted efforts, American rebels failed to make major inroads into the hearts and minds of the Quebeçois during their revolution, though Carleton was rather disappointed by what he perceived as feeble habitant loyalty.

The creation of the United States left a stream of people heading north into British Quebec—where these Loyalist refugees, as they were called, ironically found themselves living under the Quebec Act and its French orientation. They demanded British institutions for a British colony—particularly after fighting and losing to defend them south of the border. Quebec's British administrators wanted to oblige, but tinkering with the Quebec Act remained unacceptable to the ever-vigilant and suspicious Quebeçois. The solution to this impasse was the Constitution Act of 1791 which split the land into two colonies, Upper and Lower Canada, the former enjoying traditional British rule, the latter the Quebec Act—but with an elected Assembly based upon male representation by population.

Thus the socio-political battle lines emerged in Lower Canada: the Anglos and their supposedly co-opted "friends" the seigneurs and clergy, versus the habitants now lead by a small cohort of up-and-coming young middle-class French-Canadian patriots. If Britain's wish was for a peaceable colony on the other side of the Atlantic, it was sorely disappointed. Canada continues to live the legacy of this turbulent era, and two referenda on separation at the end of the twentieth century, plus another promised, surely prove that resolution still eludes us and that we live on as two solitudes.

## Discussion Points

1. Were French-Canadians better off or not under British rule?
2. British visitors such as Murray, Lambert, and Selkirk were outsiders commenting upon a culture and people with whom they did not identify. In what respects, if any, did they demonstrate an ethnocentric bias?
3. Why did French-Canadian nationalism emerge in this period?
4. Did members of the Catholic clergy such as Plessis "sell out" to the British?

## Documents

### 1. General James Murray, "Report of the State of the Government of Quebec in Canada," June 5, 1762.

The Canadians may be ranked under four different classes

1st The Gentry or what they call Nobility
2d The Clergy
3d The Merchants or trading part
4th The Peasantry or what is here stilled, Habitant.

1st The Gentry. These are descended from the Military and Civil officers, who have settled in the Country at different times and were usually provided for in the Colony Troops; These consisted formerly of 28 afterwards 30 and had been lately augmented to 40 Companys. They are in general poor except such as have had commands in distant posts where they usually made a fortune in three or four Years. The Croix de St Louis quite completed their happiness. They are extremely vain and have an utter contempt for the trading part of the Colony, tho' they made no scruple to engage in it, pretty deeply too, whenever a convenient opportunity served; They were great Tyrants to their Vassals who seldom met with redress, let their grievances be ever so just.

This class will not relish the British Government from which they can neither expect the same employments or the same douceurs, they enjoyed under the French.

2d The Clergy. Most of the dignified among them are French, the rest Canadians, and are in general of the lower class of People, the former no doubt will have great difficulty to reconcile themselves to us, but must drop off by degrees. Few of the latter are very clever ... they would soon become easy and satisfied, their influence over the people was and is still very great, but tho' we have been so short a time in the Country, a difference is to be perceived, they [the people] do not submit so tamely to the Yoke, and under sanction of the capitulation they every day take an opportunity to dispute the tythes with their Curés.

These were moved from their respective parishes at the Bishop's pleasure, who thereby always kept them in awe, it may not be perhaps improper to adopt the same Method, in case His Majesty should think right, for the sake of keeping them in proper subjection, to nominate them himself or by those who act under his authority....

3d The Traders of this Colony under the French were either dealers in gross or retailers, the former were mostly French and the latter in general natives of this Country all of whom are deeply concerned in the letters of Exchange; many are already gone to solicit payment and few of those who have any fund of any consequence in France remain here.

4th ... The 4th Order is that of the Peasantry, these are a strong healthy race, plain in their dress, virtuous in their morals and temperate in their living: They are in general extremely ignorant, for the former government would never suffer a printing press in the Country, few can read or write, and all receive implicitly for truth the many arrant falsehoods and atrocious lies, industriously handed among them by those who were in power.

They took particular pains to persuade them, the English were worse than brutes, and that if they prevailed, the Canadians would be ruled with a rod of Iron, and be exposed to every outrage, this most certainly did not a little contribute, to make them so obstinate in their defence. However ever since the Conquest, I can with the greatest truth assert, that the Troops have lived with the Inhabitants in a harmony unexampled even at home. I must here, in justice to those under my command in this Government, observe to Your Lordship, that in the Winter which immediately followed the reduction of this Province, when from the Calamities of War, and a bad harvest, the inhabitants of these lowest parts were exposed to all the horrors of a famine, the Officers of every rank, even in the lowest generously contributed towards alleviating the distresses of the unfortunate Canadians by a large subscription, the British Merchants and Traders readily and cheerfully assisted in this good work, even the poor Soldiers threw in their mite, and gave a day's provisions, or a day's pay in the month, towards the fund, by this means a quantity of provisions was purchased and distributed with great care and assiduity to numbers of poor Families, who, without this charitable support, must have inevitably perished;

such an instance of uncommon generosity towards the conquered did the highest honor to their conquerors and convinced these poor deluded people, how grossly they had been imposed upon; the daily instances of lenity, the impartial justice which has been administer'd, so far beyond what they had formerly experienced, have so alter'd their opinion with regard to us, I may safely venture to affirm for this most useful Order of the state, that far from having the least design to emigrate from their present habitations into any other of the French Colonies, their greatest dread is lest they should meet with the fate of the Acadians and be torn from their native Country.

Convinced that this is not to be their case and that the free exercise of their religion will be continued to them once Canada is irrecoverably ceded by a Peace the people will soon become faithful and good subjects to His Majesty, and the Country they inhabit within a short time prove a rich and most useful Colony to Great Britain....

With a very slight cultivation all sorts of grain are here easily produced, and in great abundance, the inhabitants are inclinable enough to be lazy, and not much skilled in Husbandry, the great dependencies they have hitherto had on the Gun and fishing rod, made them neglect tillage beyond the requisites of their own consumption and the few purchases they needed, the Monopolies that were carried on here in every branch, made them careless of acquiring beyond the present use, and their being often sent on distant parties and detachments, to serve the particular purposes of greedy and avaricious Men without the least view to public utility, were circumstances under which no country could thrive; As they will not be subject to such Inconveniences under a British Government, and being necessarily deprived of arms they must of course apply more closely to the culture of their Lands.

The mines already discovered, and the mineral and sulphurous waters in many parts of this Country leave no room to doubt, nature has been bountiful to it in this respect, and that further discoveries and improvements are likely to be made with regard to these, whenever it becomes more populous. Notwithstanding the waste of war, which they have much more severely felt from pretended friends, than from their declared foes, the Country will abound in three or four Years with all kind of provisions, sufficient not only to answer their home consumption, but even to export if a Market can be procured....

The present state of population may be easily seen for the annexed Account of the number of people in this Government taken about a twelve month ago.

There is great reason to believe this Colony has been upon the decrease in this respect for near twenty Years past, the Wars which they have been almost constantly carrying on, the strictness with which Marriages within a certain degree of consanguinity were forbidden except by dispensation, the obliging Strangers inclined to engage in that state, previously to prove their not being married before, and the prohibition of intermarriages between protestants and Roman Catholics were so many bars to the propagation of the Species, these difficulties are now in a good measure removed; the men are an active, strong, and healthy race, the Women are extremely prolifick and in all human probability the next twenty Years will produce a vast increase of People.

The French bent their whole attention in this part of the World to the Fur Trade, they never enter'd heartily or with any spirit into the fisheries: most of what was done in this way was by adventurers from the ports of France; some Fish indeed Lumber and provisions were exported to the French islands. Had this trade been opened and agriculture promoted here with any degree of warmth, this branch of Commerce must have become both valuable and extensive, but it was monopolized into the hands of a few, by the connivance and management of the Chiefs, the sole view of these being to enrich themselves by every means. The interest of the State could not fail to be sacrificed upon all occasions....

## 2. Joseph-Octave Plessis, Bishop of Quebec, "Sermon on Nelson's Victory at Aboukir," 1799.

… What sort of government, Gentlemen, is the best suited for our happiness? Is it not the one marked by moderation, which respects the religion of those it rules, which is full of consideration for its subjects, and gives the people a reasonable part in its administration? Such has always been the British government in Canada. To say this is in no way to practise the flattery that cowards use to bless the powers that be. God forbid, my brothers, that I should profane this holy pulpit by base adulation or interested praise. This testimony is demanded by truth as well as gratitude, and I have no fear of being contradicted by anyone who knows the spirit of the English government. It always proceeds with wise deliberation; there is nothing precipitous in its methodical advance. Do you see in its operations any of the delusive enthusiasm, the thoughtless love of novelty, the liberty without limits or restraints that, before our very eyes, is destroying certain malconstituted states? What care it takes for the property of its subjects! What skillful efforts are made to arrange the public finances so that its subjects are scarcely aware of the burden! Have you heard any complaints, these past forty years under their rule, of the poll-taxes, the tariffs, the head taxes under which so many other nations groan? What of those arbitrary requisitions of

immense sums that unjust conquerors arrogantly impose on the unhappy conquered? Have you been reduced, by their lack of foresight, to those famines that
formerly afflicted our Colony, which we still recall with horror and shuddering?
Have you not seen, on the contrary, that in years of scarcity the government
wisely prohibits the export of grain until enough has been put aside for your
own needs? Have you been subjected to military service since the Conquest,
obliged to leave your wives and children destitute in order to go to some far-off
place to attack or repulse some enemy of the State? Have you contributed a
penny to the expenses of this costly war that Great Britain has been waging for
almost six years? Almost the whole of Europe has been given over to carnage and
destruction, the holiest cloisters have been violated, virgins dishonoured, mothers and children slaughtered in several places. Is it not evident, and can it not be
said, that at the height of this war you enjoy all the advantages of peace? To
whom, my brothers, aside from God, do you owe these favours, if not to the
paternal vigilance of an Empire which, in peace as in war, I dare to say, has your
interests closer to its heart than its own? In every field I see evidence of this
partiality. Your criminal code, for example, was too severe; it provided no sufficiently reliable rule for distinguishing the innocent from the guilty, and it
exposed the weak to the oppression of the strong. It has been replaced by the
criminal law of England, that masterpiece of human intelligence, which checks
calumny … which convicts only those whose guilt is obvious, which gives the
accused every means of legitimate defence, and which, leaving nothing to the
discretion of the judge, punishes only in accordance with the precise provisions
of the law. Finally, what about the common law? While in France all is in disorder, while every Ordonnance bearing the stamp of Royalty is proscribed, is it not
wonderful to see a British Province ruled by the common law of Paris and by the
Edicts and declarations of the kings of France? To what are we to attribute this
gratifying peculiarity? To the fact that you wanted to maintain these ancient
laws; to the fact that they seemed better adapted to the nature of real property in
this country. There they are, then, preserved without any alterations except those
that provincial Legislation is free to make. And in that Legislation you are represented to an infinitely greater degree than the people of the British Isles are in
the Parliaments of England or Ireland.

Do such benefits, Gentlemen, not demand from us some return? A lively
feeling of gratitude towards Great Britain; an ardent desire never to be separated
from her; a deep conviction that her interests are no different from our own; that
our happiness depends upon hers; and that if sometimes it has been necessary to
grieve over her losses, we must, by the same principle, rejoice today in the glory

she has won and regard her latest victory as an event no less consoling for us than it is glorious for her.

Where do we stand, Christians, if we add to these political considerations another that, above all else, makes this empire worthy of your gratitude and praise? I mean the liberty left our religion and guaranteed by law; the respect shown to those in our monasteries; the unbroken succession of Catholic Bishops, who have so far enjoyed the favour and confidence of the King's Representatives; the unfailing support our curés have enjoyed in the villages and countryside in their efforts to conserve faith and morals. If this faith is growing weaker among us, my brothers, if morality is becoming more lax, it is not because of any change of government; it is to you yourselves that this disorder must be attributed; to your lack of submission to the teaching of the Gospels; to your foolish pursuit of a liberty you already enjoy without knowing it; to the poisonous harangues of those dishonest and unprincipled men, those perpetual grumblers who are offended by order, humiliated by obedience, and outraged by the very existence of religion.

Alas! Where would we be, my brothers, if such men should ever get the upper hand, if their desires should be fulfilled, if this country, by a grievous misfortune, should return to its former masters? This house of God, this august temple, would soon be converted to a den of thieves! Ministers of religion—you would be displaced, banished, and perhaps decapitated! Fervent Christians— you would be deprived of the ineffable consolations you enjoy in the accomplishment of your religious duties! Your land, consecrated by the sweat and tears of so many virtuous missionaries who have planted the faith here, would, to a religious eye, display nothing but a vast, melancholy solitude. Catholic fathers and mothers, under your very eyes, in spite of yourselves, you would see your beloved children nursed on the poisoned milk of barbarism, impiety, and dissoluteness! Tender children, whose innocent hearts still manifest only virtue, your piety would become prey to these vultures, and a savage education would soon obliterate the pleasing sentiments that humanity and religion have engraved on your souls!

*Conclusion.* — But what am I saying? Why dwell on such sad reflections on a day when all ought to be joy? No, no, my brothers. Fear not that God will abandon us if we remain faithful. What he has just done for us should inspire only comforting thoughts for the future. He has struck down our perfidious enemies. Let us rejoice in this glorious event. Everything that weakens France tends to draw us away from it. Everything that separates us from her assures our lives, our liberty, our peace, our property, our religion, and our happiness. Let us give everlasting thanks to the God of victories. Let us pray that He will long preserve the bountiful and august Sovereign who governs us, and that he will continue to lavish on Canada his most abundant blessings.

## 3. Selkirk, "Diary," February 10, 1804.

... There is but one opinion as to the universal disaffection of the French Canadians to the British Government, & it seems scarcely to be more questioned than their repugnance is unconquerable.... —They have never been reconciled to the British institutions that have been introduced among them—Even the trial by Jury & Criminal procedure are approved only by a few of the most enlightened men—

The English at Quebec & Montreal cry out in the true John Bull style against their obstinate aversion to institutions which they have never taken any pains to make them understand—& are surprized at the natural & universally experienced dislike of a conquered people to their conquerors & to every thing which puts them in mind of their subjection.... The English Govt. certainly seems never to have acted with any system as to Canada—the only chance of reconciling the people would have been either to use every effort to change them entirely in language & institutions & make them forget that they were not English—or keeping them as French to give a Government adapted to them as such, & keep every thing English out of sight—neither of these plans has been followed, & the policy of Govt. has been a kind of vibration between them—at first after 3 or 4 years hesitation it was decided in 1764 to introduce the English Law—the French Lawyers did not like the trouble of learning their trade anew, & found pretexts for remonstrating & stating pretexts of hardships—they were listened to, & from the subsequent contradictory determinations at different times has resulted a complete jumble of Laws & a total uncertainty in many what Law is to be ruler....

The present system of Militia has been established (after a considerable interval) after the model of the States, merely requiring 12 days attendance of each man when called out at separate detached days—by which they have not sufficient opportunity for discipline & the old system of subordination being broken this is not easily renewed:—nor does that seem to be the object of the present system—No arms are put into the hands of the Canadian Militia—a precaution which is just sufficient to insult them, without being any security as most of the peasantry have guns of their own.—In addition to this Ld. Dorchester in organizing the Quebec Militia instituted a British Regt. entirely separate from the Canadian.

The dislike of the Canadians to the English is enhanced by the superiority of fortune which the E. are acquiring by Commerce—this the French do not succeed in—it is not their turn (nor have they sufficient Education). The Law of inheritance (ab intestato) divides the Seigneuries among the family—the Eldest Son has half—the rest goes equally among the other children—this has reduced many families to insignificance—dissipation has forced others to sell their properties & these have all fallen into English hands—as the Canadians have few means of acquiring new fortunes—Indeed except the Bar it may be said none—perhaps half the Seigneuries of Canada now belong to English proprietors—a mistake— ...

The Seigneurs who still remain have not much influence with the country people—the Habitant has no intercourse with his Seigneur but what is of an unpleasant nature—holding his land on perpetuity he is under no dependance & has no favours to ask—but he is called upon annually for his Rent—for his multure—& occasionally for his Lods & Ventes, which appear to him unreasonable taxes & burdens on his industry—Consequently tho' both Ld. Dorchester & Sr Robt. Milnes have been partial to the Canadian gentry & given them almost every office under Govt. to which they were competent this has not had any effect in conciliating the people in general.

The most likely channel to influence the common peasants would perhaps be thro' the Clergy—but this hold has been almost thrown away, by devolving the entire patronage of the Curés to the Catholic Bishop.—In addition to this, the law which allows them no tythes from lands held by protestants, operates to give them a needless jealousy, perhaps the silly parade with which a Protestant Bishoprick & Cathedral have been set up at Quebec, may add to this.—

The Ch. Justice & Bishop Mountain both accuse the Curés of throwing from jealousy of Protestantism every opposition in the way of parochial Schools which Govt. have been desirous of instituting—Education in general is very much neglected—few of the Habitants can write their name—the women have all the little Education that is in the country. Lanaudiere & other Canadian gentlemen ascribe the want of Parish Schools to the people being scattered & not collected in villages—so that the children would have too far to go—an objection certainly groundless as the Canadian Settlements are incomparably thicker than those in New England.

The finishing stroke to the impolitic management of Canada has been the establishment of the Constitution of 1791—this modelled on the British Constitn—was meant as a boon—but the people neither understanding nor ripe for it have not taken it as such—& the Assembly having within 3 or 4 years laid on several new taxes, goes currently by the name of the Maudite Chamber.

This Establishment coming just at the time that some vague rumours of the French Revolution had reached them set their heads agog & the greatest part of the members thought they might do as they pleased, & even to be established wholly independant, & being thwarted in this by the English members, have established what was naturally to be expected—an English & a French party— the great majority of Members of the Assembly are French, & from the unpopularity of the Seigneurs, mostly Habitants of low origin—some were pointed out to me who could not write, the leading men are lawyers who find this a convenient theatre for making themselves known. The proceedings are carried on both English & French—almost every speech & every motion etc is translated—the same is done in the Courts of Justice. The French have contended strongly to have a preference for their language but this is resisted. This is one of the questions which in prudence ought to have been kept asleep, but which the Establishment of a popular Assembly necessarily brought into discussion.—The French party have attempted to fix Salaries for the Members of Assembly—this is opposed because the Salary would be an inducement for more French Candidates who would carry the elections against the few English who are now members—Govt. keeps a majority by means of some official persons in the Assembly—they have also a majority of English in the Upper House—the Canadian members of which are also men of more respectability & education, mostly persons who were of rank & consequence before the Conquest & who either are (or persuade the Government that they are) reconciled completely to the British system.—It is remarked even in private society how much the English & Canadians draw asunder.—At Montreal where the English have everything there are scarcely any genteel French to be met in society—the gentry of the place & neighbourhood hold Assemblies of their own at Boucherville a few miles off where no English intrude.—At Quebec the example & influence of the Govr has tended to prevent that total separation, but even there they do not appear to live to-gether or amalgamate.—While I was there the Govr gave a ball on Mardi gras—the room held two country dances—nine tenths of the company in the one dance was French—in the other English.— ....

## 4. Anglo-Canadiensis, "To the Editor of the *Quebec Mercury*," *Le Canadien*, November 29, 1806.

Sir:

...That the rising flood of French ambition must be opposed, no worthy subject would deny; all those who love freedom must agree with that sentiment; and a truth so widely recognized is universally felt; but to argue that this opposition should be carried out, even in part, through a change of language and way of life in Canada, and therefore, that Canada must be relieved of its Frenchness, is a proposition that, while itself ridiculous, will, I think, appear equally impolitic, in light of the following comments....

So what is the policy that can force Anglicanus to *de-Frenchify Canada*? *The time has come*, says he, *for this Province, after 47 years of possession, to be English*, but might that end not be achieved without leaving behind the way of life and the language of the French? Might a Canadien not be, and is not he, truly English, by reason of his love for English freedoms, his commitment to the English Government, and his aversion to the principles of the French? Does loyalty lie in similarity of language? If not, and if it is only to be found in similarity of principles, then why *de-Frenchify* Canada? On what essential point do Canadien subjects differ from their English counterparts? If such a difference exists, why then did the Americans, whose language, religion, and way of life were those of the English, break free of their governance, and call on the French for assistance? Why have the inhabitants of Guernsey, who are French-speaking, remained loyal to the Crown of England for so long? Why did those of Jersey, French-speaking as well, give asylum to Charles II at a time when no part of the British Empire dared recognize him? Those islands have belonged to the English for more than 47 years, and they are still not English! Still not de-Frenchified! They even now retain their customs, their Norman laws, their feudal system, and their State assemblies! So how foolhardy would Edward I have been to recognize these rights, and how much more so would our minister have been to conserve them. Anglicanus knows all that (if he knows anything), he knows how close those islands are to France, our mortal enemy; he knows that nothing untoward has come of that proximity, of the language, laws, or way of life of those peoples, and he claims that Canada, as far from France, in principle, as the breadth of the sea that separates them, must be *anglicized—that we must raise a rampart against French ambition, by propagating the English language!!*

In vain was Wolfe victorious, in vain did the consideration and magnanimity of the English nation earn the affection of the Canadiens—it is left, so Anglicanus claims, to an army of English grammarians to clear away prejudice, impose British influence, and strengthen the bonds of union.

Can he not see the want of justice in these thoughts? Would it not be more apposite to raise *a rampart* (since ramparts must be raised) against the intrigues of our neighbours, rather than facilitating communication with them, by *propagating* their language? For, following his reasoning, if the English language is a *rampart* against French ambition, why should the French language not be the same against American speculations, especially at a time when Congress, which is English-speaking, is dictating laws of commerce to our British merchants?

But Anglicanus is occupied by reflections of greater importance: according to him, we must fear French education more than any other danger, however serious it be, because the few who leave this Province (and it is, in fact, very few) will align themselves with the flag of Bonaparte and not the flag of the English. I will note here that his fears, with respect to education, are not unlike those of a certain English Theologian with respect to the Canadiens' religion. This political Theologian predicted, at the time of the conquest of this Province, that if the Canadiens were left in Popery, the Pope would dispatch his indulgences here: the Canadiens would align themselves with France, declare their independence, and cause the neighbouring Colonies to do the same. Independence has effectively taken place, based on this prediction; but to quote the illustrious Edmund Burke "it has happened in precisely the opposite direction. Every Protestant Colony has rebelled, they have joined with France, and it has happened that Papist Canada has been the one Country to remain loyal, the only one in which France has not set foot, the sole inhabited Colony of Great Britain's left today."

However, at the time of independence, the Canadiens were certainly more French than they are at present, the impressions of the French Government were more recent, the contrast with the English Government was more striking, and yet Canadien loyalty was not shaken. So why *de-Frenchify* Canada? Why abolish an education that can shape such worthy subjects? No, the Canadiens, if left with their customs and way of life, even though they speak like the French and, like them, eat soup, will never cease to be what they have been until now. The Scots have not proven unworthy subjects for having retained the dress of their forebears; the Welsh for having kept their dialect and primitive way of life, and a Canadien will be no less worthy a subject for speaking in that tongue in which he vowed eternal loyalty to the English, and in which he continues to rejoice in their success.

### 5. John Lambert, *Travels Through Lower Canada and the United States of North America in the Years 1806, 1807, and 1808.*

The suppression of the male orders was wise and politic, because, however useful the Jesuits might have been to their own government, it is hardly possible that they could have ever been reconciled to act in favor of one whose religious tenets clashed with theirs. As to the begging friars, no nation could be benefitted by them. The priests or catholic clergy at present so numerous, and who have received the support and protection of the English government, are entitled to particular notice. From the great influence which they possess over the minds of the Canadians, their importance cannot be questioned....

The Habitants content themselves with following the footsteps of their forefathers. They are satisfied with a little, because a little satisfies their wants. They are quiet and obedient subjects, because they feel the value and benefit of the government under which they live. They trouble themselves not with useless arguments concerning its good or bad qualities, because they feel themselves protected, and not oppressed by its laws. They are religious from education and habit, more than from principle. They, observe its ceremonies and formalities, not because they are necessary to their salvation, but because it gratifies their vanity and superstition. They live in happy mediocrity, without a wish or endeavour to better their condition, though many of them are amply possessed of the means. Yet they love money, and are seldom on the wrong side of a bargain. From poverty and oppression they have been raised, since the conquest, to independent affluence. They now know, and feel the value of money and freedom, and are not willing to part with either. Their parsimonious frugality is visible in their habitations, their dress, and their meals; and had they been as industrious and enterprizing as they have been frugal and saving, they would have been the richest peasantry in the world....

As agriculture and commerce have increased, the British settlers have risen into consequence, and men of respectability been sent over to govern the country. The French inhabitants have however degenerated in proportion as the British have acquired importance. The noblesse and seigniors have almost dwindled into the common mass of the vulgar; their estates and seigniories have been divided among the children, or have fallen into the hands of the opulent British merchants. The few who still possess an estate or seigniory seldom live upon it, but reside wholly in the towns, equally adverse to agriculture, commerce, and the arts. They visit their estates merely to pick up their rents; and in collecting these, often have many broils with their tenants, whose contributions in kind, are not always of the best quality; and so far do they sometimes carry their contempt of their seignior,...

The general deficiency of education and learning among the great body of the people in Canada has been long a subject of newspaper-complaint in that country. But it is extremely doubtful whether the condition of the people would be ameliorated or the country benefitted by the distribution of learning and information among them. The means of obtaining instruction, at present, are undoubtedly very limited; but it is occasioned, in a great measure, by their own parsimonious frugality; for if they were willing to spare a sufficient sum for the education of their children, plenty of masters would be found and plenty of schools opened. The British or American settlers in the back townships teach their own children the common rudiments of education; but the Canadians are themselves uneducated, and ignorant, even of the smallest degree of learning; therefore they have it not in their power to supply the want of a school in their own family, and thus do they propagate from age to age, the ignorance of their ancestors....

With respect to their obtaining a knowledge of the English language, I agree with those who are of opinion that so desirable an object might, to a certain extent, be attained by the interference of the government, and the establishing of parochial Sunday schools. The number who understand, or speak, English in Lower Canada, does not amount to one fifth of the whole population, including the British subjects. Few of the French clergy understand it, for in the seminary at Quebec, where it ought to form an indispensable part of the student's education, it is totally neglected; in consequence of which, a great many French children who are educated there, besides those that are designed for the church, lose a favourable opportunity of becoming acquainted with it; and that which is omitted in youth is neither easily, nor willingly, acquired in manhood. It is possible that the French clergy may look with jealousy upon the diffusion of the English language among their parishioners; they may think that as the intercourse between the British and French Canadians will be facilitated by such a measure, the eyes of the latter would be opened to many of the inconsistencies and defects of their religion; and that, in consequence, they may be induced to change their faith, and throw off the dominion of their priests. These, however, are but groundless fears, for as long as vanity retains its hold in the breasts of the Canadians, and while the clergy continue that indefatigable perseverance in their ministry, and that unblemished character and reputation, which distinguish them at present, it is not probable that their parishioners will depart from the religion of their forefathers. The instruction of the French children in the English language, is, therefore, neither difficult, nor liable to any serious objection. That it is a desirable object, and highly necessary for political as well as private reasons, is without doubt: that it is necessary for the dispatch of business, and for the impartial administration of justice, every man, who has been in a Canadian court of law, must acknowledge without hesitation.

Upon a review of the preceding sketch of the character and manners of the Habitants, who constitute the great body of the Canadian people, it will be found that few peasantry in the world are blest with such a happy mediocrity of property, and such a mild form of government as they universally enjoy. They possess every necessary of life in abundance, and, when inclined, may enjoy many of its luxuries. They have no taxes to pay, but such as their religion demands. The revenues of the province are raised, in an indirect manner, upon those articles which are rather pernicious than beneficial to them; and therefore it is their own fault if they feel the weight of the impost. They are contented and happy among themselves, and protected by a well regulated government. The laws are severe, but tempered in their administration with so much lenity and indulgence for human failings, that it has occasioned a singular proverbial saying among the people, that "it requires great interest for a man to be hung in Canada"; so few in that country ever meet with such an ignominious fate.

They have now enjoyed an almost uninterrupted peace for half a century, for they were so little disturbed in the American war, that that event can hardly be considered as an interruption. This has increased the population, agriculture, commerce, and prosperity of the country; and while it has raised the people to all the comforts of moderate possessions, of freedom, and independence, it has strengthened their attachment to the constitution and government under which they have thus prospered....

The Canadians have no reason to complain of the change of government. Before the conquest they were often unacquainted with that protection which the laws now afford them....

The lawyers who practise in Lower Canada, are nearly all French; not more than one-fifth at most, are English. They are styled advocates, and in the double capacity of counsellor and attorney: ...Lawsuits are numerous, and are daily increasing....

The French lawyers are not possessed of very shining abilities. Their education is narrow and contracted, and they have but few opportunities of becoming acquainted with those intricacies and nice discriminations of the law, that prevail in the English courts. The English advocates are generally better informed, and some of them either study law in England, or under the attorney and solicitor-generals, in Canada, who are generally men of considerable ability, and extensive practice. The Canadian lawyers are not excelled in the art of charging, even by their brethren in England. Their fees are high, though regulated, in some measure, by the court.... Tenacious as the Habitants are of their money, they are often involved in litigation, and the young advocates know how to avail themselves of the ignorance of their clients....

A very small proportion of the British Canadians were born in the colony, and consequently very little difference in person, dress, or manners, is discernible between them and the inhabitants of the mother-country. The French have also assimilated themselves so nearly to the British in dress, manners, and amusements, especially the younger branches, that if it was not for their language, there would be little to distinguish their respective coteries....

The Catholics of Canada, are a living evidence of the beneficial effects of religious toleration, regulated by the prudent measures of a mild and liberal government, though professing a contrary faith, and one too that was formerly viewed by the Papists with as much horror, as we looked upon theirs. But the Canadian Catholics never concern themselves about the religion of those who hold the reins of government. It is sufficient for them that they are allowed every privilege which the Protestants enjoy; that they sit in the executive and legislative councils, in the House of Assembly, and upon the Bench....

For fifty years the Roman Catholics of Canada have lived under a Protestant government.—They have been dutiful and obedient subjects, and when our other colonies shook off the yoke of Great Britain, they remained true and faithful notwithstanding great inducements were held out to them, by their neighbours, to follow their example. This steady adherence of the Canadians to their conquerors, can be attributed only to their due sense of the benefits they had received from them; and to the firm attachment of the clergy to the British government; for had the latter been inimical, either from religious or political causes, they could with the greatest ease have stirred up the whole body of the people to rebellion....

## 6. Hugh Gray, *Letters from Canada Written During a Residence There in the Years 1806, 1807 and 1808*, 1809.

The Canadians are legitimate Frenchmen,—the descendants of the worshippers of Louis the Fourteenth and of Cardinal Richelieu,—the descendants of men who never once formed an idea, themselves, of the nature of civil and religious liberty, and who, of course, would not be likely to impress it on the minds of their children. The authoritative mandates of the French king have never sounded in their ears in vain;—they were issued with all the arrogance of despotism, and received with implicit and passive obedience. Even now, to reason with the great bulk of the Canadians on the measures of government, is what they never look for; they have no idea of questioning their propriety;—command them *au nom du Roi*, and you will be obeyed.

The government of Britain have thought fit to give to Canada a constitution upon the same principles as their own; and have given to the Canadians the right of electing, and being elected members of the legislature.... Is it clear, that the British form of government is fitted for Canada, and that the Canadians are in a state to be benefited by being allowed a share in the government? Does their knowledge, their education, the whole train and direction of their ideas, prejudices, and passions, fit them for being legislators? I suspect that the answer must be in the negative. How can those men attain a knowledge of the principles of government, and of civil and religious liberty, who can neither read nor write, which is the case with the great mass of the people, and however strange it may appear, is the case with many of the members of the House of Assembly. This must seem incredible, but is however strictly true; and is of itself a most convincing proof that it was too soon to give them a share in the government. The state of the country is so low as to arts and letters, that it is impossible to find in the counties, and even sometimes in the towns, men, who in any respect are capable of taking a part in the legislature. Let knowledge be more generally spread through the country; let the people be taught to read and to reason, which Englishmen had long been habituated to before they received their constitution, and then, and not till then, ought they to have a voice in the deliberations of government.

The division of Canada into two provinces ... must allow that union gives strength and vigour; by the union of Scotland and Ireland with England, the strength of the whole is generally allowed to be increased. The same principle will apply to the Canadas. They should not have separate legislatures, because it will in time engender separate interests, real or supposed; and produce a jarring in their co-operation for the general good of the colony, and in promoting the interests of the mother country.

Quebec, March, 1807. There is a great deal of misapprehension in Britain relative to this country. It is naturally concluded that, in a British colony such as Canada, a conquered country, those who govern and who give law to it, would be Englishmen. This, however, is by no means the case; for though the governor and some of the council are English, the French Canadians are the majority in the house of assembly; and no law can pass, if they choose to prevent it. The English (supposing the governor to exert all the influence he possesses) cannot carry one single question; and the Canadians have been in the habit of shewing, in the most undisquised manner, the power of a majority, and a determination that no bill should pass contrary to their wishes. They carry things with a high hand; they seem to forget that the constitution under which they domineer over the English, was a free gift from Britain; and that what an act of parliament gave, an act of parliament can take away.

You will naturally imagine also, that in a British colony, the English language would be used in the house of assembly, public offices, and courts of justice. No such thing; the French language is universally used, and the record is kept in French and in English. That Canadians will not speak English; and Englishmen are weak enough to indulge them so far as to speak French too, which is much to their disadvantage; for though they may speak French well enough to explain themselves in the ordinary affairs of life, they cannot, in debate, deliver themselves with that ease, and with the same effect as in their native language.

I really do not see what they have to complain of; and yet they are very much dissatisfied.

Their dissatisfaction has lately had vent through the medium of a newspaper edited at Quebec in the French language. I have taken notice of it in a previous letter. They call it "Le Canadien." It affords to a certain class of the community a mode of expressing their feelings, to which they wish to give as extensive a circulation as possible. If one were really to believe that there are grounds for all that has appeared in this paper against the English, it would be concluded that the Canadians are the most oppressed people in the world.

I have taken pains to find out if they have any real cause of complaints — if they are oppressed or maltreated in any one way; but I have looked for it in vain. I have every wish to do them justice, and would gladly state to you any circumstance to justify their apparent dissatisfaction; but really, I cannot find any. I am afraid I must look for it only in their own tempers and dispositions, influenced by the peculiarity of their situation, as descendants of those who formerly had entire possession of the country, and of its government, civil and military; and who feel sore at being deprived of any part of the inheritance of their fathers.

It is to be regretted that those amongst the Canadians who are looked up to by their countrymen, and whose opinions pass current under the idea of their having been formed after due deliberation, and after having well studied the matter, should be so negligent of their duty to their countrymen, as to publish opinions, and make assertions not well founded, and without having duly considered and well understood the subject; such men do great injury to society. If any discontent exists in the country, any idea of oppression, or mal-administration in government, such men are the cause of it.

Government, from the beginning, instead of shewing a decided preference to their own language, adopted a temporising system, which left the Canadians without a motive to learn English. Had the knowledge of the English language always been held out as a recommendation to favour, and a preference given on that account, where other qualifications were equal—had English alone prevailed in the courts of justice, and in all departments of state, and public offices; it is highly probable that it would have been the general language of the country at the present moment: at least, it would have become a necessary part of the education of the better sort of people; as they could not have appeared at the governor's without it, nor have had any thing to say, either in the provincial parliament, or courts of justice. Had the leading men of the country been Englified, their influence would have been felt by the lower classes; and you might now, in a great measure, have had a colony of Englishmen, instead of Frenchmen. I may be told that language is only sound, and that a man may have good principles, whatever language he speaks. All that may be very true; but I deny that the descendants of Frenchmen, retaining the French language, manners, and customs, and constantly talking of the French as their progenitors, can ever be good British subjects, or enter heartily into her interests. The French man's *amor patriae* is not easily rooted out; may, nor any other man's *amor patriae*. It can only be done by giving a proper direction to the minds of young people; to accomplish which not the least pains are taken in Canada.

I have no hesitation in saying, that I think it would have been a fortunate thing for the country, if the English civil laws had been also firmly and permanently established; not on account of its own superior excellence, which the Canadians might justly question, but because it would have been understood by the judges, and uniformly and properly interpreted. A proper line of proceeding would, by this time, have been fixed upon; the practice and rules of court would have been ascertained and determined; the decisions would have been uniform; the laws would have been strictly enforced; and the minds of the people kept alive to proper notions of right and wrong....

Previous to the conquest by the English, I am told that the Canadians were an upright, honest people, fulfilling every engagement, and punctual in the performance of their various duties....

After the conquest, the people of greatest respectability both civil and military, retired to France—judges, counsellors, great landholders, governors, and rulers of all sorts; all those who, by example, precept, or authority, were qualified to keep good order in the country, who knew the people, their prejudices, and wants: almost all such left it. In their room came English governors and judges, who, though well meaning and just men, yet knew neither the people, nor their laws, language, nor customs; and (from not being brought up in the country) they were unacquainted with the thousand minute and undescribable impressions and notions acquired in childhood, which have a strong influence on our character and conduct through life. They could not, in the nature of things, preserve that check on the people to which they had been accustomed under the judges of their own nation....

Nothing debases a people so soon or so effectually as bad laws, or a bad administration of laws, in themselves good: the latter more frequently occurs than the former....

Here it is that Canada is defective; the courts are ill arranged; the forms of proceeding, vague and undefined. The French and English laws and forms, though good by themselves, have made a very bad mixture. There is, in short, something so bad in these matters, that the ends of justice are completely defeated. In Quebec, civil justice is really laughed at. A man who pays his debts here, has greater merit than in most other countries; he need not do it unless he thinks proper; he has only to entrench himself behind the forms and quibbles of the law, and laugh at his creditors....

In Canada there are no bankrupt laws; and you cannot arrest your debtor, unless you can swear that he is about to leave the country. You cannot put his property in trust for the benefit of his creditors, or deprive him of the power of disposing of it. You may easily conceive what an opening is thus given to those who are fraudulently inclined....

One of the principal causes of the poverty, not only of the Canadian farmer, but also of all ranks amongst them, is the existence of an old French law, by which the property of either a father or mother is, on the death of either, equally divided amongst their children. Nothing seems more consonant to the clearest principles of justice than such a law; yet it assuredly is prejudicial to society....

This division of property is extremely prejudicial to the interest not only of the landholder but also to that of the merchant, shopkeeper, and mechanic....

One effect of this law, and not only of the least material, is, that the affection between parents and children is likely to be destroyed by it: and, in fact, it is remarked, that in this country the instances of unfeeling conduct between parents and children are extremely frequent, and a spirit of litigation is excited amongst them. One is at a loss to account for such unnatural conduct, until an acquaintance with the laws and customs of the country gives a clue to unravel the mystery.

The law, making marriage a co-pathership, and creating a *communité de bien*, is sanctioned by the code of French law, called *Coutume de Paris*, which indeed is the text book of the Canadian lawyer; the wife being by marriage invested with a right to half the husband's property; and being rendered independent of him, is perhaps the remote cause that the fair sex have such influence in France; and in Canada, it is well known, that a great deal of consequence, and even an air of superiority to the husband, is assumed by them. In general (if you will excuse a vulgar metaphor), the grey mare is the better horse....

However, I believe I can safely say, that nowhere do the Roman Catholics and Protestants live on better terms than here. They go to each other's marriages, baptisms, and burials without scruple; nay, they have even been known to make use of the same church for religious worship, one party using it in the forenoon, and the other in the afternoon. There is something truly Christian in all this; it evinces a meekness of spirit, and degree of charitable forbearance with one another, which greatly promote general happiness....

### 7. P-S. Bédard, "Memorandum In Support of the Petition of the Inhabitants of Lower Canada," 1814.

The ideas that those of the English party are striving to keep alive, namely, that the Canadiens are less suited to filling positions of trust because they are too concerned for their own country and have less interest in and affection for the mother country, are less than sound. A Canadien is more attached to his country than to any other part of the Empire, the way a Scot is more attached to Scotland, or an Englishman is more attached to England, and he is no less capable, for that, of holding positions of trust in his own land. The honour or even the risk of losing his place will have no less influence on him than on any other, assuming the mistaken principle of there being a difference between the mother country's interests and those of his own land. It is true that a former subject is bound to be more attached to the Empire; but he also has less aversion to the people and Government of the United States, and if everything is taken into account, it will be seen that a Canadien is far more strongly attached to the interests of the mother country, in respect to the preservation of this land.

The Canadiens unable to protect themselves have only the mother country to protect them. Once this country is lost, they no longer have a homeland they can turn to; an Englishman still has his homeland.

If the Canadas pass under the authority of the United States, their population will be overwhelmed by that of the United States, and they will become nothing, without influence whatever in their Government; unable to protect their religion, which will only render them offensive to all the other sects that abound in the United States, and which, while tolerant of one another, all agree in their abhorrence of this one.

No fathers attached to their religion could think with anything but horror of dying and leaving their children under such domination. While the country remains under the British Empire, they need not fear the same dangers; they need not dread that a population hostile to their religion will emigrate from the mother country; they have hopes that their population will always be the largest in the country, and that with a constitution such as has been granted by the mother country, they will have the means of keeping their religion and all that is dear to them, provided that the mother country truly wishes to allow them the enjoyment of that constitution without its serving to render them offensive, and provided that the encouragement given to the American population in this country by the English party's administration ceases to bring about the evil they must fear.

Those of the English party are hostile to their concerns, in that, having far more affinity with the Americans in terms of customs, religion, and language, they encourage the American population, as a means of ridding themselves of the Canadiens whom they still regard as an alien population, as a French and Catholic population, with the same prejudice that the general population in the mother country harbours for the French and for Catholics, they cannot keep from seeing themselves in a foreign country, in a province in which the (French) Canadien population is predominant; a colony peopled by Americans seems to them more English, and in it, they would not see themselves as being so much in a foreign land. These effects are further compounded by the fact that perhaps the greater part of the Government's officials have become personally involved in introducing the American population to this country, through Crown land concessions granted to them in proximity to the United States; thus, the English party is at odds with the Canadien party, precisely on the point at which the latter's life and existence as a people is affected.

All that remains to the Canadiens in their present circumstances is their hope that the mother country will ultimately find that their interests converge with her own in terms of the preservation of the country, that the swallowing up of the Canadien population by the American population will be the swallowing up of the mother country's authority over this land, and that the loss of political life of the Canadiens, as an incipient people, will also be the loss of political life of the whole country.... They hope that these things will be perceived by the mother country, and that there, a good enough opinion will be formed of their interest, if not their loyalty, to judge them worthy of enjoying the use of their constitution, in common with His Majesty's other subjects without distinction whatsoever, and failing this good fortune, they see themselves, based on their present situation, destined to become, in the eyes of the mother country, an offensive and endlessly suspect people, preparing to be swallowed up by the abyss that awaits them.

We beseech Your Lordship to believe that His Majesty's Canadien subjects are true and loyal subjects; called up by His Majesty, they have already saved their country at a time when His Majesty's other subjects have shown less loyalty, they are still being called up by His Majesty to defend it; if their small efforts can bear sufficient witness to their loyalty, they hope that His Royal Highness will be so good as to take their situation under consideration, and grant them such remedy as he deems suitable.

## Readings

Bernier, G., and D. Salee. *The Shaping of Quebec Politics and Society: Colonialism, Power and the Transition to Capitalism in the 19th Century*. New York: Crane Russak, 1992.

Brunet M., *Les Canadiens apres la Conquete, 1759–1775*. Montreal: Fides, 1969.

Brunet M., "Les Canadiens et la France Revolutionnaire," *Revue d'Historie l'Amerique Francaise*, 13 (1960).

Cook, R. "Some French-Canadian Interpretations of the British Conquest," in *Historical Papers*. Ottawa: Canadian Historical Association, 1966.

Greenwood, F. *Legacies of Fear: Law and Politics in the Era of the French Revolution*. Toronto: University of Toronto Press, 1993.

Greer, A. *Peasant, Lord and Merchant: Rural Society in Three Quebec Parishes, 1740-1840*. Toronto: University of Toronto Press, 1985.

Igartua, J. "A Change in Climate: The Conquest and the Merchants of Montreal," *Historical Papers*. Canadian Historical Association, 1974.

Lawson, P. *The Imperial Challenge: Quebec and Britain in the Age of the American Revolution*. Montreal: McGill-Queen's University Press, 1989.

Miquelon, D., ed. *Society and Conquest: The Debate on the Bourgeoisie and Social Change in French Canada 1700–1850*. Toronto: Copp Clark, 1977.

Neatby, H. *Quebec: The Revolutionary Age, 1760–1791*. Toronto: McClelland and Stewart, 1966.

Neatby, H. *The Quebec Act: Protest and Policy*. Toronto: Prentice Hall, 1972.

Nish, C., ed. *The French Canadians, 1759–1766: Conquered? Half-conquered? Liberated?* Toronto: Copp Clark, 1966.

Ouellet, F. *Economic and Social History of Quebec, 1760–1850: Structures and Conjunctures*. Ottawa: Gage, 1980.

Smith, "Le Canadien and the British Constitution 1806–1818," *Canadian Historical Review* Vol XXXVIII (June, 1957).

Standen, S. "The Debate on the Social and Economic Consequences of the Conquest: A Summary," in P. Boucher, ed., *Proceedings of the Tenth Meeting of the French Colonial Society*. New York: University Press of America, 1985.

Tousignant, P. "The Integration of the Province of Quebec into the British Empire," in F. Halpenny, ed., *Dictionary of Canadian Biography*, Vol IV. Toronto: University of Toronto Press, 1978.

*Chapter Six*

# "Our Robinson Crusoe Sort of Life": Three Women in Upper Canada

1. Susanna Moodie, *Roughing It in the Bush*, 1852.
2. Anna Brownell Jameson, *Winter Studies and Summer Rambles*, 1838.
3. Catharine Parr Traill, *The Backwoods of Canada*, 1836.

## Introduction

Did women experience early Canada differently from men? Did they have a unique culture? Some historians argue that the colonies offered women far greater opportunities to demonstrate their ability and exercise authority. Opponents disagree, asserting that male domination in the new world was as stultifying as in the old.

Upper Canada in the early part of the nineteenth century remained a frontier backwater. Few roads linked the dusty little settlements, and these became impassable in both spring and fall, and in winter too when the snow flew. Thus most new settlers lived in deeply isolated "bush farms" hacked from the virgin land and often many kilometres from the nearest neighbour, let alone village. Life was tough, often teetered on the impossible, and required enormous stamina, perseverance, and ingenuity. The few towns of any consequence, such as Toronto or Kingston, remained rustic outposts with muddy streets and few trappings of European sophistication—despite their citizens' insistence to the contrary. Upper Canada did, however, hold out the promise of boundless opportunities to emigrants fleeing economic and social trauma in the British Isles. A person could own land and, with a bit of luck and a great deal of hard work, make an independent life far more lucrative than anything available in the "Old Country."

Women like Susanna Moodie and her older sister Catharine Parr Traill, wrote for personal satisfaction, profit, and to provide cautionary tales to others contemplating immigration to the "backwoods of Canada." Their accounts were naturally directed toward their own kind: the upper and upper middle class English families unable to keep up with their peers and anxious to avoid social humiliation by emigrating. That was, after all, why Moodie and her husband left England. Her brother, who lived in Upper Canada, encouraged them by sending glowing reports of economic prosperity and high social status and they followed him there in 1832. Susanna's husband invested much of their precious money on dubious stocks that inevitably crashed. That, plus limited farming experience, lost them two farms and made them all but destitute in a land that Susanna increasingly called her "prison house."

Moodie eventually petitioned the Lieutenant Governor of Upper Canada for help, and in 1839 he secured her husband an appointment as sheriff. She probably wrote *Roughing It in the Bush* during the depths of their troubles, but it was not published until 1852, by which time the Moodies enjoyed modest prosperity. They owned a stone house instead of their earlier crude log structures, there were schools for their children, they bought a piano, and hired several servants. This was not the genteel England for which Susanna always pined, but it was a far cry from the grim days when there was not enough money to provide shoes for their children, let alone hire maids.

Anna Brownell Jameson was already a well established author by the time she arrived in Toronto for an eight-month stay in 1836. She had little wish to come, but did so to save her marriage to a husband who arrived three years earlier and was by then Attorney General for Upper Canada. She failed in her primary objective, but did leave an invaluable study of society in Upper Canada during the early part of the nineteenth century. Brownell Jameson visited several communities in the area, found few attractions, and hated the unsophisticated pretensions of Upper Canada's urban upstarts. This was not pure snobbery on her part because she clearly sympathized with ordinary settlers creating new lives in tough environments. Her book on Upper Canada is generally bleak and probably discouraged a number of would-be immigrants. It sold well in England after publication in 1838, perhaps to people willing to move anywhere but Canada.

Catharine Parr Traill could have been writing about a different colony altogether—which makes comparisons with her sister so intriguing. She arrived in Upper Canada in the same year as Susanna and established a bush farm close by. She came from the same upper middle class background, and had similar financial worries. She too was a writer, with several published children's books to her credit. Her husband, Thomas, also had little practical farming experience. Repeated crop failures brought them, like the Moodies, to the precipice of bankruptcy. Through it all, however, Catharine maintained a sense of wonder at her new world and remained enthusiastic about life in the backwoods, especially the natural beauty of the countryside. But it was not easy. Her husband hated the isolation of the backwoods and suffered from acute depression. This left her to sustain the family, which she did with aplomb: she lived and wrote into her nineties and gave birth to nine children. Though she never made much money from her writing, her many articles did establish her as a distinguished natural-ist. The following account, published in 1836, comes from a series of eighteen letters describing her experiences in the backwoods of Upper Canada.

## Discussion Points

1. If a working class woman, born in Canada, recorded her expe-riences of early Upper Canada, how would it differ from the accounts by Moodie, Brownell Jameson, and Traill?
2. Is it obvious that these accounts were written by women?
3. One Canadian novelist referred to Moodie as "a snob, a liar ... a self-righteous, egotistical woman who writes self-indulgently to make herself look great." Was he right?
4. Moodie and Traill, sisters with remarkably similar backgrounds and who experienced all-but-identical conditions, came to wildly different conclusions about Upper Canada. What does this say about historical evidence? How can one resolve blatant contra-dictions between two sources?
5. What qualities would an immigrant have needed in order to prosper in Upper Canada? Would sustained effort and good faith have been enough to guarantee success?

## Documents

### 1. Susanna Moodie, *Roughing It in the Bush*, 1852.

In most instances, emigration is a matter of necessity, not of choice; and this is more especially true of the emigration of persons of respectable connections, or of any station or position in the world. Few educated persons, accustomed to the refinements and luxuries of European society, ever willingly relinquish those advantages, and place themselves beyond the protective influence of the wise and revered institutions of their native land, without the pressure of some urgent cause. Emigration may, indeed, generally be regarded as an act of severe duty, performed at the expense of personal enjoyment, and accompanied by the sacri-fice of those local attachments which stamp the scenes amid which our childhood grew, in imperishable characters upon the heart. Nor is it until adversity has pressed sorely upon the proud and wounded spirit of the well-educated sons, and daughters of old but impoverished families, that they gird up the loins of the mind, and arm themselves with fortitude to meet and dare the heart-breaking conflict.

The ordinary motives for the emigration of such persons may be summed up in a few brief words—the emigrant's hope of bettering his condition, and of escaping from the vulgar sarcasms too often hurled at the less wealthy by the purse-proud, commonplace people of the world. But there is a higher motive still, which has its origin in that love of independence which springs up spontaneously in the breasts of the high-souled children of a glorious land. They cannot labour in a menial capacity in the country where they were born and educated to command. They can trace no difference between themselves and the more fortunate individuals of a race whose blood warms their veins, and whose name they bear. The want of wealth alone places an impassable barrier between them and the more favoured offspring of the same parent stock; and they go forth to make for themselves a new name and to find another country, to forget the past and to live in the future, to exult in the prospect of their children being free and the land of their adoption great.

The choice of the country to which they devote their talents and energies depends less upon their pecuniary means than upon the fancy of the emigrant or the popularity of a name. From the year 1826 to 1829, Australia and the Swan River were all the rage. No other portions of the habitable globe were deemed worthy of notice. These were the El Dorados and lands of Goshen to which all respectable emigrants eagerly flocked. Disappointment, as a matter of course, followed their high-raised expectations. Many of the most sanguine of these adventurers returned to their native shores in a worse condition than when they left them. In 1830, the great tide of emigration flowed westward. Canada became the great landmark for the rich in hope and poor in purse. Public newspapers and private letters teemed with the unheard-of advantages to be derived from a settlement in this highly favoured region.

Its salubrious climate, its fertile soil, commercial advantages, great water privileges, its proximity to the mother country, and last, not least, its almost total exemption from taxation—that bugbear which keeps honest John Bull in a state of constant ferment—were the theme of every tongue, and lauded beyond all praise. The general interest, once excited, was industriously kept alive by pamphlets, published by interested parties, which prominently set forth all the good to be derived from a settlement in the Backwoods of Canada; while they carefully concealed the toil and hardship to be endured in order to secure these advantages. They told of lands yielding forty bushels to the acre, but they said nothing of the years when these lands, with the most careful cultivation, would barely return fifteen; when rust and smut, engendered by the vicinity of damp over-hanging woods, would blast the fruits of the poor emigrant's labour, and almost deprive him of bread. They talked of log houses to be raised in a single day, by the generous exertions of friends and neighbours, but they never ventured upon a picture of the disgusting scenes of riot and low debauchery exhibited during the raising, or upon a description of the dwellings when raised—dens of dirt and misery, which would, in many instances, be shamed by an English pig-sty. The necessaries of life were described as inestimably cheap; but they forgot to add that in remote bush settlements, often twenty miles from a market town, and some of them even that distance from the nearest dwelling, the necessaries of life which would be deemed indispensable to the European, could not be procured at all, or, if obtained, could only be so by sending a man and team through a blazed forest road—a process far too expensive for frequent repetition.

Oh, ye dealers in wild lands—ye speculators in the folly and credulity of your fellow-men—what a mass of misery, and of misrepresentation productive of that misery, have ye not to answer for! You had your acres to sell, and what to you were the worn-down frames and broken hearts of the infatuated purchasers? The public believed the plausible statements you made with such earnestness, and men of all grades rushed to hear your hired orators declaim upon the blessings to be obtained by the clearers of the wilderness.

Men who had been hopeless of supporting their families in comfort and independence at home, thought that they had only to come out to Canada to make their fortunes; almost even to realize the story told in the nursery, of the sheep and oxen that ran about the streets, ready roasted, and with knives and forks upon their backs. They were made to believe that if it did not actually rain gold, that precious metal could be obtained, as is now stated of California and Australia, by stooping to pick it up.

The infection became general. A Canada mania pervaded the middle ranks of British society; thousands and tens of thousands, for the space of three or four years, landed upon these shores. A large majority of the higher class were officers of the army and navy, with their families—a class perfectly unfitted by their previous habits and education for contending with the stern realities of emigrant life. The hand that has long held the sword, and been accustomed to receive implicit obedience from those under its control, is seldom adapted to wield the spade and guide the plough, or try its strength against the stubborn trees of the forest. Nor will such persons submit cheerfully to the saucy familiarity of servants, who, republicans in spirit, think themselves as good as their employers. Too many of these brave and honourable men were easy dupes to the designing land-speculators. Not having counted the cost, but only looked upon the bright side of the picture held up to their admiring gaze, they fell easily into the snares of their artful seducers.

To prove their zeal as colonists, they were induced to purchase large tracts of wild land in remote and unfavourable situations. This, while it impoverished and often proved the ruin of the unfortunate immigrant, possessed a double advantage to the seller. He obtained an exorbitant price for the land which he actually sold, while the residence of a respectable settler upon the spot greatly enhanced the value and price of all other lands in the neighbourhood....

Many a hard battle had we to fight with old prejudices, and many proud swellings of the heart to subdue, before we could feel the least interest in the land of our adoption, or look upon it as our home.

All was new, strange, and distasteful to us; we shrank from the rude, coarse familiarity of the uneducated people among whom we were thrown; and they in turn viewed us as innovators, who wished to curtail their independence by expecting from them the kindly civilities and gentle courtesies of a more refined community ... The semi-barbarous Yankee squatters, who had "left their country for their country's good," and by whom we were surrounded in our first settlement, detested us, and with them we could have no feeling in common. We could neither lie nor cheat in our dealings with them; and they despised us for our ignorance in trading and our want of smartness.

The utter want of that common courtesy with which a well-brought-up European addresses the poorest of his brethren, is severely felt at first by settlers in Canada. At the period of which I am now speaking, the titles of "sir," or "madam," were very rarely applied by inferiors....

Why they treated our claims to their respect with marked insult and rudeness, I never could satisfactorily determine, in any way that could reflect honour on the species, or even plead an excuse for its brutality, until I found that this insolence was more generally practised by the low, uneducated emigrants from Britain, who better understood your claims to their civility, than by the natives themselves. Then I discovered the secret.

The unnatural restraint which society imposes upon these people at home forces them to treat their more fortunate brethren with a servile deference which is repugnant to their feelings, and is thrust upon them by the dependent circumstances in which they are placed. This homage to rank and education is not sincere. Hatred and envy lie rankling at their heart, although hidden by outward obsequiousness. Necessity compels their obedience; they fawn, and cringe, and flatter the wealth on which they depend for bread. But let them once emigrate, the clog which fettered them is suddenly removed; they are free; and the dearest privilege of this freedom is to wreak upon their superiors the long-locked-up hatred of their hearts. They think they can debase you to their level by disallowing all your claims to distinction; while they hope to exalt themselves and their fellows into ladies and gentlemen by sinking you back to the only title you received from Nature—plain "man" and "woman." ...

But from this folly the native-born Canadian is exempt; it is only practised by the low-born Yankee, or the Yankeefied British peasantry and mechanics. It originates in the enormous reaction springing out of sudden emancipation from a state of utter dependence into one of unrestrained liberty....

And here I would observe, before quitting this subject, that of all follies, that of taking out servants from the old country is one of the greatest, and is sure to end in the loss of the money expended in their passage, and to become the cause of deep disappointment and mortification to yourself.

They no sooner set foot upon the Canadian shores than they become possessed with this ultra-republican spirit. All respect for their employers, all subordination is at an end; the very air of Canada severs the tie of mutual obligation which bound you together. They fancy themselves not only equal to you in rank, but that ignorance and vulgarity give them superior claims to notice. They demand the highest wages, and grumble at doing half the work, in return, which they cheerfully performed at home. They demand to eat at your table, and to sit in your company, and if you refuse to listen to their dishonest and extravagant claims, they tell you that "they are free; that no contract signed in the old country is binding." ...

When we consider the different position in which servants are placed in the old and new world, this conduct, ungrateful as it then appeared to me, ought not to create the least surprise....

The serving class, comparatively speaking, is small, and admits of little competition. Servants that understand the work of the country are not easily procured, and such always can command the highest wages....

The Canadian women, while they retain the bloom and freshness of youth, are exceedingly pretty; but these charms soon fade, owing perhaps, to the fierce extremes of their climate....

The early age at which they marry and are introduced into society takes from them all awkwardness and restraint....

To the benevolent philanthropist, whose heart has bled over the misery and pauperism of the lower classes in Great Britain, the almost entire absence of mendicity from Canada would be highly gratifying. Canada has few, if any, native beggars; her objects of charity are generally imported from the mother country, and these are never suffered to want food or clothing. The Canadians are a truly charitable people; no person in distress is driven with harsh and cruel language from their doors; they not only generously relieve the wants of suffering strangers cast upon their bounty, but they nurse them in sickness, and use every means in their power to procure them employment. The number of orphan children yearly adopted by wealthy Canadians, and treated in every respect as their own, is almost incredible.

It is a glorious country for the labouring classes, for while blessed with health, they are always certain of employment, and certain also to derive from it ample means of support for their families....

It has often been remarked to me by people long resident in the colony, that those who come to the country destitute of means, but able and willing to work, invariably improve their condition and become independent; while the gentleman who brings out with him a small capital is too often tricked and cheated out of his property, and drawn into rash and dangerous speculation which terminate in his ruin. His children, neglected and uneducated, but brought up with ideas far beyond their means, and suffered to waste their time in idleness, seldom take to work, and not infrequently sink down to the lowest class....

The clouds of the preceding night, instead of dissolving in snow, brought on a rapid thaw. A thaw in the middle of winter is the most disagreeable change that can be imagined. After several weeks of clear, bright, bracing, frosty weather, with a serene atmosphere and cloudless sky, you awake one morning surprised at the change in the temperature; and, upon looking out of the window, behold the woods obscured by a murky haze—not so dense as an English November fog, but more black and lowering—and the heavens shrouded in a uniform covering of leaden-coloured clouds, deepening into a livid indigo at the edge of the horizon. The snow, no longer hard and glittering, has become soft and spongy, and the foot slips into a wet and insidiously-yielding mass at every step. From the roof pours down a continuous stream of water, and the branches of the trees, collecting the moisture of the reeking atmosphere, shower it upon the earth from every dripping twig. The cheerless and uncomfortable aspect of things without never fails to produce a corresponding effect upon the minds of those within, and casts such a damp upon the spirits that it appears to destroy for a time all sense of enjoyment. Many persons (and myself among the number) are made aware of the approach of a thunderstorm by an intense pain and weight about the head; and I have heard numbers of Canadians complain that a thaw always made them feel bilious and heavy, and greatly depressed their animal spirits.

I had a great desire to visit our new location, but when I looked out upon the cheerless waste, I gave up the idea, and contented myself with hoping for a better day on the morrow; but many morrows came and went before a frost again hardened the road sufficiently for me to make the attempt.

The prospect from the windows of my sister's log hut was not very prepossessing. The small lake in front, which formed such a pretty object in summer, now looked like an extensive field covered with snow, hemmed in from the rest of the world by a dark belt of sombre pine-woods. The clearing round the house was very small, and only just reclaimed from the wilderness, and the greater part of it was covered with piles of brush-wood, to be burnt the first dry days of spring.

The charred and blackened stumps on the few acres that had been cleared during the preceding year were everything but picturesque; and I concluded, as I turned, disgusted, from the prospect before me, that there was very little beauty to be found in the backwoods. But I came to this decision during a Canadian thaw, be it remembered, when one is wont to view every object with jaundiced eyes.

Moodie had only been able to secure sixty-six acres of his government grant upon the Upper Katchawanook Lake, which, being interpreted, means in English, the "Lake of the Waterfalls," a very poetical meaning, which most Indian names have. He had, however, secured a clergy reserve of two hundred acres adjoining; and he afterwards purchased a fine lot, which likewise formed part of the same block, one hundred acres, for £150. This was an enormously high price for wild land; but the prospect of opening the Trent and Otonabee for the navigation of steamboats and other small craft, was at that period a favourite speculation, and its practicability, and the great advantages to be derived from it, were so widely believed as to raise the value of the wild lands along these remote waters to an enormous price; and settlers in the vicinity were eager to secure lots, at any sacrifice, along their shores.

Our government grant was upon the lake shore, and Moodie had chosen for the site of his log house a bank that sloped gradually from the edge of the water, until it attained to the dignity of a hill. Along the top of this ridge, the forest road ran, and midway down the hill, our humble home, already nearly completed, stood, surrounded by the eternal forest. A few trees had been cleared in its immediate vicinity, just sufficient to allow the workmen to proceed, and to prevent the fall of any tree injuring the building, or the danger of its taking fire during the process of burning the fallow.

A neighbour had undertaken to build this rude dwelling by contract, and was to have it ready for us by the first week in the new year. The want of boards to make the divisions in the apartments alone hindered him from fulfilling his contract. These had lately been procured, and the house was to be ready for our reception in the course of a week. Our trunks and baggage had already been conveyed thither by Mr D——; and, in spite of my sister's kindness and hospitality, I longed to find myself once more settled in a home of my own....

The snow had been so greatly decreased by the late thaw, that it had been converted into a coating of ice, which afforded a dangerous and slippery footing. My sister, who had resided for nearly twelve months in the woods, was provided for her walk with Indian moccasins, which rendered her quite independent; but I stumbled at every step. The sun shone brightly, the air was clear and invigorating, and, in spite of the treacherous ground and my foolish fears, I greatly enjoyed my first walk in the woods. Naturally of a cheerful, hopeful disposition, my sister was enthusiastic in her admiration of the woods. She drew such a lively picture of the charms of a summer residence in the forest, that I began to feel greatly interested in her descriptions, and to rejoice that we, too, were to be her near neighbours and dwellers in the woods; and this circumstance not a little reconciled me to the change.

Hoping that my husband would derive an income equal to the one he had parted with from the investment of the price of his commission in the steamboat stock, I felt no dread of want. Our legacy of £700 had afforded us means to purchase land, build our house, and give out a large portion of land to be cleared, and, with a considerable sum of money still in hand, our prospects for the future were in no way discouraging....

The house was made of cedar logs, and presented a superior air of comfort to most dwellings of the same kind. The dimensions were thirty-six feet in length, and thirty-two feet in breadth, which gave us a nice parlour, a kitchen, and two small bedrooms, which were divided by plank partitions. Pantry or storeroom there was none; some rough shelves in the kitchen, and a deal cupboard in a corner of the parlour, being the extent of our accommodations in that way....

The first spring we spent in comparative ease and idleness. Our cows had been left upon our old place during the winter. The ground had to be cleared before it could receive a crop of any kind, and I had little to do but to wander by the lake shore, or among the woods, and amuse myself.

These were the halcyon days of the bush. My husband had purchased a very light cedar canoe, to which he attached a keel and a sail: and most of our leisure hours, directly the snows melted, were spent upon the water.

These fishing and shooting excursions were delightful. The pure beauty of the Canadian water, the sombre but august grandeur of the vast forest that hemmed us in on every side and shut us out from the rest of the world, soon cast a magic spell upon our spirits, and we began to feel charmed with the freedom and solitude around us. Every object was new to us. We felt as if we were the first discoverers of every beautiful flower and stately tree that attracted our attention, and we gave names to fantastic rocks and fairy isles, and raised imaginary houses and bridges on every picturesque spot which we floated past during our aquatic excursions. I learned the use of the paddle, and became quite a proficient in the gentle craft.

It was not long before we received visits from the Indians, a people whose beauty, talents, and good qualities have been somewhat overrated, and invested with a poetical interest which they scarcely deserve. Their honesty and love of truth are the finest traits in characters otherwise dark and unlovely. But these are two God-like attributes, and from them spring all that is generous and ennobling about them.

There never was a people more sensible of kindness, or more grateful for any little act of benevolence exercised towards them. We met them with confidence; our dealings with them were conducted with the strictest integrity; and they became attached to our persons, and in no single instance ever destroyed the good opinion we entertained of them.

The tribes that occupy the shores of all these inland waters, back of the great lakes, belong to the Chippewa or Missasagua Indians, perhaps the least attractive of all these wild people, both with regard to their physical and mental endowments.

The men of this tribe are generally small of stature, with very coarse and repulsive features. The forehead is low and retreating, the observing faculties large, the intellectual ones scarcely developed; the ears large, and standing off from the face; the eyes looking towards the temples, keen, snake-like, and far apart; the cheek bones prominent; the nose long and flat, the nostrils very round; the jaw-bone projecting, massy, and brutal; the mouth expressing ferocity and sullen determination; the teeth large, even, and dazzlingly white. The mouth of the female differs widely in expression from that of the male; the lips are fuller, the jaw less projecting, and the smile is simple and agreeable. The women are a merry, light hearted set, and their constant laugh and incessant prattle form a strange contrast to the iron taciturnity of their grim lords....

The summer of '35 was very wet; a circumstance so unusual in Canada that I have seen no season like it during my sojourn in the country. Our wheat crop promised to be both excellent and abundant; and the clearing and seeding sixteen acres, one way or another, had cost us more than fifty pounds; still we hoped to realize something handsome by the sale of the produce; and, as far as appearances went, all looked fair. The rain commenced about a week before the crop was fit for the sickle, and from that time until nearly the end of September was a mere succession of thunder showers; days of intense heat, succeeded by floods of rain. Our fine crop shared the fate of all other fine crops in the country; it was totally spoiled; the wheat grew in the sheaf, and we could scarcely save enough to supply us with bad sickly bread; the rest was exchanged at the distillery for whiskey, which was the only produce which could be obtained for it. The storekeepers would not look at it, or give either money or goods for such a damaged article.

My husband and I had worked hard in the field; it was the first time I had ever tried my hand at field-labour, but our ready money was exhausted, and the steamboat stock had not paid us one farthing; we could not hire, and there was no help for it. I had a hard struggle with my pride before I would consent to render the least assistance on the farm, but reflection convinced me that I was wrong—that Providence had placed me in a situation where I was called upon to work—that it was not only my duty to obey that call, but to exert myself to the utmost to assist my husband and help to maintain my family.

Ah, poverty! thou art a hard taskmaster, but in thy soul-ennobling school I have received more god-like lessons, have learned more sublime truths, than ever I acquired in the smooth highways of the world!

The independent in soul can rise above the seeming disgrace of poverty, and hold fast their integrity, in defiance of the world and its selfish and unwise maxims. To them, no labour is too great, no trial too severe; they will unflinchingly exert every faculty of mind and body before they will submit to become a burden to others....

The misfortunes that now crowded upon us were the result of no misconduct or extravagance on our part, but arose out of circumstances which we could not avert nor control. Finding too late the error into which we had fallen, in suffering ourselves to be cajoled and plundered out of our property by interested speculators, we braced our minds to bear the worst, and determined to meet our difficulties calmly and firmly, nor suffer our spirits to sink under calamities which energy and industry might eventually repair. Having once come to this resolution, we cheerfully shared together the labours of the field. One in heart and purpose, we dared remain true to ourselves, true to our high destiny as immortal creatures, in our conflict with temporal and physical wants.

We found that manual toil, however distasteful to those unaccustomed to

;r all such a dreadful hardship; that the wilderness was not without
iard face of poverty without its smile. If we occasionally suffered
ve as often experienced great pleasure, and I have contemplated a
dge of potatoes on that bush farm with as much delight as in years
long r— iad experienced in examining a fine painting in some well-appointed
drawing-room.

I can now look back with calm thankfulness on that long period of trial
and exertion—with thankfulness that the dark clouds that hung over us, threatening to blot us from existence, when they did burst upon us, were full of blessings.
When our situation appeared perfectly desperate, then were we on the threshold
of a new state of things, which was born out of that very distress.

In order more fully to illustrate the necessity of a perfect and childlike
reliance upon the mercies of God—who, I most firmly believe, never deserts
those who have placed their trust in Him—I will give a brief sketch of our lives
during the years 1836 and 1837.

Still confidently expecting to realize an income, however small, from the
steamboat stock, we had involved ourselves considerably in debt, in order to pay
our servants and obtain the common necessaries of life; and we owed a large sum
to two Englishmen in Dummer, for clearing ten more acres upon the farm. Our
utter inability to meet these demands weighed very heavily upon my husband's
mind. All superfluities in the way of groceries were now given up, and we were
compelled to rest satisfied upon the produce of the farm. Milk, bread, and potatoes during the summer became our chief, and often, for months, our only fare.
As to tea and sugar, they were luxuries we would not think of, although I missed
the tea very much; we rang the changes upon peppermint and sage, taking the
one herb at our breakfast, the other at our tea, until I found an excellent substitute for both in the root of the dandelion....

Necessity has truly been termed the mother of invention, for I contrived to
manufacture a variety of dishes almost out of nothing, while living in her school.
When entirely destitute of animal food, the different varieties of squirrels supplied us with pies, stews, and roasts. Our barn stood at the top of the hill near
the bush, and in a trap set for such "small deer," we often caught from ten to
twelve a day.

The flesh of the black squirrel is equal to that of the rabbit, and the red,
and even the little chipmunk, is palatable when nicely cooked. But from the
lake, during the summer, we derived the larger portion of our food. The children
called this piece of water "Mamma's pantry", and many a good meal has the
munificent Father given to his poor dependent children from its well-stored

depths. Moodie and I used to rise by daybreak, and fish for an hour after sunrise, when we returned, he to the field, and I to dress the little ones, clean up the house, assist with the milk, and prepare the breakfast.

Oh, how I enjoyed these excursions on the lake; the very idea of our dinner depending upon our success added double zest to our sport!

One morning we started as usual before sunrise; a thick mist still hung like a fine veil upon the water when we pushed off, and anchored at our accustomed place. Just as the sun rose, and the haze parted and drew up like a golden sheet of transparent gauze, through which the dark woods loomed out like giants, a noble buck dashed into the water....

That winter of '36, how heavily it wore away! The grown flour, frosted potatoes, and scant quantity of animal food rendered us all weak, and the children suffered much from the ague....

On the 21st of May of this year, my second son, Donald, was born. The poor fellow came in hard times. The cows had not calved, and our bill of fare, now minus the deer and Spot, only consisted of bad potatoes and still worse bread. I was rendered so weak by want of proper nourishment that my dear husband, for my sake, overcame his aversion to borrowing, and procured a quarter of mutton from a friend. This, with kindly presents from neighbours—often as badly off as ourselves—a loin of a young bear, and a basket containing a loaf of bread, some tea, some fresh butter, and oatmeal, went far to save my life.

Shortly after my recovery, Jacob—the faithful, good Jacob—was obliged to leave us, for we could not longer afford to pay wages. What was owing to him had to be settled by sacrificing our best cow, and a great many valuable articles of clothing from my husband's wardrobe. Nothing is more distressing than being obliged to part with articles of dress which you know that you cannot replace. Almost all my clothes had been appropriated to the payment of wages, or to obtain garments for the children, excepting my wedding dress, and the beautiful baby-linen which had been made by the hands of dear and affectionate friends for my first-born. These were now exchanged for coarse, warm flannels, to shield him from the cold.

Moodie and Jacob had chopped eight acres during the winter, but these had to be burnt off and logged up before we could put in a crop of wheat for the ensuing fall. Had we been able to retain this industrious, kindly English lad, this would have been soon accomplished; but his wages, at the rate of thirty pounds per annum, were now utterly beyond our means....

Reader! it is not my intention to trouble you with the sequel of our history. I have given you a faithful picture of a life in the backwoods of Canada, and I leave you to draw from it your own conclusions, To the poor, industrious working man it presents many advantages; to the poor gentleman, none! The former works hard, puts up with coarse, scanty fare, and submits, with a good grace, to hardships that would kill a domesticated animal at home. Thus he becomes independent, inasmuch as the land that he has cleared finds him in the common necessaries of life; but it seldom, if ever, in remote situations, accomplishes more than this. The gentleman can neither work so hard, live so coarsely, nor endure so many privations as his poorer but more fortunate neighbour. Unaccustomed to manual labour, his services in the field are not of a nature to secure for him a profitable return. The task is new to him, he knows not how to perform it well; and, conscious of his deficiency, he expends his little means in hiring labour, which his bush-farm can never repay. Difficulties increase, debts grow upon him, he struggles in vain to extricate himself, and finally sees his family sink into hopeless ruin.

If these sketches should prove the means of deterring one family from sinking their property, and shipwrecking all their hopes, by going to reside in the backwoods of Canada, I shall consider myself amply repaid for revealing the secrets of the prison-house, and feel that I have not toiled and suffered in the wilderness in vain.

## 2. Anna Brownell Jameson, *Winter Studies and Summer Rambles*, 1838.

… Their deportment was taciturn and self-possessed, and their countenances melancholy; that of the chief was by far the most intelligent. They informed me that they were Chippewas from the neighborhood of Lake Huron; that the hunting season had been unsuccessful; that their tribe was suffering the extremity of hunger and cold; and that they had come to beg from their Great Father the Governor rations of food, and a supply of blankets for their women and children. They had walked over the snow, in their snow-shoes, from the lake, one hundred and eighty miles, and for the last forty-eight hours none of them had tasted food. A breakfast of cold meat, bread, and beer, was immediately ordered for them; and though they had certainly never beheld in their lives the arrangement of an European table, and were besides half-famished, they sat down with unembarrassed tranquillity, and helped themselves to what they wished, with the utmost propriety—only, after one or two trials, using their own knives and fingers in preference to the table knife and fork. After they had eaten and drunk sufficiently, they were conducted to the government-house to receive from the governor presents of blankets, rifles, and provisions, and each, on parting, held

out his hand to me, and the chief, with grave earnestness, prayed for the blessing
of the Great Spirit on me and my house. On the whole, the impression they left,
though amusing and exciting from its mere novelty, was melancholy. The sort of
desperate resignation in their swarthy countenances, their squalid, dingy
habiliments, and their forlorn story, filled me with pity, and, I may add, disappointment; and all my previous impressions of the independent children of the
forest are for the present disturbed.

These are the first specimens I have seen of that fated race, with which I
hope to become better acquainted before I leave the country. Notwithstanding
all I have heard and read, I have yet but a vague idea of the Indian character; and
the very different aspect under which it has been represented by various travellers, as well as writers of fiction, adds to the difficulty of forming a correct estimate
of the people, and more particularly of the true position of their women. Colonel Givins, who has passed thirty years of his life among the north-west tribes,
till he has become in habits and language almost identified with them, is hardly
an impartial judge. He was their interpreter on this occasion, and he says that
there is as much difference between the customs and language of different nations, the Chippewas and Mohawks, for instance, as there is between any two
nations of Europe.

*January 16*
... The cold is at this time so intense, that the ink freezes while I write, and my
fingers stiffen round the pen; a glass of water by my bed-side, within a few feet
of the hearth (heaped with logs of oak and maple kept burning all night long), is
a solid mass of ice in the morning. God help the poor emigrants who are yet
unprepared against the rigor of the season!—yet this is nothing to the climate of
the lower province, where, as we hear, the thermometer has been thirty degrees
below zero. I lose all heart to write home, or to register a reflection or a feeling;—
thought stagnates in my head as the ink in my pen—and this will never do!—I
must rouse myself to occupation; and if I cannot find it without, I must create it
from within. There are yet four months of winter and leisure to be disposed of.
How?—I know not; but they *must* be employed, not wholly lost....

*February 17*
"There is no *society* in Toronto," is what I hear repeated all around me—even by
those who compose the only society we have. "But," you will say, "what could be
expected in a remote town, which forty years ago was an uninhabited swamp,
and twenty years ago only began to exist?" I really do not know what I expected,

but I will tell you what I did not expect. I did not expect to find here in this new capital of a new country, with the boundless forest within half a mile of us on almost every side—concentrated as it were the worst evils of our old and most artificial social system at home, with none of its *agrémens*, and none of its advantages. Toronto is like a fourth- or fifth-rate provincial town with the pretensions of a capital city. We have here a petty colonial oligarchy, a self-constituted aristocracy, based upon nothing real, nor even upon anything imaginary; and we have all the mutual jealousy and fear, and petty gossip, and mutual meddling and mean rivalship, which are common in a small society of which the members are well known to each other, a society composed, like all societies, of many heterogeneous particles; but as these circulate within very confined limits, there is no getting out of the way of what one most dislikes: we must necessarily hear, see, and passively endure much that annoys and disgusts anyone accustomed to the independence of a large and liberal society, or the ease of continental life. It is curious enough to see how quickly a new fashion, or a new folly, is imported from the old country, and with what difficulty and delay a new idea finds its way into the heads of the people, or a new book into their hands. Yet, in the midst of all this, I cannot but see that good spirits and corrective principles are at work; that progress is making: though the march of intellect be not here in double quick time, as in Europe, it does not absolutely stand stock-still.

There reigns here a hateful factious spirit in political matters, but for the present no public or patriotic feeling, no recognition of general or generous principles of policy: as yet I have met with none of these. Canada is a colony, not a *country;* it is not yet identified with the dearest affections and associations, remembrances, and hopes of its inhabitants: it is to them an adopted, not a real mother. Their love, their pride, are not for poor Canada, but for high and happy England; but a few more generations must change all this.

We have here Tories, Whigs, and Radicals, so called; but these words do not signify exactly what we mean by the same designations at home.

You must recollect that the first settlers in Upper Canada were those who were obliged to fly from the United States during the revolutionary war, in consequence of their attachment to the British government, and the soldiers and non-commissioned officers who had fought during the war. These were recompensed for their losses, sufferings, and services, by grants of land in Upper Canada. Thus the very first elements out of which our social system was framed, were repugnance and contempt for the new institutions of the United States, and a dislike to the people of that country—a very natural result of foregoing causes; and thus it has happened that the slightest tinge of democratic, or even liberal principles in politics, was for a long time a sufficient impeachment of the loyalty, a stain upon the personal character, of those who held them. The Tories have therefore been hitherto the influential party; in their hands we find the government patronage, the principal offices, the sales and grants of land, for a long series of years.

Another party, professing the same boundless loyalty to the mother country, and the same dislike for the principles and institutions of their Yankee neighbors, may be called the Whigs of Upper Canada; these look with jealousy and scorn on the power and prejudices of the Tory families, and insist on the necessity of many reforms in the colonial government. Many of these are young men of talent, and professional men, who find themselves shut out from what they regard as their fair proportion of social consideration and influence, such as, in a small society like this, their superior education and character ought to command for them.

Another set are the Radicals, whom I generally hear mentioned as "those scoundrels," or "those rascals," or with some epithet expressive of the utmost contempt and disgust. They are those who wish to see this country erected into a republic, like the United States. A few among them are men of talent and education, but at present they are neither influential nor formidable.

There is among all parties a general tone of complaint and discontent—a mutual distrust—a languor and supineness—the causes of which I cannot as yet understand. Even those who are enthusiastically British in heart and feeling, who sincerely believe that it is the true interest of the colony to remain under the control of the mother country, are as discontented as the rest: they bitterly denounce the ignorance of the colonial officials at home, with regard to the true interests of the country: they ascribe the want of capital for improvement on a large scale to no mistrust in the resources of the country, but to a want of confidence in the measures of the government, and the security of property.

In order to understand something of the feelings which prevail here, you must bear in mind the distinction between the two provinces of Upper and Lower Canada. The project of uniting them once more into one legislature, with a central metropolis, is most violently opposed by those whose personal interests and convenience would suffer materially by a change in the seat of government. I have heard some persons go so far as to declare, that if the union of the two provinces were to be established by law, it were sufficient to absolve a man from his allegiance. On the other hand, the measure has powerful advocates in both provinces. It seems, on looking over the map of this vast and magnificent country, and reading its whole history, that the political division into five provinces, each with its independent governor and legislature, its separate correspondence with the Colonial office, its local laws, and local taxation, must certainly add to the amount of colonial patronage, and perhaps render more secure the subjection of the whole to the British crown; but may it not also have perpetuated local distinctions and jealousies—kept alive divided interests, narrowed the resources, and prevented the improvement of the country on a large and general scale?

But I had better stop here, ere I get beyond my depth. I am not one of those who opine sagely, that women have nothing to do with politics. On the contrary; but I do seriously think, that no one, be it man or woman, ought to talk, much less write, on what they do not understand. Not but that I have my own ideas on these matters, though we were never able to make out, either to my own satisfaction or to yours, whether I am a Whig, or Tory, or Radical....

*February 18*
Toronto is, as a residence, worse and better than other small communities—worse in so much as it is remote from all the best advantages of a high state of civilization, while it is infected by all its evils, all its follies; and better, because, besides being a small place, it is a *young* place; and in spite of this affectation of looking back, instead of looking up, it must advance—it may become the thinking head and beating heart of a nation, great, wise, and happy; who knows? And there are moments when, considered under this point of view, it assumes an interest even to me; but at present it is in a false position, like that of a youth aping maturity; ... With the interminable forests within half a mile of us—the haunt of the red man, the wolf, the bear—with an absolute want of the means of the most ordinary mental and moral development, we have here conventionalism in its most oppressive and ridiculous forms. If I should say, that at present the people here want cultivation, want polish, and the means of acquiring either, *that* is natural—is intelligible—and it were unreasonable to expect it could be otherwise; but if I say they want honesty, you would understand me, *they* would not; they would imagine that I accused them of false weights and cheating at cards. So far they are certainly "indifferent honest" after a fashion, but never did I hear so little truth, nor find so little mutual benevolence. And why is it so?—because in this place, as in other small provincial towns, they live under the principle of fear—they are afraid of each other, afraid to be themselves; and where there is much fear, there is little love, and less truth....

*February 21*
... Fires are not uncommon in Toronto, where the houses are mostly wood; they

have generally an alarum once or twice a week, and six or eight houses burned in the course of the winter; but it was evident this was of more fearful extent than usual. Finding, on inquiry, that all the household had gone off to the scene of action, my own maid excepted, I prepared to follow, for it was impossible to remain here idly gazing on the flames, and listening to the distant shouts in ignorance and suspense. The fire was in the principal street (King-street), and five houses were burning together. I made my way through the snow-heaped, deserted streets, and into a kind of court or garden at the back of the blazing houses. There was a vast and motley pile of household stuff in the midst, and a poor woman keeping guard over it, nearly up to her knees in the snow. I stood on the top of a bedstead, leaning on her shoulder, and thus we remained till the whole row of buildings had fallen in. The Irishmen (God bless my countrymen! for in all good—all mischief—all frolic—all danger—they are sure to be the first) risked their lives most....

*March 28*
There is yet no indication as the approach of spring, and I find it more than ever difficult to keep myself warm. Nothing in myself or around me feels or looks like *home*. How much is comprised in that little word! May it please God to preserve to me all that I love! But, O absence! how much is comprised in *that* word too! it is death of the heart and darkness of the soul; it is the ever springing, ever-dying hope; the ever-craving, never-having wish; it is fear, and doubt, and sorrow, and pain;—a state in which the past swallows up the present, and the future becomes the past before it arrives! ...

*April 1*
So, there is another month gone; and the snows are just beginning to disappear, and the flocks of snow-birds with them; and the ice is breaking up at the entrance of the bay, and one or two little vessels have ventured as far as the King's Wharf; and the wind blows strong to dry up the melting snow, and some time or other, perhaps, spring will come, and this long winter's imprisonment will be at an end....

This is the worst season in Canada. The roads are breaking up, and nearly impassable; lands are flooded, and in low situations there is much sickness, particularly ague. We have still sixteen square miles of ice within the bay.

The market at Toronto is not well supplied, and is at a great distance from us. The higher class of people are supplied with provisions from their own lands and farms, or by certain persons they know and employ. With a little management and forethought, we now get on very well; but at first we had to suffer great inconvenience. Quantities of salted provisions are still imported into the country for the consumption of the soldiers and distant settlers, and at certain seasons—at present, for example—there is some difficulty in procuring anything else.

Our table, however, is pretty well supplied. Beef is tolerable, but lean; mutton bad, scarce, and dearer than beef; pork excellent and delicate, being fattened principally on Indian corn. The fish is of many various kinds, and delicious. During the whole winter we had black-bass and white-fish, caught in holes in the ice, and brought down by the Indians. Venison, game, and wild fowl are always to be had; the quails, which are caught in immense numbers near Toronto, are most delicate eating; I lived on them when I could eat nothing else. What they call partridge here is a small species of pheasant, also very good; and now we are promised snipes and woodcocks in abundance. The wild goose is also excellent eating when well cooked, but the old proverb about Heaven sending meat, &c. &c. is verified here. Those who have farms near the city, or a country establishment of their own, raise poultry and vegetables for their own table. As yet I have seen no vegetables whatever but potatoes; even in the best seasons they are not readily to be procured in the market. Every year, however, as Toronto increases in population and importance, will diminish these minor inconveniences.

The want of good servants is a more serious evil. I could amuse you with an account of the petty miseries we have been enduring from this cause, the strange characters who come to offer themselves, and the wages required. Almost all the servants are of the lower class of Irish emigrants, in general honest, warm-hearted, and willing; but never having seen anything but want, dirt, and reckless misery at home, they are not the most eligible persons to trust with the cleanliness and comfort of one's household. Yet we make as many complaints, and express as much surprise at their deficiencies, as though it were possible it could be otherwise. We give to our man-servant eight dollars a month, to the cook six dollars, and to the housemaid four; but these are lower wages than are usual for good and experienced servants, who might indeed command almost any wages here, where all labor is high priced....

Apropos to newspapers—my table is covered with them. In the absence or scarcity of books, they are the principal medium of knowledge and communication in Upper Canada. There is no stamp-act here—no duty on paper; and I have sometimes thought that the great number of local newspapers which do not circulate beyond their own little town or district, must, from the vulgar, narrow tone of many of them, do mischief; but on the whole, perhaps, they do more good. Paragraphs printed from English or American papers, on subjects of general interest, the summary of political events, extracts from books or magazines, are copied from one paper into another, till they have travelled round the country. It is true that a great deal of base, vulgar, inflammatory party feeling is also circulated by the same means; but, on the whole, I should not like to see the number or circulation of the district papers checked. There are about forty published in Upper Canada; of these, three are religious, viz. the "Christian Guardian," "The Wesleyan Advocate," and "The Church;" a paper in the German language is published at Berlin, in the Gore district, for the use of the German settlers; "The Correspondent and Advocate" is the leading radical, "The Toronto Patriot," the leading Conservative paper. The newspapers of Lower Canada and the United States are circulated in great numbers; and as they pay postage, it is no inconsiderable item in the revenue of the post-office. In some of these provincial papers I have seen articles written with considerable talent; amongst other things, I have remarked a series of letters signed Evans, addressed to the Canadians on the subject of an education fitted for an agricultural people, and written with infinite good sense and kindly feeling; these have been copied from one paper into another, and circulated widely; no doubt they will do good. Last year the number of newspapers circulated through the post-office, and paying postage, was

| Provincial papers | 178,065 |
| United States and foreign papers | 149,502 |

... There is a commercial news-room in the city of Toronto, and this is absolutely the only place of assembly or amusement, except the taverns and low drinking-houses. An attempt has been made to found a mechanics' institute and a literary club; but as yet they create little interest, and are very ill supported.

If the sympathy for literature and science be small, that for music is less. Owing to the exertions of an intelligent musician here, some voices have been so far drilled that the psalms and anthems at church are very tolerably performed; but this gentleman receives so little general encouragement, that he is at this moment preparing to go over to the United States. The archdeacon is collecting subscriptions to pay for an organ which is to cost a thousand pounds; if the money were expended in aid of a singing-school, it would do more good.

The interior of the episcopal church here is rather elegant, with the exception of a huge window of painted glass which cost £500, and is in a vile, tawdry taste.

Besides the episcopal church, the Presbyterians, Methodists, Roman Catholics, and Baptists have each a place of worship. There is also an African church for the negroes.

The hospital, a large brick building, is yet too small for the increasing size of the city. The public grammar-school, called the "Upper Canada College," forms a cluster of ugly brick-buildings; and although the system of education there appears narrow and defective, yet it is a *beginning*, and certainly productive of good.

The physician I have mentioned to you, Dr. Rees, entertains the idea of founding a house of reception for destitute female emigrants on their arrival in Canada—a house, where, without depending on *charity*, they may be boarded and lodged at the smallest possible cost, and respectably protected till they can procure employment. You may easily imagine that I take a deep interest in this design....

I have not often in my life met with contented and cheerful-minded women, but I never met with so many repining and discontented women as in Canada. I never met with *one* woman recently settled here, who considered herself happy in her new home and country: I *heard* of one, and doubtless there are others, but they are exceptions to the general rule. Those born here, or brought here early by their parents and relations, seemed to me very happy, and many of them had adopted a sort of pride in their new country, which I liked much. There was always a great desire to visit England, and some little airs of self-complacency and superiority in those who had been there, though for a few months only; but all, without a single exception, returned with pleasure, unable to forego the early habitual influences of their native land....

I know it has been laid down as a principle, that the more and the closer men are congregated together, the more prevalent is vice of every kind; and that an isolated or scattered population is favourable to virtue and simplicity. It may be so, if you are satisfied with negative virtues and the simplicity of ignorance. But here, where a small population is scattered over a wide extent of fruitful country, where there is not a village or a hamlet for twenty or thirty or forty miles together—where there are no manufactories—where there is almost entire equality of condition—where the means of subsistence are abundant—where there is no landed aristocracy—no poor laws, nor poor rates, to grind the souls and the substance of the people between them, till nothing remains but chaff,— to what shall we attribute the gross vices, the profligacy, the stupidity, and basely vulgar habits of a great part of the people, who know not even how to enjoy or to turn to profit the inestimable advantages around them?—And, alas for them! there seems to be no one as yet to take an interest about them, or at least infuse a new spirit into the next generation. In one log hut in the very heart of the wilderness, where I might well have expected primitive manners and simplicity, I found vulgar finery, vanity, affectation, under the most absurd and disgusting forms, combined with a want of the commonest physical comforts of life, and the total absence of even elementary knowledge. In another I have seen drunkenness, profligacy, stolid indifference to all religion; and in another, the most senseless fanaticism. There are people, I know, who think—who fear, that the advancement of knowledge and civilization must be the increase of vice and insubordination; who deem that a scattered agricultural population, where there is a sufficiency of daily food for the body; where no schoolmaster interferes to infuse ambition and discontent into the abject, self-satisfied mind; where the labourer reads not, writes not, thinks not—only loves, hates, prays, and toils— that such a state must be a sort of Arcadia. Let them come here!—there is no march of intellect here!—there is no "schoolmaster abroad" here! And what are the consequences? Not the most agreeable to contemplate, believe me.

I passed in these journeys some school-houses built by the wayside: of these, several were shut up for want of schoolmasters; and who that could earn a subsistence in any other way, would be a schoolmaster in the wilds of Upper Canada? Ill fed, ill clothed, ill paid, or not paid at all—boarded at the houses of the different farmers in turn, I found indeed some few men, poor creatures! always either Scotch or Americans, and totally unfit for the office they had undertaken. Of female teachers I found none whatever, except in the towns. Among all the excellent societies in London for the advancement of religion and education, are there none to send missionaries here?—such missionaries as we want, be it understood—not sectarian fanatics. Here, without means of instruction, of social amusement, of healthy and innocent excitements—can we wonder that whiskey and camp meetings assume their place, and "season toil" which is unseasoned by anything better.

## 3. Catharine Parr Traill, *The Backwoods of Canada*, 1836.

*November the 20th, 1832*

... We begin to get reconciled to our Robinson Crusoe sort of life, and the consideration that the present evils are but temporary goes a great way towards reconciling us to them.

One of our greatest inconveniences arises from the badness of our roads, and the distance at which we are placed from any village or town where provisions are to be procured.

Till we raise our own grain and fatten our own hogs, sheep, and poultry, we must be dependent upon the stores for food of every kind. These supplies have to be brought up at considerable expense and loss of time, through our beautiful bush-roads; which, to use the words of a poor Irish woman, "can't be no worser." ...

This is now the worst season of the year—this, and just after the breaking up of the snow. Nothing hardly but an ox-cart can travel along the roads, and even that with difficulty, occupying two days to perform the journey to and fro, and the worst of the matter is, that there are times when the most necessary articles of provisions are not to be procured at any price. You see, then, that a settler in the bush requires to hold himself pretty independent, not only of the luxuries and delicacies of the table, but not unfrequently even of the very necessaries.

One time no pork is to be procured; another time there is a scarcity of flour, owing to some accident that has happened to the mill, or for the want of proper supplies of wheat for grinding; or perhaps the weather and bad roads at the same time prevent a team coming up, or people from going down. Then you must have recourse to a neighbour, if you have the good fortune to be near one, or fare the best you can on potatoes. The potato is indeed a great blessing here; new settlers would otherwise be often greatly distressed, and the poor man and his family who are without resources, without the potato must starve....

*November the 2nd, 1833*

... We had a glorious burning this summer after the ground was all logged up; that is, all the large timbers chopped into lengths, and drawn together in heaps with oxen. To effect this the more readily we called a logging-bee. We had a number of settlers attend, with yokes of oxen and men to assist us. After that was over, my husband, with the menservants, set the heaps on fire; and a magnificent sight it was to see such a conflagration all around us. I was a little nervous at first on account of the nearness of some of the log-heaps to the house, but care is always taken to fire them with the wind blowing in a direction away from the building. Accidents have sometimes happened, but they are of rarer occurrence than might be expected when we consider the subtlety and destructiveness of the elements employed on the occasion.

If the weather be very dry, and a brisk wind blowing, the work of destruction proceeds with astonishing rapidity; sometimes the fire will communicate with the forest and run over many hundreds of acres. This is not considered favourable for clearing, as it destroys the underbrush and light-timbers, which are almost indispensable for ensuring a good burning. It is, however, a magnifi-

cent sight to see the blazing trees and watch the awful progress of the conflagration, as it hurries onward, consuming all before it, or leaving such scorching
mementos as have blasted the forest growth for years.

When the ground is very dry the fire will run all over the fallow, consuming the dried leaves, sticks, and roots. Of a night the effect is more evident;
sometimes the wind blows particles of the burning fuel into the hollow pines
and tall decaying stumps; these readily ignite, and after a time present an appearance that is exceedingly fine and fanciful. Fiery columns, the bases of which are
hidden by the dense smoke wreaths, are to be seen in every direction, sending up
showers of sparks that are whirled about like rockets and fire-wheels in the wind.
Some of these tall stumps, when the fire has reached the summit, look like gas
lamps newly lit. The fire will sometimes continue unextinguished for days....

Our crops this year are oats, corn, and pumpkins, and potatoes, with some
turnips. We shall have wheat, rye, oats, potatoes and corn next harvest, which
will enable us to increase our stock. At present we have only a yoke of oxen
(Buck and Bright, the names of three-fourths of all the working oxen in Canada),
two cows, two calves, three small pigs, ten hens, and three ducks, and a pretty
brown pony....

A small farmer at home would think very poorly of our Canadian possessions, especially when I add that our whole stock of farming implements consists
of two reaping-hooks, several axes, a spade, and a couple of hoes. Add to these a
queer sort of harrow that is made in the shape of a triangle for the better passing
between the stumps: this is a rude machine compared with the nicely painted
instruments of the sort I have been accustomed to see used in Britain. It is
roughly hewn, and put together without regard to neatness; strength for use is all
that is looked to here. The plough is seldom put into the land before the third or
fourth year, nor is it required; the general plan of cropping the first fallow with
wheat or oats, and sowing grass-seeds with the grain to make pastures, renders
the plough unnecessary till such time as the grasslands require to be broken up.
This method is pursued by most settlers while they are clearing bushland; always
chopping and burning enough to keep a regular succession of wheat and spring
crops, while the former clearings are allowed to remain in grass....

On first coming to this country nothing surprised me more than the total
absence of trees about the dwelling-houses and cleared lands; the axe of the
chopper relentlessly levels all before him. Man appears to contend with the trees
of the forest as though they were his most obnoxious enemies; for he spares
neither the young sapling in its greenness nor the ancient trunk in its lofty pride;
he wages war against the forest with fire and steel.

There are several sufficient reasons to be given for this seeming want of taste. The forest-trees grow so thickly together that they have no room for expanding and putting forth lateral branches; on the contrary, they run up to an amazing height of stem, resembling seedlings on a hot-bed that have not duly been thinned out. Trees of this growth when unsupported by others are tall, weak, and entirely divested of those graces and charms of outline and foliage that would make them desirable as ornaments to our grounds....

*Lake Cottage, March 14, 1834*
... You say you fear the rigours of the Canadian winter will kill me. I never enjoyed better health, nor so good, as since it commenced. There is a degree of spirit and vigour infused into one's blood by the purity of the air that is quite exhilarating. The very snow seems whiter and more beautiful than it does in your damp, vapoury climate. During a keen bright winter's day you will often perceive the air filled with minute frozen particles, which are quite dry, and slightly prick your face like needle-points, while the sky is blue and bright above you. There is a decided difference between the first snow-falls and those of mid-winter; the first are in large soft flakes, and seldom remain long without thawing, but those that fall after the cold has regularly set in are smaller, drier, and of the most beautiful forms, sometimes pointed like a cluster of rays, or else feathered in the most exquisite manner....

The swarthy complexions, shaggy black hair and singular costume of the Indians formed a striking contrast with the fair-faced Europeans that were mingled with them, seen as they were by the red and fitful glare of the wood-fire that occupied the centre of the circle....

The hymn was sung in the Indian tongue, a language that is peculiarly sweet and soft in its cadences, and seems to be composed with many vowels. I could not but notice the modest air of the girls; as if anxious to avoid observation that they felt was attracted by their sweet voices, they turned away from the gaze of the strangers, facing each other and bending their heads down over the work they still held in their hands. The attitude, which is that of the Eastern nations; the dress, dark hair and eyes, the olive complexion, heightened colour, and meek expression of face, would have formed a study for a painter, I wish you could have witnessed the scene; I think you would not easily have forgotten it. I was pleased with the air of deep reverence that sat on the faces of the elders of the Indian family as they listened to the voices of their children singing praise and glory to the God and Saviour they had learned to fear and love.

The Indians seem most tender parents; it is pleasing to see the affectionate manner in which they treat their young children, fondly and gently caressing them with eyes overflowing and looks of love....

*September 20, 1843*

... Canada is the land of hope; here everything is new; everything going forward; it is scarcely possible for arts, sciences, agriculture, manufactures, to retrograde; they must keep advancing; though in some situations the progress may seem slow, in others they are proportionately rapid.

There is a constant excitement on the minds of emigrants, particularly in the partially settled townships, that greatly assists in keeping them from desponding. The arrival of some enterprising person gives a stimulus to those about him: profitable speculation is started, and lo, the value of the land in the vicinity rises to double and treble what it was thought worth before; so that, without any design of befriending his neighbours, the schemes of one settler being carried into effect shall benefit a great number. We have already felt the beneficial effect of the access of respectable emigrants locating themselves in this township, as it has already increased the value of our own land in a three-fold degree....

Our society is mostly military or naval; so that we meet on equal grounds, and are, of course, well acquainted with the rules of good breeding and polite life; too much so to allow any deviation from those laws that good taste, good sense, and good feeling have established among persons of our class.

Yet here it is considered by no means derogatory to the wife of an officer or gentleman to assist in the work of the house, or to perform its entire duties, if occasion requires it; to understand the mystery of soap, candle, and sugar-making; to make bread, butter, and cheese, or even to milk her own cows, to knit and spin, and prepare the wool for the loom. In these matters we bush-ladies have a wholesome disregard of what Mr and Mrs So-and-so think or say. We pride ourselves on conforming to circumstances; and as a British officer must needs be a gentleman and his wife a lady, perhaps we repose quietly on that incontestable proof of our gentility, and can afford to be useful without injuring it.

Our husbands adopt a similar line of conduct: the officer turns his sword into a ploughshare, and his lance into a sickle; and if he be seen ploughing among the stumps in his own field, or chopping trees on his own land, no one thinks less of his dignity, or considers him less of a gentleman, than when he appeared upon parade in all the pride of military etiquette, with sash, sword, and epaulette. Surely this is as it should be in a country where independence is inseparable from industry; and for this I prize it.

Among many advantages we in this township possess, it is certainly no inconsiderable one that the lower or working-class of settlers are well disposed, and quite free from the annoying Yankee manners that distinguish many of the earlier-settled townships. Our servants are as respectful, or nearly so, as those at home; nor are they admitted to our tables, or placed on an equality with us, excepting at "bees," and such kinds of public meetings; when they usually conduct themselves with a propriety that would afford an example to some that call themselves gentlemen, viz., young men who voluntarily throw aside those restraints that society expects from persons filling a respectable situation.

Intemperance is too prevailing a vice among all ranks of people in this country; but I blush to say it belongs most decidedly to those that consider themselves among the better class of emigrants. Let none such complain of the airs of equality displayed towards them by the labouring class, seeing that they degrade themselves below the honest, sober settler, however poor. If the sons of gentlemen lower themselves, no wonder if the sons of poor men endeavour to exalt themselves above him in a country where they all meet on equal ground and good conduct is the distinguishing mark between the classes....

*November the 28th, 1834*
You will have been surprised, and possibly distressed, by my long silence of several months, but when I tell you it has been occasioned by sickness, you will cease to wonder that I did not write.

My dear husband, my servant, the poor babe, and myself, were all at one time confined to our beds with ague. You know how severe my sufferings always were at home with intermittents, and need not marvel if they were no less great in a country where lake-fevers and all kinds of intermittent fevers abound.

Few persons escape the second year without being afflicted with this weakening complaint; the mode of treatment is repeated doses of calomel, with castor-oil or salts, and is followed up by quinine. Those persons who do not choose to employ medical advice on the subject dose themselves with ginger-tea, strong infusion of hyson, or any other powerful green tea, pepper, and whiskey, with many other remedies that have the sanction of custom or quackery.

I will not dwell on this uncomfortable period further than to tell you that we considered the complaint to have had its origin in a malaria, arising from a cellar below the kitchen. When the snow melted, this cellar became half full of water, either from the moisture draining through the spongy earth, or from the rising of a spring beneath the house; be it as it may, the heat of the cooking and Franklin stoves in the kitchen and parlour caused a fermentation to take place in

the stagnant fluid before it could be emptied; the effluvia arising from this mass
of putrefying water affected us all. The female servant, who was the most exposed to its baneful influence, was the first of our household that fell sick, after
which we each in turn became unable to assist each other....

I lost the ague in a fortnight's time—thanks to calomel and quinine; so did
my babe and his nurse: it has, however, hung on my husband during the whole
of the summer, and thrown a damp upon his exertions and gloom upon his
spirits. This is the certain effect of ague, it causes the same sort of depression on
the spirits as a nervous fever. My dear child has not been well ever since he had
the ague, and looks very pale and spiritless....

I have stood of a bright winter day looking with infinite delight on the
beautiful mimic waterfalls congealed into solid ice along the bank of the river;
and by the mill-dam, from contemplating these pretty frolics of Father Frost, I
have been led to picture to myself the sublime scenery of the arctic regions.

In spite of its length and extreme severity, I do like the Canadian winter: it
is decidedly the healthiest season of the year; and it is no small enjoyment to be
exempted from the torments of the insect tribes, that are certainly great drawbacks to your comfort in the warmer months....

Not to regret my absence from my native land, and one so fair and lovely
withal, would argue a heart of insensibility: yet I must say, for all its roughness,
I love Canada, and am as happy in my humble log-house as if it were courtly
hall or bower; habit reconciles us to many things that at first were distasteful. It
has ever been my way to extract the sweet rather than the bitter in the cup of life,
and surely it is best and wisest so to do. In a country where constant exertion is
called for from all ages and degrees of settlers, it would be foolish to a degree to
damp our energies by complaints, and cast a gloom over our homes by sitting
dejectedly down to lament for all that was so dear to us in the old country. Since
we are here, let us make the best of it, and bear with cheerfulness the lot we have
chosen. I believe that one of the chief ingredients in human happiness is a capacity for enjoying the blessings we possess.

Though at our first outset we experienced many disappointments, many
unlooked-for expenses, and many annoying delays, with some wants that to us
seemed great privations, on the whole we have been fortunate, especially in the
situation of our land, which has increased in value very considerably; our chief
difficulties are now over, at least we hope so, and we trust soon to enjoy the
comforts of a cleared farm.

My husband is becoming more reconciled to the country, and I daily feel
my attachment to it strengthening. The very stumps that appeared so odious,

through long custom seem to lose some of their hideousness; the eye becomes familiarized even with objects the most displeasing till they cease to be observed. Some century hence how different will this spot appear! I can picture it to my imagination with fertile fields and groves of trees planted by the hand of taste. All will be different; our present rude dwellings will have given place to others of a more elegant style of architecture, and comfort and grace will rule the scene which is now a forest wild....

## *Readings*

Atwood, M. "Introduction," in S. Moodie, *Roughing It in the Bush*. London: Virago, 1986.

Ballstadt, C., E. Hopkins, and M. Peterman. "'A Glorious Madness': Susanna Moodie and the Spiritualist Movement," *Journal of Canadian Studies* 17, 4 (Winter 1982–83).

Ballstadt, C., E. Hopkins, and M. Peterman, eds. *I Bless You in My Heart: Selected Correspondence of Catharine Parr Traill*. Toronto: University of Toronto Press, 1995.

Ballstadt, C., E. Hopkins, and M. Peterman, eds. *Letters of Love and Duty: The Correspondence of Susanna and John Moodie*. Toronto: University of Toronto Press, 1993.

Ballstadt, C., E. Hopkins, and M. Peterman, eds. *Susanna Moodie: Letters of a Lifetime*. Toronto: University of Toronto Press, 1985.

Buss, H. *Mapping Ourselves: Canadian Women's Autobiography*. Kingston and Montreal: McGill-Queen's University Press, 1993.

Errington, J. *Wives and Mothers, Schoolmistresses and Scullery Maids: Working Women in Upper Canada, 1790–1840*. Montreal and Kingston: McGill-Queen's University Press, 1995.

Errington, J. "A Woman is a Very Interesting Creature: Some Women's Experiences in Upper Canada," *Historic Kingston* 38 (1990).

Fowler, M. *The Embroidered Tent: Five Gentlewomen in Early Canada*. Toronto: Anansi, 1982.

Gairdner, W. "Traill and Moodie: The Two Realities," *Journal of Canadian Fiction* 2 (1973).

Gerson, C. "Nobler Savages: Representations of Native Women in the Writings of Susanna Moodie and Catharine Parr Traill," *Journal of Canadian Studies* 32, 2 (Summer 1997).

Gray, C. *Sisters in the Wilderness: The Lives of Susanna Moodie and Catharine Parr Traill*. Toronto: Viking, 1999.

Hopkins, E. "A Prison-House for Prosperity: The Immigrant Experience of the Nineteenth-Century Upper Class British Woman," in J. Burnet, ed., *Looking into My Sisters Eyes: An Exploration in Women's History*. Toronto: Multicultural History Society of Ontario, 1986.

Light, B., and A. Prentice, eds. *Pioneers and Gentlewomen of British North America*. Toronto: New Hogtown Press, 1980.

Mathews, R. "Susanna Moodie, Pink Toryism, and the Nineteenth Century Ideas of Canadian Identity," *Journal of Canadian Studies* 10, 3 (August 1975).

McKenna, K. "Options for Elite Women in Early Upper Canada Society: The Case of the Powell Family," in J. Johnson and B. Wilson, eds., *Historical Essays on Upper Canada: New Perspectives*. Ottawa: Carleton University Press, 1989.

McDonald, T. "'Come to Canada While You Have a Chance': A Cautionary Tale of English Emigrant Letters in Upper Canada," *Ontario History* 91, 2 (Autumn 1999).

Morgan, C. *Public Men and Virtuous Women: The Gendered Languages of Religion and Politics in Upper Canada, 1791–1850*. Toronto: University of Toronto Press, 1996.

Peterman, M. *This Great Epoch in Our Lives: Susanna Moodie's Roughing It in the Bush*. Toronto: ECW Press, 1996.

Potter-MacKinnon, J. *While the Women Only Wept: Loyalist Refugee Women in Eastern Ontario*. Montreal and Kingston: McGill-Queen's University Press, 1993.

Shields, C. *Susanna Moodie: Voice and Vision*. Ottawa: Borealis, 1977.

Thomas, C. *Love and Work Enough: The Life of Anna Jameson*. Toronto: University of Toronto Press, 1967.

Thurston, J. *The Work of Words: The Writing of Susanna Strickland Moodie*. Montreal and Kingston: McGill-Queen's University Press, 1996.

*Chapter Seven*

# "THE LONG AND HEAVY CHAIN OF ABUSE": POLITICAL CRISIS IN LOWER CANADA

1. Etienne Parent, "Address to the Canadien Public," *Le Canadien*, May 7, 1831.
2. Etienne Parent, "Concerning the 92 Resolutions," *Le Canadien*, February 26, 1834.
3. "The Six Counties Address," Montreal, *The Vindicator*, October 31, 1837.
4. Robert Nelson, "Declaration of Independence," February 22, 1838.
5. Lord Durham, "To Lord Glenelg," August 9, 1838, in *Imperial Blue Books Relating to Canada*, 1839.
6. Lord Durham, "Report on the Affairs of British North America," 1840.
7. Louis-Joseph Papineau, "The Story of Canada's Insurrection in Refutation of Lord Durham's Report," *La Revue*, 1839.

## Introduction

Canadians pride themselves on their "peaceable kingdom," a country that resists the political and social violence of the United States. This was not always the case. 1837 was a turbulent year that saw both Upper and Lower Canada erupt in violence as bands of desperate men sought to overthrow the British administration in favour of an American-style republican structure. Though rebel support was far from unanimous and their attempts ultimately failed, there was widespread dissatisfaction with colonial rule. The crux of the issue was over who should have the right to legislate. In Britain the bulk of power rested with the elected members of the House of Commons. However, her colonies retained a unique system where elections were held but the popular representatives sitting in the legislative assemblies had virtually no power. Instead governors and their councillors carried out the policies of the British Colonial Office. Local democrats took their inspiration from the U.S., arguing that those in positions of legislative power for the colonies should be account-

able and responsible to local people through election, and should not be aristocratic appointees serving at London's pleasure.

The St. Lawrence River region was not alone in its rebellious spirit. Politically motivated violence erupted in Upper Canada, and the Maritmes also saw
the rise of movements dedicated to political reform. But no other British North
American colony exploded like Lower Canada. This resulted from a number of
unique factors.

First, Lower Canada sank into recession in the mid-1830s and an already
impoverished habitant population feared for its future as seigneurs squeezed
them for ever more money. Fiercely autonomous rural French-Canadian communities also felt threatened by English and urban meddling in their affairs.
Greater local democracy, they believed, would prevent their subjugation by "foreign" vested interests. Many French-Canadian urbanites, especially the politically
astute professional classes, saw themselves as becoming increasingly assimilated
and under the control of an Anglo dominated colonial bureaucracy and economic elite, derisively referred to as the Chateau Clique. Increasingly the Parti
Canadien came to believe that only full democratic citizenship rights through a
system of responsible government or total independence could check British
cultural dominance. Demographic trends also caused concern for many French-
Canadians. While the French-speaking majority remained intact, their
percentage of the total population dwindled as thousands of British immigrants annually arrived at the port of Quebec. It looked as if French-Canadians
were inevitably doomed to drown in a sea of Anglo-domination.

The Catholic Church, that institution fundamental to French-Canadian
life, found itself on the horns of a dilemma as tensions mounted in the colony.
Like the political reformers, it sought to preserve French-Canadian culture but it
was also a staunchly conservative and anti-democratic institution with no patience for republicanism. In the end it threatened the rebels with excommunication
thus forcing many French-Canadians to choose between their church and their
independence.

Push as they might for greater democracy, the Patriotes could not budge a
fortified and deeply entrenched British political structure that held to the belief
that colonies existed to serve the mother country and not local interests. After
years of petitions, resolutions, and attempts at persuasion, the crisis came to a
head with the drafting of the "Six Counties Address": Lower Canada's equivalent to the American Declaration of Independence. The Address won mass support
at a meeting in St. Charles, a farming community outside Montreal, on October
24, 1837. Flushed with political passion, some Patriote leaders prepared for

battle against the British colonial government. However, their chief spokesman, Louis-Joseph Papineau, quickly fled to the United States before any armed confrontations began.

British authorities quickly crushed the rebellion, arresting thousands of participants, and put the torch to much of the pro-Patriote rural countryside of Lower Canada. There would to be no repetition of the American Revolution. The rebellion had made it clear that serious problems existed with the administration of the British North America colonies. It became Durham's task to discover what exactly was wrong and draw up a series of recommendations to prevent further troubles. Many contend that his final report only served to exacerbate an already difficult situation.

## Discussion Points

1. Did the situation in Lower Canada justify rebellion?
2. For the most part it was the more articulate Canadiens, newspaper editors, doctors, lawyers, and other professional men knocking at the doors of power, who expressed discontent. Did they describe the grievances of society as a whole, including those of women and men from other occupations such as farmers, artisans, lumberjacks, and fishers?
3. If Durham was right, that this was a war between races, how can one explain the presence of leaders like Wolfred and Robert Nelson?
4. The 1830s was a time of political upheaval in various areas in Europe. Canadians also looked over their shoulders to conditions in the United States. To what extent were British North American reform ideas locally, as opposed to internationally, based?

## Documents

**1. Etienne Parent, "Address to the Canadien Public," *Le Canadien*, May 7, 1831.**

We cannot go before the members of the public without first thanking them for the generally favourable reception they have given to the patriotic enterprise we embark on today; and their having shown themselves since to be well-disposed toward the proposal to establish a French paper in Québec gives us great hopes of success. It seems that this success must now depend entirely upon ourselves, on our efforts and zeal in carrying out the important task we have set ourselves, and in satisfying the expectations of a liberal public. This goal we will strive to achieve; everything beckons us on, our self-interest, our honour, our reputation, and our sentiments.

Our slogan, in the campaign we are about to launch, we will draw from the hearts of all those for whom love of country is not an empty phrase; from those who in life cast their eyes beyond the details of their personal existence, who have a sense of nationhood, that fine virtue without which societies would be but collections of isolated beings incapable of those grand and noble acts, which build great nations, and which render those nations worthy in God's eyes; this watchword that will guide us in the thorny course on which we take our first step is *"our institutions, our language, and our laws!"* For it is the destiny of the Canadien people not only to preserve civil liberty, but also to fight for their existence as a people; it is thus that history represents our forebears, steering the plough with one hand and warding off attacks of barbarous natives with the other. It was with such heroic efforts and steadfastness that our first ancestors created the name Canadien. That name bequeathed to us, unsullied, by our forebears; that name whose honour they upheld on the field of battle, and whose existence they preserved in our councils against the continual pressures of blind and self-interested policy, it is up to the rising generation to pass on a legacy as fine as the one they received. This is the noble task of these fine youths who speak with the people's voice, who have lately joined the venerable ranks of our former defenders, they who steered until now, past the pitfalls, the ark of Canadien freedom. Along with these youths we have applauded the efforts, we have admired the virtues and talents of those veteran patriots, and along with them we will labour to follow in their footsteps, and finish the work they started.

Guiding us on the road to freedom we will have the example of the two finest nations on the globe, to one of which we are attached by ties of blood, and to the other, by those of an honourable and, for us, advantageous, adoption. We will be followed on our way by the good wishes and approbation of the entire civilized world. For all peoples are simultaneously driven by the same spirit, the same desire, that of participating in their own governance, so that ancient prejudices, tired maxims and private interests cannot deprive them of institutions made necessary by fresh needs, or prevent them from exercising rights essential to their happiness. This is what the English call *self-government*. It was the need for such government that, during those three memorable days of July, brought about repeated marvels in the heart of Paris, and that in the words of a patriotic poet, encompassed three centuries in three days; it is this same need that now prompts calls for reform in all parts of England; it is this pressing need that today causes a worthy people to confront imminent danger of destruction, that kindles in Poland an almost miraculous courage, at the approach of the Russian colossus; once again it is this noble need that has lately caused Belgium to be counted among the nations. Come closer to our own hemisphere and we will see before our eyes this self-government in practice, offering to the world the beautiful sight of civilization marching with giant steps, and renewing and multiplying in our own time the marvels of Orpheus's lyre.

Canadiens, will we, with such noble examples before us, prove apathetic? Will we deserve to become the dregs of a nation, a herd of slaves, serfs of a glebe we will till for the profit of whomever pleases to make himself our master? And yet this is the fate that awaits us, if we do not grasp the sole means we have of escaping it, namely, to learn to govern ourselves. There is no middle course; if we do not govern ourselves, we will be governed. The whole difference (and it is huge) between the subjects of the King of England and those of the Sultan derives from this: that the former participate in their government, while the latter are too unaware, too demoralized even to wish to do so.

But it is not enough to wish it; one must be capable of it. South America had the desire, but having stagnated for centuries in ignorance fuelled by a greedy and despotic government, she is tearing herself apart with the chains she has just broken. Could we not, without exaggeration, compare Canada with South America? Like her, we have passed, almost instantly, from the most despotic of governments to the most liberal. The Canadien people's long indifference to affairs of state has allowed a petty class of men to pile up to their advantage abuses under which we have nearly been crushed, and which only efforts verging on the superhuman on our part will rid us of. Fortunate we are that our union with a generous, free, and powerful nation has spared Canadien blood! Fortunate that that great nation has listened to the account of close to half a century of suffering, abuse, and injustices, and has promised us justice; but once dispensed, what permanent good will come of it, if we know not how to prevent a recurrence of those ills of which we complained? what will it serve us to have seen our present enemies routed, if we do not acquire the means of preventing others from taking their place amongst us?

So what are these means, what is this palladium of our social and political happiness? Canadiens, you hold the secret within you. Who amongst you, who, to save himself from discord would wish to entrust the conduct of his domestic affairs to his neighbour? you would fear, no doubt, and rightly so, that your heritage would be plundered and misappropriated by those to whom you had abandoned all control. Well! and yet this is what all men do who, under a constitution such as ours, pay no heed to the public business of their country. Under English government, it is public opinion that does everything; the authorities would like to deny its power, but in vain; they are forced to submit to it. But this opinion can only take shape in the light; to be strong it must be enlightened, and never will there be such opinion amongst a people unwilling to make the effort to follow and study the affairs of its government; witness Spain and Portugal, where the ignorance and mindlessness of the people have, in our time, frustrated every effort of a far-too-small number of patriots. If during the invasion by the Duc d'Angoulème, the people of London or Paris had been in Madrid, would he have as easily rivetted together the irons that bind Spain today?

Of all the available means, after that of regular study, which can be undertaken by only a few, we are offering to the public, in the present publication, the most efficient and most advantageous, and perhaps the least costly. *Le Canadien*, being published for a new people, and one as yet not much advanced in its knowledge of public affairs (and that is not the least ill of which the country must accuse the administration), we will endeavour most particularly to spread knowledge of constitutional right and practice, by way of extracts and précis of the best works of their kind, and by letting pass no occasion for debate, either by ourselves, or by cleverer pens, on any topic of public interest; and in short, by any other means that present themselves; and not the least of it will be the publication of the debates in the Legislature, especially those of the House of Assembly, which we will not fail to provide while in session. Nor will we neglect the political news from abroad, for in this time of general unrest, leading to a better order of things, in this time of despotism on trial and of the inherent rights of peoples, no mail coach arrives that does not provide some useful lesson, an example to follow, or a mistake to avoid.

To sum up: it is our policy, our aim, our feeling, wish and desire, to preserve all that constitutes for us our existence as a people, and as a means of achieving that end, to preserve every civil and political right that is an English country's prerogative. It is with these sentiments that we introduce ourselves, it is with these sentiments that we will act, it is with them that we will prosper or that we will sink.

Should it be necessary for us, in order to spark the attention of our fellow citizens, to prove that our institutions have been endangered, and that an axe has more than once been taken to the tree, we would remind them of the removal and pillage of the Jesuits' possessions, those handsome endowments made in aid of our Canadien youth, and the deprivation of which has been keenly felt in a setback in education; we would remind them of the covert and repeated attacks against the religion of the inhabitants of this country, and the endowment of a *Protestant clergy* with this country's very lands, and what is more flagrant yet, the attempt to subject our clergy to the *bon plaisir*, that Machiavellian creation recently taken to such extremes as to make utter laughingstocks of its perpetrators. On a different matter we seem to be seeing the scaling-back in practice of the insulting and impolitic assumption that the prince, when dispensing justice, must speak a language foreign to that of his subjects; do not these people, who at the call of their sovereign have gone bravely to the field of battle, deserve to be addressed by their sovereign in words intelligible to them? This is the way in which deluded ministers work to break the bonds that attach a royalist people to their king. But let us overcome our repugnance and cast our eyes on a still more abhorrent measure; we have just seen our language chased from the courts, now see our laws cast out, see ourselves driven out of a goodly portion of the country for which we twice paid with our blood. We will say nothing of our very real financial straits; they would always have existed, had we been Protestants or Jews, under English or under Scottish laws, speaking Spanish or speaking German. Love of people's money is the overriding passion of all administrations, and we suffer from it here just as others suffer from it elsewhere, and in time we will manage to curb it; England is after showing us the way.

Canadiens of all classes, all trades, all professions, with cherished laws, customs, and institutions to preserve, allow us to repeat that a Canadien press is the most powerful measure you can put in place. The celebrated Canning said somewhere that, when writing about the English constitution, were he to omit the part played by the press, he would be giving a very imperfect idea of the constitution. Montesquieu goes further yet, saying that if freedom of the press were introduced into Turkey, it would soon produce civil and political freedom there. Of all the presses, the periodic press is the one best suited to the people, it is in fact the sole library of the people. But in a new country such as ours, for the press to succeed and do all the good it is capable of, all those acquainted with its benefits must take a special interest in it, they must endeavour, each in his own sphere of influence, to procure readers, and in doing so they can take pride in working for the good of their country; for knowledge is power, and every new reader adds to the people's strength.

## 2. Étienne Parent, "Concerning the 92 Resolutions," *Le Canadien*, February 26, 1834.

RESOLVED, 50: That under the following terms of one of the aforementioned dispatches: "if unfortunate events should force Parliament to exercise its supreme authority to calm internal dissensions in the colonies, my object, as well as my desire, would be to submit to parliament such modifications to the Canadas charter, as might tend, not to introduce institutions incompatible with the existence of a monarchical government, but whose effect would be to uphold and cement the union with the Mother Country, while strictly adhering to the spirit of the British constitution, and upholding, in their genuine prerogatives, and within acceptable limits, the mutual rights and privileges of all His Majesty's classes, if they involve some threat of change, other than that asked for by the majority of the people of this province, whose sentiments can be legitimately expressed by no authority but that of its representatives, this House would believe itself failing the English people, if it hesitated to point out that, in under twenty years' time, the population of the United States of America will be as great as or greater than that of Great Britain; and that of English America will be as great as or greater than was that of the former English colonies when they judged it time to decide that the inestimable advantage of self-government over being governed must encourage them to repudiate a colonial regime which, generally speaking, was far better than that of English America today."

However much we might wish to present, as soon as possible to our readers, the result of the important debates that have marked the house of assembly sessions for some time, a wish that has often prevented us from laying out for the public, at greater length than we have done, our own ideas, our own feelings about the significant measures that currently preoccupy our representatives, we cannot resist the urge today to protest against the way in which a number of our contemporaries, among them the *Gazette de Québec*, are representing several of the resolutions on the state of the province, and in particular, the one that heads up this article.

These gentlemen see in this resolution a threat, a boast. Such comments would not be remotely surprising in those short-lived papers born of a seditious mind, and whose tone and style clearly indicate their origin and aim; but that serious newspapers, in such grave circumstances, over such serious matters, which are bound to be followed by equally serious consequences, should resort to such weak measures to counter their adversaries, and this, especially, when comments such as theirs can create, abroad, disastrous impressions of the country towards

which these gentlemen profess such strong interest and attachment; it is a striking example of the differences that vexation over a defeat can induce, fruit of the
most inexplicable defection. No matter how much the House declares that it
neither can nor wishes to make threats, they close their eyes, block their ears,
and cry at the top of their lungs that it is making threats, that it is calling
foreigners to its aid; then backed by these false premises, they revel in qualifying
as empty and ridiculous boasts, near-treason they say, that which is, on the part
of the representatives, but the perfect fulfilment of a sacred duty to the Mother
Country, vivid proof of the high price it places on its union with her, and of its
keen desire to see this union bound by liberal and conciliatory policy. If the
representatives sincerely wished for a sudden scission between this colony and
England, the surest way of securing it would indeed be by letting the government commit itself more and more to the ruin it is heading towards; by letting
it fill the cup of injustice, by giving it its head in the course of the arbitrary, until
the people, no longer able to bear the weight of the chains, would spontaneously
shake them off and overwhelm their tyrants. And in this instance they would
have no fear, as had the European peoples, as had the former Spain, as has Italy
today, that legions of soldiers would come pouring in from neighbouring countries, to rebuild the altar of despotism they had just overthrown. This then would
be the surest policy to follow for the foes of British allegiance.

No, it is not a threat to England to lay before her the facts, the circumstances and the probabilities that must necessarily have an inevitable influence
on the destiny of this country, and whose oversight on the part of the Mother
Country could yield bitter fruits for her and her colony. Since time immemorial, this has been the stumbling block of all home countries, in their lack of
awareness, from where they stand, of the condition and mood of their colonies.
Read the famous debates that took place in the British upper house over the
coercive measures against the former colonies, today the flourishing United
States; you will see there the greatest ignorance regarding them, and out of it,
the succession of measures and senseless steps that removed an empire from the
crown of England. It appears that the same ignorance, the same want of thought
exists today in the Sovereign's councils, with respect to Canada, and there seems
to be an obstinate closing of eyes to our social condition, our geographic position and the deepest feelings of the human heart. It is in the very nature of man
to be free, absolutely free, to have to answer for his actions to none but his
Creator, to enjoy the full fruits of his labours, and if, to secure more fully the
enjoyment of the fruit of this labour, he consents to give up a part of it; if in
order to enjoy his natural liberty peacefully he is happy to sacrifice a part of it;

if in a word he consents to live in society to enjoy the benefits it offers, it is clear that he means to have these benefits in the best conditions possible, which is to say by sacrificing his freedom and possessions to the smallest degree possible. For example, if a people sees that its possessions and liberty can be protected efficiently, or in other words, that it can obtain good government at far better value than it now has, and while giving up far less freedom, can one assume that this people will not seek a way to improve its lot? Can one assume that this people would be insensitive to its own interests, to the noble propensity for perfectionism that the finger of God has engraved in the hearts of men? Can one assume that it would tear claims of sovereignty from its brow, which is not made to bear the yoke: *os sublime dedit cælumque tueri jussit*. The people of this country, the social man of Canada, sees today that in America one can have a good, an excellent government, at a far better price than he pays for his own, and while giving up far less freedom than he does now; he has a shining, timeless example before his eyes. The despotic governments of Europe are so aware of the irresistible force of liberal ideas that they close their doors to liberal newspapers, and keep their presses under strictest surveillance.

As early as 1828 our delegates declared before a committee of the house of commons that we were starting to look at what was going on next door to us; and this was what England's greatest statesmen foresaw at the time of the passage of the constitutional act, saying that we should have nothing to envy with respect to our neighbours. It is in these circumstances that a colonial Minister, who himself recognized these truths, sends a dispatch that causes us to lose hope of his co-operation in advancing an undertaking he himself had encouraged when but a mere member of the House of Commons; it is in these circumstances that far from consenting to move our political institutions closer to those of the other American peoples, he announces in a threatening tone that his opposite intention is to make them more and more like those of Europe. At this moment, what is the duty of the representatives of the country, called to advise the government for the well-being and peace of the people? Is it not to demonstrate to the sovereign and parliament the injudiciousness, indeed the folly of this colonial minister, by laying before them the important facts and circumstances that this civil servant cannot have considered? The House of Assembly sees in the policy Mr Stanley is announcing the inevitable loss of this loyal colony; it sees there a violent, premature scission, would it not be negligent towards its country, its king, and the Mother Country, if it failed to show them the calamitous abyss an unthinking minister is about to excavate? And this will be called a threat, a boast, a sign of revolution? Let it be remembered, that this was the language so-called loyalists used half a century ago with respect to the anglo-American people, and history has already proclaimed the justice of their cause. Let care be taken that in another half-century history does not proclaim the justice of Canada's cause. Loyalists of today, this will be your doing, just as the independence of the United States was that of people like you in a previous age. Colonial Ministers, this will be your doing, if listening to empty clamour, you insist on making Americans live under a European régime. As well transplant to the tropics the produce of Siberia.

### 3. "The Six Counties Address," Montreal, *The Vindicator,* October 31, 1837.

Fellow Citizens:

When a systematic course of oppression has been invariably harassing a People, in despite of their wishes expressed in every manner recognized by constitutional usage; by popular assemblies, and by their Representatives, in Parliament, after grave deliberation; when their rulers, instead of redressing the various evils produced by their own misgovernment, have solemnly enregistered and proclaimed their guilty determination to sap and subvert the very foundations of civil liberty, it becomes the imperative duty of the People to betake themselves to the serious consideration of their unfortunate position—of the dangers by which they are surrounded—and by well-concerted organization, to make such arrangements as may be necessary to protect, unimpaired, their rights as Citizens and their dignity as Freemen.

The wise and immortal framers of the American Declaration of Independence, embodied in that document the principles on which alone are based the Rights of Man; and successfully vindicated and established the only institutions and form of government which can permanently secure the prosperity and social happiness of the inhabitants of this Continent, whose education and habits, derived from the circumstances of their colonization, demand a system of government entirely dependent upon, and directly responsible to, the People.

In common with the various nations of North and South America who have adopted the principles contained in that Declaration, we hold the same holy and self-evident doctrines: that God created no artificial distinctions between man and man; that government is but a mere human institution formed by those who are to be subject to its good or evil action, intended for the benefit of all who may consent to come, or remain under, its protection and control; and therefore, that its form may be changed whenever it ceases to accomplish the ends for which such government was established; that public authorities and men in office are but the executors of the lawfully-expressed will of the community, honoured because they possess public confidence, respected only so long as they command public esteem, and to be removed from office the moment they cease to give satisfaction to the People, the sole legitimate source of all power.

In conformity with these principles, and on the faith of treaties and capitulations entered into with our ancestors, and guaranteed by the Imperial Parliament, the People of this Province have for a long series of years complained by respectful petitions, of the intolerable abuses which poison their existence and paralyse their industry. Far from conceding our humble prayers, aggression has followed aggression, until at length we seem no longer to belong to the British Empire for our own happiness or prosperity, our freedom or the honour of the British Crown or people, but solely for the purpose of fattening a horde of useless officials, who not content with enjoying salaries enormously disproportioned to the duties of their offices, and to the resources of the country, have combined as a faction, united by private interest alone, to oppose all reforms in the Province, and to uphold the iniquities of a Government inimical to the rights and liberties of this colony.

Notwithstanding the universally admitted justice of our demands, and the wisdom and prudence of remedying our complaints, we still endure the misery of an irresponsible Executive, directed by an ignorant and hypocritical Chief; our Judges, dependent for the tenure of their office on the mere will and pleasure of the Crown, for the most part the violent partisans of a corrupt administration, have become more completely the tools and mercenaries of the Executive, by accepting the wages of their servility, in gross violation of every principle of Judicial independence, from foreign authority, without the intervention of the people to whom, through their Representatives, belongs the sole right of voting the salaries of their public servants; the office-holders of the Province devour our revenues, in salaries so extravagant as to deprive us of the funds requisite for the general improvement of the Country, whereby our public works are arrested, and the navigation of our rivers obstructed; a Legislative Council appointed by men resident three thousand miles from this country, and systematically composed so as to thwart and oppose the efforts of our freely-chosen Representatives in all measures for the promotion of the public good, after continuing unchanged during the present administration, thereby depriving the country of the advantages of domestic legislation, has at length been modified in a manner insulting to all classes of society, disgraceful to public morality, and to the annihilation of the respect and confidence of all parties in that branch of the Legislature, by the introduction of men for the most part notorious only for their incapacity, and remarkable alone for their political insignificance, thus making evident, even to demonstration, to all, whatever may be their preconceived ideas, the propriety and urgent necessity of introducing the principle of election into that body, as the only method of enabling the Provincial Legislature to proceed beneficially to the despatch of public business.

Our municipalities are utterly destroyed; the country parts of the Province, as a disgraceful exception to the other parts of this Continent, are totally deprived of all power of regulating, in a corporate capacity, their local affairs, through freely elected Parish and Township Officers; the rising generation is deprived of the blessings of education, the primary schools, which provided for the instruction of 40,000 children, having been shut up by the Legislative Council, a body hostile to the progress of useful knowledge, and instigated to this act by an Executive inimical to the spread of general information among the people—the Jesuits' College founded and endowed by the provident government which colonized this Province for the encouragement and dissemination of learning and the sciences therein, has, with a barbarism unworthy the rulers of a civilized state, disgraceful to the enlightened age in which we live,... been converted into, and is still retained, as a barrack for soldiery, whilst the funds and property devoted to the support of this and similar institutions have been, and continue to be, squandered and maladministered for the advantage of the favourites, creatures and tools of the Government; our citizens are deprived of the benefits of impartially chosen juries, and are arbitrarily persecuted by Crown officers, who to suit the purposes of the vindictive Government of which they are the creatures, have revived proceedings of an obsolete character, precedents for which are to be found only in the darkest pages of British history. Thus our Judiciary being sullied by combined conspiracies of a wicked Executive, slavish Judges, partizan Law Officers, and political Sheriffs, the innocent and patriotic are exposed to be sacrificed, whilst the enemies of the country, and the violators of all law, are protected and patronized, according as it may please the administration to crush and destroy; to save and protect. Our commerce and domestic industry are paralysed; our public lands alienated, at a nominal price, to a company of speculators, strangers to the country, or bestowed upon insolent favourites, as a reward for their sycophancy; our money is extorted from us without our consent, by taxes unconstitutionally imposed by a foreign Parliament, to be afterwards converted into an instrument of our degradation by being distributed among a howling herd of officials, against our will, without our participation, and in violation of all principles of constitutional law.

In the midst of their honest and unwearied efforts to procure a redress of the foregoing grievances, our fellow citizens have been insolently called on to give an account of their public conduct, for which they were responsible to no individual, least of all to the person whom chance or ministerial patronage may place for a season at the head of our Provincial Government. They have been harassed and annoyed by dismissals from offices of mere honour, held for the benefit and at the request of their own immediate neighbours, because they vindicated the rights of their country, like American Freemen; and as an index of further intended aggression, armed troops are being scattered in time of profound peace throughout the country, with the presumptuous and wicked design of restraining by physical force the expression of public opinion, and of completing by violence and bloodshed our slavery and ruin, already determined upon beyond the seas.

Such an aggression as this might justify the recourse, on the part of an outraged people, to all and every means to preserve the last of their insulted privileges—the right to complain. But, thanks to the blindness of the aggressors, the wickedness of the measure will be providentially neutralized by its folly. The regiments about to be quartered among us are composed of men sprung from, and educated with, the Democracy of their country. They, for the most part, entered on their present profession, not from choice, but because they could not find any other employment in their native land. Instead of being stimulated to good conduct by the hope of promotion, too poorly paid, they are exposed to every sort of petty tyranny, and if a murmur escape their lips, they are subjected, like the bonded slave, to the ignoble punishment of the lash. [Contrast] this hard fate with the freedom, content, employment and high wages to be obtained in the United States....

The long and heavy chain of abuses and oppressions under which we suffer, and to which every year has only added a more galling link, proves that our history is but a recapitulation of what other Colonies have endured before us. Our grievances are but a second edition of their grievances. Our petitions for relief are the same. Like theirs, they have been treated with scorn and contempt, and have brought down upon the petitioners but additional outrage and persecution. Thus the experience of the past demonstrates the folly of expecting justice from European authorities.

Dark, however, and unpromising as may be the present prospects of this our beloved country, we are encouraged by the public virtues of our fellow citizens to hope that the day of our regeneration is not far distant. Domestic manufactures are springing up amongst us, with a rapidity to cheer us in the

contest. The impulse given but a few short months ago by the example of generous and patriotic minds, of wearing domestic cloths, has been generally followed,
and will shortly be universally adopted. The determination not to consume duty-
paying merchandise, and to encourage Free Trade with our neighbours, matters
of vital importance, is daily becoming more general, resolute and effective. The
people are everywhere being duly impressed with the conviction that the sacrifices to be made must bear some proportion to the glorious object to be achieved,
and that personal inconvenience for the good cause must therefore be not only
freely, but readily, endured.

Fellow-countrymen! Brothers in affliction! Ye, whatsoever be your origin,
language or religion, to whom Equal Laws and the Rights of Man are dear;
whose hearts have throbbed with indignation whilst witnessing the innumerable
insults to which your common country has been exposed, and who have often
been justly alarmed whilst pondering over the sombre futurity [being prepared]
by misgovernment and corruption for this Province and for your posterity; in
the name of that country, and of the rising generation, now having no hope but
in you, we call upon you to assume, by systematic organization in your several
Townships and Parishes, that position which can alone procure respect for yourselves and your demands. Let Committees of Vigilance be at once put in *active*
operation throughout your respective neighbourhoods. Withdrawing all confidence from the present administration, and from such as will be so base as to
accept office under it, forthwith assemble in your Parishes and elect Pacificator
Magistrates, after the example of your brother Reformers of the County of Two
Mountains, in order to protect the people at once from useless and improvident
expense, and from the vengeance of their enemies. Our Young Men, the hope of
the country, should everywhere organize themselves, after the plan of their brothers, 'The Sons of Liberty' in Montreal, in order that they may be prepared to act
with promptitude and effect as circumstances may require; and the brave Mili-
tiamen, who by their blood and valour have twice preserved this country for
ungrateful rulers, should at once associate together, under officers of their own
choice, for the security of good order and the protection of life and property in
their respective localities. Thus prepared, Colonial Liberty may haply be yet
preserved.

In this hope, and depending, for a disenthralment from the misrule under
which we now groan, on the Providence of God, whose blessing on our disinterested labours we humbly implore; relying on the love of liberty which the free air
and impregnable fastnesses of America should inspire in the hearts of the People
at large, and upon the sympathy of our Democratic neighbours who in the

establishment of arbitrary rule on their borders, wisely and clearly [will foresee] the uprearing of a system which might be made a precedent and instrument for the introduction of the same arbitrary rule into other parts of the American Continent, and who can never consent that the principles for which they successfully struggled in the Eighteenth, shall, in our persons, be trampled in the dust in the Nineteenth century, We, the Delegates of the Confederated Counties of Richelieu, St Hyacinthe, Rouville, L'Acadie, Chambly and Verchères, hereby publicly register the solemn and determined resolution of the People whom we represent, to carry into effect, with the least delay possible, the preceding recommendations, and never to cease their patriotic exertions until the various grievances of which they now complain shall have been redressed; and We hereby invite our fellow-citizens throughout the Province to unite their efforts to ours to procure a good, cheap and responsible system of government for their common country.

Signed for, and on behalf of, the Confederation of the Six Counties, this 24th day of October, 1837.

W.F.D. Nelson, President
J.T. Drolet,
F.C. Duvert, Vice Presidents
A. Girod,
J.P. Boucher-Belleville, Secretaries

## 4. Robert Nelson, "Declaration of Independence," February 22, 1838.

DECLARATION

In view of the fact that the formal treaty signed between the People of Upper and Lower Canada ... has been constantly infringed by the British government ... and in view of the fact that we no longer wish to suffer the repeated infringements of our most cherished rights or to patiently endure the numerous and recent insults and acts of cruelty perpetrated by the government of Lower Canada, we, in the name of the people of Lower Canada, worshipping the decree of divine providence that entitles us to overthrow a government that has ignored the purpose and intent of its creation, and to choose the most suitable form of government to establish justice ... and guarantee to us and our descendants the benefits of civil and religious Freedom,

SOLEMNLY DECLARE:

1. That as of today, the People of Lower Canada are ABSOLVED from any allegiance to Great Britain, and that any political link between that power and Lower Canada CEASES from this day forward.

2. That Lower Canada must take the form of a REPUBLICAN government and now declare itself, de facto, a REPUBLIC.

3. That under the free Government of Lower Canada, all citizens will have the same rights; the natives will cease to be subject to any civil disqualification whatsoever, and will enjoy the same rights as those of other citizens of the State of Lower Canada.

4. That the union of Church and State is declared abolished in its entirety, and each person has the right to practise freely the religion and faith dictated by his conscience.

5. That Feudal or Seigneurial Tenure is, de facto, abolished, as if it had never existed in this country.

6. That all persons bearing or who will bear arms, or will provide assistance to the Canadien People in their fight for emancipation are released from all debts and obligations real or assumed, to the seigneurs, for arrears by virtue of the formerly existing Seigneurial Rights.

7. That the "Customary Jointure" is henceforth wholly abolished and banned.

8. That imprisonment for debts will no longer exist, except in the case of obvious fraud as will be specified in an Act of the Legislature of Lower Canada for that purpose.

9. That the death penalty will be pronounced in cases of murder only, and not otherwise.

10. That every Mortgage on Real Estate shall be specific, and to be valid, shall be registered with the Offices set up for that purpose by an Act of the Legislature of Lower Canada.

11. That there will be full and complete freedom of the Press on all public matters and affairs.

12. That trial by JURY is guaranteed to the People of the State, to the most liberal extent in criminal trials, and in civil affairs to a total sum to be established by the Legislature of the State of Lower Canada.

13. That as a necessity and a duty of the Government to the People, universal public education will be put in place and particularly encouraged, as soon as circumstances will allow.

14. That to ensure elective frankness and freedom, all elections will be conducted by means of a BALLOT.

15. That as soon as circumstances will allow, the People will choose Delegates according to the current division of the country into Cities, Towns, and Counties, who will constitute a Convention, or Legislative Body, to found and establish a Constitution, according to the country's needs, and in con-

formance with the clauses of this Declaration, subject to modification in accordance with the People's will.

16. That every male person over the age of twenty will have the right to vote under the conditions as set out above, for the election of the aforementioned Delegates.

17. That all the Lands known as Crown Lands, as well as those called clergy reserves, and those that are nominally in the possession of a certain company of speculators in England, called the "British American Land Company," become by right, the property of the State of Canada, save for such portions of the said lands as may be in the possession of farmers, who hold them in good faith, for whom we guarantee title in virtue of a law that will be passed to legalize the possession of such plots of land, located in the "Townships" which are now under cultivation.

18. That the French and English languages will be used in all public matters.

AND to support THIS DECLARATION, and the success of the Patriotic cause, which we uphold, WE, confident of the Almighty's protection and of the justice of our actions, hereby mutually and solemnly pledge, one to the other, our life, our fortunes and our most sacred honour. By Order of the Provisional Government ...

## 5. Lord Durham, "To Lord Glenelg," August 9, 1838, in *Imperial Blue Books Relating to Canada,* 1839.

My Lord,

The first point to which I would draw your attention, being one with which all others are more or less connected, is the existence of a most bitter animosity between the Canadians and the British, not as two parties holding different opinions and seeking different objects in respect to Government but as different races engaged in a national contest.

This hatred of races is not publicly avowed on either side: on the contrary, both sides profess to be moved by any other feelings than such as belong to difference of origin.... If the difference between the two classes were one of party or principles only, we should find on each side a mixture of persons of both races, whereas the truth is that, with exceptions which tend to prove the rule, all the British are on one side, and all the Canadians are on the other. What may be the immediate subject of dispute seems to be of no consequence; so surely as there is a dispute on any subject, the great bulk of the Canadians and the great bulk of the British appear ranged against each other. In the next place, the mutual dislike of the two classes extends beyond politics into social life, where, with some trifling exceptions again, all intercourse is confined to persons of the same origin. Grown-up persons of a different origin seldom or never meet in private society; and even the children, when they quarrel, divide themselves into French and English like their parents. In the schools and the streets of Montreal, the real capital of the province, this is commonly the case. The station in life, moreover, of an individual of either race seems to have no influence on his real disposition towards the other race; high and low, rich and poor, on both sides— the merchant and the porter, the seigneur and the habitant—though they use different language to express themselves; yet exhibit the very same feeling of national jealousy and hatred. Such a sentiment is naturally evinced rather by trifles than by acts of intrinsic importance. There has been no solemn or formal declaration of national hostility, but not a day nor scarcely an hour passes without some petty insult, some provoking language, or even some serious mutual affront, occurring between persons of British and French descent. Lastly, it appears, upon a careful review of the political struggle between those who have termed themselves the loyal party and the popular party, that the subject of dissension has been, not the connexion with England, nor the form of the constitution, nor any of the practical abuses which have affected all classes of the people, but simply such institutions, laws, and customs as are of French origin, which the British have sought to overthrow and the Canadians have struggled to preserve, each class assuming false designations and fighting under false colours— the British professing exclusive loyalty to the Crown of England, and the Canadians pretending to the character of reformers. Nay, I am inclined to think that the true principles and ultimate objects of both parties, taken apart from the question of race, are exactly the reverse of what each of them professes, or, in other words, that the British (always excluding the body of officials) are really desirous of a more responsible Government, while the Canadians would prefer the present form of Government, or even one of a less democratic character.... Such a contradiction between the real and avowed principles of each party could not have occurred if all the people had been of one race, or if every other consideration had not given way to the sentiment of nationality.

This general antipathy of the Canadians towards the British, and of the British towards the Canadians appears to have been, as it were, provided for at the conquest of the province, and by subsequent measures of the British Government. If Lower Canada had been isolated from other colonies, and so well peopled as to leave little room for emigration from Britain, it might have been right at the conquest to engage for the preservation of French institutions, for the existence of a "Nation Canadienne"; but, considering how certain it was that, sooner or later, the British race would predominate in the country, that engagement seems to have been most unwise. It insured such a strife as has actually taken place; for, notwithstanding the division of Canada into two provinces, for the purpose of isolating the French, the British already predominate in French Canada, not numerically of course, but by means of their superior energy and wealth, and their natural relationship to the powers of Government.

It was long before the Canadians perceived that their nationality was in the course of being over-ridden by a British nationality. When the Constitutional Act bestowed on them a representative system, they were so little conversant with its nature, and so blind to the probable results of British emigration, that they described the constitution as a "machine Anglaise pour nous taxer," and elected to the House of Assembly almost a majority of Englishmen. But with the progress of British intrusion they at length discovered, not only the uses of a representative system, but also that their nationality was in danger; and I have no hesitation in asserting that of late years they have used the representative system for the single purpose of maintaining their nationality against the progressive intrusion of the British race. They have found the British pressing upon them at every turn, in the possession of land, in commerce, in the retail trade, in all kinds of industrious enterprize, in religion, in the whole administration of government, and though they are a stagnant people, easily satisfied and disinclined to exertion, they have naturally resisted an invasion which was so offensive to their national pride.

The British, on the other hand, impeded in the pursuit of all their objects, partly by the ancient and barbarous civil law of the country, and partly by the systematic opposition of the Canadians to the progress of British enterprize, have naturally sought to remove those impediments, and to conquer, without much regard to the means employed, that very mischievous opposition. The actual result should have seemed inevitable. The struggle between the two races, conducted as long as possible according to the forms of the constitution, became too violent to be kept within those bounds. In order to preserve some sort of government, the public revenue was disposed of against the will of the Canadian people represented by their Assembly. The consequent rebellion, although precipitated by the British from an instinctive sense of the danger of allowing the Canadians full time for preparation, could not, perhaps, have been avoided; and the sentiment of national hostility has been aggravated to the uttermost, on both sides, by that excessive inflammation of the passions which always attends upon bloodshed for such a cause, and still more by this unusual circumstance that the victorious minority suffered extreme fear at the beginning of the contest, and that the now subdued majority had been led to hope everything from an appeal to force.

Supposing my view of that subject to be correct, your Lordship will readily understand that the bulk of the Canadian people are as disaffected as ever, and that the British part of the population regard the Canadians with vindictive jealousy. The Imperial Government is distrusted by both parties; by the Canadians because they fear, or rather expect in gloomy silence, that advantage will be taken of their late rebellion to remove the very causes of dissension, by giving a British character to the institutions and laws of the province, so that there shall no longer be any serious impediment to British colonization and enterprize; and by the British, on the other hand, because they doubt whether the Imperial Government will ever sufficiently understand the state of parties here, to approve of the great changes which must inevitably take place, if another period of legislative strife, and perhaps another rebellion, are to be averted.

And here I must notice a fact of great importance. The more discerning of the Canadians are perfectly aware that if the authority of the United States should ever extend to this country, whether by means of war or of a peaceful union, the peculiar institutions, and even the language, of French Canada would be extinguished as soon as possible, yet are they willing, with the exception perhaps of a considerable portion of the clergy, to incur the loss of all that they have held most dear, in order to gratify the sentiment of vengeance that has now got possession of them. I would not exaggerate the amount of the sacrifice that they are willing to make for the sake of revenge....

But be this as it may, whether they are moved by a sentiment of mere vengeance, or by revenge mixed with despair, I am well convinced that an American invasion of this province would be highly acceptable to most of them.

That this should be the case is really not surprising when one discovers how all the powers of Government have been neglected and abused for many years past in this colony. Not to go further back than the commencement of serious differences between the Canadians and British as such; since, when the two branches of the legislature have neglected their proper functions to pursue the contest between races, a long time has passed without anything like beneficial legislation, and not a few of the many evils resulting from this perversion of legislative powers have, by a very natural mistake, been attributed to neglect and corruption in the Executive. At the same time it must be confessed, that the Executive has been both neglectful and corrupt. I need not remind your

Lordship of those flagrant instances in which the Imperial Government has been led to interfere for the correction of administrative abuses, nor is this a fit occasion for entering on that subject in detail; but I am bound to add, that the Government of this province, including the administration of justice, has not obtained the respect of the people, and that, according to all my information, there has been ample ground for the distrust and suspicion with which authority is regarded.

This leads to another feature in the disposition of that portion of the British inhabitants which may be termed "independent." Their main object, as I have before explained, has been to remove the obstacles which the ignorance, the apathy, and the ancient prejudices of the Canadians opposed to the progress of British industry and enterprize; to substitute, in short, for Canadian institutions, laws and practices, others of a British character. In this pursuit they have necessarily disregarded the implied, not to say precise, engagement of England to respect the peculiar institutions of French Canada. But the Imperial Government, on the contrary, never quite forgetting that ancient pledge, has rather extended its protection to the Canadians than espoused the cause of the British settlers. It were to be wished, perhaps, that this policy had been consistently pursued from the beginning, as in that case a British community might not have grown up here with feelings, wants, and a degree of power which make it simply impossible to pursue such a policy now. But it has not been consistently pursued. By a variety of measures, and especially by promoting emigration to this colony, the Imperial Government have really undermined the Canadian nationality which they perhaps intended to preserve. A similar contradiction may be observed in their treatment of the national struggle which has ended in civil war. Never taking a decided part with either section in the colony, they have wavered between them, now favouring the one and then the other, but neither decidedly, and finally displeasing both sections in about the same degree. Under such a system, if it may be called one, no governor could have pursued a consistent course, or have attached either the Canadians or the British to the Imperial Government....

## 6. Lord Durham, "Report on the Affairs of British North America," 1840.

... A plan by which it is proposed to ensure the tranquil government of Lower Canada, must include in itself the means of putting an end to the agitation of national disputes in the legislature, by settling, at once and for ever, the national character of the Province. I entertain no doubts as to the national character which must be given to Lower Canada; it must be that of the British Empire; that of the majority of the population of British America; that of the great race which must, in the lapse of no long period of time, be predominant over the whole North American Continent. Without effecting the change so rapidly or so roughly as to shock the feelings and trample on the welfare of the existing generation, it must henceforth be the first and steady purpose of the British Government to establish an English population, with English laws and language, in this Province, and to trust its government to none but a decidedly English Legislature.

It may be said that this is a hard measure to a conquered people; that the French were originally the whole, and still are the bulk of the population of Lower Canada; that the English are new comers, who have no right to demand the extinction of the nationality of a people, among whom commercial enterprize has drawn them. It may be said, that, if the French are not so civilized, so energetic, or so money-making a race as that by which they are surrounded, they are an amiable, a virtuous, and a contented people, possessing all the essentials of material comfort, and not to be despised or ill-used, because they seek to enjoy what they have, without emulating the spirit of accumulation, which influences their neighbours. Their nationality is, after all, an inheritance; and they must be not too severely punished, because they have dreamed of maintaining on the distant banks of the St. Lawrence, and transmitting to their posterity, the language, the manners, and the institutions of that great nation, that for two centuries gave the tone of thought to the European Continent. If the disputes of the two races are irreconcileable, it may be urged that justice demands that the minority should be compelled to acquiesce in the supremacy of the ancient and most numerous occupants of the Province, and not pretend to force their own institutions and customs on the majority.

But before deciding which of the two races is now to be placed in the ascendant, it is but prudent to inquire which of them must ultimately prevail; for it is not wise to establish to-day that which must, after a hard struggle, be reversed to-morrow. The pretensions of the French Canadians to the exclusive possession of Lower Canada, would debar the yet larger English population of Upper Canada and the Townships from access to the great natural channel of that trade which they alone have created, and now carry on. The possession of the mouth of the St. Lawrence concerns not only those who happen to have made their settlements along the narrow line which borders it, but all who now dwell or will hereafter dwell, in the great basin of that river. For we must not look to the present alone. The question is, by what race is it likely that the wilderness which now covers the rich and ample regions surrounding the comparatively small and contracted districts in which the French Canadians are located, is eventually to be converted into a settled and flourishing country? If this is to be done in the British dominions, as in the rest of North America, by some speedier process than the ordinary growth of population, it must be by immigration from the English Isles, or from the United States,—the countries which supply the only settlers that have entered, or will enter, the Canadas in any large numbers. This immigration can neither be debarred from a passage through Lower Canada, nor even be prevented from settling in that Province. The whole interior of the British dominions must ere long, be filled with an English population, every year rapidly increasing its numerical superiority over the French. Is it just that the prosperity of this great majority, and of this vast tract of country, should be for ever, or even for a while, impeded by the artificial bar which the backward laws and civilization of a part, and a part only, of Lower Canada, would place between them and the ocean? Is it to be supposed that such an English population will ever submit to such a sacrifice of its interests?

I must not, however, assume it to be possible that the English Government shall adopt the course of placing or allowing any check to the influx of English immigration into Lower Canada, or any impediment to the profitable employment of that English capital which is already vested therein. The English have already in their hands the majority of the larger masses of property in the country; they have the decided superiority of intelligence on their side; they have the certainty that colonization must swell their numbers to a majority; and they belong to the race which wields the Imperial Government, and predominates on the American Continent. If we now leave them in a minority, they will never abandon the assurance of being a majority hereafter, and never cease to continue the present contest with all the fierceness with which it now rages. In such a contest they will rely on the sympathy of their countrymen at home; and if that is denied them, they feel very confident of being able to awaken the sympathy of their neighbours of kindred origin. They feel that if the British Government intends to maintain its hold of the Canadas, it can rely on the English population alone; that if it abandons its colonial possessions, they must become a portion of that great Union which will speedily send forth its swarms of settlers, and, by force of numbers and activity, quickly master every other race. The French Canadians, on the other hand, are but the remains of an ancient colonization, and are and ever must be isolated in the midst of an Anglo-Saxon world. Whatever may happen, whatever government shall be established over them, British or

American, they can see no hope for their nationality. They can only sever themselves from the British Empire by waiting till some general cause of dissatisfaction alienates them, together with the surrounding colonies, and leaves them part of an English confederacy; or, if they are able, by effecting a separation singly, and so either merging in the American Union, or keeping up for a few years a wretched semblance of feeble independence, which would expose them more than ever to the intrusion of the surrounding population. I am far from wishing to encourage indiscriminately these pretensions to superiority on the part of any particular race; but while the greater part of every portion of the American Continent is still uncleared and unoccupied, and while the English exhibit such constant and marked activity in colonization, so long will it be idle to imagine that there is any portion of that Continent into which that race will not penetrate, or in which, when it has penetrated, it will not predominate. It is but a question of time and mode; it is but to determine whether the small number of French who now inhabit Lower Canada shall be made English under a Government which can protect them, or whether the process shall be delayed until a much larger number shall have to undergo, at the rude hands of its uncontrolled rivals, the extinction of a nationality strengthened and embittered by continuance.

And is this French Canadian nationality one which, for the good merely of that people, we ought to strive to perpetuate, even if it were possible? I know of no national distinctions marking and continuing a more hopeless inferiority. The language, the laws, the character of the North American Continent are English; and every race but the English (I apply this to all who speak the English language) appears there in a condition of inferiority. It is to elevate them from that inferiority that I desire to give to the Canadians our English character. I desire it for the sake of the educated classes, whom the distinction of language and manners keeps apart from the great Empire to which they belong. At the best, the fate of the educated and aspiring colonist is, at present, one of little hope, and little activity; but the French Canadian is cast still further into the shade, by a language and habits foreign to those of the Imperial Government. A spirit of exclusion has closed the higher professions on the educated classes of the French Canadians, more, perhaps, than was absolutely necessary; but it is impossible for the utmost liberality on the part of the British Government to give an equal position in the general competition of its vast population to those who speak a foreign language. I desire the amalgamation still more for the sake of the humbler classes. Their present state of rude and equal plenty is fast deteriorating under the pressure of population in the narrow limits to which they are confined. If they attempt to better their condition, by extending themselves over the neighbouring country, they will necessarily get more and more mingled with an English population: if they prefer remaining stationary, the greater part of them must be labourers in the employ of English capitalists. In either case it would appear, that the great mass of the French Canadians are doomed, in some measure, to occupy an inferior position, and to be dependent on the English for employment. The evils of poverty and dependence would merely be aggravated in a ten-fold degree, by a spirit of jealous and resentful nationality, which should separate the working class of the community from the possessors of wealth and the employers of labour....

There can hardly be conceived a nationality more destitute of all that can invigorate and elevate a people, than that which is exhibited by the descendants of the French in Lower Canada, owing to their retaining their peculiar language and manners. They are a people with no history, and no literature. The literature of England is written in a language which is not theirs; and the only literature which their language renders familiar to them, is that of a nation from which they have been separated by eighty years of a foreign rule, and still more by those changes which the Revolution and its consequences have wrought in the whole political, moral and social state of France. Yet it is on a people whom recent history, manners and modes of thought, so entirely separate from them, that the French Canadians are wholly dependent for almost all the instruction and amusement derived from books: it is on this essentially foreign literature, which is conversant about events, opinions and habits of life, perfectly strange and unintelligible to them, that they are compelled to be dependent. Their newspapers are mostly written by natives of France, who have either come to try their fortunes in the Province, or been brought into it by the party leaders, in order to supply the dearth of literary talent available for the political press. In the same way their nationality operates to deprive them of the enjoyments and civilizing influence of the arts. Though descended from the people in the world that most generally love, and have most successfully cultivated the drama—though living on a continent, in which almost every town, great or small, has an English theatre, the French population of Lower Canada, cut off from every people that speaks its own language, can support no national stage.

In these circumstances, I should be indeed surprised if the more reflecting part of the French Canadians entertained at present any hope of continuing to preserve their nationality. Much as they struggle against it, it is obvious that the process of assimilation to English habits is already commencing. The English language is gaining ground, as the language of the rich and of the employers of labour naturally will. It appeared by some of the few returns, which had been received by the Commissioner of the Inquiry into the state of Education, that there are about ten times the number of French children in Quebec learning English, as compared with the English children who learn French. A considerable time must, of course, elapse before the change of a language can spread over a whole people; and justice and policy alike require, that while the people continue to use the French language, their Government should take no such means to force the English language upon them as would, in fact, deprive the great mass of the community of the protection of the laws. But, I repeat that the alteration of the character of the Province ought to be immediately entered on, and firmly, though cautiously, followed up; that in any plan, which may be adopted for the future management of Lower Canada, the first object ought to be that of making it an English Province; and that, with this end in view, the ascendancy should never again be placed in any hands but those of an English population. Indeed, at the present moment this is obviously necessary: in the state of mind in which I have described the French Canadian population, as not only now being, but as likely for a long while to remain, the trusting them with an entire control over this Province, would be, in fact, only facilitating a rebellion. Lower Canada must be governed now, as it must be hereafter, by an English population: and thus the policy, which the necessities of the moment force on us, is in accordance with that suggested by a comprehensive view of the future and permanent improvement of the Province....

But the period of gradual transition is past in Lower Canada. In the present state of feeling among the French population, I cannot doubt that any power which they might possess would be used against the policy and the very existence of any form of British government. I cannot doubt that any French Assembly that shall again meet in Lower Canada will use whatever power, be it more or less limited, it may have, to obstruct the Government, and undo whatever has been done by it ... nor co-operation to be expected from a legislature, of which the majority shall represent its French inhabitants. I believe that tranquillity can only be restored by subjecting the Province to the vigorous rule of an English majority; and that the only efficacious government would be that formed by a legislative union.

If the population of Upper Canada is rightly estimated at 400,000, the English inhabitants of Lower Canada at 150,000, and the French at 450,000, the union of the two Provinces would not only give a clear English majority, but one which would be increased every year by the influence of English emigration; and I have little doubt that the French, when once placed, by the legitimate course of events and the working of natural causes, in a minority, would abandon their vain hopes of nationality. I do not mean that they would immediately give up their present animosities, or instantly renounce the hope of attaining their end by violent means. But the experience of the two Unions in the British Isles may teach us how effectually the strong arm of a popular legislature would compel the obedience of the refractory population; and the hopelessness of success would gradually subdue the existing animosities, and incline the French Canadian population to acquiesce in their new state of political existence.

## 7. Louis-Joseph Papineau, "The Story of Canada's Insurrection in Refutation of Lord Durham's Report," *La Revue*, 1839.

... Well! I challenge the English government to contradict me, when I affirm that none amongst us had prepared for, wanted, or even foreseen, armed resistance. But the English government was resolved to rob the Province of its revenue, its representative system; it was resolved to condemn some of us to death, others to exile; and it was with that objective that it proposed to proclaim martial law, and bring citizens to judgment via court-martial for acts that, only weeks earlier, it had acknowledged gave no grounds for indictment, basing the necessity of establishing military tribunals on the impossibility of obtaining death warrants from the civil courts! Yes, once again, the executive power has implemented, against innocent men, misunderstanding the home country's interest, inhumane schemes it had recognized it had no right to indulge in; there is where the provocation came from.

Consequently, among the actors of this bloody drama, not one repents of having attempted resistance; and among their citizens, not one in a thousand reproaches them for having done so. Except, that in every heart there is deep sorrow that this resistance was unsuccessful, and at the same time great hope that it will be resumed and will prevail.

This is not to say that the insurrection was unjustified, but we had resolved not to resort to such actions yet. This is what our confiscated papers made known to a slanderous government intent on persecution.

And when I make this statement, it is for the sole purpose of restoring the historical truth and not in the least to repudiate the moral responsibility of a government in rebellion against the enshrined rights of human beings, in rebellion also against, as the jurisconsults of Great Britain say, "the inalienable birthright of English subjects," a mocking expression with regard to the colonies and devised to provide Spartan pleasures to the English aristocracy, such as that of giving chase to the islets of Ireland, the Canadas, Jamaica, and every one of their foreign possessions, any time the serfs who inhabit them decide they no longer wish to be ruthlessly exploited at will.

... But such is the impiety of English tyranny that, even shielded from its poisonous influence and its choking grip, the historian of the Canadas cannot speak freely during the military occupation of those pillaged, burnt, and decimated provinces. For the government has indulged in such orgies there that it is drunk on them. Tell it of its crimes: far from getting out of them, it plunges in, only surfacing to go straight from torpor to drunken frenzy, to strike even harder at the country it hates and in which it is hated everywhere. Tell it the names of men loyal to their country: you are one of those denouncers filling up the dungeons, one of those savage spectators refusing clemency so that Christians might be thrown to the beasts.

So one can only cite facts and public documents, familiar in America, unknown, or what is worse, distorted, in Europe. For the English government has taken care to place under lock and key, along with the publishers and printers, all the type and printing presses that were not for sale; it has bought up everything it has not locked away; and undoubtedly in order to give advice to the imperial parliament on Canada's future governance so as to inform English public opinion, and, in this way, enlighten the world as to the virtues of the governors and the ingratitude of the governed, it reshaped those raw materials, men, and typefaces bought in laid-out pages of contemporary history. The measures known, the aim is revealed. By way of the English press, you have learned nothing but official lies.

It is no longer up to me to stand as the English government's accuser, as it has been my duty to do through thirty years of public life. That government has admitted its guilt in the hundred-and-twenty-page folio just published by Lord Durham. The systematic corruption, the shameful misappropriation of public funds, the hostility toward the people, the appalling examples of irresponsibility on the part of government officials, the monopolization of the public domain, nothing is missing from this picture, so hideous that its counterpart could only be found in the history of another English possession, Ireland.

And yet, the author has consistently toned down his accusatory statements against the authority whose representative he is, and of which he wishes to retain his leaden sceptre over the colonies by such pitiful means that he has lost his reputation as a statesman.

Desirous of proving that only his favourite race, the Saxon race, is worthy of being in command, Lord Durham has untruthfully painted it fair, and he has darkened with the blackest colours the false portrait he has drawn of French Canadians. But despite this shameful bias, I confidently send impartial readers back to that peculiar report, fully convinced that they will draw this conclusion from it, that the Canadiens can expect no justice from England; that for them, submission would be a stain and a death warrant, and independence, on the contrary, an assumption of revival and life. More than that, it would be a rehabilitation of the French name, terribly compromised in America by the shame of the Treaty of Paris of 1763, by the mass banishment of more than twenty thousand Acadians driven from their homes, and last, by the lot of six hundred thousand Canadiens governed for the past eighty years with unremitting injustice, decimated today, condemned tomorrow to political inferiority, out of hatred of their French origins.

Right in what it says when it blames the government, wrong in what it says when it blames the people....

... Adam Thom was his table companion and counsellor.

This man, who was nothing but an impassioned partisan, of mediocre talent, always worked up over the abuse of strong liquor when he dealt with English policy, became a madman when he spoke of French Canadians. Fired by the thirst for blood, his hatred then knew no bounds. Over a number of years, affronts against the nation as a whole and repeated calls for the assassination of the most popular representatives daily sullied the pages of his newspaper; he figured, as the leader of a gang, in a number of riots that broke out in Montreal in the past four years; riots led by English magistrates against those citizens who, in elections or in the Chamber of Deputies, had come into conflict with the executive power. Were those acts of violence ever curbed? Were their perpetrators hunted down even once? No. Troops at the magistrates' disposal bathed our villages in blood; they desecrated the court of justice so as to bar victims' relatives from exercising their sacred right to seek punishment for the crime in the courts, and they took over the proceedings so as to shield the guilty, with simulated trials, from any sentences.

Adam Thom had set up the Doric Club, an armed company with the avowed aim of doing away with French Canadians should the government ever grant the latter the object of their incessant demands: an elected legislative council. Five months before his promotion as Lord Durham's advisor, and while prisons were filling up with Canadiens, he was writing: "Punishing the leaders, however agreeable it might be to the English inhabitants, would not make as deep or as useful an impression on the minds of the people as would the sight of foreign farmers placed on the lands of every agitator in every parish. The sight of widows and children parading their misery before the expensive homes of which they were dispossessed, would be most effective. There must be no wavering in carrying out this measure. Special commissioners must be appointed immediately and charged with the task of bringing to conclusion the trial of that batch of traitors in prison. It would be ludicrous to fatten up this lot all winter only to lead them to the gallows later on."...

Against the disturbances of which Lord Durham has rolled out the endless list, against the more numerous, more serious disturbances that he has not even mentioned, what barrier does he mean to erect? He reports on the good that freedom has brought to the independent Americans, the bad that despotism has brought to the English Americans; he shows how prolonging England's governance of Canada is impossible, and he concludes that this state of affairs must be maintained. What disastrous inconsistency! ...

Yet it is from these alleged grievances that comes the great, the only measure of legislative reform that Lord Durham recommends: the assimilation of the French population by the English population by means of a union of the two Canadas....

The Saxon race is far better suited to governing than could you yourselves be. Upper Canada is crippled by debts, you have none. So! we are going to create one big and beautiful province that will no longer owe anything, after full and empty have been mixed together. You will then have a viceroy, and to her title of Queen of the United Kingdom of Great Britain and Ireland, our gracious sovereign will add: and of British North America. Renounce a narrow nationality. Don a larger and more noble one. Give up your Canadien name and take on that of British North Americans!

Alas! if our name, erased by an act of parliament, was too short, is not the one replacing it too long? and is not that of the independent Americans of sounder proportions?

An historical account, impartial and succinct, of the events that have taken place in my country over the past two years will prompt the conviction in every mind that it is not English statutes that will determine the future of Canada; but that this future is written in the declaration of the rights of man and in the political constitution that our good, wise, and contented neighbours, the independent Americans, have given themselves....

## Readings

Azjenstat, J. *The Political Thought of Lord Durham.* Kingston and Montreal: McGill-Queen's University Press, 1988.

Bernard, J-P. *Les Rebellions de 1837–1838. Les Patriotes dans la Memoire Collective et chez les Historiens.* Montreal: Boreal Express, 1983.

Bernard, J-P. *The Rebellions of 1837 and 1838 in Lower Canada.* Ottawa: Canadian Historical Association, 1996.

Bernier, G. and D. Salee. "Les Insurrections de 1837–1838. Remarques Critiques en Marge de l'Historiographie," *Canadian Review of Studies in Nationalism* 13, 1 (1986).

Buckner, P. *Transition to Responsible Government: British Policy in British North America, 1815 to 1850.* Westport: Greenwood Press, 1985.

Burroughs, P. *The Canadian Crisis and British Colonial Policy, 1828–1841.* Toronto: Macmillan, 1972.

Burroughs, P., ed. *The Colonial Reformers and Canada, 1830–1849.* Toronto: McClelland and Stewart, 1969.

Greer, A. *The Patriots and the People: The Rebellion of 1837 in Rural Lower Canada.* Toronto: University of Toronto Press, 1993.

Greer, A. "Rebellion Reconsidered," *Canadian Historical Review* 76, 1 (March 1995).

Kenny, S. "The Canadian Rebellions and the Limits of Historical Perspective," *Vermont History* 58, 23 (Summer 1990).

Manning, H. *The Revolt of French Canada, 1800–1835.* Toronto: Macmillan, 1962.

Martin, G. *The Durham Report and British Policy: A Critical Essay.* Cambridge: Cambridge University Press, 1972.

Monet, J. *The Last Canon Shot: A Study of French Canadian Nationalism 1837–1850.* Toronto: University of Toronto Press, 1969.

Ouellet, F. *Lower Canada 1791–1840: Social Change and Nationalism.* Trans. P. Claxton. Toronto: McClelland and Stewart, 1980.

Ouellet, F. "La Tradition Revolutionaire au Canada. A Propos de L'Historiographie des Insurrections de 1837-1838 dans le Bas-Canada," *University of Ottawa Quarterly* 55, 2 (April-June 1985).

Schull, J. *Rebellion: The Rising in French Canada.* Toronto: Macmillan, 1971.

Senior, E. *Redcoats and Patriotes: The Rebellions in Lower Canada 1873–38.* Ottawa: Canada's Wings, 1985.

Verney, J. O'Callaghan. *The Making and Unmaking of a Rebel.* Ottawa: Carleton University Press, 1994.

*Chapter Eight*

# "An Unwanted Ebullition of Commercial Rivalry": North West Company vs. Hudson's Bay Company

1. Thomas Douglas Earl of Selkirk, *The Memorial of Thomas Earl of Selkirk*, 1819.
2. William McGillivray, "To Sir G. Drummond," June 24, 1815.
3. William McGillivray, "Deposition," March 14, 1818.
4. W.B. Coltman, "Report," May 14, 1818.

## Introduction

After a brief but intense firefight, 21 corpses, some mutilated and stripped, lay where they had fallen on the hard prairie; and the grieving knot of Selkirk settlers once again prepared to flee Red River. The bloodshed know as the "Seven Oaks Massacre" had been the culmination of many factors.

By the late eighteenth century, landowners in the Scottish highlands proceeded to evict their tenants in favour of more lucrative and less labour intensive sheep herding. These highland clearances, as they were called, left thousands of destitute and rootless Scots casting around Scottish and English cities. Thomas Douglas, the Scottish Earl of Selkirk was one of those rare aristocrats who combined capitalism with humanitarianism. His plan was to obtain land in British North America, and relocate homeless Scottish paupers. This, he argued, would benefit the dispossessed, eliminate potential rabblerousers from the United Kingdom, strengthen the Britishness of the empire, and make him money. He began two such schemes, both with limited success: one on Prince Edward Island; the other in Upper Canada, before planning the third at Red River in what is now Manitoba—and for which he did not have official British government sanction.

Red River formed part of the lands chartered to the Hudson's Bay Company as part of its 1670 title. Once a major shareholder of the HBC, Selkirk convinced the company to grant him 300,417 square kilometres of land stretching along the Red River and into what is today North Dakota and Minnesota as a new colony independent of the Company, but which would in future supply the HBC with food. Selkirk would annually import 200 settlers via Hudson's Bay, despite the colony's remoteness and the fact that it lay in the heart of land used by the local Metis population and its rival North West Company. The vanguard of the first settlers arrived in 1812.

The North West Company was an amalgam of independent Montreal-based fur traders, who realized that their only hope of competing with the giant HBC was by uniting, which they did in the 1780s. The Company aggressively sought fur trading areas in the Athabasca country, beyond what they accepted as the HBC's scope, and soon developed a thriving business rivalling their arch foe. The Company's biggest single impediment was its lack of proximate access to a deep-water port for exporting furs and importing trade goods, something the HBC already had, and which it jealously guarded. North Westers compensated for this by creating a transcontinental transportation system whereby furs from the Athabasca were marketed in China and trade goods brought from Europe through Montreal and then westward.

And what of Selkirk's new colony? Could the HBC even grant him the land in the first place? Not according to the North West Company which refused to accept the HBC's monopoly over the area and, on the contrary, claimed it *de facto* as their own. Indians and Metis already lived there, many of them making pemmican for the NWC, or hired on as paddlers for the Company's cargo canoes. Furthermore, this area was geographically and strategically sensitive, acting as the sole conduit through which North West traders must travel on their annual trek.

Natives, Metis, and Montreal traders obviously looked upon Selkirk's new settlers with deep suspicion, suspecting that the Earl's real agenda was not creating a colony, but to sever the NWC's east-west transportation artery in a bid to defeat the company. Selkirk vehemently denied the charge. Distance exacerbated the problem: Montreal and London, the respective companies' headquarters, were months away at best, and their agents on the ground therefore had to take matters into their own hands, responding to evolving conditions as they saw fit.

Relations between the two groups deteriorated when the Earl's chosen governor, Miles Macdonell, issued the Pemmican Proclamation in January, 1814. It placed an embargo on exporting any food produced at Red River, the rationale being the very real danger of starvation, particularly since Macdonell expected a new group of settlers and the fledgling colony lacked the resources to feed them. This, of course, meant that pemmican would not reach the North West Company—a serious liability to both the company and to the local producers who depended on the trade. The arbitrary and perceived capriciousness of the Proclamation added fuel to the fire of the "pernicious HBC conspiracy" theorists—who hardly needed persuading in the first place. The predictable results pitted the tiny group of settlers against the Metis and Montrealers—who apparently managed to divide and conquer Selkirk's people through intimidation and by convincing them of the hopelessness of their settlement venture. They did, however, promise to ship the settlers to Upper Canada where land grants supposedly awaited. The colony disbanded in 1815 when most of Selkirk's small and disheartened band accepted the offer.

Selkirk fretted in Britain and realized he must personally take the colony's reins if it was to survive. He set out to do so in 1816, arriving at Montreal, and launching an expedition back to Red River where a few of his colonists had reestablished his colony and had even captured a number of North West Company posts. Selkirk believed justice was on his side and that the NWC's actions were indefensibly criminal. If the government of Canada would not uphold the law and arrest the Montrealers as he requested, Selkirk would do so himself, and employed a group of disbanded Swiss soldiers as his mercenary "army."

Selkirk heard of the "massacre" as he neared the North West Company's depot at Fort William on the western edge of Lake Superior. He and his "soldiers" took the law into their hands, believing they had the right to do so after Seven Oaks, and captured the fort after arresting the Montreal traders inside, including William McGillivray, the NWC's director. Selkirk then seized goods from the fort and held them as future compensation for the "massacre." Eventually he proceeded west to reclaim his Red River Colony—but not before refusing two warrants for his arrest issued by the Canadian government as a result of his unilateral actions at Fort William. What Selkirk failed to realize was the antipathy many powerfully placed eastern Canadians felt toward his adventures. He also chose to ignore the shaky legal basis of the Red River Colony's very existence. That legality was in itself a conundrum: which court had the right to establish its legitimacy? By the Canada Jurisdiction Act of 1803, the colony of Canada, not the HBC, enjoyed jurisdiction over criminal matters in the Hudson Bay Company's territory. Furthermore, the Company's land claims, particularly its expansion, remained highly contentious and legally untested. Selkirk soon found himself embroiled in a litigious battle that tarnished his image, all but bankrupted him, eventually broke his health, and contributed to his early death from tuberculosis in 1820.

The Canadian press and public figures initially vilified Selkirk as, at best, a misguided romantic out of touch with reality who descended into criminal activity when others thwarted his way. At worst, they cast him as a conniving HBC agent gunning for a rival by using innocent immigrants and taking the law into his own hands. Montreal-based North West Company executives and senior colonial staff, who did not like Selkirk, certainly pushed this interpretation, both privately and publicly. The pendulum swung over time, and by the mid-nineteenth century writers increasingly portrayed Selkirk's efforts as an idealistic and altruistic crusade to pacify and Europeanize the Canadian west in the face of opposition from "savages" and "uncivilized half-breeds." Seven Oaks, in this interpretation, became an integrally linked precursor to events of both 1870 and 1885, and later helped justify government suppression of the Natives and Metis under Louis Riel. Selkirk's image received a boost while the North Westers became the villains—especially over their actions at Seven Oaks, and despite evidence that suggests the marksmen acted on their own volition and without NWC sanction. Coltman's analysis of 1818 appears to be the most objective report on the event but was later ignored, buried beneath a mountain of mythology eulogizing Selkirk. Perhaps Coltman's ambiguous conclusions did not sit well with those later nation-builders who wished to justify subsequent exclusion of Natives and Metis from large tracts of prairie land, and who revere Selkirk as a founding father of the Canadian west. In the end, guilt for the deaths at Seven Oaks remained unproven and the Crown charged no one.

### Discussion Points

1. Was the North West Company justified in resisting the Selkirk Colony?
2. Metis celebrate Seven Oaks as a landmark in their evolution as a distinct people and object to the term "massacre." Was this really their victory against unauthorized intruders?
3. How should we commemorate this complex historical event? Can we regard Selkirk as a "founder" of Canada?

### Documents

**1. Thomas Douglas Earl of Selkirk, *The Memorial of Thomas Earl of Selkirk*, 1819.**

...That in the year 1811, your memorialist obtained from the Hudson's Bay Company for a valuable consideration a conveyance of a tract of land situated on

Red River, being a part of the Territory granted to that Company by Royal Charter: your memorialist had previously consulted several of the most eminent Counsel in London, who concurred in opinion, that the title was unquestionably valid; and he had good reason to believe that a similar opinion has been expressed to His Majesty's Government by the Attorney and Solicitor General of England.

By the terms of the conveyance, your memorialist was bound to settle a specified number of families on the tract of land conveyed to him: and your memorialist as well as all persons holding lands under him were debarred from interfering in the fur trade. Notwithstanding this restriction, your memorialist was early apprized that any plan for settling the country in question, would be opposed with the most determined hostility by the North West Company of Montreal; and threats were held out by the principal partners of that association in London, that they would excite the native Indians to destroy the settlement. In order to obviate this danger, your memorialist instructed his agents to use their utmost endeavours to conciliate the good will of the native Indians, to make a purchase from them of the land requisite for the settlement, and also to abstain from all interference with the servants of the North West Company, except in so far as it should be unavoidable in self-defence. But as it was probable that the influence of the North West Company might be sufficient to mislead the native Indians, it was thought necessary to provide the settlers with the most effectual means of defence, which the local situation of the country would admit.

In pursuance of the condition of his grant, your memorialist sent out a small party of men to commence a settlement. They reached the Red River in autumn of the year 1812, and were followed shortly after, by several families of emigrants. These people were under the direction of Miles Macdonell, Esq. who had been appointed Governor of the District under a provision of the Charter of the Hudson's Bay Company. From the circumstances under which the settlement had been undertaken, an intercourse of mutual accommodation naturally arose between the settlers and the traders of the Hudson's Bay Company; but the establishment was in every respect, completely distinct from the trade of that Company. During the first two years after the arrival of the settlers, various clandestine machinations were carried on by the partners and clerks of the North West Company to excite the jealousy of the Indians, to debauch the servants employed on the establishment, to stir up discontent among the settlers, and to prevent them from obtaining supplies of provisions from the natural produce of the country. There can be no doubt that this was done by desire of the partnership, not only from the continued and systematic manner in which the intrigues were carried on, but also from direct evidence of these instructions given by some of the partners, and from a letter of one individual of the greatest influence among them then residing in London, pointing out to his associates in the interior of this Continent, the absolute necessity of preventing the colonization of Red River—The obstructions thus superadded to all the usual difficulties of an infant settlement, would have been sufficient to defeat the undertaking entirely, if the natural advantages of the country had not been very great. But in spite of every obstacle, the establishment was on the point of taking firm root.

Within a few months after the arrival of Mr. Miles Macdonell, the jealousy which had been instilled into the minds of the Indians, was entirely removed, and they became zealously attached to the settlement. In the second year after the arrival of the settlers, their crops (though sown under very unfavorable circumstances) were so abundant as to leave no probability of their being forced to abandon the country from want of provisions—another year of uninterrupted industry would have rendered them independent of any resources except the produce of their own farms. At the same time the favorable reports which they had sent home to their friends as to the fertility and salubrity of the country, the abundance of game, and the facility of cultivation, had operated to attract other settlers, and in the course of the ensuing year, there was reason to expect a considerable increase of numbers, so that the establishment would have become too strong to be attacked by open violence with any prospect of success.

It was in these circumstances that the partners of the North West Company at their annual meeting in the year 1814, determined to adopt more effectual measures for destroying the settlement, before it should be too late to make the attempt. For this purpose they sent instructions to collect from various quarters a set of men whom they judged fit instruments for acts of violence, viz: the sons of their Canadian, and other servants by Indian women, a great number of whom are reared about their trading posts. These men are bred up in the most entire dependence on the Company, and had been always employed in their service in the same manner as their Canadian servants from whom they were never distinguished till the period alluded to. It was then for the first time that they were taught to consider themselves a separate tribe of men, and distinguished by a separate name, with the view of ascribing their violences to the native Indians. These half-breeds (or Bois Brulés as they were now to be called) have been described as a Nation of independent Indians: but they are in fact with very few exceptions in the regular employment and pay of the North West Company, mostly as canoemen, some as interpreters and guides, and a few of better education as clerks. The latter are the progeny of partners of the Company, at whose expence most of them have been brought up, and through whose influence they may look to be themselves partners. These are the chiefs of this "New Nation."

These men being accustomed to live at a distance from the restraints of civilized society, were ignorant of any law but that of the strongest: or, if they had any idea of the punishments denounced by law against robbers and murderers, the mode of life to which they were habituated, led them to feel confident of escaping from the hand of justice. But they were not allowed to entertain any apprehension on this head, as their superiors constantly inculcated on their minds, that the North West Company had sufficient influence with his Majesty's Government, to screen from punishment any persons who might commit crimes by their direction. They have even been led to believe, that the Company had authority for all that they did, and were actually identified with the Government.

A great number of these half-breeds were collected at Red River in the spring of the year 1815, and were led on from one act of violence to another, till they ended in hostile attacks, openly and regularly carried on against the colonists, and repeated until they succeeded in driving them away from the place, and effecting the destruction of the settlement. As a preparatory step to these measures, Mr. Duncan Cameron, the partner of the North West Company in charge of their affairs on Red River, took his station in the immediate vicinity of the settlement, and laboured assiduously through the whole of the winter, to seduce the settlers to desert their engagements and go to Canada, where they were assured that the North West Company would procure for them gratuitously, not only lands, but also provisions, tools, cattle and every other accommodation they could desire. He gained over some leading individuals by the promise of direct pecuniary rewards, and used every artifice to gain popularity with the others, and to excite discontent against the gentlemen in charge of the settlers. When bribery and flattery would not prevail, intimidation was resorted to. Stories were invented and circulated to terrify the ignorant strangers, with the idea that the Indians had expressed the most vehement hostility, and were determined to assemble in the spring to massacre all those who should not avail themselves of the opportunity of escaping in the canoes of the North West Company.

By the assiduous use of these means of corruption and intimidation, a majority of the settlers were gained over to enter into the views of the North West Company, and their ringleaders were then secretly instructed to avail themselves of a favourable opportunity, to carry off some swivels and other small pieces of artillery. By this robbery the settlement was deprived of the only means of defence by which superior numbers could have been repelled, and the North West Company, being then confident in the indisputable superiority of their force, commenced a train of undisguised violence, which continued without interruption for nearly three months, directed against all the settlers who did not choose to join their party, and which ended in driving them away from Red River, burning their houses, and laying waste their fields.

Among the pretexts for these violences, it had been alleged that they were justifiable on the principle of retaliation, because the Governor of the settlement had, in the preceding year, seized a quantity of provisions belonging to the North West Company. Though it can hardly require any argument to demonstrate the injustice of retaliating upon the innocent settlers, for any act of their Governor, yet, as the seizure in question has been much misrepresented, and great importance has been ascribed to the occurrence, it may be proper to explain the circumstances under which it took place.

In all the British Colonies, Governors have occasionally exercised the power of laying an embargo on the exportation of provisions, in cases of urgent necessity in order to obviate the danger of famine. In the month of January 1814, Mr. Miles Macdonell deemed it necessary to adopt this measure, and to prohibit, for a period of twelve months, the exportation of provisions from the District over which he had been appointed Governor. He had reason to believe that, in addition to the settlers then under his charge, a considerable number of emigrants were to arrive from Europe in the course of the ensuing season, and he had ascertained that the people, then at the place, had not the means of raising a crop sufficiently abundant for the wants of all these additional inhabitants. It was therefore evident that it would be necessary still to have recourse to the natural resources of the country, and of these, the North West Company were endeavouring to deprive the settlers. For the purpose of distressing them and creating an artificial scarcity, the servants of the North West Company, being well supplied with fleet horses, were ordered to drive away the Buffaloe from the hunters of the settlers, who not being well mounted were in the habit of hunting these animals on foot, by cautiously approaching them unobserved. These orders were given soon after the canoes of the North West Company arrived from Fort William in autumn, and were acted upon through the whole course of the winter. The settlers had experienced these obstructions continually for several, months before Mr. Macdonell resolved upon the embargo.

When he issued his Proclamation on the subject, in the month of January

1814, the North West Company avowed their detemination to disregard it, and to carry out their provisions by force, treating the authority of the Governor with derision. The latter had no alternative but to enforce his orders, and to seize the provisions which their servants were employed in carrying out of his district. As soon however as the partners in the country had adopted a more becoming language, he evinced in the clearest manner that he had no view to distress them, or to injure their trade; for, upon the proposal of a conciliatory arrangement made by some of the partners, and on their agreeing to acquiesce in his authority, even under protest, he consented to do every thing necessary for their accommodation, and in fact restored, and allowed them to export out of the district, as much of the provisions which had been seized, as they considered necessary for their trade for twelve months, engaging at the same time to pay for the remainder. Whether Mr. Macdonell's conduct was right or wrong, he alone was responsible for it. The seizure was made under regular warrants issued in his official capacity as Governor of the district, and if he acted wrong, those who were injured had a legal remedy open to them, and might have obtained his removal by Petition to the King in Council. Instead of resorting to this plain and obvious course of proceeding, the only legal and constitutional mode of bringing the question to issue, they availed themselves of their superiority of numbers, to which they attempted to give a shew of legal authority by the help of a warrant issued by one of their own partners, a Magistrate for the Indian Territories, for the arrest of Mr. Macdonell. The sole purpose of this arrest was to remove him from the establishment under his charge, and to leave the settlers a more easy prey to the violence which was meditated against them. This warrant, originally issued by Archibald Norman Macleod, did not even profess to be grounded on the seizure, or (as it has since been called) the robbery of provisions belonging to the North West Company, but was simply for having worn arms, and this too, in a country where it is not only the general custom to wear arms, but where the partners and clerks of the North West Company in particular, are never seen without them.

... While the North West Company were congratulating themselves on the idea of having finally destroyed the settlement of Red River, the people, who had been driven away, were joined in their place of refuge by some other settlers, with whose assistance they returned and re-occupied their farms. In this undertaking they put themselves under the guidance of Mr. Colin Robertson, a gentleman who had been employed by the Hudson's Bay Company for other objects, but who, in this case of unforeseen exigency, undertook the arduous charge of re-establishing the settlement. The circumstances did not admit of his waiting for instructions from your memorialist, who did not receive any information of the state of affairs, till many months afterwards. Mr. Robertson was joined in the beginning of winter, by a considerable number of families who had sailed from Scotland before any intelligence of these disturbances. At the same time Mr. Robert Semple arrived in the country, having been recently appointed by the Hudson's Bay Company, Governor of their Territories and invested with all the authority which their charter confers.

Notwithstanding the devastation which had been effected the preceding spring, Mr. Robertson found means of procuring subsistence for the people of whom he had taken charge, and of putting the settlement in a respectable state of defence. He was welcomed with the strongest demonstrations of joy by the Indian natives, and found no difficulty in conciliating the good will of the Canadians, of whom several reside in the country in a wandering manner, and, from not being in the regular service of any traders, are called free Canadians. Among these people were several half-breeds, who, not being in the immediate employment of the North West Company, did not express the slightest disinclination to the colonization of the country.

At the time of Mr. Robertson's arrival, there were but few of the servants of that Company in the neighbourhood, as their canoes had not yet returned from Fort William, and during this interval there was every appearance of peace and harmony. But on the arrival of Mr. Duncan Cameron and Mr. Alexander Macdonell, by whom the outrages of the preceding spring had been conducted, a great change was immediately observed, and it soon appeared that new preparations had been set on foot, to accomplish in a more effectual manner the extermination of the settlement.

The crimes, which had been committed by Duncan Cameron during the preceding season, had been of the most flagrant description: On evidence of these transactions, bills of indictment have been found against him in the Courts of Montreal for three capital felonies, besides other crimes and misdemeanours. These crimes were of sufficient notoriety, to justify any individual, who might think fit to incur the responsibility in arresting and sending him in custody to this Province....

Three days after the date of this letter, his half-breeds attacked the servants of the Hudson's Bay Company by force of arms, took them prisoners, and seized the whole of the property under their charge, and in particular, the provisions on which the subsistence of the settlers depended.

After this blow, Macdonell no longer disguised his intentions to destroy the settlement. He invited the Indians to join his expedition, and declared that if the Settlers dared to resist, the ground should be drenched with their blood. He encouraged his men by the prospect of plunder, and even promised to give up the women of the settlement to gratify their brutal lusts. His whole force being assembled, he proceeded in military array from Qu'appelle towards the settlement. The half-breeds on horseback, passed through the plains along the rivers, escorting the boats which conveyed the provisions, and other property of which he had robbed the Hudson's Bay Company, as well as that which he had obtained by trade from the Indians. On the 1st June, he arrived at Brandon House, a post of the Hudson's Bay Company, where he sent a party of his men to force their way into the fort, to seize the property it contained, and carry it to a neighbouring post, occupied by one of his clerks. Of this plunder, some trifles were distributed among his men, but all the most valuable articles were deposited in the stores of the North-West Company. From thence Macdonell proceeded on his march to a place called Portage des Prairies, where he remained with most of the Canadians in his service; while he sent forward sixty or seventy half-breeds on horseback to the settlement, under the command of Cuthbert Grant, a clerk of the North-West Company who had acted a conspicuous part in all the violences of the preceding year, and who was now brought forward in the character of the "great Chief of the new Nation."

Before the taking and plundering of Brandon House, Governor Semple could hardly be inducted to believe, that the North-West Company would venture to set the laws of their country so completely at defiance, as to make an open attack on the settlement; but after receiving that intelligence, he could no longer doubt that such an attack was determined on: and in order that his attention might not be distracted, and his force divided by the necessity of maintaining two separate posts, he resolved to demolish that which had lately been occupied by the North-West Company, and to employ the materials in rendering his own more tenable. This work was but partially effected when intelligence was brought by an Indian, that Grant and his party were on their way, and would attack him in the course of two days. A considerable body of native Indians of the Sauteux or Chippawa tribe, who were encamped in the neighbourhood, on hearing this intelligence came and offered to take up arms in defence of the settlement; but Governor Semple declined their services, being unwilling under any circumstances to employ Savages against his countrymen.

The intelligence brought by the Indian proved to be correct, and at the time that he had predicted in the afternoon of the 19th June, a party of horsemen were observed marching directly towards the middle of the settlers' habitations, which began at the distance of a mile from the fort and extended two or three miles along the river. Most of the families had removed to the fort upon the alarm given by the Indian; but many of the men were averse to quit their agricultural labours, and still remained on their farms. The Governor having expressed his anxiety about these people, took his fowling piece and was preparing to go out. All the men in the fort, by a spontaneous movement, and without any orders, were taking their arms to follow him, when he desired them to remain, telling them that he was not going to fight, but merely to see what were the intentions of these horsemen, and that it would be sufficient that twenty men should follow him. Twenty five was the number that actually went out with him, including seven of the gentlemen who usually messed at his own table. They had not gone far, when they met some of the settlers flying in terror towards the fort, and learnt that the half-breeds had taken some of their friends prisoners. In their alarm they said that the half-breeds had carts and cannon, and at the suggestion of one of the settlers, the Governor sent to the fort for a field piece. Anxious however to come to a parley with the half-breeds, and to enable the rest of the settlers to escape, he continued to advance, still under the unfortunate mistake of supposing that these people might listen to reason.

Grant in the mean time perceiving this small party, collected his men, and dividing them into two bodies, gallopped up with one division directly against Semple; while he ordered the other to make a circuit in the plain, so as to cut off his retreat to the fort. The two parties of horsemen closing in from opposite sides, surrounded him in the form of a semicircle, leaving no opening except towards the river. At this moment Grant sent a Canadian of the name of Boucher to summon the Governor to surrender, Boucher accosted him with the most insulting language and gestures, which even in that perilous situation, Semple could not brook. With an expression of indignation, he took hold of the bridle of Boucher's horse: the latter leaped down, and ran off towards his comrades, who immediately commenced firing, by which Semple himself and a great proportion of his party were wounded, and several killed on the spot. A few straggling shots only were returned, and as the half-breeds still continued to keep up a constant fire, Semple called out to his men to provide for their own safety: three only succeeded in making their escape, some others made the attempt, but were shot in their flight. The wounded men were lying on the field incapable of resistance, and calling out for mercy, when the half-breeds came up, and butchered them with the most horrid imprecations, stripping them of their bloody clothing, and in several instances, mangling the bodies in wanton cruelty. The half-breeds were not the only men engaged in this massacre: a Canadian of the name of Francois Deschamps was among the most active, and collected a large booty from the person of those he had despatched. One gentleman only, of the name of Pritchard, who had formerly been in the service of the North West Company, was saved through the interference of a Canadian, who had great difficulty in protecting him. This was the scene which has been called "a battle," "an affray," "an unfortunate occurrence."

In the course of the same evening, Mr. Pritchard was sent by Grant, to summon the settlers at the fort to surrender. With no small difficulty he had obtained a promise that their lives should be spared, and that they should be allowed to leave the country, provided they would give up all the property belonging to your memorialist, or to the Hudson's Bay Company. The settlers saw that resistance would be unavailing, and on the day following the massacre, Grant, at the head of the murderers, took possession of the fort and the property it contained, in the name of the North West Company. It was not long before his masters arrived to sanction his proceedings, and appropriate the plunder to their own use.

The news of the victory obtained by Grant, with the slaughter of more than twenty of the "English," was speedily communicated to Macdonell, at Portage des Prairie, and was received by him, and the clerks under his command, with shouts of joy and exultation. Having thus "cleared the way," as he termed it, Macdonell proceeded with the remainder of his men, to receive possession of his conquest, and was soon after joined at the fort, lately occupied by the settlers, by an assemblage of partners and clerks of the North West Company, coming from various and distant quarters, with great numbers of armed men. At their head, was Mr. Archibald Norman Macleod, who is not only a partner, but one of the agents, or (as their own publications have lately announced, as the more proper appellation,) directors of the North West Company of Montreal; and being deputed by Mr. William McGillivray, and the other heads of the "concern," had set off at the first opening of the navigation, and travelled with the utmost possible expedition, with the view of completing the work of destruction, before any intelligence could reach the settlers, of the arrival of your memorialist in Canada, or of his intention to visit Red River....

The conduct of Macleod was imitated by his partners in the other parts of Athabasca, where undisguised acts of robbery and arson were committed, all under pretext of retaliation, a pretext for which the North West Company are never at a loss, when a crime is to be committed. It is an established maxim among them, that they have a right to take redress at their own hands for any act of which they think fit to complain, and this principle is not only acted upon by the subordinate partners, but systematically prescribed as their rule of conduct, by the head of the "concern," a member of the Legislative Council of this Province. It certainly cannot require much comment, to shew the consequences which are to be expected, when a body, so powerful as the North West Company, are allowed to determine at their own pleasure, the proper measure of compensation for any injury which they may suppose, or alledge to have been committed against them, and to give the name of retaliation to any crime, which they may find it for their interest to perpetrate: to devastation, to robbery, to arson, and to murder.

The outrages which have been detailed, are so extraordinary, that some hesitation may naturally be felt, in supposing them possible. It may seem incredible, that such a tissue of atrocities, should be the work of men professing the christian religion, and enjoying the respectable character of British merchants. The Indian trade, as it has been hitherto carried on from Canada, though certainly contemptible as a national object, is the whole fortune of those who are engaged in it, and among those who profit the most by the present system, are several individuals of the highest station in this Province. But the impressions which have been diffused, as to the extent and importance of the trade of the North West Company, and their services to the British Government, are extremely mistaken. It is only by a constant use of the arts of deception, and much arrogance of pretension, that they preserve an external appearance, calculated to impose upon strangers. If, however, the North West Company were all they wish to be thought, no one would put them in comparison with the East-India Company of Amsterdam, under whose auspices, and for whose benefit, the massacre of Amboyna was perpetrated. The motives for the massacre of Red River were precisely the same; to maintain by means of violence and intimidation, a monopoly which is not yet secured by law, yet a monopoly by which the native Indians are held in worse than Turkish slavery, and an extensive and valuable country is condemned to endless sterility. The North West Company, though invested with no right but those common to every British subject, have succeeded for more than thirty years past, in excluding all others from the extensive countries to the North and West of Lake Superior. All the Indian countries, the North West Company arrogate to themselves as their own territories, and consider the entrance of any others of His Majesty's subjects, from whatsoever quarter, as an invasion of their rights. In order to repress such attempts, open violence is systematically employed against every intruder, with no other reserve than the caution necessary to avoid committing the principals of the "concern." From the immense distance of any courts of justice, the subordinate agents in these acts of violence have hitherto been assured of impunity, but it is evident, that as soon as agricultural settlements shall be firmly established in these countries, together with those institutions of religion, law, and police, which must accompany a civilized population, such a system of ferocious violence will no longer be practicable....

The North West Company, though well aware that the settlement at Red River, has always been an undertaking completely separate from the trade of the Hudson's Bay Company, yet in order to give greater scope to their detestable principle of retaliation, have attempted to identify these establishments. Even his Majesty's Government, by lending too ready an ear to these misrepresentations, has been induced to believe, that all the crimes which have been committed in the Indian countries, have only been the result of mutual violence between contending parties of traders. But from the statement which is now submitted to your Grace, it cannot but be evident, that this opinion is completely erroneous. The question now at issue is not whether this or that Company shall engross the fur trade:—But whether the British Government, does or does not afford protection to its subjects: Whether the strong may be permitted to trample upon the weak without restraint, to expel the tillers of the earth from their habitations, to lay waste their fields, to reduce their cottages to ashes, to drive their helpless wives and children into the desert, and to commit every species of enormity, in furtherance of their criminal views: Whether this extensive and valuable Province is to have a system of judicature, calculated only to crush obnoxious men, while those who are in favor, may commit the most attrocious crimes, with impunity: Whether to promote the sordid purposes of individual gain or illegal monopoly, murder may be systematically organized, and the blood of British subjects remain unattoned, because some of those who profit by it, are members of the Executive and Legislative Councils of Lower Canada, and reputed to be under the special protection of His Majesty's Government.

2 OCTR. 1818.

## 2. William McGillivray, "To Sir G. Drummond," June 24, 1815.

My dear Sir,
I cannot but express the feelings of indignation to which this calumny gives rise. I deny, in the most solemn manner, the allegations whereon this shameful accusation is founded: so far from their having any existence in truth, the contrary is the fact; for it can be proved, that the first year of his Lordship's settlement, the innocent people who had been enticed from their homes by his golden but delusive promises, and misrepresentations, had no other means of avoiding starvation, but the supplies which they derived from the stores of the North-West

company; therefore had the principles of the body, or of those employed by them, been such as the Earl of Selkirk has been pleased to impute to them, there was no need of hostile Indians to interfere in the destruction of the settlement: hunger alone would speedily have accomplished the work.

... I therefore declare, that I am an utter stranger to any instigation, or any determination of the Indian nations to make any attack on the settlement in question; but I will not take upon me to say, that serious quarrels may not happen between the settlers and the nations, whose hunting grounds they have taken possession of, in the American style of injustice and land pillage, exclusive of the danger they run from the vicinity of the Sioux nation, who from time immemorial have made it a practice to make war on the Indians on the Red River, their permanent enemies, and upon the whites who are found in that country; many instances of which can be adduced, because the Indian nations, when in a state of hostility, consider the whites found in the country of their enemy, as being in his interest, and to be treated accordingly.

The arrogant and violent conduct of Lord Selkirk's agents, cannot well fail to produce such a result as the quarrels above mentioned. The Indians require no instigation to commit violence, where they consider their own interests as concerned, for notwithstanding the influence which it is supposed the North-West company has over them, within a few years, a brigade of boats coming down the Red River was attacked without any apparent previous cause or provocation, and several men killed or wounded; lives are occasionally lost in like manner in every part of the North-West country.

The influence, whatever it may be, which the North-West company possess over the Indians, has been exerted in a manner essentially different from the false and atrocious idea of intending to be instrumental in the massacre of Lord Selkirk's helpless and deluded settlement ... and it is strange that at the time the exertion of this influence occasioned that company to be identified by the enemy with the government, and their property at Saint Mary's in consequence plundered and destroyed, as belonging to government, the agents of his Lordship should, under a pretended, but usurped authority, with force and arms have plundered the company of their property on the banks of the Red River, which actually took place in the Spring of the year 1814, when their depôt of provisions, which had been collected during the preceding winter, and which was the only supply they had for their canoe men in their voyage from the interior to their place of rendezvous on Lake Superior, was forcibly seized, and the greater part feloniously retained.... Consequently this act of robbery was committed with the express intention of either starving the North-West canoe men, or putting a total stop to the exit of the company's returns. Insinuations against the

North-West company, and pretended alarms brought forward by persons capable of such acts, come indeed from them with an ill grace; but the motives are manifest, and meant to anticipate or counteract the feelings which their own conduct, when known, would naturally produce.

The robbery above mentioned might have been prevented, or his lordship's agents made to pay dear for their unjustifiable conduct, had the North-West company's people availed themselves of what was in their power, and been as regardless of consequences as their opponents appeared to be; but all aid from the nations was refused, and other means avoided, which in strict justice they had a right to resort to in defence of their property and right, as British subjects. His Excellency has been misinformed in regard to our being the only people who had intercourse with the Indian nations; there are great numbers of hunters, Canadians and others, who are to be found in many parts of the North-West country, and particularly on the Red River, who live among the Indians and not being in the company's service are not subject to their control. Besides the Hudson's Bay company as traders (of which company Lord Selkirk is now an associate) have their posts close to those of the North-West company, in every part of the country eastward of the rocky mountains, excepting Athabasca, which forms no portion of the alleged Hudson's Bay territory; and as they supply the natives to the extent of their means in like manner as the North-West company; therefore it is presumed, that with equal justice and good faith in their dealings they must possess the same influence.

It would indeed be extraordinary if the North-West company, who cannot always save their own people from violence, should be held responsible for whatever misfortune may happen to Lord Selkirk's, or to the servants of the Hudson's Bay company; against such doctrines I most solemnly protest. Individuals in the Indian country are personally responsible for their own criminal acts, in like manner as elsewhere; and an act of the British parliament (43d of His Majesty) was passed for this express purpose. The British government has not only an influence, but a legal authority over the community; but does this make the members thereof personally responsible for the murders and robberies committed in the United Kingdom? His Excellency may rest assured that the North-West company will never instigate, nor authorize any of their servants to instigate, the Indian nations to commit murder, were they even as void of humanity as the Earl of Selkirk seems to consider them; they know too well the consequences to themselves of encouraging disorders of any kind in the Indian country. The Indians, once roused to arms, would hardly distinguish between an Highlander or Canadian from the shores of Hudson's Bay, and people of the same country coming from Canada. I beg leave to inclose some documents which may be considered as referred to in this letter. I wish his Excellency to be possessed of facts, in order to remove from his mind any unfavourable impression which the unfounded and self-interested calumnies, raised and propagated against us by the Earl of Selkirk and his agents and partizans are calculated to produce. That nobleman has thought proper lately to become the rival of the North-West company in the trade which they have carried on for upwards of thirty years with credit to themselves, and it is hoped with benefit to their country. Under the guise and cloak of colonization, he is aiming at ... an exterminating blow against their trade. Insinuations of alarm and false accusations form part of the system, and his agents and servants are probably instructed to bring them artfully forward, to raise prejudices against us; surely interested representations from such a quarter should be received with caution, and be better supported than the correspondence of his Lordship's agent sent to Canada, who collects and reports his pretended information as derived from a common Canadian whom he does not name. It is matter of astonishment, that the idea of colonization in the Indian country, at the distance of 2,000 miles from home, should be tolerated by His Majesty's government, and its consequences not seen through. If it fail, as it must and ought, numerous innocent individuals will fall a sacrifice to his Lordship's visionary pursuits; and if it succeeds, it must infallibly destroy the Indian trade in the result: as experience proves, that when colonization advances, Indians and their trade disappear. Thus his Lordship is contributing towards Indian extermination. Besides the planting of colonies so far in the interior, where they are placed out of the reach and control of the mother country, is, as it were, transferring them and their future interests to the United States, in whose territory, by the terms of the late treaty of peace, they will most probably be found; and thus a strength is raising up to be hereafter employed in aid of American ambition against British interests. In a fair commercial competition, we have no objection to enter the lists with his Lordship, but we cannot remain passive spectators of the violence used to plunder or destroy our property, under any pretended or usurped authority as was assumed by Mr. Miles McDonnell, who styles himself governor, but whose proclamation resembles that of a bashaw, respecting our depôts or collection of provisions for the trade as above stated. In all such attempts hereafter, the North-West company would assuredly be justified in repelling force by force; at all events, I cannot but consider the rights and property of that body as equally entitled to the protection of His Majesty's government as the Earl of Selkirk's....

### 3. William McGillivray, "Deposition," March 14, 1818.

Sir,

... In the commencement of the recent disturbances in the Indian country, and when the first aggressions were committed upon us, we did not see in the measures of Lord Selkirk any other than the effects of an enthusiastic prosecution of his Lordship's visionary schemes, which, however disastrous to the persons engaged in them, and injurious to us, might perhaps be ascribed to laudable motives; nor did we see, in the increasing activity of the Hudson's Bay company's traders, any thing more than an unwonted ebullition of commercial rivalry, which, however much it was our interest to counteract, we never could entertain thoughts of repressing, by any other means than by a commensurate increase of energy and of industry in the operations of our trade; but the experience we have acquired, by the development of his Lordship's views from their early bud, the wily purchase of so large a part of the Hudson's Bay stock, to their full bloom of maturity, the sack of Fort William, has convinced us that the measures of Lord Selkirk have been undeviatingly intended to produce the utter destruction of our trading concern, and the ruin of our fortunes and characters, and that the active co-operation of the Hudson's Bay company was an engine put in motion by his Lordship to assist in accomplishing those ends, ultimately thereby to raise himself upon the ruins of the North-West company into a monopolizer of the fur trade of the whole continent, in addition to his ambition of becoming lord paramount of the soil, through an immense tract of the country....

Before beginning the summary of the events immediately connected with the disputes in question, it may be well to direct your attention to the circumstance that the North-West company have never acknowledge the exclusive rights, either of trade, or of territorial property and jurisdiction, claimed by the Hudson's Bay company under their obsolete charter. It was indeed, at times, considered as good policy in the Canadian traders, to seem to respect those rights, in order to deter more active rivals from stepping over the heads of the sluggish factors who crept about the shores of the bay, and sometimes by a great effort, followed the tracts of the adventurous Canadians into some parts of the interior. But at no time was ever done any overt act of acknowledgment of such rights; ...

Lord Selkirk denies being individually a *fur trader*; but what must that person be called who is a partner to the amount of nearly one-half of the whole trading stock of a *fur trading* company, who directs their affairs, engages their servants, and in the Indian country, at Fort William to wit, has actually in his own person traded with the Indians for furs? Who plans an establishment in the interior of the country, for the purpose of raising recruits of servants fit to be employed in the trade of the Hudson's Bay company, whose own servants are engaged under the express stipulation of being liable to be drafted into the trading service of that company; and who, in fine, instructs his agent to establish as soon as possible, distilleries in his colony, for the purpose of supplying the company's trade with spirituous liquors?

... But had Lord Selkirk's primary object been that of colonization, still the establishment of a settlement known to be intended as a hot-bed, out of which our rivals were to be provided with full grown trading servants, and in the heart of a country whence our people derived by far the greater part of their provisions; a country, the extensive inclosure and cultivation of which, would destroy or remove to a most inconvenient distance, the hunting grounds on which we chiefly depended for the means of subsisting our numerous voyageurs, would of itself have been pregnant with distress and injury to our trade. It became still more an object of jealousy and alarm, when we considered the undisguised designs entertained by the Hudson's Bay committee, under the impulse of their noble dictator to revive, or rather for the first time to put in force, in their most hateful shape, the extensive and undefined privileges granted under a stretch of prerogative to a set of court-favourites; and when it was openly stated that the North-West company, who were the legitimate successors of the first discoverers and possessors of the country, which they have since explored from sea to sea, were poachers and interlopers, and should be dealt with accordingly, that their buildings should be razed to the foundation, and their persons and property subjected to the operation of that most preposterous and oppressive clause in the Hudson's Bay company's pretended charter, by which they were empowered to levy war, and to right and recompense themselves upon the persons and property of those whom they caught within the hallowed confines of their sacred territories.

Early did we predict that the formation of a settlement, in its ostensible objects of cultivation, so diametrically opposed to the habits and prejudice of the natives of the soil, would produce dissatisfaction, disturbance and bloodshed, between the newcomers and the native inhabitants; and our prediction has been too mournfully fulfilled. Early did we declare, that such a heterogeneous community in the centre of our trading grounds, would be withal productive of insubordination and desertion amongst our servants, and this has been convincingly brought home to your own knowledge, Sir, by the numerous warrants you have yourself granted at Red River against our engagés for desertion. And early and candidly did we state, both to Government and to our opponents, that we, in consequence, viewed this projected settlement as in its essence, both injurious to our trading interests, and pregnant with the seeds of its own dissolution.

This was the light in which we saw the matter, even while we supposed it to be merely a colonizing speculation; and much more strongly would our suspicions and alarms have been excited, had we then known what has since been so forcibly thrust upon our conviction, that this pretended scheme of a colony was no other than a cloak thrown over the avaricious designs of the Earl of Selkirk to become a monopolizer of the fur trade, and one of the steps by which he meant to climb into the sanctuaries of our commercial secrets, to ransack our stores, to steal our account-books, (we beg pardon, we should have said, to bribe a needy dependent to steal his employer's books,) and meanly to pry into the private ledgers of his competitors in trade....

Lord Selkirk, or rather his judicious friend, who has vamped up the "Statement," gives the North-West company's partners and people, then on the spot, very little credit for the fostering humanity with which they sheltered, fed, and clothed his deluded settlers, and is most appropriately severe upon what he calls the canting compassion of the North-West company. The uniformity of all the depositions that are before you on that subject, is more than a sufficient answer to these very charitable insinuations.

This leads us to the second epoch of these transactions, when Miles McDonnell, the *soi-disant* governor of Assiniboine ... issued his proclamation of the 8th January 1814. The cloven foot had before appeared by the assertion of his dominion, as well over the Indians, as over the other inhabitants of the country, of his having the right to interdict them both from fishing and hunting at his pleasure, and requiring them to bring their provisions to him alone for sale; and still more by the pains taken to impress upon the minds of the natives and of the North-West company's servants, that the ruin of that association was at hand, and that their traders would soon be compelled to leave the country, the whole soil of which was arrogantly asserted to belong to the Hudson's Bay company, and under him to their grantee, the Earl of Selkirk.

The seizures of provisions at Turtle River, at Rivière la Sourie, and on the Assiniboine River, the interruption of the navigation, the taking of our people prisoners, the notices to quit, the arming and training of the settlers to war, the arrogant and despotic tone assumed by Miles McDonnell, styled by himself "Civil Governor," but uniformly designated by his own people under his *military* title of Captain, are all so fully stated by oral and written evidence, produced to you, that we will do no more in this place than point out to your more particular attention, that passage in the journal of Mr. Peter Fidler, one of their chief factors, under date the 21st June 1814, where he says, "*had the Captain* persevered, they would all have been starved out in two days more," as showing the spirit which actuated the author of these proceedings against the North-West company.

So far there appears nothing but aggressions on the part of our opponents, without, on our side, the adoption of a single defensive measure.

That the settlers were trained and exercised in arms, for the purpose of forcibly putting into executions the plans of Lord Selkirk, for the expulsion of our people from Red River, and eventually from the whole of the North-West, could not be doubted; and the use made of the cannon and fire-arms supplied by Government for the protection of the colony, but which were directed to the purposes of outrages upon our people, confirmed it. Hence it was perfectly fair and justifiable in Mr. Duncan Cameron, to take advantage of the spirit of discontent and desertion which began to prevail amongst the colonists, from the miseries they had suffered, and the arbitrary conduct of their commander. By facilitating the passage of all who chose to proceed to Canada, the North-West company were diminishing the numerical force of those by whom they expected to be encountered in arms and subjected to further pillage; and had the encouragement given in this way been carried much farther than it was, it would still have been merely in *self-defence*, by reducing the physical means of annoyance possessed by our antagonists....

You are well aware too, Sir, from the evidence before you, that in no case did the North-West company's people ever fire a first shot. The extracts from their own (Mr. Fidler's) journal, show that Lord Selkirk's partizans were always the first aggressors, and with the various other depositions filed with you, constitute irrefragable proofs of the systematic plan of mere defence which the North-West company's people have all along pursued....

... by the arrest and prosecution of Miles McDonnell and John Spencer, for their illegal proceedings. It was not to the law of the strongest, nor to the Indian law of the tomahawk, that we had recourse on that occasion, but to the regular proceedings of law, and the warrants granted against McDonnell and Spencer were issued by a magistrate duly qualified....

The assemblage of the half-breeds requires a little further comment; we need not dwell here upon the organization of that class of men. You are yourself, Sir, personally aware, that although many of them, from the ties of consanguinity and interest, are more or less connected with the North-West company's people, and either as clerks or servants, or as free hunters, are dependent on them; yet they one and all look upon themselves as members of an independent tribe of natives, entitled to a property in the soil, to a flag of their own, and to protection from the British Government.

It is absurd to consider them legally in any other light than as Indians; the British law admits of no filiation of illegitimate children but that of the mother; and as these persons cannot in law claim any advantage by paternal right, it follows, that they ought not to be subjected to any disadvantages which might be supposed to arise from the fortuitous circumstances of their parentage.

Being therefore Indians, they, as is frequently the case among the tribes in this vast continent, as *young men* (the technical term for warrior) have a right to form a new tribe on any unoccupied, or (according to the Indian law) any conquered territory. That the half-breeds under the denominations of *bois brulés* and *metifs* have formed a separate and distinct tribe of Indians for a considerable time back, has been proved to you by various depositions.

Now, if a person is aggrieved or in imminent danger, will not the law of nature, which is the foundation of all other law, both bid and entitle him to seek for aid and protection against the injuries and dangers with which he is threatened, amongst those who are able and willing to assist him? And who more able, who more willing, who more bound to assist their relations, their friends, their employers, than those contemned half-breeds?—Those whom the liberal book-maker in Lord Selkirk's half-pay (see Statement, page 17) terms "a lawless banditti," the illegitimate "progeny chiefly of the Canadian traders by Indian women." These, whom the unfortunate Semple in his letters contemptuously calls "your *black-breed* allies." Seeing then that the menaces of his opponents were fulfilling, that the capture of Fort Gibraltar, and of the post of Pambina, and the attempt to get possession of his own post and person, would be followed up by every possible measure of violence to cut off all communication between him, the northern departments and Fort William; and well knowing the salvation of the North-West company depended on getting out their provisions from Assiniboine River, to prevent the distress and probable starvation of all the brigades coming through Lake Winnipic, it was prudent, it was politic, it was just, it was the bounden duty of Mr. Alexander McDonnell to avail himself of the proffered assistance of the half-breed tribe, to make common cause with them, and to secure the protection of their physical strength, both to save the persons and property of the North-West company from further outrage and pillage, and to carry out the provisions so indispensable for their existence.... Steadily therefore pursuing these measures of self-defence, the bringing so many of the half-breeds together into one body was necessary and laudable; and although it was found, that by giving so much consequence to the new nation, they were led to consider themselves as beyond control, and were occasionally objects of alarm and uneasiness to the North-West people themselves; yet we do not hesitate to avow, that under such circumstances, to avail of their services for the protection of our property and our trade, was not only what we were justified in doing, but what we must of necessity repeat, if compelled to it by similar dangers. But these very people who are so vilified by our opponents were always courted by them, particularly by Mr. Semple and his coadjutor, Colin Robertson, and were endeavoured to be gained over by flattering promises of superior advantages, beyond any they could get from the North-West company. A cavalry body-guard of them (and none more active in the saddle, more expert with the firelock, or more warlike in deportment, could be found in this hemisphere, as you yourself, Sir, who have seen them in a body, will allow) was even considered as an appendage that would add dignity and strength to the government of Assiniboine, could such a body of household troops have been procured; ... Mr. Alexander McDonnell, with a prudence and foresight, justified both by the past occurrences and the events that ensued, collected and combined these allies in one focus, and entrusted to part of them the execution of a material part of his plan, for extricating the North-West company from the snares in which they were sought to be entangled. The prudence, the coolness, the forbearance, and, when the trial came, the fortitude and generalship with which these men conducted themselves on the lamentable occasion that ensued,—now that prejudice ought to have passed away—now that truth is about to dispel the mist of falsehood, scurrility and calumny which hung over the affray of the 19th of June 1816—now that you have yourself on the spot narrowly investigated all that related to it, must be subjects of approval; and boldly will we venture to predict, that the stricter the inquiry, the more certain it will appear that Mr. Semple and those who perished with him, fell sacrifices to their own illegal and inconsiderate aggression....

The engagement by Lord Selkirk at Montreal, of about 140 of the disbanded soldiers of the late De Meuron and Watteville regiments ... and a necessary compliment of officers, his obtaining a body guard of a detachment of the 37th regiment, and the embarkation of the force collected at La Chine, with heavy artillery, in the beginning of June 1816, where they were marshalled in full uniform to the sound of the drum and the bugle, are events of proof before you, which need only be mentioned to show how unequivocally they indicate the long previous premeditation of the blow....

## 4. W.B. Coltman, "Report," May 14, 1818.

Sir,

... Whilst such appears to me to be the case, established by the evidence against the Hudson's Bay company, that against the North-West company is still more strong and clear; as their violations of law have evidently been much greater, and attended with results shocking to the feelings of humanity; at the same time that they have no pretexts of legal rights, by which they may have been misled, nor any claims upon Government, for more than the ordinary protection of law; any pretension they might have made, as a body, for the enterprize and vigour with which they pursued and extended a trade, beneficial to themselves and the empire, being completely destroyed by the vices inherent to the system on which they conducted their affairs, and which have during the late disturbances been brought forward in so conspicuous a light, and produced events so fatal, as to appear imperatively to call for the interference of Government. The foundation of the whole evil, is probably to be traced to that violent spirit, which is nurtured by the species of monopoly that the North-West company has established, and continues to maintain, in the Indian territories; still more by physical force than by any fair advantage, derived from capital or connection; the various illegal measures adopted to crush minor adventurers who have attempted to oppose this monopoly, are recorded in the courts of Montreal, and are of public notoriety, whilst the pernicious effects produced on the character of individuals, employed to maintain the same, have been exhibited in strong colours, by the late events.

By the arrangements of the North-West company, a strong stimulus is held out to the junior members of this association, in the considerable share of profits reserved to reward their successful exertions in the service of the company; this, whilst it has produced those results, which are so creditable to their character as a trading body, has at the same time given rise to an "esprit de corps," little attentive to the rights and claims of others, and accustomed to consider an exclusive devotion to the interests and honour of the company, as a primary duty, dignified in some of their intercepted letters, by the appellation of "loyalty to the concern;" to this feeling is added a spirit much more disposed to inflict, than submit to acts of injury and insult, formed originally perhaps by the local circumstances of the parties, far removed from the protection and control of civilized society, and where every man must to a certain degree, feel his life to be in his own keeping, and to be best secured by a constant and open preparation for self-defence. These circumstances tending naturally to produce habits of overbearing violence, left unchecked by any salutary regulations, or rather indeed encouraged, as far as they tended to promote the interests of the association, have at length formed the general character of its members, as exhibited in the evidence before me, in their violent and oppressive conduct towards the natives of the country, frequently to their own servants, and still more so to their opponents in trade. To this last point my inquiries have of course been chiefly directed, as being one of the immediate objects of my mission; and it appears to me, that a short review of the conduct of both parties, will be sufficient to show, that although the Hudson's Bay company may have been the first aggressors, the retaliatory measures of the North-West company have so much exceeded all lawful or reasonable bounds of self-defence, and been carried to such violent extremes, as to render the proceedings of their party, beyond comparison, the most criminal....

Beginning however from this period, it appears to me that there can be no doubt the Hudson's Bay company's servants must be considered as the first aggressors; the fact indeed, although a good deal of contradictory evidence had previously been collected ...

From this correspondence, your Excellency will perceive, that exclusive of individual offences on each side, the North-West company impute to the Earl of Selkirk a criminal conspiracy, in the view of forcibly and illegally driving them out from the Indian territories; whilst it is well known, that a similar charge of conspiracy, "for the purpose of destroying the Red River colony," is the principal offence which his Lordship now attaches to the North-West company, as a body. The substance of most of the principal facts that have been established before me, in evidence against the Earl, has already been stated, in speaking of his proceedings in connection with the governors and other agents of the Hudson's Bay company; but although these may involve great moral responsibility, and as it appears to me, make out a case seriously affecting the chartered rights of the company, yet I do not see how they can be deemed sufficient, even with the addition of the very illegal and unjustifiable proceedings of the Earl at Fort William, to support a criminal charge of so serious a nature as conspiracy. With regard to the partners of the North-West company also, I am doubtful how far such a charge, if at all made out; can apply to any number of them, as it appears to me, they will be found in general to have acted under a sense of injury and insult, (a submission to which might often be inconsistent, in the Indian territories with personal safety,) and under some pretext of self defence, although pushed by their habitual system of violence, far beyond all grounds of law or reason. From the evidence before me, it appears certainly, that a very great jealousy was expressed against the colony from its first establishment, especially by the partners in London; of this the most striking evidence is afforded by a letter of Mr. Simon McGillivray, dated London, 9th April 1812, to the wintering partners of the North-West company, in which, speaking of the Earl of Selkirk's plans of colonization, he says, "it will require some time, and I fear cause much expense to us as well as to himself, before he is *driven to abandon* the project, and yet *he must be driven to abandon* it, for his success would strike at the very existence of our trade;" but these feelings do not appear to have given rise to any violent or illegal proceedings, till after the forcible seizure of the provisions on the Red River, by Miles McDonnell. On the occurrence of this event, however, alarming as it might be to the North-West company, from the state of the war, and at the same time as indicative of a future intention to give practical effect by force, to the exclusive rights of territory, which had been publicly claimed from the first settlement of the colony, measures of retaliation were adopted far beyond what it appears to me the case could be supposed to justify; for independent of the warrants issued against Miles McDonnell and other officers of the colony, and the offer of free passages to Canada, to any of the settlers or servants, who chose to quit the place, measures which are avowed by the North-West company, there can scarcely be a doubt, that if actual orders were not given at the general meeting of the partners at Fort William, the Summer in question, for the entire expulsion of the colony, (of which there is certainly no proof,) that such sentiments of hostility and desire of revenge, for the injuries and insults supposed to have been inflicted, were loudly expressed, as to satisfy all the junior members of the association, that the complete breaking up of the colony would be a measure most acceptable to their superiors, and to the company at large; and that the means adopted to accomplish the same, would not be very scrupulously examined.

With respect to the charges against the North-West company, of having adopted at this meeting measures for the destruction of the colony, by means of the Indians, no proof has been produced of any combined plan, to which the agents or leading partners had given their sanction, and but slight and second-hand evidence, even that any measures of the kind had been discussed amongst individuals; to men indeed of the characters, and actuated by the motives which have been already mentioned, a more direct appeal than that which I have stated, was probably unnecessary. On the return of the partners and servants of the North West company, in the Autumn, from Fort William to the neighbourhood of Red River, they induced the natives before mentioned, to quit their different posts, which of course added to the irritation already existing on their minds, and confirmed any hostile views they might previously have entertained; these notices, it appears evident from their intercepted letters, they apprehended would be practically acted upon, and from the same source, it is indisputably established, that in the course of the ensuing winter, most, if not all, the partners of the company, with many of their inferior partizans in the neighbourhood of Red River, had become parties to plans for driving off the colonists, and for employing the aid of the Indians for that purpose, although resolved however, to hazard this measure with all its consequent dangers, it appears to have been done rather with a view of alarming the settlers, and thereby inducing them to leave the country, than for the purpose of direct attacks, with any design of their general destruction; ...

Persons who could, however, make up their minds to the employment of Indians in any shape, against their fellow subjects, were not to be expected to hesitate about that of the less savage force of half-breeds; of this class of persons, some few who have received their education in Canada, and are employed by the North-West company, as clerks, are nearly as much civilized as the traders themselves, a few others on the contrary, are scarcely removed from the savage state, and the greater bulk fill the various gradations between these two; the connection between this class of people and the North-West company, (from the former partners, clerks, or servants, of which company, those now on Red River are chiefly descended,) is naturally very intimate, and is further kept up by the number of them whom the company constantly employ as clerks, exclusive of frequently engaging the remainder as hunters and canoe-men. These men, who form for their number, a formidable force, being habituated to all the arts of Indian warfare, and at the same time possessed of a considerable portion of the energy of the whites, Miles McDonnell had most injudiciously offended, by some restrictions on what they conceived their natural rights, about the same time that he commenced his system of aggression on the North-West company.

By the partizans of this latter company, the ill-will thus excited was sedulously kept alive; their proceedings in this and other respects, during the Winter and following Spring, in the course whereof considerable violence was exhibited on both sides, although beyond comparison the greater on behalf of the North-West company, will be found fully detailed in my statement. The result was, that after inducing more than three-fourths of the settlers and servants to abandon the colony, and accept their offers of a passage to Canada, and arresting and taking down Miles McDonnell, and Spencer, the sheriff, as prisoners, the North-West company were enabled by secretly instigating the half-breeds, to succeed in driving away the remaining settlers; and by the burning of their houses, to destroy nearly every vestige of the colony, without themselves taking an open part in the more violent proceedings. At the meeting at Fort William, the ensuing Summer, when Mr. Simon McGillivray appears to have replaced his brother, as principal agent of the company, the parties from Red River were all received with unqualified approbation; to the half-breeds, in particular, praises and rewards were given, consisting (exclusive of a public feast) of a suit of clothes each, and presents of arms to a few of the leaders; and evidence has been produced, that they were at the same time told by Mr. Simon McGillivray, that they had done well in defending their lands; and that if the colonists attempted to return, they should drive them away again, and should be supported by the North-West company.... For the numerous and mutual violences of the ensuing Winter and Spring, I must again refer to the Statement, observing, that in the seizure of Duncan Cameron's person and post at the forks of Red River, and the pertinacious retention of this latter, the Hudson's Bay company's party, so far exceeded any legitimate measures of defence, that they must I think be considered as aggressors, in most of the occurrences previous to the 19th June; although at the same time there can be no doubt that the half-breeds, acting at the instigation of the North-West company, (by whom they were collected, and furnished with supplies of food and ammunition,) had early in the year resolved on again attempting to drive off the colonists. On the 19th June, when the unfortunate affray took place in which Governor Semple lost his life, the two parties seem to have met accidentally, and with arms in their hands, and mutually irritated feelings; that the action took place without previous design on either side; the first shot appears, next to a certainty, to have been fired by the Hudson's Bay company's party, at the moment that Governor Semple, enraged by the insolent address of Boucher, (the messenger sent forward by the half-breeds,) attempted to snatch away his gun; the savage massacre of the wounded, and the inhuman plundering and butchering of the dead bodies after the action, appears therefore to form the most aggravated part of the proceeding. This, Grant, their leader, states, he endeavoured in vain to prevent; and the total absence of any accusation against him on this score, and the numerous testimonies to his general humanity, leave little doubt of the truth of this assertion; if admitted, however, it furnishes only an additional proof of the ferocity of a part of the body, and shows in the stronger point of view, the dangerous course adopted by the North-West company, in employing so ungovernable and almost savage a force. This indeed forms the great offence of the company as a body, and has, together with the melancholy consequences which have followed therefrom, naturally and justly excited a strong public feeling against them; it is true, that few comparatively of the partners of the company appear to have actually taken part in the assembling of the half-breeds this year, but a similar measure had been universally approved the preceding one, and a large number of the partners who arrived at Red River shortly after the 19th June, with the mixed views of liberating Duncan Cameron, retaking their own post, and revenging these and the other violences they attributed to their opponents, appear to have given an unqualified approbation to all the proceedings of the half-breeds, and many of them to have expressed their triumph and joy on viewing the scene of action; if one witness who speaks to this particular fact (my doubts respecting whose testimony will be found fully explained in my statement) could be fully credited, in terms and with circumstances of ferocity scarcely human; at all events, it is clearly established, that about forty suits of clothes which Mr. Archibald Norman McLeod, the principal agent of the company, then present, had brought up, were distributed amongst the half-breeds, including those present on the 19th June, as a recompence for their services to the company, and that further rewards of the same kind were found prepared at Fort William, on the Earl of Selkirk's taking possession of that post, for such as had not received them in the first instance. It is on these proceedings at Red River, that Archibald Norman McLeod and so many other of the partners of the North-West company, are indicted as accessaries to the murder of Governor Semple; and it is chiefly for the approval of the proceedings of the half-breeds, implied by further rewards prepared at Fort William, at a period when Mr. William McGillivray was residing there as principal agent, that the same charge is expected to be made out against him....

The observations relative to this last occurrence, apply equally or perhaps more strongly to the half-breeds, in respect to the greater part of whom there are also many other circumstances of extenuation; they evidently acted in the first instance under a mistaken sense of right, and an impression that the settlers were invaders of the natural rights of themselves and the North-West company; their claim to the soil, jointly with the Indians (in favour of which the evidence before me shows that plausible grounds might be assigned,) was evidently strongly impressed on them by the partners of the North-West company, to whose opinions they naturally looked up, and during the contest, many circumstances of mutual irritation had occurred; yet their final plan of attack appears to have bene confined to the expulsion of the colonists, without further violence than might be unavoidable in the accomplishment of that object; the affray of the 19th of June, melancholy as it was in its result, seems clearly to have been unpremeditated, and it appears that but few individuals amongst the half-breeds partook of the massacre that succeeded it. Of the sincerity of the half-breeds in the opinions they profess to have acted upon, strong presumptive proof is afforded by the openness with which they generally avowed their intentions, by their address to Government, (which there can be little doubt was sent, although probably in one way or other suppressed by the North-West company,) and in the final voluntary submission of its principal leaders to public authority.

After this long detail of the final impressions remaining upon my mind, on the coolest and most deliberate consideration of the evidence before me, I deem it right to state, that I now feel more strongly convinced than ever, of the general correctness of the opinion, which I had the honour of submitting to your Excellency on my return from the Indian country, as the result of my inquiry, as far as it had then gone; namely, "that the moral character of most of the offences, was, that of each party instead of appealing to the laws of their country, endeavouring to enforce the rights to which they conceived themselves entitled, or to redress their supposed injuries by force;" ...

## Readings

Brown, J. *Strangers in the Blood: Fur Trade Families in Indian Country.* Vancouver: University of British Columbia Press, 1980.

Brown, J., and J. Peterson, eds. *The New Peoples: Being and Becoming Métis in North America.* Winnipeg: University of Manitoba Press, 1985.

Bumsted, J. "Introduction" to J. Bumsted, ed., *The Collected Writings of Lord Selkirk 1810-1829* Vol 2. Winnipeg: Manitoba Record Society, 1987.

Bumsted, J. "The Quest for a Usable Founder: Lord Selkirk and Manitoba Historians," *Manitoba History* 2 (1981).

Burley, E. *Servants of the Honourable Company: Work, Discipline, and Conflict in the Hudson's Bay Company 1770-1879.* Toronto: Oxford University Press, 1997.

Carlos, A. "The Birth and Death of Predatory Competition in the North American Fur Trade, 1810-1821," *Explorations in Economic History* 19, 2 (1982).

Dick, L. "The Seven Oaks Incident and the Construction of a Historical Tradition," *Journal of the Canadian Historical Association* 2 (1991).

Foster, J. "The Origins of Mixed Bloods in the Canadian West," in L. Thomas, ed., *Essays on Western History.* Edmonton: University of Alberta Press, 1976.

Gray, J. *Lord Selkirk of Red River.* Toronto: Macmillan, 1963.

Gressley, G. "Lord Selkirk and the Canadian Courts," in J. Bumsted, ed., *Canadian History Before Confederation.* 2nd edition. Toronto: Gage, 1979.

Kaye, B. "The Red River Settlement: Lord Selkirk's Isolated Colony in the Wilderness," *Prairie Forum* 11, 1 (Spring 1986).

Mcleod, M., and W. Morton. *Cuthbert Grant of Grantown.* Toronto: McClelland and Stewart, 1974.

Moodie, D. "The Trading Post Settlement of the Canadian Northwest, 1774-1821," *Journal of Historical Geography* 13, 2 (October 1957).

Morton, A. *A History of the Canadian West to 1870-71.* 2nd edition. Toronto: University of Toronto Press, 1973.

Morton, W. "The North West Company: Pedlars Extraordinary," *Minnesota History* (Winter 1966).

Pannekoek, F. *The Fur Trade in Western Canadian Society*. Ottawa: Canadian Historical Association, 1989.

Podruchny, C. "Unfair Masters and Rascally Servants? Labor Relations Among Bourgeois Clerks and Voyageurs in the Montreal Fur Trade, 1760-1821," *Labour* 43 (Spring 1999).

Ray, A. *Indians in the Fur Trade*. Toronto: University of Toronto Press, 1974.

Rich, E. *The Fur Trade and the North West to 1857*. Toronto: McClelland and Stewart 1967.

Rich, E. *The History of the Hudson's Bay Company, 1670–1870*. London: Hudson's Bay Record Society, 1959.

*Chapter Nine*

# "SICILY OF NORTH AMERICA":
# THE LAND ISSUE IN PRINCE EDWARD ISLAND

1. John Lewellin, *Emigration*, 1826.
2. George R. Young, *A Statement of the 'Escheat Question' in the Island of Prince Edward*, 1838.
3. B. Sleigh, *Pine Forests and Macmatak Clearings*, 1853.
4. "Report of the Commissioners Appointed to Inquire into the Differences Prevailing in Prince Edward Island Relative to the Rights of Landowners and Tenants With a View to the Settlement of the Same on Fair and Equitable Principles," July 18, 1861.
5. Charles Mackay, "A Week in Prince Edward Island," *Fortnightly Review*, 1866.

## *Introduction*

A typical Canadian will likely imagine PEI as a bucolic land, home to that feisty but insufferably wholesome little girl from Green Gables. And if not Anne Shirley, then the island is perceived as a tranquil and pastoral farmscape producing potatoes or lobsters. But historically PEI and Newfoundland's colonial histories were perhaps the most unusual of Britain's North American possessions, each for its own peculiar reason. In Prince Edward Island's case, the issue of land ownership tainted settlement and colonial development from the colony's inception, leading to acrimony and sometimes violence between land owners and tenants during the first half of the nineteenth century. Whatever measure of tranquillity that came later, arrived at the cost of considerable hardship, suffering, and anxiety.

France claimed and settled Île Saint Jean, as they named it, in the 1720s. Though the population remained very small, isolated, and dependent upon the great French fort at Louisburg on Cape Breton Island, it swelled briefly to some 5000 souls during the Seven Years' War and particularly after the Acadian expulsion and Louisburg's defeat. Britain captured the island in 1758 and British military commanders, who could not abide a sizable French population in the area, soon "encouraged" most to leave—despite not taking formal possession until the Treaty of Paris and the fall of New France in 1763.

In 1765, Captain Samuel Holland surveyed the island and divided it into 67 township lots of some 20,000 acres each. Then things took a novel turn. Rather than hold the lots as Crown land to be given out in small freeholds to prospective settlers, as normally occurred in newly surveyed colonies, the British government in 1767 held a lottery among military officers and others to whom it owed favours and awarded the lots according to the results. Thus there was no Crown land apart from lot 66 and a few areas surrounding proposed towns. No consideration whatsoever was given to the original Native inhabitants. The lucky lottery winners faced only two caveats: to settle one Protestant from outside Britain for every 200 acres within ten years; and to pay an annual quitrent. Quitrents were to supply capital for local improvements so the British treasury would not bear the expense.

The new proprietors persuaded London to grant the island colonial status in 1769 but settlers ceased arriving, some who did left, and markets dried up. Thus the proprietors, the vast majority of whom lived in England and never ever stepped ashore in PEI, felt little incentive to seek settlers, improve their holdings, or pay the annual quitrents—to which the British government acquiesced, funding the limited local development taking place. The proprietors who did pay justly accused local island officials of squandering the quitrents. In any case, PEI remained woefully undeveloped, lacking even rudimentary versions of the societies developing elsewhere in North America.

Small numbers of settlers did immigrate to PEI throughout this period, the vast majority at their own expense. Perhaps naively, most new settlers simply squatted on whatever patch they chose and set about creating farms from the bush. Some remained as squatters for decades, others eventually drafted contracts with the proprietors: leases that required rents based upon the land value plus their portion of the proprietor's quitrent. This, needless to say, remained highly unpopular with tenants who resented increased rents from hardwrought improvements they made, but which also drove the proprietor's land values upward. So why negotiate leases at all? Without them squatters had no legal rights whatsoever and could be evicted, which would be particularly galling for a squatter on a thriving farm built over two or three generations of family. Lease holding farmers were not necessarily in the clear either. Falling in arrears of the annual rent could, and did, result in eviction, or at least in long term debt to the proprietor. The one glimmer of hope, and one to which increasing numbers of settlers clung, was to invoke the centuries-old law of squatting which gave settlers clear title to their land if they could prove twenty years of continual farming without ever paying rent. This became a very real factor by the 1830s by which time many settlers approached the required number of years, which in turn brought out rent-collecting landlords, or their hated agents, seeking to avoid losing chunks of their land. Settlers hid from proprietors, agents "disappeared" or were brutalized, proprietors received threats, and the island lurched toward a showdown between the 30,000 odd islanders against the handful of proprietors and their representatives.

The picture was, of course, not entirely one-sided and landlords, too, held valid grievances. Just as many proprietors failed to pay quitrent or fulfill their other obligations to the Crown, evidence suggests that many, if not most, tenants equally reneged on their obligations to their landlords—and got away with it, sometimes for generations. Why? Possibly because proprietors realized that one cannot get blood from a stone and that one shirking tenant improving the land is better than no tenant at all. Perhaps they also let things slide for the prosaic reason that tracking down errant tenants from the other side of the Atlantic was simply too bothersome for the meagre results. Certainly neither party in the argument held a monopoly on moral righteousness—though both claimed it. As historian J.M. Bumsted stated: "the lines of conflict had been plainly drawn between Islanders and proprietors. Islanders were scoundrels, proprietors were parasites."

For islanders, the issue coalesced into the escheat movement of the 1830s. "Escheating," was the legal term for the Crown's right to repossess land given to a landlord for failure to meet his obligations. In the Prince Edward Island context, this meant that a proprietor could see his land escheated had he not settled, at his expense, the requisite settler-per-200-acres. There might even be grounds, in strictly legal terms, for repossessing land had the proprietor settled it with non-Protestants, or with people from Britain. Very few, if any, proprietors had fulfilled those original obligations. The Escheat Party of the 1830s further argued that escheated land should automatically revert, in free title, from the Crown to those living upon it. Islanders certainly supported the movement, and the almost universal male franchise allowed the budding Escheat Party an astonishing three-to-one victory in the 1838 election for the Island Assembly. The movement was wildly optimistic, but unrealistic since it struck at the very heart of the right of private property, which most British parliamentarians fervently supported—perhaps because they were property owners. Enacting escheats required approval from London, and in some instances from the very people who would be escheated. The attempt was therefore bound to remain stillborn, despite its tremendous popularity. Landlords also argued that it was hardly fair for them to lose their lands and tenants to gain theirs gratis when both stood guilty of the same misdeed: failing to fulfill obligations. The escheat movement crumbled in the face of formidable opposition in England and its failure quickly doused the radical flame, but it was the first agrarian protest movement in Canada and it did sow the seeds for moderate reformers and their call for responsible government as a solution. It also fostered what ultimately became the Land Commission of the 1860s which called for voluntary sale of proprietorial land and purchase at reasonable cost by those actually residing upon it. The following documents illustrate the thrust-and-parry of the land arguments.

## Discussion Points

1. Who had the better case—landowners or tenants?
2. To what extent were the labels "scoundrels" for Islanders and "parasites" for landlords appropriate?
3. Leasehold tenure was the norm throughout the British Isles. Was it a legitimate problem holding back the development of PEI, or simply an excuse—a scapegoat—to explain unfulfilled expectations? Would land owners have fared differently from renters?

## Documents

### 1. John Lewellin, *Emigration*, 1826.

... Mode of Tenure.—Upon the conquest of the Island from the French, about 70 years since, it was granted by the British Government, in Townships of 20,000 acres each; whereby the Colony sustained a deep and lasting injury. Had so fertile a country continued Crown land, and been granted to actual settlers in quantities of land equal, or proportioned to their means of improvement, the greater part of it would now be occupied by men of talent and capital, and in a high state of improvement—what might not the Island in such circumstances have done!

The Proprietors themselves, also, have been too generally negligent of their property. Living commonly in Britain, and possessing other means, they generally have given too little attention to their Estates in Prince Edward Island; neglected to make the Colony more known; and committed a mistake in leasing rather than selling lands—not considering that it is from the number and respectability of the body of small proprietors, or occupying yeomen, that the improvement of a new county must spring, and the rapidly increasing value of its unoccupied lands arise....

Dry goods, or British merchandise and manufactures, bore very high prices some few years since. At the present time they may be obtained very reasonable in Charlotte-Town for prompt cash payment. In many country places great prices are still charged; but should a fishery be established, trade extended, or the land better cultivated and its surplus produce sent to a cash market, either of which would introduce money into the Colony, goods will be sold still lower; and should all these branches of national industry and national wealth prosper—and prosper they must; I had almost said, with my Uncle Toby, prosper they shall— then some of the superabundant capital of Britain will no doubt find profitable employment here; and what ardent and enthusiastic mind will then fix the limits of the advancement of the Colony? The Island Prince Edward has long since been described as the Garden of Canada. It has lately been designated the Sicily of North America. In some future period it may become the emporium of an extensive commerce. At present there are a great number of vessels, from 60 to 100 tons and upwards, built in the Colony, every season, and sold in Newfound-land for the seal fishery.

There are no manufactures carried on in the Colony, except domestic ones for the use of the farmer's family. The settlers generally make of their wool a very useful cloth, called homespun, worth from 4s. 6d. to 5s. per yard, which serves the men for jackets and trowsers, whilst a finer sort supplies the females with gowns for winter use; they also manufacture blankets, stockings or socks, and mittins. The wool is simply dyed with indigo. Some families make the greater part of their table, bed, and personal linen from flax, often using with it cotton warp of American manufacture. Leather is tanned by most settlers from their own hides; and there is need of it, shoes being very expensive to purchase. The Colonists make a great part of the soap and candles they use, but the greater number burn fish oil for light. People generally do not procure for themselves half the comforts they might enjoy with a little more exertion and perseverance. All that a Farm will produce in England for the farmer's table may be produced here, and of excellent quality; but in the country parts there are no butchers' or bakers' shops, yet the settlers sometimes sell part of what meat they kill, and sometimes lend. Indeed, there is amongst them a great deal of that spirit of hospitality which is pleasing in every country, and more particularly grateful and needful in a young one. Gardens and Orchards are much neglected, although apples, and other fruits, thrive well, and no country can boast of finer vegetables, which are not so early as in England.

Many of the Settlers live very much on Fish (herring, mackerel, cod, lobsters, &c.) and potatoes, oatmeal porridge and milk, but people generally are getting into more expensive habits in food, dress, dwellings, and furniture. Tea may be purchased from 3s. 6d. to 5s. per lb. Sugar 6d. Rum 3s. 9d. to 5s. per gallon.

Here we may pause and exclaim—Verily, this is a good poor man's country! Here a settler may begin farming without a shilling in his pocket, and obtain employment at such wages as will not only enable him to live, but also to proceed with his farm—a country where the unfortunate but industrious may find a refuge, with a certainty of food and raiment, and save himself from being brought to day-labour or forced to seek parochial relief in the place which once witnessed his prosperity. It might answer also for persons with small means and large families, if they could purchase partly cleared farms, and were willing to labour a part of their time. Officers on half-pay might find it a retreat not to be despised. It is a growing country—growing in value, in importance, in power to yield the comforts of life, and in the respectability of its society, to which every creditable emigrant would be a valuable addition: and it may be an inducement to some minds that a man of moderate attainments shines like a little star in new and small communities, who would be unregarded in any well improved circle in Britain.

Emigrants may enjoy in the Island advantages in many respects preferable or superior to what they would meet with in Upper Canada, where British goods are dearer and produce cheaper. Here would be no long journey to perform after the voyage, requiring a considerable expenditure, but the settler can go upon a farm immediately on his arrival; and this is a great convenience to those who bring their furniture, implements, a few goods, &c.; and all who can should do so. We have a greater choice of markets; the Canadian settler must sell to the merchant or storekeeper; the Prince Edward Island farmer can ship his productions to Halifax, Newfoundland, Miramichi, &c. and a trade to the West Indies has been commenced, which would absorb all our surplus beef, pork, butter, hams, flour, oats, and other articles, should it be found desirable to prosecute this commerce....

## 2. George R. Young, *A Statement of the 'Escheat Question' in the Island of Prince Edward,* 1838.

To the Tenantry and the other Inhabitants of the Island of Prince Edward,
The affairs of the Island have now reached a crisis. It is admitted that they are in
a state of lamentable embarrassment and confusion.... The dormant question of
escheat has been revived; the payment of rents has been resisted; the sheriff has
been assaulted in the execution of his duty; strangers entering Belfast, because
suspected to be bailiffs, have been fired at by a mob; public meetings have been
held, inflammatory resolutions have been passed, and addresses, got up in the
same spirit, presented to the Lieutenant Governor. An Island blessed with a
fertile soil, a favorable climate, excellent harbours, free fisheries, and a healthy
and active population,with every requisite, in short, to make a country prosperous and a people contented and happy,—has been placed in such a position that
the rights of property are endangered, the peace of society disturbed, and an
exigency created in which the authority of the Government must soon be exercised to enforce the laws, by resort to force, if the people themselves have not the
prudence and good sense to return to tranquillity and to good order.... The past
agitation can end in no beneficial result, but will only embarrass the Government, and interfere with your own prosperity and future welfare....

It would be in vain at the present moment to inquire into the policy of a
past Government, by which the Island was parcelled out into large tracts, some
of which have since passed into the possession of British proprietors. It is clear
that these titles now rest upon the King's grant, which is the best, because the
highest title known to the law. If any one of these could be disturbed, if a
proprietor holding under this title, confirmed as it is by the royal seal, could be
deprived of his property, there is not a farmer or freeholder in the Island who
would be secure in the ownership of his own land. Every freeholder holds under
one of these original grants, and to uphold them is to uphold your own leases
and your own title deeds; to abrogate them would not only be a gross violation
of the law and of the honour of the Crown, but disturb every man in his possession, and reduce the affairs of the Island into a state of inextricable and
irremediable confusion.

But however much the policy above referred to may be disapproved of, it is
to be recollected that many of the past proprietors have dealt liberally with their
estates—that they have sent out a valuable class of settlers—have given them advantageous leases—have in many cases received no rents—and even, after a period
of years of non-payment, have released their tenantry from all the arrears of rents

which were due. Many of them enjoy now the character of being good land-lords—their tenants make no complaints—they are contented and happy— ...

Before quitting the subject of the rights of the proprietors, it ought not to be forgotten, however, that some of them have acquired and now hold their title by purchase—that they have paid for their lands with money—that they were no parties to the ancient grants of 1767—and that to deprive them of their property so held and so acquired would, in plain language, be an act of robbery; and has been so characterised in the debates in the House of Assembly. The proprietors are as clearly entitled to the quiet and peaceable possession of their estates, as any of you are to your houses, the fields which you have cultivated, the crops you have raised, or the cattle you have reared; and the Government could deprive them of their estates with as little justice as you, by the same exercise of power, could be ejected from your farms or stripped of your property. In short, the conditions contained in these grants are as binding upon the Crown, as the terms contained in your leases or deeds are binding upon the propri-etors.... Upon what principle can it be said that rents payable under leases, and which you voluntarily have entered into, can be compared to taxes imposed by the Government? Leases are strictly private contracts—bargains between man and man. The Government neither created, nor has it the power to interfere with them. Would you submit to any law, passed either by the Government at home or the Island legislature, requiring that you should pay to the proprietor one shilling and sixpence per acre, in place of your present rents of one shilling? Have either the right to do so? Now, if they cannot make you pay more, neither have they the power to compel the proprietor to take less. The whole argument is a fallacy....

Having placed these view before you, having thus addressed your good sense and your feelings of justice, we come now to touch upon the question of escheat, and to inquire what you or the Legislature can hope to gain, if the prayer of the agitators were actually conceded, and a Court of Escheat estab-lished. We are satisfied there is not an honest man amongst you, who, if the question were submitted to him, would be prepared to say that a proprietor should be deprived of his property contrary to the law; that is to say, if he had complied with all the terms imposed by the Crown when the grant was con-ferred upon him, or upon the person from whom he has bought his estate. A Court of Escheat could only re-invest the lands in the Crown, upon clear proof being given that the conditions, as modified by the King's Ministers, had not been performed. And it may be pressed upon your consideration, whether any of those who agitate this question have proved to you a single case, in which, if acting as a juror under the solemn sanction of an oath, you would be prepared to say that the estates stood liable to forfeiture. Do not be led away by general declamation; do not yield to specious and unfounded hopes or promises; but bring to this question the same sound understanding and honesty of purpose which you apply to the other and the ordinary transactions of life—the same rule of right and of justice which you would seek for yourselves.

But the question remains, whether it is the interest of the present tenantry and the settlers that the lands they now occupy should be escheated, and pass into the hands of the Crown. Some of the persons who have agitated upon this question have endeavoured to inflame your minds by holding out this prospect,—that if the estates of the proprietors were forfeited, they would be granted unconditionally by Her Majesty to those who occupied them—that from being tenants, without paying for your lands, you would become freeholders, and thus be released for the future from the payment of rents. Now ask yourselves if the Government has held out any such promise—have these hopes the shadow of a foundation from the language of any person in authority? ...

The proprietors, although they have been, and still are, disposed to comply with every lawful demand, and to pay the quit rents due upon their lands, are of opinion that they have just cause of complaint in the severity with which their collection has been pressed, when abandoned in other colonies, and in the ruinous law expenses incurred when they were not paid within the period prescribed. Many of them complain of the rigour with which the law has been enforced upon all occasions against them; to repeat the language employed by some of them to the writer, they say, "The majesty of the law appears then in its full might: but the moment we appeal to it for protection, and seek to recover our rents, it is allowed to become a dead letter, its arm sleeps nerveless; and we have been told that it cannot be enforced by those whose duty it is to persuade or to compel obedience. The quit rents are exacted from us with severity, and unless immediate payment be made, our property is wantonly sacrificed by the very parties who, if they do not actually refuse justice, dole it out with an apathy and tardiness which render it a mockery. Can it be just, can it be reasonable, that the proprietors should be called upon to pay quit rents, not only for the wilderness land (of that they do not complain), but for the occupied and cultivated land, whilst the tenantry are persuaded by agitators, free from punishment, not to pay the rents which are due to us? What would those in authority say if we, by the same means as are employed against us, endeavoured to resist the payment of our rents? If we pay, ought not the tenants? If the law be rigidly administered to us, why not to them? While exacted to the last shilling from us for every acre, whether barren or swamp, is it just that the resident freeholder and farmer should be allowed to refuse payment for the rents due on their cultivated lands, as they have done for a series of years?" This language is quoted that you may comprehend the view they take of the question, that you may inquire into the truth of these complaints, and if true, that, as honest men, you may correct this injustice, and apply to the proprietors that golden rule which is the basis of all sound morality.

### 3. B. Sleigh, *Pine Forests and Macmatak Clearings,* 1853.

... But for seven months of the year impenetrable masses of ice choke up those openings for commerce, while icebergs and vast fields of constantly moving ice roll on with fearful rapidity through the narrow pass of the capes, rendering the passage across a work of imminent peril to life.

This is not the only drawback to the progress of the Colony. The winter sets in early in December, and continues in intensity until the following June; nay, snow is often to be found in the woods as late as July. When once the season of more genial warmth commences, the rapidity of vegetation exceeds belief. Providence, in his goodness, enables the crops speedily to fructify, and the ploughman is quickly followed by the reaper. The fertility of the soil is not to be found equalled in any other portion of North America: the whole island, to the water's edge, is capable of cultivation; the land is easily cleared of the forest, and its prolific nature grants to the husbandman the means of subsistence.

But this happy state of existence has barely three month's duration, within which period are to be reckoned the Spring, the Summer, and the Autumn of this evanescent climate. The expense of supplying fodder for the seven dreary months of winter bears heavily upon the farmer, and in countless instances cattle are actually destroyed in preference to keeping them. The result is, that the people of the Island are decidedly the poorest, as far as pecuniary means are concerned, to be found in the British Provinces. It is a well-known though vulgar saying in the Island, that "the sight of a shilling acts as an onion on a farmer's eyes."

The tenure of land in the island is chiefly proprietary, owned in blocks from 20,000 to 50,000 acres. It is no uncommon occurrence for seven townships to belong to one proprietor....

The settlers in the Island, who form the chief bulk of the population, are those who have been, either themselves or their fathers, sent over wholesale by the landlords, from heavily-populated estates in Scotland or Ireland. The people who permitted themselves to be thus unceremoniously expatriated as a burden from the soil of the Mother-country were, as a matter of course, composed of the lowest and most degraded class. The sentiments of attachment to the land of their birth could never, under such circumstances, have been remarkable for an excessive display of warmth, nor has any one ever accused them of any stronger love of loyalty. Poverty, and its accompaniment, vice, nurtured by ignorance and petty cunning, did not form a favourable school whence the young islander could draw wholesome example from the sire....

Distinct from this class are to be found (and their position is greatly to be pitied) the minority, composed of numbers of high-minded, honourable men, to whom the well-known cheapness of living, and the unrivalled healthiness of the climate, notwithstanding its winter rigour, offered strong inducements to settle there. Then there are a few resident proprietors, gentlemen by birth, education, and feeling, and several retired officers from the Army.

The introduction—most unadvisedly, into an island barely numbering 70,000 inhabitants, nine-tenths of whom are ignorant labourers—of the principle of Responsible Government, has ended, as might have been foreseen, by the powers of government passing into the hands of the lower orders, to the total exclusion of the educated class. It will hardly be believed in England, that the highest Member in the Executive Council keeps a grog-shop; ...

With such a party managing the affairs of the Colony, the rights of property ... are, as may be supposed, most grievously tampered with. The grand aim of the present Government is to annihilate the proprietary interest; and most warmly are they supported in these their views by the Governor. They have commenced their operations with that subtle cunning, derived, it may be conjectured, from the example of their respectable sires; which operations, unless arrested in time, will result in the loss of every acre in the island, owned by a proprietor....

To render the position of landlord and tenant even more complicated, a Bill has been introduced, designated "The Tenants' Compensation Bill," the main feature of which consists in obliging the proprietor, if he distrain for rent, to allow to the tenant the full value of all improvements made by him on the property distrained. This Bill in full operation, and adieu to all rents, or arrears of rent, for a half-century to come. It, in fact, will operate as a grant of a virtual freehold to every tenant, and rob the proprietor of his land, under the plausible pretext of a just and equitable legal enactment.

These are the sentiments of the inhabitants of King's County, embracing twenty townships, of seven of which I was once foolish enough to become proprietor, embracing about 100,000 acres.

## 4. "Report of the Commissioners Appointed to Inquire into the Differences Prevailing in Prince Edward Island Relative to the Rights of Landowners and Tenants With a View to the Settlement of the Same on Fair and Equitable Principles," July 18, 1861.

May it please Your Majesty;

... From the issuing of the grants, in 1767 down to the present time, every Secretary of State for the Colonies, and every Governor, has been perplexed by the questions arising out of that ill-advised exercise of the Royal prerogative.

The amount of money and time wasted in public controversy, no man can estimate; and the extent to which a vicious system of colonization has entered into the daily life of this people, and embittered their industrial and social relations, it is painful to contemplate and record.

The past is beyond remedy; but the undersigned have felt that if tranquility and mutual co-operation among its people could be hereafter secured to the Island, such a consummation could only result from a searching review of all the questions which there touch the tenures of the land.

The undersigned have also felt that as the case of Prince Edward Island was exceptional, so must be the treatment. The application of the Local Government for a Commission, and the large powers given to it by the Queen's authority, presupposed the necessity of a departure from the ordinary legal modes of settling disputes between landlords and tenants, which the experience of half a century had proved to be inadequate. Finding, therefore, that it was impossible to shut out of their inquiry while on the Island, the questions of escheat, quitrents, the fishery reserves, the claims of the descendants of the original French inhabitants, Indians, and loyalists, they have thought it quite within the range of their obligations to express their opinions freely upon those branches of the general subject.

The opposition of some of the proprietors who had not become parties to the arbitration, and who seemed to regard the Commissioners as intruders upon their property, and willing violators of their rights, was apparent. These persons appeared to forget that the Commissioners did not seek the duties imposed upon them, that they had no personal interests in the inquiry, that the grievances of Prince Edward Island grew out of no neglect of theirs. These persons appeared also to forget, that, though the rights of property have ever been sacredly guarded by the law, whenever the possession or abuse of property becomes prejudicial to the public interests, the rights and prejudices of individuals can be constitutionally controlled for the public good. The protesting proprietors of

Prince Edward Island have no better titles to their properties than had the Seigneurs of Canada, the owners of the encumbered estates in Ireland, or the slave-holders in the West Indies. They have none so good, because every acre they own is held by the generous forbearance of the British Government, after breach of conditions over and over again. Were these people, in view of the distracted condition of the Colony, dealt with by specific legislation, or were they now compelled to accept the conditions of this award, they would only be treated as large classes of their fellow subjects have been under the pressure of similar exigencies, and, for the reasons stated, would have but little right to complain.

Looking back at the origin of these unhappy disputes, it is apparent that the granting of a whole Colony in a single day, in huge blocks of 20,000 acres each, was an improvident and unwise exercise of the prerogative of the Crown. Had the proprietors, however, formed themselves into an Emigration Society, and commenced the colonization of the Island, on a rational plan for their mutual advantage, there is every reason to believe that, with the surplus population of the British Islands to draw upon, they might have fully peopled Prince Edward Island in a few years. But there was no plan, and no co-operative movement among the grantees. Some of them early entered upon the duties of colonization in a spirit of judicious enterprize, and with a liberal expenditure; but others did little, and that little often unwisely, while the majority did nothing. The emigrants sent out by the few were disheartened by the surrounding wilderness owned by the many, who made no effort to reclaim it, or were tempted to roam about or disregard the terms of settlement, by the quantity of wild land with no visible owner to guard it from intrusion. By mutual co-operation and a common policy, the proprietors might have redeemed the grants of the Imperial Government from the charge of improvidence. The want of these indispensable elements of success laid the foundation of all the grievances which subsequently afflicted the Colony....

The most simple remedy for the evils which actually exist at the present time, would seem to be suggested by the operation of the Land Purchase Act, so far as the Commissioners have been able to estimate the results of its operations. Under that Act the Worrell and Selkirk estates have been purchased, covering 140,000 acres. No injustice has been done to the proprietors, who have cheerfully accepted the sums offered by the Government. They have been promptly paid, and at once relieved from all uncertainty as to the future, from the risk of unpaid rents and the heavy expenses of management and collection. The estates thus purchased *en bloc*, have been bought at prices so low, that the Government has been enabled to re-sell the lands in fee, at such an advance as not only meets the outlay, but all the expenses of management and distribution By this system, it is apparent that three signal advantages are secured, that are not presented by any other.

1st. The proprietors are dispossessed by their own consent.

2dly. The tenants are enabled to purchase their holdings and improvements, not necessarily at a price so high as to represent the rents stipulated to be paid, but at the lowest price which the expenses of management, added to the aggregate cost of the estate, will warrant.

3dly. The wild lands are at once rescued from the operation of the leasehold system and are subjected to the wholesome control of the Local Government, to be hereafter disposed of in fee simple, at moderate prices, as they are in all the other North American provinces....

It is clear that the local Government cannot generally apply the principles of the Land Purchase Act, without the assistance of the Imperial Parliament. To complete the purchases already made their resources have been strained; and even if the money paid could be at once collected the Government could only purchase two other estates at one time, so that many years must elapse before any large measure of relief could be given to the great body of the tenantry, whose complaints have led to this inquiry.

The Commissioners are expected to propose a remedy, and discharge themselves of that duty, entirely conscious that the slightest modification or compromise of his legal rights will be regarded as spoliation by the landlord, while anything short of confiscation will scarcely satisfy the tenant. Their duty is not to satisfy either; but with all the elements of a sound judgment before them, to do substantial justice to both.

It is difficult for an European to understand why almost every man in America considers it a personal degradation to pay rent. In the British Islands leasehold tenure is the general rule, and freehold the exception. A wealthy man pays rent with no more sense of inferiority than he feels when he pays his taxes. A poor man lives and dies without any hope of owning land, often without any desire to become a freeholder. On this side of the Atlantic a very different sentiment grew out of the discovery and settlement of a boundless continent, where the best land could be seized upon, or bought for a trifle, in the early stages of colonization; and where even now, after two centuries of occupation, land is so easily obtained, at prices so low that almost every industrious man may own a freehold; if he does not, in the agricultural districts, something discreditable to his character or his capacity is assumed; and even in the towns a man prefers to own the house he lives in, though the amount of interest he would pay upon a mortgage may be quite equal to his rent.

The tenantry of Prince Edward Island share the common sentiment of the continent which surrounds them. The prejudice in favor of a freehold tenure, if it is one, is beyond the power of reason. The proprietors cannot change the sentiment, the local government have no power to resist it; and the Imperial Government, having become weary of collecting rents and supporting evictions in Ireland, can hardly be expected to do for the landlords in Prince Edward Island what has ceased to be popular or practicable at home.

It is, therefore, imperative upon all the parties concerned to convert this tenure. Agrarian questions now occupy the public mind incessantly in this fine Colony, to the exclusion of all sound politics. A public man is valued in proportion as he is subservient to the proprietors, or friendly to the tenants, not for the measures of internal improvement or intercolonial policy he may propound; and the intellectual and social life of this people is exhausted and frittered away by disputes and contentions detrimental to the interests of all parties.

Should the general principles, propounded in this report, be accepted in the spirit which animates the Commissioners, and be followed by practical legislation, the Colony will start forward with renewed energy, dating a new era from 1861. The British Government will have nobly atoned for any errors in its past policy. The Legislature will no longer be distracted with efforts to close the Courts upon proprietors, or to tamper with the currency of the Island. The cry of "tenant right" will cease to disguise the want of practical statesmanship, or to overawe the local administration. Men who have hated and disturbed each other will be reconciled, and pursue their common interests by mutual co-operation. Roads will be levelled, breakwaters built, the river beds will be dredged, and new fertilizers applied to a soil, now annually drained of its vitality. Emigration will cease, and population, attracted to the wild lands, will enter upon their cultivation unembarrassed by the causes which perplexed the early settlers. Weighed down by the burden of this investigation, the undersigned have sometimes felt doubtful of any beneficial results. But they now, at the close of their labours, indulge the hope that if their suggestions are adopted, enfranchised and disenthralled from the poisoned garments that enfold her, Prince Edward Island will yet become, what she ought to be, the Barbadoes of the St. Lawrence.

## 5. Charles Mackay, "A Week in Prince Edward Island," *Fortnightly Review*, 1866.

The Land and Rent question touched them more nearly. The tenants all over the island made up their minds half a century ago that the lands they occupied were their own; that their landlords had no title; and that consequently the exaction of rent was an act of oppression which they were bound to resist. As this opinion had brought many of them into collision with the sheriff and his courts of law, the island at the time of my visit to Charlottetown was in a state of commotion.

The dispute had reached its crisis. The farmers had formed themselves into a "Tenants' League," the object of which was to resist the payment of the rents they had bound themselves to pay by the terms of their leases, and virtually to confiscate the property of the landowners. When the sheriff appeared in any district to serve his writs upon the defaulters a signal was blown upon a long tin trumpet, with one of which every farmer in the island was supplied, and at the well-known sound the people gathered from far and near, as they did in olden times in England and Scotland on the alarm of invasion, by the beacon-fire or the tocsin, and took effectual means to prevent the service of the writs by the assault and battery or forcible detention of the officers. Six weeks before my arrival the state of affairs in the island was so threatening that the Administrator and his Prime Minister, the Colonial Secretary, unable to rely upon the special constabulary for any assistance in the preservation of the peace, and in view of the fact that the Tenant Leaguers had sometimes appeared in armed gangs of 100 or 200 at a time, and that the lives of the sheriffs and their officers were endangered, deemed it their duty to send to Major-General Doyle at Halifax for military assistance. The request was complied with, and 200 men of the 16th Regiment were sent to the island with all possible speed. Their arrival changed the aspect of affairs. Whenever the sheriff had to serve a writ he was accompanied by twenty or thirty soldiers, and the Tenant Leaguers, not being desperate enough to risk a battle with the military, "accepted the situation."

## Readings

Baglole, H., ed. *Exploring Island History: A Guide to the Historical Resources of Prince Edward Island*. Belfast: Ragweed, 1977.

Bitterman, R. "Agrarian Protest and Culural Transfer: Irish Emigrants and the Escheat Movement on Prince Edward Island," in T. Power, ed., *The Irish in Atlantic Canada*. Fredericton: 1991.

Bitterman, R. "Women and the Escheat Movement: The Politics of Everyday Life on Prince Edward Island," in J. Guildford and S. Morton, eds., *Separate Spheres: Women's Worlds in the 19th-Century Maritimes*. Fredericton: Acadiensis Press, 1994.

Bolger, F., ed. *Canada's Smallest Province: A History of P.E.I*. Charlottetown: Prince Edward Island 1973 Centennial Commission, 1973.

Buckner, P., and D. Frank, eds. *The Atlantic Provinces before Confederation*. Fredericton: Acadiensis, 1985.

Buckner, P., and J. Reid, eds. *The Atlantic Region to Confederation: A History*. Toronto: University of Toronto Press, 1994.

Bumsted, J. *Land, Settlement, and Politics on Eighteenth-Century Prince Edward Island*. Kingston and Montreal: McGill-Queen's University Press, 1987.

Bumsted, J. "Settlement by Chance: Lord Selkirk and Prince Edward Island," *Canadian Historical Review* 59, 2 (June 1978).

Clark, A. *Three Centuries on the Island: A Historical Geography of Settlement and Agriculture in Prince Edward Island, Canada*. Toronto: University of Toronto Press, 1959.

Day, D., ed. *Geographical Perspectives on the Maritime Provinces*. Halifax: St. Mary's University, 1988.

Hatvany, M. "Tenant, Landlord and Historian: A Thematic Review of the 'Polarization' Process in the Writing of 19th-Century Prince Edward Island History," *Acadiensis* 27 (1997).

MacNutt, W. *The Atlantic Provinces: The Emergence of Colonial Society, 1712–1857*. Toronto: McClelland and Stewart, 1965.

McCallum, M. "Title, Entitlement and the Land Question in P.E.I." in G. Baker and J. Phillips, eds., *Essays in the History of Canadian Law* Vol VIII. Toronto: University of Toronto Press, 1999.

Rawlyk, G., ed. *Historical Essays on the Atlantic Provinces*. Toronto: McClelland and Stewart, 1967.

Robertson, I. *The Tenant League of Prince Edward Island, 1864–1867: Leasehold in the New World*. Toronto: University of Toronto Press, 1996

Robertson, I. "Highlanders, Irishmen, and the Land Question in Nineteenth Century Prince Edward Island," in J. Bumsted, ed., *Interpreting Canada's Past* Vol. 1. Toronto: Oxford University Press, 1996.

*Chapter Ten*

# "Undue Credit and Overwhelming Charges": Commerce in Newfoundland

1. Edward Kemp, "To Geo. and Jas. Kemp and Co.," February 25, 1817.
2. J.H. Attwood, "Deposition to the Select Committee on Newfoundland Trade," 1817.
3. Edward Chappell, *Voyage of His Majesty's Ship Rosamond to Newfoundland and the Southern Coast of Labrador,* 1818.
4. Committee of Inhabitants, "Report to Earl Bathurst," December 6, 1822.
5. R. McCrea, *Lost Amid the Fogs,* 1869.

## Introduction

That Newfoundland enjoys a distinct and unique culture in modern Canada is hardly surprising considering its unusual development within the British Empire. Here was an island that England claimed as long ago as 1583, earlier than anywhere else in what is now Canada. Humphrey Gilbert established a tiny settlement there and declared it English in the name of Elizabeth I—despite the annual presence of Portuguese, Spanish, and French fishing ships. This territorial claim, under traditional circumstances, should have resulted in slow but steady settlement under the steady gaze of British administrators. This would normally lead to colonial status for the land, then eventually to the establishment of representative government, and finally to some sort of independence within the empire. That was certainly the scenario played out in the rest of present day Canada, but not in Newfoundland.

Despite Britain's ownership of the land and the fact that other European nations except France accepted its claim, colonization took an opposite course to the norm. Firstly, where else would an imperial nation designate chunks of its own shoreline for the exclusive use, though not settlement, of one of its competitors? England did that in Newfoundland, creating the "French Shore" and tolerating the presence of Portuguese, Basque, Breton, and Spanish fishers as well. English officials, in a unique twist to normal imperial development, discouraged settlement by its own people, even banning it. Why? Chiefly because the ocean, not the land, held value by providing a bountiful source of fish. The island served no other purpose than to provide ground for curing the cod before fishers packed it aboard the homebound ships at the end of each summer. So why not leave a small coterie of settlers to legitimize English jurisdiction? Newfoundland also served as a naval nursery, the annual fishery graduating a steady stream of green young men into seasoned sailors fit for her majesty's Royal Navy at a time when ships required hundreds of highly skilled sailors. Britain needed its able seamen close to home in case of emergency, not on the far side of the Atlantic, which meant ensuring the entire fleet, with its crew, returned to Poole and other West Country ports every year. There was also a well-founded fear that settlers would be a financial liability over the difficult winter months when food and supplies dwindled to nothing. Newfoundland's poor agricultural potential added credence to this argument until the potato arrived on "the Rock" in the middle of the eighteenth century. Even it struggled to survive in the meagre soil and barely augmented the subsistence lives of those eventually wintering over.

Thus Newfoundland indeed developed oddly. A decree in 1634 empowered the first sea captain arriving each season to act as *de facto* governor and fleet admiral, and to rule accordingly. "Law" therefore depended on the capriciousness of that particular individual, leading to gross inconsistencies from year to year except when it came to ousting the handful of squatters eking out lives on shore. They found themselves mercilessly hounded, and when caught, faced lashings, house burnings, and even hanging. Things improved in 1729, after London appointed the first admiral to oversee the territory, but even he remained on site only for the four summer months, leaving the island ungoverned and lawless for most of the year. Sanctions against settlement were finally lifted when Britain recognized the impossibility of enforcement and colonial status followed shortly thereafter in 1824.

Most eighteenth- and nineteenth-century sea captains engaged in the Newfoundland fishery operated under charter to one of the merchant families in the West Country of England, particularly from the city of Poole. Captains recruited young men as crew, retaining a percentage of their wages as a bond for their return at the end of the summer. Each spring they sailed to the rich fishing grounds of the Grand Banks. Ships carried two teams: a fishing crew that caught the fish; and one for shore which prepared the catch by filleting the cod and spreading it on raised wooden drying racks called flakes. After curing, the shore men barrelled or stacked the fish in readiness for shipment back to Europe where Spain served as England's largest single market.

It did not take long before West Country merchants established semi-permanent quarters on Newfoundland's shores. Nor did it take long for hired men and shore crew to jump ship and establish themselves as settlers employed as seasonal fishers. By 1827, some 60,000 people called Newfoundland home. These permanent and semi-permanent residents tended to originate from either the West Country or from Ireland, and were roughly evenly split between Protestants and Catholics, though merchants were largely Protestant. This created a very clear class division between the tiny group of merchants who owned and managed virtually everything, and everyone else—who tended to be divided by sectarianism. Because merchants controlled imports and exports to the Rock, it was to them that the majority of people had to turn, both to sell their catch and to procure supplies. This quickly led to a new pattern of social and economic interaction known as the "truck" system whereby the economy ran on credit. Poor planters, as individual boat owners were known, obtained supplies in advance and on credit from merchants, and paid off their tab from their catch—in a good season. In bad times, when the value of the cod did not match what they owed, they went further into debt. By the late eighteenth century, a disproportionate percentage of the settled population found itself permanently indebted to the handful of merchants.

Settlers accused the merchants of charging extortionate prices for supplies and unfairly lowering the value of the cod catch. Evidence supports this parasitical interpretation and led generations of historians, to cast the merchants as evil money-grubbers. Closer examination, however, now suggests a more complex and ambiguous pattern. Merchants, after all, took all the financial chances in a harsh environmental, economic, and social milieu, and frequently ended up out of pocket when times were tough—as they often were. The number of high profile merchant bankruptcies certainly supports this. Where else, merchants argued, did workers receive pay *in advance* of their labour, as planters and their fisher servants did in Newfoundland. This, they further pointed out, tied merchants to the planters in hope of recouping their losses. Nor did good times necessarily mean vast profits for the merchants as mythology indicates. Planters all too often unscrupulously sold their fish to fly-by-night offshore American cash buyers for a quick buck rather than pay down their debts to the merchants in port, as the law required. Then there is the thorny issue of the single resource economy. Settlers accused merchants of discouraging diversification, particularly into agriculture, by making it impossible to obtain land; an accusation previously accepted. Revisiting the evidence, however, now suggests that agriculture may have failed as much for environmental and other reasons than from merchant bullying.

Other issues exacerbated the tense relationship, issues that ostensibly remained beyond the merchant's control. There were, by the nineteenth century, simply too many merchants, too many fishers and planters, too many year-round residents, and a glut of fish on the international market. This meant more and more people scrabbling for diminishing resources, which of course resulted in hardship for the entire community. Since merchants were perceived as heartless amid acute privation, planters and fishers consequently banded together and a tradition of collective action emerged, with gangs of men marching on the merchants, uttering threats, rioting, and sometimes looting warehouses. Merchants, who lacked the collective numbers to resist, often gave in to the mob as they struggled to cope in a land largely without the rule of law.

On the other hand, life was far better for the average merchant than for anyone else in Newfoundland. Many merchants did generate considerable fortunes and did send their locally made profits to the Old Country, which was very detrimental to Newfoundland's future economic growth. And while merchants tended not to flaunt their wealth, everyone knew their status, and evidence certainly suggests that merchants found it convenient to have planters and fishers in their debt. Finally, the polarized nature of the society encouraged merchants to thwart efforts at political change, fearing it might diminish their considerable power which, of course, simply increased tension and animosity between the two groups.

## Discussion Points

1. In what respects did the fishing industry determine Newfoundland's development?
2. Was Newfoundland a classic case of the evils of capitalism?
3. Why couldn't the local fishing population break the cycle of dependency and underdevelopment?

## Documents

### 1.  Edward Kemp, "To Geo. and Jas. Kemp and Co.," February 25, 1817.

Brigus, 25ᵗʰ February 1817.

... "I am happy to say we have been tolerably tranquil, so far at least as to be free from any violence on the stores, although we are daily besieged by importunate and unprincipled claimants for provisions, who have developed still further the disorderly state of the times, and show the strongest inclinations to plunder and distress the merchants stores.

"All these people are moneyless, and almost all are entirely strangers to the house, yet make their demands in the most authoritative and insolent manner, holding forth, 'That while the stores contain a biscuit they will have it.' Now we have barely enough to maintain our own crew till the 1ˢᵗ May, and whatever is taken will occasion us a proportionate distress; and I am thinking, that bye and bye we shall be forced to quarter ourselves about the harbour for a meal.

"The most of these ruffians are without any shadow of claim upon our house, some undertake schemes owing to distress; but they are joined by great numbers who do not want, and who only engage with them for their own safety, or as in many cases to promote uproar and confusion.

"The country is overrun with such dangerous characters; and if they are not sent from us next season, I believe no merchant will do well to leave much property here the following winter; but the nearer prospect of the spring gives much cause of apprehension.

"From the probable state of such a population, in another month, from their known disposition to plunder in bodies, and from intimations already made, I have every reason to fear the first arrival in Brigus, will be in serious danger of capture by a lawless mob, who would either demand purchase without intention or perhaps ability to pay, or would unceremoniously take what they want by force of numbers. In such an affair, a few might be known amongst them; but their poverty would preclude any recovery of payment for the wrong done us, whilst the far greater part would be dispersed during the next Summer, and leave us not even the satisfaction of making an example of one of them, or the means of supplying our own regular dealers.

"I think that whatever provisions come next Spring to Brigus, will stand in the most imminent danger of nearly total loss, for it seems morally certain they will become the object of immediate tumultuous attack. We have no military or civil power near us to overawe, nor would the harbour people, if they were all home from the ice, and so disposed, be able to resist the force we may expect against us. In this case of extremity, I feel it my duty to propose, that no supplies whatever shall be here, until the advance of next summer shall disclose the eligibility of receiving a further stock for the subsequent fall.

"I hope this letter will reach you in time, for a consideration of its subjects, before the supplies are sent off. If they be already provided, but not gone from the port, it were better they should remain in your stores until the storm be overpast, than that they come here; and be assured I shall be ever watchful of renewing the course of business as soon as it can be done safely."

## 2. J.H. Attwood, "Deposition to the Select Committee on Newfoundland Trade," 1817.

I left Newfoundland myself on the 12th day of February last, after having been an eye-witness of greater general distress in the town of St. John's that I have ever heard of having existed in any other British community; thousands at that period of hardy industrious men were daily walking the streets, without money, without provisions, without lodgings, and without employment; they were depending on casual charity for their daily sustenance, and generally had no other lodgings that the snow covered bounds of the merchants wharfs, or the bare shelter of old hulks of boats hauled up on the beach, during the oldest nights of the severest winter that has been experienced in the memory of man, in that inhospitable climate; and it is my firm belief, that not half of the population of St. John's, Conception Bay, and all the district to the southward, had either provisions of their own, or money to buy them, or property, on the credit of which they could be obtained; and I am consequently of opinion, that more than half the population of Newfoundland have all this winter been maintained either by public charities, or private charities: this evil was certainly aggravated by the scarcity of provisions. Early in November, it was ascertained by a general inspection and inquiry into the quantity of provisions in St. John's, that there was only bread and flour sufficient for one month's supply for the population to support them through a period of five months winter, all the neighbouring parts to the southward were found to be in as bad or a worse state. At the time when this state of things was discovered, the governor had no authority to grant licences for the importation of provisions from America; and but for a supply, which was most humanely afforded by the commander of the forces from the King's stores, the state of famine and wretchedness would have been still more dreadful. If it is asked, what brought so great a number of persons so destitute, before much could have been suffered from French competition in foreign markets, I answer, that the losses in the trade have been most enormous; that a large proportion of the merchants, I think about fourteen in the town of St. John's alone, and nearly all the shopkeepers and planters, have been already ruined. I am satisfied that not less than 100 shopkeepers have been reduced to a state of insolvency in St. John's in the course of the last two years; I do not think I should much exceed if I said 150; I am satisfied not five of them remaining perfectly solvent. These people flourished up to the year 1814, and imported from 1,500 *l.* to 15,000 *l.* per annum each, principally of manufactured goods, which they chiefly vended among the planters from the outports and their servants; but a great proportion of the servants not being employed on wages last year, and wages of the others being so greatly reduced, that they had nothing to spare for the purchase of dry goods; the sales of the shopkeepers either declined to nothing, or they gave their goods on credit to the persons who could get no means of paying for them.

I content it is quite impossible for the trade to support the excessive population over another winter unless the trade is supported; they positively have not the means. The starving multitude have no where to look for relief but to His Majesty's Government. The ship owners, who originally took them out, are no way connected with the trade, and are not to be found; the planters who hired them originally, and the merchant who received the produce of their labours, have all become insolvent, and need that relief which they would otherwise have been expected to afford. The merchants who yet remain unruined in the trade, have more than they can do in providing sustenance and employment for those who have all along been dependent upon them.

The fourth and last difficulty under which the trade labours, I would mention, is the operation of the law of the 49th Geo. III. so far as it relates to the distribution of the effects of insolvents. In cases of the insolvency of planters now, the servant is paid 20 s. in the pound of his wages, in preference to all other creditors, not only out of the produce of the voyage, but also out of the other effects, as boats, crafts, stages, houses, &c. if the fish and oil be not sufficient. The consequence of this is, that the servants have no inducement to labour after they have caught so much fish as, together with the other effects of the planter, will be sufficient to pay their wages; and thus, having no motive for exertion, and having, in the common course of the fishery, no master present to overlook them, they neglect their duty, and report to their planter that fish was scarce; whereas they have probably been sleeping in their boats three-fourths of the day without trying for it.

### 3. Edward Chappell, *Voyage of His Majesty's Ship Rosamond to Newfoundland and the Southern Coast of Labrador,* 1818.

... In order to procure for themselves a passage across the Atlantic, they enter into a bond with the master of a trading-vessel; whereby they stipulate to pay him a certain sum as passage-money, immediately subsequent to their having obtained employment in St. John's. The emigrants are compelled to find securities in Ireland, for the due observance of their agreement; and when the vessel reaches Newfoundland, they are suffered to go at large, in search of an employer. It must be allowed, that many of them are not over scrupulous in returning to fulfil their contract; as they hope, by absenting themselves, to avoid paying their passage-money. In such cases, the master of the trading-vessel publishes the names of the absentees; with an intimation, that, on the failure of appearance, their Irish securities will be sued for the amount of the debt, costs of the suit, and interest. The fear of involving their parents, or other relations, in a law process, seldom fails to draw forth the fugitives; when their employer instantly pays down the amount of their passage-money, and places the sum to his new servant's account.

From this moment the unfortunate emigrants become the vassals of their employers; as it is but rarely that they can succeed in working out their emancipation: for the slavery of the Newfoundland fishermen, thus commenced upon their first entering the country, is perpetuated by a system of the most flagrant and shameful extortion. Every merchant, the master of a fishery, is the huckster of his whole establishment; and the servants are compelled to purchase their supplies of food, raiment, and every trifling necessary, of the person in whose service they may chance to be engaged. No money passes between them; but the account of every article that is supplied to the fishermen is entered in the books of their masters. The prices are so enormous, that the original debt due for the passage-money of the emigrants, instead of being diminished by the hardest and most faithful servitude, continues rapidly to increase. It is in vain that the unfortunate debtor complains of the barefaced imposition, by which he is forced to pay three times the value of the most trivial article: having no money, he cannot go elsewhere to obtain what he may want, nor can he subsist without the necessaries of life. Thus, then, the Newfoundland fisherman toils from day to day, with no relaxation for the present, and without the least hope for the future. His exertions, labours, and industry, serve but to swell the purse and the pride of a rapacious master; until death happily intervenes, and cancels all the accounts betwixt them.

The capital of *Newfoundland* consists of one very narrow street, extending entirely along one side of the port. The houses are principally built of wood and there are very few handsome or even good-looking edifices in the place. This street stands upon very irregular ground, and is not paved; therefore, in wet weather, it is rendered almost impassable, by mud and filth. There are a great number of small public-houses, but scarcely one tolerable inn: the *London Tavern*, however, has a good billiard-room attached to it. Shops of all descriptions are very numerous; but most commodities are extravagantly dear, particularly meat, poultry, and vegetables, as the town receives all its supplies of those articles from *Nova Scotia*. The number of wharfs for lading ships is remarkable: almost every petty merchant, indeed, possesses one of his own: and there is, besides these, a fine broad quay, called the government wharf, which is open for accomodation of the public....

It would be very difficult to form the least calculation respecting the population of *St. John's*; as no computation, however accurate, can be considered as correct beyond the instant of time in which it is made. During the height of the fishery, it appears to be overflowing with inhabitants; but most of the people employed therein return to *Europe* in the autumn....

The trading commodities of *Newfoundland* are so well known, that it will only be requisite to say, the *exports* consist of *fish, oil,* and a very few *furs*: the *imports* are, *provisions, clothing, salt, fishing-gear,* and some *India* goods....

*Broyle Bay* is a deep inlet: its entrance lies at the foot of the Cape before mentioned. The depth of water is sufficient for vessels of almost any size, and the harbour is sheltered from all winds....

There are not more than five or six families settled within this bay; who, of course, obtain their livelihood by the curing of cod: and they afterwards carry the product of their labour to *St. John's*, where they dispose of it to the merchants, in exchange for provisions and necessaries; but they very seldom receive specie in return for their *fish*. From this it will appear evident, that those merchants, who reside constantly at *St. John's*, receive a double profit: the first arising from their foreign exports of salted *cod*; and the second, from the articles which they supply to the *out-harbour* settlers in return for this commodity. It follows, therefore, as a natural consequence, that the principal mercantile men of this country, by monopolizing almost the whole of the external and internal trade, are thereby enabled to amass the most splendid fortunes with an inconceivable rapidity; whilst the middling and lower classes of fishermen may toil from year to year, with patient and unremitted industry, and yet find themselves in their old age, many degrees worse off than when first they crossed the *Atlantic*, as wretched emigrants from their native country....

### 4. Committee of Inhabitants, "Report to Earl Bathurst," December 6, 1822.

The committee consider it a duty they owe the petitioners and themselves, thus far to explain their statements; they now beg leave to call the attention of your Lordship to the present state of Newfoundland, a country of great extent, the oldest of the British settlements in America, placed nearly in the same latitude as England, with a climate peculiarly favourable to the health of its inhabitants, possessing more of the elements of commerce than any other of the colonies of North America, and of the greatest importance to the parent state, not only as a valuable acquisition to the commercial interests of the empire, but as the best nursery for seamen to support the naval ascendancy of the empire; now, after the lapse of near three centuries, being almost in the same state as when first discovered by Cabot. With a population of one hundred thousand persons, without any certain mode of employment or subsistence, without a government efficient for any local purpose, without roads, without means of education for the people, without any of those institutions which are necessary for the government of every civilized country. The trade and fisheries, hitherto the chief support of the people, languishing for want of due encouragement....

From the earliest period, the attention of the settlers, as well as transient persons, were exclusively turned towards the fisheries, and the commercial pursuits connected with them. They were the only source which the inhabitants looked up to for support, consequently they were subject to the vicissitudes of such uncertain employments; when the fisheries flourished, the inhabitants were enabled to obtain a comfortable subsistence; when they declined, they suffered in exact proportion to that decline; such have invariably been the situation of the people; and such ever will be their state, until they can get more certain means of employment than can be afforded by the fisheries. Merchants will only employ their capital as long as there is a fair prospect of gain; if that prospect be reversed, they will withdraw from the trade; and it forms no principal of mercantile economy to enquire how the people are to exist, by whose labour and industry in more prosperous times, they gained all their wealth and importance. If this mode of reasoning be true, in reference to trade in general, how much more applicable is it to the uncertain trade carried on in the fisheries in Newfoundland.

From the earliest period, the affairs of Newfoundland were mainly influenced by merchants residing in England, the trade and fisheries were a monopoly in their hands, to preserve which they exerted all their influence to prevent the improvement or settlement of the country, apprehensive that it would be fatal to their monopoly. They represented the soil as barren and incapable of improvement; the climate so extremely severe, as to render it uninhabitable; aware that it was a favourite object with government to increase the naval strength of the empire by the extension of the fisheries, they stated the moveable fishery carried on by themselves as the best to promote that object, and that the sedentary fishery of the natives would defeat it.

The parties thus interested in the trade, influenced government to second all their views; every obstacle was thrown in the way of settlement; a policy was pursued, and laws were formed, that had the direct tendency of preventing the cultivation of the soil, to which justly may be attributed the present wretched state of the island.

The government of Newfoundland was in a great degree placed in the hands of a few merchants, and it is not at all surprising that they were influenced by the same principles which had invariably governed merchants, in every age and country, to sacrifice every other interest to their own. Their object was to make money, and in the shortest time possible; this facility they found, during a long period of a profitable trade and successful fishery, to realize large fortunes, made them consider their residence in Newfoundland merely as a probation of a few years, after which they expected to be able to retire, and enjoy the fruits of their prosperous industry in other countries. Within the last thirty or forty years, a great number of persons have retired from this country, carrying with them large sums realized out of the trade and fisheries. Fortunes, of from 50, 100, 200 and 300,000 pounds, have been made by individuals who came to the island without a shilling, and who are now removed to other countries. It must appear evident, that such a continual drain of capital must have been most injurious to its interests; and it was only a country possessing an inexhaustible mine of wealth in her fisheries, that could permit such to take place.

The peculiar state of Newfoundland, where the labour and skill of the people being exclusively turned towards the fisheries, every other interest being sacrificed to them, permitted the adventurer to accumulate a fortune without making the slightest improvement. He remained in the country only a few months in the summer, he had no object in making improvements beyond what was necessary to protect his goods from the weather, until they were shipped off. It is well known, that the houses in which many of the persons lived, who made the largest fortunes in Newfoundland, were so mean, that the cottage of an English peasant would be considered a palace in comparison. These kind of houses are the improvements, if improvements they can be called, made in Newfoundland by the most wealthy merchants in the trade.

A variety of causes have operated within these few years, to interfere with the monopoly of the merchants. Notwithstanding the impediments thrown in the way, the population has very much increased; so many hands being employed in the fishery, cause the supply of fish very much to exceed the demand; the trade is very much divided, which keeps up a spirit of competition unfavourable to the old state of things. The important privileges granted to the French and Americans, to fish on the best part of our coasts, with the bounties and other encouragement they obtain from their respective governments, enable them to supply the foreign markets at a price much lower than the British, which cause a rivalship that our merchants cannot contend with. These causes have very much interfered with the monopoly so long in the hands of the merchants in the trade.

If the great body of the people of Newfoundland remain in their present state of beggary and want, it is an illusion if the trading part of the community expect to be much better in their condition. To enable the people to buy and pay for their goods, a proportion of their labour must be turned into some more productive channels than the fisheries can afford. The experience of the last eight years ought to be sufficient to convince the few merchants who remain in the country, and who were able to stem the overwhelming torrent which brought destruction on so many respectable houses, that the trade and fisheries of the country are not alone adequate to the support of the people; and if they follow up the old system of supplying in the fishery, their ruin is equally certain.

To enable the merchants of Newfoundland to cope with their rivals in foreign markets, fish must be catched at much less expense than hitherto, which cannot be done as long as every thing necessary for the maintenance of the people must be imported from distant countries. By the more general cultivation of the soil, the people would be enabled to raise a great proportion of their food; it would afford profitable employment for that part of the population who cannot be employed in the fishery; and it would be far the most effectual and best auxiliary to it. It is well worth the trial.

It has been said, that the people of Newfoundland are not in a situation to pay the expenses necessarily attending a local government. The committee have no hesitation in saying, that such is not the case; and have not the slightest doubt of the competency of the country, even in its present depressed state, without inconvenience, to bear all the expenses necessary for that purpose. It has been a favourite object with interested persons to throw a cloud of misrepresentation on every thing connected with the country; its resources were little known, except to those who were making them subservient to their interest.

If Newfoundland have not possessed the means of paying the expense of a civil government, it must appear extraordinary that so many persons who came there without a shilling in their pockets were able, in the course of a few years, to realize fortunes, to retire from the island, and live in splendor in other countries. The committee can now point out to your Lordship individuals residing in London, Poole, Dartmouth, Bristol, Edinburgh, Greenock, Cork, and Waterford, and other parts not alone of the United Kingdom, but even in the United States of America, who made their properties in Newfoundland. If individuals could in few years realize from the labour and industry of the people sufficient to enable them to retire from the country to live independently in other countries, surely it is not too much for the committee to say, that the same people can pay the expenses of their government which would revert back on themselves with manifold advantages.

To prove the ability of the inhabitants to pay the expense of their government, the committee beg to state a few well known facts: The town of St. John's is the capital of the island, and the principal depositary for the supplies and productions of the fishery; the ground on which the stores, wharfs and dwelling-houses are erected, is chiefly owned by persons residing in Great Britain, whose ancestors gained a title to it merely by occupying it for the purposes of the fishery; in consequence of the great increase of trade and population, the ground has become valuable, and the rent now charged for that situate at the waterside of Saint John's, is from 20 to 40 s. per foot, on which large sums have been expended by the tenants in making the necessary erections; a sum not less than 30,000 l. is annually remitted from the town of Saint John's for rents; can it then be doubted that a people, who pay such large sums to absentee landlords, who do not contribute in the slightest degree to the support of the country, could pay the expenses of a civil government?

It is well known, that the mercantile houses, which accumulated all their capital in this trade, have in prosperous times, made profits of from 20 to 30,000 pounds in one year, a sum more than adequate to the support of a civil government.

Local governments have been ceded to the Canadas, Nova Scotia, Prince Edward Island, Bermuda, and some of the most inconsiderable islands in the West Indies, while Newfoundland, of equal importance to the parent state, the most ancient of her possessions in America, is deprived of its advantages.

## 5. R. McCrea, *Lost Amid the Fogs,* 1869.

... The merchant is really no merchant here,—that is, no fair speculator, under the usual and proper understanding of that term in trade; he is simply a great commercial gambler. The planter or middleman imitates his superior on a smaller scale; and the ignorant fisherman follows suit as a matter of course. This system of trade, between the supplier and supplied, began in the first days of the settlement as a fishing-colony, when goods, only to be procured from a few rich merchants at the summer-stations, were necessarily taken in advance by the fishermen; and, unhappily, the same plan of barter still exists, to the detriment of the morality and prosperity of the community. In short, the workman eats his bread before it is earned by the sweat of his brow; and it is not difficult to arrive at the result of such a plan. The merchant, with his stores full of provisions, clothing, fishing-gear, and household goods, like a spider in his parlour, awaits the approach of the hungry fisherman, his legitimate fly. In the spring, before the seal-fishery commences,—in May, when the cod are coming in,—in November—no matter whether the season has been favourable or not—the fisherman must have supplies for his family; his children must be fed. The merchant, once embarked in such a business, has no choice but to continue, or lose all. He must, therefore, charge awful profits, to remunerate himself against such an awful risk. Accordingly, while he sells a barrel of flour to the cash-customer (when he gets one) for 30s., he books it to the fisherman (who may or may not pay him) for £3, 10s.; a pair of boots worth, perhaps 17s., are put down £2, 5s.; a gridiron, worth 2s. 6d., is noted at 9s.; a Jersey, 7s. 6d., at 25s., and so on. This is but a moderate estimate of this iniquitous barter; it being by no means an uncommon thing, when the risk is greater, to book the same barrel of flour at £6, and all other things at a thousand per cent in proportion.

Iniquitous barter, be it well understood, on both sides; and let us see how it acts. The fisherman, in the majority of cases, little he cares on the matter. The system descended to him from his fathers; they rubbed on and lived under it, and so will he. So he travels home with his goods, eats and rejoices, caring nothing for the evil day of reckoning, which comes when the fishing is over: the fish delivered at so much on one side of the ledger, and the outrageous credit he has taken balanced on the other. Rarely, indeed, is there a residue in his favour, but enough still owing to bring him back to the spider's parlour again, and, in most cases, keep him in the meshes all his life. The consequences to the man and his family are easily understood. Economy, order, cleanliness, education, prosperity, are practically to them unknown. As he gains his money in a chance-like, gambling fashion, so he spends it recklessly, without a thought for the morrow.

Let us look at the results which bad fisheries, for a few consecutive years, engendered. Latterly, no less than one-third of the whole revenue of the colony has been spent in pauper-relief, failing which a great part of the labouring population would have perished. And, traced back to the origin of this outlay, this enormous sum was simply a tax or penalty, paid by the whole public, on the pernicious system adopted by the merchants in their business transactions.

There is yet a worse evil than this. The fisherman looks round, and sees in the ocean a great gambling-pool, from which he may, perhaps, in some very favourable season, without great trouble, draw a famous lottery-ticket. On the other side, he sees round his door abundance of land, which, with toil, will yield him sustenance, in turnips, potatoes, hay, barley, fodder, and garden-stuff. But is it in poor, ignorant, human nature to labour and sweat, when—oh! so easily—all its wants can be supplied without the toil?—when the simple credit at the merchant's enables all to eat to-day, and to pay when Providence is pleased to send the fish? So the patient earth is left, year after year, untouched; and the greasy fisherman, leaning idle, in the precious spring-time, against the merchant's store in Water Street, hugs himself with the cherished idea, that his ticket this year in the great fish-lottery will surely turn up a tremendous prize. Thus slow and sure, against chance and luck, have little hope of winning. But it must be understood that this is a way of existence emmently suited to the Irish character, luxuriantly developing the richest traits of that unstrung nationality, which forms the majority in this most ancient, yet still untilled, offshoot of the British crown.

There is something to be said on the other side of a question involving such lamentable consequences to the welfare of a people. There is some truth in asserting that the merchant of the present day cannot help the mischief; that he does his best with the disastrous legacy of his forefathers; that he could not begin a new and healthy system without the concurrence of all his compeers, involving the risk of immediate collapse to many of them. He is obliged to charge the fisherman exorbitantly for his credit, for the risk is tremendous—out of all proportion to anything else known in trade—not only on account of bad seasons, but also from the bad faith of the men to whom he has given supplies, year after year, with scarcely any return, yet waiting, hoping, praying, believing in an eventual turn of luck. Yes, luck!—the whole business of the colony is absolutely concentrated in that word. At last the prospect of a brimming year arrives, and all looks hopeful. The merchant hears great accounts of the catch and of the quality of the fish; indeed he sees, here and there, his neighbours' wharves begin to groan with ocean-fruit. He begins to hug himself with the belief that, at last, his books are not only to be balanced, but that large profits will enable him to realise the dearest wish of his heart—a country-house near Liverpool or Greenock.

But, alack-the-day! to his intense disgust, many of the fishermen begin to come to his office with long faces and tales of *bad* luck; to be turned away with threats and curses, of little avail, indeed, for he understands only too well the lying lips the ill-taught fellows open. How is the enigma to be explained? for fish in abundance there is, without a shadow of doubt. It is all sold, as soon as caught, for *cash down*, to other parties. The fisherman, on the Banks, with his boat loaded to the brim with fish day after day, makes a simple reflection, that, if he sends up too much of his labour to the merchant, it will just be wiping off old scores, and be paying for bread eaten long ago. So, in the gray of the morning, it happens that a fore-and-aft schooner comes booming along, the skipper of which, backing her sails among the little crafts, soon fills up his venture, at a moderate expense, when away he bowls to Halifax or Boston, to join the Yankee or blue-nosed cuckoo-traders in growing fat over the helpless sparrows of Newfoundland. Up go the iron shutters before the warehouse doors and windows; and one hears, every now and then, of £20,000 worth of book-debts sold by auction, in the Commercial Rooms, for £20, and at another, of £15,600 for a five-pound note!

The signs of these things are about us and around us as we walk on. The success or failure of mercantile speculations cannot be altogether hid behind the baize-doors of the counting-house. The prosperity or poverty of a British city must be, at any rate, stamped plainly on its face; for British merchants, when fortune smiles, button not up their pockets; and, from within, their good-will, loyalty, pride if you please, but honest pride withal, pour forth large blessings on all around. In their own homes of plenty they pluck freely of the fruit and flowers, and scatter them generously abroad. Yet, could any stranger, knowing this, traverse this great commercial city from one end to the other, and not draw the conclusion that something at the root of its business was wrong and rotten,—some trust, which had failed to establish itself between man and man,—a want of faith between employer and employed? He will be told, on the one hand, that, in proportion to its inhabitants, a larger business is done here than at any other colonial city; and he will look about on the strength of this, and see not a trace of that pride.... Standing on the flat flakes echelloned on every cranny of the rocks are the women and children, ready to catch the fish as they are pitchforked up out of the boats, and place them ready for the splitter. Alack, the evil time! they have not long to wait; for like the disciples of old, many of them have toiled all day and caught nothing. In former years, when there were fewer fishermen, fewer planters, fewer murderous dodges against the fish, these flakes of an evening could scarcely bear the tremendous weight of the great ocean harvest. Now happy is the planter who sees his flakes occasionally covered with fish. Yet there cannot be an effect without a cause, and why the poor fishermen's families starve in winter, and why the merchant has to wait so many more years before he can hope to build that house in Greenock or Liverpool, must now needs be told or guessed at.

In the first place, there are now many more merchants, many more planters or middlemen, many more fishermen to divide the catch which has averaged pretty much of a muchness for many years past. In the second, the new styles of fishing, introduced on the principle of quick returns and devil take the hindmost, have done vast injury to the fisheries. In the good old times—really good in this wise—the proper sized fish only were taken with hook and line, at no injury to other fish in the waters. But, to carve a short road out to riches, first of all was brought in the cod-seine, which utterly destroys the chances of the legitimate hook and liners, if used anywhere near their ground; and by it, moreover, tons of young small fish, useless for commerce, are cast out and thrown aside. Next came in the bultow, which swept into its maw numbers of heavy mother-fish, at a consequence to the future which needs no further explanation. And lastly was introduced the infernal jigger, which, barbing and tearing among a shoal of fish, like a Malay running a-muck in a crowd, for every fish taken by it, possibly injures half a dozen others cruelly, and finally drives the whole lot, thoroughly frightened, from the bank. Verily, the goose with the eggs of gold is killed and cooked to perfection.

Thus, it is not difficult to perceive that, in the cod-fishery—the great harvest and business of the country—it is, from first to last, a sort of pull-devil, pull-baker sort of system, the evils of which, accumulating for years, have now begun to be seriously felt. The fisherman, with his family, eats his bread long before it is earned, and then struggles against nature to win a hopeless victory. Just as in the gambler's game of *rouge et noir*, every now and then great coups by a few individuals are made, exciting hundreds of others to try their luck; yet the chances, as a standing quantity, being ever in favour of the "hell," the victims sooner or later are all cleaned out. So, under this sad system of undue credit and overwhelming charges, the very first hint of a falling house is the signal for the fisherman's revenge upon his creditor; and, like the rats in the sinking ship, he turns tail at once, and transfers his fish (already mortgaged) to another merchant, without scruple, for cash prices or a new credit, or sells it to the cute Yankee ever on the watch along the banks for such a chance....

Even apart from all other consideration of eventual good, little pity on account of the failure of their trade do the merchants of Fish-and-fog-land deserve. For years and years they have drawn away their wealth and influence from the place, returning few tithes of gratitude to the Great Giver of their prosperity; doing little or nothing for the public good, and separating themselves as from a contaminated community as soon as possible. Thus while men of any education fly to happier lands, you may see here a good many with thousands upon thousands who cannot even write their own names; and the great masses of the fish gamblers, poverty-stricken from the first check, unable to rise in the great human scale generation after generation. The system strikes at the root of all that is right or elevating, and keeps the standard of public opinion, if indeed such a thing can be said to exist at all, at its very lowest mark.

## *Readings*

Alexander, D. "Literacy and Economic Development in Nineteenth Century Newfoundland," *Acadiensis* 10, 1 (Autumn 1980).

Alexander, D. "Newfoundland's Traditional Economy and Development to 1934," *Acadiensis* 5, 2 (Spring 1976).

Anthler, S. "The Capitalist Underdevelopment of Nineteenth Century Newfoundland," in R. Brym and R. Sacouman, eds., *Underdevelopment and Social Movements in Atlantic Canada.* Toronto: New Hogtown Press, 1975.

Buckner, P., and D. Frank, eds. *The Atlantic Provinces before Confederation.* Fredericton: Acadiensis Press, 1985.

Buckner, P., and J. Reid, eds. *The Atlantic Region to Confederation: A History.* Toronto: University of Toronto Press, 1994.

Cadigan, S. *Hope and Deception in Conception Bay: Merchant-Settler Relations in Newfoundland, 1785–1855.* Toronto: University of Toronto Press, 1995.

Candow, J. *Of Men and Seals: A History of the Newfoundland Seal Hunt.* Ottawa: Environment Canada, 1989.

Cadigan, S. "Merchant Capital, the State, and Labour in a British Colony: Servant-Master Relations and Capital Accumulation in Newfoundland's Northeast Coast Fisher, 1775–1799," *Journal of the Canadian Historical Association* 3 (1991).

Cadigan, S. "The Moral Economy of the Commons: Ecology and Equity in the Newfoundland Cod Fishery, 1815–1855," *Labour* 43 (Spring 1999).

Cadigan, S. "Planters, Households and Merchant Capitalism: Northeast-Coast Newfoundland, 1800–1835," in D. Samson, ed., *Counted Countryside: Rural Workers and Modern Society in Atlantic Canada, 1800-1950.* Fredericton: Acadiensis Press, 1994.

Cadigan, S. "The Staple Model Reconsidered: The Case of Agricultural Policy in Northeast Newfoundland, 1785–1855," *Acadiensis* 21, 2 (Spring 1992).

Crowley, E. "Empire versus Truck: The Official Interpretation of Debt and Labour in the Eighteenth-Century Newfoundland Fishery," *Canadian Historical Review* 70, 3 (September 1989).

Day, D., ed. *Geographical Perspectives on the Maritime Provinces.* Halifax: St. Mary's University, 1988.

Greene, J. *Between Damnation and Starvation: Priests and Merchants in Newfoundland Politics, 1745–1855.* Kingston-Montreal: McGill-Queen's University Press, 1999.

Gunn, G. *The Political History of Newfoundland, 1832–1864.* Toronto: University of Toronto Press, 1966.

Handcock, W. *'Soe longe As there comes noe women': Origins of English Settlement in Newfoundland.* St. John's: Breakwater Press, 1989.

Head, C. *Eighteenth-Century Newfoundland: A Geographer's Perspective.* Toronto: McClelland and Stewart, 1976.

Hiller, J., and P. Neary, eds. *Newfoundland in the Nineteenth and Twentieth Centuries.* Toronto: University of Toronto Press, 1980.

Innis, H. *The Cod Fisheries: The History of an International Economy.* Rev. Ed. Toronto: University of Toronto Press, 1954.

Little, L. "Collective Action in Outport Newfoundland: A Case Study from the 1830s," *Labour* 26 (Fall 1990).

Matthews, K. *Lectures on the History of Newfoundland.* St John's: Breakwater Press, 1988.

MacNutt, W. *The Atlantic Provinces: The Emergence of Colonial Society, 1712–1857.* Toronto: McClelland and Stewart, 1965.

Mannion, J. "Irish Merchants Abroad: The Newfoundland Experience, 1750–1850," *Newfoundland Studies* 2, 2 (1986).

Mannion, J., ed. *The Peopling of Newfoundland: Essays on Historical Geography.* St John's: Institute of Social and Economic Research Memorial University, 1977.

McCann, P. "Culture, State Formation and the Invention of Tradition: Newfoundland 1832–1855," *Journal of Canadian Studies* 23, 1-2 (Spring and Summer 1988).

Moyles, R. *"Complaints Is Many and Various, But the Odd Divil Likes It": Nineteenth Century Views of Newfoundland.* Toronto: Peter Martin and Associates, 1975.

O'Flaherty, P. "Government in Newfoundland before 1832: The Context of Reform," *Newfoundland Quarterly* 84, 2 (Fall 1988).

O'Flaherty, P. *Old Newfoundland: A History to 1843.* St. John's: Long Beach Press, 1999.

Ommer, R., ed. *Merchant Credit and Labour Strategies In Historical Perspective.* Fredericton: Acadiensis Press, 1990.

Rowe, F. *A History of Newfoundland.* Toronto: McGraw Hill, 1980.

Ryan, S. "Fishery to Colony: A Newfoundland Watershed, 1793–1815," *Acadiensis* 12, 2 (Spring 1983).

Ryan, S. *Fish Out of Water: The Newfoundland Saltfish Trade, 1814–1914.* St. John's: Breakwater Press, 1986.

Ryan, S. *The Ice Hunters: A History of Newfoundland Sealing to 1914.* St. John's: Breakwater Press, 1994.

Sager, E. "The Merchants of Water Street and Capital Investment in Newfoundland's Traditional Economy," in L. Fischer and E. Sager, eds., *The Enterprising Canadians: Entrepreneurs and Economic Development in Eastern Canada, 1820–1914.* St. John's: Maritime History Group, 1979.

Vickers, D., ed. *Marine Resources and Human Societies in the North Atlantic since 1500.* St. John's: Memorial University, 1997.

*Chapter Eleven*

# "The Very Vitals Are Chilled": Lumbering in New Brunswick

1. Peter Fisher, *Sketches of New Brunswick,* 1825.
2. J. McGregor, *Historical and Descriptive Sketches of the Maritime Colonies of British America,* 1828.
3. Anonymous, *Letters from Nova Scotia and New Brunswick Illustrative of their Moral, Religious and Physical Circumstances in the Years 1826, 1827 and 1828,* 1829.
4. Abraham Gesner, *New Brunswick,* 1847.
5. James Johnson, *Notes on North America: Agricultural, Economic and Social,* 1851.

## Introduction

New Brunswick was regarded as the quintessential "timber colony" whose economy rose and fell with its forest production and English demand for lumber. Yet most accounts about the men who worked in the woods portray them as an unsavoury lot of speculating scoundrels who swore, drank, brawled, and then spent their way into debt before dying loveless and crippled in early age. Critics worried that much of this activity took place beyond "civilization's gaze" without the softening influence of female nurturing; that it tended to lead to cyclical feast-and-famine among the workers; that it was based upon speculation; and that it encouraged transience instead of settlement. Lumberjacks were not, in other words, a good example of Victorian morality with its emphasis on hearth and home, rigid social decorum, hard work, and thrift. Overall New Brunswickers quickly developed an uneasy ambivalence toward their main industry.

By the beginning of the nineteenth century, New Brunswick was a new and largely undeveloped colony. Some 14,000 Loyalists, streaming north from the United States after the Revolution, increased the population of Nova Scotia to the point where the British government decided in 1784 to divide the colony and create a new one on the north shore of the Bay of Fundy. The original intent was to focus upon agricultural land since farming was perceived as wholesome, encouraging self-reliance and supporting permanent family based communities.

That is perhaps how New Brunswick would have developed had world politics not interceded. Napoleon Bonaparte had, by 1805, conquered much of continental Europe. Unable to engage Britain in battle, Napoleon instead waged economic warfare by creating the Continental System that closed continental Europe to England—thereby eliminating Britain's supply of Baltic timber, for which the country had an insatiable appetite. Britain turned elsewhere and New Brunswick, because of its relative proximity, fine pine forests, suitable natural harbours, and excellent river network, became the obvious new supply depot. At first local families and friends, often impoverished immigrants eking out lives on bush farms, entered the trade to supplement their meagre incomes. The process was relatively easy since Crown forests remained unregulated until 1817 so anyone could cut anywhere and licences, once introduced, remained readily available and inexpensive. The timber trade quickly became the leading industry and the officially blessed and encouraged agricultural economy barely survived. Larger communities ended up importing virtually all their food from the United States.

How did the industry function? Every autumn, thousands of men left their families and headed into the bush to join impromptu work camps carving up New Brunswick's Crown land. Most camps were small, usually fewer than fifteen men, operated by private individuals who contracted to supply a coastal merchant with a specified amount of timber—for which they often received supplies, or "truck," in advance. The merchant, meanwhile, typically created an export contract with a British importer. Once in the bush, and after building a log hut for themselves and a shelter for their draft animals, the men divided into three teams: the fallers; the hewers who cut up the logs; and the transporters who dragged them to the nearest frozen watercourse. All winter they toiled, warmed by huge quantities of rum which sustained them against the constant cold. A St. Croix river crew of some 500 men, for example, supposedly consumed 16,000 litres in 1832 alone.

Spring thaws created "freshets," little runoffs that were used to float logs downstream. This was the most dangerous and uncomfortable time as lumberers spent days chasing errant logs, pushing them around obstacles, and unsnarling deadly logjams. They had to work quickly too, because all the wood had to reach a major watercourse before levels dropped and stranded valuable logs until the following year. Once on a river of sufficient size, such as the Miramichi, the lumberers chained their logs into huge booms which they then floated to the coastal mills and waiting ships. Finally paid off, lumberers then supposedly spent their hard-earned cash on a debauched orgy of wine, women, and song until nothing remained and they had to eke out an existence until the following autumn when they repeated the process. According to many puritanically-minded souls, the lumbering lifestyle led young men to hell—in spite of creating considerable wealth for the colony as a whole.

And generate wealth it did. Despite efforts to diversify the economy and encourage agriculture, lumber products constituted almost 75 per cent of the value of New Brunswick's exports in 1826. In good years, some 600 ships left New Brunswick for Britain and elsewhere, heavily laden with wood products and valued at some £200,000 per annum. But periodic economic downturns could wreak havoc in the timber trade, often leading moral crusaders to crow self-righteously. These cyclical recessionary periods were all the worse because of their unpredictability, and inevitably resulted from the vagaries of international rather than local conditions. Napoleon's defeat, for example, annulled the advantages created by the embargo on Baltic timber. Britain's flirtation with free trade in the 1840s led New Brunswick timber suppliers to assume they could no longer compete and exports indeed tumbled by as much as 50 per cent—though the bust proved short lived. Nonetheless, sudden downturns in overseas demand sometimes led to a glut of timber on the international market, which in turn forced prices down, bankrupted merchants, and created serious unemployment in New Brunswick's backwoods. New Brunswick rode an economic roller-coaster, especially in the second quarter of the nineteenth century, which was hard on local communities and made long-term planning difficult, all the while encouraging the wrath and condemnation of the industry's opponents.

### Discussion Points

1. Considering the male companionship, lifestyle, high wages, and limited commitment, couldn't an agrument be made in favour of working in the woods over the isolated, boring, climate dependent life of a farmer?
2. Since cutting timber took place in the winter when agriculture came to a stand still, was it not likely that these many people worked at both activities? In other words, lumbering and farming were not mutually exclusive.
3. The economies of both New Brunswick and Newfoundland depended upon a single natural resource. In what respects did this make these two colonies similar?
4. Of all the Maritime colonies, would New Brunswick have offered the best economic opportunities for immigrants?

*Documents*

### 1. Peter Fisher, *Sketches of New Brunswick*, 1825.

The genius of these people differ greatly from Europeans—the human mind in new countries left to itself exerts its full energy; hence in America where man has in most cases to look to himself for the supply of his wants, his mind expands, and possesses resources within itself unknown to the inhabitants of old settled countries, or populous cities. In New-Brunswick, a man with his axe and a few other simple tools, provides himself with a house and most of his implements of husbandry,— while an European would consider himself as an outcast, he feels perfectly at home in the depth of the forest. In new countries likewise the mind acquires those ideas of self-importance and independence so peculiar to Americans. For the man who spends the greater part of his time alone in the forest, as free as the beasts that range it without controul, his wants but simple and those supplied from day to day by his own exertions, acquires totally different habits of acting and thinking, from the great mass of the people in crowded cities, who finding themselves pressed on all sides, and depending on others from day to day for precarious support, are confirmed in habits of dependence.

Hence the inhabitants of this Province are men who possess much native freedom in their manners. This, from their veneration to their King makes them faithful subjects and good citizens, not blindly passive, but from affection adhering to that Government under which they drew their first breath and under which they have been reared....

Upwards of three hundred sail load annually at Miramichi. The timber is paid for part in specie, and part in British and West-India goods and provisions.

A stranger would naturally suppose, that such a trade must produce great riches to the country; and that great and rapid improvements would be made. That large towns would be built—that the fair produce of such a trade would be seen in commodious and elegant houses, extensive stores and mercantile conveniences, in public buildings for ornament and utility, good roads and improved seats in the vicinity of the sea-ports, with Churches, Kirks, Chapels, &c.: All these with many other expectations would be but a matter of course. But here he would not only be disappointed, but astonished at the rugged and uncouth appearance of most part of this extensive county. There is not even a place that can claim the name of a town. The wealth that has come into it, has passed as through a thoroughfare to the United States, to pay for labour or cattle. The persons principally engaged in shipping the timber have been strangers who have taken no interest in the welfare of the country; but have merely occupied a spot to make what they could in the shortest possible time. Some of these have done well, and others have had to quit the trade: but whether they won or lost the capital of the country has been wasted, and no improvement of any consequence made to compensate for it, or to secure a source of trade to the inhabitants, when the lumber shall fail. Instead of seeing towns built, farms improved, and the country cleared and stocked with the reasonable returns of so great a trade; the forests are stripped and nothing left in prospect, but the gloomy apprehension when the timber is gone, of sinking into insignificance and poverty. Formerly the woods swarmed with American adventurers who cut as they pleased. These men seeing the advantages that was given them, and wishing to make the most of their time, cut few but prime trees, and manufactured only the best part of what they felled, leaving the tops to rot: by this mode more than a third of the timber was lost. This with their practice of leaving what was not of the best quality after the trees were felled, has destroyed hundreds of thousands of tons of good timber: And when this was stopped by permitting none but British subjects and freeholders to obtain licences, the business was not much mended as any person wishing to enter into the trade could, by purchasing a small sterile spot for a small trifle (provided he was a British subject) get in the way of monopolizing the woods. These are some of the causes that have and still do operate against the prosperity of the country. Men who take no interest in the welfare of the province, continue to sap and prey on its resources.

From the foregoing statement it plainly appears that chief of the export trade of this Province consists of timber, which is its natural stock or capital; and as there are many articles taken in exchange from the mother country, which are indespensibly necessary to the inhabitants of this Province; it points out the necessity of paying strict attention to its preservation. In this Country there is no article, or articles, that can in any degree furnish exports equal to the pine, which is manufactured in the simplest manner, and got to market with but little trouble. So simple is the process that most settlers who have the use of the axe can manufacture it: the woods furnishing a sort of simple manufactory for the inhabitants, from which, after attending to their farms in the summer, they can draw returns during the winter for those supplies which are necessary for the comfort of their families. This being the case, the preservation of our forests becomes of prime importance to the prosperity of the Province.

The evils that must arise to the Province, by allowing the timber to be monopolized and hastily cut off are many. The timber standing in the Country, particularly on the Crown Lands, may be considered as so much capital or stock, to secure a permanent trade, and promote the solid improvement of the Country. Most of the lands in this Province where pine is found are intermixed with other timber, and although the precise spots on which the pine grows, are unfit for Agriculture, without much labour; yet there are most always spots adjoining, where a settler may cultivate with success: so that in a lot of two or three hundred acres, there is generally enough for tillage, and a man settling on such land could always choose his spot for farming, and keep his timber to cut at his leisure. His pine so reserved would as long as it lasted serve him as a resource, from whence, after attending to his farming in the summer, he could draw returns during the winter, for such supplies as would be necessary for his family, and for improving his farm.

To make this more evident, we will suppose a man settling on a wilderness lot—like most settlers he has but little save his own labour—perhaps he has a small family—he commences with cutting down a small spot, and erecting a hut—say in the summer or fall—he then moves on his family, and looks round for sustenance till he can raise his first crop—in doing this his funds are exhausted, and he wants by his own labour to replenish them during the winter, and provide a few implements of husbandry, and nails, &c. for building a barn— now supposing his lot to be back from the river, and at a distance from old settlements where labour is wanted—what does he do?—why he resorts to his pine—to the simple manufactory before noticed, and makes a few tons, say twenty, thirty, forty, or fifty, according to his ability—carefully cutting the under brush and timber, so as to put his land where he is working in a fair train for clearing—this timber he probably gets hauled to the water on shares, if he is very poor and has no team; the returns for which the next spring, furnishes him with supplies, and enables him to continue on his land and prosecute his farming. If he cannot do without the return of his timber till spring, he applies to a merchant, who if the man is of good fame, advances him such articles as may be particularly necessary for his family. This enables him to find labour on his own lot, and stay with his family: whereas if he has no such resource, he must leave his home, and go to a distance from his family, seeking labour; and probably they may be so circumstanced as not to be left safely alone, and he has to take them with him, which breaks up his family and prevents him from settling.

If a number of families commence a settlement together, where the timber has not been destroyed, but where a fair proportion is still growing on the land, they exchange labour with each other, and by their joint exertions, manufacture and transport their own lumber to market. In this way they are enabled from year to year to prosecute their settlement and pay for their grants: the timber answering as a first crop fully grown, and a resource to make returns for necessaries.—By this method, as the pine disappears, houses and barns will rise in its

place, and the country, instead of a barren waste, will exhibit flourishing settlements, peopled with a race who will know the value of their improvements; and
feel their interest identified with the country: and whose attachment to the Government will increase with their growing possessions. Their children, raised on
the soil, from the strong principles of early association, will feel that interest in
the welfare of the country, that no transient advantage can produce; and grow
up an ornament and strength to the Province. On the contrary, if the lumber is
cut off by mere speculators, the land will be left in an impoverished state, much
valuable timber will be wantonly destroyed, and the places from whence the
timber is taken will be left an uncultivated waste; settlers will neither have the
inclination or ability to occupy them. While the major part of the men employed in getting the lumber for the merchants, instead of making a comfortable
provision for their families, will wear out the prime of their days without making any permanent establishment; and keep their families shifting about the
country like vagrants. Their children, for the want of employment, and the
direction of their fathers, brought up in idleness—their education and morals
neglected, and bad habits acquired, will be the reverse of those before noticed:
and many of them will become a vagrant race, unconcerned or uninterested in
the welfare of the country, and in many instances a nuisance to it. While their
parents, after they get unfit for the business, will be turned off in debt.

In short, it will be the most direct way to prevent the settlement of the
back lands, and to produce (what is the bane of all countries) a race of inhabitants who have no interest in the soil or welfare of the Province....

The preceding statement points out the necessity of adopting a more prudent system in conducting the timber business. Not to push the trade to such an
extent—to retrench the expenses, by raising the heavy parts of the supplies near
the timber districts; and to follow up the timber trade with the improvement of
the country and cultivation of the soil.

Another great drawback to the prosperity of the Province is the great consumption of ardent liquors—partly occasioned by the present mode of conducting
the timber business. The amount of spiritous liquors imported and consumed in
the Province in 1824, at the least calculation was £120,000, exclusive of the
County of Charlotte; and add to this amount the cost of the transport of the
liquor to the interior and the enormous charges on the article in the distant parts
of the Province, the cost to the consumer may be fairly reckoned at treble the
amount, making in the whole the gross sum of £360,000 for ardent liquors
alone, consumed by the inhabitants of the Province, being near twenty gallons
on an average for every male over sixteen years of age.

## 2. J. McGregor, *Historical and Descriptive Sketches of the Maritime Colonies of British America,* 1828.

*New Brunswick.*

The timber trade has no doubt been one, if not the principal, cause of the rapid growth of St. John. Great gains were at first realized, both by it and ship-building; and although the merchants and others immediately concerned in these pursuits were nearly ruined afterwards by the extent of their undertakings and engagements; yet, it must be recollected, that each of those trades has enabled New Brunswick to pay for her foreign imports, and with the timber trade she has built St. John, Fredericton, and St. Andrew. To the settler on new lands it presented a ready resource; and if he only engaged in it for a few winters it was wise to do so; as by the gains attending it, he was put in possession of the means of stocking his farm and clothing himself and family. The province, therefore, gained great advantage by this trade; and, although it is not less certain that it has been prosecuted to more than double the extent of the demand for timber, it would, notwithstanding, be extreme folly to abandon it altogether. Two-thirds of the people engaged in the timber trade and ship-building have only to give their industry another direction, and the remainder may work to advantage. In this view agriculture offers the most alluring, and at the same time most certain, source of employment. The fisheries follow next. Let the industry of the inhabitants be but divided between agriculture, the timber trade, and the fisheries, and this beautiful and fertile province will probably flourish beyond any precedent. But the farmer must adhere to agriculture alone; the lumberer will do better, or at least he will realize more money, by following his own business, and those engaged in the fisheries will find it best to confine themselves chiefly to this pursuit....

The principal settlements are along the River St. John, and its lakes; on the north banks of the St. Croix; on the Gulf of St. Lawrence; on the River Miramichi; and on the shores of the Bay de Chaleur. The spirit of agriculture is beginning to diffuse itself rapidly through all, even the most northerly and coldest, parts of the province. Hitherto the timber trade and shipbuilding, by engaging a great part of the labour of a population so very small in proportion to the extent of the country, have retarded the cultivation of the soil and the improvement of the country. None of the North American colonies are more in want of settlers of steady and rural habits....

[F]ertile tracts of intervale land abound, which might be cultivated to profitable advantage, if the country were once settled with people of steady rural habits. The lumberers, who compose probably more than half the population, never will become industrious farmers; and the cultivation of the soil is consequently neglected.

The timber trade, which, in a commercial as well as political point of view, is of more importance in employing our ships and seamen, than it is generally considered to be, employs also a vast number of people in the British Colonies, whose manner of living, owing to the nature of the business they follow, is entirely different from that of the other inhabitants of North America.

Several of these people form what is termed a "lumbering party," composed of persons who are all either hired by a master lumberer, who pay them wages, and finds them in provisions; or, of individuals, who enter into an understanding with each other, to have a joint interest in the proceeds of their labour. The necessary supplies of provisions, clothing, &c., are generally obtained from the merchants on credit, in consideration of receiving the timber which the lumberers are to bring down the river the following summer. The stock deemed requisite for a "lumbering party," consists of axes, a cross-cut saw, cooking utensils; a cask of rum; tobacco and pipes; a sufficient quantity of biscuit, pork, beef, and fish; pease and pearl barley for soup, with a cask of molasses to sweeten a decoction usually made of shrubs, or of the tops of the hemlock tree, and taken as tea. Two or three yokes of oxen, with sufficient hay to feed them, are also required to haul the timber out of the wood.

When thus prepared, these people proceed up the rivers, with the provisions, &c., to the place fixed on for their winter establishment; which is selected as near a stream of water, and in the midst of much pine timber, as possible. They commence by clearing away a few of the surrounding trees, and building a camp of round logs; the walls of which are seldom more than four or five feet high; the roof is covered with birch bark, or boards … These men are enormous eaters, and they also drink great quantities of rum, which they scarcely ever dilute. Immediately after breakfast, they divide into three gangs; one of which cuts down the trees, another hews them, and the third is employed with the oxen in hauling the timber, either to one general road leading to the banks of the nearest stream, or at once to the stream itself: fallen trees and other impediments in the way of the oxen are cut away with an axe.

The whole winter is thus spent in unremitting labour: the snow covers the ground from two to three feet from the setting in of winter until April; and, in the middle of fir forests, often till the middle of May. When the snow begins to dissolve in April, the rivers swell, or, according to the lumberers' phrase, the "freshets come down." At this time all the timber cut during winter is thrown into the water, and floated down until the river becomes sufficiently wide to make the whole into one or more rafts. The water at this period is exceedingly cold; yet for weeks the lumberers are in it from morning till night, and it is seldom less than a month and a half, from the time that floating the timber down the streams commences, until the rafts are delivered to the merchants. No course of life can undermine the constitution more than that of a lumberer and raftsman. The winter snow and frost, although severe, are nothing to endure in comparison to the extreme coldness of the snow water of the freshets; in which, the lumberer is day after day, wet up to the middle, and often immersed from head to foot. The very vitals are thus chilled and sapped; and the intense heat of the summer sun, a transition, which almost immediately follows, must further weaken and reduce the whole frame.

To stimulate the organs, in order to sustain the cold, these men swallow immoderate quantities of ardent spirits, and habits of drunkenness are the usual consequence. Their moral character, with few exceptions, is dishonest and worthless. I believe there are few people in the world, on whose promises less faith can be placed, than on those of a lumberer. In Canada, where they are longer bringing down their rafts, and have more idle time, their character, if possible, is of a still more shuffling and rascally description. Premature old age, and shortness of days, form the inevitable fate of a lumberer. Should he even save a little money, which is very seldom the case, and be enabled for the last few years of life to exist without incessant labour, he becomes the victim of rheumatisms and all the miseries of a broken constitution.

But notwithstanding all the toils of such a pursuit, those who once adopt the life of a lumberer seem fond of it. They are in a great measure as independent, in their own way, as the Indians. In New Brunswick, and particularly in Canada, the epithet "lumberer" is considered synonymous with a character of spendthrift habits, and villainous and vagabond principles. After selling and delivering up their rafts, they pass some weeks in idle indulgence; drinking, smoking, and dashing off, in a long coat, flashy waistcoat and trousers, Wellington or hessian boots, a handkerchief of many colours round the neck, a watch with a long tinsel chain and numberless brass seals, and an umbrella. Before winter they return again to the woods, and resume the pursuits of the preceding year. Some exceptions, however, I have known to this generally true character of lumberers. Many young men of steady habits, who went from Prince Edward Island, and other places, to Miramichi, for the express purpose of making money, have joined the lumbering parties for two or three years; and, after saving their earnings, returned and purchased lands, &c. on which they now live very comfortably.

From 800 to 1,000 cargoes of timber have been imported annually for some years from British America, and this trade employs about 6,000 seamen, who are exposed to every variety of climate. The timber trade is very important as a nursery for sailors, and it is besides of great value to England, in the value of freights and timber, which are principally paid for by the production of British labour. On the most convenient streams, there are several saw mills, from which the quantity of boards and deals required are brought down the river for shipping. Ship building has also occupied the attention of the merchants, about twenty large vessels having been built on the river.

In October, 1825, upwards of a hundred miles of the country, on the north side of Miramichi river, became a scene of the most dreadful conflagration that has perhaps ever occurred in the history of the world. In Europe, we can scarcely form a conception of the fury and rapidity with which the fires rage through the American forests during a dry hot season; at which time, the underwood, decayed vegetable substances, fallen branches, bark, and withered trees, are as inflammable as a total absence of moisture can render them. When these tremendous fires are once in motion, or at least when the flames extend over a few miles of the forest, the surrounding air becomes highly rarefied, and the wind naturally increases to a hurricane. It appears that the woods had been, on both sides of the North West branch, partially on fire for some time but not to an alarming extent, until the 7th of October, when it came on to blow furiously from the north-west, and the inhabitants on the banks of the river were suddenly alarmed by a tremendous roaring in the woods, resembling the incessant rolling of thunder; while at the same time, the atmosphere became thickly darkened with smoke. They had scarcely time to ascertain the cause of this phenomenon before all the surrounding woods appeared in one vast blaze, the flames ascending more than a hundred feet above the tops of the loftiest trees, and the fire, like a gulf in flames, rolling forward with inconceivable celerity. In less than an hour Douglastown and Newcastle were enveloped in one vast blaze, and many of the wretched inhabitants, unable to escape, perished in the midst of this terrible fire....

The ravages of the fire extended as far as Fredericton, on the River St. John, where it destroyed the Governor's residence, and about eighty other houses; and to the northward, as far as the Bay de Chaleur. At the lowest computation, five hundred lives were lost.

If the benevolence and charity of mankind were ever manifested in a more than common degree of feeling for their fellow-men, it was assuredly on this memorable occasion. Clothing and provisions were sent from the neighbouring colonies immediately on the accounts of the distress arriving. Sir Howard Douglas, the Governor, crossed the country at once, to ascertain the full extent of the calamity. Subscriptions for the relief of the sufferers were raised to an amount hitherto unexampled, in Great Britain, in the United States, and in all the British American Colonies.

Miramichi may now be said to have completely surmounted the misery and loss occasioned by the ravages of so terrible a calamity. Newcastle is again rising from its ashes, and will in a few years likely contain as many houses, and as large a population as formerly. The country laid waste by the insatiate element is of little value, it is true, in comparison with its former worth. The timber has been destroyed, and the land impoverished, on which, trees common to sterile soils are springing up. I have often heard it observed by people unacquainted with America, that the land would become valuable by being cleared of the woods by fire, and that immense labour in reclaiming the forest lands would thus be saved; but no opinion can be more erroneous. Settlers who know the value of wilderness lands always choose those covered with the heaviest and largest trees; and the strongest objection that can be made to a piece of land, is its having been subjected to fire, which withers the trees, and effectually exhausts the soil, in consequence of its producing afterwards two or three crops of tall weeds, which require more nourishment than the same number of corn crops would. If the land were, immediately after a fire, brought under cultivation, they would then be equally valuable to those cleared in the usual way; but as these great fires seldom level the large trees, they are in consequence of losing the sap, much harder and more difficult to cut down than green wood; and, by being all charred, exceedingly disagreeable to work among. The clearing of ground, on which the trees are all in a fresh growing state, is therefore preferred to that which has been subjected to fires, which seldom consume effectually more than the underwood, decayed fragments, and the branches of the large trees. The trees cut down for the timber of commerce, are not of the smallest importance in respect to clearing the lands; although I have heard it urged in England as an argument in favour of the timber trade. The lumberers choose the trees that they consider the most suitable, and not one in ten thousand is esteemed so. Almost every description of forest trees would be valuable for different purposes, if once landed in the United Kingdoms; but the principal part of the cost is the freight across the Atlantic, and in order, therefore, that a ship may carry the greatest possible quantity, the largest and straightest trees are hewn square, and not brought round to market as the trees cut down in England are. The timber trade of America has been attended with loss to almost every merchant engaged in it.

The causes of which are numerous, but principally arising, first, from the low price of labour and naval stores in the northern kingdoms of Europe, enabling the people of those countries to export timber to Great Britain at extremely low prices; and secondly, from the lumberers not being able, or indeed willing, to pay the debts they contracted with the merchants, in consequence of the depreciated value of timber. Many adventurers, also, without any capital, from witnessing extraordinary gains having been occasionally made by the merchants, entered into this business, and who, having nothing to lose, ventured into daring speculations, which were exceedingly injurious to regularly established merchants....

**3. Anonymous, *Letters from Nova Scotia and New Brunswick Illustrative of their Moral, Religious and Physical Circumstances in the Years 1826, 1827 and 1828,* 1829.**

LETTER XVIII
*Jan.* 3, 1828.
My Dear Sir: New Brunswick depends almost wholly upon timber, and, therefore, its trade experiences fluctuations, to which Nova Scotia is a stranger, and its agricultural resources have not been explored to the same extent. Those beautiful rivers, which fertilize its vallies, display vast quantities of the finest trees upon their banks, and afford an easy and expeditious journey for the product of the *lumberer* to the wharves, where numberless vessels are to be found at all times, ready to waft it to foreign shores.

"To consider its hardships and privations," said I, yesterday, as we passed a few woodsmen at work, to my friend Mr.——, "one would not believe that any man would be a lumberer, except from necessity." "Oh!" said he, "there are thousands who prefer it to all other employments whatsoever. If the life of the woodsmen has its miseries, then, like those of the sailor, they make his enjoyments more exquisite. If the work be heavy, and the hardships many, yet, by one of heaven's beautiful provisions, the pleasures are precisely in the same ratio....

"The life of the woodsman, like that of the mariner, is precarious and uncertain; and, therefore, like him, he is heedless of to-morrow, and enjoys the present. You cannot wonder, then, that the lumberers have a strong similarity to the sailors, and are wholly different from all around them in the forest.

"From the beginning to the end of winter they may be said to have their feet perpetually wet, for generally they work knee-deep in snow. Their camp keeps out the rain with difficulty; their bed is of the boughs of the trees in the neighbourhood. In drifting the logs down the stream, the woodsman is some-times carried off on one of them. Sometimes he stands on a rock while the waters are sweeping by, washing the half of his body; and sometimes he is carried head-long by the fury of the torrent, and his cries, mixing with the loud roar of the current, proclaim his doom to his companions." "What a life, my dear Sir," said I. "Oh! but then, to countervail these evils, if he master them,—and if he sink under them, all is peaceful in the grave, whether it be dug by the hands of men, or by the attrition of the waters,—he goes into his tent at night, lights his fire of faggots, cooks his provision, drinks his grog, sings himself to sleep, enjoys a profoundness of slumber, which is wholly a stranger to the less adventurous, and rises to his next day's labour in the full buoyancy of health and spirits."

"All these farms along our path belong to lumberers. The soil is excellent, but how bleak they look. What small comfort about their houses! These persons are all in debt. Perhaps a third of them are in prison, or fugitives from the sheriff."...

"That man," said he, "is a lumberer. I will tell you his history. His father and mother were emigrants from Ireland. They got a grant of land, twenty or thirty years ago, from the government of New Brunswick. He embarked in tim-ber speculations, and, instead of cultivating his farm and improving its resources, became a lumberer. He acquired habits of drunkenness from his mode of life, for previously he appeared to be a sober and industrious man, and was obliged before his death to mortgage his property. He died about two years ago, and, as was generally believed, in solvent circumstances. He left a large family, and the man in the custody of the sheriff, is his eldest son. He had been engaged in the timber business for many years along with his father, and three or four of his brothers, and, though a few months ago he told me that it had been ruinous to him, and that the only prospect of relief was in its abandonment, and in becom-ing a farmer, yet he could not possibly emancipate himself from its fascinations. There is his farm. See how poor and desolate it is." "What folly," said I. "You are right. They act foolishly. Yet we ought not to sit in judgment upon others. We are curious creatures—the slaves of habit—and the creatures of circumstances. Consider the drunkard. I am sorry to say, that drunkenness, the mother of all vices, has augmented its votaries immensely among us, within the last few years. The cheapness of all sorts of spirituous liquors, operates, indeed, as a sort of bounty upon their consumption, and, consequently, upon the demoralization of the people's habits; the destruction of their constitutions, and the waste of their money....

"Wherever the inhabitants are lumberers, the country wants all the evidences of agricultural development. Camping for four months among snows, and *felling* or *drifting* the whole time, day after day, wholly unfit them for farm operations. They may work stoutly indeed, for two or three weeks, till they have ploughed and sown what is sufficient for the supply of their respective families; but then they apprehend that their toils are ended. They journey to the city that they may have a settlement of their accompts with their wood-merchants, and enjoy themselves or *have a frolic*, as they call it, before the coming on of the hay harvest. These visits are fearful drawbacks upon their farm operations. Who can doubt," said he, "that the timber business unfits a population, not only for agricultural operations, and, in this way, checks the gradual development of the physical resources of the country, but also generates habits exceedingly prejudicial to their morality and happiness?"

## 4. Abraham Gesner, *New Brunswick*, 1847.

The period is rapidly advancing when agriculture must form the essential pursuit of the chief part of the population of New Brunswick. The demand for timber has heretofore led thousands of the most active inhabitants into the forests, and saw-mills for the manufacture of wood for exportation have been erected by them upon almost every stream and rivulet. The facilities of procuring timber, the abundance of fish on the coasts and in the rivers, and plenty of game, directed the attention of the early inhabitants away from the tillage of the soil, and agriculture has been considered an inferior occupation. It is natural enough in all new countries, that the objects of commerce most readily obtained without the aid of science or skill, and such as meet with a ready demand, should first employ the inhabitants. The system of industry is only changed by necessity; and no sooner will the pineries of New Brunswick disappear, or the lumbermen be driven so far from the rivers that their employment will cease to be profitable, or an unfavourable change take place in the timber market, than he will leave his occupation and engage in another.

  It has been supposed by many, that by drawing the population away from husbandry, lumbering pursuits have been disadvantageous to the country. To certain limits, such an opinion may be in some degree correct: but it should be considered, that the lumbermen have discovered and explored new districts; they have opened the winter roads, cleared the rivers of obstructions, and been the pioneers of many flourishing settlements. From the timber trade, a number of small towns have sprung up, commerce has received its chief support, and the Province derived a large revenue. Any attempt to check the enterprise of the people, or to turn it from one pursuit to another, would be fruitless; they will direct their labours into channels that seem to them most inviting and profitable. Every country has its epochs of industry: the present, in New Brunswick, is the timber period, which will be followed by the agricultural, fishing, and, finally, the manufacturing eras.

To the immigrant, the vast forest presents at first a gloomy spectacle. When he enters upon his ground, he finds not a spot where food can be raised, and the entire surface of the earth is covered by innumerable trees, that have stood for ages, and still seem to bid defiance even to armies of axemen. The axe must be applied to every tree; for every attempt to root them out, except by cutting, and their subsequent decay, has proved abortive. The trunk is cut from two to three feet above the ground—the tree staggers, and falls with a loud crash. The axeman watches the direction taken by the falling wood, calling to his companions, if he have any, to "stand by." Here "man appears to contend against the trees of the forest as though they were his most obnoxious enemies; for he spares neither the young sapling in its greenness, nor the ancient trunk in its lofty pride—he wages war against the forest with fire and steel."

From the great extent of water communication in the Province, much of the common timber on the wild lands is valuable, as it may be readily transported and sold for fuel. The St. John and other rivers are navigated by numbers of wood-boats, which supply the towns with great quantities of cheap wood. The bark of the hemlock tree, extensively employed in tanning, is also an object of some importance.

The erection of a saw and grist mill in a new settlement is always looked forward to with much anxiety, and the inhabitants frequently bestow their labour gratuitously for the construction of the necessary dams. The best pine and spruce are made into shingles, or sawed into boards to cover their houses.

The time in which all these operations are performed is comparatively short, and the changes they produce in the features of the country seem like the work of magic rather than of ordinary industry. Nor are the comforts enjoyed by the inhabitants less than the appearance of their lands would indicate. Thousands of those who carried their first supplies into the woods upon their shoulders, now enjoy all the comforts and many of the luxuries of life. Even the once most destitute emigrant, who upon his arrival in the country was unacquainted with its peculiar mode of industry, has gained an honest independence, and many of such have lived to see their children established around them upon valuable farms. By such operations, the forests are levelled, and their solitudes are cheered by the light of day; the swamps and bogs are redeemed to the plough, the scythe

and the sickle, and hill and valley resound with human labour and happiness,—
until the land is filled with villages, towns and cities; turnpikes, canals and railways
succeed, and transmit the rewards of labour for the support of commerce—the
command to "increase and multiply" is obeyed, and many of the objects for
which man was placed upon the earth are fulfilled.

The felling and hewing of the timber for the British market are generally
performed by parties of men hired by the timber-merchant or dealer for the
purpose. In the autumn, they are despatched into the woods, with a supply of
provisions, axes, horses, or oxen, and everything requisite for the enterprise.
Their stores are conveyed up the larger streams, in tow-boats drawn by horses, or
in canoes paddled by men; and in winter they are transported over the ice. Hay
for their teams is procured from the nearest settlements, and is frequently purchased at £6 per ton. The site for operations having been selected by the leader of
the party, a camp is erected, and covered with the bark of trees. The floor of the
shanty is made of small poles, and a sort of platform is raised for the general bed,
which is composed of evergreen boughs or straw. The fireplace is opposite the
sleeping-floor; and that part of the smoke that escapes, ascends through a hole in
the roof. In this rude dwelling the food is cooked, and the lumbermen rest at
night.

A hovel is also built for the oxen, and the hay secured against rain. The
party is usually divided into three gangs: one cuts down the trees, another hews
them, and the third draws the timber to the nearest stream. They begin their
work at daylight in the morning, and seldom return to the camp until evening,
when they find their supper prepared. During the night, the fire is replenished
with wood by the cook and teamster; and it is a common remark among them,
that while the head is freezing, the feet are burning. I have passed several nights
with these people in the backwoods, and always found them remarkably kind
and hospitable. They are ever cheerful and contented; and a more hardy, laborious, and active class of men cannot be found in any part of the world. Formerly,
a certain quantity of rum was supplied to each individual; but since the introduction of Temperance Societies, the practice is less common.

The avocation of the lumberman is not altogether free from danger. Many
lives have been lost by the falling of trees, and the business of forking timber is
sometimes very hazardous.

In the mountainous districts, it is necessary that the timber should be
conducted over the steep precipices and high banks along the borders of the
rivers. Having been collected on the tops of the cliffs, the square blocks are
launched endwise, over rollers, either into the water below, or on the ice, which

is frequently broken by the concussion. In its descent, the passage of the timber is occasionally arrested by trees or brushwood: the lumberman then descends, and, holding on to the brushes of doubtful foothold, he cuts away the impediments. This mode of launching timber is called "forking,"—from which may have originated the substitution of the phrase "forking over," for the payment of a debt, as expressed by some of the inhabitants.

By the latter part of April, the melting ice and snow, with heavy rains, swell the streams and produce freshets. The lumbermen commence "stream-driving." The timber on the rivulets is now floated downwards to the deep rivers; each log is launched, and, when stranded, it is again rolled into the current—and their manner of urging the enormous pieces of pine over the rapids is alike creditable to their courage and patience. Still pushing the rafts of timber downwards, and moving with the current that daily transports the bark that covers their movable camps—stung by swarms of insects both day and night, these men possess more patience under their hardships and sufferings than those of any other class in the country. Half-a-dozen of them will frequently navigate the stream astride a log of timber, which they paddle along with their legs in the water; and they will force the light skiff or canoe up a perpendicular fall of three feet, where the roaring of the water is truly deafening, and where there there is constant danger of being plunged into some whirlpool, or dashed against the rocks. Although they are frequently rendered giddy by the revolving motion of the eddies, they fix the poles upon the bottom, and move away against the foaming torrent, or cross the stream on slippery blocks of pine. Such is the force of habit, that these men view the forest as their home, and the river as their turnpike: constantly exposed to the inclemency of the weather, and the water of the rivers, they appear contented, and seem to regret when the labour of the season is ended. In situations where the water is more tranquil, a singular spectacle is sometimes presented: each of the drivers mounts a log or piece of timber, and, with their pikes in hand, the party move along like a floating regiment, until some fall or rapid warns them to re-embark. Not unfrequently, a rapid is blocked up with timber in such quantities, that it refuses to pass. This is called a "jam." The clearing away of these jams is the most dangerous part of the stream-drivers' employment, and who are sometimes thrown down a fall or rapid into the boiling pool beneath.

The quantity of timber in one of these drives is enormous: its progress along the river where the timber gets entangled among the rocks is therefore slow, especially when the summer is advanced, and the volume of the water consequently diminished. In order to deepen the water, "wing dams" are sometimes constructed on the sides of the most troublesome rapids. The depth and velocity being thus increased, the floating timber passes along more readily: but these dams greatly impede the passage of canoes in ascending the streams. Like the employment of the sailor, the work of the lumberman is peculiar: he requires much practice and experience; and it may be safely asserted, that should any unfavourable change take place in the home timber trade, thousands of men will be thrown out of employment, who have as little disposition to engage in agriculture as those who have been employed as sailors or fishermen.

The timber and logs having been collected, are formed into large flat rafts, and floated down to their place of shipment, or to saw-mills, where the logs are manufactured into deals, boards, planks, &c. The lumbermen then receive their pay, which they too often spend in extravagant festivity, until the period arrives when they again depart for the wilderness: yet there are many who take care of their money, purchase land, and finally make good settlers. Timber is collected by farmers, new settlers, and squatters, who also procure great numbers of logs for the saw-mills; but the greatest supplies are brought down by the lumbermen from the interior forests.

Mills for the manufacture of timber have greatly multiplied within a few past years. The removal of the exterior parts of the logs, by saws, is favourable to the preservation of the wood, and by it a great saving is effected in the freight. The saws, however, are chiefly applied to spruce, while the pine is shipped in squared logs.

|      | | Number of Sawmills | Value | Persons Employed |
|------|---|---|---|---|
| 1831 | — | 229 | £320,030 | 3,798 |
| 1836 | — | 320 | 420,000 | 4,200 |
| 1840 | — | 574 | 740,000 | 7,400 |
| 1845 | — | 640 | 900,000 | 8,400 |

The present flourishing state of the trade has arisen from the high duties imposed on Baltic timber. In 1791, when the export of timber from New Brunswick had only commenced, the duty on Baltic timber was only 6s. 8d. per load; that duty was gradually raised, and in 1812 amounted to £2 14s. 8d. per load. In 1820 it was £3 5s. per load; but in 1821 it was reduced to £2 15s., and, for the first time, a duty of 10s. per load was laid on American timber. By the financial system of Sir Robert Peel introduced into Parliament in 1842, it was proposed to reduce the duty on foreign wood to 30s. on squared timber, and 35s. per load on deals, according to their cubic contents; and after one year, to make a farther reduction to 25s. and 30s. respectively, and to levy 1s. a load upon timber and 2s. a load on Colonial deals. The tidings of this movement were met in the Province by strong petitions and remonstrances against the measure, which was afterwards carried by a large majority, with a change in favour of Colonial deals of 2s. per load of 50 cubic feet; the duty on foreign being 38s., and on Colonial 2s. This change in the timber duties took place on the 10th of October following, and the apprehensions of its injurious effects upon the trade of the Colonies have proved to be groundless. The removal of all duty on Baltic timber would almost annihilate the Colonial trade....

The equalisation of the duties on timber has afforded a subject of much discussion and debate—and certainly the gradual extension of the principles of free trade is very desirable: at present the British consumer is paying a higher price for his timber than it would be supplied for if the duties on foreign timber were removed. The importance of the article for ship-building, machinery, and the ordinary purposes of life, for which vast quantities are required, form a strong argument in favour of allowing it to be imported from all countries duty-free; yet it must be conceded that, under the present Colonial system, a great amount of capital has been invested in the erection of saw-mills and machinery, which would be rendered almost valueless by a sudden reduction in the protective duties of the British Colonial subject. Many thousands of men would also be deprived of employment; and although some of them would engage in agriculture, a great number of this part of the labouring population would depart for the United States. The Colonial trade, as it now exists, trains a great number of hardy seamen, who in any emergency would be ready for defence or conquest. The consumption of British manufactured goods is also far greater in the Colonies than it would be in a decline of the timber trade, which now enables the inhabitants to pay not only for the necessaries, but likewise for many of the luxuries of life.

The timber trade has been the handmaid of emigration; and although the greater number of immigrants into New Brunswick by the timber ships depart for the United States, the few that remain are greatly aided in the settlement of wild lands by the ready market created by the lumberman and timber-dealer.

The changes of duty on Baltic timber, and the high prices given in Great Britain, in 1824, gave rise to great speculations. The market was soon overloaded with Colonial ships and timber. The result was, that the price of wood fell one-half—many persons were ruined, and the most cautious merchants sustained severe losses....

Ship-building has been followed with much spirit, and still forms an important branch of industry in New Brunswick. An opinion has prevailed in Great Britain, and not without just foundation, that the ships built in the Province are imperfectly constructed and insufficiently fastened. Ships are frequently built by contract for from £4 to £7 per ton: the result has been that many of them have not been faithfully and substantially put together, and the discovery of their imperfections has injured the reputation of all the vessels of the Colony. Since 1840, a successful effort has been made to improve the ship-building, and the vessels now built by the merchants under proper inspection are equal, if not superior, to any ever launched. The abundance and good quality of the wood give New Brunswick an advantage in the building of ships and other vessels.

### 5. James Johnson, *Notes on North America: Agricultural, Economic and Social,* 1851.

The commercial, and I may say the entire internal and social condition of the province of New Brunswick, is in a transition state; and as all transitions occasion embarrassment and distress more or less general, wherever they occur, it has been the fate of this province to suffer a temporary check in its progress, in consequence of this transitionary state of things.

New Brunswick contains an area of eighteen millions of acres, of which about five millions are at present unfit for agricultural purposes. Its population is estimated at two hundred and ten thousand. With twice the geographical extent of the province of Nova Scotia, it has still a population about one-third less. It is therefore in a considerable less advanced condition than the latter province. Indeed, it was not till 1784 that it was separated from Nova Scotia, and formed into a distinct government.

The earliest inland trade of these northern provinces was confined in a great measure to the purchase, by way of barter, of the furs of wild animals collected by the native Indians in their hunting excursions. Next, and as settlers increased, the timber, or lumber trade as it is called, sprang up, and an apparently inexhaustible article of export was drawn from the boundless forests which stretched uninterruptedly over the entire surface of the province. The cutting of the trees, and the haulage and floating of them down the rivers, gave healthy employment to many men; the raising food for these men called agricultural industry into play; the export of the timber employed shipping, and afforded the means of paying for the British manufactures and West India produce imported in return; while the profits of the merchants erected towns and public buildings, improved harbours and internal communications, tempted foreign capital into the province, and generally sustained and carried it forward to its actual condition.

But, like other branches of industry, the lumber trade has always had its periods of activity and depression. When the demand was brisk and prices good, the trade was pushed eagerly forward; lumberers went into the woods by droves, and timber was shipped to England in quantities which over-loaded the market. Prices in consequence fell—those who were obliged to realise were compelled to sacrifice capital as well as profit; and thus mercantile crises, and many failures, periodically occurred among the colonial merchants. It was the over-trading of our own manufacturers in another form. The merchants of St John and the other lumbering ports were subject to these vicissitudes, not from any interference of home regulations, but through excessive individual competition among themselves. Still, on the whole the colonies gained, though many individuals were constantly suffering. And if home capital was lost to those who embarked it; it was a gain to the colony, inasmuch as it had been expended in paying for colonial labour, by which, directly or indirectly, colonial land had been cleared and prepared for the plough.

But such an export trade in the large could only be temporary. Land cleared of timber does not soon cover itself again with a new growth of merchantable trees. Every year carried the scene of the woodmen's labours farther up the main rivers, and into more remote creeks and tributaries, adding to the labour of procuring and to the cost of the logs when brought to the place of shipment. Hence, prices must rise at home, or profits must decline in the colony, and the trade gradually lessen. All these had already taken place to a certain extent, when the further increase of home prices was rendered almost impossible by the equalisation of the timber duties. In this alteration of our British laws, a large number of those engaged in the timber trade have been inclined to see the sole cause of the comparatively unprosperous circumstances in which they have recently been placed.

In so far as I have myself been able to ascertain the facts of the case, I think, with many patriotic colonists, that the welfare of these North American provinces would on the whole, and in the long run, have been promoted by a less lavish cutting and exportation of the noble ship-timber which their woods formerly contained, and which has already become so scarce and dear. Home bounties have tempted them to cut down within a few years, and sell at a comparatively low price, what might for many years have afforded a handsome annual revenue, as well as an inexhaustible supply of material for the once flourishing colonial dockyard.

At the same time, it is useless to lament over past mismanagement. It is easier to discern evils and their causes, after they have occurred, than to prevent even their recurrence. The cream of the timber trade being fairly skimmed off, the question, on my arrival in the colony, had assumed the matter-of-fact form— "How are we colonists in future to make our butter?"

It was an acknowledged evil of the lumber trade, that, so long as it was the leading industry of the province of New Brunswick, it overshadowed and lowered the social condition of every other. The lumberer, fond as the Indian of the free air and untrammelled life of the woods, receiving high wages, living on the finest flour, and enjoying long seasons of holiday, looked down upon the slavish agricultural drudge who toiled the year long on his few acres of land, with little beyond his comfortable maintenance to show as the fruit of his yearly labour. The young and adventurous among the province-born men were tempted into what was considered a higher and more manly, as well as a more remunerative line of life; many of the hardiest of the emigrants, as they arrived, followed their example: and thus not only was the progress of farming discouraged and retarded, but a belief began to prevail that the colony was unfitted for agricultural pursuits. The occasional large sums of money made by it induced also vast numbers of the farmers themselves to engage in lumbering—as a lucky hit in a mining country makes many miners—gradually to involve themselves in debts, and to tie up their farms by mortgages to the merchants who furnished the supplies which their life in the woods required. Thus not only were large numbers of the young men demoralised by their habits in the woods, trained to extravagant habits, and rendered unfit for steady agricultural labour, but very many of the actual owners of farms had become involved in overwhelming pecuniary difficulties, when the crisis of the lumber trade arrived, and stopped all further credit.

What added to the apprehension of the colonists at this time was the comparatively extensive emigration which began to take place when the demand for timber became less, and, consequently, for labourers to procure it. Undisposed to continuous farm-work, the lumberer left the province—as our navigators wander from country to country—to seek employment in Maine or elsewhere towards the West, where their peculiar employment was to be obtained. Even the pine forests of Georgia were not too distant for their love of free adventure. Unable to shake off their encumbrances at home, many of the embarrassed owners of farms also hastened to leave them—some in the hands of their creditors, without even the form of a sale—and made for the new states of the West, under the idea that in a new sphere they would be free men again, and that probably a less degree of prudence or industry might there secure them the competence which their own neighbourhood had denied them. No love of home, or attachment to the paternal acres, restrained either class of men; for these Old World feelings or notions have scarcely yet found a place among the Anglo-Saxons of any part of North America.

That such native-born and old settlers were leaving the province in considerable numbers, was construed into an indication that the province was inferior, as a place of residence, to the states and provinces to which they emigrated. Alarmists made it a topic of melancholy lamentation and gloomy forebodings; and, as in similar cases at home, party feelings laid hold of the emigration as a demonstration of the correctness of special party views, and exaggerated its evil effects. The departure of the working lumberers was a necessary consequence of the cessation of their favourite employment; and it was not considered that the moral character and habits of these men as a body, and the disheartened and embarrassed condition of the owners of the encumbered farms, rendered the departure of neither class a real loss to the population of the province; that the departure of both, in fact, was necessary, in order that the social state might have a fair chance of returning to a healthy, cheerful, energetic, and prosperous condition.

But if lumber, as a staple export, was to be insufficient to supply the future wants of the colony, in the way of paying for the necessary imports of West India product and of flour, upon what were the colonists to fall back? Were the hitherto undervalued agricultural resources of the colony greater than they had been supposed? Could these 18,000,000 of acres really be made to support a population of 210,000 inhabitants, and thus enable them to dispense at least with the large importation of bread stuffs for which they had hitherto been yearly indebted to the United States, to Prince Edward's Island, and to Canada? Or were the mines of the country of such value as to make up for the failure both of lumber and of corn, and to enable New Brunswick to keep pace in future progress with the adjoining states and provinces?

Such were the ideas and questions which had been passing through men's minds when I was honoured with the request to visit the colony, and give an opinion upon its agricultural capabilities. I trust that the result of my tour has been to inspire new hopes and awaken new confidence in the food-producing and population-sustaining powers of the land of this valuable colony, though it has lessened very much in my mind the opinion I had previously derived from books as to the extent of its mineral resources.

The city of St John is situated at the mouth of the river of the same name, which falls into the Bay of Fundy. It has a safe, though not extensive harbour, the entrance of which is defended by Partridge and other small islands. The principal part of the town is situated upon a rocky peninsula, which stretches into the harbour, but it is now extending itself in various directions over the adjoining crags and hollows. Notwithstanding the depression of trade which had for some time prevailed, the surface of naked rocks was, at the time of my visit, selling at the rate of £100 an acre for building purposes; and tasteful cottages, on picturesque sites, were springing up in the neighbourhood of the city. The older inhabitants of the city, the descendants of American loyalists, have many interesting facts to relate regarding its growth, upon what, sixty years ago, was a rocky headland, skirted by cedar swamps; and, considering the still generally uncleared condition of the province, and the position of the city itself, its progress has been at least as rapid as that of any of the greater cities on the Atlantic border of the North American continent.

Yet that there has been a serious change for the worse....

On our way we saw fires burning in the woods in many places, which, in this dry season, only required a little wind to spread in one blaze over the whole forest. At one spot, where the road ran along the edge of the forest, separating it from the cleared land, which lay between the road and the river, we passed six or eight men employed in watching for the fall of sparks, and extinguishing any which might come over from the burning woods, to the imminent danger of their crops.

In a country like this, one learns to look upon trees in a new light. Not only are they an obstacle to cultivation, which must therefore be cut down and burnt; but, so long as natural woods are near, it is dangerous to leave any about the dwelling-house for shelter or ornament. During this summer's tour, I was shown places where the spreading of fire from the forest to a few ornamental trees had caused the destruction of the whole farm buildings, to the almost total ruin of the proprietor. Thus a reason appears for the nakedness which an Englishman almost feels when in the midst of a large clearing. An unsheltered house appears, while the stumps of magnificent trees all around show how well it might have been protected from wind and sun.

Except upon the immediate banks of the river, there are few settlements along this road; and, in general, the upland is very poor until we descend to within twenty or thirty miles of the mouth of the Miramichi. About a dozen miles from Boistown, I had a conversation with a small farmer, Irish by birth, but resident from his infancy in this country. He had been in his farm only three years. By hiring himself as a working lumberer, he had saved £80, and with this he bought his present farm. It contains two hundred acres, and had ten acres cleared upon it, and a small log-house, but no barn. He has built a barn and added to his clearing, and if seasons come round, he should do well.

We passed houses and clearings, however, which were altogether deserted. This was partly owing to the failures in the crops, which have ruined so many of all classes in Ireland as well as here; partly to the failure of the lumber-trade, and to the debts and mortgages in which the small farmers, by engaging in this trade, had gradually become involved.

A stranger does not readily comprehend how a depression in the lumber-trade should seriously affect the interests of the rural population in any other way than in lessening the demand for produce, and in lowering prices. And it was not till I had been longer in the country, and conversed with many persons on the subject, that I was enabled clearly to separate, in my own mind, the evils which this trade had brought upon the rural population from those which were necessarily attendant upon the calling of a farmer.

In lumbering, a man goes into the woods in winter, cuts down trees, and hauls them to a brook, down which, when the spring freshets come, he can float them to the main river, and then to the saw-mills of the merchant to whom he sells them. If a man does this upon his own farm, or at no great distance from it, and by the aid of his own family only, all he gets for his wood is pure gain—if, in the mean time, he has been living on the produce of his own farm.

But if he goes to a distance from his own farm, and has been obliged to hire labourers, or has done so with the view of enlarging his operations, he must apply to the merchant for an advance of stores adequate to the winter's consumption. The cost of these stores, and the wages of his men, are deducted from the value of the wood he has obtained; and if the price of wood be not very low, he may still have a handsome surplus.

Such circumstances lure him on till an unfavourable winter comes, and he is not successful in cutting as good lumber, or in as large a quantity as usual, or in hauling it to the floating place; or a very late spring, or very shallow water, prevents him from getting it to market. Then his debt to the merchant for stores, and for money to pay his men, must stand over to another year; and his farm is mortgaged as security for the payment.

Meanwhile this farm has been more or less neglected, and has been every year growing less produce. His wood must be floated in spring, when his crops ought to be put into the ground. He has been absent in winter, when new land might have been cleared. His mind is occupied with other cares: he does not settle to his agricultural pursuits, and they are therefore badly conducted, even when he is at home to superintend them. And, lastly, while living in the woods, both employer and employed live on the most expensive food. They scorn anything but the fattest pork from the United States, and the finest Genessee flour.

The more homely food, therefore, which their own farms produce, becomes distasteful to them; and thus expensive and sometimes immoral habits are introduced into their families, which cause more frequent demands upon the merchant, and a consequent yearly increase of the unpaid bills.

In such a state of things, the foreclosing of mortgages, the sale of farms, and the emigration of ruined families, must necessarily be of occasional occurrence. But if the price of lumber fall very much at any period, they must become more frequent; or, if a merchant who holds many of these mortgages himself fails, a common ruin will involve all. Both of these evils have at once befallen the lumbering farmers on the Miramichi, and much distress has been the result. To this cause was owing the abandonment of farms by persons who, leaving both debts and mortgages behind, and taking with them any capital they could secure, had moved west to lumber on the Aroostook, or to begin life anew in the far off Wisconsin....

## *Readings*

Acheson, T. *Saint John: The Making of a Colonial Urban Community.* Toronto: University of Toronto Press, 1985.

Buckner, P., and D. Frank, eds. *The Atlantic Provinces Before Confederation.* Fredericton: Acadiensis Press, 1985.

Buckner, P., and J. Reid, eds. *The Atlantic Region to Confederation: A History.* Toronto: University of Toronto Press, 1994.

Condon, A. *The Envy of the American States: The Loyalist Dream for New Brunswick.* Fredericton, New Ireland Press, 1984.

Day, D., ed. *Geographical Perspectives on the Maritime Provinces.* Halifax: St. Mary's University, 1988.

Lower, A. *Great Britain's Woodyard: British North America and the Timber Trade, 1763–1867.* Montreal: McGill-Queen's University Press, 1973.

MacNutt, W. *New Brunswick: A History 1784–1867.* Toronto: Macmillan, 1963.

MacNutt, W. "The Politics of the Timber Trade in Colonial New Brunswick, 1825–1840," *Canadian Historical Review* 30 (March 1949).

Rawlyk, G., ed. *Historical Essays on the Atlantic Provinces.* Toronto: McClelland and Stewart, 1967.

Sager, E., and G. Ponting. *Maritime Capital: The Shipping Industry in Atlantic Canada, 1820–1914.* Montreal and Kingston: McGill-Queen's University Press, 1990.

Wynn, G. "'Dark and Demoralized Lumberers': Rhetoric and Reality in Early Nineteenth-Century New Brunswick," *Journal of Forest History* (October 1980).

Wynn, G. *Timber Colony: A Historical Geography of Early Nineteenth Century New Brunswick.* Toronto: University of Toronto Press, 1981.

*Chapter Twelve*

# "THEY THINK THEY KNOW EVERYTHING": NOVA SCOTIA'S IDENTITY

1. John Robinson and Thomas Ripin, *A Journey Through Nova Scotia*, 1774.
2. Peleg Wiswall, "To S. Archibald," March 14, 1818.
3. John Marshall, *A Patriotic Call to Prepare for A Season of Peace...*, 1819.
4. Thomas Haliburton, *The Clockmaker*, 1836.
5. William Young, "To Lord Durham," 1838.
6. Joseph Howe, "To Lord John Russell," September 18th, 1839.
7. Abraham Gesner, *The Industrial Resources of Nova Scotia*, 1849.

## Introduction

If Prince Edward Island was synonymous with agriculture, Newfoundland with fishing, and New Brunswick with lumber; what distinguished Nova Scotia?

Jutting out upon the bosom of the Atlantic ensured that Nova Scotia was among the first landfalls for Europeans exploring the Americas, and one of the first locations for settlement efforts. According to pre-Confederation nineteenth-century Nova Scotian thinkers, the colony rose from a rich cultural amalgam of American, British, and British North American stock—which gave them a peculiarly unique culture and people. Yet the specific definition and elaboration of what it meant to be a Nova Scotian caused considerable anguish, particularly in the first half of the nineteenth century. All they really agreed upon was that Nova Scotia was a Maritime culture with its gaze across the Atlantic to mother England, and southward to the United States. They ignored the fact that indigenous people and Acadians also formed part of the equation.

After the Acadian expulsion and its decisive victory over France in North America, Britain encouraged New Englanders to settle the recently vacated Acadian lands. Some 8000 "Planters" took up the offer and brought with them strong notions of participatory democracy and fundamentalist religion. The American Revolution had an enormous impact on Nova Scotian society, as thousands of British loyalist refugees poured into the colony. These people were North

Americans, by birth, sentiment, and despite their pro-Britishness. In Nova Scotia they set about recouping their material and psychological losses, healing their wounded pride and creating a colony which would prove to the Americans and to themselves that they had done the right thing by being Loyalists. Many of those Loyalist newcomers came from solid middle class backgrounds, with their abiding belief in family, commerce, education, community, and tempered sense of democracy—which they set about infusing into Nova Scotian society. Their skills and attitudes were, however, often at odds with what it took to overcome the hardships of pioneer life. Their expectations of compensation, their dislike of republicanism, and their sense of social superiority set them on a collision course with local inhabitants who resented and mistrusted the new arrivals. Governor Parr referred to the Loyalists as pretentious and a "cursed set of dogs." Eventually apprehension diminished especially after the partition of Nova Scotia in 1784 when two new colonies were created for the exclusive use of the Loyalists.

In the first half of the nineteenth century, Nova Scotia became the intellectual hub of British North America and created an education system unrivalled elsewhere—including a much lauded and comprehensive university system. Despite these great educational advances, Nova Scotia experienced considerable transiency as thousands of immigrants passed through on their way to more appealing destinations in Upper Canada or the United States. An unstable economy coupled with limited agricultural prospects contributed to visions of "going down the road." Even an expanding ship-building industry which would eventually achieve a measure of international reputation did not prevent Thomas Haliburton from suggesting that Nova Scotia was "a grand country to leave."

Nova Scotians suffered from that peculiarly Canadian syndrome: an inferiority complex that stunted the creation of a strong sense of identity. Some complained that Nova Scotians, particularly the Loyalists, lived beyond their means in order to maintain an artificial facade of sophistication. Others characterized all Nova Scotians as lazy and even dissolute, though writers levelling these accusations rarely offered concrete proof. Nova Scotians also felt ambivalent about democracy and what their rights should be in governing the colony. Then there was the general issue of where Nova Scotia should fit in the Empire. Some argued that quiet obscurity offered the best approach since it reflected reality and encouraged a submissive demeanour appropriate to a small sibling in a large Imperial family. Others demanded a much greater level of equality with Britain and railed against the negative image of Nova Scotia that commonly existed in the motherland. This group of thinkers hoped to correct what they considered the woeful ignorance among Englishmen of their colony—ignorance to the point where British descriptions of the place had the Nova Scotia heart-land filled with wolves that climbed trees while pursuing their victims.

## Discussion Points

1. What did it meant to be a Nova Scotian?
2. Wiswall believed that strength lay in obscurity, while Howe supported self-promotion for Nova Scotia. Which was a better policy?
3. While Haliburton's *The Clockmaker* is classified as fiction, some content reveals a "higher truth." In other words, fiction allows authors to say things that would normally not be acceptable as non-fiction. Would this apply to Haliburton or was he simply trying to be humorous?

## Documents

### 1. J. Robinson and T. Ripin, *A Journey Through Nova Scotia,* 1774.

... Money is indeed very scarce in this part of the world, so that trade is chiefly carried on by the bartering of their goods, which is undoubtedly a great disadvantage to the country, and on account of which they labour under the greatest inconveniencies. What they purchase at present, is for the most part on a year's credit, and they do not pay less than a hundred per cent interest. Their payments are made at the end of the year, with wheat, butter, cheese, beasts and horses, or whatever is convenient for them. There are merchants, whom they call store-keepers, who derive great advantage, by supplying them with all sorts of cloths, linen as well as woollen, and wearing apparel; also rum, sugar, molasses, &c. imported from Boston and the West Indies; for which they receive the produce of the country, and export it in return for the merchandize they receive from abroad. By this profitable traffic, many of them concerned in it have made for-tunes in a few years. We knew some that had not been in business above four or five years, and begun trade with a mere trifle, at this time worth fourteen or fifteen hundred pounds; notwithstanding they did not seem to be acquainted with the best markets either to buy or sell at. Were a few substantial men, who understand business of this kind, to engage in the above branch; the articles in which the above persons trade might be imported at half the price that is paid for them at present, and their money kept at home.

It is the due improvement of the land in this country, on which its best and most lasting interest depends, and without which it can never be wealthy or flourishing; the exportation of its crops would bring in a return of money, that, at present, as was observed before, is much wanted.

It is, indeed, surprising what chemerical notions many persons entertained of Nova-Scotia, previous to their leaving this country, with a view of settling at that place. They imagined that they should find lands cultivated, fields sown, and houses built ready to their hands; and that they would have nothing to do, but to take possession, and reap. Not finding things in quite so favourable a situation as they foolishly expected, and having no inclination, by diligence and industry, to render them so, they return, and, by way of excuse for themselves, represent it as a miserable country, and the inhabitants in a starving condition. However, the truth is, it is a very extensive country, abounding with fine navigable rivers, and is as well situated for trade as any place in the world. At present they consume the greatest part of their produce at home, but, by a judicious improvement of their lands, which might easily be effected, they would raise such stocks of cattle, and crops of grain, as would enable them to supply the West India markets, from whence they would have their return in ready money.

They have good land that will grow any sort of corn, flax and hemp; and pastures that will feed any kinds of cattle. Their woods produce timber, fit both for ships and house building, and supply them with pitch and tar; also, with fire wood: And they have coals for getting. They have great plenty of iron in New England. In short, they have all kinds of naval stores, as well as every necessary of life within themselves, without being beholden to any power upon earth.

The greatest disadvantage this country at present labours under is, that its inhabitants are few; and those in general, ignorant, indolent, bad managers, and what is the natural consequence of such qualities, the greatest part of them are poor. They have neither inclination nor industry to make great improvements. Can it then be wondered at, that a country so poorly, so thinly, and so lately inhabited, should have rather an unfavourable appearance, especially to those who have lived in the finest and best cultivated counties in England, where neither pains nor expence has been spared to improve their lands to the utmost advantage? Besides, where there is a want of proper management, have we not seen, even in our own country, men that occupied estates of their own, and could not make a living of them, but when the same farm has fallen into the hands of a skilful, industrious farmer, he has both paid the rent, and lived better on it than the owner could.

John Robinson, one of the persons by whom the foregoing remarks and observations were made, is of opinion, that not any of the persons who have returned from Nova-Scotia, whether farmers or labourers, but had a better opportunity of supporting themselves more comfortably there, than they are ever likely to have in England. With respect to himself, he has not the least doubt of making a much better provision for his family upon the land which he has purchased in Nova-Scotia, than it is possible to make on the best farm in the county of York. Who then, as he observes, would continue here to be racked up till bread can scarce be got to supply the wants of their children? A large sum of money would not induce him to stay any longer in this country; nor does he doubt, should it please God to continue his life twenty years longer, of seeing as great improvements in the uncultivated lands of Nova-Scotia, as has been made within these few years in the barren, winney commons of England, and at as small an expence; the land being equally as good and as capable of improvement. Besides, the improvers of land in Nova-Scotia have greatly the advantage of those in England, as the land cleared and improved by the former, is generally their own property, while the latter are for the most part tenants, and, as is too frequently the case, after all the pains and expence they have been at for the improvement of their farms, are deprived of the enjoyment of the fruits of their industry.

Many persons seem desirous to know the reason why some of the inhabitants of Nova-Scotia are selling their lands, and several of those who were not satisfied with that country, on their arrival there, and immediately returned, have given out, that such land-sellers were also about to quit it. The real truth of the matter is, that large tracks of ground, chiefly wood-land, were granted to the first settlers, who, in general, were very poor; yet, by a persevering industry and good management, they have cleared great quantities, which they occasionally sell off, in order that they may be the better enabled to proceed in the improvement and stocking of the remainder of their lands.

A poor man may take a farm, stocked by the landlord for which the latter receives for the rent, half its produce; or, for every cow, thirty pounds of butter, half the cheese, and so in proportion of whatever else the farm produces.

Nova-Scotia extends five hundred miles in length, and four hundred in breadth. There are vast tracks of land at present unoccupied; and, in general, their large marshes are but thinly peopled. As mentioned before, it is extremely well situated for trade; and the number of navigable rivers that run through it, renders land carriage unnecessary.

The inhabitants are of different countries, though chiefly from New England, Ireland and Scotland. The New Englanders are a stout, tall, well-made people, extremely fluent of speech, and are remarkably courteous to strangers. Indeed the inhabitants, in general, poor as well as rich, possess much complacence and good manners, with which they treat each other as well as foreigners. To the honour of this country, we may say, that abusive language, swearing and profaneness, is hardly known amongst them, which is the great scandal and reproach of Britain.

The Sabbath is most religiously observed; none of them will do any business, or travel, on that day; and all kinds of sports, plays and revels, are strictly prohibited. They take great care to educate their children in the fear of the Lord, and early to implant in them a right notion of religion, and the great duty they owe to God and their parents. The children have a very engaging address, and always accompany their answers, with "Yes, Sir; or, No, Sir;" or, "Yes, Ma'am; or, No, Ma'am," &c. to any questions that are asked them; and, on passing their superiors, always move the hat and foot.

The men wear their hair queu'd, and their cloathing, except on Sundays, is generally home-made, with checked shirts; and, in winter, they wear linsey-woolsey shirts, also breeches, stockings and shoes: instead of which, in summer, they have long trowsers, that reach down to their feet. They dress exceedingly gay on a Sunday, and then wear the finest cloth and linen. Many of them wear ruffled shirts, who, during the rest of the week, go without shoes or stockings; and there is so great a difference in their dress, that you would scarce know them to be the same people.

The women, in general, (except on Sundays) wear woolseys both for petticoats and aprons; and, instead of stays, they wear a loose jacket, like a bedgown. It is owing to the high price of stays, and not to any dislike they have to them, that they are not worn in common. The few that are used, are imported either from New or Old England, as they have not any staymakers amongst them. The women, in summer, in imitation of the men, usually go without stockings or shoes, and many without caps. They take much pains with their hair, which they tie in their necks, and fix it to the crown of their heads. Nor are they on the Sabbath less gay than the men, dressing for the most part in silks and callicoes, with long ruffles; their hair dressed high, and many without caps. When at Church, or Meeting, from the mistress to the ... girl, they have all their fans. We even thought, in the article of dress, they outdid the good women of England.

Nothing can be said in favour of the inhabitants, as to their management in farming. They neither discover judgment or industry. Such of the New Englanders, into whose manners and characters we particularly inspected, appeared to us to be a lazy, indolent people. In general, they continue in bed till seven or eight o'clock in the morning; and the first thing they do, after quitting it, is to get a glass of rum, after which they prepare for breakfast, before they go out to work, and return to dinner by eleven. They go out again about two, and at four return to tea. Sometimes they work an hour, or two after, and then return home, both masters and their servants, amongst whom there seems to be no distinction; and you scarce can know one from the other.

## 2. Peleg Wiswall, "To S. Archibald," March 14, 1818.

Annapolis
Dear Sir,
... Although the view I take of the situation and prospects of this Colony does not picture them in a flattering light, yet I see no cause of discouragement to those who can be content with very moderate wealth, acquired gradually by habits of industry & oeconomy—To those, who enjoying liberty and security, can be content to be humble *even in their taste*—In fine it is a comfortable good country for those who are wholly ignorant of the *Great*,—the *Learned* or the *Gay* worlds—The acquisition of great power & wealth,—proficiency in the sciences— and the refinements of fashionable life, are what Nova Scotia has no more pretensions to in reason, than Norway or Finland—To live in comfortable coarse plenty—To have our relations & friends comfortable about us—To feel no extreme sollicitude about "what we shall eat or wherewithal we shall be clothed"—To be civilised but not over refined—To have as much learning as can be carried into practical use in the common affairs of life; and sense to buy a *pennyworth* more from other countries when we want it—is, enough to make us as happy *as we can be*— ...

Although Nova Scotia has nothing favorable in its clime— little in its soil & productions, and less still in its local situation, yet it has natural constitution sufficient to bring it forward to buxome healthy puberty, if not overstrained, poisoned, dandled and debauched in its present child-hood—But it is time to have done with figurative language—What I shall add will be plain enough— Some of it may at first astonish you—...

The true present interest of Novascotia depends upon our being *obscure and unoticed*—Our Commercial Gentlemen are wonderfully anxious that we should be thought of importance to the Mother Country both in a political and commercial point of view,—That we should even be thought to possess a *formidable mercantile* body of men owning a large disposable capital!!!—Traders are very apt to imagine that all the politics of the world turn upon bargain and sale, profit and loss—But few notions are worse grounded than this—History gives it no countenance;—And untill human nature be wholly altered it never can—...

I do aver that in *obscurity* lies our value and our strength;—And that we all want of the Mother Country is her *good natured negligence*—...

We are intrinsically poor and nothing but what is Super-human can prevent our remaining so for a long time to come—But we may nevertheless be happy, and we ought to be contented—I may again occasionally glance upon this subject of our insignificance; but, to pursue this head, which relates to our dependance upon the Parent Kingdom, I do pronounce that, any change in that way, would bring upon us utter distress and ruin—It would throw us in the back ground as far as Newfoundland or Labrador. And we should long (perhaps forever) remain a bleak, barbarous collection of oppressed fishermen and potatoe planters—To avoid this direful state, we must not affect an importance which may eventuate in our being detected as cheats—Our hold upon the Mother Country should be upon her magnanimity her generosity—her kind attatchment; and perhaps, upon her pride—It is in our power to win the hearts of the Governors and other principal officers she sends amongst us, by a kind, frank and respectful demeanor—Avoiding flattery and servility—We should pride ourselves upon the glories of Britain—Her Colonies her Insignia of every kind; and be as like Englishmen as possible in all matters of external appearance. In matters however of interior jurisprudence, police and regulation, we must not copy after the institutions of any part of Europe—Those of England are clumsy, complex, expensive and awkward—They have been simplified, refined and improved on this side the Atlantic—

Beyond all doubt the ambitious days of Great Britain are now past—She has run a glorious Career, and laid up a sufficient stock both of reputation and wealth—Upon that stock she can subsist with dignity for a long time to come— If we are not fools or knaves we may repose under her laurels and partake of her goodly treasure—But it will not be wise to pester her often with lists of grievances, troublesome petitions and *special agents*—... Before closing this head, I have to say a word of what ought to be our conduct towards the United States— To call them names, and to affect to sneer at them is, *in us*, of all people under Heaven, the most contemptibly ridiculous—No individual—no society, resorts to blackguarding but from conscious inferiority and utter despair of emulation—Dont *let us* place ourselves so low, and dont *let us* provoke either recrimination or enquiry—Our interest is to make friends not to make enemies—There is, and always will be, in the body of the United States, a great many absolute British Subjects there resident from choice—There is also a large and respectable body of American citizens connected by the ties of blood and friendship, as well as of interest, with families in Great Britain and Ireland—If we have no regard to our own dignity it is nevertheless *not prudent* to wound the feelings of these persons,—When speaking of the United States,—Their Measures—Institutions—principal men etc, the language (written or verbal) of our Courts of Law—of our Legislative Assemblies—of all public societies and private genteel companies, should be, decent and respectful—...

Our relation to the Canadas may be dispatched in a few words—They are close and near neibours to the United States,—Nature has placed insuperable bars to their ever becoming neibours of ours—They care little about us, and we need not trouble ourselves much about them—As fellow subjects of the same Great Empire, we should wish them to go right, and rejoice in their fair success & prosperity—But our fates and fortunes are not necessarily blended either now or ultimately—Those countries and their populations are made of quite different materials from ours—They have different views,—different pursuits—They will soon grow to be great and to be saucy—With us they will have but little connection either in trade or otherwise—Our near friends, and true and lasting associates, "through all the changing scenes of life," must be the people of N Brunswick, Cape Breton, and Prince Edward Island.

Having looked abroad, as far as a Nova-Scotian is bound to look, We will now look at home—And the first subject that requires consideration is, our *population*—I think there is a present disposition amongst us to force that beyond our means—From the Nature of Our soil and clime we do not, and without a miracle we cannot, get on rapidly in providing the means of subsistence—*This is not a provision Country*—It is a country of great consumption—We use an extraordinary proportion of food, cloathing—and fuel—For both man and beast we require a great expence in the article of Shelter—We have very short Summers in which to provide for long winters—our wild lands are long in reclaiming—and our crops, especially of bread-corn, are very uncertain—the labor of a family for five years exclusively employed upon the vast wilderness lands we have (supposing no assistance from fishery or from natural meadows and the rearing of cattle) would not place it in a situation to secure the possessors *the bare necessaries of life*—The first settlers although they had great advantages from the *cream & choice of all the lands—from the disproportioned abundance of the River fish to the paucity of the then colonists—from game in the forests—and from the unrestrained use of wood and timber,* yet had many difficulties and suffered many hardships—Many of them were discouraged—Such as persevered, by gaining from the failure and expenditures of others,—by various adventitious aids (not like to occur again)—and above all, by the accumulated product of sixty years labour and savings, have acquired to the Province a considerable stock in improved lands, buildings, cattle and other valuables—But by no means such a stock as has anything to spare, or such an one as, considering what has been acquired by other colonies in the like time, can be anyways boasted of—It is in truth a *hard* and a *slow* country—Its means for feeding and cloathing its inhabitants, aided by all the strength of its present capital stock, will be found adequate to provide but for a very few beyond its own natural increase—Nature has adapted it only for a comparatively thin population—And, its own *natural increase* will in 30 years, or 40 at most,—bring the number of its inhabitants to the point where (as far as the *general* comfort and happiness are concerned) the maximum of population ought perhaps to be fixed—

If we could indeed entice some *rich* people from other countries (not however in such numbers as to disturb our present state of society which is yet forming and hardly settled and coagulated) to come amongst us, I should not object to their bringing a reasonable number of poor adventurers with them—But in my 35 years of experience in this country, I have found no persons rich either in pocket, character or brains that have come to settle amongst us as of *choice*—Here and there one has occasionally been *entrapped* for years or for life—I think however the time *may* come, when this Province will prove an inviting one to respectable persons of moderate wealth who from particular events or circumstances shall have a country to chuse—This generation however will never see that time if we get over-run with Maroons—Chesepeak negroes,—cast-off-Fishermen, or even with too many *poor* Scotch, Irish or English emigrants, let them be ever such useful and worthy persons *in themselves and in their proper place*—It is impossible to push on a colony advantageously beyond the course of Nature—Every thing to be good must have its time to grow,—and should not be forced—Let *us* have time to unite,—to civilize, and to organize—To become a people, ie, a community understanding each other and interested in each other—Let us not *over* leap that blessed period in the progress of a growing people which is attended with cheapness and plenty,—when there is enough for all,—and the means yet unoccupied of adding more—It is somewhat surprizing to hear our larger *selfish farmers* supported by men of sense (but certainly I think not men of consideration) in crying out about the price of labour—Labour must be at a high price in Novascotia if the labourer gets sufficient to cloath and feed himself and family comfortably through the Year—If he does not, God knows it is a bad country for him,—And, as he ought, as he certainly will, quit it for a better as soon as he can—But either the importation or even retention of many *poor settlers* at a time, will only have a transient effect upon the price of labour—It will however have a lasting effect in filling the Poor-houses,—raising the price of provisions,—increasing crimes,—bringing down the character of the Province, and eventually, furnishing recruits to the American Army & Navy—Upon this head do not let us be cajoled by land-jobbers—visionary speculators in trade,—selfish farmers or political quacks—The present interest of the Province requires that *none* should be *invited* to it—Such few as voluntarily or casually get amongst us (having decent habits and apparent capacity for earning a livelihood) will find their way to employment and encouragement—But *Hords* of Paupers and Lazzaroni, only come here to distress us and freeze and starve themselves—

*"Our agriculture must be encouraged"*—What encouragement does it want? The farmers are generally Tenants in fee simple—They do not pay the most trifling quit-rent—They pay no taxes but parish rates, and these very small—They sell every species of their produce one third higher than the like is sold for in any part of North America—*"But our farmers are not as rich as Carolina Planters"*—They are not, nor can they ever expect to be—They are however, at this very period, more wealthy than they could reasonably have expected, considering the nature of the soil and climate, and the poverty with which they all commenced—They are not to be sure more than half as rich as they assume to be, because they foolishly overvalue their lands—And this false estimate of the value of our lands, is the true cause why so many have incurred debts which they now find difficult to pay, and make an outcry for *paper-money*—...

I do not believe that the whole civilized World affords another instance of a community like ours—A population of 80,000 persons scarcely making an attempt to manufacture the simplest and coarsest articles of necessary domestic use—Such enormous buyers as we are from abroad, must needs become poor and insolvent although we used the strictest oeconomy—The attempts to be made in the way of manufactures should all be *on a small scale*—Such as an individual could support and maintain, through a course of several years, against the stream of adverse circumstances, without incuring the risque of any loss beyond what he could fear without a complaint—Away with all our magnificent projects!—We have attended too many Mountains in labour with mice—There is room for rational pursuits in this way accompanied with a reasonable prospect of moderate advantage either direct or collateral—...

It is a sad melancholy truth that no people deal less upon good faith than our own blue-nosed countrymen in general—and I think it will be some time before Novascotians will deserve and obtain a character for manly uprightness and fair dealing—There are physical—moral—political and even legal hindrances in the way of improvement—Nothing however is to be despaired of in a community that is yet growing and forming. A word may be added here about *Smuggling* which, is most certainly in itself, and in most of its bearings, a very bad thing. But I fear it is a thing (as our coasts are situated) not to be prevented either by laws or by officers—Out of Halifax and St. John it will not be undertaken in the gross or at any great risque of loss, but it is, and will be pursued in detail—There is, and will be a constant little smuggling traffick carried on from day to day by a hundred little channells—The settlers round our extensive shores find an advantage in it—And it is not in the power of all the ingenious Committees of Trade in the world to convince them that they can get articles of like value with those they smuggle on anything near such good terms from those who call themselves our *fair traders*—It were well if all temptation to smuggling could be removed—

### 3. John Marshall, *A Patriotic Call to Prepare for A Season of Peace...,* 1819.

In addition to all these considerations, let those who may feel the indifference which has been spoken of, be assured that we are considered by Great-Britain of too much importance, for her to permit us to be finally wrested from under her dominion; and therefore, that should the government of the United States, even succeed at any time in obtaining a temporary possession of the Colony, such vigorous and powerful exertions would be made to regain it; and such determined resistance throughout would be made by all truly loyal subjects among us, that they would not be able to maintain that contemptible neutrality they would wish. They would quickly be discovered; and any backwardness or reluctance they might show to stand forward and exert themselves in defence of the country, would eventually meet with the treatment it deserved. Let such therefore, in time be warned of the consequences of cherishing that disposition, let them instantly determine to maintain their allegiance through every vicissitude; and reflecting on the many blessings they at present enjoy, resolve that if ever the hour of trial should arrive, they will show the sense they entertain of their value, by their vigorous efforts to ensure their continuance.

Here, our attention may naturally enough be directed to the conduct of those, who professing themselves to be British subjects, and being under the ties of allegiance as such, are satisfied to remain under the government of that country which entertains such a hostile disposition towards us. Not only while amicable relations in profession subsist, are great numbers of those persons, there to be found, contributing by their pursuits to increase its wealth and resources; but there did many of them willingly continue, doing the same, while open hostilities prevailed, and were to all outward appearance espousing and supporting its cause. Such persons are not worthy of belonging to any government whatever. They must be conscious that no confidence is placed in them where they are, and their shallow professions of attachment to the British government, cannot shield them from the contempt of all its truly loyal and dutiful subjects.

Complaints, have we also frequently heard, and still do we continue to hear, of the defect of patriotism and public spirit, ...

Our present trade with the people of the United States, it is much to be feared, will tend to continue us in that state of dependance upon them, for flour and grain of various descriptions, under which we have so long unfortunately remained. The ground of this apprehension, is, the facility with which those articles may now be procured from thence, in the greatest abundance; from which it is but too probable, we will be prevailed on to relax our exertions for obtaining among ourselves, a supply of them adequate to our wants.

Of those, who came here as mentioned to prosecute trade, but very few have contributed their exertions.... It would appear from their conduct, as though they considered themselves while here, in a state of exile or banishment. They have in general, seemed to care very little about the prosperity of the Province; but have merely attended to the advancement of the particular pursuits in which they were engaged; and more especially to the acquisition of individual gain. For acquiring this, they have indeed been sufficiently attentive to employ all the means within their power; and from time to time as they obtained it, have been full as careful, to hasten it away to some other country. Thither, after securing the amount, which probably they had limited themselves here to acquire, they have speedily followed, to consume or enjoy it.

What numbers might been named, who have acted in this manner, and who having amassed large fortunes within the Colony, have quitted it, with the declared intention of never returning. These persons, may say in their justification, if any justification is deemed requisite—that by such conduct, they have not committed any violation of the amor patriae, for that, they never professed or entertained any attachment to this country, any farther than their own interest was concerned. It may surely then on the other hand be remarked—that they were not the persons who while here, were entitled to the first degree of consideration and attention.

If instead of thus quitting the Province, they had removed from the capital, to other parts of it, and had been satisfied, to enjoy the tranquility, the moderation, and happiness of a rural life, and to endeavour by their example, and influence, to improve and to forward our Agriculture; they would have effected more for the promotion of our general prosperity, than could have been accomplished by all other means. If they had gone still further, and loaned out their money judiciously to the farmers around them, who might have required it; or had employed it immediately themselves, in making Agricultural improvements, they would have contributed yet more to the public welfare; and through these means alone, the Province would long ere this, have been in a highly prosperous state; and quite independent of every other country for most of the chief necessaries of life. The exertions, and the example of those persons, in forwarding the Agricultural occupations in which they themselves were engaged, would have aroused, and stimulated those of inferior means and information around them; and the general extension and improvement of those occupations would have followed of course.

Having, however, from the first, been determined on quitting the country, as soon as they had acquired the limited portions of wealth, it was not to be expected, that they would have placed it out upon interest here; or have suffered any part of it which they could possibly bear away, to remain here after their departure.—The sole object of most of them, was, to drain the vitals of the colony as effectually as they could, to aggrandize and enrich themselves; and they have but too extensively, and too wofully for us, succeeded in doing it.

Even, many of those in the capital, who have grown rich by their pursuits, and are satisfied to remain in the Province, continue in the same place, either lavishing away their wealth in rounds of folly and dissipation, or having placed it in the British funds, or in those even of the United States, seem to care very little about the advancement of our general welfare.

### 4. Thomas Haliburton, *The Clockmaker*, 1836.

"... They do nothing in these parts but eat, drink, smoke, sleep, ride about, lounge at taverns, make speeches at temperance meetings, and talk about 'House of Assembly.' If a man don't hoe his corn, and he don't get a crop, he says it is owing to the bank; and if he runs into debt and is sued, why, he says the lawyers are a curse to the country. They are a most idle set of folks, I tell you."

Mr Slick looked at me with a most ineffable expression of pity and surprise. "Depend on it, sir," said he, with a most philosophical air, "this Province is much behind the intelligence of the age. But if it is behind us in that respect, it is a long chalk ahead on us in others. I never seed or heerd tell of a country that had so many natural privileges as this. Why, there are twice as many harbours and water-powers here, as we have all the way from Eastport to New Or*leens*. They have all they can ax, and more than they desarve. They have iron, coal, slate, grindstone, lime, fire-stone gypsum, free-stone, and a list as long as an auctioneer's catalogue. But they are either asleep, or stone blind to them. Their shores are crowded with fish, and their lands covered with wood. A government that lays as light on 'em as a down counterp'in, and no taxes....

"Do you know the reason monkeys are no good? because they chatter all day long; so do the niggers, and so do the Bluenoses of Novia Scotia; it's all talk and no work. Now with us it's all work and no talk; in our shipyards, our factories, our mills, and even in our vessels, there's no talk; a man can't work and talk too....

"Now the folks of Halifax take it all out in talking. They talk of steamboats, whalers, and railroads; but they all end where they begin—in talk. I don't think I'd be out in my latitude if I was to say they beat the women kind at that....

"When we want folks to talk, we pay 'em for it, such as ministers, lawyers, and members of Congress; but then we expect the use of their tongues, and not their hands; and when we pay folks to work, we expect the use of their hands, and not their tongues. I guess work don't come kind o' natural to the people of this Province, no more than it does to a full-bred horse. I expect they think they have a little too much blood in 'em for work, for they are near about as proud as they are lazy....

"That's partly the case here. They are becalmed, and they see us going ahead on them, till we are e'enamost out of sight; yet they hain't got a steamboat, and the hain't got a railroad; indeed I doubt if one half of 'em ever seed or heerd tell of or t'other of them. I never seed any folks like 'em except the Indians, and they won't even so much as look; they haven't the least morsel of curiosity in the world....

"This Province is like that 'ere tree: it is tapped till it begins to die at the top, and if they don't drive in a spile and stop the everlastin' flow of the sap, it will perish altogether. All the money that's made here, all the interest that's paid in it, and a pretty considerable portion of rent too, all goes abroad for investment, and the rest is sent to us to buy bread. It's drained like a bog; it has opened and covered trenches all through it, and them there's others to the foot of the upland to cut off the springs.

"Now you make even a bog too dry; you take the moisture out to that degree that the very sile becomes dust, and blows away. The English funds, and our banks, railroads, and canals, are all absorbing your capital like a sponge, and

will lick it up as fast as you can make it. That very bridge we heerd of at Windsor
is owned in New Brunswick, and will pay toll to that Province. The capitalists of
Nova Scotia treat it like a hired house: they won't keep it in repair; they neither
paint it to preserve the boards, nor stop a leak to keep the frame from rottin': but
let it go to wrack, sooner than drive a nail or put in a pane of glass. 'It will sarve
our turn out,' they say.

"There's neither spirit, enterprise, nor patriotism here; but the whole country
is as inactive as a bear in winter, that does nothin' but scroutch up in his den...."

"I think," said I, "this is a happy country, Mr. Slick. The people are fortu-
nately all of one origin; there are no national jealousies to divide, and no very
violent politics to agitate them. They appear to be cheerful and contented, and
are a civil, good-natured, hospitable race. Considering the unsettled state of
almost every part of the world, I think I would as soon cast my lot in Nova
Scotia as in any part I know of."

"It's a clever country, you may depend" said he, "a very clever country; full
of mineral wealth, aboundin' in superior water privileges and noble harbours, a
large part of it prime land, and it is the very heart of the fisheries....

"This Province is better as it is, quieter and happier far; they have berths
enough and big enough; they should be careful not to increase 'em; and if they
were to do it over ag'in, perhaps they'd be as well with fewer. They have two
parties here, the Tory party and Opposition party, and both on 'em run to extremes. Them radicals, says one, are for levellin' all down to their own level,
though not a peg lower; that's their gauge, just down to their own notch and no
further; and they'd agitate the whole country to obtain that object, for if a man
can't grow to be as tall as his neighbour, if he cuts a few inches off him, why, then
they are both of one heighth. They are a most dangerous, disaffected people;
they are etarnally appealin' to the worst passions of the mob. Well, says t'other,
them aristocrats, they'll ruinate the country; they spend the whole revenue on
themselves. What with Bankers, Councillors, Judges, Bishops, and Public Officers, and a whole tribe of Lawyers, as hungry as hawks, and jist about as marciful,
the country is devoured, as if there was a flock of locusts a-feedin' on it. There's
nothin' left for roads and bridges. When a chap sets out to canvass, he's got to
antagonize one side or t'other. If he hangs on to the powers that be, then he's a
Council-man; he's for votin' large salaries, for doin' as the great people at Halifax
tell him. He is a fool. If he is on t'other side, a railin' at Banks, Judges, Lawyers,
and such cattle, and bawlin' for what he knows he can't get, then he is a rogue.
So that, if you were to listen to the weak and noisy critters on both sides, you'd
believe the House of Assembly was one half rogues and t'other half fools. All this
arises from ignorance. *If they knew more of each other, I guess they'd lay aside one*

*half their fears and all their abuse. The upper classes don't know one half the virtue that's in the middlin' and lower classes; and they don't know one half the integrity and good feelin' that's in the others and both are fooled and gulled by their own noisy and designin' champions....*

*"... Now, as a disinterested man, I say if the members of the House of Assembly, instead of raisin' up ghosts and hobgoblins to frighten folks with, and to show what swordsmen they be, a-cuttin' and a-thrustin' at phantoms that only exist in their own brains, would turn to, heart and hand, and develop the resources of this fine country, facilitate the means of transport, promote its internal improvement, and encourage its foreign trade, they would make it the richest and greatest, as it now is one of the happiest sections of all America....*

*"...They buy more nor they sell, and eat more than they raise,* in this country. What a pretty way that is, isn't it? If the critters knew how to cipher, they would soon find out that a sum stated that way always eends in a naught.

"Agriculture is not only neglected but degraded here. What a number of young folks there seem to be in these parts, a-ridin' about, titivated out real jam, in their go-to-meetin' clothes, a-doin' nothin'. It's melancholy to think on it. That's the effect of the last war. The idleness and extravagance of those times took root, and bore fruit abundantly, and now the young people are above their business. They are too high in the instep, that's a fact.

"I ALLOT," said Mr. Slick, "that the Bluenoses are the most gullible folks on the face of the airth—rigular soft horns, that's a fact. Politics and such stuff set 'em a-gapin', like children in a chimbley corner listenin' to tales of ghosts, Salem witches, and Nova Scotia snowstorms; and while they stand starin' and yawpin', all eyes and mouth, they get their pockets picked of every cent that's in 'em. One candidate chap says, 'Feller citizens, this country is goin' to the dogs hand over hand; look at your rivers, you have no bridges; at your wild lands, you have no roads; at your treasury, you hain't got a cent in it; at your markets, things don't fetch nothin'; at your fish, the Yankees ketch 'em all. There's nothin' behind you but sufferin', around you but poverty, afore you but slavery and death. What's the cause of this unheerd-of awful state of things, aye, what's the cause? Why, Judges, and Banks, and Lawyers, and great folks, have swallered all the money. They've got you down, and they'll keep you down to all etarnity, you and your posteriors arter you. Rise up, like men! Arouse yourselves like freemen, and elect me to the legislatur', and I'll lead on the small but patriotic band; I'll put the big wigs through their facins, I'll make 'em shake in their shoes, I'll knock off your chains and make you free.' Well, the goneys fall tu and elect him, and he desarts right away, with balls, rifle, powder, horn, and all. *He promised too much....*

"I mean what I say," he replied. "... No, sir, the Halifax folks neither know nor keer much about the country; they wouldn't take hold on it, and if they had a waited for them, it would have been one while afore they got a bridge, I tell you. They've no spirit, and plaguy little sympathy with the country, and I'll tell you the reason on it. There are good many people there from other parts, and always have been, who come to make money and nothin' else, who don't call it home, and don't feel to home, and who intend to up killoch and off, as soon as they have made their ned out of the Bluenoses. They have got about as much regard for the country as a peddler has, who trudges along with a pack on this back. He *walks,* 'cause he intends to *ride* at last; *trusts,* 'cause he intends to *sue* at last; *smiles,* 'cause he intends to *cheat* at last; *saves all,* 'cause he intends to *move all* at last. It's actilly overrun with transient paupers, and transient speculators; and these last grumble and growl like a bear with a sore head, the whole blessed time, at everything; and can hardly keep a civil tongue in their head, while they're fobbin' your money hand over hand. These critters feel no interest in anything but cent per cent; they deaden public spirit; they hain't got none themselves, and they larf at it in others; and when you add their numbers to the timid ones, the stingy ones, the ignorant ones, and the poor ones, that are to be found in every place, why, the few smart-spirited ones that's left are too few to do anything, and so nothin' is done. It appears to me if I was a Bluenose I'd—but thank fortin' I ain't, so I says nothin'; but there is somethin' that ain't altogether jist right in this country, that's a fact....

"It's a most curious, unaccountable thing, but it's a fact,' said the Clockmaker, "the Bluenoses are so conceited, they think they know everything; and yet there ain't a livin' soul in Nova Scotia knows his own business real complete, farmer or fisherman, lawyer or doctor, or any other folk....

"The Bluenoses, Squire, they think they know everything, but they get gulled from year's eend to year's eend. They expect too much from others, and do too little for themselves...."

"Well," said I, "I will tell you what I mean. Draw a line from Cape Sable to Cape Cansoo, right through the Province, and it will split in two, this way"; and I cut an apple into two halves; "now," says I, "the worst half, like the rotten half of the apple, belongs to Halifax, and the other sound half belongs to St. John. Your side of the province on the seacoast is all stone; I never seed such a proper sight of rocks in my life; it's enough to starve a rabbit. Well, t'other side, on the Bay of Fundy, is a superfine country; there ain't the beat of it to be found anywhere. Now, wouldn't the folks living away up to the Bay be pretty fools to go to Halifax, when they can go to St. John with half the trouble? St. John is the natural capital of the Bay of Fundy; it will be the largest city in America, next to

New York. It has an immense back country as big as Great Britain, a first chop river and amazin' sharp folks, most as cute as the Yankees, it's a splendid location for business."

## 5. William Young, "To Lord Durham," 1838.

... Abuses in Nova Scotia have never reached the same irritating or fearful height which we have witnessed in other provinces. The substantial blessings of an enlightened, and, upon the whole, an impartial and upright administration of the law, of perfect freedom of conscience, and the unfettered exercise of industry, of the absence of oppression in every form, have been long enjoyed by us, and have doubtless largely contributed in fostering that ardent attachment to the British Crown and institutions, which may be fairly said to be an universal feeling. I know not of a single individual of influence or talent, who would not regard a severance of our connection with the mother country, and our incorporation, which would soon follow, into the American Union, with its outrages on property and real freedom, its growing democratic spirit and executive weakness, as the greatest misfortune that could befall us. Let not your Lordship, then, or the British Ministry, be misled into a belief, that there is any party in Nova Scotia which does not reverence the name, and would not uphold, at every hazard, the supremacy of England. True, we admire the enterprise, activity and public works of the United States, and would wish that they were more largely imitated in our own possessions; but the people of Nova Scotia have no desire to purchase these or any other advantages, by deserting their constitution. They do, however, desire that our public affairs in some respects should be more economically and wisely managed: and it is to these that I have now respectfully to solicit your Lordship's most favourable attention.

First. The administration of the Crown Lands is universally and most justly complained of.... The Young men of the colony, unable to purchase the wild lands on the terms now imposed, and who would constitute our most valuable and hardy settlers, are leaving us by hundreds, and the clearing and improvement of the country is greatly retarded....

Secondly. The oppressive and systematic encroachments of the Americans upon our fisheries have attracted universal attention, and exasperated all classes....

Thirdly. The expense of our customs' establishment is regarded as a serious evil....

Fourth. The Assembly has long been solicitous that every port in the province where there is a customhouse officer, should be declared a free port. The present system fosters the illicit trade which so injuriously affects our revenue, and cripples the activity of our foreign commerce. The Assembly have declared that they can see no reason to fear an equal open competition between the industry of their constituents and that of any other nation, and have earnestly petitioned the Home Government, and supported the application by very cogent arguments, that every port where a custom-house officer is stationed may be permitted to enjoy the privileges of a free port.

Fifth. The emoluments and salaries of some of the officers of government, not under the control of the legislature, are disproportioned to the means of the colony, and engender habits of expense which re-act upon the manners of the people, and hinder the accumulation of capital....

Sixth. The majority of the House of Assembly is dissatisfied with the composition of the Executive and Legislative Councils, and the preponderance in both of interests which they conceive to be unfavourable to reform. This is the true ground, as I take it, of the discontent that is felt. The respectability and private virtues of the gentlemen who sit at the two Council Boards are admitted by all; it is of their political and personal predilections that the people complain. They desire reforming and liberal principles to be more fully represented and advocated there, as they are in the Assembly. The majority of the House, while they appreciate and have acknowledged the anxiety of his Excellency the Lieutenant-Governor to gratify their just expectations, have also expressed their dissatisfaction that the Church of England should have been suffered to retain a majority in both Councils, notwithstanding the remonstrances of the House, and the precise and explicit directions of the Colonial Secretary. Religious dissensions are happily unknown among us, and the true way to prevent their growth and increase, is to avoid conferring an inordinate power on anyone sect, however worthy it may be of respect or favour....

### 6. Joseph Howe, "To Lord John Russell," September 18th, 1839.

Halifax, Nova Scotia

My Lord,—I share with my countrymen their solicitude on this subject; I and my children will share their deep disgrace, if the doctrines recently attributed to your Lordship are to prevail; to the utter exclusion of us all from the blessings and advantages of responsible government, based upon the principles of that Constitution which your Lordship's forefathers laboured to establish and ours have taught us to revere....

You ask me for the remedy. Lord Durham has stated it distinctly; the Colonial Governors must be commanded to govern by the aid of those who possess the confidence of the people and are supported by a majority of the representative branch. Where is the danger? Of what consequence is it to the people of England whether half-a-dozen persons, in whom that majority have confidence, but of whom they know nothing and care less, manage our local affairs; or the same number selected from the minority and whose policy the bulk of the population distrust? Suppose there was at this moment a majority in our Executive Council who think with the Assembly, what effect would it have upon the funds? Would the stocks fall? Would England be weaker, less prosperous or less respected, because the people of Nova Scotia were satisfied and happy?

But, it is said, a colony being part of a great empire must be governed by different principles from the metropolitan state; that unless it be handed over to the minority it cannot be governed at all; that the majority, when they have things their own way, will be discontented and disloyal; that the very fact of their having nothing to complain of will make them desire to break the political compact and disturb the peace of the empire. Let us fancy that this reasoning were applied to Glasgow or Aberdeen or to any other town in Britain which you allow to govern itself. And what else is a Province like Nova Scotia than a small community, too feeble to interfere with the general commercial and military arrangements of the Government; but deeply interested in a number of minor matters, which only the people to be affected by them can wisely manage; which the ministry can never find leisure to attend to and involve in inextricable confusion when they meddle with them? ... Give us this truly British privilege, and colonial grievances will soon become a scarce article in the English market.

The planets that encircle the sun, warmed by its heat and rejoicing in its effulgence, are moved and sustained, each in its bright but subordinate career, by the same laws as the sun itself. Why should this beautiful example be lost upon us? Why should we run counter to the whole stream of British experience; and seek, for no object worthy of the sacrifice, to govern on one side of the Atlantic by principles the very reverse of those found to work so admirably on the other. The employment of steamers will soon bring Halifax within a ten days' voyage of England. Nova Scotia will then not be more distant from London than the north of Scotland and the west of Ireland were a few years ago. No time should be lost, therefore, in giving us the rights and guards to which we are entitled; for depend upon it the nearer we approach the mother country, the more we shall admire its excellent constitution and the more intense will be the sorrow and disgust with which we must turn to contemplate our own....

If, my Lord, in every one of the three great kingdoms from which the population of British America derive their origin, the evils of which we complain were experienced and continued until the principles we claim as our birthright became firmly established, is it to be expected that we shall not endeavour to rid ourselves, by respectful argument and remonstrance, of what cost you open and violent resistance to put down? Can an Englishman, an Irishman or a Scotchman, be made to believe, by passing a month upon the sea, that the most stirring periods of his history are but a cheat and a delusion; that the scenes which he has been accustomed to tread with deep emotion are but mementoes of the folly and not, as he once fondly believed, of the wisdom and courage of his ancestors; that the principles of civil liberty, which from childhood he has been taught to cherish and to protect by forms of stringent responsibility, must, with the new light breaking in upon him on this side of the Atlantic, be cast aside as an useless incumbrance? No, my Lord, it is madness to suppose that these men, so remarkable for carrying their national characteristics into every part of the world where they penetrate, shall lose the most honourable of them all, merely by passing from one portion of the empire to another. Nor is it to be supposed that Nova Scotians, New Brunswickers and Canadians—a race sprung from the generous admixture of the blood of the three foremost nations of the world— proud of their parentage and not unworthy of it, to whom every stirring period of British and Irish history, every great principle which they teach, every phrase of freedom to be gleaned from them, are as familiar as household words, can be in haste to forget what they learnt upon their parents' knees; what those they loved and honoured clung to with so much pride and regarded as beyond all price. Those who expect them thus to belie their origin or to disgrace it, may as soon hope to see the streams turn back upon their fountains. My Lord, my countrymen feel, as they have a right to feel, that the Atlantic, the great highway of communication with their brethren at home, should be no barrier to shut out the civil privileges and political rights, which more than anything else, make them proud of the connection; and they feel also, that there is nothing in their present position or their past conduct to warrant such exclusion. Whatever impression may have been made by the wholesome satire wherewith one of my countrymen has endeavoured to excite the others to still greater exertions, those who fancy that Nova Scotians are an inferior race to those who dwell upon the ancient homestead or that they will be contented with a less degree of freedom, know little of them. A country that a century ago was but a wilderness and is now studded with towns and villages, and intersected with roads, even though more might have been done under a better system, affords some evidence of industry. Nova Scotian ships, bearing the British flag into every quarter of the globe, are some proofs of enterprise; and the success of the native author, to whom I have alluded, in the wide field of intellectual competition, more than contradicts the humorous exaggeration by which, while we are stimulated to higher efforts, others may be for a moment misled. If then our right to inherit the constitution be clear, if our capacity to maintain and enjoy it cannot be questioned, have we done anything to justify the alienation of our birthright? Many of the original settlers of this Province emigrated from the old colonies when they were in a state of rebellion—not because they did not love freedom, but because they loved it under the old banner and the old forms; and many of their descendants have shed their blood, on land and sea, to defend the honour of the Crown and the integrity of the empire. On some of the hardest fought fields of the Peninsula, my countrymen died in the front rank, with their faces to the foe. The proudest naval trophy of the last American war was brought by a Nova Scotian into the harbour of his native town; and the blood that flowed from Nelson's death wound in the cockpit of the *Victory* mingled with that of a Nova Scotian stripling beside him, struck down in the same glorious fight. Am I not then justified, my Lord, in claiming for my countrymen that constitution, which can be withheld from them by no plea but one unworthy of a British statesman—the tyrant's plea of power? I know that I am; and I feel also, that this is not the race that can be hoodwinked with sophistry, or made to submit to injustice without complaint. All suspicion of disloyalty we cast aside, as the product of ignorance or cupidity; we seek for nothing more than British subjects are entitled to; but we will be contented with nothing less....

### 7. Abraham Gesner, *The Industrial Resources of Nova Scotia,* 1849.

It has been frequently imputed to the inhabitants of Nova-Scotia that they have less perseverance, enterprize, and industry, than the Americans of the republic. Admitting the correctness of this opinion, it should be remembered that very many of her early settlers were several years engaged in the defence of their country; and many of them, on account of their loyalty, abandoned the cultivated fields of their forefathers in the now United States, to cut down the forest a second time in order to win a living. They were an exiled people, who had to encounter all the difficulties of colonization in a climate unmodified by the spreading out of cleared fields and the redemption of extensive marshes. The soldier had to lay down his musket and seize the axe. The citizen was driven from his town luxuries to the hard fare of the backwoodsman; and the brave officer who had fought his score of battles, hung his sword against the wall and laid his hand to the plough. That the services of such men have not been duly respected by the British government, is a painful and humiliating fact.—

There is yet another and most obvious reason why Nova-Scotia has not advanced in a degree proportionate to her resources. Up to the present time, the extent and value of the natural productions of the province are almost unknown in every part of Europe.—The current of emigration has been directed to Canada and the United States: and volume after volume has been published in praise of those countries....

To such countries the tide of emigration has been directed, and still continues to flow, while from Nova-Scotia, where there is a lack of labor, many of the young native-born farmers and mechanics annually depart, to seek a living farther west....

The prodigious undertakings of the Americans in canals, railways, electric telegraphs, and other public works; and also the rapid increase of manufactures in the western States, have created an extraordinary demand for labor. The cleverness and skill of the provincial are equal to the wants of his neighbours over the boundary, with whom he finds ready employment, high wages, and prompt payment; the result is that the young men of the province emigrate to the United States as soon as they are of age, and much of the bone and sinew of the country is transferred over to a foreign power. Many whole families also remove annually from Nova-Scotia to the American far west....

In this fine province there is neither a canal, nor a railway, excepting six miles of the latter at Picton, laid down for mining purposes. Nova-Scotia is rivalled in steam navigation by the sister province New Brunswick, where the coal employed is imported from Great Britain. She is also far behind that province in manufactures, mills, and sawing machinery. It is universally admitted that her fisheries are neglected; and her most valuable mines, with one exception only, remain unopened. From the cost and scarcity of labor, the want of markets, lack of proper means of transportation, and other causes, the agriculture of the province is retarded, manufactures improve but slowly, and the clearing of the wilderness advances at a tardy rate; notwithstanding the legislature readily opens roads to new settlements, and wild lands may be obtained at three shillings and three pence per acre. Nor is the state of education what it should be in a province that abounds in colleges and public seminaries. There is little enterprize in any pursuit. A spirit of extreme caution influences the rich; men of medium wealth are discouraged; and to this may be added a lack of general and persevering industry, with a desire for ease and extravagance....

Now the resources of Nova-Scotia are richer, more varied and inexhaustable, than those of any of the western republican districts; and they contain within themselves materials, that by being improved, would soon elevate the province to her proper position, and even above the neighbouring colonies....

They cannot be won without the aid of the Government, directed by a sound colonial system. If these colonies are worth defending they are worth improving. The inhabitants have heretofore been proverbial for their loyalty, but their attachment to the Mother country will be influenced by the protection afforded their commerce—their institutions, fisheries, and general industry. The now flourishing condition of the neighbouring States, to which many of the young and active part of the population constantly emigrate, is viewed with a restlessness dangerous to that fidelity, which can only be secured by a wise and well-timed policy, and which to the loyalty of the inhabitants shall unite their interest by improving the industrial resources of the country.

## Readings

Beck, J. *Joseph Howe*. Kingston and Montreal: McGill-Queen's University Press, 1982–1983.

Bell, W. *The Foreign Protestants and the Settlement of Nova Scotia*. Toronto: University of Toronto Press, 1961.

Bitterman, R. "Farm Households and Wage Labour in the Northeastern Maritimes in the Early 19th Century," *Labour* 31 (Spring 1993).

Brookes, A. "The Golden Age and the Exodus: The Case of Canning, King's County," *Acadiensis* 11, 1 (Autumn 1981).

Buckner, P., and D. Frank, eds. *The Atlantic Provinces before Confederation*. Fredericton: Acadiensis Press, 1985.

Buckner, P., and J. Reid, eds. *The Atlantic Region to Confederation: A History*. Toronto: University of Toronto Press, 1994.

Conrad, M., ed. *Making Adjustments: Change and Continuity in Planter Nova Scotia*. Fredericton: Acadiensis Press, 1991.

Davies, R., ed. *On Thomas Chandler Haliburton: Selected Criticism*. Ottawa: Tecumseh, 1979.

Day, D., ed. *Geographical Perspectives on the Maritime Provinces*. Halifax: St. Mary's University, 1988.

Donovan, K., ed. *The Island: New Perspectives on Cape Breton History 1713–1990*. Fredericton and Sydney: University College of Cape Breton Press, 1990.

Fingard, J. *The Dark Side of Life in Victorian Halifax*. Potters Lake: Pottersfield Press, 1989.

Gwyn, J. *Excessive Expectations: Martime Commerce and Economic Development of Nova Scotia, 1740–1870*. Montreal: McGill-Queen's University Press, 1998.

Gwyn, J. "Golden Age or Bronze Moment? Wealth and Poverty in Nova Scotia: The 1850s and 1860s," D. Akenson, ed., *Canadian Papers in Rural History* Vol 8. Gananoque: Langdale Press, 1992.

Gwyn, J. "'A Little Province Like This': The Economy of Nova Scotia under Stress, 1812–1853," in D. Akenson, ed., *Canadian Papers in Rural History* Vol 6. Gananoque: Langdale Press, 1988.

Harvey, D. "History and Its Uses in Pre-Confederation Nova Scotia," Presidential Address, *Canadian Historical Association,* 1938.

Harvey, D. "The Intellectual Awakening of Nova Scotia," *Dalhousie Review* 13 (April 1933).

Hornby, S. *Nineteenth Century Cape Breton: A Historical Geography.* Kingston and Montreal: McGill-Queen's University Press, 1992.

Mackinnon, N. *The Unfriendly Soil: The Loyalist Experience in Nova Scotia, 1783–1791.* Kingston and Montreal: McGill-Queen's University Press, 1986.

MacNeil, A. "Cultural Stereotypes and Highland Farming in Eastern Nova Scotia, 1827–1861," *Social History* 19, 37 (May 1986).

MacNutt, W. *The Atlantic Provinces: The Emergence of Colonial Society, 1712–1857.* Toronto: McClelland and Stewart, 1965.

Rawlyk, G., ed. *Historical Essays on the Atlantic Provinces.* Toronto: McClelland and Stewart, 1967.

Sager, E., and G. Ponting. *Maritime Capital: The Shipping Industry in Atlantic Canada, 1820–1914.* Montreal and Kingston: McGill-Queen's University Press, 1990.

Taylor, M. *Promoters, Patriots and Partisans: Historiography in Nineteenth Century English Canada.* Toronto: University of Toronto Press, 1989.

Tierney, F. *The Thomas Chandler Haliburton Symposium.* Ottawa: University of Ottawa Press, 1985.

## Chapter Thirteen

# "MOST HORRIBLE AND HEARTLESS": IRISH IMMIGRATION

1. Stephen De Vere, "To the Committee," November 30, 1847.
2. Dr. G. Douglas, "To Hon. D. Daly," December 27, 1847.
3. Mayor W. Boulton, "To Earl of Elgin, Governor General of British North America," 1847.
4. H. Perley, "To Sir William Colebrooke, Lieutenant-Governor of the Province of New Brunswick," December 31, 1847.
5. A. Hawke, "To T. Campbell," October 16, 1847.

## Introduction

When Canada became part of the Empire in the mid-eighteenth century, Britain preferred to populate its new colonies with citizens from the British Isles. This policy held distinct advantages for England: it made British North America more British, less French, and therefore presumably more loyal; it strengthened the connection between the mother country and its new imperial possessions; and colonies like British North America, by acting as dumping grounds of the dispossessed, addressed the problem of a large and troubling poor population back home. Most newcomers therefore came from the poorest classes: those most susceptible to the pitfalls of industrialization, urbanization, intolerance, and starvation. These economic refugees shared the pain of losing familiar surroundings, friends, and family, plus the shock of integrating into a new and often strange society at the other end—a process inevitably exacerbated by their landing in Canada at the bottom of the social heap. Many faced downright hostility and suspicion as they stepped onto Canadian quaysides after two, often miserable, months at sea.

Politics, religion, a population explosion, and famine conspired to make the situation in Ireland particularly volatile in the mid-nineteenth century. Protestant England originally conquered Catholic Ireland in the sixteenth century and established it as a colony to supply agricultural produce for burgeoning England. To facilitate this, and to ensure Ireland's future loyalty, London imported

Protestant Scottish farmers into the northeast counties of Ulster, and divided much of the rest of the island into large estates for loyal English nobleman. The local Irish became a population of repressed and subjugated tenant farmers with few rights and onerous obligations. England strengthened its hold over Ireland by annexing it in the early nineteenth century, making it an actual part of Great Britain rather than a mere colony. The new English-owned agricultural estates produced food for English tables, but a population explosion in Ireland made agriculture inefficient, both in spatial and production terms. Part of the solution was to wean the peasantry from its traditional grain diet to the highly nutritious potato, which took up little space, and thus the New World tuber became the staple for millions of poor Irish.

This functioned until a deadly blight, an airborne fungus, all but destroyed the crop for several years running during the 1840s. Millions of farmers faced one of two choices: stay and die; or take a chance by struggling to a coastal port such as Cork, Limerick, Dublin, or even Liverpool in England, find passage on a ship, and leave that living hell. Landlords and the British government used the potato famine as a pretext to encourage mass migration of tenant farmers, thereby freeing up land and lessening long-term financial obligations. Ironically, these starving souls fled amid plenty: grain production in Ireland increased during the famine, but it belonged to the landlords and was for export, not to support an indigent population of Irish. The catastrophe was so great that Ireland's population fell from 8 to 4 million, either from death or emigration. Most who fled were Catholics from what is today the Republic of Ireland, and a disproportionate number were young children, widows, the aged, and other less independent individuals. There were, however, Protestant emigrants too, largely from Ulster. The two groups generally did not mix, feared each other, and periodically clashed violently.

Many migrants died long before sighting the New World and many more, who survived the trek to the emigration ports and the voyage to North America, never made it farther than the quarantine island of Grosse-Île in the St. Lawrence River. There thousands died, packed cheek by jowl in the unspeakable squalor of the quarantine sheds, tents, and makeshift shelters, at least partly because the sudden influx of immigrants overwhelmed ill-prepared Canadian authorities. The Canadian public was not particularly sympathetic to the Irish plight. Disease, after all, soon wafted from immigrant ships to land, striking without warning, often with deadly results in an age without effective medicinal remedies. Locals came to fear and hate the disease-ridden Irish, shunning them, and forcing them out of range. This was not a new attitude. The stereotypical Irishman was a drunken, brawling, lazy, stupid, papist "Paddy." Thus new Irish immigrants, usually destitute and weak, survived as best they could, picking up tough labouring jobs on the canals, getting marginal work doing what others refused, or by breaking the law. For most of these people, the land of opportunity was, at best, a sick joke.

## Discussion Points

1. What factor was chiefly responsible for mortality among Irish immigrants travelling to Canada? To what extent were the Irish immigrants responsible for their own plight?
2. Was Canada negligent in its treatment of the Irish? Should more government assistance have been forthcoming?
3. Since the bulk of these immigrants were women and children, one could argue that Ireland was actually taking advantage of Canada by shipping out its most dependent and unwanted people. Was it really in the interest of the inhabitants of British North America to receive Irish immigrants during this period?

## Documents

### 1. Stephen De Vere, "To the Committee," November 30, 1847.

London, Canada West,

My DEAR SIR

I have to thank you for sending me the Report of the Colonization Committee of last year, the evidence contained in which (though I have not yet had time fully to go through it) proves to one the value of emigration at home, and confirms the opinions I had already formed of the benefit likely to result to the colonies from it.

The emigration of the past year was enormous, though deriving no assistance from Government until its arrival here. The mortality also was very great. During the next year, the number of emigrants will probably be still larger; and I fear we shall have a repetition of the mortality if the errors which experience has detected be not promptly and liberally corrected. I shall not regret the disasters of the last two years if their warning voice shall have stimulated and enabled us to effect a system of emigration *leading to future colonization*, which shall gradually heal the diseased and otherwise incurable state of society at home, and, at the same time, infuse a spirit into the colonies, which shall render them the ornament, the wealth, and the bulwark of the parent country.

We have no right to cure the evil of over-population by a process of decimation, nor can emigration be serviceable in Canada unless the emigrants arrive in a sound state, both of body and mind. I say "both of body and mind," because clamour in Canada has been equally directed against the diseased condition and the listless indolence of this year's emigrants; but, while I admit the justice of that clamour to a certain extent, I must protest against the injustice of those here who complain that the young and vigorous should be accompanied by the more helpless members of their families whom they are bound to protect; and I cannot but remember that famine and fever were a divine dispensation inflicted last year upon nearly the whole world, and that the colony could not reasonably expect to be wholly exempt from the misfortunes of the parent state.

The fearful state of disease and debility in which the Irish emigrants have reached Canada, must undoubtedly be attributed in a great degree to the destitution and consequent sickness prevailing in Ireland; but has been much aggravated by the neglect of cleanliness, ventilation, and a generally good state of social economy during the passage, and has been afterwards increased, and disseminated throughout the whole country by the mal-arrangements of the Government system of emigrant relief. Having myself submitted to the privations of a steerage passage in an emigrant ship for nearly two months, in order to make myself acquainted with the condition of the emigrant from the beginning, I can state from experience that the present regulations for ensuring health and comparative comfort to passengers are wholly insufficient, and that they are not, and cannot be enforced, notwithstanding the great zeal and high abilities of the Government agents.

Before the emigrant has been a week at sea he is an altered man. How can it be otherwise? Hundreds of poor people, men, women, and children, of all ages from the drivelling idiot of 90 to the babe just born; huddled together, without light, without air, wallowing in filth, and breathing a fetid atmosphere, sick in body, dispirited in heart; the fevered patients lying between the sound, in sleeping places so narrow as almost to deny them the power of indulging, by a change of position, the natural restlessness of the disease; by their agonized ravings disturbing those around and pre-disposing them, through the effects of the imagination, to imbibe the contagion; living without food or medicine except as administered by the hand of casual charity; dying without the voice of spiritual consolation, and buried in the deep without the rites of the Church. The food is generally ill-selected, and seldom *sufficiently cooked*, in consequence of the insufficiency and bad construction of the cooking places. The supply of water, hardly enough for cooking and drinking, does not allow washing. In many ships the filthy beds, teeming with all abominations, are never required to be brought on deck and aired; the narrow space between the sleeping berths and the piles of boxes is never washed or scraped, but breathes up a damp and fetid stench, until the day before arrival at quarantine, when all hands are required to "scrub up," and put on a fair face for the doctor and Government inspector. No moral restraint is attempted; the voice of prayer is never heard; drunkenness, with its consequent train of ruffianly debasement, is not discouraged, because it is profitable to the captain who traffics in the grog.

In the ship which brought me out from London last April, the passengers were found in provisions by the owners, according to a contract, and a furnished scale of dietary. The meat was of the worst quality. The supply of water shipped on board was abundant, but the quantity served out to the passengers was so scanty that they were frequently obliged to throw overboard their salt provisions and rice (a most important article of their food), because they had not water enough both for the necessary cooking, and the satisfying of their raging thirst afterwards.

They could only afford water for washing by withdrawing it from the cooking of their food. I have known persons to remain for days together in their dark close berths, because they thus suffered less from hunger, though compelled, at the same time, by want of water to heave over-board their salt provisions and rice. No cleanliness was enforced; the beds never aired; the master during the whole voyage never entered the steerage, and would listen to no complaints; the dietary contracted for was, with some exceptions, nominally supplied, though at irregular periods; but false measures were used (in which the water and several articles of dry food were served), the gallon measure containing but three quarts, which fact I proved in Quebec, and had the captain fined for; once or twice a week ardent spirits were sold indiscriminately to the passengers, producing scenes of unchecked blackguardism beyond description; and lights were prohibited, because the ship, with her open fire-grates upon deck, with lucifer matches and lighted pipes used secretly in the sleeping berths, was freighted with Government powder for the garrison of Quebec.

The case of this ship was not one of peculiar misconduct, on the contrary, I have the strongest reason to know from information which I have received from very many emigrants well-known to me who came over this year in different vessels, that this ship was better regulated and more comfortable than many that reached Canada.

Some of these evils might be prevented by a more careful inspection of the ship and her stores, before leaving port; but the provisions of the Passenger Act are insufficient to procure cleanliness and ventilation, and the machinery of the emigration agencies at the landing ports is insufficient to enforce those provisions, and to detect frauds. It is true that a clerk sometimes comes on board at the ship's arrival in port; questions the captain or mate, and ends by asking whether any passenger means to make a complaint; but this is a mere farce, for the captain takes care to "keep away the crowd from the gentleman." Even were all to hear the question, few would venture to commence a prosecution; ignorant, friendless, pennyless, disheartened, and anxious to proceed to the place of their ultimate destination.

Disease and death among the emigrants; nay, the propagation of infection throughout Canada, are not the worst conseqences of this atrocious system of neglect and ill-usage. A result far worse is to be found in the utter demoralization of the passengers, both male and female, by the filth, debasement, and disease of two or three months so passed. The emigrant, enfeebled in body, and degraded in mind, even though he should have the physical power, has not the *heart*, has not the *will* to exert himself. He has lost his self-respect, his elasticity of spirit—he no longer stands erect—he throws himself listlessly upon the daily dole of Government, and, in order to earn it, carelessly lies for weeks upon the contaminated straw of a fever lazaretto.

I am aware that the Passengers' Act has been amended during the last Session, but I have not been yet able to see the amendments. They are probably of a nature calculated to meet the cases I have detailed; but I would earnestly suggest the arrangement of every passenger ship into separate divisions for the married, for single men, and for single women; and the appointment, from amongst themselves, of "monitors" for each ward; the appropriation of an hospital ward for the sick; the providing of commodious cooking stoves and utensils, and the erection of decent privies; and the appointment, to each ship carrying more than 50 passengers, of a surgeon paid by Government, who should be invested during the voyage with the authority of a Government emigration agent, with power to investigate all complaints at sea on the spot, and at the time of their occurrence to direct and enforce temporary redress, and to institute proceedings on arrival in port, in concert with the resident emigration agent. He ought, for this purpose to have authority to detain witnesses, and to support them during the prosecution at Government expense. I would also suggest the payment of a chaplain of the religion professed by the majority of the passengers.

The sale of spirituous liquors should be prohibited except for medicinal purposes, &c., the minimum supply of water enlarged from three to four quarts.

I believe that if these precautions were adopted, the human cargoes would be landed in a moral and physical condition far superior to what they now exhibit, and that the additional expense incurred would be more than compensated by the saving effected in hospital expenses and emigrant relief.

The arrangements adopted by the Government during the past season, for the assistance of pauper emigrants after their arrival in Canada, were of three sorts, hospitals, temporary sheds, and transmission. These measures were undertaken in a spirit of liberality deserving our best gratitude; and much allowance ought to be made for imperfections of detail, which it was not easy to avoid under the peculiar and unexpected exigencies of the case; but I think I can demonstrate that much of the mortality which has desolated as well the old residents as the emigrants, may be attributed to the errors of those arrangements.

In the quarantine establishment at Grosse Isle, when I was there in June, the medical attendance and hospital accommodations were quite inadequate. The medical inspections on board were slight and hasty; hardly any questions were asked; but as the doctor walked down the file on deck, he selected those for hospital who did not look well, and, after a very slight examination, ordered them on shore. The ill-effect of this haste was two-fold:—some were detained in danger who were not ill, and many were allowed to proceed who were actually in fever. Of the management of the hospitals in general I do not feel myself qualified to speak; and I have no doubt that you are in possession of reports which will enable you to draw your own conclusions.

The sheds were very miserable; so slightly built as to exclude neither the heat nor the cold. No sufficient care was taken to remove the sick from the sound, or to disinfect and clean the building after the removal of the sick to hospital. The very straw upon which they had lain was often allowed to become a bed for their successors; and I have known many poor families prefer to burrow under heaps of loose stones which happened to be piled up near the shore, rather than accept the shelter of the infected sheds.

It would, I am aware, have been difficult to have provided a more substantial shelter for the amount of destitution produced by the peculiar circumstances of the past year; but I hope that, in future, even though the number or emigrants should greatly exceed that of last year, so large an extent of pauper temporary accommodation may not be necessary, and that a better built, and better regulated house or refuge, may be provided.

Of the administration of temporary relief by food to the inmates of the sheds, I must speak in terms or the highest praise. It was a harassing and danger-ous duty, and one requiring much judgment on the part of the agent, and it was performed with zeal, humanity, and good sense....

## 2. Dr. G. Douglas, "To Hon. D. Daly," December 27, 1847.

Sir,

... These returns will show that, while the emigration of this year has been more than double that of any previous year, the sickness and deaths have been in a much greater proportion.

In the conclusion of my Annual Report of last season, I remarked, that "from the experience of many years of the causes which produce disease among emigrants, I am persuaded that next season the number of sick will exceed that of any previous year. The partial failure of the potatoe crop last season (1845) caused much sickness; its almost total failure in that country and the north of Scotland this season (1846) will have the effect of pouring upon our shores thousands of debilitated and sickly emigrants." The result of the past season's emigration has more than fulfilled my prediction. Two causes, which could not have been foreseen, have conspired to augment beyond all calculation the num-ber of destitute and diseased emigrants.

The first of these was the enactment of a law by the general government of the United States, which, by limiting the number which each passenger vessel could carry, made the cost of a passage so high as virtually to exclude all but those having a certain amount of means of their awn. A law previously in exist-ence in the State of New York, which obliged the master or owner of a vessel bringing passengers to give bonds, that no emigrant brought out by them be-came chargeable to the commonwealth for a period of two years after their arrival, was more strictly enforced.

The effect of these laws was to turn the stream of pauper emigration to the British provinces. I estimate the accession to our emigration this year through the operation of this cause at from 30,000 to 40,000.

Another cause of the increase this season has been the application to Ire-land of a poor-law. To avoid the enormous expense which will attend its execution in some parts of the country where destitution abounds, may landlords have given free passages to those having claims on the land. In selecting these, they have, naturally enough, abstained from choosing the young, strong able-bodied labourer, but have sought to rid their estates of helpless widows with large fami-lies, cripples unable to work, aged persons, the confirmed idle and lazy, and those whose constitutions had been enfeebled by previous sickness and destitution. Such was the character and description of many of the settlers sent out from the ports of Liverpool, Dublin, Cork, and Limerick, as more particularly described in my official reports at different times during the past season.

I will enter upon a detailed statement of the operations of the season.

On the 4th of May, the usual hospital staff left for the island, with the addition to the establishment of an hospital steward, one orderly, and one nurse, the duty of the apothecary and steward having previously been performed by the same person, 50 new iron beds were ordered, and double the quantity of straw used in former years for bedding was purchased before leaving town. An additional building was ordered and commenced immediately. These preparations were deemed sufficient for the commencement, as the greatest number of sick had in former years arrived in the months of July and August. The hospital accommodation, as it then existed, was amply sufficient for 200 sick, the average of former years never having attained half that number requiring admission at one time.

On the 14th of May, the barque "Syria" arrived from Liverpool, which port she left on the 28th of March, with 243 passengers. On mustering them for inspection at Grosse Isle, I found that nine had died on the voyage, and 52 were lying ill with fever and dysentery. The sick were landed at once and placed in hospital, and the seemingly healthy were landed with the baggage at the sheds. The day after they were landed it was found necessary to send 21 of these to hospital, and each day others fell ill until the 28th, on which day 125 were patients in hospital.

On the 19th of May, five days after the arrival of the "Syria," the barque "Perseverance" and ship "Wandsworth," both from Dublin, arrived, the former having 62 and the latter 78 cases of fever and dysentery out of 310 and 527 respectively; these were all landed, the sick placed in hospital, and the healthy in the sheds to wash and purify. The passengers of both these vessels were principally tenants from the estates of William Wandesford in Kilkenny. In the "Perseverance" nine had died on the passage, and in the "Wandsworth" 45; being in one vessel about 3 per cent., and in the other 10 per cent. The passengers of both ships were from the same estates, equally provisioned, and I can only account for the greater mortality in the "Wandsworth" from the circumstance of the master of this vessel being unused to the conveyance of passengers, and unacquainted with the necessity of enforcing cleanliness and regularity, he was in all respects a steady, careful seaman. The sickness in both these ships was said by the masters to have been caused by their passengers ravenously devouring the bread-stuffs supplied by the vessel, having previous to their embarkation suffered from starvation. The sick from these two vessels, with those admitted from the "Syria," and a few from the "Jane Black" from Limerick, filled our hospitals at once to overflowing, and afforded just grounds for apprehending that sickness would prevail to an alarming extent in every vessel with Irish passengers.

Two days after the arrival of these vessels four more came in, viz., the barque "John Francis," ship "Agnes" from Cork, and barques "George" and "Royalist" from Liverpool. These four vessels had lost on the passage, which had been short, 112 of their passengers, and had more than double that number lying ill with fever and dysentery. Having no room in our crowded hospitals to accommodate this number, I resolved at once to convert the sheds used for healthy passengers into hospitals, by which additional accommodation was at once obtained for 600. I reported this arrangement for the approval of his Excellency the Governor-General on the 21st of May, asking at the same time for additional medical aid, and hospital attendants, proportioned to the increase of sick. I reported at the same time that I had taken upon me to employ Dr. Benson, a passenger by the "Wandsworth," as an assistant. On the two days following this arrangement, 200 sick were landed from the "George," "Agnes," "John Francis," and "Royalist," and placed in these sheds. I sent up express to Quebec, and obtained the assistance of Drs. Jacques and M'Grath, and a large supply of bedding, and cooking utensils. These were received the following day, and I forthwith proceeded to land other sick, making up the total number under treatment on shore to 530 on the 23rd of May, being just nine days from the first admission. From this time to the end of the month passenger vessels continued to arrive, each one more or less sickly. As far as possible, the worst of the sick were landed at once, and the others received medicine, &c., on board.

On the 27th I received by steamer a large number of tents and hospital marquees, with an additional supply of hospital bedding. I received at the same time instructions to detain all passengers where fever had prevailed for a period of ten days. With some difficulty the marquees and tents were pitched, as few men could be found to engage in any work which brought them near the hospitals, and the regular hospital attendants were overworked in their attendance on the sick and in burying the dead.

On the 30th of the month four large hospital marquees; were pitched and fitted with 64 beds each, and a large number of bell-tents were also fitted with beds, and that evening 400 more sick were landed, increasing our number to 1200. But there still remained 35 vessels in quarantine, having on board 12,175 souls, and great numbers of these were falling ill and dying daily. It was with much difficulty that people could be found to make coffins, dig graves, and bury the dead, as already observed, all our regular hospital servants were either ill or exhausted by fatigue. Dr. Benson, the gentleman engaged to assist, took fever and died after a short illness. On the 1st of June, I received the aid of two other medical assistants, in addition to Drs. Jacques and M'Grath; and the Superintendent of the Board of Works was employed to erect new hospitals, and to build cook-houses for the passengers' sheds used as temporary hospitals, and now crowded in every part.

On the fourth of this month his Excellency the Governor-General was pleased to appoint a commission of three medical gentlemen to visit, examine, and report upon the means to be adopted to relieve the distress. Upon the report of these gentlemen, orders were sent to permit the healthy passengers of all vessels detained ten days at the station to embark on board steamers sent to convey them direct to Montreal. On the 6th, the passengers from 11 vessels were embarked on board three steamers, and the day following the passengers of seven other vessels were transhipped by two steamers. A few days previous to this a small steamer had been chartered specially by the chief agent to ply daily among the vessels in quarantine, and supply the passengers with fresh provisions and comforts. An additional boat's crew was also employed in visiting vessels in quarantine with a medical man and a supply of medicine.

On the 8th of this month another of the medical gentlemen was attacked with fever, and three days previous the Rev. Mr. Gauvran, the Roman Catholic chaplain, who had been unwearied in his attendance upon the sick and dying, was down with the same disease. On the 10th of June, our number of sick had reached to 1800, who were crowded into every place that could afford shelter, hospitals, sheds, tents, and churches; these last, through the kindness of the Lord Bishop of Montreal, and his Grace the Roman Catholic archbishop, were given up for the use of the sick. In the mean time the greatest exertions were being made to put up new buildings; contracts were entered into by the Board of Works for the creation of two, capable of accommodating 120 sick each. Two others of equal size were building, under the immediate direction of the active superintendent of the Board, and a fifth was contracted for in Quebec by the Chief Agent for Emigrants, to be sent down in frame ready to be put up.

On the 11th of June, the healthy passengers from those vessels where fever had prevailed, where landed at the east end of the island, where tents had been pitched on the cleared land, capable of lodging 3000 to 4000. The most destitute of these were supplied with fresh meat and soft bread, under the controul of the Commissariat Department, an officer from which was stationed permanently on the island, with a sergeant issuer, by and through whom the whole expenditure of the establishment was made.

The police of the station was increased to ten men, and a detachment of troops was stationed on the island to aid in preserving order, and to prevent intercourse between the healthy in the tents and the sick in hospital. A medical assistant resided permanently at the east end, to afford aid to those taken ill, and to pass them over to the hospitals, for which purpose a horse and vehicle was expressly kept to convey them. A deputy agent, from the Emigrant Department, and a clerk resided also at the tents to afford assistance and advice, and to forward by steamer to Montreal those unable to pay for their passage.

In the hospitals, the number of sick continued to increase, being limited only by the amount of accommodation.

The accumulation of so vast a multitude of fever cases in one place generated a miasma so virulent and concentrated, that few who came within its poisonous atmosphere escaped. The clergy, medical men, hospital attendants, servants, and police, fell ill one after another. With respect to the clergymen, a judicious plan was adopted of retaining them for a week only, by this means many escaped; but, with medical men and attendants, this could not be done. The average period of time which a medical man withstood the disease was from 18 to 21 days; out of 26 employed during the season in the hospitals and visiting the vessels, two and myself alone escaped the fever, though otherwise severely affected in general health from breathing the foul air of the vessels and tents.... I experienced much difficulty at one time in retaining any nurses or attendants, and on those days of the week, when an opportunity of leaving the island offered by the arrival of the steamer, great numbers of servants came forward and insisted upon their discharge. I found myself obliged firmly to refuse all such applications, unless the applicant could produce a substitute. It is needless to observe, that many so retained against their will neglected their duty to the sick, and sought by every means to provoke their dismissal. Those sent down to be engaged were, in many cases, the vilest and most profligate of both sexes, and were influenced by the most sordid motives.

On the 12th of June a new hospital, capable of accommodating 120 sick was completed and occupied; two others of the same size and dimensions were finished by the end of the month. From the 19th to 26th of this month, much rain fell, with a high temperature and fog; this had a most pernicious effect upon the sick under canvas, though the tents were, in the first instance, floored with boards, after which iron bedsteads were substituted as soon as a supply of the same, was obtained from the barrack department, yet they afforded but insufficient protection from the weather when wet, and the mortality was, in consequence, much greater among the sick in tents than in the hospitals.

During the prevalence of this rain it was found impossible to wash or dry the vast quantities of hospital bedding.

The great number of sick in the early part of this month whom it was found impossible to land from want of accommodation rendered it necessary to employ two of the medical assistants to visit and prescribe for them on board.

Throughout the following months of July and August passenger vessels continued to arrive in great numbers, each more sickly than the other. The calm, sultry weather of these two months increased the mortality and sickness on board to an appalling extent, some vessels having lost one-fourth, and others one-third of their passengers, before arriving at the quarantine station. Of these I may cite the ship "Virginius," from Liverpool; this vessel left with 476 passengers, of whom 158 died before arrival at Grosse Isle, including the master, mate, and nine of the crew. It was with difficulty the few remaining hands could, with the aid of the passengers, moor the ship and furl the sails. Three days after her arrival there remained of the ship's company only the second mate, one seaman, and a boy, able to do duty; all others were either dead or ill in hospital. Two days after the arrival of this ill-fated ship, the barque "Naomi" arrived, having left Liverpool with 334 passengers, of whom 110 died on the passage, together with several of the crew. The master was just recovering from fever, on his arrival. The barque "Sir Henry Pottinger" arrived about this time from Cork, which port she had left with one cabin and 399 steerage passengers, of whom 106 died, including the master's son and several of the crew. The passengers of the two first of these vessels were sent out at the expense and from the estates of the late Major Mahon, in county Tyrone, and the survivors were, without exception, the most wretched, sickly, miserable beings I ever witnessed.

I would cite, as a further instance of the extent to which sickness and mortality prevailed about this time, the case of five vessels, viz., the "Sarah," "Erin's Queen," "Triton," from Liverpool, and "Jessie" and "Avon" from Cork. These vessels left their respective ports with an aggregate of 2235 passengers, exclusive of infants under 12 months; of this number 239 died at sea before arriving at Grosse Isle. A great number were sent to hospital, and the apparently healthy were landed at the tents where those who fell ill were passed over to hospital. After a detention of 13 days the whole number able to leave the island was 915, and of this comparative small number I am convinced a great proportion would fall ill at various places on their route.

Those who were landed at the tents in comparative good health, fell ill from the exciting causes of change of air and diet, and many died suddenly before they could be transferred to the hospitals.

By the end of August, however, long ranges of sheds had been erected, with berth-places, capable of lodging 3500 people, at the east end of the island. These buildings enabled us to dispense with all the tents.

The completion of five new hospitals, in addition to the three alluded to, enabled us to remove all the sick from the marquees and bell tents, and to restore the churches to their former use. The sickness and mortality was sensibly diminished from this period. Notwithstanding, from this to the final closing of the establishment, on the 3rd of November, every vessel coming with passengers from Liverpool, Cork, Dublin, Sligo, or other ports in the south and west of Ireland, had more or less sick. The greatest number was invariably found, as in former years, in vessels from Liverpool. The overwhelming number of sick Irish who crowded every part of this town has earned for it this year the appellation of the hospital and cemetery of Ireland. Cork and Dublin rivalled Liverpool in sending out sickly emigrants.

I have had occasion to observe in former reports, that emigrants who come from distant country places to large sea-ports, there to await the sailing of a vessel, living in the meantime in crowded cellars and lodging-houses, invariably suffer more from illness during the voyage, and arrive in a more unhealthy condition than those who have but a short distance to come, and little delay at the port of their embarkation.

I have heard fewer complaints from passengers this year of the quality of the ship's stores. I think, upon the whole, these were better than past seasons. No Indian corn meal was issued, and the biscuit and oatmeal was in most cases good and sound. The only exception to this remark was the use in some vessels, chiefly from Sligo and Killala, of what was called *whole meal*, a kind of coarse flour made from wheat, barley, rye, and pease, ground together, and not bolted; this, though a good article of food when freshly ground, and properly baked into bread, speedily attracts moisture on shipboard, where it heats and becomes caked into a solid mass, requiring to be broken down with an axe before using. In some of the vessels supplied with this article, I was assured by both captain and passengers that it was sweet and sound when inspected by the emigrant agent before leaving port. An inconvenience attending the use of this meal as food, is the impossibility of using it in any form but made into bread, and from the limited extent of the cooking places allotted to passengers it is difficult for each individual to get the use of the fire long enough to thoroughly bake the thick cakes into which it is made; hence it is frequently eaten when half baked, in which state it is sodden and indigestible. It would be desirable in all cases that one half at least of the rations furnished by the vessel should consist of oatmeal. The class of people who usually emigrate are accustomed to this food. In stormy weather, when the fires cannot be made (an occurrence which often takes place in the smaller class of vessels), it can be eaten mixed with water, in which state it is neither unpalatable nor unwholesome.

It would conduce much, however, to the health of passengers if a small portion of animal food was issued three times a week during the voyage.

The great mortality and sickness this season cannot be attributed either to a deficiency of food or over-crowding. In support of this opinion I would beg to instance the fact that, out of 7500 German settlers who arrived this season, there was not during the voyage, or on arrival at Grosse Isle, as many sick as are usually found in a like number of the same class living in their native villages. The same remark applies to the English settlers from the ports of Hull, Plymouth, Padstow, and Penzance; and to the Scotch settlers from Aberdeen, Dundee, and Leith, among whom few or no sick were found. Though in the case of these emigrants (the Germans especially) they were more crowded from having a much greater quantity of baggage. And as another proof that a sufficiency of food, good medical attendance, and comforts, do not suffice to protect Irish passengers from disease and death on the voyage, I would cite the case of the pensioners and their families who came out in the transports "Blenheim" and "Maria Somes," from Cork. The passengers of these vessels were under military discipline, had the medical attendance of a staff surgeon; they received daily rations of the best of provisions, issued under the direction of the transport agent; yet fever and dysentery prevailed throughout the voyage among the passengers and among the crew after arriving at Quebec. The "Blenheim" lost 12 passengers, and had 17 sick; and in the "Maria Somes" 17 died, and from 40 to 50 were admitted to hospital.

The disease which proved so fatal was, in most cases, brought on board, and many masters of vessels would, on going into the hold, point out to me the particular berth, place, or places, where the disease originated, and the direction in which it spread; in all such cases it was ascertained that the family occupying this berth had come on board diseased or convalescent from fever with foul and unwashed clothes.

The total number of passenger vessels inspected at the station this year has been 400, being about double the number of any previous year, the number of passengers being also double that of any former season. Of these vessels, the large number of 129 have had fever and dysentery among their passengers; 20 have had small-pox, and nine have had both fever and small-pox. 5293 passengers have died on ship board ... upon the whole number of passengers; of these, 11 were women in child-birth.

The sickness and mortality of the masters, mates, and seamen of emigrant vessels has been proportionably great. Few of those who had fever among their passengers escaped an attack of the disease, and many died, The great demand for passages to America induced many owners of vessels to fit them out whose masters were ignorant of the trade, and of the means to be adopted to preserve the health of their passengers. When fever once broke out they became alarmed for their own safety, and would not go down into the hold, which from neglect of cleanliness soon became one vast reeking pest-house; the vitiated and contaminated air of which soon enfeebled those who were of necessity obliged to breathe it, even when not struck down with fever, and rendered them indifferent to all exertion, even to the preservation of life itself, that first law of nature. In some vessels where great mortality prevailed this apathy was so great, that difficulty was experienced by the masters in inducing the passengers to remove the dead. In one vessel, the "Sisters," from Liverpool, Captain Christian, had to bring up the bodies of the dead from the hold on his shoulders; neither passengers nor seamen could be induced to assist. This humane and excellent man, whose attention to his sickly passengers was beyond all praise, fell a victim to fever a few days after the arrival of his vessel in Quebec. In another vessel, the "Erin's Queen," the master could only get the dead brought up by paying his seamen a sovereign for such body.

I regret that it is not in my power to suggest any means by which the great sickness and mortality among emigrants on their voyage out may be avoided. Much may be done by strict attention to cleanliness and ventilation as far as this is practicable, in the hold of a ship, by having the berth places and new wood-work of the 'tween-decks, whitewashed with quick lime at least once a-week during the voyage, and by obliging the bedding and clothes of passengers to be taken on deck whenever the weather will permit. And, in the fitting up of the sleeping berths, the accumulation of much filth might be prevented if the lower boards were carried down flush to the main deck. It is customary, to leave the few inches of space which they are obliged by the Passenger Act to have from the deck, open, this enables the passengers to keep their pots and vessels under the berths, which, in the rolling of the ship, get capsized, and the place becomes a receptacle of filth and dirt, which remains undisturbed as it is not seen, and cannot be readily got at to clean out. As I have already observed, the health of passengers would be better if a small quantity of animal food was issued three times a week in addition to the usual allowance of bread stuffs.

All the remedial means that may be adopted, however, will not prevent the occurrence of sickness and death to a fearful extent on ship-board so long as fever and destitution prevail in Ireland as it now does. Some one of the many passengers is sure to embark either just recovering from fever, with foul clothes and bedding, or with the seeds of the disease latent in his system, which the change of life and the discomforts of a sea voyage rapidly develop in so favourable a locale as the hold of a vessel.

Medical men are generally agreed, that the three grand measures to be taken to prevent the spread of fever, are *separation, ventilation,* and *cleanliness,* from the nature of things the two first of these are rendered impracticable in a crowded passenger-ship, and the last, of difficult attainment. Sea-sickness and the mental depression which usually attends it render it a matter of extreme difficulty to induce people to practice a virtue which they have never been accustomed to. Hence there is much reason to apprehend that next season will bring with it a recurrence of the sickness and mortality of this year, limited only in extent by the numbers who may emigrate.

It is gratifying to know, however, that there now exists hospital accommodation at Grosse Isle, with bedding, and every requisite for 2000 sick; and there are two convalescent hospitals at the east end of the island, containing 150 beds each, together with sheds capable of lodging 3500 emigrants, with cook-houses, wash-houses, police barracks, and dwelling-house for medical officer, and deputy agent for emigration. The only requisite necessary to render the establishment complete, is a landing-place near these sheds, where emigrants may land and embark with their baggage, to wash and purify. And to enable the feather beds and woollen clothes to be more effectually purified, I would suggest the erection of a large oven, where these might be subjected to dry heat, which is generally admitted to be the readiest and most effectual means of freeing feather beds and woollen garments from febrile miasma. If, in connexion with this, there could be an apparatus for cleaning the hospital bedding, by subjecting them to the action of a stream of hot vapour, it would save many valuable lives lost every year, in the disgusting and dangerous work of washing articles saturated with the ejecta of the sick and dying. I have witnessed the use of an apparatus of this kind in the Hanwell Lunatic Asylum, near London, by which the clothes and bedding of 1200 pauper lunatics are washed, and by another machine are wrung out of the water with comparative little labour or handling by the servants. To show the necessity of some such means, I would mention that, at one period last season there had accumulated upwards of 5000 pieces of hospital bedding, consisting of blankets, rugs, paillasses, which it was found impossible to get anyone to undertake the dangerous duty of washing. I was obliged, in consequence, to adopt a plan suggested by Mr. Julyan, the Commissariat officer, of making a wicker-work in the tide-way of the river; in this, the foul bed-clothes were placed, and allowed to steep for 24 hours, from thence they were carted to the wash-house, and lowered into large boilers by means of a frame-work moved by pulleys; after being thus boiled, the articles were spread out, partially dried and washed. But this was a work necessarily tedious, and still exposed those engaged in the labour more than they would be by the means above suggested. On closing the station there still remained upwards of 4000 articles of soiled bedding to be washed, which is now being done by a washer woman and two assistants, who remain on the island during the winter for the purpose.

Though perhaps uncalled for in a report of this nature, I cannot conclude without adverting to the devotion shown by the clergy, both Protestant and Roman Catholic, in their attendance upon the sick and dying throughout the trying scenes of the past year. His Lordship the Bishop of Montreal visited the island two different periods, and passed several days each time in unremitting attendance in the tents, sheds, and hospitals, when most crowded.

### 3. Mayor W. Boulton, "To Earl of Elgin, Governor General of British North America," 1847.

MAY IT PLEASE YOUR EXCELLENCY,

WE, the inhabitants of the city of Toronto, in public meeting assembled, respectfully invite the attention of your Excellency to the consideration of a subject, the urgency and importance of which will warrant our pressing it most earnestly on your Excellency's earliest notice.

During the past season the city of Toronto, in common with several other parts of Canada, has been the recipient of a very large body of emigrants from the British Isles, landed on our shores in a state, beyond all description, of lamentable and almost hopeless destitution, and bearing with them a pestilence of the most virulent and destructive character.

Out of the 100,000 emigrants landed in Quebec, nearly 40,000 were forwarded to this city; and from the month of June to the present time, the city has exhibited an amount of pauperism, suffering and disease unparalleled in her annals, and tolerable only from the belief of its having been utterly unforeseen, and from a trust in the mercy of Providence that it will not be suffered again to occur.

During the same period the hospitals appropriated to the suffering emigrants have, including the sick and convalescent divisions, been generally filled to overflowing with a number of patients often nearly reaching 1000 souls.

In addition to this mass of sickness and wretchedness, the number of persons, men, women, and children, begging from street to street for relief, has been fearfully on the increase; and a large mendicant population, once unknown to our Canadian towns, has rapidly sprung into existence.

Your Excellency must be already familiar with the terrible statistics of death, sorrow, and destitution consequent on the reckless and unguided emigration of 1847. Our object at the present time is not to dwell upon the past, further than may be necessary to suggest such a different course for the future, as may save us from a possible repetition of horrors which, if they can be or could have been averted by human precautions, would reflect deep and lasting disgrace on those who neglect the means of prevention or alleviation.

If the wide-spread suffering of the past year were a dispensation from the chastening hand of Providence, unaffected and uncaused by human agency, the city of Toronto would willingly or at least silently bear their portion of the general loss and misery.

Sincerely believing it to have arisen in a very serious degree from neglect, indifference, and mismanagement, we respectfully venture to press on your Excellency the absolute necessity that exists for the adoption of prompt remedial measures.

The dreadful sufferings from want of wholesome food, ventilation room, and decent clothing on board the emigrant vessels—the startling fact of many thousands having found a grave in the ocean, that they thought was to bear them to a land of peace and plenty—the apparently total disregard of any inspection of the vessels, at the British ports—the neglect of salutary regulations as to the number of passengers proportioned to the size of the vessels, or the providing of a sufficient supply of food—the manner in which the healthy and the sick were shipped up the river and the lakes, and the catalogue of deaths at the numerous hospitals from Grosse Isle to Sandwich—all these are now matters of history, and are, doubtless, fresh in your Excellency's recollection.

We now most earnestly request your Excellency, without waiting for any action on the part of the Provincial Legislature, to aid the inhabitants of Canada in procuring from Her Majesty's Home Government such a vigorous interposition in the conduct of the anticipated emigration of 1848 as may ensure, so far as human precautions may extend, the nonrecurrence of the melancholy and revolting sufferings of the past season. A watchful and complete system of inspection of every emigrant vessel previous to its being allowed to leave port—due attention to the clothing and provisions of the passengers—strict rules as to the number allowed to be carried—all these can avail much to diminish the risk of pestilence. Above all, the fact cannot be too widely promulgated in Great Britain and Ireland, that the throwing of a half-clad and penniless emigrant on the shores of the St. Lawrence, may be the means of ridding an estate of a burdensome tenant; but it is an almost hopeless method of providing for a fellow-Christian.

This city has already lost some of her best and most valued citizens by the malignant fever introduced by the emigrants last season. Universal alarm has pervaded the community, and considerable interruption to business and travelling has been caused by the general state of the great thoroughfares of the province, from the prevalence of disease.

Most respectfully, but firmly, do the citizens of Toronto protest, through your Excellency, against their hitherto healthy and prosperous country being made the receptacle for the cast-off pauperism and disease of another hemisphere. To those already among us, without reference to national origin or other distinction, we trust we shall ever be ready to extend a helping hand and an active charity; but we look upon it as unjust and intolerable that the neglect and misconduct of others are to be the means of impoverishing and infecting our young country.

A well regulated emigration from the British Isles will confer inestimable advantages on the North American provinces, and on this city and its environs in particular. An emigration, such as has made memorable the season of 1847, must ever prove the opposite of a blessing to all concerned in it.

We feel persuaded that Her Majesty's Government will take such necessary precautions as to relieve the province at large, and its municipalities in particular, from the most painful, but most imperative duty of adopting such stringent measures as the exigency of the crisis may require for their own preservation.

Again most earnestly and respectfully entreating your Excellency's earliest attention to this all-important subject, we beg to renew to your Excellency our assurance of respect for your Excellency's person and government.

### 4. H. Perley, "To Sir William Colebrooke, Lieutenant-Governor of the Province of New Brunswick," December 31, 1847.

May It Please Your Excellency,

I have the honour to submit, for the information of Her Majesty's Government, the annual report from this office, together with the returns (in duplicate) for the quarter, and for the year, ending 31st December, 1847.

The return for the year shows the total number of emigrants landed in New Brunswick, during the past season, to have been 16,251, being an increase on the previous year's emigration of 6486, equal to 66 per cent. Of the whole number of vessels with emigrants, 99 came direct from Ireland; and although the other seven vessels sailed from Liverpool, yet the passengers were very nearly, without exception, all from Ireland also. The immigration of the season was confined almost solely to the humblest class of Irish peasantry, chiefly from the south and west of Ireland, who, long prior to embarkation, had suffered from every species of privation, and had become enfeebled by disease. Some thousands consisted of those who had been tenants holding less than five acres of land, and of mere cottiers, who had never held land at all, sent out at the expense of the landlords, or proprietors of the soil, on which they had lived, to relieve the estates from the expense of their support. They landed in New Brunswick in the greatest misery and destitution; so broken down and emaciated by starvation, disease, and the fatigues of the voyage, as to be, in a great measure, incapable of performing sufficient labour to earn a subsistence, and they became a heavy burthen upon private charity, as well as upon the public funds.

Of 17,074 who embarked this season for New Brunswick, 823 died on ship-board, 96 in the lazaretto at Miramichi, 601 in the lazaretto at St. John, and 595 in the hospital at the same place, making a total of 2115 deaths officially reported. The whole number of deaths for the season, up to the present date, may be safely estimated at 2400, or one-seventh of those who embarked.

Of the survivors, very nearly one half have found their way into the United States, notwithstanding the exertions used to prevent their entrance there. Of the residue, some were forwarded to the interior of this province at the public expense, and others made their way into the rural districts; but these were too feeble, and so little accustomed to work of any kind, that they were almost useless to the farmer; and I regret to say, that their course through the country was almost invariably marked by disease and death. They introduced fever into the farm-houses where they were employed, and a very general disinclination was soon manifested to receiving them as inmates on any terms.

There are at present 560 in the hospital attached to the almshouse at this place. To provide for the orphan children of deceased emigrants, an establishment has been opened in this city, into which nearly 200 children have already been received and clothed, and those of sufficient age are being instructed in schools of industry within the building. This establishment bids fair to be of a most useful character; it is to be hoped that it will be permanently sustained, and its means of usefulness increased. The sympathy of benevolent individuals has already been excited in behalf of the undertaking, and contributions have been made, to render the establishment more comfortable and beneficial for these helpless orphans. As the institution advances, charitable assistance will, no doubt, be afforded on an enlarged scale; still a very considerable sum will be required from the public funds for this asylum, which it is trusted will be forthcoming for an object so necessary and so laudable.

Among the emigrants of this season there was an unusual proportion of aged and infirm people of both sexes, and of widows, and deserted wives, with large families of children. Several instances came under my notice, where aged grandfathers and grandmothers arrived with a swarm of young and helpless grandchildren, the intermediate generation having remained in Ireland.

The expenses connected with the emigration of this year have already far exceeded the grant of 3000*l.*, made in anticipation by the provincial legislature at its last session, and the head money collected during the season; and as expenses are now being incurred in various parts of the province for the care and support of emigrants, which must be continued for some time, it becomes matter of grave consideration how the amount is to be met....

The number of able-bodied labourers, such as were able and willing to work, was this year unusually small; in fact, far less than the business of the country required. While this city was literally crowded with emigrants, and others were daily arriving, the rate of wages for good labourers steadily advanced, and the average for the season was as high as it ever was before. But few employers could be found who would incur the trouble of teaching men who were willing to work, but who were wholly unaccustomed to continuous labour, whose strength was unequal to any but light work; whose diet and management required great attention, or they fell ill directly, and with whom there was the constant risk of infectious fever, the seeds of which appeared to lurk in the constitutions of all, without exception....

The corporation return which is enclosed shows that, in the year 1844, only 2,500 emigrants landed at this port, and that the number has steadily advanced since then, until in the past season it reached 15,000. In former years, also, there was a very small amount of sickness, and the hospital accommodations at the quarantine station on Partridge Island were considered quite sufficient. But they were altogether inadequate to the emergency of the past season, when cargo after cargo of sick, filthy, and miserable wretches, had to be landed in rapid succession, infecting the medical men, the nurses and attendants, and nearly all who in any way had communication with them....

As great numbers have been buried on the island during the past season, in trenches imperfectly covered with soil, some expense must be incurred in covering these trenches with lime, sea-sand, and soil, to prevent the unpleasantness and injurious effects of the cadaverous exhalations.

No time should be lost in making these preparations, as the brief space until the arrival of emigrants in the spring, will barely admit of the necessary buildings being erected, and other arrangements made in due season.

The following prosecutions were instituted during the past season for violations of the Passengers' Act, in every one of which a conviction was obtained:—Austin Yorke, master of the "Lindon," from Galway, for insufficient issues of provisions and water to passengers, convicted in the penalty of 20*l.* sterling, and costs, which have been paid.

Samuel Fox, master of the Brigantine "Susan Anne," from Beerhaven, for carrying passengers without beams for a lower deck, convicted in the penalty of 20*l.* sterling, and costs, which have been paid.

The same Samuel Fox, master of the "Susan Anne," for an excess of passengers, convicted in the penalty of 5*l.* Sterling, and costs, which were paid.

Michael Brown, master of the schooner "Lady Dombrain," from Killybegs, for carrying passengers without permanent beams for a lower deck, convicted in the penalty of 20*l.* sterling, and costs, which were paid.

Patrick Beegan, master of the schooner "Bloomfield," from Galway, for insufficient issues of provisions and water, convicted in the full penalty of 50*l.* sterling, and costs, not yet paid....

The issues of the "Eliza Liddell," at Shippegan, and of that unfortunate vessel, the "Looshtank," at Miramichi, having been thoroughly investigated, I have only now to refer to my special reports on those cases, dated 18th and 19th October last.

I observed, during the season, that in those ships which had ample height between decks, and sufficient means of ventilation, there was less sickness and a smaller number of deaths than in others not possessing those advantages. In all cases, cleanliness, regular issues of provisions at short intervals, and the encouragement of active exercise on deck were most beneficial. The good effects of air and exercise were always evident in inspecting the emigrants upon their arrival. The use of Sir William Burnett's disinfecting fluid (chloride of zinc) was also highly advantageous. In the case of the brig "St. Lawrence," from Cork to St. Andrews, the passengers embarked with several cases of fever, yet from good management on the voyage, and the free use of this chloride, they landed at St. Andrews in better health than when they embarked.

The provision of the Passengers' Act, in reference to good sound boats, of suitable size, is in many cases shamefully evaded, and more attention to their inspection is absolutely requisite. Some of the boats attached to passenger ships this season were mere baskets, an incumbrance to the ship and nothing more. Anything boat-shaped is deemed sufficient by some masters and owners, if the necessary certificates for clearance can be obtained. After such certificate and safe voyage across the Atlantic, it would be difficult to procure a conviction here for this violation of the Act, more especially as it is easy to allow boats to be stove by a sea....

The use of biscuit in the Irish passenger trade should be limited as much as possible, as also the issue of "whole meal" made from wheat without any sifting, which is passed as wheat flour. In some cases, biscuit only was furnished to the passengers, to which they were wholly unaccustomed, and they nearly starved in consequence. It is difficult to make the whole meal into palatable bread, even when of the best quality; and with the imperfect means of working on board a passenger vessel at sea, it is quite out of the question. In the absence of potatoes, oatmeal should be strictly insisted upon, as a species of food to which the Irish peasantry are accustomed, and which they can prepare in any weather, and under all circumstances. The destitute emigrants of this season relied almost wholly upon the supply of provisions furnished by the ship, and many suffered greatly in consequence of the food not being such as they could prepare or use.

During the past season no money whatsoever has been remitted to this office by landholders or others in Ireland, to be paid to passengers on their arrival here; and although various noblemen and gentlemen have sent out pauper emigrants this year, no money, to my knowledge, has been paid to them, on or after arrival here. All were left to shift for themselves, or become a burthen upon the revenues of the colony, or else to subsist upon charitable institutions, or the assistance of the benevolent.

The character of the emigration during the past year having been altogether different from any that has preceded it, no comparison can be drawn between it and that of any former year. Heretofore sturdy labourers and farmers have arrived, very often possessed of some means, however small, and all looking forward to becoming settlers and proprietors of the soil by their energy and industry; but a large proportion of the emigrants of this season will require time and training to become even useful labourers....

### 5. A. Hawke, "To T. Campbell," October 16, 1847.

Emigrant Office, Kingston, 16 October 1847.
... Up to this period, about 92,000 emigrants are reported to have been landed at Grosse Island, Quebec and Montreal. Of this number, It appears that 18,960 merely passed through our navigable waters en route to the adjoining and Western States, leaving the immigration to Canada via the St. Lawrence, a little over 74,000. To which must be added for immigrants who entered Upper Canada by our frontier ports, nearly 3,000 more, making the grand total 77,000.

It is the opinion of the immigrant agents, as well as my own, that two-thirds—in round numbers 50,000—have settled, and are now employed in various parts of Canada; and according to the latest information that I am in possession of, 5,136 are sick in the various hospitals, leaving 21,861 unaccounted for. The deaths, according to Mr. Taylor's return to the 19th ultimo, on the passage out and at the Grosse Isle, Quebec and Montreal hospitals, amount to 11,396, to which must be added 3,650 who have died in this section of the province, making the total 15,046, and leaving nearly 7,000 still unaccounted for. They will be found, with few exceptions, hanging loose upon society, especially about the towns, where by short jobs of work, and occasional charity, they manage to pick up a precarious subsistence....

With reference to the assertion so frequently made in the public prints, that many aged and infirm people have been sent to this colony, who could not, under any circumstances, earn a livelihood. I would beg to add, that in addition to this burthen, many widows with large families, whose husbands died in Ireland, and who have no friends in America have also been landed in Canada during the current season. I have as yet received returns from only three places out of eight; viz. Kingston, Cobourg and Bytown, and these returns contain lists of the names of 108 widows, having 321 children. Forty-two of these widows, having 127 children dependent upon them, lost their husbands in Ireland, and were sent out, as they declare, by the landlords upon whose estates they resided, and the relief committees. As soon as these returns are complete, I shall transmit them to your address.

Upon the whole I am obliged to consider the immigration of this year a calamity to the province. It has no doubt been the cause of much benefit to the ship and steam-boat proprietors, as well as to those interested in furnishing supplies for the subsistence of the immigrants. But, on the other hand, there is no denying; that they have scattered disease and death, to a fearful extent, wherever they have congregated in any considerable numbers. Added to this, they are generally dirty in their habits and unreasonable in their expectations as to wages. They appear to possess but little ambition or desire to adapt themselves to the new state of things with which they are surrounded. The few who possess any money invariably secrete it, and will submit to any amount of suffering, or have recourse to begging in the streets, and the most humiliating and pertinacious supplications to obtain a loaf of bread from Boards of Health or the emigrant agents, rather than part with a shilling.

## Readings

Akenson, D. *Being Had: Historians, Evidence and the Irish in North America.* Pt. Credit: P. D. Meany, 1985.

Akenson, D. *The Irish in Ontario: A Study in Rural History.* Montreal and Kingston: McGill-Queen's University Press, 1984.

Cowan, H. *British Emigration to British North America: The First Hundred Years.* Revised edition. Toronto: University of Toronto Press, 1961.

Duncan, K. "Irish Famine Immigration and the Social Structure of Canada West," *Canadian Review of Anthropology and Sociology* (February 1965).

Elliot, B. *Irish Migrants in the Canadas: A New Approach.* Montreal and Kingston: McGill-Queen's University Press, 1988.

Grace, R. *The Irish in Quebec: An Introduction to the Historiography.* Quebec: Institute Quebecois de Recherche sur la Culture, 1993.

Houston, C., and W. Smyth. *Irish Emigration and Canadian Settlement: Patterns, Links and Letters.* Toronto: University of Toronto Press, 1990.

Houston, C., and W. Smyth. *The Sash Canada Wore: A Historical Geography of the Orange Order in Canada.* Toronto: University of Toronto Press, 1980.

King, J. "The Colonist Made Exile: Stephen De Vere, 'Famine Diary' and Representations of the Famine Irish in Canada," *Irish Centre for Migraton Studies.*

Lockwood, G. "Irish Immigrants in the 'Critical Years' in Eastern Ontario: The Case of Montague Township, 1821–1881," in J. Johnson and B. Wilson, eds., *Historical Essays on Upper Canada: New Perspectives.* Ottawa: Carleton University Press, 1989.

Mackay, D. *Flight from Famine: The Coming of the Irish to Canada.* Toronto: McClelland and Stewart, 1990.

Mannion, J. *Irish Settlement in Eastern Canada: A Study of Cultural Transfer and Adaptation.* Toronto: University of Toronto Press, 1974.

O'Driscoll, R., and C. Reynolds, eds. *The Untold Story: The Irish in Canada.* Toronto: Celtic Arts of Canada, 1988.

Parr, J. "The Welcome and the Wake: Attitudes in Canada West Toward the Irish Famine Migration," *Ontario History* (1974).

Power, T., ed. *The Irish in Atlantic Canada, 1780–1900.* Fredericton: New Ireland Press, 1991.

Quigley, M. "Grosse Isle: Canada's Irish Famine Memorial," *Labour* 39 (Spring 1997).

See, S. *Riots in New Brunswick: Orange Nativism and Social Violence in the 1840s.* Toronto: University of Toronto Press, 1990.

See, S. "'An Unprecedented Influx': Nativism and Irish Famine Immigration to Canada," *American Review of Canadian Studies* 30 (Winter 2000).

Senior, H. *Orangism: The Canadian Phase.* Toronto: McGraw-Hill Ryerson, 1972.

Shea, D. "The Irish Immigrant Adjustment to Toronto, 1840–1860," *Canadian Catholic Historical Association*, Study Sessions, 39 (1972).

Stewart, W. *Life on the Line: Commander Pierre-Etienne Fortin and his Times.* Ottawa: Carleton University Press, 1997.

Toner, P., ed. *New Ireland Remembered: Historical Essays on the Irish in New Brunswick.* Fredericton: New Ireland Press, 1988.

## Chapter Fourteen

# "A GREAT HUMBUG": BRITISH COLUMBIA'S GOLD RUSHES

1. C. Gardiner, "To the Editor of *The Islander*," November 17, 1858.
2. Charles Major, "News from British Columbia," *The Daily Globe*, January 2, 1860.
3. S.G. Hathaway, Journal, 1862.
4. Matthew MacFie, *Vancouver Island and British Columbia*, 1865.

## Introduction

British Columbia remained largely untouched by Europe until the latter part of the nineteenth century. Geography perhaps played the greatest single role in BC's slow colonization: the area was simply too far removed from eastern Canada to be accessible; and once there, the topography and vegetation made settlement and communication all but impossible. If it was not the impassable mountain ranges, it was the treacherous river gorges. Much of the interior was too arid for crops, and trees too enormous to hew covered the tiny belt of fertile land along the coast. Why bother—especially since plenty of arable land, thriving communities, and far better communications existed in the eastern part of British North America? British Columbia offered too few rewards for too great an effort and Europeans stayed away until this changed in the latter part of the eighteenth century when Russian, American, and English ships ventured along the coast to reap the bountiful sea otter for its pelt. Then traders from the North West Company, which merged with the Hudson's Bay Company in 1821, sought routes from their trapping grounds in the Athabasca country to the west coast. The British government sent expeditions led first by Captain Cook and later by his garrulous successor, George Vancouver, to map the coast and to assert claim over the land. But by the mid-nineteenth century, the European presence in BC still remained minuscule, with small fur trade posts the most prominent at Victoria. All of this changed in the late 1850s with the discovery of gold.

Gold fever could drive the most upstanding and conservative individuals to ridiculous and dangerous ends chasing that seductive yellow glow. The earlier

California gold rush attracted every sort: naive city boys, hardened criminals, prostitutes, people down on their luck, shrewd businessmen and women, new immigrants without better prospects, genuine miners, and a myriad of others. The boom, of course, inevitably became a bust, leaving many dreamers high and dry, often in debt, and casting about for a new Eldorado. By the mid-nineteenth century, San Francisco teemed with luckless miners looking for new prospects.

Vague reports of gold along the Fraser River filtered south to California as early as 1855, and rumours became reality by the fall of 1857. Fortune hunters packed onto ships or came overland via Whatcom Trail through the Washington territory. Ft. Victoria, the sleepy Hudson's Bay Company trading post of some 300 people, groaned under the strain of a transient and enthusiastic throng of some 30,000 miners who descended upon the unprepared village. Most miners remained just long enough to buy provisions at grossly inflated prices before setting off for the sand bars along the Fraser, or later, to instant towns like Barkerville in the Cariboo. What they lacked in experience, they made up for in tenacity and enthusiasm—and they needed both. Mining the bars along the Fraser was either relatively easy or impossible. At low water, in the summer and autumn, anyone with a gold pan and a bit of patience could strike it rich—at least so the story went among the uninitiated. Gold-seekers, many believed, required neither skills nor investment capital. Theoretically, one simply registered a claim for a sandbar, scooped up pans full of gravel and water, gingerly sloshing the debris over the edge until nothing remained but the heavy gold settled on the bottom. Winter time and spring runoff, however, covered the sandbars with turbulent and frigid water that made panning infeasible, or at least desperately dangerous. Frustrated miners camped along the banks and prayed for levels to recede, worrying whether money and supplies would last until they could pan again. Many, if not most, found their prayers unanswered.

The British government worried about so many Americans in the interior of present-day British Columbia. Colonial officials feared the presence of large numbers of American miners would encourage the American annexation of this territory. Only Vancouver Island had colonial status and James Douglas, its governor, did not wait for official consent before asserting direct British authority over the mainland in 1858. This, however, was easier said than done, particularly after many miners moved from the Fraser and Thompson rivers further north into the distant and isolated Cariboo.

Why did miners specifically follow the rivers toward their source rather than look elsewhere once sand bar yields declined? Logic dictated that the gold dust on the river originated upstream where floodwaters scoured it from solid rock. Thus a miner could theoretically follow the trail of dust to the "mother lode." New Cariboo strikes occurred at Keithly, Antler, Williams, and Lightning Creek. Instant towns like Barkerville sprang up almost overnight. Unlike panning sandbars, however, this new chapter in British Columbia's mining history required plenty of capital to cover the costs of boring shafts deep into the ground, refining the ore, and then transporting it to the coast. Unless a miner had money, he inevitably had to create partnerships or give up, drifting to the next gold discovery, ever hopeful of getting there early in the game. Shaft mining also required skill and at least rudimentary geological knowledge, which few possessed. And what were the chances of success? A handful, usually those staking early claims, made famous fortunes. Billy Barker, who gave his name to Barkerville, was one exception. The vast majority eked out bare subsistences or drifted back to Victoria, broke and broken. Many never survived to tell their tales.

Communities in the mining areas often disappeared as quickly as they emerged. Barkerville virtually overnight became the biggest city west of Chicago and north of San Francisco. Ten years later it was all but abandoned. Neither education nor religion, two hallmarks of stable communities, usually existed. The lack of families made the social structure even less stable and predictable. Life in the little towns also tended to be very seasonal with frenzied summer activity tapering off to somnolent and frigid winter boredom.

## Discussion Points

1. Why was British Columbia not a land of opportunity?
2. How were the colonies of Vancouver Island and British Columbia different from their counterparts in eastern British North America?
3. Anti-Oriental discrimination became common in late nineteenth-century British Columbia. In what respects is this reflected in MacFie's account?
4. If you were a would-be miner desperate to beat the crowds and make a lucky strike, how would you describe British Columbia to those with whom you corresponded back home? Is there any indication that some of the negative images could have been deliberately designed to discourage competition?

*Documents*

## 1. C. Gardiner, "To the Editor of *The Islander*," November 17, 1858.

... No doubt you are aware that about the 1st of May last a great excitement arose, and spread quickly over the lands of California, Oregon and Washington Territories, proving equally infectious to men of all vocations—the merchant, the farmer, the mechanic and miner—that gold in abundance was found on the Fraser and Thompson Rivers. I being, perhaps, like many others, of somewhat an excitable disposition, left, on the 20th May [1858], a mining town in the interior of California, and proceeded to San Francisco, where I found the excitement even more intense than in the mountains—the greatest credence being given to the stability of the reports, they going unanimously to prove the country could not be surpassed in richness with gold.

... Some thousands men were waiting there at that time in the greatest dilemma not knowing which way to proceed to the new mines. Fraser River being so high could not be ascended for two months, a sufficient distance to reach the main diggings, on account of the current running so swiftly through the Big Canyon, forming rapids, which would be impossible to navigate at that stage of water. Nevertheless, many would form in companies, buy a canoe, lay in from three to six months' provisions, and start, working their way as far as possible, until the river fell. Others would assert they would wait for the trail, which was then in operation of being cut through the country, across the Cascade Mountains to Thompson River, at the expense of some Land and Town Lot speculators, who were determined to have the great depot and centre of trade, effected by the new mines, on American soil. The balance of the men were divided in opinion, the weaker, or perhaps I may now justly allow, the wiser, being disgusted with the chances of getting to the New Eldorado, resolved to return to California.

... The upsetting of our canoe was nothing more than an accident, which most every company experienced, many not only losing their grub, but their lives. We very nearly lost two of our men, but were providentially saved by catching hold of the branches of a leaning tree, as the current was taking them swiftly down.

... Every day of the 23 [days to get up the river] we were in the cold water most of the time, with our heads out, but very frequently with them under, an unpleasantness which could not be avoided, in passing the line outside the trees and brush which grew on the banks of the river, when the water was low, but were now submerged half way to their tops. Those nights we passed in sleeping in our wet clothes, or part of them only, as each in his turn had to keep watch, with revolver in hand, that the Indians did not steal our provisions, as well as Mamaloose [kill] us while asleep. Notwithstanding our guard, every few mornings one or the other of the companies would have something missing that the Red Skin had stolen at night. Indeed it is considered as impossible to keep them from or detect them stealing....

We found quite a number of men camped on the river banks, the most of whom had come by trail from the Colville Mines in Washington Territory, and who were forced to kill their horses and mules, the flesh of which they had been subsisting on for the last 4 weeks. Flour we soon ascertained (if there was any for sale) was worth $125 per 100 lb., meat of all kinds $1.75, beans $1.00, and everything else in proportion.

Fraser River was still very high, and the miners informed us they could only make from two to five dollars per day, that not being sufficient to grub them the way provisions sold, and there was not a probability of it getting much cheaper for some time.

Five of us in Company pitched our tent, fixed up our mining tools, and went to work. We prospected up and down the river a distance of 40 miles each way, and could find gold in small quantities most anywhere on the surface of the bars, which were then getting bare, as the river fell. The gold is much finer than any found in California, and found in a different deposit. On Fraser River what has been dug has been found within three to eighteen inches of the surface, in a kind of sand being underneath a very pretty gravel, but no gold in it. In this country it is just the reverse, in sand like on Fraser, we can find nothing in California, but in the gravel, and the nearer we approach the bed rock, the coarser the gold, and the richer it pays. We found a bar which prospected better than any other in that section, and set in to try our luck. We worked early and late, averaging from $3 to $5 per day. We washed out dirt in rockers, using quick silver, not then being able to save all the gold, it being so fine, much would float off, and some rusty that would not amalgamate. After working there about six weeks our stock of provisions was getting nearly exhausted, and we concluded to pack up and start down stream. I for one was getting tired of living on bread and water alone, for long since the Indians had stolen the coffee. Not any of the miners within fifty miles of us at this time were making grub, at the price of provisions; indeed it was hard to get it at any price, as few had it to spare. The river had fallen quite low, and where we expected, as in California, to find it rich, we could make nothing. Men began to think it a great humbug, and the glowing accounts of Fraser River became gradually pronounced a fiction. The natives there were all so very troublesome, stealing and pointing guns at men was a prominent feature of their character....

I am afraid, Mr. Editor, I have taken up too much space in your columns, and shall conclude by saying I should not advise anyone from P. E. Island to come to Fraser River, with the intention of making his fortune; and I'm quite sure, speaking from experience, nothing will be gained by going for anything else, as the trip is a very expensive and laborious one.

Michigan Bluffs, Placer County, California.

## 2. Charles Major, "News from British Columbia," *The Daily Globe*, January 2, 1860.

Fort Hope, Frazer River
Sept. 20th, 1859
Dear Sir: I am afraid you will think I had forgot my promise,—but I wanted to know something about the country before writing to you. In the first place, do not think that I have taken a dislike to the country because I am not making money; the dislike is general all over the country. To give you anything like a correct idea of it would take more paper than I have small change to purchase, and more time than I could spare, and then it would only be commenced.

The country is not what it was represented to be. There is no farming land in British Columbia, as far as I can learn, except a very small portion joining Washington Territory, and on Vancouver's Island, where there is one valley of 20,000 acres; but that cannot be sold until Col. Moody's friends come out from the old country, and get what they want.

It never can be a place, because there is nothing to support it, except the mines, and just as soon as they are done the place goes down completely, for there is absolutely nothing to keep it up; and I tell you the truth the mines are falling off very fast. There is nothing in this country but mines—and very small pay for that; they are you may say, used up. We have been making two, three and four dollars per day, but it would not last more than two or three days; and so you would spend that before you would find more. There has been great excitement about Fort Alexander, three hundred miles above this, and also about Queen Charlotte's Island. They have both turned out another humbug like this place. A party arrived here yesterday from Alexander, and they are a pitiful looking lot. They are what the Yankees call dead broke. They have been six hundred miles up the river. When they got down here they had no shoes to their feet.

Some had pieces of shirt and trowsers, but even these were pinned together with small sharp sticks; and some had the rim of an old hat, and some the crown. They had nothing to eat for one week, and not one cent in money. This is gold mining for you!

I expect the Frazer River fever has cooled down by this time, at least I hope so; for I do pity the poor wretches that come out here to beg. They can do that at home; as for making money, that is out of the question. Since we came here (to use the miners' term) we have been making grub; and those who can do that, think they are doing well. If there are any making arrangements to come to this place, let them take a fool's advice and stay at home. I would just about as soon hear that anyone belonging to me was dead, as to hear they had started to come here. They say it wants a man with capital to make money here; but a man with money in Canada will double it quicker than he will here. And if I, or any other, was to work as hard and live as meanly, I could make more money in Canada than I can here. Since we have been on the River we have worked from half-past two and three o'clock in the morning till nine and ten o'clock at night (you can see the sun twenty hours out of the twenty-four in the summer season) and lived on beans! If that is not working, I don't know what it is. Besides this you go home to your shanty at night, tired and wet, and have to cook your beans before you can eat them. And what is this all for? For gold of course; but when you wash up at night, you may realize 50 cents, perhaps $1.

There have been some rich spots struck on this river, but they were very scarce, and they are all worked out; and the miners are leaving the river every day, satisfied there is nothing to be made. But now that I am in the country I will remain for a year or so, and if nothing better turns up by that time, I think I will be perfectly satisfied. I have met with some that I was acquainted with, and it is amusing to see those who felt themselves a little better than their neighbors at home, come here and get out of money, and have to take the pick and shovel, perhaps to drag firewood out of the woods and sell it, or make pack-mules of themselves to get a living. I do not mean to say that it is so all over the Colony, but it is from one end of Frazer River to the other. I dare anyone to contradict what I say; and I have good reason to believe it is as bad all over the country. I saw a patch of oats here the other day. They were out in head, only four inches in height, yellow as ochre, and not thick enough on the ground to be neighbours. Vegetables and other things are as poor in the proportion; and as for the climate, it is just as changeable as in Canada, if not more so. I can't say much about the climate on Vancouver's Island, but I think it is rather better.

I met T.G., the carpenter, from Sarnia, who left there about a year ago. He went round the Horn, and he was ten months and fifteen days in coming here. He is cutting saw logs making a little over grub. He says he is going to write to the Sarnia Observer, and give this place a cutting up! There are a great many Canadians here, and they would be glad to work for their board. A man could not hire out to work a day if he was starving. I have seen some parties from California; they say times are very hard there. There are just three in our party now, H.H., J.R., and myself. There were two of the H's; one was taken sick and had to leave the river; he is in Victoria, and is quite recovered again; has been there two months, and has not got a day's work yet. I was very sick myself when I just came here, but am quite healthy now, and so fat I can hardly see to write. The rest are quite well.

The Indians are not very troublesome at the mines; they are kept down pretty well. They are very numerous here and on the Island, the lowest degraded set of creatures I ever saw.

It is estimated that the number of miners who make over wages, is one in five hundred; and the number that do well in the mines is one in a thousand. So you see it is a very small proportion. If you know anyone that wants to spend money, why, this is just the place. Anyone bringing a family here would require a small fortune to support them in this horrible place, hemmed in by mountains on all sides, and these covered with snow all the year.

I have lived in a tent since I came up the river, and I have to lie on the ground before the fire and write; it gives a very poor light, so excuse the writing. It has been raining here steady one week, and the mountains are all covered with snow; for when it rains here it is snowing upon the mountains. It is a wild looking place. You will please tell our folks you hear from me, and that we are all well. I will write to some of them in about two weeks or so. I have wrote five letters already, but I have not heard from any of them; so many letters go astray in coming here and going from this place, that perhaps they do not get them at all. Give my respects to old friends, and tell them to be contented and stay at home.

### 3. S.G. Hathaway, *Journal*, 1862.

British Columbia, June 20.
On the 3rd June I left San Francisco in Steamship Brother Jonathan for Victoria. On the way up we went into the Columbia River up to Portland, Oregon. Remained there from Saturday noon till Monday morning, then out to sea again & on to Victoria arriving there Tuesday afternoon, June 10—just one week on

the trip. We pitched our tent in the edge of the woods, half a mile out of town & began camp life at once. We found that, owing to the snow still lying up in the mountains we were still early & so concluded to wait a while & learn more of the country before starting. On the 17 I and two other young men—one from Maine, the other from New Hampshire—concluded to try our luck as partners; so we bought a mule together & a load of provisions—enough to last six weeks at least—& on the 18th took another step for Cariboo, taking a steamboat for New Westminster on the Fraser River—Got in at evening & had to lie over till this morning, waiting for another boat to take ... and here we are now steaming along in a bright, warm day against a rushing, boiling current, winding this way & that through a rugged chain of snowy mountains, many of them rising up for thousands of feet so steep that no living thing can climb.... There are numbers of Indians all through this region, & we see an encampment now & then, & see them paddling their eggshell canoes. They are peaceable & depend much upon trade with the whites for their living—

Monday—June 23—Little Lillooet Lake — after sailing up the Fraser river about 45 miles we turned into Harrison river, & 5 miles brought us to where it widened into a beautiful lake from one to 6 or 8 miles wide & 45 miles long. I wish you could see it. Snowy mountains & rocky cliffs rising straight up from the water, shutting out all the world but the blue sky overhead; islands & sharp points running out into the lake—making a picture of wild grandeur different from anything I ever saw before. We got to the upper end at 10 o'clock at night, where there is a shanty village called Port Douglas. Got our things ashore & blundered around in the dark to find a spot to camp, which we did without much trouble. From Douglas there is 29 miles of land travel to the next lake, where we are now. The next morning after landing we loaded the mule & made up packs for ourselves, each one carrying from 30 to 40 pounds, & away we went. It was very warm, my pack bore down heavy & my boots—iron heeled, soles nearly an inch thick & driven full of round headed nails—gave my poor feet a sorry rasping. I had too much clothing, & was soon drenched in sweat. We staggered along some 4 miles & stopped for dinner & a few hours rest; then we bucked to it again & stopped for the night after making altogether about 10 miles. The next day we did better—making 14 miles—though it was a rainy day and we were all sore—my feet the worst in the lot. We stopped at a wayside shanty for the night, paying two dollars apiece for our supper & breakfast. This morning we made the 5 miles to this lake in less than two hours, & here we must wait most of the day for a chance to sail up the lake to the next portage, as the strips of land separating the chain of lakes are called. We meet many men returning already. Most of them have not been through to Cariboo, but far enough to find out that they have not money enough to stand it. Most of those who have been there give the same reason for coming back—too early in the season & not money enough to be able to wait till the ground is in a fit state to work. For myself I expect nothing, & try to think as little as possible about it. I am in for it now & must see it out now if it takes my last dollar & leaves me "dead broke" in a foreign land—

June 26—Anderson Lake—We came up Lillooet Lake on Monday evening in a big clumsy boat, sending the mule around by a trail. It was a short trip—only 7 miles, & we got through & crossed the land portage—less than 2 miles —to Pemberton Lake before dark. Made camp for the night. Next morning bundled aboard a ricketty little steam boat & came to Pemberton City about 2 o'clock. Got dinner & started on the 30 mile portage to Lake Anderson, getting here early this morning—Thursday. & we are wasting a few hours for the boat to be loaded—

June 27—Seaton Lake—Made the trip down to Anderson— about 16 miles—packed up & hurried across the narrow portage—less than 2 miles—to catch the Seaton lake boat, but found they had only waited for those who had horses to ride, & she was a quarter of a mile off when we got to the landing. We sent some hearty curses after them for the scurvy trick & camped to lie over till today. There are many Indians all along the route. They work pretty well, packing over the portages, loading wagons & boats, &c & the squaws bring us branches of grass to sell—They have some customs different from Indians I have seen before. They bury their dead up in the air!—that is, they build a crib & stick it up on poles 15 to 30 feet high, sometimes leaning it against a large tree, and they put the bodies in these. Over & around them they hang flags, blankets, kettles—sometimes a gun—whatever belonged to them when alive, I suppose —I have seen quite a number of these burial places during the last few days, almost always in some place overlooking the water. The water through the whole country here is cold as ice water from the melting of the snows from every hill. I went in for a wash today. One plunge was enough.

July 4—well up on the Brigade route for Cariboo. No holiday for us, we must keep moving, though we would lie by & rest if the mosquitoes would not torment us. Night & day, at all times & all places they swarm upon us,—millions upon millions of all kinds. We are all but eaten by them, & yet we are told they are worse ahead—God pity us!—Came down Seaton Lake June 27— Next morning on to Lillooet City. Here we had to cross the Fraser river— more than 1/4 of a mile wide & boiling & surging along at the rate of 20 miles an hour.

Nothing larger than a whale boat to cross in. Took our load in, hitched poor mule to the stern, & away we went, my heart in my throat through fear of losing Billy. But we made the other shore all safe, half a mile or so further down, paid 25 cts apiece, & a dollar for the mule, & we were off at last, free from steamboats & dependent only on ourselves & Billy Mule. Every day we push ahead, over mountains, through green valleys, along lakes, & we have come at last into a region where we see no snowy mountains, nothing but low hills, grassy plains, & a great many ponds & small lakes. The days are very long—twilight till after 9 o'clock, & we travel early & late, resting 3 or 4 hours in the middle of the day. I have suffered much with my feet, but they are doing better now, & my health otherwise would be excellent, were it not for the colds I have caught, which have settled down to a troublesome cough.

My long spell in the printing office made me tender; but I think I shall soon harden to it.

Going to Cariboo is no play. We expect to be two weeks longer yet, & the worst of the road comes last. We still meet many poor fellows going back, a sorrowful looking set. They all went up too soon, & with too little money, so that high prices drove them back before the weather would allow them to prospect.

July 15—Almost in the diggings—Dragging along day by day—wet, tired, hungry & sleepy, I felt hardly able to write a full description of our journey as I had meant to do at first.

Today we draggled along in the rain over a miry trail till we got well soaked, when we made camp for the afternoon and dried out by a rousing fire—From all the accounts we hear from those going back the prospect is a gloomy one—but on we go to try our luck. Provisions are very dear—at Williams Lake, nearly a hundred miles back we bought 50 lbs flour, 18 lbs Bacon, 32 lbs Beans—100 lbs in all, for which we paid $90—The next we buy will be a dollar a pound we expect.

Aug. 6.—Nelson Creek—Cariboo—Got in to the new town of Van Winkle on Lightning Creek, on Saturday, July 18th. Provisions dear & scarce. Flour $1.25 a pound—tea $3.00, salt $5 for a 3 pound bag, nails $3 a pound & hardly any to be had. My partners growled all the way up because I thought best to bring some nails along,—they wish now we had brought all nails! Sold Billy Mule at once for $140, & I found on dividing our goods that I had provision enough to last me 5 or 6 weeks. Next day, Sunday, we rested, & on Monday I took blanket & grub for two weeks, stored the rest in a cabin at $1 a week, & came over to Nelson Creek to prospect for diggings. First bought a license to mine, good for a year—$5 for that. My partners got discouraged in a day or two & went off, & I expect they are out of Cariboo by this time. I then went in with two sailor boys from Martha's Vineyard who travelled part of the way up with us & came over to Nelson at the same time. Found some men who have been prospecting on the creek for 2 months, sinking shafts (wells, you would call them) trying to hit upon the deepest part of the channel where the gold always settles. They have the best looking chance on the creek, & as they had just got out of money & provision, they offered us an equal share with them if we would join them & feed two of them two weeks. We concluded to do so; so here we are, hard at work, the two weeks nearly up, & nothing certain known as yet. Yesterday I went back to Van Winkle & packed over all my things—70 pounds. If anybody thinks that it is fun let them try it—8 miles & back, over a mountain, deep sloppy mud nearly every foot of the way, & big logs to straddle & climb at every ten steps, it seems, & sometimes two or three of them together at that. Walk over that road in the morning & stagger back with a load of 70 pounds in the afternoon, & almost any lazy man would be satisfied with his day's work.

I am afraid Cariboo will swamp me as it has thousands of others. There are some few men who are getting out gold very fast. Some few claims are yielding as high as 150 pounds a week—report says more; but the great majority are getting nothing, most of the crowd, in fact, have been driven back by the high prices eating their money up before they had a chance to try for diggings. I have almost a mind to go back to California if I find nothing where we now are, but I hate to give up while there is yet a chance, however slight—I have still about $440, left out of $613 that I had on leaving Suisun, & I can manage to stand it here for the balance of the season & have enough left to pay my way back to California & there begin anew. Not a pleasant prospect at that, but I suppose I shall have to stand it. However, if I stay here I shall not fail through lack of trying.

Aug 10. Sunday. Broke down yesterday as far as this creek is concerned. Water came into the bottom of our shaft so fast that we cannot dig deeper without making a wheel & pump, & the prospects are not good enough to satisfy us in going to the expense. Today the two men we have been feeding start out for Cala. together with one of the sailor boys, who leaves so that his partner may have money enough to stay longer. As for me I don't know what to do. Inclination & judgment, too, as far as that goes say "Go back to Cal." God knows this is a hateful country—rain nearly all the time & all the country covered with a thick, heavy growth of gloomy firs, with the swampy, miry ground buried under fallen trees so that it is almost impossible to get along. Everybody

I see looks gloomy & discouraged, & it really seems hopeless to try to do more in Cariboo. In all my trials I never saw a darker time.

Sept. 8.—Still on Nelson—concluded to try to pick up a few dollars here, by scratching around where men worked last year rather than run around. Have made about $100 clear of expenses in the last month—rather slow for Cariboo. Today we have had snow & I suppose we must soon leave. I have little hope of now getting back the cost of the trip to say nothing of pay for my time, but I am thankful that I have not lost all like so many others. I am working very hard, every day, Sundays & all, & I shall be glad when forced to give it up. I do not know that I can earn anything here more than a few days longer, & I think I shall go to Williams' Creek, where there are very rich diggings & new discoveries being made. Some of the claims there pay twenty-five pounds of gold a day to each man working! More money in one day than I want to make me happy for life. Well I must grind along till my lucky day comes, & gather in my slow dollars one by one, only too happy if old age don't nip me before I get a little resting place in this wide world.

Sept. 28—On Nelson yet. Been scratching around steadily. Am now even on the cost of the trip & enough besides to take me back to Cala. Bad weather now—snowing & freezing nearly all the time. Most of the men have left the creek—only four left here now, & each one working & living by himself about a quarter of a mile from each other. Today my cabin mate went away. We started in to work together but he soon bought a bit of ground that was paying well—about $50 a day—giving $500. It fizzled out completely before he got half his money back, & now he strikes out for Williams' Creek. Would go myself & try for big diggings, but I cannot feel justified to leave $10 a day, & I am making that now with a fair show of doing so as long as I dare stay here—That cannot be many weeks more—Looks dubious now—If a deep snow comes on it will be a serious matter for me to get out. But my chief fear is of being robbed on my way down—many have been robbed and some murdered on the down trails. This country is all a wilderness & it is very easy for robbers to escape. No doubt there are many lying in wait for the big purses that have been growing fat up here & will soon be on the way out for the winter.

Oct. 5. Nelson Creek—Bad weather lately. The sun is fast working south & we see but little of it even when fair. It is freezing cold & scarce an hour without a snow squall.

Have been troubled with a nervous fear lest I should get snowed in, but at last concluded to take the chance & brave it out. I got the man working alone above to join me & prospect a place on the hill high above the creek. I think it will pay & if it will we shall have a good claim for next year. So I went over to Lightning today after more grub & got enough to stand me two weeks. Let in to snow in the morning & has been at it hard & steady ever since. It rather frightens me, but I am in for it now & must take the chances whether I will or not. We have got to dig a ditch & bring water on the ground we wish to prospect, & it will take us three or four days to test it, if it looks dangerous then to stay longer we will make a break out, if not we shall stay till our grub is nearly gone.

Found the town today nearly deserted, most of the men having gone below for the winter. I expect hard times getting out, but that don't scare me—it is the chance of getting blocked in & frozen or starved that makes me fearful. Wish now that instead of going for grub today I had packed up & got safely over the mountain that we have to cross at the head of Nelson. If it keeps on snowing this way there will be three feet of snow there tomorrow, & when we go we have to carry a load of blankets & grub. Hard to get in & harder to get out, this Cariboo.

Oct. 13. It was a bad night to us that of last date. Snow fell heavily & steadily all night. Could not sleep for nervousness, & about midnight the overloaded trees began to fall crashing down all around us. Went out & roused new partner Martin in cabin close by. Stood outside watching, & before he could find his boots a large tree which threatened us gave way by the roots. Yelled the alarm and out came Martin bare footed for dear life. He ran directly under the course of the tree, stumbled & fell & the tree crashed in the snow directly at his heels. A narrow escape & it seemed to frighten me more than it did him. After that we sat up till day in my cabin, rushing out at every crack & warning sound. I think we heard the fall of fifty trees & eight or nine fell that might have crushed us, but luckily they leaned the other way. The storm held up during the day & we went on with our work.

We got about discouraged on Tuesday the 7th & were about to make ready to leave, when we were surprised by the unexpected coming back of my old cabin mate from Williams Creek. He encouraged us to stand out a while longer, so we pitched in till yesterday, Sunday, & then went out after more grub, intending to stay ten days longer if possible. Most of last week we had snow & cold weather—& on Friday it began to rain, & on Saturday there was a heavy freshet. Sunday was a fine day but we had a hard time breaking a trail out to Lightning. The rain seemed to have packed it hard & made it worse. Today Monday, it has set in to rain again so that after getting well drenched we quit work about the middle of the afternoon. This weather is a surprise all around. Almost everybody has left the country believing that everything would be frozen by this time. So far I am loser by staying. Have spent about $50 for grub since Sunday before last

& have made nothing for it yet. We are trying a place now where we did expect to make $20 a day, but it does not look good now since we started in. Thought last evening when we got back to camp faint & worn out that I could never get out of this if another heavy snow should come, but after supper felt stronger & am taking the chances, now quite unconcernedly. By the way, the night of the great storm closed on the morning of my birthday I shall hardly forget it—

Oct. 17. Friday. Mild weather has held on till the snow is nearly gone. Diggings still turn out poorly—have not got our grub money back yet.... I am in a bad fix just now—got a raging boil coming—just at this particular time, & on my foot, too!—It seems as if the devil must have had a hand in it. Could not get out to work today—tried it—took me nearly an hour to get on my boot & hobble off 50 yards, then I just crawled back again. Right among the cords at the bend of the foot just above the instep—Who ever heard of such a thing—It is very late in the season for Cariboo, & if a big snow comes within a few days, how shall I, a cripple, get out? A serious question with me now.

Oct. 26. Sunday. Have had a sorry time since last date. My boil does not work well. Poulticed for 8 days till nothing more would run but blood & now I am dressing with salve. The skin has come off from a spot the size of a half dollar, leaving the raw flesh still swelled, hard, and sore. Pulled on my rubber boot yesterday for a trial, but was glad to squirm out of it again pretty quickly. Have suffered as much in my mind as in my body through fear of snow setting in. It holds off beyond all expectation. We have had some light falls, & Thursday & Friday last very cold, making anchors ice in the swift water. Yesterday was rainy clearing off in the night with a light snow—today as usual, cold gray clouds threatening snow. The sun runs so low here now that we can see it only about two hours at & near midday even when fair. Don't remember seeing the sun three times in the last three weeks. O, that I were out of this gloomy wretched country! Were I not a cripple I should feel at ease, for if snow set in steadily I could pack up & leave, sure of being able to fight my way out, but now my fears get the better of me.

[Note in pencil by another hand: "From all accounts lost trying to make Williams Creek. R.C.S. Randall."]

## 4. Matthew MacFie, *Vancouver Island and British Columbia,* 1865.

... Between March and June, in 1858, ocean steamers from California, crowded with gold-seekers, arrived every two or three days at Victoria. This place, previously a quiet hamlet, containing two or three hundred inhabitants, whose shipping had been chiefly confined to Indian canoes and the annual visit of the company's trading ship from England, was suddenly converted into a scene of bustle and excitement. In the brief space of four months 20,000 souls poured into the harbour. The easy-going primitive settlers were naturally confounded by this inundation of adventurers.

Individuals of every trade and profession in San Francisco and several parts of Oregon, urged by the insatiable *auri sacra fames*, threw up their employments, in many cases sold their property at an immense sacrifice, and repaired to the new Dorado. This motley throng included, too, gamblers, 'loafers,' thieves, and ruffians, with not a few of a higher moral grade. The rich came to speculate, and the poor in the hope of quickly becoming rich. Every sort of property in California fell to a degree that threatened the ruin of the State. The limited stock of provisions in Victoria was speedily exhausted. Flour, which on the American side sold at 2L. 8s. per barrel, fetched in Vancouver Island 6L. per barrel. Twice the bakers were short of bread, which had to be replaced with ship biscuit and soda crackers. Innumerable tents covered the ground in and around Victoria far as the eye could reach. The sound of hammer and axe was heard in every direction. Shops, stores, and 'shanties,' to the number of 225, arose in six weeks.

Speculation in town lots attained a pitch of unparalleled extravagance. The land-office was besieged, often before four o'clock in the morning, by the multitude eager to buy town property. The purchaser, on depositing the price, had his name put on a list, and his application was attended to in the order of priority, no one being allowed to purchase more than six lots. The demand so increased, however, that sales were obliged to be suspended in order to allow the surveyor time to measure the appointed divisions of land beforehand....

The bulk of the heterogeneous immigration consisting of American citizens, it was not wonderful that they should attempt to found commercial depots for the mining locality in their own territory. Consequently, they congregated in large numbers at Port Townsend, near the entrance to Puget Sound and at Whatcom in succession. Streets were laid out, houses built, and lots sold in those places. But inconveniences of various kinds hindered their success. Semiahmo, near the mouth of Fraser River, was next tried as the site of a port; but this rival city never had existence except on paper. These foreign inventors of cities obstinately refused to acknowledge the superior natural advantages of Victoria compared with the experimental ports they had projected. It is not speculators in new towns, however, but merchants and shippers that determine the points at which trade shall centre; and it is only that harbour which combines the greatest facilities for commerce, with the fewest risks to vessels, which is patronised by them. Victoria, judged by these tests, was found most eligible of all the competing places of anchorage in the neighbourhood....

While the majority—comprising Jews, French cooks, brokers, and hangers-on at auctions—stayed in Victoria for the purpose of ingloriously improving their fortunes, by watching the rise and fall of the real-estate market, several thousands, undismayed by dangers and hardships incident to crossing the gulf and ascending the river, proceeded to the source of the gold. When steamers or sailing-vessels could not be had, canoes were equipped by miners to convey them to British Columbia; but this frail means of transit, unequal to the risks of the passage, sometimes occasioned loss of life.

A monthly licence had to be taken out by all bound for the mines, and this gave them the right to take whatever provisions were required for individual use. At the outset steamers on the river allowed miners 200 lbs. and subsequently 100 lbs. free of charge; but they preferred in general to join in the purchase of canoes for sailing up the river as well as across the gulf.

The country drained by the Fraser resembles mountainous European countries in the same latitude, where streams begin to swell in June and do not reach their lowest ebb till winter. Those, therefore, who happened to enter the mining region in March or April, when the water was very low, succeeded in extracting large quantities of gold from the 'bars' or 'benches' not covered with water. The mass of immigrants not having arrived till a month or two later, found the auriferous parts under water. Ignorant of the periodic increase and fall of the stream to which I have adverted, their patience was soon exhausted waiting for the uncovering of the banks. Not a few, crestfallen and disappointed, returned to Victoria.

A gloomy impression began to prevail among the less venturesome spirits that tarried in this scene of morbid speculation. Gold not coming down fast enough to satisfy their wishes, thousands of them lost heart and went back to San Francisco, heaping execrations upon the country and everything else that was English; and lacing the reported existence of gold in the same category with the South Sea bubble. The rumour took wing that the river never did fall; and as placer-mining could only be carried on rivers, the state of the river became the barometer of public hopes, and the pivot on which everybody's expectations turned. This preposterous idea spread, was readily caught up by the press of California, and proved the first check to immigration. Another impediment was the commercial restrictions imposed by the Hudson's Bay Company in virtue of the term of their charter for exclusive trade in the interior not having yet expired.

A few hundred indomitable men, calmly reviewing the unfavourable sea-

son in which they had commenced mining operations, and the difficulties unavoidable to locomotion in a country previously untrodden for the most part by
white men, resolved to push their way forward, animated by the assurance that
they must sooner or later meet the object of their search and labour. Some settled
on the bars between Hope and Yale, at the head of navigation; others advanced
still higher, running hair-breadth escape, balancing themselves in passing the
brink of some dangerous ledge or gaping precipice encumbered with provisions
packed on their backs.

A new route was proposed via Douglas, at the head of Harrison Lake and
Lilloet, that should avoid the dangers and obstructions of the river trial. But this
did not at first mend matters; for the intended road lay through a rugged and
densely-wooded country, and much time and money required to be consumed
before it could be rendered practicable. Before the line for the Lilloet route was
generally known, parties of intrepid miners, anxious to be the first to reap its
benefits, tried to force their way through all the difficulties opposed to them.
The misery and fatigue endured by them was indescribable. They crept through
underwood and thicket for many miles, sometimes on hands and knees, with a
bag of flour on the back of each; alternately under and over fallen trees, scram-
bling up precipices, or sliding down over masses of sharp projecting rock, or
wading up to the waist through bogs and swamps. Every day added to their
exhaustion; and, worn out with privation and sufferings, one knot of adventurers after another became smaller and smaller, some lagging behind to rest, or
turning back in despair. The only thought seemed to be to reach the river ere
their provisions should give out. One large party was reduced to three, and when
they came to an Indian camp where salmon was to be had, one of these hardy
fellows made up his mind to return....

Nor was this case an uncommon one. Gold there was in abundance, but
want of access prevented the country from being 'prospected'; and reckless men,
without stopping to take this into account, condemned the mines and everything connected with them without distinction.

If the commerce of the interior had been thrown open, and private enterprise allowed to compete with the natural difficulties of the country, these would
have soon been overcome. Forests would have been opened, provisory bridges
thrown over precipices, hollows levelled, and the rush of population following
behind, the country would have been rapidly settled, and the trader have brought
his provisions to the miner's door.

Affairs in Victoria, meanwhile, grew yet more dismal. The 'rowdy' element
that had assembled in the city, finding no legitimate occupation to employ their
idle hands, were under strong temptation to create such disturbances as they had

been accustomed to get up in California. Losing, for the moment, that wholesome dread of British rule which that class usually feel, a party of them rescued a prisoner from the hands of the police, and actually proposed to hoist the American flag over the old Hudson's Bay Company's fort. But the news that a gunboat was on her way from Esquimalt to quell the riot, soon calmed alarm and restored peace.

Large sums of money, sent up from San Francisco for investment, were shipped back again; and whole cargoes of goods, ordered during the heat of the excitement, were thrown upon the hands of merchants. Jobbers had nothing to do but smoke their cigars or play at whist. Some accused the company; others complained of the Government; others sneered at 'English fogyism;' and others deplored the want of 'American enterprise.' 'Croaking' was the order of the day.

The Governor, seeing the tide of immigration receding, managed to control his prejudice against the 'foreigners' from a neighbouring state, so far as to moderate the severe restrictions he had put upon goods imported to British Columbia, and adopted more active measures in opening trails to the mines. But his tardy decision came too late to be attended with immediate benefit.

At length, however, the river did fall, and the arrival of gold-dust foreshadowed a brighter future. But sailing vessels left daily, crowded with repentant and dejected adventurers, whose opposition to the country had become so inveterate, that they could not now be made to believe in the existence of gold from Fraser River, though proved by the clearest ocular demonstration. The old inhabitants imagined that Victoria was about to return to its former state of insignificance.

Yet it is asserted, on reliable authority, that in proportion to the number of hands engaged upon the mines—notwithstanding the unequalled drawbacks in the way of reaching them—the yield during the first six months was much larger than it had been in the same period and at the same stage of development in California or Australia....

For a few intelligent and persevering men these facts and figures had weight. But amateur miners, romantic speculators, and 'whiskey bummers,' could not, by the most attractive representations, be detained in the country ... For such scouts of civilisation—had the 'castles in the air' which they built not been demolished—would have reenacted in our colonies such scenes of riot and bloodshed as disgraced California nine years previously. It was well that we should get rid of all who wanted impossibilities and indulged exaggerated hopes. The few hardy and enterprising settlers who remained ceased to pursue Will-o'-the-wisps, and composed themselves to the sober realities of life.

In September '59, when I first set foot in Victoria, the process of depopulation was still going on, though it soon after reached its lowest point. A healthy relation between supply and demand in every department was being effected. The tens of thousands that had pressed into the city in '58 were diminished to not more than 1,500, embracing 'the waifs and strays' of every nationality, not excepting a good many whose antecedents were not above suspicion.

Apart from the Government buildings, two hotels, and one shop, all the dwellings and houses of business were at that time built of wood. Many stores were closed and shanties empty. There was little business doing, and no great prospect ahead. This stagnant condition continued with but little abatement till the close of 1860, when intimations came of eminently productive mines being discovered at the forks of Quesnelle, which at that time seemed as difficult of access as the Arctic regions. A few scores of miners, arguing from the fineness of the gold dust found near Hope, Yale and the forks of the Thompson, that it was washed down from some quartz formation in the north, penetrated to the spot just referred to. Language fails to describe the trials these men endured from the utter absence of paths of any kind, the severity of winter climate, and often the scant supply of provisions. The theory by which the daring pioneers were guided was remarkably verified, and the toils of many of them were abundantly rewarded.

Their return to Victoria with bags of dust and nuggets rallied the fainting hopes of the community, and they were regarded as walking advertisements that the country was safe. Business immediately improved, the value of town property advanced; some who had been hesitating about erecting permanent buildings caught inspiration and at once plunged into brick-and-mortar investments.

The few scores that had worked on Antler Creek in '60 increased, in the spring of '61, to 1,500. Some addition to our population in the latter year came from California, and every man who could possibly make it convenient to leave Victoria for the season went to the new diggings. Of those who went, one-third made independent fortunes, one-third netted several hundreds of pounds, and one-third, from a variety of causes were unsuccessful....

The chief misfortune connected with the influx of population at this period was that it comprised an excessive proportion of clerks, retired army officers, prodigal sons, and a host of other romantic nondescripts, who indulged visions of sudden wealth obtainable with scarcely more exertion than is usually put forth in a pleasure excursion to the continent of Europe. These trim young fellows exhibited a profusion of leather coats and leggings, assuming a sort of defiant air, the interpretation of which was, 'We are the men to show you "Colonials" how to brave danger and fatigue!' But their pretensions generally evaporated with the breath by which they were expressed, and many that set out with this dare-all aspect were soon thankful to be permitted to break stones, chop wood, serve as stable-boys, or root out tree-stumps. The vague imaginations with which they left home were soon dissipated, when, on the termination of the voyage, they discovered that 500 miles lay between them and Cariboo— a distance which must be passed over muddy roads and frowning precipices, with whatever necessaries might be required for the trip strapped to their shoulders. Hundreds went half way to the mines, and returned in despondency; hundreds more remained in Victoria, and were only saved from starvation by the liberality of more prosperous citizens. A much larger number came than the country, with a deficient supply of roads, was prepared to receive. Still a considerable number made large amounts of money, and the majority of those who have possessed sufficient fortitude to bear inconveniences and battle against discouragements are in a fair way for speedily acquiring a competency....

It was remarked by an intelligent shipmaster, whom I met in Victoria, that he had not found in any of the numerous ports he had visited during a long sea-faring career, so mixed a population as existed in that city. Though containing at present an average of only 5,000 or 6,000 inhabitants, one cannot pass along the principal thoroughfares without meeting representatives of almost every tribe and nationality under heaven. Within a limited space may be seen— of Europeans, Russians, Austrians, Poles, Hungarians, Italians, Danes, Swedes, French, Germans, Spaniards, Swiss, Scotch, English and Irish; of Africans, Negroes from the United States and the West Indies; of Asiatics, Lascars and Chinamen; of Americans, Indians, Mexicans, Chilanos, and citizens of the North American Republic; and of Polynesians, Malays from the Sandwich Islands....

In description of resources Vancouver Island may resemble the parent country, and thus merit the proud title of 'the England of the Pacific.' But the peculiar elements composing the nucleus of the population render it physically impossible for that exact form of national character we have been accustomed to ascribe to Great Britain to be perpetuated in the island of the Far West. Does the presence, so largely, of inferior races forbode the fatal tainting of the young nation's blood and signal its premature decay, or will the vitality of the governing race triumph over the contamination with which more primitive types threaten to impregnate it? This is the important enquiry that engrosses the attention of ethnological speculators in the nascent communities of the North Pacific....

It is maintained also, that while by intermarrying with descendants of Europeans we are but reproducing our own Caucasian type, by commingling with eastern Asiatics we are creating debased hybrids; that the primary law of nature teaches self-preservation; and that such protective enactments as have been referred to are essential to the perpetuation and advancement of the nation.

Happily both these coloured races are admitted to the enjoyment of civil privileges in these colonies upon terms of perfect equality with white foreigners, and are alike eligible for naturalisation. Yet even on the British side of the boundary there is a disposition to look coldly upon the immigration of Celestials. It is alleged that so large an amount of Chinese labour must have the effect of reducing the price of white labour. But such an opinion is without foundation; for those Chinamen, who arrive without capital, are only capable of engaging in menial employments, such as cooking, hawking tea, and keeping laundries. It is but few skilled labourers, I presume, that would desire to compete with them in these callings. Nor can their presence at the mines at all interfere with the enterprises of the superior race; for it is well known that they are unable to resort to those mechanical appliances requisite in the working of rich diggings; that they always keep at a respectful distance from the whites, and are content with such small returns as may be yielded by abandoned 'claims,' from which the whites have already taken the cream.

As to the fear that, if access to the country were not made strait for them, they might ultimately overrun and devastate it like a plague of locusts, nothing could be more groundless. No people have a more intelligent acquaintance with 'the law of supply and demand.' They are generally under the direction of shrewd merchants among their own countrymen, who never encourage the poorer classes to leave China without being certain that a fair prospect of occupation exists for them in the parts to which they are imported; and in this respect the judgment of those leading Chinamen is rarely at fault. It must be acknowledged to their credit that in California, British Columbia, and Vancouver Island, an unemployed Chinaman is seldom to be met with, and a more industrious and law-abiding class does not reside in these dependencies. In their social and domestic habits, however, I frankly admit there is room for much improvement as far as cleanliness is concerned.

It is natural that a race so exclusive and so much avoided by their white fellow-citizens on the coast, should give preference to the manufactures of their own country. Much of the clothing they wear and many of their articles of food come from China. They contrive, it is true, to spend as little of their earnings as possible on their adopted soil—most of the money made by the humbler classes among them being remitted home for the laudable object of contributing to the support of needy relatives. But it is a mistake to regard the trade done and the capital acquired by them as so much wealth diverted from the channels of white industry, since but for their presence in the country the greater part of that trade would not have been created; nor would that capital have been accumulated. They cannot prevent commercial advantage accruing to the colonies from their influence, if they would. It is often British bottoms that convey them from China, and they are obliged to buy hardware, waterproof boots, and pork from us. Poultry, too, being esteemed a great luxury, is in great demand among them. When they have lived among the civilised for a time, it not unfrequently happens that they adopt the European and American costume entire....

The Chinese of Vancouver Island and British Columbia, only numbering at present about 2,000, have not yet attempted the erection of any places of devotion. But when attracted in greater force, the pious among them, according to the Buddhist standard, may be expected to erect fanes in which to celebrate traditional rites....

Whether, therefore, we consider the antiquity of these Mongols, their natural ingenuity, or the encouragement afforded by their national institutions to talent, integrity, and industry, the most cogent reasons exist for our extending to them a cordial welcome. Let the colonists show the fruits of a superior civilisation and religion, not in ridiculing and despising these Pagan strangers, but in treating them with the gentle forbearance due to a less favoured portion of the family of mankind, and they will continue to be useful and inoffensive members of society. The prejudice which characterises race or colour as a disqualification for the exercise of civil rights reflects dishonour upon the civilised community that indulges it.

The descendants of the African race resident in the colonies are entitled to some notice. About 300 of them inhabit Victoria, and upwards of 100 are scattered throughout the farming settlements of the island and British Columbia. The chief part came to the country some time previous to the immigration of '58, driven from California by social taboo and civil disabilities. They invested the sums they brought with them in land, and by the sudden advance in the value of real estate which followed the influx of gold seekers, most of them immediately found themselves possessed of a competency. It was not surprising, under these circumstances, that some, formerly habituated to servitude or reproached as representatives of a barbarous race, should, on being delivered from the yoke of social oppression, fail to show much consideration for the indurated prejudices of the whites, most of whom at that period were either Americans or British subjects, who sympathised with the ideas prevailing in the United States respecting the social status of the coloured people.

Whereas they had been restricted in California to worship Almighty God in their own churches or in a part of those frequented by whites, designed for the exclusive accommodation of persons of colour, they were permitted on coming to Vancouver Island free range of unoccupied pews, in the only church then erected in the colony. The church-going immigrants in the mass wafted to our shores in '58 were at once brought into a proximity with coloured worshippers which was repugnant to past associations. It is difficult to analyse this social prejudice between the races, and impossible to defend it. But I have been astonished to observe its manifestations in Christian gentlemen whose intelligence and general consistency were exemplary. The negro supporters of the church, regarding themselves as the 'old families' of the country and the monied aristocracy, and wincing under the recollection of social wrongs endured by them under the American flag, were not disposed to give way in the slightest to the whims and scruples of the whites. Many of the latter remonstrated with the clergyman against allowing the congregation to assume a speckled appearance—a spectacle deemed by them novel and inconvenient. They insisted that they were prepared to treat the "blacks" with the utmost humanity and respect, in their own place; but that the Creator had made a distinction which it was sinful to ignore, that the promiscuous arrangement might lead to the sexes in both races falling in love with each other, entering into marriage, and thus occasioning the deterioration of the whites without the elevation of the negroes being effected. The worthy parson, being direct from the parent country, and till then wholly inexperienced in the social relations of the conflicting races, felt at liberty to take only philanthropic and religious ground in dealing with the question. He maintained that the stains of men's sin, in common, were so dark, that mere difference in colour was an affair of supreme insignificance before the Almighty, in comparison, and that the separation desired by the whites was of carnal suggestion, which Christianity demanded should be repressed. He is said even to have gone so deeply into the subject in a particular sermon as to assert that the disposition of nerves, tendons, and arteries, and the essential faculties of the soul were alike in white and black—the sole distinction between them consisting of colouring matter under the skin, the projection of the lower jaw, and the wool by which the scalp was covered....

The same prejudice of race continues, unfortunately, to interfere with harmony in social gatherings for the purposes of amusement. More than once has the presence of coloured persons in the pit of the theatre occasioned scenes of violence and bloodshed, followed by litigation. When, a few years since, a literary institute was attempted to be formed, and the signatures of one or two respectable negroes appeared in the list of subscribers, the movement came to an untimely close. A white member of a temperance society, which was eminently useful In the community, proposed the name of a coloured man for admission, intentionally avoiding to disclose at the time any information as to his race, and when it was discovered that the society had been beguiled, ignorantly, into accepting a negro as a brother teetotaller, it broke up.

There is nothing in the constitution of the colony to exclude a British born negro from the municipal council or the legislature, and yet, however well qualified he might be by talent and education for the honour, his election could not be carried in the present state of public feeling. The negroes are perfectly justified in claiming those civil rights which British law confers upon them, and they are resolved not to desist struggling till these are fully achieved.

Having by commendable zeal succeeded in organising a rifle corps and a brass band, they expressed a wish to appear in uniform, on occasion of a public procession formed to escort the present Governor to his residence on landing in the colony. But the prejudice of the whites ruled it otherwise. When they sought an opportunity of showing esteem for the retiring Governor at a banquet given to that gentleman, admission was refused them. When the 'common-school' system is introduced, in which the families of both races are equally entitled to participate, I foresee that storms will arise.

Many of this people in the country are necessarily endowed with very limited intelligence, while some are well-informed, and eloquent in speech. But, as a race, they compare favourably with whites of corresponding social position, in industry and uprightness....

The Government officials constitute the centre of the social system (still in a formative state), and around it multitudes of broken-down gentlemen and certain needy tradespeople rotate. The most wealthy members of the community have, in general, more money than culture—a condition of things always incident to the early stage of colonial development. Many of them owe their improved circumstances simply to being the lucky possessors of real estate at a time when it could be bought for a nominal amount. Some who eight years ago were journeymen smiths, carpenters, butchers, bakers, public-house keepers, or proprietors of small curiosity shops in San Francisco or Victoria, are now in the receipt of thousands of pounds a year. Among this class there are those who bear their prosperity with moderation, while others indicate the limited extent of their acquaintance with the world by an air of amusing assumption.

There is a resident in the country who, in consideration of his past official relation to it, as first Governor of British Columbia, deserves passing notice in this place. I refer to Sir James Douglas. This gentleman is completely unknown in England, except at the Colonial Office and to a few directors of the Hudson's Bay Company. But being a local celebrity, the reader may not object to be introduced to so interesting a character. In stature he exceeds six feet. His countenance, by its weather-beaten appearance, still tells of many years spent in fur-trapping adventure, in the wilds of the interior. Introduced at the age of fifteen or sixteen from the West Indies, the reputed place of his birth, into the service of the company, and deprived, during the greater part of his life, of the advantages of society, except that of Indians, half-breeds, and persons like himself occupying humble situations in the employ of the company, every praise is due to him for not being indifferent to mental culture in those mountain solitudes in which the flower of his manhood was passed. The stateliness of his person—of which he always seems proudly conscious—and his natural force of character suggest the reflection to an observer, how vastly more agreeable would have been his address and powerful the influence of his character and abilities had he enjoyed in early life a liberal education and intercourse with persons of refinement and culture....

His efforts to appear grand, and even august, were ludicrously out of proportion to the insignificant population he governed—numbering less than the inhabitants of many a country town in England. When he spoke to anyone within the precincts of the Government House, his Quixotic notions of his office, which he evidently thought splendid, prompted him to make choice of the sesquipedalian diction he employed in his despatches. The angle of his head, the official tone, the extension of his hand, the bland smile which never reached beyond the corners of his mouth—all these stiff and artificial arrangements were carefully got up and daily repeated by him under the delusion that the public imagined him to be natural and a perfect Brummell in politeness. His manners always gave one the impression that to make up for early disadvantages he had religiously adjusted his whole bearing to the standard of Lord Chesterfield, and it is needless to say how amusing was the combination of his lordship and this dignified old furtrapper.

His attitude toward the officials serving under his government was austere and distant. This he had acquired under the sort of military regime observed between the officers and servants of the Hudson's Bay Company. I have heard magistrates addressed by him in a pompous manner that no English gentleman would assume toward his porter. But Sir James solemnly felt that 'the machine of state' could only be kept in motion by his delivering commands, with head erect, and with that rotund and peremptory utterance which at once betrayed and excused vulgarity.

He was rarely visible at his desk or in the street without being arrayed in semi-military uniform; but the climax of his extravagance was probably capped by his being followed perpetually, whether taking an airing in the country or going to visit, by an imposing orderly, duly armed and in uniform. In so small and practical a town as Victoria, the temptation of the local wits to satirise so preposterous a spectacle was irresistible.

Petty diplomacy was a passion with Sir James—doubtless developed, from his youth, in the wheedling mode of transacting business with the Indians, adopted by the company in the interior. He never sent away any suppliant for governmental favours without holding out some hope, which, at the same moment, he, in many cases, determined to frustrate. A favourite plan of his with any whom he thus sought to keep in good humour was to exhaust their patience by expedient and indefinite postponement of the object desired....

If the character of people is respectable, humble origin is felt to be much less a barrier to advancement in the colonies than in England. But in no part of the empire are shams so readily detected.

Let it not be supposed, however, that our female society is entirely composed of this or of any other class that is doubtful. It must be confessed, that there are too many females in both colonies as everywhere else, that reflect as little credit upon the land of their adoption as they did on the land of their birth. Still, we have among us ladies of birth and education, and, what is yet more important, of moral qualities that would render them an ornament to their sex in any part of the world.

Refugees from bankruptcy, disgrace, or family strife, suffered in some other part of the world, are to be met with in Victoria every few yards. But among the unfortunate are some of the most estimable men I have ever seen.

The tone of society has become decidedly more British since 1859; but still, as then, the American element prevails. Citizens of the United States may easily be known by their spare, erect, and manly figure. The business men among them are, for the most part, attired in superfine cloth, most frequently of a dark colour, and highheeled, broad-toed boots, of admirable fit. The coloured shooting-jacket, so frequently worn by Englishmen in the colony during the week, has no attraction for Americans.

For ethereal beauty, handsomeness, liveliness, and general intelligence, American ladies must be allowed to be eminently distinguished. That high refinement, which can only result from breeding and education, and is to be found in the foremost rank of British society, is without parallel among Americans. But it is my impression that the average of educated American ladies cannot be equalled, in interesting expression of countenance and brightness of intellect, by English ladies of the middle-class generally. The charming sweetness of the American beauty, however, fades prematurely, and at the age of 30, when a well-developed English lady is but in her prime, the smooth visage and transparent complexion of our fair cousin have been for years invaded by wrinkles.

Americans appear to me defective in conversational power. However rapid and distinct their speech may be, the diction employed by them is so stilted, and their forms of expression are so elaborate, as to contrast unfavourably with the terse idiomatic phraseology used by those Englishmen who are competent to wield their own language....

The intense pitch to which the feelings of people are strung in a gold-producing country is a frequent cause of insanity. Whether that malady exist in a greater degree in this community than in one of a more settled description, I am not sufficiently versed in the statistics of the subject to aver. But certainly a much larger proportion of cases have been personally known to me here than in the same period I ever saw in the much denser populations of England. I can reckon up eight persons—all of whom I have been on speaking terms with, and most of whom I knew intimately, who, in four years and a half, have become lunatics, and as such are either living or dead....

The immigrant accustomed to the distinctions of class obtaining in settled populations of the old world, will be struck to observe how completely the social pyramid is inverted in the colonies. Many persons of birth and education, but of reduced means, are compelled, for a time after their arrival, to struggle with hardship, while the vulgar, who have but recently acquired wealth, are arrayed in soft clothing and fare sumptuously. Sons of admirals and daughters of clergy-men are sometimes found in abject circumstances, while men only versed in the art of wielding the butcher's knife, the drayman's whip, and the blacksmith's hammer, or women of low degree, have made fortunes....

Society in the interior is very depraved. In Yale, Douglas, Lytton, Lilloet, Forks of Quesnelle, and the mining towns, little trace of Sunday is at present visible, except in the resort of miners on that day to market for provisions, wash-ing of dirty clothes, repairing machinery, gambling, and dissipation. Out of the 5,000 souls in Victoria, a few may be found who respect the ordinances of reli-gion. But at the mines, adherents of religious bodies have hitherto been numbered by scores and units.

Up to the present there have been but two places of worship in Cariboo—one connected with the Church of England, and the other with the Wesleyan Methodists. Till the fall of 1863, when these were built, the services of public worship were conducted in a bar-room and billiard-saloon. At one end of the apartment was the clergyman, with his small congregation, and at the other were desperadoes, collected unblushingly around the faro or pokah table, staking the earnings of the preceding week.

Profane language is almost universal, and is employed with diabolical ingenuity. The names of 'Jesus Christ' and the 'Almighty' are introduced in most blasphemous connections. Going to church is known among many as 'the religious dodge,' which is said to be 'played out,' or, in other words, a superstition which has ceased to have any interest for enlightened members of society....

The slang in vogue in the mining regions is imported mainly from California, and is often as expressive as it is original. 'Guessing' and 'calculating' are exercises of perpetual occurrence. If one have the best of a bargain, he is said to have got 'the dead wood' on the other party in the transaction. A mean and greedy man is 'on the make;' and where a 'claim' is to be disposed of, the proprietor is 'on the sell.' A conceited man thinks himself 'some pumpkins;' and when any statement is made, the exact truth of which is doubted, it is said to be 'rayther a tall story.' When a claim disappoints the hopes of those interested in it, it has 'fizzled out.' Credit is 'jaw-bone;' and in one store on the road to Cariboo, the full-sized jaw-bone of a horse is polished, and suspended on the wall, with the words written under: 'None of this allowed here.' The ground of the allusion is evident, the product resulting from the motion of the jaw being the only security a needy purchaser has to offer. Another expression for wanting credit is 'shooting off the face.' Deceit in business is 'shananigan.' A good road, steamboat, plough, dinner, or anything else you please, is 'elegant.' When one has run off to avoid paying his debts, he has 'skedaddled,' or 'vamoosed the ranch;' or if hard-up, he wants to 'make a raise.' Owing to the remoteness of British Columbia from other centres of British population, it is called the 'jumping-off place'—another phrase for the end of the world. Any issue likely to arise from a given chain of events, is seen 'sticking out.' When two parties are playing into each other's hands, with a sinister object in view, it is a case of 'logrolling.' When the conduct of any one renders him liable to a whipping or something worse, he is 'spotted.'

Among the roughest of professional miners, exhibitions of kindness occur fitted to shame many of more moral pretensions. As a class, they are not avaricious. It is not so much the possessing of money, as the excitement attending the acquisition of it, that affords them satisfaction. It were more conducive to their welfare could they be induced to cultivate more thrifty habits. If the patronage they recklessly bestow upon public-houses were withdrawn, and the vast sums thus squandered diverted into productive channels, the spirit of legitimate enterprise would be fostered, and the resources of the country be more rapidly developed.

The sentiment of 'pure and undefiled religion' does not flourish at present in the colonies. In the Protestant world on the Pacific coast, the religious sect to which a man is attached may commonly be determined by the extent of his business. Small retailers and mechanics swarm among the Methodists; jobbers, who break packages, and the larger class of store-keepers, frequent the Presbyterian and Congregational chapels; and the bankers, lawyers, and wholesale dealers prefer the Church of England. Just as with their augmented resources they erect comfortable houses, so they seek to provide themselves with a church suited to their advanced social position. The utilitarian tendencies of the people are such, that eloquent or spiritual preaching by itself will not attract worshippers. Their comfort must be consulted, as it respects the place of worship erected, and their emotions must be appealed to through the medium of an organ and an efficient choir.

Religious scepticism prevails to a remarkable extent, as it does in all new countries. I have known cases in which Christian pastors have been turned away from the bedside of the dying colonist, and forbidden by him either to offer prayer to Almighty God for his restoration to health, or administer the consolations of the Gospel. But I trust such cases of extreme obduracy are not common....

In a country where so many are governed by impulse, and rendered desperate by losses sustained in speculation, it is not surprising that instances of highway robbery and murder should occasionally happen. The commission of these crimes, however, as in California and Australia, has been hitherto confined to solitary intervals, between the towns of British Columbia, on the way to the mines. The proportion of crime, at present, is decidedly small, considering the character and number of the population....

## Readings

Bescoby, I. "Society in Cariboo During the Gold Rush," in T. Thorner, ed., *Sa Ts'E: Historical Perspectives on Northern British Columbia*. Prince George: College of New Caledonia Press, 1989.

Careless, J. "The Business Community in the Early Development of Victoria, British Columbia," in D. Macmillan, ed., *Canadian Business History: Selected Studies, 1497–1971*. Toronto: McClelland and Stewart, 1972.

Careless, J. "The Lowe Brothers, 1852–70: A Study in Business Relations on the North Pacific Coast," in W. Ward and R. McDonald, eds., *British Columbia: Historical Readings*. Vancouver: Douglas and McIntyre, 1981.

Clark, S. "Mining Society in British Columbia and the Yukon," in P. Ward and R.

McDonald, eds., *British Columbia: Historical Readings*. Vancouver: Douglas and McIntyre, 1981.

Fisher, R. *Contact and Conflict: Indian European Relations in British Columbia, 1774–1890*. Second edition. Vancouver: University of British Columbia Press, 1992.

Gough, B. "The Character of the British Columbia Frontier," *BC Studies* 32 (1976–77).

Gough, B. *Gunboat Frontier: British Maritime Authority and the Northwest Coast Indians, 1846–1890*. Vancouver: University of British Columbia Press, 1984.

Gough, B. "'Turbulent Frontiers' and British Expansion: Governor James Douglas, the Royal Navy and the British Columbia Gold Rushes," *Pacific Historical Review* 41 (1972).

Gresko, J. "'Roughing It in the Bush' in British Columbia: Mary Moody's Pioneer Life in New Westminster, 1859–1863," in G. Creese and V. Strong-Boag, *British Columbia Reconsidered: Essays on Women*. Vancouver: Press Gang, 1992.

Harris, R. *The Resettlement of British Columbia: Essays on Colonialism and Geographical Change*. Vancouver: University of British Columbia Press, 1997.

Karr, C. "James Douglas: The Gold Governor in the Context of His Times" in B. Norcross, ed., *The Company on the Coast*. Nanaimo: Nanaimo Historical Society, 1983.

Loo, T. *Making Law, Order and Authority in British Columbia 1821–1871*. Toronto: University of Toronto Press, 1994.

Mackie, R. "The Colonization of Vancouver Island, 1849–1858," *BC Studies* 96 (1992–93).

Marshall, D. "Rickard Revisited: Native 'Participation' in the Gold Discoveries of British Columbia," *Native Studies Review* 11, 1 (1996).

Roy, P. *A White Man's Province: British Columbia Politicians and Chinese and Japanese Immigrants 1858–1914*. Vancouver: University of British Columbia Press, 1989.

Sterne, N. Fraser. *Gold 1858! The Founding of British Columbia*. Pullman: Washington State University Press, 1998.

Ward. P. *White Canada Forever: Popular Attitudes and Public Policy Toward Orientals in British Columbia*. Second edition. Montreal: McGill-Queen's University Press, 1990.

Williams, D. "The Administration of Criminal and Civil Justice in the Mining Camps and Frontier Communities of British Columbia," in L. Knafla, ed., *Law and Justice in a New Land: Essays in Western Canadian Legal History*. Toronto: Carswell, 1986.

Williams, D. '...The Man for a New Country': Sir Matthew Baillie Begbie*. Sidney: Gray Publisher, 1977.

Woodward, F. "The Influence of the Royal Engineers on the Development of British Columbia," *BC Studies* 24 (Winter 1974–1975).

Van Kirk, S. "A Vital Presence: Women in the Cariboo Gold Rush, 1862–1875," in G. Creese and V. Strong-Boag, *British Columbia Reconsidered: Essays on Women*. Vancouver: Press Gang, 1992.

## Chapter Fifteen

# "The Sweet Zephyrs of British Land": The Black Experience

1. Jehu Jones, "To Charles Ray," August 8, 1839.
2. Mary Ann Shadd Cary, *Plea for Emigration*, 1852.
3. Samuel Ward, "To Messrs. Bibb and Holly," October 1852.
4. Fielding Smithea, "Mr. Editor," *British Colonist*, June 10, 1859.
5. William Brown, "The Colored People of Canada" *Pine and Palm*, September–December 1861.
6. S. Howe, *The Refugees from Slavery in Canada West: Report to the Freedman's Inquiry Commission*, 1864.

## Introduction

If there is one thing that Canadians believe that sets them apart, particulary from the United States, it is our tolerance and inclusiveness of visible minorities and different cultures. Today, government sanctioned multiculturalism encourages the celebration of diversity. But the historical record suggests that we have been anything but tolerant. What happened to blacks in British North America in the pre-Confederation era is a prime example.

The black presence in Canada goes back almost to the beginning of European settlement though their number remained small and relegated to a very few domestic slaves owned by wealthy French-Canadians. This situation was very different from the southern New England colonies where thousands of slaves constituted a large percentage of the population and formed an integral part of the agricultural economy.

The first large group of free blacks to arrive in British North America in any number came as Loyalists fleeing the American Revolution. Britain had promised them freedom if they revolted against their American pro-revolutionary masters and supported the English cause. While they received land and provisions like other Loyalists, "Nova Scarcity" turned out to be a bitterly cold and painful experience. In 1782, Canada's first race riot occurred at Shelburne. Life in New Brunswick turned out even worse with its restrictions on where blacks could fish, settle, with whom they could consort, and a myriad of other colour-based discriminatory laws. It made life very tough indeed, and ensured that many newly freed slaves failed to cope.

Many people considered slavery both natural and vital, abolitionist sentiments did gain momentum in Britain toward the end of the eighteenth century, but not without considerable controversy. Pro-slavery advocates contended that blacks were inherently inferior and incapable of either handling freedom or of integrating into society. The anti-abolitionist faction dismissed these claims, arguing that a slave's shortcomings sprang from bondage. Though it existed, racial-based prejudice was certainly muted in Upper Canada compared to in the United States. Then, in 1793, John Graves Simcoe, the governor of the new colony, convinced the Assembly to pass a bill outlawing the importation of slaves and providing for the gradual emancipation of those already in bondage.

The second major influx of blacks arrived in the new colony of Upper Canada after the War of 1812 and did so as a result of changing conditions in the Northern United States. Free blacks and runaway slaves settled in relatively large numbers in northern slave-free states after America's independence, particularly in urban centres. Integration proceeded reasonably peaceably. Then, after about 1820, the United States experienced economic woes, a wave of new European immigrants, and a commensurate scramble for a diminishing number of jobs. Blacks lost the contest to a series of new rules and regulations that increasingly marginalized and persecuted them. Anti-black riots, violence, and harassment became common in many northern American cities. The new anti-black sentiment culminated in the federal Fugitive Slave Law of 1850, which allowed Southern slave owners to track down runaway slaves seeking sanctuary in northern slave-free states. Slave hunting became a lucrative business, and many an ex-slave, some with years of liberty, found himself kidnapped back to Kentucky and bondage.

Slavery remained legal in Britain, and thus in British North America, until the Emancipation Bill of 1833 formally abolished it and codified the notion that "every man is free who reaches British soil." This bill, plus the implications of the Fugitive Slave Law, gave great impetus for blacks to flee to Canada and freedom. Southern American slave owners, needless to say, resented this shift, particularly in the face of a steady flow of slaves escaping via the underground railway that emerged to secret them to safety. They pressured the American federal government to push for an extradition treaty with Canada, but British administrators concluded that slavery was inconsistent with British law and therefore demurred. Virtually no slave who reached Canada faced deportation.

Canada, and particularly Upper Canada, not surprisingly gained mytho-
logical status among slaves, as exemplified by abolitionist George W. Clark's
song "The Free Slave":

> *I'm on my way to Canada*
> *That cold and distant land*
> *The dire effects of slavery*
> *I can no longer stand—*
> *Farewell, old master,*
> *Don't come after me.*
> *I'm on my way to Canada*
> *Where coloured men are free.*

And the myth held truth. Runaway slaves and free blacks arriving on the
Upper Canadian frontier generally received generous support from a network
of black and white abolitionists, including material assistance and welcome
into the community. Courts in most instances acted impartially, even prosecut-
ing those harassing the newcomers. Many blacks found themselves invited to
local churches and their children attended publicly funded schools without
colour bars.

However, all was not sweetness and light. Though Upper Canadian laws
were supposedly colourblind, local citizens often were not. This was perhaps the
greatest problem blacks faced upon arrival. Racism tended to be covert rather
than overt, and thus beyond the impartiality of the legal system. Many Upper
Canadian whites feared the black presence and reacted by ostracizing black newcomers—which was perfectly legal and considered normal behaviour. Many did
not wish their children educated among blacks, arguing that proximity begged
trouble, especially considering rumours of black sexual promiscuity and allure.
In some regions parents successfully lobbied for legislation to create separate
schools for black children. Churchgoers in other areas called for distinct churches
for blacks, or at least segregated pews within the building. Public snubbing remained perhaps the greatest visible indicator that, the law aside, many whites in
Canada did not consider the newcomers as equal brethren at all. The hundreds
of minor racial slurs cumulatively made life unpleasant and difficult for many
black newcomers, and also gave rise to the notion of Canadians as a "politely
racist" people— a far cry from the myth of tolerance.

The black community itself remained divided on how best to develop a
peaceful coexistence in the new land, or at least what to do next. Integrationists

believed that blacks must abandon black culture and meld into mainstream society in every way if they were to become genuinely equal partners in the Canadian fabric. Segregationists, on the other hand, contended that black salvation lay in distancing the community from white society by creating separate settlement lands, churches, schools, and other social institutions. They, as a group, supported white bids for separate schools. A third organization of blacks argued that Canada should be a mere transit point en route to Sierra Leone or Liberia, two new states bought in West Africa with philanthropic abolitionist money. Haiti, the first independent black nation in the Americas, also beckoned, as did Jamaica. All four destinations, but particularly the two African nations, attracted considerable numbers of immigrants.

Blacks in Canada never amounted to more than one per cent of the population, but there were areas where concentrations rose to as high as thirty-three per cent. In all, some 62,000 blacks called British North America home, two thirds of whom settled in what is today southern Ontario. Though approximately two thirds of the black population arrived in the decades after the 1830s, many newcomers saw Canada as a temporary sanctuary rather than as "home," and pined for the day when they could safely return to the United States. This occurred after the Emancipation Proclamation in 1863, by which the Americans made slavery illegal. Canada experienced a large exodus of blacks who returned to their native lands. Canada West (Ontario), for example, saw its black population decline from a peak of 40,000 in 1859 to some 15,000 by 1871.

## Discussion Points

1. To what degree, if any, can Canada boast about its tolerance for ethnic diversity? Were Canadians actually less racist than Americans?
2. What were the greatest obstacles that blacks faced within Canada?

## Documents

### 1. Jehu Jones, "To Charles Ray," August 8, 1839.

Toronto, U[pper] C[anada]
My dear sir:
I am persuaded that you will be pleased to know, that, under the blessings of

Divine Providence, I enjoy good health, and what are the impressions that was first made upon my feelings, which have been actively engaged for seven years in the States, carefully looking out for a home, but without success, to more favorable prospects under the crown of Great Britain....

Rev. Mr. Miller and myself were also invited to a tea party at Mrs. Wilson's in Elizabeth Street, got up by the ladies of Toronto, in honor of the day. I scarcely need to add that the ladies sustained themselves, and the company in one of the neatest and social entertainment, that I ever had the pleasure to witness; at a late hour, worn down with the fatigue, incident to the occasion, I returned to my lodgings to contemplate on the magnanimity of the British nation, who under God, have given liberty to all her slaves. So, sir, you can readily perceive, that since first I inhaled the sweet zephyrs of British land, that it has made deep Impressions upon my heart, not easily to be forgotten—having been introduced to his honor the Mayor, who received and welcomed me in the most cordial, and friendly manner; I visited the city, public buildings, barracks, and the soldiers....

There is a regiment composed entirely of colored men—the commissioned officers are white. I have seen several of the members in this city—the corps are stationed on the Frontier. Great confidence is reposed in this regiment, and they have the most important post, in consequence of their acknowledged loyalty to the British Crown. When I reflect upon the known and acknowledged advantages to be derived by colored men, emigrating into the British provinces, where all distinction of caste is despised, and man known by his merits and loyalty to the Queen and country, I cannot but enquire how is it, that my brethren of the Northern States, who have the advantages of coming over, to examine the province for themselves, and to scrutinize the state of society, and report the result of their investigation in this matter have neglected to do so, it appears that our attention has never been properly directed or we have failed to accomplish any good end, can we always remain in a country, where prejudice against our complexion—which God and nature gave us—operates with violent and unholy hands upon us, to frown—wither and crush us for ever—even the prospects of comfortable living in security of the person and property of colored men are doubtful, and although there are no positive legislative enactments in the professedly free States, to deny us the privileges of advancing in knowledge and understanding of mechanical business and trades; still the blighting influence of prejudice, is so extraordinarily great, that it triumphs over every attempt as yet that has been made to give correct instructions to colored youths, in various & useful branches of mechanicism. I must confess and acknowledge it is passing strange, that there should be so many intelligent and some learned men, residing in the Northern States, that are in possession of ample wealth for any good purpose—still as if infatuated, remain there deprived of every political and of many moral and religious liberties; whilst the kingdom of Great Britain is open to all men where life, liberty, and the pursuits of happiness, without dissimulation, is distributed with an equal hand, to all men, regardless of the country or condition of any. This province especially, seems to invite colored men to settle down among the people, and enjoy equal laws. Here you need not separate into disgusting sect of caste. But once your elastic feet presses the provincial soil of her Britannic Majesty, Queen Victoria, God bless her, you become a man, every American disability falls at your feet—society—the prospects of society, holds out many inducements to men of capital; here we can mingle in the mass of society, without feeling of inferiority; here every social and domestic comforts can be enjoyed irrespective of complexion. Tell my young countrymen this subject requires their most profound consideration—the subject of being in reality free men....

## 2. Mary Ann Shadd Cary, *Plea for Emigration*, 1852.

In Canada, as in other recently settled countries, there is much to do, and comparatively few for the work. The numerous towns and villages springing up, and the great demand for timber and agricultural products, make labour of every kind plentiful. All trades that are practised in the United States are there patronized by whomsoever carries on: no man's complexion affecting his business. If a coloured man understands his business, he receives the public patronage the same as a white man. He is not obliged to work a little better, and at a lower rate. There is no degraded class to identify him with, therefore every man's work stands or falls according to merit, not as is his colour. Builders and other tradesmen of different complexions work together on the same building and in the same shop, with perfect harmony, and often the proprietor of an establishment is coloured, and the majority of all of the men employed are white....

In the large towns and cities, as in similar communities in other Christian countries, the means for religious instruction are ample. There are costly churches in which all classes and complexions worship, and no "negro pew," or other seat for coloured persons, especially. I was forcibly struck, when at Toronto, with the contrast the religious community there presented, to our own large body of American Christians. In the churches, originally built by the white Canadians, the presence of coloured persons, promiscuously seated, elicited no comment whatever. They are members, and visitors, and as such have their pews according to their inclination, near the door, or remote, or central, as best suits them. The number of coloured persons attending the churches with whites constitutes a minority, I think. They have their "own churches."

That that is the feature in their policy, which is productive of mischief to the entire body, is evident enough; and the opinion of the best informed and most influential among them, in Toronto and the large towns, is decided and universal. I have heard men of many years residence, and who have, in a measure, been moulded by the better sentiment of society, express deep sorrow at the course of coloured persons, in pertinaciously refusing overtures of religious fellowship from the whites; and in the face of all experience to the contrary, erecting Coloured Methodist, and Baptist, and other Churches. This opinion obtains amongst many who, when in the United States, were connected with coloured churches. Aside from their caste character, their influence on the coloured people is fatal. The character of the exclusive church in Canada tends to perpetuate ignorance, both of their true position as British subjects, and of the Christian religion in its purity....

The refugees express a strong desire for intellectual culture, and persons often begin their education at a time of life when many in other countries think they are too old. There are no separate schools. At Toronto and in many other places, as in the churches, the coloured people avail themselves of existing schools; but in the western country, in some sections, there is a tendency to "exclusiveness." The coloured people of that section petitioned, when the School Law was under revision, that they might have separate schools. There were counter-petitions by those opposed, and to satisfy all parties, twelve freeholders among them, can, by following a prescribed form, demand a school for their children; but if other schools, under patronage of Government, exist, (as Catholic or Protestant), they can demand admission into them, if they have not one. They are not compelled to have a coloured school....

Much has been said of the Canadian coloured settlements, and fears have been expressed by many that by encouraging exclusive settlements, the attempt to identify coloured men with degraded men of like colour in the States would result, and as a consequence, estrangement, suspicion, and distrust would be induced. Such would inevitably be the result, and will be, shall they determine to have entirely proscriptive settlements. Those in existence, so far as I have been able to get at facts, do not exclude whites from their vicinity; but that settlements may not be established of that character, is not so certain.

Dawn, on the Sydenham River, Elgin, or King's Settlement, as it is called, situated about ten miles from Chatham, are settlements in which there are regulations in regard to morals and the purchase of lands bearing only on the coloured people; but whites are not excluded because of dislike. When purchase was made of the lands, many white families were residents; at least, locations were not selected in which none resided. At first, a few sold out, fearing that such neighbours might not be agreeable; others, and they the majority, concluded to remain, and the result attests their superior judgement. Instead of an increase of vice, prejudice, improvidence, laziness, or a lack of energy, that many feared would characterize them, the infrequency of violations of law among so many, is unprecedented. Due attention to moral and intellectual culture has been given; the former prejudices on the part of the whites have given place to a perfect reciprocity of religious and social intercommunication. Schools are patronized equally; the gospel is common, and hospitality is shared alike by all....

The coloured subjects of Her Majesty in the Canadas are, in the general, in good circumstances, that is, there are few cases of positive destitution to be found among those permanently settled. They are settled promiscuously in cities, towns, villages, and the farming districts; and no equal number of coloured men in the States, north or south, can produce more freeholders. They are settled on, and own portions of the best farming lands in the Province, and own much valuable property in the several cities. There is, of course, a difference in the relative prosperity and deportment in different sections, but a respect for, and observance of the laws, is conceded to them by all. Indeed, much indifference on the part of whites has given place to genuine sympathy, and the active abolitionists and liberal men of the country look upon that element in their character as affording ground for hope of a bright future for them, and as evidence that their sympathy for the free man is not misplaced, as more than compensation for their own exertions for those yet in bonds....

Notwithstanding the prosperity and liberal sentiment of the majority, there is yet a great deal of ignorance, bigotry, prejudice, and idleness. There are those who are only interested in education so far as the establishment of separate schools and churches tends to make broad the line of separation they wish to make between them and the whites. They are active to increase their numbers, and to perpetuate, in the minds of the newly arrived emigrant or refugee, prejudices, originating in slavery, and as strong and objectionable in their manifestations as those entertained by whites toward them.

## 3. Samuel Ward, "To Messrs. Bibb and Holly," October 1852.

Messrs. Bibb & Holly

Gentlemen:

... I now proceed to my second point, the comparing of Canada, with Yankee negro hate.

1. Canadian Negro Hate, is incomparably MEANER than the Yankee article. The parties who exhibit most of this feeling, are as poor, as ignorant, as immoral, as low, in every respect as the most degraded class of negroes. In numerous instances, are they very far below them. No one can visit Canada, or any part of Canada, without seeing this, if his eyes be open. Our recently arriving slaves, are, in all respects quite equal to our newly arrived emigrants from Europe, and the free blacks coming from the United States are quite comparable to any class of whites, coming from the same country. The meanness of negro hate, therefore, is greater and lower, than that of the United States, as it is the setting up of one class of poor ignorant people, against another, by themselves, with just nothing under the moon, to boast of. In the United States, we are slaves, and but demi-freemen, if not all slaves. Here we all stand on a legal and political equality. The blacks [are] as free as the whites, and in law and in fact quite equal to them. Hence the greater meanness of Canadian than American Negro Hate.

Again Canadian Negro Hate is NOT ORIGINAL. Copied aped deviltry is always meaner than the original diabolism. But the negrophobia of Canada, is a poor pitiable, brainless, long eared imitation of Yankeeism, certain parties, go to Yankeedom to work. They return with Yankee cash, and Yankee ideas, and deal out both, in small quantities around their respective neighborhoods. In other cases, Yankees come here to reside. They bring their negrophobia with them. Canadians of the smaller sort catch the infection, straight way, go to aping their Yankee neighbors in this thing, in an awkward manner, and upon a very small scale. All they know is what they have heard, all they feel is second-handed. A meaner set of negro haters, God in his inexplicable mercy, does not suffer to live, than these poor fools of Canadian second-handed imitations.

But the greater meanness of this feeling, here, is also, in the fact that it is *gratuitous*. The whole world despise[s] gratuitous deviltry. A Yankee, commends himself to his richer more aristocratic neighbors, by his negrophobia. He puts himself on the side of Yankee fashion, by it. He sells more of his wares, in this way: he gets trade with men-stealers, and women-whippers, and human flesh mongers by it. If he be a priest he renders himself more acceptable to the occupants of the *front pews*, by it. If a politician he gets more votes, because he better pleases his slave-holding masters, by it. It is to him, therefore, a fair matter about which to *"calculate."* But not one word of this, applies to the Canadian. All he does, in this matter, is gratuitous: a devil serving without reward, in any possible shape. Bad and mean as is Yankee Negro Hate, it cannot be called as the Canadian article can *disinterested deviltry.* Be sure, as Hiram Wilson says, "it came from Hell by way of the United States," but it was *damaged* terribly in the passage hitherwards.

It should be added that the Yankees who bring this thing with them, and *peddle* it about the province appear meaner than they do at home, inasmuch as they come here for the same reason as we blacks come, to better our conditions. I look upon them just as I look upon an Irishman in the United States, who tramples upon blacks who helped to fight for the very liberties which these Irish paupers enjoy, and of which they seek to deprive the blacks.

2. Unlike the Yankee product of the same name, Canadian Negro Hate, here has neither the current religion, nor the civil law, to uphold it. Steam-boat Captains, and Hotel keepers referred to above would be fined if brought before our courts, for their maltreatment of black persons. The British law knows no man by the color of his skin. In Yankeedom, negroes have no legal protection against such outrages. I never knew of but one instance, of a colored person receiving damages against a Steam-boat, for maltreatment in the United States. Instances here are numerous. A Hotel in Canada, forfeits its licence by treating a man as Mr. O'Banyan was treated. Trustees, who deny a black child the right of attending school, forfeit £5, each, and lose the Government money for their school. In Boston, no such punishment can be brought upon the white trustees, who exclude black children from the school.

Not a single denomination, have we in Canada, where ministers uphold or sanction this illegal and unchristian treatment of black persons. I have travelled much, and mingled freely with all sects, and I find it invariably true that in their places of worship and in their religious devotions whites and blacks, are on a common footing. The Holy Trinity, is the richest Episcopal church in Canada, equality—prevails there. Knox's church is the largest Free Presbyterian church in Canada, the same is true there. So in the Congregational church, so in the Methodist, so also in the Roman Catholic. Individuals belonging to each of these communions, ministers and laymen, may and do *enjoy* this beautiful brotherly negro hate. But the thing is far from being general. Indeed on this part of all denominations I have received uniformly, the treatment of a christian gentleman. There are not one dozen places in the United States, where so much can be said.

You will readily judge from the last point, that Canadian Negro Hate can not be eternal. The labors of the anti-slavery society, the improvement, progress, and good demeanor of the black people will, in a very short time, undermine and destroy this abomination, unless, certain things, to which I shall presently refer, exert an unhappy influence. Having law, religion, and British example at headquarters against it, Canadian negrophobia, cannot long abide. When publicly attacked, it hides its head from the indignant gaze of a condemning community. The pulpit, in ninety-nine cases of an hundred could be marshalled against it, at any time. The Press (which in too many instances is far from being what it should be) condemns it, through the most influential papers in our Province. It is therefore, quite destitute of the influences which keeps it alive in our native land, let a hundredth part, of as much be done, here, against it as in the United States, in the shape of direct attack and it would disappear altogether.

There is this to be said, however, touching this feeling here. Ours is an aristocratic country. We make here, no pretentions to "social equality," "Republicanism," "Democracy" all that. Many blacks come here, and finding that they are not treated as equals by the better classes, attribute the treatment they receive, to the prejudice. The mistake, is [i]n not looking at society as it really is. A black gentleman of good education, polite manners, and courtly address, would be received as a gentleman, while a white man destitute of these would not be so received. Then too, as wealth enters largely into a man's position, here, it is not to be wondered at, that our people should be treated, in Canada as are other poor people....

The only thing to be feared, is, that some of the black people will act in such a manner as to increase, rather than diminish the prejudice against us. We have separate and distinct black churches, schools and preachers, whose existence and influence are much against us. Some of our preachers of the Methodist and Baptist denomination, are really too ignorant to instruct any body. The noisy behaviour of some women among whom was a female preacher in one of the Toronto churches not long since, was any thing but creditable or elevating. But if we act rightly, all will be well.

### 4. Fielding Smithea, "Mr. Editor," *British Colonist*, June 10, 1859.

Victoria, V[ancouver] I[sland]
Mr. Editor:
Have the colored people realized their fond anticipations in coming to Vancouver's Island? I answer no. And if not, what is the position they occupy in this colony? I answer decidedly a degrading one, and certainly one not to be borne by men of spirit.

It is a fact generally known that in the United States of America, the colored people labor and live under many disadvantages, the result of prejudice. Yet while this is a truth, there are many States in which colored men vote and enjoy all the rights of citizens! Hence we have in many of the northern States colored men practicing the law, medicine, and many other professions. We enter their colleges, and graduate in common with white students. In many of these colleges they have colored gentlemen professors and teachers. This state of things has been brought about by the untiring efforts of our friends, whose name is legion, and forming a connecting link with such men as Clarkson, Burke, and Wilberforce.

Finally, we went to California in common with others, to make money, and very many were successful. In the early history of California, the very worst men, shoulder-striking, devil-daring fellows, fought their way into office, and when in, they tried to pass a law prohibiting any more colored persons and Chinamen from emigrating thither, and those already there must register their names in a Recorder's office, and though they did not accomplish their diabolical purpose, yet we took the will for the deed and considered ourselves, not only outraged, but more degraded than ever. Hence we held mass meetings, and discussed the question of where we should go. Some said to Sonora in Lower California, others into Central America; but just at that time there was some talk about Vancouver's Island, where the majority concluded to go. A Roman general said "Veni, Vidi, Vici," and I can say, we came, we saw, and even conquered difficulties, but we have not conquered that mildew-like feeling that lurks in the hearts of our enemies, i.e., prejudice. Having from early boyhood cherished a friendly feeling for the British Government, which was the result of her liberal policy towards the colored people generally, we had hoped on coming here to occupy this virgin soil; that we would enjoy all the rights and privileges enjoyed by others, but how sadly have many of us been disappointed. All the hotels, inns, and whiskey shops, are closed against us, and a colored gentleman was ordered out of the cabin of the steamer *Gov. Douglas*, the other day—he had a cabin ticket. They shut us out from their concerts, and a member of the church says give him $500 and he will build a gallery in the English Church, in which to huddle us together; I know nothing of English law, yet I believe the course these men pursue is contrary to all law, human or Divine.... So I am informed that there is in town a secret association of wicked white men (I wonder if any are good singers), whose ostensible purpose is to keep colored men out of the jury box, and from serving on the Grand Jury. Now for myself, I care not if I never fill any office here, but in the language of one, "Fiat justitia, ruat coelum."

... Some of our people whose susceptibilities are not so keen upon the subject of human rights, say having the law in our favor we ask no more. It is well said, "if ignorance is bliss." But when I consider how many ways there are to evade the law, I subscribe to no such doctrine, for there is a power behind the throne stronger than the throne itself, and that power is public opinion. Were it not so, men would have no regard for human society.

In view of these facts, I contend that the position we hold in this colony, is not only humiliating in the extreme, but degrading to us as a class. I will not now stop to enquire why it is that we are thus treated, hated and despised. Enough to know that it is so. I know some among us are inclined to whitewash these matters over, saying there will be a better state of things hereafter. But the obnoxious seeds of prejudice are so deeply rooted in the white man's heart, which he directs against us with such burning force, biting like an adder and stinging like an asp, that we naturally suffer from its deadly effects.

It is said that in war colored men make good and brave soldiers but I think in the common walks of life they are viewed through different glasses. I believe it utterly impossible for the African and the Anglo-Saxon races ever to live together on terms of equality. *I am as firmly fixed in this opinion as I am that some day I shall go to judgement.* I am not alone in this feeling, for I reflect the views of very many of our people, even In Victoria, unless they say one thing and mean another.

When I contemplate the vast multitude of colored people scattered throughout the United States of America, the Canadas, and the West Indies, my heart yearns for the day when God, in his providence will gather us together in some favored country, where we cannot only be men without any restraint, but grow and become a great nation like others; this inward desire does not only predominate over all others, but it does in very deed *consume me gradually away....*

## 5. William Brown, "The Colored People of Canada," *Pine and Palm,* September–December 1861.

No section of the American Continent has been watched with so much interest, both by the oppressor, the oppressed, and the friends of freedom and civilization, as the Canadas. The only spot in America, where every child of God could stand and enjoy freedom, and the only place of refuge for the poor whip-scarred slave of the Southern plantation, it has excited the malignant hate of all slaveholding Americans, while it shared the sympathy and approving interest of the friends of the African race everywhere. The colored population of the Canadas have been largely overrated. There are probably not more than 25,000 in both Provinces, and by far the greater number of these are in Canada West, and in a section of country lying west of Toronto, and near Chatham....

PREJUDICE AGAINST COLOR. Canada has so long been eulogized as the only spot in North America where the Southern bondsman could stand a freeman, and the poetical connection of its soil with the fugitive, the "North Star," and liberty, had created such an enthusiastic love in my heart for the people here, that I was not prepared to meet the prejudice against colored persons which manifests itself wherever a member of that injured race makes his appearance.

That old, negro hating cry of "Crow, crow," which used to greet the well dressed colored person on the other side of the line twenty years ago, and which I had not heard for a long time, sounded harshly upon my sensitive ears as I passed through the streets of this city. Indeed, in none of the States, not even in Pennsylvania, is the partition wall between the blacks so high as in Canada. Amongst the colored men here, are some first class mechanics, yet none of these can get employment in shops where white men are at work. I have been informed by the best authority, in every place through which I have passed, that the introduction of a colored mechanic in any establishment here, would be taken as an insult by the white men, who would instantly leave their work. A splendid carpenter has just gone by with his whitewash bucket and brush; unable to get employment at his trade, he resorts to the latter for a livelihood. The equality meted out to colored persons in the hotels of New England, are unknown in Canada. No where here, are our people treated with any kind of respect in the hotels; they are usually put off into inferior rooms by themselves, fed at separate tables from the whites, and not permitted to enter the common sitting rooms of the inn. Most of the towns have excluded the colored children from the common schools....

I think that the prejudice against the colored people in Canada, arises mainly from the following causes: First, the colored inhabitants withdrawing themselves from the whites, forming separate churches, taking back seats in public meetings, and performing the menial offices of labor, and thereby giving the whites an opportunity to regard them with a degree of inferiority.

Second, the main body of the population of Canada appears to be made up of the lower class of the people of England, Scotland, and Ireland. As I walk the streets here, I look in vain for that intelligent portion of the middle classes that I used to meet in London, Edinburgh, and Dublin. This lower stratum, coming from the old world, and feeling keenly their inferiority in education and refinement, and being vulgar and rude themselves, try ... to draw attention from their own uncouthness, by directing the public eye to the other degraded class. It would, however, be doing injustice to the cause of Reform, to say that the entire population of Canada is of the class above mentioned....

Notwithstanding there is so much prejudice, and the colored people are shut out from the more profitable employments, they are nevertheless thrifty, and doing well. Although bad beer and poor whiskey appear to be in good demand in this city, and I have met several persons who seemed to have an over stock on hand, I have not yet seen a colored inhabitant intoxicated. In the vicinity of London there are many of our race who own good farms and carry them on in the best manner. A man I once knew at the South as a slave, now resides upon a beautiful place of sixty acres in a high state of cultivation, fine grafted fruit on it, a well finished house, and large, comfortable barns, all of which he owns himself, without a single debt. Although there seems to be such hatred of the negro here if one is known to be wealthy, the whites vie with each other to see which shall do him the most honor....

The past history and present condition of the colored population of Canada, differ widely from that of any other race in the world. Brought up under the strong arm of oppression, bought, sold, made to toil without compensation, from early dawn till late at night; the tenderest ties of nature torn asunder, deprived of all the rights of humanity, by both law and public opinion, at the South, they escape to Canada with all the hope and enthusiasm that such a long-dreamed of change can bring. On arriving here they are met by two classes; the mongrel whites, half French, Indian and Spanish on the one side, and Irish, Scotch, German and English, on the other. These natives, employ the fugitive, work him late and early, and pay him off in old clothes and provisions, at an exorbitant price, or cheat him entirely out of his wages. If he is so fortunate as to slip through the fingers of these, he then falls into the hands of another class, a set of land speculators, under the guise of philanthropy, owning large tracts of wild, heavy timbered, and low, wet land, which has been purchased for a shilling an acre, or thereabouts, and is importuned to "come and buy yourself a home; you can have ten years to pay for it in. Come now, get you a farm and be independent." The land is bought, the contract duly signed, and the poor man with his family settles in a log hut, surrounded by water a foot deep, in the spring of the year. By hard work, and almost starvation, they succeed in making their annual payments, together with the interest. The "Benevolent Land Association" has its Constitution and By-Laws, with any number of loop-holes for itself to get out at, but none for the purchaser. The fugitive is soon informed that he must fulfil certain obligations, or he will forfeit his claim. Unable to read, he takes his paper, goes to a lawyer, pays a fee, and is told that it is all right, he is bound by the contract. This unexpected stipulation is scarcely settled, ere he is again informed that if he does not comply with another oppressive act, he will forfeit his claim. Away he starts to the lawyer; another fee, and he returns with a flea in his ear. The last requirement is fulfilled with a sigh and a heavy heart. After years of toil, he has paid all that he agreed to, and demands his deed, when he is met with the reply that the "Association" has passed an act that every settler shall erect a frame house, twenty-four by thirty feet, must put a post and paling fence in front, and must ditch his land, or he cannot get his deed. Once more he goes to the lawyer, pays a fee, and then begins to think that "all that glitters is not gold," and gets upon his knees and prays to the Lord to give him patience to bear up under his multitude of misfortunes, or damns the "Benevolent Land Society," and swears that philanthropy in Canada is a humbug. Should he have health, strength, religion, and physical courage enough to pass safely through the meshes of the "Land Society," he then falls into the hands of the political jugglers. In Canada, one must possess a certain amount of property, or pay rent in a given sum, to entitle him to a vote for a member of Parliament. On the "Refugee Home" lands the colored residents voted for the candidates, at the election preceding the last, when it was found that they held the balance of power in their district, and at once it was resolved to disfranchise them. Consequently, at the last election, these people were assessed so low, that they fell under the required sum, and lost the right to vote. Still their taxes are just the same as they were when exercising the franchise. Thus, the names of more than fifty persons in one town were struck from the voters' list, on account of color.

The more I see of Canada, the more I am convinced of the deep-rooted hatred to the negro, here. In no hotel, can a colored person receive the respect given to the same class in New England. In every place except Toronto and Hamilton, they are excluded from the public schools, and in one district, where there were not enough colored children to entitle them to a separate school, the district school was abolished entirely rather than permit the colored children to attend it. One of the wealthiest and most influential colored farmers, and almost white, too, was lately refused a membership to a county agricultural society. Whenever a colored man is employed by a white man, the former is invariably put to a side table to take his meal; in the farming districts it is the same; and even when a white man works for a colored person, he demands a side-table, for he feels himself above eating with his master....

### 6. S. Howe, *The Refugees from Slavery in Canada West: Report to the Freedman's Inquiry Commission,* 1864.

... So the colored people of Canada say the climate suits them; that they are very well; that they bear as many children as whites do, and rear them as well. But the opinion of the most intelligent white persons is different.

Many intelligent physicians who have practised among both classes, say that the colored people are feebly organized; that the scrofulous temperament prevails among them; that the climate tends to development of tuberculous diseases; that they are unprolific and short-lived.

From an abundance of such testimony, the following, given by two eminent physicians, one in the West, the other in the eastern part of Upper Canada, is selected as among the most reliable. Dr. Fisher, physician at the Provincial Lunatic Asylum, says:—

"I think the colored people stand the climate very badly. In a very short time lung disease is developed, and they go by phthisis. The majority do not pass forty years. Of course, there are exceptions. They die off fast. I suppose I have had thirty colored people here with little children, with scrofulous disease, extending as far as ulceration of the temporal bone. Then they are a good deal subject to rheumatism. They bear a great many children, but raise only about one-half of them, I think. The children are generally weakly and puny; not so strong as our white children. A great many of them die in childhood. The principal disease is tubercular deposition of the stomach and intestines."

Dr. T. Mack, of St. Catherines, says:—

"It strikes me that the mixed races are the most unhealthy, and the pure blacks the least so. The disease they suffer most from is pulmonary—more than general tubercular; and where there is not real tubercular affection of the lungs, there are bronchitis and pulmonary affections. I have the idea that they die out when mixed, and that this climate will completely efface them. I think the pure blacks will live. I have come to this conclusion, not from any statistics, but from personal observation. I know A, B, and C, who are mulattoes, and they are unhealthy; and I know pure blacks, who do not suffer from disease, and recover from the smallpox, and skin diseases, and yellow fever, which are very fatal to mulattoes. I think there is a great deal of strumous diathesis developed in the mixed race, produced by change of climate." ...

However, let the rationale of prejudice against the negroes be what it may, it surely does not become the English to reproach the Americans, as a people, with the sin of it; for they themselves have quite as much of it; and their people show it whenever the negroes come among them in sufficient numbers to compete for the means of living, and for civil rights. Whenever circumstances call it forth among the coarse and brutal, they manifest it just as brutally as Americans do. They have done so in Canada; and would doubtless do so in England.

If the French people are, as they boast to be, above this prejudice, (which is improbable,) it must be because they have greater moral culture, (which is more improbable;) or else that the Celtic element in their blood has closer affinity with the African than ours has.

The English Canadians try to persuade themselves that when this malady of prejudice does occasionally appear among them, they do not have it in the natural way, but catch it from the Americans; and that it breaks out in its worst form in towns where Americans most abound.

The colored people, however, say, that this theory of contagion is not sustained by facts; and the bulk of the evidence shows that they are right.

The truth of the matter seems to be that, as long as the colored people form a very small proportion of the population, and are dependent, they receive protection and favors; but when they increase, and compete with the laboring class for a living, and especially when they begin to aspire to social equality, they cease to be "interesting negroes," and become "niggers."

The words of Mr. Meigs, of Malden, expressed the truth; but the contemptuous tone in which he uttered the last sentence, gave it additional force. Said he:

"I have been here for twenty-three years. The feeling against the colored people has been growing ever since I came here, and more particularly since your President's Proclamation. They are becoming now so very haughty that they are *looking upon themselves as the equals of the whites!*"

This prejudice exists so generally in Canada, that travellers usually form an unpleasant and unjust opinion of the colored refugees, because it is usually strong and bitter in that class of persons with whom travellers come most in contact. For instance, the head-clerk in the————hotel at————in answer to our inquiries about the condition of the colored people, broke out as follows:—

"Niggers are a damned nuisance. They keep men of means away from the place. This town has got the name of 'Nigger Town,' and men of wealth won't come here. I never knew one of them that would not steal, though they never steal any thing of any great amount. Chickens have to roost high about here, I tell you. The Grand Jury of this county has just indicted seven persons, and every one of them was black. They will steal a little sugar, or a pound of butter, and put it in their pockets. But perhaps they are not to blame for it, for they have been trained to steal in slavery."

This sort of evidence forms the staple out of which newspaper reporters manufacture articles, and form the public opinion about the Canadian refugees. Now, in this very hotel, the head waiter, an intelligent man, who enjoyed the respect and confidence of the household, clerks included, was a colored man— one who bought himself for $1,000, saving, with singular persistency and resolution, $50 a year for twenty years, for that purpose. His place was one of considerable consequence, requiring capacity and integrity; and he seemed to fill it to general satisfaction.

It is not, however, hotel clerks alone, but grave officials, Mayors and others, who, when first addressed, are apt to speak contemptuously of the colored people; though they usually do them more justice upon reflection; especially in those cities where the negro vote is large enough to turn an election....

The Hon. Isaac Buchanan, M.P., of Hamilton, said to us:—

"I think we see the effects of slavery here very plainly. The children of the colored people go to the public schools, but a great many of the white parents object to it, though their children do not, that I know of. I suppose, if the question was put to vote, the people would vote against having the negroes remain here."

Hon. George Brown, M.P., of Toronto, said:—

"I think the prejudice against the colored people is stronger here than in the States. To show you the prejudice that exists against them, I will mention one fact. When I was a candidate for Parliament in Upper Canada, 150 people signed a paper, saying that if I would agree to urge the passage of a law that the negro should be excluded from the common schools, and putting a head-tax upon those coming into the country, they would all vote for me; otherwise they would vote for my opponent. There were 150 men degraded enough to sign such a paper and send it to me."

Mr. McCullum, principal teacher of the Hamilton High School, says:—

"Up at the oil springs, the colored people have quite a little town. The white people were there, and they had all the work. They charged six shillings for sawing a cord of wood. The colored people went up there from Chatham, and, in order to get constant employment, they charged only fifty cents a cord. What did the white people do? They raised a mob, went one night and burned every shanty that belonged to a colored person, and drove them off entirely. Well, it was a mob; it was not society at all; it was but the dregs of society who did this. They took a quantity of the oil, and while some of their number were parleying with the colored people in front of their doors, they went behind, threw the oil over their shanties, set it on fire, and the buildings were in flames in a moment. The parties were arrested, and two of them sent to the penitentiary for seven years."

Rev. James Proudfoot, of London, says:—

"You will find a great many colored people about Chatham—too many. It has produced a certain reaction among the white people there. The white people do not associate much with them; and even in the courts of justice, a place is allotted to the colored people—they are not allowed to mix with the whites. A number of gentlemen have told me that."

Mayor Cross, of Chatham, says:—

"The colored people generally live apart. There has been, hitherto, a very strong prejudice against them, and the result is that they are, generally speaking, confined to a particular locality of the town."

Rev. Mr. Geddes, of Toronto, says:—

"The great mass of the colored population will be found in the West; and where they go in any great numbers, the people acquire a strong prejudice against them."

Mr. Sinclair, of Chatham, says:—

"Our laws know nothing about creed, color, or nationality. If foreign-born, when they take the oath of allegiance, they are the same as natives. But in regard to social prejudice, that is something we cannot help. The colored people are considered inferior, and must remain so for many years, perhaps forever, because their color distinguishes them. One or two colored men are constables here, but that is all.

"Many of the colored people, even in this town, say that if they could have the same privileges in the States that they have here, they would not remain a moment. The prejudice is not so strong in this town, where they have been so long known, and where the people see they can be improved and elevated; but even in this county, there is one township where no colored man is allowed to settle. One man has tried to build a house there, but as fast as he built it in the day time, the white people would pull it down at night. No personal violence was done to him. That was in the township of Orford. In the township of Howard, I think there are only four colored families, and they are a very respectable class of people. In that township, there was as much prejudice as anywhere, fourteen years ago; but two colored families, very respectable and intelligent people, settled there—they were rather superior in those respects to the neighborhood generally—and they did a vast amount towards doing away with the prejudice. They were intelligent, cleanly, moral, and even religious; so that ministers of the gospel would actually call and take dinner with these people, as they found every thing so nice, tidy and comfortable, and the poor colored people so kind, and so ready to welcome any decent person who came. So that a good deal depends upon the first samples that go into a town."

The testimony of the colored people is still more striking. Mrs.———— Brown (colored), of St. Catherines, says:—

"I find more prejudice here than I did in York State. When I was at home, I could go anywhere; but here, my goodness, you get an insult on every side. But the colored people have their rights before the law; that is the only thing that has kept me here."

Dr. A.T. Jones (colored), of London, says:—

"There is a mean prejudice here that is not to be found in the States, though the Northern States are pretty bad."

Rev. L.C. Chambers (colored), of St. Catherines, says:

"The prejudice here against the colored people is stronger, a great deal, than it is in Massachusetts. Since I have been in the country, I went to a church one Sabbath, and the sexton asked me, 'What do you want here to-day?' I said, 'Is there not to be service here to-day?' He said, 'Yes, but we don't want any niggers here.' I said, 'You are mistaken in the man. I am not a "nigger," but a negro.'"

Mrs. Susan Boggs (colored), of St. Catherines, says:—

"If it was not for the Queen's law, we would be mobbed here, and we could not stay in this house. The prejudice is a great deal worse here than it is in the States."

G.E. Simpson (colored), of Toronto, says:—

"I must say that, leaving the law out of the question, I find that prejudice here is equally strong as on the other side. The law is the only thing that sustains us in this country."

John Shipton (colored), of London, says:—

"I never experienced near the prejudice down there, (in the States,) that I have here. The prejudice here would be a heap worse than in the States, if it was not that the law keeps it down."

It would be easy to show how the natural sympathy and compassion which is felt for the exiles on their first arrival by all, and which continues to be felt by people of Christian culture, is converted into antipathy and animosity among the vulgar. The teachers in the pulpit, and the teachers of public schools, have much to answer for in this matter. The clergy of the Church of England are generally staunch friends of the negro. Rev. Mr. Geddes, of Hamilton, said:—

"There are several colored people belonging to my church. I have them also in the Sunday school, and have always taken an interest in the improvement of their condition, socially and religiously. There are two young colored women also in the Sunday school, who teach white children of respectable parents."

He related to us a case of two young ladies who were sent to Hamilton for education, and who joined his Sunday school. Their parents, on learning that colored children attended the school, sent a remonstrance, saying that their children must not be associated with negroes. His answer was:—

"I am sorry that any persons belonging to the Church of England are so narrow-minded as to suppose their children will be injured because there are a few colored persons in the same school; but of course we cannot change our principle, and the young ladies must leave."

Many Presbyterian clergymen are equally humane and just; but there are those of all denominations who refrain from rebuking by their example the intolerant and unchristian spirit which prevails among their people.

So some of the teachers in public schools, rising to the dignity of their high calling, see in their colored pupils poor and friendless children, who have most need of sympathy and encouragement, and therefore they bestow them freely, careless whether committee-men and the public approve or not.

Mr. McCullum, principal of the well-appointed High School in Hamilton, says:—

"I had charge of the Provincial Model School at Toronto for over ten years, and I have had charge of this school over four years, and have had colored children under my charge all that time. They conduct themselves with the strictest propriety, and I have never known an occasion where the white children have had any difficulty with them on account of color. At first, when any new ones came, *I used to go out with them in the playground myself, and play with them specially,* just to show that I made no distinction whatever; and then the children made none. I found this plan most healthy in its operation.

"Little white children do not show the slightest repugnance to playing with the colored children, or coming in contact with them. I never knew of a case. But sometimes parents will not let their children sit at the same desk with a colored child. The origin of the difficulty is not being treated like other children. We have no difficulty here. We give the children their seats according to their credit-marks in the preceding month, and I never have had the slightest difficulty. The moral conduct of the colored children is just as good as that of the others."

In London, the head-master of the High School manifested a different spirit: he said—

"It does not work well with us to have colored children in school with the white. In our community, there is more prejudice against the colored people, and the children receive it from their parents. The colored children must feel it, for the white children refuse to play with them in the playground. Whether it is a natural feeling or not I cannot tell, but it shows itself in the playground and in the class-room."

One of the teachers said:—

"I think that the colored children would be better educated, and that it would be more conducive to the happiness both of colored and white children if they were in separate schools. The colored children would not be subjected to so much annoyance. Some white children of the *lower orders* don't mind sitting by them in school; but there are others who are very particular, and don't like it at all."

Now, this head-master is a man of vigorous nature, who makes his influence felt widely; and should he exert that influence as Mr. McCullum does, then perhaps "*it would work well* to have colored children in school with the whites;" then perhaps his sub-teachers would not show such lack of sympathy with the little colored children committed, in the providence of God, to their charge; then perhaps there would be no such sad sight as we saw in the playground, where colored children stood aside, and looked wishfully at groups of whites playing games from which they were excluded. Such scenes do not occur in the playground at Hamilton, because the teacher takes care, by showing *personal interest* in the colored children, to elevate them in the eyes of their comrades. Moreover, it is not likely that the school committee of London would persist in efforts to expel colored children from the public schools, and so degrade them in the public eye, if one humane master should publicly protest against it, as any citizen has a right to do.

Toronto and Hamilton are distinguished among the populous places of Canada West for the comparative liberality and kindness towards colored people. London is not; and the difference arises in some degree, doubtless, from the different spirit which children imbibe in the public schools under different head masters. At any rate, this accounts for the difference better than the theory of "contagion" from Americans does.

The Canadians constantly boast that their laws know no difference of color; that they make blacks eligible to offices, and protect all their rights; and the refugees constantly admit that it is so. The very frequency of the assertion and of the admission, proves that it is not considered a matter of course that simple justice should be done. People do not boast that the law protects white men.

After making all due allowance for the fact that the lack of culture disqualifies most of the refugees for many offices to which they are legally eligible, and also for refined society, there is manifest injustice done to them in various ways by reason of a vulgar and bitter prejudice, which defeats the benevolent purposes of the law. For instance, they are practically kept off the juries. The testimony of Mr. A. Bartlett, town clerk of Windsor, shows one way in which it is done. He says:—

"The selection of the jury is a simple thing. We begin with the man who is assessed the highest on the roll, and we go down to half the names on the roll; then the amount paid by that person who is lowest on the first half forms the amount of property qualification for that jury. Then we take two-thirds of that number, and of course the selectors have it in their power to say what two-thirds shall be taken; and of course the colored man is cut off, because they don't want him on."

It happens sometimes that a sturdy Englishman, seeing only his duty, insists upon its being done legally and impartially, and then colored men are drawn.

Such a case happened recently. A black man was drawn and duly summoned. He appeared in court, and was placed upon the jury, to the consternation of some snobs, who refused to sit in the box with him. The Judge had the manliness to reprimand them, then to fine them, and finally to imprison them; which at last brought them to what senses they had.

There is the same practical difficulty with regard to

### Public Schools

The Canadian law makes no distinction of color. It proposes that common schools shall be beneficial to all classes alike. Practically, however, there is a distinction of color, and negroes do not have equal advantage from public instruction with whites. The law allows colored people to send their children to the common schools, or to have separate schools of their own. They have asked for and obtained such separate schools in Chatham, Malden, and Windsor. Now, there is a growing feeling among the whites that they made a mistake in giving the blacks their choice; and a strong disposition is manifested in many places to retract it, and to confine colored children to separate or caste schools.

On the other hand, there is a growing feeling on the part of the colored people that they made a mistake in asking for separate schools; and a strong disposition is manifested to give them up; but the whites will not allow them to do so.

This again shows how surely the natural sympathy for the refugee is converted into antipathy or prejudice whenever, by increase in number, they come into antagonism with the dominant class. By such antagonism, the natural affinities between the whites become intensified, and they desire to keep the blacks in a separate caste, because they feel that it must be a lower one. Many colored people see this also, and they desire to prevent the establishment of such caste. Each party begins to see that the democratic tendency of the common school is to prevent or weaken castes, while the inevitable tendency of the separate schools is to create and to strengthen them.

The struggle has already commenced in several places. The school committee of London has shown its purpose of removing the colored children from the common school to a separate school; and the colored people have declared their purpose of resisting it. Most active among them is Dr. A.T. Jones, a very black man, and a very intelligent one also; although he was a slave during the first twenty years of his life. He testified as follows:—

"The people here won't make the separate schools go. When they try it, they will have trouble. I will tell you precisely what I tell them. I tell them—'I have eight children, who were all born in this town,—British subjects, as much as the whitest among you; and they don't believe in any thing else but the Queen. Now, instead of leaving these children to grow up with that love for the country and the Queen, you are trying to plant within them a hatred for the country; and they day may come when you will hear them saying, "This is the country that disfranchises us, and deprives us of our rights;" and you may see them coming back here from the United States with muskets in their hands.' I don't believe that in ten years from this time you will see a colored man in this country. We won't stay here after this war is decided; for I have my opinion in which way it is to be decided. I have told my children to stay in school until they are put out. 'If they tell you to go,' I have said to them, 'don't go, but wait until they lay hands on you to put you out; and then you come quietly home, and I will attend to it.' I have four children in the school, who go regularly, and are getting on very well; there is no complaint of them. I told the trustees if there was any complaint of their not behaving well, or any thing of the kind, to expel them from the school, or let me know."

This struggle between a fugitive slave and the school trustees of the city of London involves a great principle, and the decision of the Court will be looked for with interest, not only by the parties immediately concerned, but by multitudes in Canada. Nor should the interest be confined to that country; for the same question and the same struggle will arise in this.

Meantime, the question has been decided in favor of the right of the school trustees of London to establish a separate school for colored children by the highest authority short of the Court,—Dr. Ryerson, the Chief Superintendent of Public Instruction in Canada West. He said to us:—

"It is within the power of the school trustees in cities and towns to make a distinction between colors, for there they have the direction of all the schools; but in country places, where there are distinct school municipalities, it is at the option of the colored people to have separate schools or not. In some country places, the trustees have refused to admit colored children to the schools; the parents have appealed to me; I have referred them to the courts; and the courts have always given decisions in their favor."

It is conceded that the law authorizes the school trustees to establish separate schools for colored people upon their asking for them; it also authorizes school trustees in cities and towns to establish *separate* schools without such restriction. The obvious intent of giving this latter power was to meet the wants of Roman Catholics, who congregate in towns and cities. But notwithstanding this intent, the Chief Superintendent decides that, under the law, the trustees may establish separate schools for colored children, and exclude them from the schools for whites. This seems, to a layman, an extraordinary decision, however it may strike lawyers. It seems extraordinary, because the whole people, speaking through the laws, not only declared against distinctions which lead to the establishment of castes, but purposely ignored distinction of color among citizens. They established a government to carry out their will; and yet a subordinate branch of this government may use power derived from it to defeat that will, and to degrade part of the citizens on account of their color!

Moreover, it would seem that by permitting the School Trustees to establish separate schools upon the petition of colored people, the legislature did not contemplate the establishment of such schools *against* their will.

The spirit of the law clearly contemplated *common* schools, not compulsory *caste* schools; and if these can be established in virtue of any *by*-law, then verily, the letter killeth the spirit....

It would be easy and agreeable to cite cases in which not only justice but good will is manifested towards the refugees. It is usually done in the towns where they make a very small proportion of the population. It is done in the University of Toronto, and in some other literary educational institutions. But upon the whole, there is a strong popular prejudice against the colored people, which operates greatly to the disadvantage of the refugees.

Then another disadvantage is to be considered. Emigrants going to a new country, especially to a cold one, need to make some preparation, and to take with them a little property. These refugees, however, could do neither. Those from the Slave States landed in Canada penniless, and without change of raiment. Those from the Free States brought small sums which they had earned;

but very few had money enough for a month's subsistence. The Provincial Government did nothing for them; and the local authorities made no provision for employing them. Some money, indeed, has been raised by contribution in England and the United States, but most of this has been expended (with questionable wisdom) for establishing several communities, or agricultural colonies; for building up churches; and for supporting white agents in comfort. Very little of this money has been applied directly to the aid of the refugees.

Notwithstanding all these disadvantages, they have shown the will and the ability to work and to support themselves.

### Disposition to Work

No sensible people in Canada charge the refugees with slothfulness. The only charge worth notice is that they "shirk hard work." This charge is made thoughtlessly by most people; wrathfully by those who have to do the heavy drudgery. The gist of the matter, however, is this: In every civilized community there is a certain amount of hard work, requiring muscular effort, to be done by somebody. In Canada, as elsewhere, this work, instead of being made a blessing to all by fair and equal distribution, is made a grievous burden to one class, by being thrown exclusively on their shoulders, while another class suffers from lack of it.

Each white man tries to spare his own muscles, and to make some of his neighbors do his share of manual labor. If he must work, he prefers the lightest kind of labor. The negro stands by, and imitates the white man. Work he must; but, like his fugleman, he prefers the light kind; and he contrives to get it.

Men want to be shaved, and to have their boots blacked. They want also to have heavy hods carried up ladders; and wet mud shovelled out of ditches. There stand Irishmen, Germans, and negroes, seeking work. Each would prefer the lighter kind, especially as it is best paid. Each would prefer to exercise his fingers rather than his arms; and to wait and tend, rather than strain his back and weary his muscles. But the employer prefers the nimble-fingered negro for his light work, and the brawny-armed Irishman for his heavy work. So the negro shaves, and brushes, and tends, and frisks about; while his competitor delves, and swears that "a nigger is too lazy to work."

Sometimes the competition and contrast are very striking, as in hotels and boarding-houses. Here the colored men abound; but in these very houses, the porterage, and all heavy work and dirty work, are done by white men. If you ring your bell, the nimble mulatto who skips up to you in his white linen jacket, does not soil his dainty fingers by bringing the coal which you ask for, but sends a stalwart fireman, a traditionary white man, but so black and begrimed by coal, that in the South he might need free papers to prove his lineage....

But mulattoes dislike hard manual labor, not only because it is held less respectable than light work or no work, but because by their very organization,—by their lymphatic temperament, and lack of animal vigor, they are less adapted to prolonged muscular effort than full breeds. That they do not lack industry and thrift, the condition of those in Canada proves clearly, for thousands and tens of thousands of colored people have there worked hard for a living, and have earned it.

First, there is negative proof of this, in the fact that they do not beg, and that they receive no more than their share of public support, if even so much. We traversed the whole length of Canada West three times, stopping at the places where colored people most abounded; going into their quarters in the cities, and visiting their farm-houses by the wayside; yet we met no beggars; and although there were evident signs of extreme poverty among those recently arrived, we did not see such marks of utter destitution and want, as may be found in the lower walks of life in most countries. The following are fair specimens of the testimony given by intelligent white persons upon this point.

Hon. George Brown, M.P., of Toronto, says:—

"One thing about the colored people here is quite remarkable; they never beg. They only ask for work; and when they get work, if they have borrowed any money, they will come back and pay it—a thing I never knew white men to do. Their ministers are about the only beggars with black faces I have ever seen."

Mr. Park, a merchant of Malden, says:—

"Part of them (the colored population) are disposed to be industrious, and part of them are pretty indolent. They don't take care of their own poor. We have no poor-house. The poor are relieved either by the government of the municipality, or by the people. The colored people get about the same assistance, in proportion to their numbers, that the whites do. I think they beg more than the whites do."

Mr. Brush, Town Clerk of Malden, says:—

"A portion of them (the colored people) are pretty well-behaved, and another portion not. We have a very small Irish laboring population. A great many of these colored people go and sail (are sailors) in the summer time, and in the winter, lie round, and don't do much. The upper part of this town is inhabited by French people, the worst people in the world. There is not the toss of a copper between them and the colored people We have to help a great many of them; more than any other class of people we have here. I have been Clerk of the

Council for three years, and have had the opportunity of knowing. I think the Council have given more to the colored people than to any others."

In and about Malden the colored people congregate too numerously, and do not do so well as in other places.

The Rev. James Proudfoot, of London, says:—"I don't know a beggar among the colored people."

The great mass of the colored people of Canada have been thrown entirely upon their own resources; and their history is generally like that of a fugitive whom we met, who told us that on arrival, he had to borrow twenty-five cents to buy an axe, and from that day forward had worked on without asking favors, until he had become independent and comfortable.

There is a most striking contrast between these exiles,—penniless, un-aided, in a cold climate, amid unsympathizing people,—and those who were sent, at great expense, across the ocean to an African climate, then supported entirely for six months, and afterwards aided and bolstered up by a powerful society, which still expend large sums for the support of the Colony. The first have succeeded; the latter have virtually failed. Let the lesson be pondered by those who are considering what shall be done with the negro.

But second, there is positive and tangible proof of the will and the ability of the colored people to work and support themselves, and gather substance even in the hard climate of Canada.

## Readings

Bearden, J., and L. Butler. *Shadd: The Life and Times of Mary Shadd Cary.* Toronto: NC Press, 1977.

Bode, P. *The Odyssey of John Anderson.* Toronto: Osgoode Society, 1989.

Cooper, A. "Black Women and Work in Nineteenth-Century Canada West: Black Woman Teacher Mary Bibb," in P. Bristow, ed., *'We're Rooted Here and They Can't Pull Us Up': Essays in African Canadian Women's History.* Toronto: University of Toronto Press, 1994.

Gillie, D., and J. Silverman. "The Pursuit of Knowledge Under Difficulties: Education and the Fugitive Slave in Canada," *Ontario History* 74 (1982).

Hill, D. *The Freedom Seekers: Blacks in Early Canada.* Agincourt: Irwin, 1981.

Kilian, C. *Go Do Some Great Thing: The Black Pioneers of British Columbia.* Vancouver: 1978.

Knight, C. "Black Parents Speak: Education in mid-Nineteenth Century Canada West," *Ontario History* 4 (December 1997).

Law, H. "'Self-Reliance is the True Road to Independence': Ideology and the Ex-Slaves in Buxton and Chatham," *Ontario History* 77 (1985).

Martin, G, "British Officials and Their Attitude to the Negro Community in Canada," *Ontario History* 66, 2 (June 1974).

Pachai, B. *Beneath the Clouds of the Promised Land: The Survival of Nova Scotia's Blacks.* Halifax: Black Educators Association of Nova Scotia, 1987–90.

Silverman, J. *Unwelcome Guests: American Fugitive Slaves in Canada, 1830–1860.*

Spray, W. *The Blacks of New Brunswick.* Fredericton: Brunswick Press, 1972.

Stouffer, A. *The Light of Nature and the Law of God: Antislavery in Ontario 1833–1877.* Montreal and Kingston: McGill-Queen's University Press, 1992.

Walker, J. *The Black Loyalists: The Search for a Promised Land in Nova Scotia and Sierre Leone, 1783–1870.* Reprinted. Toronto: University of Toronto Press, 1992.

Walker, J. *A History of Blacks in Canada: A Study Guide for Teachers and Students.* Hull: Queen's Printer, 1980.

Wayne, M. "The Black Population of Canada West on the Eve of the American Civil War: A Reassessment Based on the Manuscript Census of 1861," *Social History.*

Winks, R. *Blacks in Canada.* Montreal: McGill-Queen's University Press, 1971.

Winks, R. "Negro School Segregation in Ontario and Nova Scotia," *Canadian Historical Review* 50, 2 (June 1969).

Yee, S. "Gender Ideology and Black Women as Community-Builders in Ontario, 1850–1870," *Canadian Historical Review* 75, 1 (1994).

*Chapter Sixteen*

# "Like Snow Beneath an April Sun": Mid-Nineteenth Century Native Dissent

1. Pelancea Paul (François Paul) et al., "To His Excellency John Harvey, Lieut. Governor of Nova Scotia," February 8, 1849.
2. Chief Kahkewaquonaby (Peter Jones), "Answers to the Queries proposed by the Commissioners appointed to enquire into Indian Affairs in this Province," February 6, 1843.
3. Chiefs Brant Brant, Joseph Penn, and Joseph Smart, "To the Chiefs and People of the Several Tribes Assembled in General Council at Orillia," July 21, 1846.
4. Chief Peau de Chat, "Address to T.G. Anderson, vice-superintendent of Indian Affairs," Sault Ste. Marie, August 18, 1848.
5. Shinguaconse (Little Pine), 1849.
6. Chief Peguis (William King), "To the Aboriginal Protection Society," Red River, 1857.

## Introduction

Although confrontations between Native people and governments have become more common with the recent crises at Oka, Gustafsen Lake, Ipperwash, and Burnt Church, it is tempting to assume that, with some notable exceptions, Native people in early British North America did little to resist European settlement and westward expansion. But these people were never silent victims. By the nineteenth century, many Native leaders did set about addressing some of the wrongs they perceived as having been perpetrated against their people. Their voices indeed remained relatively small and muted, but they did cause a stir at the time, and arguably emerged as the precursors to modern Canadian Native militancy. Perhaps more importantly, at least in the pragmatic sense, their words not only inspired their own people, but also affected an increasing number of non-indigenous Canadians, Americans, and Europeans who felt troubled by what they heard.

The central complaint invariably revolved around the profound differences between what the British promised and what they delivered, particularly with respect to Native land ownership. The Royal Proclamation of 1763, signed by George III after Britain's victory in the Seven Years' War, recognized Native land ownership and set aside a large tract of land, in perpetuity, as "Indian Territory." This land encompassed much of present-day central Quebec and Ontario, and a huge sickle-shaped wedge encircling the New England colonies to the south. The king decreed that whites could not settle this land unless Natives first voluntarily agreed to sell it to the Crown.

Unofficially, however, Natives found themselves pushed from their lands, either physically or as a result of unfriendly encroachment in the form of unscrupulous land speculators, afflictions of hunger and disease, or the unwelcome presence of farms, villages, and towns. Colonial governments remained unsympathetic to the Native plight, despite the Proclamation, and tended to turn a blind eye to transgressions. Bit by bit, many Native bands gave up and sold out in favour of specific reserves set aside and guaranteed by colonial administrators. Thus by the nineteenth century, a huge gulf existed between what British colonial governments promised Native people via the Royal Proclamation and what they delivered. It was this inconsistency that roused the ire of indigenous people.

A few indigenous Canadians had already been published before the early nineteenth century, but their literature usually took the form of local histories, journals, travelogues, religious pamphlets, autobiography, and letters. By the 1820s, however, a handful of Native ordained ministers shifted their focus to political protest, usually in the form of letters to English, British North American, and American officials, as well as politicized sermons, tracts, petitions, and analytical reports on the appalling conditions of indigenous people. Some chiefs also joined the fight, usually concentrating on rallying their fellow chiefs rather than on admonishing non-Natives. Some preachers gained international fame and spent years spreading their message throughout eastern North America and northern Europe. Men such as Peter Jones became popular on the English social circuit, particularly when they showed up in full Native regalia, and eventually married into English society.

Their message of loss remained similar and constant: loss of land and wealth; loss of culture; and loss of direction. It was not that these Christian Natives rejected European civilization, or nostalgically pined for the past. On the contrary, people like Peter Jones endorsed European culture from its political systems to table manners, and looked forward to his own people's assimilation. What men like Jones wanted was real assistance, not just empty promises, as their people lost their traditional ways and struggled to replace them.

## Discussion Points

1. These documents are organized regionally. What differences existed between the Native situations in the Maritimes, central Canada, and Red River?
2. What remedies did Native people propose? Which were the most realistic?
3. Did the non-Native people have a unique obligation to Native people?

## Documents

### 1. Pelancea Paul (François Paul) et al., "To His Excellency John Harvey, Lieut. Governor of Nova Scotia," February 8, 1849.

To His Excellency John Harvey, K.C.R. and K.H.H., Lieut. Governor of Nova Scotia:

The Petition of the undersigned Chiefs and Captains of the Micmac Indians of Nova Scotia, for and on behalf of themselves and their tribe humbly showeth:

That a long time ago our fathers owned and occupied all the lands now called Nova Scotia, our people lived upon the sides of the rivers and were a great many. We were strong but you were stronger, and we were conquered.

Tired of a war that destroyed many of our people, almost ninety years ago our Chief made peace and buried the hatchet forever. When that peace was made, the English Governor promised us protection, as much land as we wanted, and the preservation of our fisheries and game. These we now very much want.

Before the white people came, we had plenty of wild roots, plenty of fish, and plenty of corn. The skins of the Moose and Carriboo were warm to our bodies, we had plenty of good land, we worshipped *"Kesoult"* the Great Spirit, we were free and we were happy.

Good and Honorable Governor, be not offended at what we say, for we wish to please you. But your people had not land enough, they came and killed many of our tribe and took from us our country. You have taken from us our lands and trees and have destroyed our game. The Moose yards of our fathers, where are they. Whitemen kill the moose and leave the meat in the woods. You have put ships and steamboats upon the waters and they scare away the fish. You have made dams across the rivers so that the Salmon cannot go up, and your laws will not permit us to spear them.

In old times our wigwams stood in the pleasant places along the sides of the rivers. These places are now taken from us, and we are told to go away. Upon our camping grounds you have built towns, and the graves of our fathers are broken by the plow and harrow. Even the ash and maple are growing scarce. We are told to cut no trees upon the farmer's ground, and the land you have given us is taken away every year.

Before you came we had no sickness, our old men were wise, and our young men were strong, now small pox, measles and fevers destroy our tribe. The rum sold them makes them drunk, and they perish, and they learn wickedness our old people never heard of.

Surely we obey your laws, your cattle are safe upon the hills and in the woods. When your children are lost do we not go to look for them?

The whole of our people in Nova Scotia is about 1500. Of that number 106 died in 1846, and the number of deaths in 1848 was, we believe, 94. We have never been in a worse condition than now. We suffer for clothes and for victuals. We cannot sell our baskets and other work, the times are so hard. Our old people and young children cannot live. The potatoes and wheat do not grow, and good people have nothing to give us. Where shall we go, what shall we do? Our nation is like a withering leaf in a summer's sun.

Some people say we are lazy, still we work. If you say we must go and hunt, we tell you again that to hunt is one thing and to find meat is another. They say catch fish, and we try. They say make baskets, we do but we cannot sell them. They say make farms, this is very good, but will you help us till we cut away the trees, and raise the crop? We cannot work without food. The potatoes and wheat we raised last year were killed by the poison wind. Help us and we will try again.

All your people say they wish to do us good, and they sometimes give, but give a beggar a dinner and he is a beggar still. We do not like to beg. As our game and fish are nearly gone and we cannot sell our articles, we have resolved to make farms, yet we cannot make farms without help.

We will get our people to make farms, build houses and barns, raise grain, feed cattle and get knowledge. Some have begun already. What more can we say? We will ask our Mother the Queen to help us. We beg your Excellency to help us in our distress, and help us that we may at last be able to help ourselves. And your petitioners as in duty bound will ever pray.

## 2. Chief Kahkewaquonaby (Peter Jones), "Answers to the Queries proposed by the Commissioners appointed to enquire into Indian Affairs in this Province," February 6, 1843.

*Query* No. 1.—How long have you had an acquaintance with any body of Indians?

*Answer* No. 1.— Being an Indian on my mother's side, I am well acquainted with the habits, customs, and manners, of the Chippeway nation of Indians to whom I belong. The tribe or clan with whom I have been brought up is called *Messissauga*, which signifies the eagle tribe, their *ensign* or *toodaim* being that of the eagle. I also lived for several years among the Mohawk Indians on the Grand River, by whom I was adopted. Since my entering upon the work of a missionary, I have travelled very extensively among all the Indian tribes in this country, and am therefore well acquainted with their former and present state; but, as I belong to the River Credit Indians, I intend to confine my remarks principally to them.

*Query* No. 2.—What has been their improvement during that time in their moral and religious character, and in habits of industry?

*Answer* No. 2.—Previous to the year 1823, at which time I was converted to Christianity, the Chippeway and indeed all the tribes were in a most degraded state; they were pagans, idolaters, superstitious, drunken, filthy, and indolent; they wandered about from place, living in wigwams, and subsisted by hunting and fishing. Since their conversion, paganism, idolatry, and superstition, have been removed, and the true God acknowledged and worshipped. The Christians are sober, and comparatively clean and industrious; they have formed themselves into settlements, where they have places of worship and schools, and cultivate the earth.

*Query* No. 3.—Do you find them improved in their mode of agriculture to any extent, since you first became acquainted with them?

*Answer* No. 3.—Many of them have made considerable progress in farming, but not to the extent they would have done if they had been settled on their own farm lots. The Credit Indians live in a village, and some of them have necessarily to go a mile or two to their farms, which has been a great hindrance to their improvement. Before their conversion very few of them raised even Indian corn, but now many of them grow wheat, oats, peas, Indian corn, potatoes, and other vegetables, several cut hay and have small orchards. I find the Indians at Muncey Town far behind their brethren at the Credit in agricultural industry.

*Query* No. 4.—What progress have they made in Christianity?

*Answer* No. 4.—Considerable; many of them can repeat the Lord's prayer, the ten commandments, and the Apostle's creed. They also understand the leading articles of our holy religion. I have translated the Book of Genesis, the gospels of Matthew and John, with other portions of Scripture, which they have now in their possession. They have made some proficiency in singing, are tolerably well acquainted with the rules of sacred harmony, and have a hymn-book translated into their own language, which is in constant use.

*Query* No. 5.—Since their conversion to Christianity are their moral habits improved? What effect has it had upon their social habits?

*Answer* No. 5.—Christianity has done much to improve their moral, social, and domestic habits. Previous to their conversion the women were considered as mere slaves; the drudgery and hard work was done by them; now the men treat their wives as equals, bearing the heavy burdens themselves, while the women attend to the children and household concerns.

*Query* No. 6.—Do they appear sensible of any improvement in their condition, and desirous of advancing?

*Answer* No. 6.—Very much so, and feel grateful to those who instruct them. They are still desirous of advancing in knowledge, seeing their white neighbours enjoy many comforts and privileges which they do not possess.

*Query* No. 7.—Are any of the Indians still heathens? What efforts have been made to convert them? And what obstacles have prevented their conversion?

*Answer* No. 7.—There are no heathens at the Credit, Alnwick, Rice Lake, Mud Lake, Snake Island, Balsom Lake, narrows of Lake Simcoe, Cold Water, St. Clair, and Moravian Town; but there are a number at Muncey Town, some at Sahgeeng, Big Bay, and the Grand River. I believe all the Indians at Walpool Island are pagans. There are a few among the Oneidas settled on the Thames at Muncey, and a number of Pattawatimees wandering about in these western parts who are in a most deplorable state of poverty and degradation. Efforts have been made to introduce Christianity to most of the pagans by missionaries of various denominations, but principally by native teachers. The obstacles to their conversion arise from their strong partiality to the ways of their forefathers, and their prejudices to the white man's religion. I am happy to state that the Wesleyan Missionaries, aided by native teachers, have never yet failed to introduce Christianity among a body of Indians.

*Query* No. 8.—What, in your opinion, is the best mode of promoting their religious improvement?

*Answer* No. 8.—To combine manual labour with religious instruction; to educate some of the Indian youths with a view to their becoming missionaries and school teachers, as it is a well know fact that the good already effected has been principally through the labours of native missionaries.

*Query* No. 9.—Do the children in the Indian schools shew any aptitude in acquiring knowledge?

*Answer* No. 9.—Considering they are taught in a strange language, they show as much aptitude as white children.

*Query* No. 10.—What, in your opinion, is the best mode of promoting the moral, intellectual, and social improvement of the Indians?

*Answer* No.10.—The establishment of well-regulated schools of industry, and the congregating of the several scattered tribes into three or four settlements, which would be a great saving of expense to the Government and to missionary societies, at the same time it would afford greater facilities for their instruction in everything calculated to advance their general improvement.

*Query* No. 11.—Can you offer any suggestions on the expediency and best means of establishing schools of industry for the Indian youth, and the best system of instruction to be adopted in them?

*Answer* No. 11.—I would respectfully refer the commissioners to my letter on this subject, addressed to them, dated November 21st, 1842. In addition to what is there stated, I am happy to add that most of the Indian youths who have been educated at the academies have become respectable, and are now usefully employed in instructing their countrymen.

*Query* No. 12.—Do the Indians show any aptness for mechanical arts? And if so, to what arts?

*Answer* No. 12.—I know several Indians who have become pretty good mechanics with little or no instruction. At the Credit Mission there are two or three carpenters and a shoemaker. At Muncey we have one blacksmith, and some carpenters and tailors. By a little more instruction they would soon become good workmen in any mechanical art. The only drawback which I have observed is a want of steady application to their respective trades.

*Query* No. 13.—Is the health of the Indians generally good, or otherwise, as contrasted with the white population in their neighbourhood?

*Answer* No. 13.—From observation I am led to conclude that in general they are not as healthy as the white population. I apprehend this arises from their former mode of living, when they were frequently exposed to excessive fatigue and fasting, to carrying heavy burdens, drunkenness, and injuries inflicted on each other when in this state. These things have laid the foundation of many pulmonary complaints from which the present generation are suffering.

*Query* No. 14.—Do you find the Indians on the increase or decrease in numbers, irrespectively of migration? If the latter, what, in your opinion, is the cause?

*Answer* No. 14.—Previously to their conversion to Christianity they were rapidly decreasing. Before the white man came to this country the old Indians say that their forefathers lived long and reared large families, and that their diseases were few in number. In my opinion the principal causes of their decrease have been the introduction of contagious diseases, which hurried thousands off the stage of action; their excessive fondness for the *fire-waters*, and want of proper care and food for the children and mothers. I am happy however to state that this mortality has been greatly checked since they have abandoned their former mode of life.

I have kept a register of the number of births and deaths of the Credit Indians for several years past. After their conversion they remained stationary for some years; but, latterly, there has been a small increase from actual births. I have also observed, in other tribes, that the longer they have enjoyed the blessings of civilisation, the more healthy they have become, and the larger families they have reared.

*Query* No. 15.—Is there in your opinion any means of checking the excessive mortality among the Indians, if such prevails?

*Answer* No. 15.—In my opinion the best means is to promote industry and regular habits amongst them, and to have a good medical man stationed at or near each Indian settlement. I have known many of them suffer much, and die for the want of medical aid. It is also my opinion that intermarriages with other tribes of people would tend greatly to improve their health. Many of the small tribes are degenerating on account of their having continued for ages to marry into the same body of Indians Hence the necessity of concentrating the scattered tribes.

*Query* No. 16.—Do the Indian men or women frequently intermarry with the whites?

*Answer* No. 16.—When this country was first visited the whites it was a common practice for white men to take Indian wives, but at present it seldom occurs. As far as my knowledge extends, there are only three or four white men married to Indian women, and about the same number of Indian men married to white women.

*Query* No. 17.—Is there any marked difference in the habits and general conduct between the half-breeds the native Indians? If so, state it.

*Answer* No. 17.—The half-breeds are in general more inclined to social and domestic habits. I have always found them more ready to embrace Christianity and civilization than the pure Indian, who, in his untutored state, looks upon manual labour as far too degrading to engage his attention.

*Query* No. 18.—In cases where intermarriages with whites have taken place, do you find the condition of the children of the marriage improved?

*Answer* No. 18.—I think they are, especially as regards their health and constitution.

*Query* No. 19.—Do the Indian women frequently live with white men, without being married?

*Answer* No. 19.—I know of no instances in all the tribes with which I am acquainted.

*Query* No. 20.—Does the birth of illegitimate children among the unmarried women occur frequently? And in what light is the circumstance viewed by the Indians?

*Answer* No. 20.—Such occurrences are not so frequent as when the Indians were in their drunken state; and when they do occur it is regarded as a great sin, and the mother loses her reputation as a virtuous woman.

*Query* No. 21.—Do any of the Indians enjoy all, or any, of the civil and political rights possessed by other subjects of Her Majesty?

*Answer* No. 21.—Not any to my knowledge; except the protection of law which I believe every alien enjoys who may visit or reside in any part of her Majesty's dominions. I am fully persuaded that, in order to improve the condition of the Indians, all the civil and political rights of British subjects ought to be extended to them so soon as they are capable of understanding and exercising such rights.

*Query* No. 22.—Are there any instances of Indians possessing such rights, besides those, of the children of educated white men married to Indian women?

*Answer* No. 22.—I know of none.

*Query* No. 23.—In your opinion have the Indians the knowledge and ability to exercise any of those rights?

*Answer* No. 23.—In my opinion, some of the Credit Indians, and a few at other settlements; are so far advanced in knowledge as to be able to exercise some of those rights, such as voting for Members of Parliament, township officers, &c., and to sit as jurors.

*Query* No. 24.—Can you offer any suggestions for the improvement of the condition of the Indians?—For the application of their presents, the expenditure of their annuities, and the proceeds of the sales of their lands?

*Answer* No. 24.—I would most respectfully suggest—

1st—The importance of establishing schools of Industry as soon as possible, that there may be no further delay in bringing forward the present rising generation.

2nd—In order to promote industry among the Indians, agricultural societies ought to be formed at each settlement, and rewards offered to such as might excel in any branch of farming. This would excite a spirit of emulation, and be productive of good results.

3rd— In forming an Indian settlement, I consider that each family ought to be located on his own farm lot, containing 50 or 100 acres of land, with the boundaries of each lot marked out and established.

4th—I am of opinion that it would have a beneficial tendency were titles given to the Indians by the Government, securing their reserved lands to them and their posterity for ever. In offering these suggestions I do not mean to say that it would be prudent to confer titles individually on the Indians, but on the whole tribe. At present they hold no written documents from Government, and they frequently express fears that they will, at some future period, lose their lands. This fear acts as a check upon their industry and enterprise. In suggesting the impropriety of giving individual titles, I consider at the same time it would be well to hold out the promise to the sober and industrious, that when they shall have attained to a good knowledge of the value of property, and have established a good character, they shall have titles given them.

5th—The power of the chiefs is very different from what it was in former times, when their advice was listened to, and their commands implicitly obeyed. Immoral acts were then punished, and the offenders submitted without a murmur. But I am sorry to say, at present, many of the young people ridicule the attempts of the chiefs to suppress vice. I would humbly suggest that the Legislature, in its wisdom, take this subject into consideration, and pass an Act incorporating the chiefs to act as councillors, and the Superintendents of the Indian department as wardens. Bye-laws could be passed for the regulation and improvement of the several communities of Indians, such as the enactment of a moral code of laws, performance of statute labour, the regulation of fences, &c.

6th—I think it very desirable that something should be done for the Pottawatimees who wander about in these parts. They are in a state of great poverty and degradation, and an annoyance to the white inhabitants wherever they go. They have no lands in this province, having recently come over from the United States. I would, therefore, suggest the propriety of locating them, and thus bring them under the influence of civilization and Christianity.

7th—Feeling a deep interest for the welfare of the Muncey Indians residing at Muncey Town, I beg to call the attention of the Commissioners to their state. They are an interesting people, strongly attached to the British Government; and during the last American war rendered essential service in the defence of this province. If the Government could do something in the way of assisting them in their farming, it would afford great satisfaction, and be the means of facilitating their civilization. They receive no annuity from Government, and consequently have no means at their command to help forward their improvements.

8th—With regard to their presents, I would respectfully suggest the propriety of issuing them at their respective settlements. This would prevent some of the tribes being obliged to leave home, very often to the great damage of their crops, in order to travel to a distant post to receive the Queen's bounty.

9th—It is my opinion that the annuities payable to the Indians for lands ceded to the Crown ought to be applied in promoting agriculture and education among them.

10th—The proceeds of the sales of their lands ought to be invested in good securities, and the interest paid annually, and applied to such purposes as may improve their condition.

11th—I would suggest the propriety of rendering annually detailed accounts of the receipts and expenditures of the annuities, and the proceeds of the sales of their lands, and that the same be laid before the Indians in council for their satisfaction and information.

All which is respectfully submitted.

### 3. Chiefs Brant Brant, Joseph Penn, and Joseph Smart, "To the Chiefs and People of the Several Tribes Assembled in General Council at Orillia," July 21, 1846.

Brothers—

We have too long been children; the time has come for us to stand up and be men. We must all join hands like one family, and help one another in the great cause of Indian improvement: this is our only hope to prevent our race from perishing, and to enable us to stand on the same ground as the white man.

Let us then sound the shell, and summon every red man from the woods; let us give up the chase of the deer and the beaver; it is unprofitable: the white man's labour is fast eating away the forest, whilst the sound of his axe and his bells is driving the game far away from their old haunts; it will soon be all gone. Let us then leave the bush to the wolves and the bears, and come forth and build our wigwams in the open fields: let us exchange the gun and the spear for the axe and the plow, and learn to get our living out of the ground, like our white brethren.

Brothers—

Many summers have passed away since our forefathers forsook a wandering life, and built settled homes in cleared places; we may therefore, as elder brothers, testify to you how great are the advantages of changing your mode of life. We confess, with sorrow, that we have not improved, as we ought, the advantages we have enjoyed; we are desirous, therefore, that you should profit by our faults and not neglect your opportunities.

Brothers—

There is no reason why we should not become an intelligent, industrious, and religious people. Experience has proved that the Great Spirit has given us powers of mind and body, not inferior to those of our white neighbours; then, why should we be inferior to them? Besides, Government has given us sufficient land to cultivate which is carefully protected from encroachment; we are supplied with clothing as presents from our Good Mother the Queen, whilst our other wants are relieved by the sale of such of our lands as we do not want to use. Good and careful Fathers are appointed to watch over our interests and attend to all our wants; they are anxious to do everything in their power to improve our people, and it is for this purpose they have called this Council.

Brothers—

Let us listen to all they have to say, with attention, and thankfulness. In all their dealings with us, though they are strong and we are weak, they never command us, they always use us like equals and brethren. In all they propose they have our good at heart; let us then meet their suggestions with generous confidence.

Brothers—

We understand one of the chief objects they have in view at present, is to improve our young people by means of Boarding Schools, at which they will not only be taught book and head knowledge, but also learn to work with their hands; in fact, to make our boys useful and industrious farmers and mechanics, and our girls good housekeepers. This seems to us very necessary, for most of our young people are both ignorant and indolent, and they must be taught and accustomed to work when young, or they will never learn it, nor like it, after they have been taught.

Brothers—

In conclusion, we congratulate you all (we hope all) that you, like ourselves, have been led by the good Spirit of God, out of the darkness of heathenism into the light and knowledge of the true religion, and that, in addition to the ties of blood and colour, we are still more closely bound together by one Faith and one Hope, as believers in our Lord, Jesus Christ. We must not forget that we are yet babes in Christ, and have tasted but slightly of the benefits of Christianity; greater blessings are in store for our race, if we only diligently seek them.

Religion and civilization must go hand in hand, and then they will greatly assist each other in raising our respective Tribes to a safe and honourable position in the scale of society. If we are only faithful to our responsibilities and to ourselves, our Tribes will soon be raised from their present degraded and helpless condition, and be alike useful and respected, both as Members of society and as Christians.

## 4. Chief Peau de Chat, "Address to T.G. Anderson, vice-superintendent of Indian Affairs," Sault Ste. Marie, August 18, 1848.

Father,
You ask how we possess this land. Now it is well known that 4000 Years ago when we first were created all spoke one language. Since that a change has taken place, and we speak different languages. You white people well know, and we Red Skins know how we came in possession of this land—it was the Great Spirit who gave it to us—from the time my ancestors came upon this earth it has been considered ours—after a time the Whites living on the other side of the Great Salt Lake, found this part of the world inhabited by the Red Skins—the Whites asked us Indians, when there were many animals here—would you not sell the Skins of these various animals for the goods I bring—our old ancestors said Yes. I will bring your goods, they the whites did not say any thing more, nor did the Indian say any thing. I did not know that he said come I will buy your land, every thing that is on it under it &c &c he the White said nothing about that to me—and this is the reason why I believe that we possess this land up to this day. When at last the Whites came to this Country where now they are numerous—He the English did not say I will after a time get your land, or give me your land, he said indeed to our forefathers, when he fought with the French and conquered them come on our Side and fight them, and be our children, they did so, and every time you wanted to fight the Big knives you said to the Indians wont you assist me, Yes! we will help you this Man (pointing to Shinguaconse) was there and he was in much misery—the English were very strong when we gave our assistance. When the war was over the English did not say I will have Your land, nor did we say you may have it—and this father You know, this is how we are in possession of this Land—It will be known every where if the Whites get it from us.

Father,
You ask in what instances the Whites prevent our Farming, there are bad

people among us who are continually saying to us don't Farm, live as Indians always did, You will be unhappy if you cultivate the Land, take your Gun go and hunt, bring the Skins to me, and leave off tilling the Soil—and the Queen says to me become Christian my children. Yes I say we will become Christians but when this bad man (the Trader) sees me he says leave it alone do as you formerly did, and this is the way he destroys my religion and farming this is the way I explain the question you have now asked me.

Father,

The miners bum the land and drive away the animals destroying the land Game &c much timber is destroyed—and I am very sorry for it—When they find mineral they cover it once with Clay so that the Indians may not see it and I now begin to think that the White man wishes to take away and to steal my land, I will let it go, and perhaps I will accomplish it. I wish to let the Governor have both land and Mineral, I expect him to ask me for it, and this is what would be for our good. I do not wish to pass any reflections on the conduct of the whites—ask me then, send some one to ask for my land my Mineral &c. I wont be unwilling to let it go to the Government shall have it if they give us good pay. I do not regret a word I have said—You Father You are a White Man make Yourself an Indian, take an Indians heart come assist me to root out the evil that has been among us and I will be glad answer me is there any thing that requires explanation.

Father,

The Indians are uneasy seeing their lands occupied by the Whites, taking away the mineral and they wish that our Great Father would at once settle the matter. Come and ask me for my land and mineral that there be no bad feelings left, I am Sorry, my heart is troubled. I dont know what would be good for us, it will not do for me an Indian to say to the Governor come buy my land, yet this is what I think would be very good, Yes very good for my people, then the White man the miner and trader could do what he liked with the land and so could the Indian on that part which we would like to reserve, when we give our land up we will reserve a picce for ourselves and we, with our families will live happily on it we will do as we please with it. There (pointing to Fort William) I will find out a place for my self. Perhaps you will come and arrange Matters it would be well if you could, and if an officer cannot come this autumn to settle our affairs I will look out for one in the Spring to do it for me and this is nearly all I have to say, tell the Governor at Montreal to send a letter and let us know what he will do and what our land is worth in the mean time I will converse with my tribe on the subject. When I am going to sell my land I will speak again and Settle Matters.

A great deal of our Mineral has been taken away I must have something for it. I reflect upon it, as well as upon that which still remains.

## 5. Shinguaconse (Little Pine), 1849.

When your white children first came into this country, they did not come shouting the war cry and seeking to wrest this land from us. They told us they came as friends to smoke the pipe of peace; they sought our friendship, we became brothers. Their enemies were ours, at the time we were strong and powerful, while they were few and weak. But did we oppress them or wrong them? No! And they did not attempt to do what is now done, nor did they tell us that at some future day you would.

Father,

Time wore on and you have become a great people, whilst we have melted away like snow beneath an April sun; our strength is wasted, our countless warriors dead, our forests laid low, you have hounded us from every place as with a wand, you have swept away all our pleasant land, and like some giant foe you tell us 'willing or unwilling, you must now go from amid these rocks and wastes, I want them now! I want them to make rich my white children, whilst you may shrink away to holes and caves like starving dogs to die!' Yes, Father, your white children have opened our very graves to tell the dead even they shall have no resting place.

Father,

Was it for this we first received you with the hand of friendship, and gave you the room whereon to spread your blanket? Was it for this that we voluntarily became the children of our Great Mother the Queen? Was it for this we served England's sovereign so well and truly, that the blood of the red skin has moistened the dust of his own hunting grounds, to serve those sovereigns in their quarrels, and not in quarrels of his own?

Father,

We begin to fear that those sweet words had not their birth in the heart, but that they lived only upon the tongue; they are like those beautiful trees under whose shadow it is pleasant for a time to repose and hope, but we cannot forever indulge in their graceful shade—they produce no fruit.

Father,

We are men like you, we have the limbs of men, we have the hearts of men, and we feel and know that all this country is ours; even the weakest and most cowardly animals of the forest when hunted to extremity, though they feel destruction sure, will turn upon the hunter.

Father,

Drive us not to the madness of despair. We are told that you have laws which guard and protect the property of your white children, but you have made none to protect the rights of your red children. Perhaps you expected that the red skin could protect himself from the rapacity of his pale faced bad brother.

## 6. Chief Peguis (William King), "To the Aboriginal Protection Society," Red River, 1857.

... Those who have since held our lands not only pay us only the same small quantity of ammunition and tobacco, which was first paid to us as a preliminary to a final bargain, but they now claim all the lands between the Assiniboin and Lake Winnipeg, a quantity of land nearly double of what was first asked from us. We hope our Great Mother will not allow us to be treated so unjustly as to allow our lands to be taken from us in this way.

We are not only willing, but very anxious after being paid for our lands, that the whites would come and settle among us, for we have already derived great benefits from their having done so, that is, not the traders but the farmers. The traders have never done anything but rob and keep us poor, but the farmers have taught us how to farm and raise cattle. To the missionaries especially we are indebted, for they tell us every praying day (Sabbath) to be sober. honest, industrious and truthful. They have told us the good news that Jesus Christ so loved the world that he gave himself for it, and that this was one of the first messages to us, "Peace on earth and good will to man." We wish to practise these good rules of the whites, and hope the Great Mother will do the same to us, and not only protect us from oppression and injustice, but grant us all the privileges of the whites.

We have many things to complain of against the Hudson's Bay Company. They pay us little for our furs, and when we are old are left to shift for ourselves. We could name many old men who have starved to death in sight of many of the Company's principal forts.

When the Home Government has sent out questions to be answered in this country about the treatment of the Indians by the Company, the Indians have been told if they said anything against the Company they would be drive away from their homes. In the same way when Indians have wished to attach themselves to missions, they have been both threatened and used badly. When a new mission has been established, the Company has at once planted a post there, so as to prevent Indians from attaching themselves to it. They have been told they are fools to listen to missionaries, and can only starve and become lazy under them. We could name many Indians who have been prevented by the Company from leaving their trading posts and Indian habits when they have wished to attach themselves to missions.

When it is decided that this country is to be more extensively settled by the whites, and before whites will be again permitted to take possession of our lands, we wish that a fair and mutually advantageous treaty be entered into with my tribe for their lands, and we ask, whenever this treaty is to be entered into, a wise, discreet, and honourable man, who is known to have the interests of the Indian at heart, may be selected on the side of the Indian to see that he is fairly and justly dealt with for his land, and that from the first it be borne in mind, that in securing our own advantage, we wish also to secure those of our children and their children's children.

I commit these my requests to you as a body now well known by us to have the welfare of the poor Indian at heart, and in committing this to you in behalf of myself do so also on behalf of my tribe, who are as one man in feeling and desires on these matters. Will you, then, use the proper means of bringing these our complaints and desires in a becoming and respectful manner both before the Great Council of the nation (Parliament and through it to our Great Mother the Queen), who will show herself more truly great and good by protecting the helpless from injustice and oppression than by making great conquests.

Wishing that the Great Spirit may give you every good thing, and warmest thanks for your friendship.

## *Readings*

Blackstock, M. "The Aborigines Report (1837): A Case Study in the Slow Change of Colonial Social Relations," *Canadian Journal of Native Studies* 20, 1 (2000).

Den Otter, A. "The 1857 Parliamentary Inquiry, the Hudson's Bay Company, and Rupert's Land's Aboriginal People," *Prairie Forum* (2000).

Getty, A., and A. Lussier. *As Long as the Sun Shines and the Water Flows: A Reader in Canadian Native Studies.* Vancouver, University of British Columbia Press, 1983.

Fisher, R. *Contact and Conflict: Indian-European Relations in British Columbia, 1774–1890.* Vancouver: University of British Columbia Press, 1977.

Hall, T. "Native Limited Identities and Newcomer Metropolitanism in Upper Canada, 1814–1867," in D. Keane and C. Reid, eds., *Old Ontario: Essays in Honour of J.M.S. Careless.* Toronto: Dundurn, 1990.

Leslie, J. "The Bagot Commission: Developing a Corporate Memory for the Indian Department," *Canadian Historical Association Papers.* Ottawa: Canadian Historical Association, 1982.

Miller, J. *Shingwauk's Vision: A History of Native Residential Schools.* Toronto: University of Toronto Press, 1996.

Miller, J. *Skyscrapers Hide the Heavens: A History of Indian-White Relations in Canada.* Toronto: University of Toronto Press, 1989.

Milloy, J. *The Plains Cree: Trade Dipomacy and War, 1790–1870.* Winnipeg: University of Manitoba Press, 1988.

Petrone, P. *First People, First Voices,* Toronto: University of Toronto Press, 1983.

Petrone, P. *Native Literature in Canada: From the Oral Tradition to the Present.* Toronto: Oxford University Press, 1990.

Rogers, E., and D. Smith. *Aboriginal Ontario: Historical Perspectives on the First Nations.* Toronto: Dundurn Press, 1994.

Schmalz, P. *The Ojibwa of Southern Ontario.* Toronto: University of Toronto Press, 1991.

Smith, D. *Sacred Feathers. The Reverend Peter Jones (Kahkewaquinaby) and the Mississauga Indians.* Toronto: University of Toronto Press, 1987.

Smith, S. "The Dispossesion of the Mississauga Indians: A Missing Chapter in the Early History of Upper Canada," *Ontario History* 73, 2 (June 1981).

Upton, F. *Micmacs and Colonists: Indian-White Relations in the Maritimes, 1713–1867.* Vancouver: University of British Columbia Press, 1979.

## Chapter Seventeen

# "THE BOLD SCHEME": CONFEDERATION

1. "Montreal Annexation Manifesto," *Montreal Gazette,* October 11, 1849.
2. Hon. Sir Etienne-Pascal Taché, Speech, February 3, 1865.
3. Hon. George Etienne Cartier, Speech, February 7, 1865.
4. Hon. George Brown, Speech, February 8, 1865.
5. Hon. Antoine Aimé Dorion, Speech, February 16, 1865.
6. "To The Queen's Most Excellent Majesty," March 6, 1865.
7. Joseph Howe, Speech, 1866.
8. Petition of the Inhabitants of Nova Scotia, "To the Honourable The Commons of Great Britain and Ireland in Parliament Assembled," August 16, 1866.
9. Petition of the undersigned Merchants, Traders, Fishermen, and other Inhabitants of Newfoundland, "To the Honourable The Commons of Great Britain and Ireland in Parliament Assembled," July 4, 1866.

## Introduction

Was it a good idea to create the Dominion of Canada in 1867? Was it even possible to fuse independent-minded British colonies into one giant nation with a tiny population spread unevenly along the southern perimeter? Canada certainly still exists as a nation state, but does that make it good, viable, or natural? Quebec clearly remains ambivalent about the national marriage, and library shelves bulge with treatises on western Canadian alienation. Perhaps Réné Lévesque, the former Quebeçois leader, was right: we should admit that Confederation was a shotgun wedding doomed to fail, get on with the divorce, and become platonic friends and good neighbours. And yet what about the unity rally in downtown Montreal in 1995 when polls suggested that the latest Quebec independence referendum might go to the "yes" side? What about those thousands of nationalists who converged on Quebec from across the country and who wept at the thought of Canada torn asunder? Our present debate on national unity rolls on, as it did during the 1860s.

To many in the nineteenth century, uniting British North American colonies was unnatural, impractical, and unpopular—but perhaps necessary. The colonies shared few things in common, other than being legally British. They had divergent agendas, religions, differing world views, and even unique cultures, dialects, and languages: Maritimers tended to look seaward and to Europe, Upper Canadians west to the new frontier, and Quebeçois inward. Their one common element was a defensive suspicion of their southern neighbours—yet even that was far from universal among citizens. Some argued that British North America, in fact, had so much in common with the Americans that their destiny lay with joining the United States. This, they argued, made eminent sense from economic, defensive, cultural, and historical perspectives. Today Molson brewery champions itself as arch-Canadian, right down to its beer name and the popular "I am Canadian" advertising, but John Molson was amongst those who signed the annexation manifesto.

Evidence in support of the theory that colonial mergers were hopeless could also be found in the newly created colony of Canada, a merger of the former Lower and Upper Canadas. It had proven as dysfunctional as opponents had predicted. The two halves eyed each other with deep suspicion, thwarted each other's agendas, and their political system perpetually teetered on deadlock—at a time when decisive action seemed critical.

Maritime provinces remained deeply skeptical about lessening ties to Britain and merging with the Canadas. Many maritimers believed they had little to gain and much to lose in a federation wherein they would be the clear minority, especially if representation by population ruled the day. Their trade lay with the eastern American states and with Europe, not with the St. Lawrence and the Great Lakes, and their colonies wanted little to do with the Canada's English-French problems or assume larger public debts. Uncertainty ruled the day. What would it mean to become a Canadian province? Status as a British colony meant belonging to the world's largest empire.

But some people still considered following the American example by creating another independent, transcontinental North American nation. Their arguments ranged from self-defence to cultural nationalism. But economic considerations took the spotlight. Great Britain abandoned much of its traditional Imperial Preference and began to buy resources from the cheapest sources, which tended to make Canadian staple exports like wheat uncompetitive. Exports dropped. In response to British actions during the American Civil War, the United States also abrogated the ten year old Reciprocity Agreement it had with Canada's eastern colonies. Nor could purely inter-colonial trade realistically replace these two markets because of the many physical, legal, and political barriers. A united

British North America might revive dwindling trade by creating an effective internal market and make possible the acquisition of the prairies. Farmland had become expensive and a commodity in short supply in most colonies. Canadians intent on careers in agriculture had been migrating to the American mid-West by the thousands. No single colony had the economic resources to buy out the Hudson's Bay Company interest in the prairies, but collectively a united Canada had hopes of raising the revenue. Some cynics have also suggested that men like MacDonald, Brown, and Cartier knew full well the significance of becoming the founders of a new nation. Americans like Washington, Jefferson and Adams had achieved almost legendary status. Ironically, today few Canadian youths can name the country's first prime minister.

## Discussion Points

1. List the reasons for and against Confederation based upon these documents. Did financial matters take precedence?
2. Were the arguments for Confederation a sufficient basis upon which to build a country? Did the Annexation Manifesto propose a more logical solution?
3. Today people distrust promises or claims made by politicians. How much credibility should we give to the speeches in this chapter?
4. Do any of the objections to Confederation in the 1860s still ring true? What promises, if any, has Confederation not fulfilled?

## Documents

### 1. "Montreal Annexation Manifesto," *Montreal Gazette*, October 11, 1849.

To the People of Canada.

The number and magnitude of the evils that afflict our country, and the universal and increasing depression of its material interests, call upon all persons animated by a sincere desire for its welfare to combine for the purposes of inquiry and preparation with a view to the adoption of such remedies as a mature and dispassionate investigation may suggest.

Belonging to all parties, origins and creeds, but yet agreed upon the advantage of co-operation for the performance of a common duty to ourselves and our country, growing out of a common necessity, we have consented, in view of a brighter and happier future, to merge in oblivion all past differences of whatever character, or attributable to whatever source. In appealing to our Fellow-Colonists to unite with us in this our most needful duty, we solemnly conjure them, as they desire a successful issue and the welfare of their country, to enter upon the task at this momentous crisis in the same fraternal spirit.

The reversal of the ancient policy of Great Britain, whereby she withdrew from the Colonies their wonted protection in her markets, has produced the most disastrous effects upon Canada. In surveying the actual condition of the country, what but ruin or rapid decay meets the eye! Our Provincial Government and Civic Corporations, embarrassed; our banking and other securities greatly depreciated; our mercantile and agricultural interests alike unprosperous; real estate scarcely saleable upon any terms; our unrivalled rivers, lakes and canals almost unused; whilst commerce abandons our shores; the circulating capital amassed under a more favourable system is dissipated with none from any quarter to replace it. Thus, without available capital, unable to effect a loan with Foreign States, or with the Mother Country, although offering security greatly superior to that which readily obtains money both from the United States and Great Britain, when other than Colonists are the applicants;—crippled, therefore, and checked in the full career of private and public enterprise, this possession of the British Crown—our country—stands before the world in humiliating contrast with its immediate neighbours, exhibiting every symptom of a nation fast sinking to decay.

With superabundant water power and cheap labour, especially in Lower Canada, we have yet no domestic manufactures; nor can the most sanguine, unless under altered circumstances, anticipate the home growth, or advent from foreign parts, of either capital or enterprise to embark in this great source of national wealth. Our institutions, unhappily, have not that impress of permanence which can alone impart security and inspire confidence, and the Canadian market is too limited to tempt the foreign capitalist.

Whilst the adjoining States are covered with a net-work of thriving railways, Canada possesses but three lines, which, together, scarcely exceed 50 miles in length, and the stock in two of which is held at a depreciation of from 50 to 80 per cent.—a fatal symptom of the torpor overspreading the land.

Our present form of Provincial Government is cumbrous and so expensive as to be ill suited to the circumstances of the country; and the necessary reference it demands to a distant Government, imperfectly acquainted with Canadian affairs, and somewhat indifferent to our interests, is anomalous and irksome. Yet, in the event of a rupture between two of the most powerful nations of the world, Canada would become the battle-field and the sufferer, however little her interests might be involved in the cause of quarrel or the issue of the contest.

The bitter animosities of political parties and factions in Canada, often leading to violence, and, upon one occasion, to civil war, seem not to have abated with time; nor is there, at the present moment, any prospect of diminution or accommodation. The aspect of parties becomes daily more threatening towards each other, and under our existing institutions and relations, little hope is discernible of a peaceful and prosperous administration of our affairs, but difficulties will, to all appearance, accumulate until government becomes impracticable. In this view of our position, any course that may promise to efface existing party distinctions and place entirely new issues before the people, must be fraught with undeniable advantages.

Among the statesmen of the Mother Country—among the sagacious observers of the neighbouring Republic—in Canada—and in all British North America—amongst all classes there is a strong pervading conviction that a political revolution in this country is at hand.—Such forebodings cannot readily be dispelled, and they have, moreover, a tendency to realise the events to which they point. In the meanwhile, serious injury results to Canada from the effect of this anticipation upon the more desirable class of settlers, who naturally prefer a country under fixed and permanent forms of government to one in a state of transition.

Having thus adverted to some of the causes of our present evils, we would consider how far the remedies ordinarily proposed possess sound and rational inducements to justify their adoption:

1.—"The revival of protection in the markets of the United Kingdom."

This, if attainable in a sufficient degree, and guaranteed for a long period of years, would ameliorate the condition of many of our chief interests, but the policy of the empire forbids the anticipation. Besides, it would be but a partial remedy. The millions of the Mother Country demand cheap food; and a second change from protection to free trade would complete that ruin which the first has done much to achieve.

2.—"The protection of home manufactures."

Although this might encourage the growth of a manufacturing interest in Canada, yet, without access to the United States market, there would not be a sufficient expansion of that interest, from the want of consumers, to work any result that could be admitted as a "remedy" for the numerous evils of which we complain.

3.—" A federal union of the British American Provinces."

The advantages claimed for that arrangement are free trade between the different Provinces, and a diminished governmental expenditure. The attainment of the latter object would be problematical, and the benefits anticipated from the former might be secured by legislation under our existing system. The markets of the Sister Provinces would not benefit our trade in timber, for they have a surplus of that article in their own forests; and their demand for agricultural products would be too limited to absorb our means of supply. Nor could Canada expect any encouragement to her manufacturing industry from those quarters. A federal union, therefore, would be no remedy.

4.—"The Independance of the British North American Colonies as a Federal Republic."

The consolidation of its new institutions from elements hitherto so discordant—the formation of treaties with foreign powers—the acquirement of a name and character among the nations—would, we fear, prove an over-match for the strength of the new Republic. And, having regard to the powerful confederacy of States conterminous with itself, the needful military defences would be too costly to render independence a boon, whilst it would not, any more than a federal union, remove those obstacles which retard our material prosperity.

5.—"Reciprocal free trade with the United States, as respects the products of the farm, the forest, and the mine."

If obtained, this would yield but an instalment of the many advantages which might be otherwise secured. The free interchange of such products would not introduce manufactures to our country. It would not give us the North American Continent for our market. It would neither so amend our institutions as to confer stability nor ensure confidence in their permanence nor would it allay the violence of parties, or, in the slightest degree, remedy many of our prominent evils.

6.—Of all the remedies that have been suggested for the acknowledged and insufferable ills with which our country is afflicted, there remains but one to be considered. It propounds a sweeping and important change in our political and social condition involving considerations which demand our most serious examination. THIS REMEDY CONSISTS IN A FRIENDLY AND PEACEFUL SEPARATION FROM BRITISH CONNECTION AND A UNION UPON EQUITABLE TERMS WITH THE GREAT NORTH AMERICAN CONFEDERACY OF SOVEREIGN STATES.

We would premise that towards Great Britain we entertain none other than sentiments of kindness and respect. Without her consent we consider separation as neither practicable nor desirable. But the Colonial policy of the Parent

State, the avowals of her leading statesmen, the public sentiments of the Empire, present unmistakable and significant indications of the appreciation of Colonial connection. That it is the resolve of England to invest us with the attributes and compel us to assume the burdens of independence is no longer problematical. The threatened withdrawal of her troops from other colonies—the continuance of her military protection to ourselves only on the condition that we shall defray the attendant expenditure, betoken intentions towards our country, against which it is weakness in us not to provide. An overruling conviction, then, of its necessity, and a high sense of the duty we owe to our country, a duty we can neither disregard nor postpone, impel us to entertain the idea of separation; and whatever negotiations may eventuate with Great Britain, a grateful liberality on the part of Canada should mark every proceeding.

The proposed union would render Canada a field for American capital, into which it would enter as freely for the prosecution of Public works and Private enterprise as into any of the present States. It would equalise the value of real estate upon both sides of the boundary, thereby probably doubling at once the entire present value of property in Canada, whilst, by giving stability to our institutions, and introducing prosperity, it would raise our public corporate and private credit. It would increase our commerce, both with the United States and foreign countries, and would not necessarily diminish to any great extent our intercourse with Great Britain, into which our products would for the most part enter on the same terms as at present. It would render our rivers and canals the highway for the immigration to, and exports from, the West, to the incalculable benefit of our country. It would also introduce manufactures into Canada as rapidly as they have been introduced into the Northern States; and to Lower Canada especially, where water privileges and labour are abundant and cheap, it would attract manufacturing capital, enhancing the value of property and agricultural produce, and giving remunerative employment to what is at present a comparatively non-producing population. Nor would the United States merely furnish the capital for our manufactures. They would also supply for them the most extensive market in the world, without the intervention of a Custom House Officer. Railways would forthwith be constructed by American capital as feeders for all the great lines now approaching our frontiers; and railway enterprise in general would doubtless be as active and prosperous among us as among our neighbours. The value of our agricultural produce would be raised at once to a par with that of the United States, whilst agricultural implements and many of the necessaries of life, such as tea, coffee and sugar, would be greatly reduced in price.

The value of our timber would also be greatly enhanced by free access to the American market, where it bears a high price, but is subject to an onerous duty. At the same time, there is every reason to believe that our shipbuilders, as well at Quebec as on the Great Lakes, would find an unlimited market in all the ports of the American continent. It cannot be doubted that the shipping trade of the United States must greatly increase.—It is equally manifest that, with them, the principal material in the construction of ships is rapidly diminishing, while we possess vast territories, covered with timber of excellent quality, which would be equally available as it is now, since under the free trade system our vessels would sell as well in England after annexation as before.

The simple and economical State Government, in which direct responsibility to the people is a distinguishing feature, would be substituted for a system, at once cumbrous and expensive.

In place of war and the alarms of war with a neighbour, there would be peace and amity between this country and the United States. Disagreements between the United States and her chief if not only rival among nations would not make the soil of Canada the sanguinary arena for their disputes, as under our existing relations must necessarily be the case. That such is the unenviable condition of our state of dependence upon Great Britain is known to the whole world, and how far it may conduce to keep prudent capitalists from making investments in the country, or wealthy settlers from selecting a fore-doomed battle-field for the home of themselves and their children, it needs no reasoning on our part to elucidate.

But other advantages than those having a bearing on our material interests may be foretold. It would change the ground of political contest between races and parties, allay and obliterate those irritations and conflicts of rancour and recrimination which have hitherto disfigured our social fabric. Already in anticipation has its harmonious influence been felt—the harbinger may it be hoped of a lasting oblivion of dissensions among all classes, creeds and parties in the country. Changing a subordinate for an independent condition, we would take our station among the nations of the earth. We have, now, no voice in the affairs of the Empire, nor do we share in its honors or emoluments. England is our Parent State, with whom we have no equality, but towards whom we stand in the simple relation of obedience. But as citizens of the United States the public services of the nation would be open to us,—a field for high and honorable distinction on which we and our posterity might enter on terms of perfect equality.

Nor would the amicable separation of Canada from Great Britain be fraught with advantages to us alone. The relief to the Parent State from the large expenditure now incurred in the military occupation of the country,—the removal of the many causes of collision with the United States, which result from the contiguity of mutual territories so extensive.—the benefit of the larger market which the increasing prosperity of Canada would create, are considerations which, in the minds of many of her ablest Statesmen, render our incorporation with the United States a desirable consummation.

To the United States also the annexation of Canada presents many important inducements. The withdrawal from their borders, of so powerful a nation, by whom in time of war the immense and growing commerce of the lakes would be jeopardized—the ability to dispense with the costly but ineffectual revenue establishment over a frontier of many hundred miles—the large accession to their income from our Customs—the unrestricted use of the St. Lawrence, the natural highway from the Western States to the ocean, are objects for the attainment of which the most substantial equivalents would undoubtedly be conceded.

FELLOW-COLONISTS,

We have thus laid before you our views and convictions on a momentous question—involving a change, which, though contemplated by many of us with varied feelings and emotions, we all believe to be inevitable;—one which it is our duty to provide for, and lawfully to promote.

We address you without prejudice or partiality,—in the spirit of sincerity and truth—in the interest solely of our common country,—and our single aim is its safety and welfare. If to your judgment and reason our object and aim be at this time deemed laudable and right, we ask an oblivion of past dissensions; and from all, without distinction of origin, party, or creed, that earnest and cordial co-operation in such lawful, prudent, and judicious means as may best conduct us to our common destiny.

## 2. Hon. Sir Etienne-Pascal Taché, Speech, February 3, 1865.

... The honorable member then referred to the artificial communications of the country, viz., our Canals, which, he said, were on a scale unequalled in America, or, indeed, in the world. Our Railway system too, in proportion to our means and population, was as extensive as could be found anywhere else; yet with all these advantages, natural and acquired, he was bound to say we could not become a great nation. We labored under a drawback or disadvantage which would effectually prevent that, and he would defy any one to take a map of the world and point to any great nation which had not seaports of its own open at all times of the year. Canada did not possess those advantages, but was shut up in a prison, as it were, for five months of the year in fields of ice, which all the steam engineering apparatus of human ingenuity could not overcome, and so long as this state of things continued, we must consent to be a small people, who could, at any moment, be assailed and invaded by a people better situated in that respect than we were. Canada was, in fact, just like a farmer who might stand upon an elevated spot on his property, from which he could look around upon fertile fields, meandering streams, wood and all else that was necessary to his domestic wants, but who had no outlet to the highway. To be sure he might have an easy, good-natured neighbor, who had such an outlet, and this neighbor might say to him, "Don't be uneasy about that, for I will allow you to pass on to the highway, through my cross road, and we shall both profit by the arrangement." So long as this obliging neighbor was in good humor everything would go on pleasantly, but the very best natured people would sometimes get out of temper, or grow capricious, or circumstances might arise to cause irritation. And so it might come to pass that the excellent neighbor would get dissatisfied. For instance, he might be involved in a tedious and expensive law suit with someone else; it might be a serious affair—in fact, an affair of life or death, and he might come to the isolated farmer and say to him, "I understand that you and your family are all sympathising with my adversary; I don't like it at all, and I am determined you will find some other outlet to the highway than my cross road, for henceforth my gate will be shut against you." In such a case what is the farmer to do? There is the air left, but until the aerostatic science is more practically developed, he can hardly try ballooning without the risk of breaking his neck. (Laughter.) Well, that was precisely our position in reference to the United States ... The people of the Northern States believed that Canadians sympathized with the South much more than they really did, and the consequences of this misapprehension were: first, that we had been threatened with the abolition of the transit system; then the Reciprocity Treaty was to be discontinued; then a passport system was inaugurated, which was almost equivalent to a prohibition of intercourse, and the only thing which really remained to be done was to shut down the gate altogether and prevent passage through their territory. Would anyone say that such a state of things was one desirable for Canada to be placed in? Will a great people in embryo, as he believed we were, coolly and tranquilly cross their arms and wait for what might come next? ...

On the whole, he thought that the Confederation of all the Provinces had become an absolute necessity, and that it was for us a question of to be or not to be. If we desired to remain British and monarchial, and if we desired to pass to our children these advantages, this measure, he repeated, was a necessity. But there were other motives and other reasons which should induce us to agree to the scheme. Every honorable gentleman in the House knew the political position of the country, and were acquainted with the feelings of irritation which have prevailed for many years. They knew it happily not by their experience in this House, but by the tone of the public press, and by the discussions in another place where taunts and menaces were freely flung across the floor by contending parties. They knew what human passions were, and how, when bitter feelings continued for a long time, the distance between exasperation and actual conflict was not very great. They had now before their own eyes an example of the effects of such disagreements. It was persistently believed by many that the rival interests would never come to a rupture, but for three years they had been waging a conflict which had desolated and ruined the fairest portion of the country, and in the course of which acts of barbarity had been committed which were only equalled by the darkest ages. We in Canada were not more perfect, and the time had arrived when, as he believed, all the patriotic men in the country ought to unite in providing a remedy for the troubles we had to contend with. It might be said that the remedy proposed was not required, but he would like to know what other could be proposed. Legislation in Canada for the last two years had come almost to a stand still, and if any one would refer to the Statute Book since 1862, he would find that the only public measures there inscribed had been passed simply by the permission of the Opposition. This was the condition of things for two years, and if this were an evil there was another not less to be deplored; he referred to the administration of public affairs during the same period. From the 21st May, 1862, to the end of June, 1864, there had been no less than five different Governments in charge of the business of the country....

Lower Canada had constantly refused the demand of Upper Canada for representation according to population, and for the good reason that, as the union between them was legislative, a preponderance to one of the sections would have placed the other at its mercy. It would not be so in a Federal Union, for all questions of a general nature would be reserved for the General Government, and those of a local character to the local governments, who would have the power to manage their domestic affairs as they deemed best. If a Federal Union were obtained it would be tantamount to a separation of the provinces, and Lower Canada would thereby preserve its autonomy together with all the institutions it held so dear, and over which they could exercise the watchfulness and surveillance necessary to preserve them unimpaired....

### 3. Hon. George Etienne Cartier, Speech, February 7, 1865.

... The question for us to ask ourselves was this: Shall we be content to remain separate—shall we be content to maintain a mere provincial existence, when, by combining together, we could become a great nation? It had never yet been the good fortune of any group of communities to secure national greatness with such facility. In past ages, warriors had struggled for years for the addition to their country of a single province ... Here, in British North America, we had five different communities inhabiting five separate colonies. We had the same sympathies, and we all desired to live under the British Crown. We had our commercial interests besides. It was of no use whatever that New Brunswick, Nova Scotia and Newfoundland should have their several custom houses against our trade, or that we should have custom houses against the trade of those provinces. In ancient times, the manner in which a nation grew up was different from that of the present day. Then the first weak settlement increased into a village, which, by turns, became a town and a city, and the nucleus of a nation. It was not so in modern times. Nations were now formed by the agglomeration of communities having kindred interests and sympathies. Such was our case at the present moment. Objection had been taken to the scheme now under consideration, because of the words "new nationality." Now, when we were united together, if union were attained, we would form a political nationality with which neither the national origin, nor the religion of any individual, would interfere. It was lamented by some that we had this diversity of races, and hopes were expressed that this distinctive feature would cease. The idea of unity of races was utopian—it was impossible. Distinctions of this kind would always exist. Dissimilarity, in fact, appeared to be the order of the physical world and of the moral world, as well as of the political world. But with regard to the objection based on this fact, to the effect that a great nation could not be formed because Lower Canada was in great part French and Catholic, and Upper Canada was British and Protestant, and the Lower Provinces were mixed, it was futile and worthless in the extreme. Look, for instance, at the United Kingdom, inhabited as it was by three great races. (Hear, hear.) Had the diversity of race impeded the glory, the progress, the wealth of England? Had they not rather each contributed their share to the greatness of the Empire? Of the glories ... how much was contributed by the combined talents, energy and courage of the three races together? (Cheers.) In our own Federation we should have Catholic and Protestant, English, French, Irish and Scotch, and each by his efforts and his success would increase the prosperity and glory of the new Confederacy. (Hear,

hear.) He viewed the diversity of races in British North America in this way: we were of different races, not for the purpose of warring against each other, but in order to compete and emulate for the general welfare. (Cheers.) We could not do away with the distinctions of race. We could not legislate for the disappearance of the French Canadians from American soil, but British and French Canadians alike could appreciate and understand their position relative to each other. They were placed like great families beside each other, and their contact produced a healthy spirit of emulation. It was a benefit rather than otherwise that we had a diversity of races....

## 4. Hon. George Brown, Speech, February 8, 1865.

... Well, sir, the bold scheme in your hands is nothing less than to gather all these countries [Newfoundland, Nova Scotia, New Brunswick, Lower Canada, Upper Canada, and British Columbia] into one—to organize them all under one government, with the protection of the British flag, and in heartiest sympathy and affection with our fellow-subjects in the land that gave us birth. (Cheers.) Our scheme is to establish a government that will seek to turn the tide of European emigration into this northern half of the American continent—that will strive to develop its great natural resources—and that will endeavor to maintain liberty, and justice, and Christianity throughout the land....

... We imagine not that such a structure can be built in a month or in a year. What we propose now is but to lay the foundations of the structure—to set in motion the governmental machinery that will one day, we trust, extend from the Atlantic to the Pacific. And we take especial credit to ourselves that the system we have devised, while admirably adapted to our present situation, is capable of gradual and efficient expansion in future years to meet all the great purposes contemplated by our scheme. But if the honorable gentleman will only recall to mind that when the United States seceded from the Mother Country, and for many years afterwards their population was not nearly equal to ours at this moment; that their internal improvements did not then approach to what we have already attained; and that their trade and commerce was not then a third of what ours has already reached; I think he will see that the fulfilment of our hopes may not be so very remote as at first sight might be imagined—...

There is one consideration, Mr. Speaker, that cannot be banished from this discussion, and that ought, I think, to be remembered in every word we utter; it is that the constitutional system of Canada cannot remain as it is now. (Loud cries of hear, hear.) Something must be done. We cannot stand still. We cannot go back to chronic, sectional hostility and discord—to a state of perpetual Ministerial crises. The events of the last eight months cannot be obliterated; the solemn admissions of men of all parties can never be erased. The claims of Upper Canada for justice must be met, and met now. I say, then, that every one who raises his voice in hostility to this measure is bound to keep before him, when he speaks, all the perilous consequences of its rejection,—I say that no man who has a true regard for the well-being of Canada, can give a vote against this scheme, unless he is prepared to offer, in amendment, some better remedy for the evils and injustice that have so long threatened the peace of our country. (Hear, hear.) ...

I am persuaded that this union will inspire new confidence in our stability, and exercise the most beneficial influence on all our affairs. I believe it will raise the value of our public securities, that it will draw capital to our shores, and secure the prosecution of all legitimate enterprises; and what I saw, while in England, a few weeks ago, would alone have convinced me of this. Wherever you went you encountered the most marked evidence of the gratification with which the Confederation scheme was received by all classes of the people, and the deep interest taken in its success....

But secondly, Mr. Speaker, I go heartily for the union, because it will throw down the barriers of trade and give us the control of a market of four millions of people. (Hear, hear.) What one thing has contributed so much to the wondrous material progress of the United States as the free passage of their products from one State to another? What has tended so much to the rapid advance of all branches of their industry, as the vast extent of their home market, creating an unlimited demand for all the commodities of daily use, and stimulating the energy and ingenuity of producers? Sir, I confess to you that in my mind this one view of the union—the addition of nearly a million of people to our home consumers—sweeps aside all the petty objections that are averred against the scheme. What, in comparison with this great gain to our farmers and manufacturers, are even the fallacious money objections which the imaginations of honorable gentlemen opposite have summoned up? All over the world we find nations eagerly longing to extend their domains, spending large sums and waging protracted wars to possess themselves of more territory, untilled and uninhabited. (Hear, hear.) Other countries offer large inducements to foreigners to emigrate to their shores—free passages, free lands, and free food and implements to start them in the world. We, ourselves, support costly establishments to attract immigrants to our country, and are satisfied when our annual outlay brings us fifteen or twenty thousand souls. But here, sir, is a proposal which is to add, in one day, near a million of souls to our population—to add valuable territories to our domain, and secure to us all the advantages of a large and profitable commerce, now existing.... [H]ere is a people owning the same allegiance as ourselves, loving the same old sod, enjoying the same laws and institutions, actuated by the same impulses and social customs,—and yet when it is proposed that they shall unite with us for purposes of commerce, for the defence of our common country, and to develop the vast natural resources of our united domains, we hesitate to adopt it! If a Canadian goes now to Nova Scotia or New Brunswick, or if a citizen of these provinces comes here, it is like going to a foreign country. The customs officer meets you at the frontier, arrests your progress, and levies his imposts on your effects. But the proposal now before us is to throw down all barriers between the provinces—to make a citizen of one, citizen of the whole; the proposal is, that our farmers and manufacturers and mechanics shall carry their wares unquestioned into every village of the Maritime Provinces; and that they shall with equal freedom bring their fish, and their coal, and their West India produce to our three millions of inhabitants. The proposal is, that the law courts, and the schools, and the professional and industrial walks of life, throughout all the provinces, shall be thrown equally open to us all. (Hear, hear.)

But, thirdly, Mr. Speaker, I am in favor of a union of the provinces because—and I call the attention of honorable gentlemen opposite to it—because it will make us the third maritime state of the world. (Hear, hear.) When this union is accomplished, but two countries in the world will be superior in maritime influence to British America—and those are Great Britain and the United States. (Hear, hear.) ... Well may [the French-Canadian people] look forward with anxiety to the realization of this part of our scheme, in confident hope that the great north-western traffic shall be once more opened up to the hardy French-Canadian traders and voyageurs. (Hear, hear.) Last year furs to the value of £280,000 ($1,400,000) were carried from that territory by the Hudson's Bay Company—smuggled off through the ice-bound regions of James' Bay, that the pretence of the barrenness of the country and the difficulty of conveying merchandise by the natural route of the St. Lawrence may be kept up a little longer. Sir, the carrying of merchandise into that country, and bringing down the bales of pelts ought to be ours, and must ere long be ours, as in the days of yore— (hear, hear)—and when the fertile plains of that great Saskatchewan territory are opened up for settlement and cultivation, I am confident that it will not only add immensely to our annual agricultural products, but bring us sources of mineral and other wealth on which at present we do not reckon. (Hear, hear.) ...

But, sixthly, Mr. Speaker, I am in favor of the union of the provinces, because, in the event of war, it will enable all the colonies to defend themselves better, and give more efficient aid to the Empire, than they could do separately. I am not one of those who ever had the war-fever; I have not believed in getting up large armaments in this country; I have never doubted that a military spirit, to a certain extent, did necessarily form part of the character of a great people; but I felt that Canada had not yet reached that stage in her progress when she could safely assume the duty of defence; and that, so long as peace continued and the Mother Country threw her shield around us, it was well for us to cultivate our fields and grow in numbers and material strength, until we could look our enemies fearlessly in the face.... But, Mr. Speaker, there is no better mode of warding off war when it is threatened, than to be prepared for it if it comes. The Americans are now a warlike people. They have large armies, a powerful navy, an unlimited supply of warlike munitions, and the carnage of war has to them been stript of its horrors. The American side of our lines already bristles with works of defence, and unless we are willing to live at the mercy of our neighbors, we, too, must put our country in a state of efficient preparation. War or no war—the necessity of placing these provinces in a thorough state of defence can no longer be postponed. Our country is coming to be regarded as undefended and indefensible....

## 5. Hon. Antoine Aimé Dorion, Speech, February 16, 1865.

... If the scheme proposed to us were an equitable one, or one calculated to meet the wishes of the people of this country; but, as I said a minute ago, the scheme was not called for by any considerable proportion of the population. It is not laid before the House as one which was demanded by any number of the people; it is not brought down in response to any call from the people; it is a device of men who are in difficulties, for the purpose of getting out of them. (Hear, hear.) ... I come now to another point, viz., is the scheme presented to us the same one that was promised to us by the Administration when it was formed? This, sir, might be but of slight importance if the manner in which this proposed Constitution was framed had not a most unfortunate bearing on the scheme itself; but it is a grave matter, since the scheme is so objectionable, especially as we are gravely told that it cannot be amended in the least, but that it is brought down as a compact made between the Government of this country and delegates from the governments of Nova Scotia, New Brunswick, Newfoundland, and Prince Edward Island—as a treaty which cannot be altered or amended in any particular.

(Hear.) The plain meaning of this is, sir, that the Lower Provinces have made out a Constitution for us and we are to adopt it....

The whole scheme, sir, is absurd from beginning to end. It is but natural that gentlemen with the views of honorable gentlemen opposite want to keep as much power as possible in the hands of the Government—that is the doctrine of the Conservative party everywhere—that is the line which distinguishes the tories from the whigs—the tories always side with the Crown, and the Liberals always want to give more power and influence to the people. The instincts of honorable gentlemen opposite, whether you take the Hon. Attorney General East or the Hon. Attorney General West, lead them to this—they think the hands of the Crown should be strengthened and the influence of the people, if possible, diminished—and this Constitution is a specimen of their handiwork, with a Governor General appointed by the Crown, with local governors also appointed by the Crown; with legislative councils, in the General Legislature, and in all the provinces, nominated by the Crown; we shall have the most illiberal Constitution ever heard of in any country where constitutional government prevails. (Hear.) The Speaker of the Legislative Council is also to be appointed by the Crown, this is another step backwards, and a little piece of patronage for the Government. We have heard in a speech lately delivered in Prince Edward Island or New Brunswick, I forget which, of the allurements offered to the delegates while here in the shape of prospective appointments as judges of the Court of Appeal, Speaker of the Legislative Council, and local governors—(hear, hear)— as one of the reasons assigned for the great unanimity which prevailed in the Conference.

... Now, sir, when I look into the provisions of this scheme, I find another most objectionable one. It is that which gives the General Government control over all the acts of the local legislatures. What difficulties may not arise under this system? Now, knowing that the General Government will be party in its character, may it not for party purposes reject laws passed by the local legislatures and demanded by a majority of the people of that locality.... But how different will be the result in this case, when the General Government exercises the veto power over the acts of local legislatures. Do you not see that it is quite possible for a majority in a local government to be opposed to the General Government; and in such a case the minority would call upon the General Government to disallow the laws enacted by the majority? The men who shall compose the General Government will be dependent for their support upon their political friends in the local legislatures, and it may so happen that, in order to secure this support, or in order to serve their own purposes or that of their supporters, they will veto laws which the majority of a local legislature find necessary and good. (Hear, hear.) We know how high party feeling runs sometimes upon local matters even of trivial importance, and we may find parties so hotly opposed to each other in the local legislatures, that the whole power of the minority may be brought to bear upon their friends who have a majority in the General Legislature, for the purpose of preventing the passage of some law objectionable to them but desired by the majority of their own section. What will be the result of such a state of things but bitterness of feeling, strong political acrimony and dangerous agitation? (Hear, hear.)

... [T]his scheme proposes a union not only with Nova Scotia, New Brunswick, Prince Edward Island, and Newfoundland, but also with British Columbia and Vancouver's Island ... I must confess, Mr. Speaker, that it looks like a burlesque to speak as a means of defence of a scheme of Confederation to unite the whole country extending from Newfoundland to Vancouver's Island, thousands of miles intervening without any communication, except through the United States or around Cape Horn. (Oh!) ...

I now come to another point. It is said that this Confederation is necessary for the purpose of providing a better mode of defence for this country. There may be people who think that by adding two and two together you make five. I am not of that opinion. I cannot see how, by adding the 700,000 or 800,000 people, the inhabitants of the Lower Provinces, to the 2,500,000 inhabitants of Canada, you can multiply them so as to make a much larger force to defend the country than you have at present. Of course the connection with the British Empire is the link of communication by which the whole force of the Empire can be brought together for defence. (Hear, hear.) But the position of this country under the proposed scheme is very evident. You add to the frontier four or five hundred more miles than you now have, and an extent of country immeasurably greater in proportion than the additional population you have gained; and if there is an advantage at all for the defence of the country, it will be on the part of the Lower Province, and not for us.... Within a period of four years the Northern States have called into the field 2,300,000 men—as many armed men as we have men, women and children in the two Canadas—and ... we hear every day of more being raised and equipped. It is stated that, in view of these facts, it is incumbent upon us to place ourselves in a state of defence. Sir, I say it here, candidly and honestly, that we are bound to do everything we can to protect the country—(Hear, hear.)—but we are not bound to ruin ourselves in anticipation of a supposed invasion which we could not repel, even with the assistance of England. The battles of Canada cannot be fought on the frontier, but on the high seas and at the great cities of the Atlantic coast; and it will be nothing but folly for us to cripple ourselves by spending fifteen or twenty millions a year to raise 50,000 men for the purpose of resisting an invasion of the country. The best thing that Canada can do is to keep quiet and give no cause for war....

### 6. "To The Queen's Most Excellent Majesty," March 6, 1865.

To the Queen's Most Excellent Majesty
Most Gracious Sovereign,

We, Your Majesty's loyal and faithful servants, the Legislative Council and House of Assembly of Prince Edward Island, having had under our consideration the resolutions or report of the Conference of delegates from the Provinces of Canada, Nova Scotia, and New Brunswick, and the Colonies of Newfoundland and Prince Edward Island, held at the city of Quebec on the 10th October 1864, upon the subject of a proposed Confederation of those Provinces and Colonies, and the Despatch of the Right Honourable Edward Cardwell, Your Majesty's Principal Secretary of State for the Colonial Department, to Lord Viscount Monck, Governor-General of Canada, dated the 3rd December 1864, relative thereto, humbly beg leave to approach Your Majesty's throne, for the purpose of conveying to Your august Majesty the expression of our desire and determination, as the constitutional representatives of the people of Prince Edward Island, in regard to the great question involved in the said report; and having after most mature deliberation arrived at the conclusion that the proposed Confederation, in so far as it is contemplated to embrace Prince Edward Island, would prove disastrous to the best interests and future prosperity of this Colony, we would humbly crave leave to state the grounds upon which that conclusion is based.

First.—Prince Edward Island, being entirely dependent on its agriculture and fisheries, has no staple commodity to export for which Canada can furnish a market (Canada being also essentially an agricultural country, and possessing valuable and extensive fisheries in the Gulf of St. Lawrence). That while such is, and ever must be, the relative commercial position of this Island and Canada, the products of our soil and fisheries, find in the extensive markets of our parent country, the United States, and the West Indies ready and profitable customers. That the proposed Union, while admitting the produce and manufactures of Canada into this Island free, would, by assimilation of taxes, enormously increase the duty to which those of Great Britain and the United States are at present subject in this Island, thereby compelling this Colony to take a large portion of its imports from Canada, making payment therefor in money, instead of procuring them from countries which would receive our produce in exchange, an arrangement so inconsistent with the fundamental principles of commerce that it would not only greatly curtail our commercial intercourse with Great Britain and the United States, but materially diminish our exports to those countries, and prove most injurious to the agricultural and commercial interests of this Island.

Second.—That if the relative circumstances of Canada and this Island rendered a Union practicable, the evident injustice of the terms agreed to by the Quebec Conference would prevent their being ratified by this Island. Without entering into full detail on this branch of the subject, or adverting to the fact that by the proposed terms of the Confederation we are called upon to transfer to the Confederate exchequer a steadily increasing revenue, and that too under our comparatively low tariff, for a fixed and settled annual subsidy of a greatly diminished amount, we would briefly notice some of the objectionable features of the said report.

And first in reference to the fundamental principle upon which the Confederation is proposed to rest, namely, representation according to population. Without admitting this principle under all circumstances to be sound or just, we consider it to be particularly objectionable as applied to this Island in connexion with Canada, from the fact that the number of our inhabitants is and must continue comparatively small, in consequence of this Island possessing no Crown lands, mines, or minerals, or other extraneous resources, and that we never can expect to become, to any great extent, a manufacturing people, by reason of our navigation being closed for nearly half the year, and all trade, and even communication with other countries (except by telegraph and the medium of a fragile ice-boat) stopped. And when we consider the provision of the said report which is intended to regulate the mode of re-adjusting the relative representation of the various Provinces at each decennial census, and reflect upon the rapid rate of increase in the population of Upper and Lower Canada, particularly the former, heretofore, and the certainty of a still greater increase therein in the future over that of the population of this Island, it follows, as a certain and inevitable consequence, if a Federation of the Provinces were consummated upon the basis of the said report, that the number of our representatives in the Federal Parliament would, in the course of a comparatively short number of years, be diminished to a still smaller number than that proposed to be allotted to us at the commencement of the Union.

Third.—In further noticing the injustice of the terms of the said report, as applicable to us, we would advert to the old imperial policy, so pregnant with ill consequences to us, by which all the lands in this Colony were granted in large tracts to absentees, and which deprives this Island of the revenue drawn by the sister colonies from these sources,—to our insular position and numerous harbours, furnishing cheap and convenient water communication, which render expensive public works here unnecessary,—to the revenue to be drawn by the proposed Federal Government from this Island and expended among the people of Canada and the other Provinces in constructing railways, canals, and other great public works, thereby creating a trade which would build up cities and enhance the value of property in various parts of those Provinces, advantages in which this Island could enjoy an very small participation;—and to our complete isolation during five months of the year, when ice interrupts our trade and communication with the mainland, and during which period this Island could derive no possible benefit from the railroads and other public works which they would equally with the people of those Provinces be taxed to construct. These and many other circumstances placing Prince Edward Island in an exceptional position in regard to the other Provinces, but which seem to have been entirely ignored, ought, in our opinion, to have produced an offer of a financial arrangement for this Island very different in its terms from that contained in the report of the said Conference.

Fourth.—That while we fully recognize it to be the duty of this Colony to use every means, to the extent of its limited resources, to aid in defending its inhabitants from foreign invasion, we cannot recognize the necessity of uniting in a Confederation with Canada for the purpose of defence upon terms, which, in other respects, are so unfair to the people of Prince Edward Island, and thereby sacrificing our commercial and financial interests for the sake of securing the co-operation of Canada in a military point of view, it being our abiding hope and conviction, that so long as we remain a loyal and attached Colony of Great Britain, under whose protecting sway and benign influence we have so long had the happiness to live, and endeavour to aid, by a reasonable contribution towards the defence of our Colony, by placing our militia service upon a sounder and safer footing that it has hitherto attained, the powerful aid of our mother country will continue, as theretofore, to be extended to us in common with the other North American dependencies of the British Crown. For the foregoing reasons, and many other which we could urge, we beg most humbly and respectfully to state to Your Majesty that we, the representatives of Your faithful subjects, the people of Prince Edward Island, in Colonial Parliament now assembled, do disagree to the recommendations contained in the said report of the Quebec Conference, and on the part of Prince Edward Island do emphatically decline a Union, which after the most serious and careful consideration, we believe would prove politically, commercially, and financially disastrous to the rights and best interests of its people.

We do, therefore, most humbly pray that Your Majesty will be graciously pleased not to give Your Royal assent or sanction to any Act or measure founded upon the resolutions or report of the said Conference, or otherwise, that would have the effect of uniting Prince Edward Island in a Federal Union with Canada, or any other of Your Majesty's Provinces in America.

## 7. Joseph Howe, Speech, 1866.

Let us see what these Canadians desire to do. They are not, as we have shown, a very harmonious or homogeneous community. Two-fifths of the population are French and three-fifths English. They are therefore perplexed with an internal antagonism which was fatal to the unity of Belgium and Holland, and which, unless the fusion of races becomes rapid and complete, must ever be a source of weakness. They are shut in by frost from the outer world for five months of the year. They are at the mercy of a powerful neighbour whose population already outnumbers them by more than eight to one, and who a quarter of a century hence will probably present sixty eight millions to six millions on the opposite side of a naturally defenceless frontier. Surely such conditions as these ought to repress inordinate ambition or lust of territory on the part of the public men of Canada.... While they discharge their duties as unobtrusive good neighbours to the surrounding populations, and of loyal subjects of the empire, Great Britain will protect them by her energy in other fields should the Province become untenable but it is evident that a more unpromising nucleus of a new nation can hardly be found on the face of the earth, and that any organized communities, having a reasonable chance to do anything better would be politically insane to give up their distinct formations and subject themselves to the domination of Canada.

Thus situated, and borne down by a public debt of $75,000,000, or about $25 in gold per head of their population, the public men of Canada propose to purchase the territories of the Hudson's Bay Company, larger than half of Europe. They propose to assume the government of British Oregon and Vancouver's Island, provinces divided from them by an interminable wilderness, and by the natural barrier of the Rocky Mountains; and they propose to

govern Nova Scotia, New Brunswick, Prince Edward Island and Newfoundland—countries severally as large as Switzerland, Sardinia, Greece, and Great
Britain, appointing their governors, senators and judges, and exercising over
them unlimited powers of internal and external taxation....

Anybody who looks at the map of British America, and intelligently searches
its geographical features in connection with its past record and present political
condition, will perceive that it naturally divides itself into four great centres of
political power and radiating intelligence. The Maritime Provinces, surrounded
by the sea: three of them insular, with unchangeable boundaries, with open
harbours, rich fisheries, abundance of coal, a homogeneous population, and
within a week's sail of the British Islands, form the first division; and the Ashburton
Treaty, which nearly severed them from Canada, defines its outlines and proportions. These Provinces now govern themselves, and do it well, and Canada has
no more right to control or interfere with them than she has to control the
Windward Islands or Jamaica. These Provinces have developed commercial enterprise and maritime capabilities with marvellous rapidity. Three of them can
be held while Great Britain keeps the sea. Newfoundland and Prince Edward
Island are surrounded by it, and the narrow isthmus of fourteen miles which
connects Nova Scotia with the mainland can be easily fortified and can be enfi-
laded by gunboats on either side. But what is more these Provinces can help
Great Britain to preserve her ascendency on the ocean. While far-seeing members of the House of Commons are inquiring into the causes which diminish the
number of her sailors and increase the difficulty of manning her fleet, is it not
strange that the great nursery for seamen which our Maritime Provinces present
should be entirely overlooked, and that flippant writers should desire to teach
60,000 hardy seafaring people to turn their backs upon England and fix their
thoughts upon Ottawa; and should deliberately propose to disgust them by
breaking down their institutions and subjecting them to the arbitrary control of
an inland population, frozen up nearly half the year, and who are incapable of
protecting them by land or sea.

Referring to the statistics of trade and commerce, it will be found that
Nova Scotia employs 19,637 mariners and fishermen; Newfoundland, 38,578;
and Prince Edward Island, 2,113. Nova Scotia alone owns 400,000 tons of
shipping.

Here are colonies within seven days' steaming of these shores, floating the
flag of England over a noble mercantile marine, and training 60,000 seamen
and fishermen to defend it, and yet the House of Commons is to be asked to
allow some gentlemen in Ottawa to draw these people away from the ocean,

which for their own and the general security of the empire they are required to protect, that their hearts may be broken and their lives wasted on interminable frontiers incapable of defence. Parliament, it is hoped, will think twice about this proposition, and of the scheme for launching a prince of the blood into a sea of troubles for the glorification of the Canadians.

Canada forms the second division of British America, in order of sequence as we ascend from the Atlantic. It is a fine country with great natural resources, and may develop into some such nation as Poland or Hungary. Hemmed in by icy barriers at the north, and by a powerful nation on the south, shut out from deep sea navigation for nearly half the year, with two nationalities to reconcile, and no coal, who will predict for her a very brilliant destiny at least for many years to come? The best she can do is to be quiet, unobtrusive, thrifty, provoking no enmities, and not making herself disagreeable to her neighbours, or increasing the hazards which her defence involves, by any premature aspirations to become a nation, for which status at present she is totally unprepared....

But it may be asked, do not the Maritime Provinces desire this union? and, if the question includes the Quebec scheme of confederation, it is soon answered. Every one of them rejected it with a unanimity and decision not to be misunderstood. In Prince Edward Island, both branches of the Legislature being elective, but five members could be got to vote for it. In Newfoundland it was condemned by the people at the polls. In Nova Scotia the leader of the Government was compelled to come down to the House and declare it "impracticable"; and in New Brunswick the electors, animated by the instinct of self-preservation, rushed to the polls, swept the delegates aside, and trampled it under their feet. Here the matter would have rested had all the Provinces been treated with the justice and impartiality to which they were entitled....

## 8. Petition of the Inhabitants of Nova Scotia, "To the Honourable The Commons of Great Britain and Ireland in Parliament Assembled," August 16, 1866.

HUMBLY SHOWETH,—

... That the people of this Province, from their maritime position, have developed the pursuits of ship building, navigation, commerce, and fishing into prosperous activity. Their agricultural resources are rich and varied, whilst the vast mineral wealth which underlies the whole area of the country is a special guarantee of its future prosperity under favourable political conditions. The gold mines of Nova Scotia, without rising to the character of dazzling lotteries to attract a promiscuous or disorderly population from abroad, have proved steadily remunerative as a regular department of native industry, and a profitable investment for foreign capital. The great iron mines already discovered give earnest, in connexion with its coal fields, of manufacturing capabilities not inferior to those of any country of similar extent. It has the thickest coal seams in the world, and their area is extensive, affording fair ground for the presumption that, for the purposes of peace or war, Nova Scotia's continued connexion with Great Britain would prove of mutual advantage. Possessed of these resources, the people desire closer relations with the Mother Country in order to be able to enjoy more largely the benefits, as well as share more fully the responsibilities, of the Empire; and already the Province has enrolled 60,000 efficient militia and volunteers to assist in the maintenance of British power on this Continent, and sends to sea 440,000 tons of shipping, built and owned within the Province, bearing the flag of England, and manned by more than 20,000 seamen.

That Nova Scotia has no controversies with the mother-country, the other Provinces, or with the population of the neighbouring United States; and highly prizes the privileges so long enjoyed of regulating her own tariffs, and conducting trade, but lightly burthened, with the British Islands and Colonies in all parts of the world and with foreign countries.

That the people of Nova Scotia are prepared to entertain any propositions by which (preserving to them the institutions they now have and the privileges they enjoy) greater facilities for commercial and social intercourse with other States and Provinces may be secured; and they are willing, whenever their own coast and harbours are safe, to aid Her Majesty's forces to preserve from agression the Provinces in the rear.

But they view with profound distrust and apprehension schemes, recently propounded, by which it is proposed to transfer to the people of Canada the control of the Government, Legislation, and Revenues of this loyal and happy Province, and they venture respectfully to crave from your Honourable House justice and protection:

That the Province of Canada lies as far from Nova Scotia as Austria does from England, and there exists no reason why a people who live at such a distance, with whom we have but little commerce, who have invested no capital in our country, who are unable to protect it, and are themselves shut off from ocean navigation by frost for five months of the year, should control our Legislation and Government:

That in 1864 the Government of Nova Scotia, without any authority from the Legislature, and without any evidence of the consent of the people, sent delegates to Canada to arrange in secret conference at Quebec a political union between the various Provinces. That these delegates concealed the result of their conference from the people until it became incidentally made public in another Province, and that, to this hour, they have never unfolded portions of the scheme having the most essential relation to the peculiar interests and local government of Nova Scotia subsequent to Confederation.

That the scheme, when at last made public, was received with great dissatisfaction in Nova Scotia; that the opposition to it has been constantly on the increase, and has been intensified by the conduct of the Government and the delegates, who now propose to call in the aid of your Honourable House to assist them to overthrow, by an arbitrary exercise of power, free institutions enjoyed for a century and never abused:

That the objections of the people to the proposed Confederation scheme affect not merely minor local details, but the radical principles of the plan. The people cannot recognize the necessity for change in their present tranquil, prosperous, and free condition. They cannot believe that the proposed Confederation with the distant Colony (Canada) will prove of any practical benefit, either for defence or trade; while, from the past history of that country, its sectional troubles, its eccentric political management and financial embarrassments, they have great reason to fear that Confederation would be to them a most disastrous change, retarding their progress, and rendering their prolonged connexion with the Crown precarious if not impossible. Forming, as she does now, a portion of the Empire, Nova Scotia is already confederated with fifty other States and Provinces, enjoys free trade with two hundred and fifty millions of people living under one flag and owning the authority of one Sovereign. She has no desire to part with her self control, or to narrow her commercial privileges, by placing herself under the dominion of a Sister Colony, with an exposed frontier, frostbound for a third of the year, and with no navy to defend the Maritime Provinces when her ports are open.

The scheme of government framed at Quebec is unlike any other that history shows to have been successful. It secures neither the consolidation, dignity, and independent power of monarchy, nor the checks and guards which ensure to the smaller States self-government and controlling influence over the Federal authorities in the neighbouring Republic. By adopting the federal principle, sectionalism in the five Provinces is perpetuated; by the timid and imperfect mode in which that principle is applied the people, whose minds have been unsettled by this crude experiment, may be driven to draw contrasts and nourish aspirations of which adventurous and powerful neighbours will not be slow to take advantage; and the people of Nova Scotia have no desire to peril the integrity of the Empire, with the blessings they now enjoy, or to try new experiments, which may complicate foreign relations, and yet add no real strength to the Provinces it is proposed to combine.

The people object also the financial arrangements, as especially burdensome and unfair to this Province. Having long enjoyed the control and benefited by the expenditure of their own revenues, they cannot approve a scheme that will wrest the greater part of these from their hands, to keep up costly and cumbrous federal machinery, and to meet the liabilities of Canada.

For many years the commercial policy of Nova Scotia has been essentially different from that of Canada. The latter country, partly from necessity arising out of financial embarrassments, and partly as an indirect premium on her own manufactures, has adopted a tariff varying from 20 to 30 per cent. on imported goods.

Almost surrounded, as Nova Scotia is, by the ocean, her people are favourably situated for enjoying free commercial intercourse with every section of the British Empire and with those foreign countries open to her commerce by the enlightened policy of the Parent State: of this privilege she has availed herself by imitating, as far as local circumstances would permit, the liberal and free trade policy of the Mother Country—ten per cent. being the ad valorem duty collected under the Nova Scotia tariff on goods imported into the Province. The proposed scheme of union will give Canada, by her large preponderance in the Legislature, the power to shape the tariff for the whole Confederacy according to her inland ideas and necessities, so as to levy the same onerous duties on British goods imported into Nova Scotia as are now exacted by Canada.

That since the Confederation scheme has been announced there have been special parliamentary elections in three out of the eighteen counties of this Province, and in all three it has been condemned at the polls.

That in 1865 the scheme was condemned at nearly every public meeting held by the delegates to discuss it, and numerous petitions against its adoption were presented to the Provincial Parliament, and only one in its favour, until the leader of the Government declared the measure to be "impracticable."

That at the opening of the late session no reference to Confederation was made in the speech of the Lieutenant Governor, and down to a late period the people of Nova Scotia were led to believe that the scheme had been abandoned. A resolution was introduced towards the close of the session, clothing the Government with power to appoint delegates, who, in connexion with delegates from the other Provinces, are to frame a scheme of government, to which it is proposed to ask the sanction of your Honourable House before it has been submitted to the Legislature that it may annihilate, or to the people whose legal and constitutional rights and powers it may transfer or circumscribe.

The undersigned, menaced by a measure that may be revolutionary, repose implicit confidence in the protection of the Imperial Parliament. They deny the authority of their own Legislature, invested with limited powers for a definite term, to deprive them of rights earned by their ancestors by the most painful sacrifices, wisely exercised and never abused for more than a century, and which they had no legitimate authority to alienate or break down. They believe that any scheme of government, framed by a committee of delegates and forced upon the Provinces without their revision or approval, would generate wide spread dissatisfaction among a loyal and contented people, who will not fail to reflect that no change can be made in the constitution of any of the neighbouring States which has not first been approved by the electors; and that important measures, affecting imperial policy or institutions, are rarely attempted till they have been submitted for acceptance or rejection by the people whose interests they are to affect.

Your petitioners therefore pray that your Honourable House will be pleased to defer all action in favour of Confederation in the Imperial Parliament until the people of Nova Scotia shall have exercised and enjoyed their constitutional privilege to express their opinions at the polls, or that your Honourable House may be pleased to direct that a special committee shall inquire into all the features of the proposed scheme of Confederation, as it is likely to affect the several Provinces in their relations to each other and to the mother-country; or that the people of Nova Scotia be permitted to appear by counsel at the bar of your Honourable House to defend their interests and institutions. And your petitioners, as in duty bound, will ever pray, &c.

9. **Petition of the undersigned Merchants, Traders, Fishermen, and other Inhabitants of Newfoundland, "To the Honourable The Commons of Great Britain and Ireland in Parliament Assembled," July 4, 1866.**

The Petition of the undersigned Merchants, Traders, Fishermen, and other Inhabitants of Newfoundland.

MOST HUMBLY SHOWETH,—

That this Colony has for many years enjoyed the blessings and privileges of self-government and local legislation, the imposition and appropriation of duties and taxes, and the general management of its local affairs:

That the sentiments of all classes of its people have been, and still are, of the most loyal and devoted character; that its necessities or demands for protection from the foreign enemy or from internal disturbance have never been a heavy burden or a serious cost to the Imperial Exchequer; while from the fact of its staple products being confined to fish and oil, and the country having limited agricultural and no manufacturing resources, its chief import trade is prosecuted and its most intimate commercial relations are held with Great Britain. Newfoundland, while holding a prominent and formidable position upon the Atlantic, as the point nearest to England, is practically more remote from the principal ports of the Canadas than from Britain itself, and has never had any political, and only minor commercial, connexion with the former—a connexion which is entirely cut off by sea for nearly six months of the year, during which time there can be no communication with Canada, except through the territories of a foreign power—the United States of America. The inhabitants of this Colony would desire to see this island always retained separately by Britain, as its ocean fortress and military outpost in this part of the world, whatever might be the future destiny of the Colonies on the mainland. But let the value attached to her position in an Imperial view be what it may, the Colony has, from its distinct trade and its different characteristics, no community of interests with Upper or Lower Canada, and little with the other Maritime Provinces.

The people regard, therefore, with grave apprehension and alarm any project which has for its object the union of the Island of Newfoundland with the other British North American dependencies of the Crown. Some reasons which might influence them to receive it with favour are just those which make it undesirable for Newfoundland. The motives which in their case have actuated the policy of Great Britain for the promotion of the scheme of Confederation are entirely wanting in ours. We are no cause of offence, we are not in the path of possible aggression or in the way of attack, unless and until the national cause of Great Britain involves us in a common fate. We are a comparatively small burthen on the Home Government; and, in the present condition of affairs, obtain those supplies from Britain which we should, under the proposed Union, have in a great measure to abandon for the inferior manufactures of colonies with which we have little trade. Under these circumstances, it has been proposed to include this Colony in a Confederation on the basis of the Quebec Convention of 1864, and by this measure to deprive her of those civil, constitutional, and territorial rights which she has so long held and so dearly prized; and for a loss so great there is no offer of a substantial return.

Our taxation, already burdensome, will be assimilated to the much higher Canadian tariff. Our revenues will go to the central exchequer, and in return we shall receive a sum far below our present income without any corresponding advantages.

No matter how a rapidly growing population, the development of our resources, or our future necessities may call for augmented supplies, not to speak of the constantly increasing demands for public improvements; no matter how large at any time our contribution to the Federal finances may be, our receipts from it are proposed to be permanently limited to 112,000*l.* per annum.

The proposed Central Government will also possess the dangerous power to levy duties upon the exports of a Colony, whose only wealth lies in them, and which, from its peculiar circumstances, will be utterly without the means of local taxation wherewith to promote public improvement or to relieve its people from a pauperism which, to some extent, is necessarily chronic and frequently widespread and disastrous.

The chief exports of Nova Scotia and New Brunswick are expressly exempt from the power of Federal taxation.

The people of Newfoundland have no interest and can derive no benefit whatever from the great public works of Canada, existing or projected. There is no provision even made in the Quebec Convention for a connexion by lines of steamers between the Colony and the other Provinces on the one hand, and Great Britain on the other; while for the North-western territory guarantees for complete territorial connexion are contained.

These are amongst the objections which apply to the Quebec Convention, even if the project of union could on any basis be made applicable and beneficial to this Colony, its trade, and people.

But the peculiar position and circumstances arising from the nature of its trade, its resources and its geography are such that the Maritime Provinces in their original project of union never contemplated the introduction of New-foundland. Even when the Canadas proposed to unite with them, this Colony was not included until after the convocation of delegates at Quebec in the autumn of 1864, when a request was made to our local Executive to send non-official delegates to be present at the proceedings.

These delegates were not clothed with any active authority.

The express terms of the convention show that Newfoundland was only provisionally referred to.

The subject had never been a matter of popular inquiry or political consideration in this Colony up to that time. Public alarm has been excited by the result of late elections in the Continental Colonies, and by the fact that delegates from them are, it is said, to proceed to Britain to negotiate a scheme of union.

It is with the view to convey to your Honourable House the aversion of this people to be considered at this time in any overtures or negotiations whatever that may be so made or had, that your petitioners on their behalf now approach your Honourable House.

If circumstances should hereafter arise to make it less objectionable than it now is for this Colony to be considered in any project of union with the rest of British North America, our people will, petitioners feel sure, lend a ready and loyal ear to the Imperial counsels.

In the meantime your petitioners believe the objections to be insuperable; but if they be wrong, the voice of all the people of the Colony may be taken at an early and convenient time.

These people are, at this time, for the most part scattered and engaged in the avocation of the fishery. And it is for this reason that at this moment of alarm these petitioners presume to give expression to an opinion, and to prefer a prayer which they believe to coincide with the wishes and feelings of the great majority of the people....

Your petitioners therefore humbly pray your Honourable House that no negotiations may be had, and that no measure or project may be entertained in Parliament, contemplating the present comprehension of this Colony in any scheme of union with the other Provinces, until this question, involving as it does the vital interests and future fate of this dependency of the Crown, shall have been definitely submitted to the people of Newfoundland at a general election of representatives to their House of Assembly. And as in duty bound they will ever pray.

## Readings

Beck, J. *Joseph Howe: Briton Becomes Canadian*. Kingston and Montreal: McGill Queen's University Press, 1982.

Bolger, F. *Prince Edward Island and Confederation, 1863–1873*. Charlottetown: St. Dunstan's University Press, 1964.

Bruckner, P., P. Waite, and W. Baker. "CHR Dialogue: The Maritimes and Confederation: A Reassessment," *Canadian Historical Review* 71, 1 (March 1990).

Careless, J. *Brown of the Globe*. Toronto: University of Toronto Press, 1964.

Cook, R., ed. *Confederation*. Toronto: University of Toronto Press, 1967.

Creighton, D. *The Road to Confederation: The Emergence of Canada 1863–1867*. Toronto: Macmillan, 1964.

Hiller, J. "Confederation Defeated. The Newfoundland Election of 1869" in J. Hiller and P. Neary, eds., *Newfoundland in the Nineteenth and Twentieth Centuries.* Toronto: University of Toronto Press, 1980.

Martin, G. *Britain and the Origins of the Canadian Confederation, 1837–1867.* Vancouver: University of British Columbia Press, 1995.

Martin, G., ed. *The Causes of Canadian Confederation.* Fredericton: Acadiensis Press, 1990.

Morton, W. *The Critical Years: The Union of British North America, 1875–1873.* Toronto: McClelland and Stewart, 1964.

Owram, D. *Promise of Eden: The Canadian Expansionist Movement and the Idea of the West, 1856–1900.* Second edition. Toronto: University of Toronto Press, 1992.

Pryke, K. *Nova Scotia and Confederation, 1867–1871.* Toronto: University of Toronto Press, 1979.

Rawlyck, G. *The Atlantic Provinces and the Problems of Confederation.* Halifax: Breakwater Press, 1979.

Silver, A. *The French Canadian Idea of Confederation, 1864–1900.* Toronto: University of Toronto Press, 1982.

Waite, P. *The Life and Times of Confederation, 1864–1867: Politics, Newspapers and the Union of British North America.* Toronto: University of Toronto Press, 1962.

Weale, D., and H. Baglole. *The Island and Confederation: The End of an Era.* Summerside: Williams and Crue, 1973.

# SOURCES

1. **"So Blind and So Ignorant": Looking into Other Eyes**

   The first two documents come from R. Thwaites (ed. and trans.), *Jesuit Relations and Allied Documents* (Cleveland: Burrows and Company, 1896–1901) Vol. 6, 19, 21. Le Clerq's comments and those of the Micmac chief appear in William Ganong (ed. and trans.), *New Relations of Gaspesia* (Toronto: The Champlain Society, 1910); for his general observations and his dialogue with Adario see Lahontan, *Some New Voyages to North America* (London: H. Bonwicke, 1703).

2. **"Advantages and Inconveniences": The Colonization of Canada**

   Champlain's account was reprinted in H. Bigger ed., *The Works of Samuel de Champlain*, Vol. 2 (Toronto: The Champlain Society, 1925); Pierre Boucher, *True and Genuine Description of New France Commonly Called Canada* (Paris: 1664) was translated and reprinted by E. Montizambert under the title *Canada in the Seventeenth Century* (Montreal: G.E. Desbarats, 1883). Talon's memoir can be found in *Rapport de l'Archiviste de la Province de Quebec 1930–31* (Québec: Imprimeur du Roi, 1931). The 1922–23 annual report of the same journal contains D'Auteuil's memoir of 1715. Duchesneau's letter appears in S. Clark, *The Social Development of Canada* (Toronto: University of Toronto Press, 1955), while Dennonville's correspondence was reproduced in E.B. O'Callaghan (ed.), *Documents Relative to the Colonial History of the State of New York,* Vol. 9 (Albany: Weed Parson and Company, 1855). P. Charlevoix, *Journal of a Voyage to North America*, Vol. 1 (London: R. and J. Dodsley, 1761). Hocquart's instructions were reproduced in Y. Zoltvany (ed.), *The French Tradition in America* (New York: Harper and Row, 1969), and his memoir can be found in J. Reid, K. McNaught, and H. Crowe (eds.), *A Source Book of Canadian History* (Don Mills: Longman, 1964).

3. **"An Afflicted People": The Acadians**

   Documents by Mascarene, Jonquiere, Galerm, and one of those by Charles Lawrence can found reproduced in N.F.S. Griffiths, *The Acadian Deportation: Deliberate Perfidy or Cruel Necessity* (Toronto: Copp Clark, 1969). The circular letter from Gov. Lawrence to the Governors on the Continent, Halifax 1755, was reprinted in Public Archives of Canada, *Report*, II (Ottawa: King's Printer, 1905). "Minutes of His

Majesty's Council...1726" are in A. McMehan (ed.), *Original Minutes of His Majesty's Council at Annapolis Royal, 1720–1739* (Halifax: Nova Scotia Archives, 1908) The Acadian Memorial is reprinted in T. Atkins (ed.), *Selections from the Public Documents of Nova Scotia* (Halifax: C. Annand, 1869).

4. **"The Ruin of Canada": Last Decades of New France**

Documents by Daine, Montcalm, Pean, and the untitled "Memoir" were reprinted in E.B. O'Callaghan (ed.), *Documents Relative to the Colonial History of the State of New York* Vol. 10 (Albany: Weed Parson and Company, 1858); de Capellis and de Beaucat's accounts were reproduced in K. MacKirdy, J. Moir and Y. Zoltvany, *Changing Perspectives in Canadian History* (Don Mills: J.M. Dent and Sons, 1971). "Narrative of the doings during the Siege of Quebec, and the conquest of Canada by a nun of the General Hospital of Quebec transmitted to a religious community of the same order, in France" was first published in English in 1826 and most recently reprinted in Jean-Claude Hebert, *The Siege of Quebec in 1759: Three Eyewitness Accounts* (Québec: Ministry of Cultural Affairs, 1974).

5. **"The Abundant Blessings of British Rule": Quebec's New Administration**

Murray's report was reproduced in A. Shortt and A. Doughty eds. *Documents Relating to the Constitutional History of Canada, 1759–1791* (Ottawa: King's Printer, 1907); the Plessis sermon appears in H. Forbes (ed.), *Canadian Political Thought* (Toronto: Oxford University Press, 1977); the Selkirk material comes from P. White (ed.), *Lord Selkirk's Diary, 1803–1804: A Journey of His Travels to British North America and the Northeastern United States* (Toronto: The Champlain Society, 1958); "To the Editor of the *Quebec Mercury*," (*Le Canadien*: November 29, 1806); John Lambert, *Travels through Lower Canada and the United States of North America in the Years 1806, 1807 and 1808,* Vol. I (London: Richard Phillips, 1810); the document by Gray appears in J. Hare and J. Wallot (eds.), *Ideas in Conflict* (Trois-Rivières: Editions Boreal Express, 1970); Memoire by Bédard is reproduced in Y. Lamonde and C. Corbo (eds.), *Le Rouge et le Bleu: Une Anthologie de la Pensée Politique au Québec de la Conquete á la Revolution Tranquille* (Montreal: Les Presses de L'Université de Montreal).

6. **"Our Robinson Crusoe Sort of Life": Three Women in Upper Canada**

Susanna Moodie, *Roughing It in the Bush* (London: Richard Bentley, 1852); Anna Brownell Jameson, *Winter Studies and Summer Rambles* (London: Saunders and Otley, 1838); Catharine Parr Traill, *The Backwoods of Canada* (London: Charles Knight, 1836).

7. **"The Long and Heavy Chain of Abuse": Political Crisis in Lower Canada**

For copies of documents by Parent and Nelson see Lamonde and C. Corbo (eds.), *Le Rouge et le Bleu: Une Anthologie de la Pensée Politique au Québec de la Conquete á la Revolution Tranquille* (Montreal: Les Presses de L'Université de Montreal); "The Six Counties Address" was reprinted in H.D. Forbes (ed.), *Canadian Political Thought* (Toronto: Oxford University Press, 1977); Lord Durham to Glenelg appears in W.

Kennedy (ed.), *Statutes, Treaties and Documents of the Canadian Constitution 1713–1929,* 2nd edition (Toronto: Oxford University Press, 1930), while the other Durham excerpts were reprinted in C. Lucas (ed.), *Lord Durham's Report on the Affairs of British North America* (Oxford: Clarendon Press, 1912); Louis-Joseph Papineau's "Historie" was reproduced in A. Ferretti and G. Miron (eds.), *Les Grands Textes Independantistes: Écrits, Discours et Manifestes Quebeçois, 1774–1992* (Montreal: L'Hexagone, 1992).

### 8. "An Unwanted Ebullition of Commercial Rivalry": North West Company vs. Hudson's Bay Company

See Thomas Douglas, Earl of Selkirk, *The Memorial of Thomas Earl of Selkirk* (Montreal: Nehum Mower, 1819); copies of correspondence by William McGillivray and E. Coltman's final report are found in Great Britain, House of Commons, *Papers Relating to the Red River Settlement* (London: 1819).

### 9. "Sicily of North America": The Land Issue in Prince Edward Island

J. Stewart, *An Account of Prince Edward Island, in the Gulf of St. Lawrence, North America* (London: W. Winchester and Son, 1806); George Young, *A Statement of the "Escheat Question" in the Island of Prince Edward; Together with the Causes of the Late Agitation and Remedies Proposed, April 1838* (London: R. and W. Swale, 1838); B. Sleigh, *Pine Forest and Macmatak Clearings* (London: R. Bentley, 1853); "Report of the Commissioners" is found in I. Robertson (ed.), *The Prince Edward Island Land Commission of 1860* (Fredericton: Acadiensis Press, 1986); the Charles Mackay article appears in P. Waite, *Pre-Confederation* (Scarbourgh: Prentice Hall, 1965).

### 10. "Undue Credit and Overwhelming Charges": Commerce in Newfoundland

Documents by Kemp and Attwood can be found in Great Britain, House of Commons, *Report of the Select Committee on Newfoundland Trade* (London: 1817); Edward Chappell, *Voyage of His Majesty's Ship Rosamond to Newfoundland and the Southern Coast of Labrador* (London: R. Watts, 1818); the Report to Earl Bathurst is reprinted in Great Britain, House of Commons, *Papers and Accounts of Newfoundland, Imports and Exports, Trade, Customs etc.* (London: 1824); R. McCrea, *Lost Amid the Fogs* (London: S. Low, Son and Marston, 1869).

### 11. "The Very Vitals Are Chilled": Lumbering in New Brunswick

Peter Fisher, *Sketches of New Brunswick* (Saint John: Chubb and Sears, 1825); John Macgregor, *Historical and Descriptive Sketches of the Maritime Colonies of British America* (London: Longman, Rees, Orme, Brown and Green, 1828); Anonymous, *Letters from Nova Scotia and New Brunswick Illustrative of their Moral, Religious and Physical Circumstances during the Years 1826, 1827 and 1828* (Edinburgh: Waugh and Innis, 1829); Abraham Gesner, *New Brunswick* (London: Simmonds and Ward, 1847); James Johnston, *Notes on North America: Agricultural, Economic and Social* (London: W. Blackwood, 1851).

## 12. "They Think They Know Everything": Nova Scotia's Identity

See John Robinson and Thomas Ripin, *A Journey Through Nova Scotia...* (York: C. Etherington, 1774); Wiswall's letter was reproduced in D. Harvey, "A Blue Print for Nova Scotia in 1818," *Canadian Historical Review* 24, 4 (1943); J. Marshall, *A Patriotic Call to Prepare in a Season of Peace...* (Halifax: A.H. Holland, 1819); Howe's address can be found in J.A. Chisholm (ed.), *The Speeches and Public Letters of Joseph Howe,* Vol. II (Halifax: 1909); Thomas Haliburton, *The Clockmaker* (London: R. Bentley, 1838); William Young's letter appears in J. Reid, K. McNaught, and H. Crowe (eds.), *A Source Book of Canadian History* (Don Mills: Longman, 1964); Abraham Gesner, *The Industrial Resources of Nova Scotia* (Halifax: A. and W. MacKinlay, 1849).

## 13. "Most Horrible and Heartless": Irish Immigration

Britain, House of Commons, *Papers Relative to Emigration* (London: 1847) contain copies of the accounts by Stephen de Vere, G.M. Douglas, W. Boulton, H. Perley, A. Buchancan, A. Hawke, and Adam Ferrie.

## 14. "A Great Humbug": British Columbia's Gold Rush

Major's account appeared in *British Columbia Historical Quarterly*, IV (July 1941), while C.C. Gardiner's is found in the same periodical I (1937); S.G. Hathaway's journal was printed in I. Bescoby, "Notes and Documents," *Canadian Historical Review* (September 1932); Matthew Macfie, *Vancouver Island and British Columbia* (London: Longman, Green, Longman, Roberts and Green, 1865).

## 15. "The Sweet Zephyrs of British Land": The Black Experience

With the exception of Mary Cary's *Plea for Emigration* (Detroit: George Patterson, 1852) and S. Howe, *The Refugees from Slavery in Canada West: Report to the Freedmen's Inquiry Commission* (Boston: Wright and Potter, 1864), copies of the other documents in this chapter can be found in C. Ripley (ed.), *The Black Abolitionist Papers,* Vol. 2 (Chapel Hill: University of North Carolina Press, 1986).

## 16. "Like Snow Beneath an April Sun": Mid-Nineteenth Century Native Dissent

The Paul et al. petition was included in R. Whitehead, *The Old Man Told Us: Excerpts from Micmac History, 1500–1950* (Halifax: Nimbus, 1991); the document by Chief Peau de Chat was found in P. Petrone (ed.), *First People, First Voices* (Toronto: University of Toronto Press, 1983); while the Shinguaconse "Little Pine" document was most recently reprinted in P. Petrone (ed.), *Native Literature in Canada: from Oral Tradition to the Present* (Toronto: Oxford University Press, 1990); P. Jones *History of the Ojebway Indians* (London: A.W. Bennett, 1861); "To the Chiefs and People of Several Indian Tribes Assembled in General Council at Orillia, July 31, 1846, *Minutes of the General Council of Chiefs and Principal Men...* (Montreal: 1846); Peguis to the Aborigines Protection Committee, 1857 appears as an appendix in Great Britain, House of Commons, *Report from the Select Committee on the Hudson's Bay Company* (London: 1857).

## 17. "The Bold Scheme": Confederation

The "Montreal Annexation Manifesto" was reprinted in A. Doughty (ed.), *Elgin-Grey Papers, 1846–1852* (Ottawa: King's Printer, 1937), while the speeches by Taché, Cartier, Brown, and Dorion were reprinted in *Canada, Confederation Debates* (Ottawa: King's Printer, 1951); Howe's address was recorded in J.A. Chisholm (ed.), *The Speeches and Public Letters of Joseph Howe,* Vol. II (Halifax: 1909); petitions from Prince Edward Island, Nova Scotia, and Newfoundland were reprinted in Great Britain, House of Commons, *Correspondence Respecting the Proposed Union of the British North American Provinces* (London: 1867).